INTERACTIVE CASEBOOK SERIES℠

LEGAL WRITING
FROM ADVICE TO ADVOCACY

A Contemporary Approach

Kristen Konrad Tiscione
PROFESSOR OF LAW, LEGAL PRACTICE,
GEORGETOWN UNIVERSITY LAW CENTER
WASHINGTON, D.C.

WEST ACADEMIC PUBLISHING

444 Cedar Street, Suite 700
St. Paul, MN 55101
1-877-888-1330

Printed in the United States of America

ISBN: 978-1-64708-420-2

To Nick, Zach, and Mike,
the three stars that light my life,

and

to Alec and Myles,
for their enthusiasm, support, and
significant contribution to this project.

Preface

When I learned to ride a bike, I did not just hop on and start pedaling. First, my father explained to me what to do and why: "You'll need to hold the wheel straight," "Pedal fast enough to keep the bike going," and "Don't slam on the brakes, or you'll go flying." When I got on the bike, he held it steady. As I started to pedal, he held on, running behind me, until I was going fast enough to keep the bike up (apparently he subscribed to the "no training wheels" philosophy). As I pedaled, I began to understand what he meant by needing to pedal fast enough. If I didn't, I started to lose balance. Once I realized he had let go, I got scared and slammed on the brakes. Then I understood what he meant by "you'll go flying."

Theory informs practice, which informs theory. The two are inseparable. Knowing the theory of bike riding helped me learn to ride a bike. Similarly, knowing the theory of legal analysis, both predictive and persuasive, will help you learn the critical skills of lawyering: giving advice to clients and advocating on their behalf. As you will learn, giving advice comes in a variety of forms, such as phone calls, email, memoranda, and opinion letters. Advocacy takes many forms in many contexts: negotiating a deal, filing a lawsuit, commenting on proposed changes to the law, arguing before a judge or jury, and writing arguments to the court, just to name a few.

This book introduces you to the what, the why, and the how of legal writing. The theory that informs our discipline is rhetoric. At its most narrow, rhetoric is the study of persuasion; at its broadest, it is the study of all communication. As a source of study, rhetoric dates back to ancient Greece, where it was used to teach argumentation for careers in law and politics. It was respected and taught all over the world for thousands of years. During the Renaissance, philosophical differences on the topics appropriate to courses in logic and rhetoric reduced rhetoric to the study of style, and its influence in the Western world began to wane. It survived during the eighteenth century, but stripped of its substance, it had disappeared in formal education by the end of the nineteenth century.

The goal of this book is to restore rhetoric to its rightful place in legal education and, as a result, hasten your learning. Becoming a good legal writer is about more than imitating samples and using good grammar. It requires a paradigm shift in the way you think about the law, the creation of law, your role in that process, and writing on behalf of others with a specific audience in mind. It also requires that you be able to speak about the law, and several chapters are devoted to client meetings, reporting to a supervisor, oral argument, and public speaking in general.

Legal writing is a skill you will develop throughout the course of your career. It takes a long time to become an expert at anything, and you will always think you have more to learn. I hope this book combines the right balance of theory, explanations, and samples to get you pedaling and in control. When your bike starts to wobble, you should have the tools necessary to decide what corrections to make and why. As you face the challenges of learning to think, write, and speak like a lawyer, you can expect to "go flying" a few times. We've all been there. Just climb back on that bike and start pedaling. It's quite a wonderful ride.

KRISTEN K. TISCIONE
Professor of Law, Legal Practice
Georgetown University Law Center

December 2020

Features of This Casebook

Throughout the book you will find various text boxes on either side of the page. These boxes provide information that will help you to understand a case or cause you to think more deeply about an issue.

For More Information These boxes point you to resources to consult for more information on a subject.

What's That? These boxes explain the meaning of special legal terms that appear in the main text. *Black's Law Dictionary* definitions may be accessed by clicking on the hyperlinked term in the text.

Take Note Here you will be prompted to take special notice of something that deserves further thought or attention.

Classroom Pointer These boxes contain information worthy of classroom discussion.

It's Latin to Me The law is fond of Latin terms and phrases; when you encounter these for the first time, this box will explain their meaning.

Go Online If there are relevant online resources that are worth consulting in relation to any matter being discussed, these boxes will direct you to them.

Food for Thought These boxes pose questions that prompt you to think about issues raised by the material.

Practice Pointer Here you will find advice relevant to legal practice typically inspired by the actions (or inactions) of legal counsel in the cases or simply prompted by an important issue being discussed.

FYI A self-explanatory category that shares useful or simply interesting information relevant to material in the text.

Hear It These boxes point you to an audio file that is relevant to the material in the text.

Bottom Line These boxes reference important takeaways from the reading.

Test Your Knowledge These boxes contain hyperlinks to online assessment questions that will help you test your understanding of the material in the part.

Acknowledgments

Two sabbaticals, two research leaves, and several summer writing grants have helped make this book possible. I am grateful to ***Deans Alexander Aleinikoff and William Treanor*** for Georgetown University Law Center's unflagging financial support of my scholarship. I am also grateful to the following faculty and colleagues, whose advice and expertise has proved invaluable:

Noelle Adgerson, Executive Assistant, Legal Research and Writing, Georgetown University Law Center

Wayne Davis, Philosophy Department Chair and Professor, Georgetown University

Jennifer Locke Davitt, Head of Faculty Services, Georgetown Law Library, Georgetown University Law Center

Frances C. DeLaurentis, Professor of Law, Legal Practice, Georgetown University Law Center

Vicki Girard, Professor of Law, Legal Practice, Georgetown University Law Center

Dee Konrad (in memoriam), Professor of English, Barat College

Betsy Kuhn, Faculty Manuscript Editor, Georgetown University Law Center

Ellie Margolis, Professor of Law, Temple University Beasley School of Law

Heather McCabe, Associate Professor, Legal Research and Writing, Georgetown University Law Center and partner, McCabe Russell, P.A.

Jarrod Reich, Professor of Legal Writing & Lecturer in Law, University of Miami School of Law

Ruth Anne Robbins, Distinguished Clinical Professor of Law, Rutgers Law

Louis Michael Seidman, Carmack Waterhouse Professor of Constitutional Law, Georgetown University Law Center

Anna Selden, Associate Director of Publications and Faculty Manuscript Management, Georgetown University Law Center

Jill A. Smith, Instructional Technology Librarian, Georgetown University Law Center

Morgan Stoddard, Director of Research Services, George Washington University Law

Robin West, Frederick J. Haas Professor of Law and Philosophy, Georgetown University Law Center

I also thank my past and present research assistants, ***Amanda Rome, Gabriel Lerner*** (in memoriam), ***Margaret Engoren, Jonathan Ammons, Rex Winter, Molly Clarke, Alec Williams*** and ***Myles Young,*** whose hard work and enthusiasm over the years have helped sustain me.

Finally, I thank my husband for his stalwart belief in me and his loving and constant support.

If ancient Greece and Rome are dust,
we are but wind to keep them aloft.

Summary of Contents

Table of Contents

Part XIII Citations and Signals

LEGAL WRITING
FROM ADVICE TO ADVOCACY

A Contemporary Approach

Part I

Introduction to Law School

Chapter 1

Welcome to the Legal Profession

A well-functioning society needs lawyers. Lawyers should be committed to the rule of law and achieving justice. But to succeed, they must also write well. The practice of law takes many different forms: prosecuting or defending an alleged criminal, drafting new laws, advising businesses on how to comply with federal and state regulations, negotiating a merger between two companies, or mediating a divorce settlement, to name a few. Each of these tasks requires that the lawyer know how to research, reason, speak, and write well in order to achieve her client's goals. Proficiency in these skills often distinguishes the great lawyer from the good one.

Whether or not you choose to practice law, your legal education will change you. You will never look the same way again at an apartment lease, an airplane ticket, a loan instrument, or a set of terms and conditions on the internet. You will feel like a whole new world has opened up for you, with its own, complicated language. Learning this language is exciting. Most first-year law students soon find themselves talking about the law constantly, even at social gatherings. You may find yourself becoming impatient with family and friends who are not immersed in the same, intensive law school experience because they do not understand what you are going through. In the end, you will come to appreciate how deeply the law influences our daily lives.

Regardless of where and why you are attending law school, you will undoubtedly learn to think differently and more analytically—like a lawyer. Thinking like a lawyer starts with a client: an individual, a corporation, or some other business entity or organization with a legal problem, lots of questions, and a story to tell. To think like a lawyer is to begin solving the problem by asking questions, enlisting the client's help to collect all pertinent facts, and reserving judgment. With perhaps only a sense of the applicable legal principles, the lawyer conducts thorough and efficient research to find and interpret the law and then apply it to the client's situation. Only then is the lawyer in a position to explain the law and predict, negotiate, or argue for a particular outcome.

A major goal of law school is to teach you this essential and unique skill set. You will learn that rules of law come from constitutions, statutes, administrative regulations, and judicial decisions on a variety of subjects ranging from property to tax to criminal law. You will also learn the rules of law in several of these areas, but law school is less about this "black letter" law than the ability to find, read, interpret, shape, and apply it in the service of your clients' goals. In that sense, it's more about the rhetoric of law than the law itself. And this book will introduce you to the core concepts of rhetoric for the purpose of advising clients and advocating on their behalf.

At first, you might find the reference to "rhetoric" here off-putting. Since the time of Plato, rhetoric has been considered by some as inferior to philosophy or science. In ancient Greece, a teacher of rhetoric was known as a sophist, which translates into a teacher of knowledge. But over time, the sophists' ability to dazzle audiences with clever and ornate speech earned them a reputation for being manipulative and deceptive. It was not a large leap to begin thinking of lawyers as masters of sophistry.[1]

Despite this negative connotation, rhetoric—as the art of persuasion—was taught throughout the world alongside logic and grammar from roughly the fifth century BCE until the late nineteenth century ACE. Today, we think of rhetoric as the study of all human communication, not just persuasion. It is a method for learning how to communicate effectively and for interpreting and analyzing language. As you will read, it was used to teach some of the greatest legal minds dating back to the ancient world, and it will inform everything you do in law school.

---

1 Unfortunately, this negative attitude towards lawyers continues to permeate Western culture. *See, e.g.,* Chaucer, *Prologue*, in Canterbury Tales, ll. 323–24 ("Nowhere a man so busy of his class, and yet he seemed much busier than he was."); Joyce Carol Oates, Rape: A Love Story 70 (2003) ("A lawyer is basically a mouth, like a shark is a mouth attached to a long gut. The business of lawyers is to talk, to interrupt one another, and to devour one another if possible."); Will Rogers, *The Lawyers Talking, in* 6 Will Rogers' Weekly Articles: The Roosevelt Years, 1933–1935, at 208 (Steven K. Gragert ed., Will Rogers Mem'l Museums rev. ed. 2011) (1982), https://perma.cc/XKN4-EMKR ("The minute you read something and you can't understand it you can almost be sure that it was drawn up by a lawyer."); William Shakespeare, The Second Part of King Henry VI act 4, sc. 2 ("The first thing we do, let's kill all the lawyers.").

NOTE: Citations throughout the book in footnotes are in law review format. Citations "above the line"in the text of the book are in practitioner format. *See infra* Part XIII.

Chapter 2

Welcome to Law School: Getting Started

Starting law school is both exciting and terrifying. There are so many opportunities opening up before you, and yet at first, you may feel like you're somewhere you don't belong, like you got lucky. You're not alone. Everyone feels unsure at times. Here's what upper class students suggest:

Be kind. The first (and arguably most important lesson) is simple: be kind to other people. Each of your classmates is seeking to better themselves, so reserve judgment. Kindness contributes to those individual goals and betterment of the whole law school. Law school is nearly impossible to get through alone. You need to be able to talk to your peers about cases, student organizations, study groups, outlining for exams, whether you want to make law review, and other important topics, like where to buy groceries.

If someone asks for your notes for a day of class, share them. If someone asks to use your outline to check theirs, collaborate. You may need the favor returned in the future. Grades are important, no doubt, but being kind and considerate will open endless doors in the legal profession. Start working today to form the kind of person you want to be as a member of the profession.

Be tolerant of viewpoints different from your own. Law school discussions may be difficult at times because they will invite strong emotions and opinions that differ from yours. Learn now to listen and respect others' experiences and views.

Find a study method that works for you. There is no "right way" to study. Throughout your first few weeks of law school, 2Ls and professors will suggest multiple approaches to studying. No one of these methods is the correct one. Some people do best studying on their own, some in a group. Let your study group form naturally as you make friends.

Some of you will prefer detailed case briefs to make the material stick, others will prefer to highlight important text in the casebook.[1] There are endless ways to approach studying, as you will soon see. Try different methods until you find the

1 For more information on how to read for class, see *infra* ch. 6.

one that works for you. There is no rush to figure it out. You will be in law school for several years.

Grab your legal education by the horns. Law school is a "seize the day" opportunity. Prepare for class, engage, and grow. Intelligence isn't fixed. If you don't understand something, work it through. Ask your professors. Discuss it with classmates. Read more about it. Instead of thinking, I "just don't get it," think "I don't get it *yet*." Open your mind to new ideas. Listen and learn. Get comfortable with confusion: it's a sign of growth. When you feel discouraged, try to remember what it's like to learn something really hard for the first time. It takes a while to get the hang of it.

Don't hesitate to speak up for fear of being wrong. You may find you learn more from answering questions incorrectly than from acing a cold call. If you have a good guess as to what the answer to a question is, raise your hand. Worst case scenario, you are wrong. Your classmates aren't going to remember your incorrect answer and neither will your professor. Your classmates are likely too worried about their own answers to be remembering yours. If you have no idea what the answer to a question is (and your professor allows it), pass. If you are having a bad day or didn't get the chance to do the reading, give yourself a break and take the pass.

Stay healthy. Study hard and take advantage of as many events and activities as you can without sacrificing your mental health. Remember, you may be a law student, but you are a person too. Take care of yourself physically and mentally. Make the time to go out, make friends, get enough sleep, and exercise. Do your best, be patient, and take one day at a time. Let that be enough.

Dream big and change the world. Law school presents you with the tools you need to make the changes you want to make. Never lose sight of why you are here. As lawyers, we have the power to impact and improve lives, whether it be through representation, drafting legislation, or any of the many other ways lawyers interact with the world on a day-to-day basis. Lawyers create and maintain the scaffolding of society, and this is the beginning of your ability to make a significant contribution. Use your legal education to better yourself so you can better the world. If you develop the tools you need to be a successful lawyer now, the options for change are endless.

Chapter 3

What Are Legal Research and Legal Writing?

The purpose of **legal research** is to find the law you need to help your client. It is both something you do and something you find.

You are already familiar with researching in print and online sources, but legal research is likely to seem very different to you. First, the sheer volume of law (that grows daily) can be overwhelming, making it difficult to be confident that you have found everything that is necessary or helpful to answer your questions. With roughly 2.65 million volumes, the Law Library of Congress,[1] has the largest legal collection in the world. Most of the resources you will need in law school will be available online.

Second, there are so many different ways to go about your research that you can find yourself going in circles, making it hard to know where you've been and when to stop. Sometimes you stop simply because you run out of time.

Third, legal research usually costs money. Some online legal resources are very expensive, some have moderate costs, and some are free (but these tend to be the least helpful for initially finding the law you need). If you have access to a good law library, print resources are almost always free. You will want to develop a technique that is cost effective both for your client and your practice. You will want to resist the urge to think of legal research as equivalent to Googling (although the web can sometimes be a great starting place).

Finally, the process of legal research is analytical, not mechanical. That means you will need to be thinking like a lawyer as you go—reading what you find, assessing its reliability, determining how it applies to your client's situation, and deciding where to turn next. Unless you know what you already have (by reading the material you've found), you won't know what you still need. If you wait to read your research until you are done, it may be too late in the process to start over again.

Like legal research, **legal writing** is something you do and find. You also create it. In some ways, lawyers even create law.

---

1 *See* https://www.loc.gov/law/.

You may be tempted to think that writing is writing, and since you are already a good writer, this part will be easy. Most second-year law students would tell you otherwise. It's not that the writing skills you bring to law school are not useful; it's that legal writing is so different from the kind of writing you likely did in college. It's also different from the kind of writing philosophers, historians, scientists, journalists, and other professionals engage in.

First, the sole purpose of legal writing is to inform and persuade the reader efficiently and effectively. You may write to advise your client on how to comply with federal regulations, form a corporation, or ask a judge to grant your client's motion. In each of these situations, the writing must be accurate, comprehensive, straightforward, and concise. Style in legal writing exists to serve its ultimate goal, not for its own sake. Second, lawyers speak a very distinct language, and the legal community has a certain way of doing things. It will take a while to learn this language. Once you begin to learn this language, you may be tempted to use it in a way that only lawyers would understand. You will learn, however, that the best legal writing is writing that *any reader* can understand.

There are many forms of legal writing, and they can be divided into three major categories: advice, advocacy, and legal instruments (e.g., contracts, deeds, securities, etc.). When a client first comes to a lawyer with a problem or goal, the lawyer collects all the pertinent facts, often conducts other factual investigation and legal research, and then advises the client on what to do next.

Written legal advice can take the form of a formal opinion letter, a legal memorandum, email, bench memoranda, and several variations on these. A lawyer might choose to send an **opinion letter** directly to the client for many reasons. The advice might be complicated and several people will be reviewing it. Perhaps the problem poses substantial risk to the client, and the legal representation is likely to be expensive and time-consuming. Or maybe the lawyer wants to create a record to avoid confusion and protect her relationship with the client (see Chapter 41).

Bottom Line

Legal advice typically takes these forms:

- opinion letters
- legal memoranda
- email
- bench memoranda

Legal memoranda (memos), on the other hand, are often written from one lawyer to another, both of whom represent the same client or clients in similar situations. Typically, in any kind of law practice, a senior lawyer will ask a junior lawyer to conduct research on a specific legal question and draft a memo that explains the law and predicts how it will apply to the client's situation. The lawyers may then use the memo for planning purposes or send it directly to the client. Although legal memos used to be commonplace in many law offices, they are increasingly too expensive to produce for client use. For that reason, as well as others, a lawyer might write an **email** instead (see Chapters 37 and 40).

Bench memoranda fall into the category of advice, but they are written by judicial clerks (law students or recent law graduates) for judges or a panel of judges. Their purpose is to inform the judge(s) about the law applicable in a pending case, anticipate the parties' arguments, and often recommend the most appropriate ruling in that case (see Chapter 42).

Written legal advocacy takes many forms too. It differs from legal advice in that its explicit purpose is to persuade the reader to adopt the writer's point of view and take some action in the client's favor. Much legal advocacy takes place in the context of civil or criminal lawsuits and administrative law proceedings.

A civil suit is a dispute between private parties, where the plaintiff claims the defendant has committed some form of legal wrong that caused the plaintiff harm. A civil plaintiff files a lawsuit by filing a complaint with the court. These and the papers filed thereafter are often referred to as **pleadings**. You will learn more about them in Civil Procedure.[2]

Bottom Line

Legal advocacy or argument typically takes these forms:

- pleadings (a generic reference to all documents filed in a lawsuit)
- motions
- memoranda of points and authorities
- briefs
- position or white papers
- comments
- agency filings

A party to a lawsuit may file a **motion**, asking a judge to make an interim or final decision with respect to the case. For example, in a civil case, a defendant might move to dismiss the complaint for failing to state a valid claim (known in federal civil procedure as a 12(b)(6) motion).[3]

In a criminal case, the defendant might seek to prevent the government from admitting evidence allegedly obtained in violation of the defendant's constitutional rights. These requests are referred to as **motions** and are often accompanied by **memoranda of points and authorities** that explain the legal reasons for granting or denying the motion (see Chapter 52).

At other points before, during, and after trial, the parties may need to present the court with their legal arguments relevant to the case. These written arguments are usually referred to as **briefs**. They too give the legal reasons why a court should rule in the party's favor (e.g., see Chapter 45 on appellate briefs).

---

2 A criminal suit is an action filed by a federal or state government alleging that a crime has been committed by the named defendant(s) against the public. A criminal action begins with the government filing a complaint, indictment, or information.

3 *See infra* ch. 52.

Position papers, sometimes called white papers when written by or for the government, are detailed statements outlining the views of a particular individual, entity, or organization. Lawyers write these in a variety of contexts. For example, a lawyer might write a position paper outlining her client's position in advance of a mediation to settle a private dispute. An association representing certain business interests might urge the legislature to enact a law granting them tax relief, or a state agency might make public its future policies on land use and development.

Both federal and state agencies engage in rulemaking and adjudication as part of their administrative duties. When agencies seek to create new regulations, they solicit input that lawyers often write in the form of **comments**. As part of enforcing their regulations, agencies often investigate and hold hearings. A lawyer representing a client in an agency investigation or hearing files documents similar to those filed in lawsuits.

Lawyers also write a wide variety of **legal instruments** unrelated to any dispute. For example, lawyers often write the laws or regulations that legislatures adopt. When you buy a house, the document that transfers ownership from the seller to you is called a deed; the document that gives the bank an interest in the house as collateral for a loan is called a mortgage or a deed of trust. Wills and trusts are used for estate planning, and leases are used to create private and commercial landlord/tenant relationships. Most of these instruments are contracts, which you will learn more about either in Contracts or upper level courses. They usually require that the lawyer have specialized knowledge in a particular area of the law.

Bottom Line

Legal instruments include:

- Deeds and mortgages
- Wills and trusts
- Leases
- Business-related agreements or contracts
- Articles of incorporation
- Bylaws
- Negotiable instruments
- Securities
- Loan documents such as notes

Chapter 4

How Do I Approach This Course?

Most of us begin law school with little or no experience reading and writing about the law. So, if you're also new to the party, welcome. When we started law school, we didn't know how to conduct legal research, read a judicial opinion, interpret a statute, or even talk about the law in a sophisticated way. That's what this course is about. But that's only the beginning. This course will teach you not only how to think like a lawyer but also how to write like one. What you learn here will serve you throughout law school and your entire career. As this course unfolds, keep these thoughts in mind:

Do not underestimate the role of this course in your legal education and your career. If you know anyone who's gone to law school and asked them about it, they probably told you that this is the most important course you will take. That's because it introduces you to law practice: the process of applying the law to specific situations in the service of clients. No other course in the first year is likely to bridge this gap between theory and practice. Your work for this course may also serve as a writing sample for prospective employers.

Even though you are already a good writer, prepare to learn to write differently. If you're in law school, you're already a good writer. But you're probably not a good *legal* writer. Not yet anyway. Maybe you majored in English and are used to writing interpretations of Shakespeare, or maybe you majored in Biology and have written mostly scientific reports. Maybe you worked for several years and haven't written much since college.

Everyone has their own writing experience and expertise, but together you and your classmates will learn how to become good legal writers. Try to remember that it takes time to develop expertise. Be patient with yourself. Resist the temptation to forget what you already know and start with a "clean slate." Take the time to understand the parallels between good legal writing and your existing writing skills. Keep what works; throw out what doesn't.

Learn the conventions of legal discourse. In the same way a scientist is expected to present conclusions based on data, a lawyer is expected to advise and argue for her client based on the law. But there is more to it than that. The scientific community expects the data to be interpreted and presented in a particular way for it to be effective or convincing. So too with the legal community. And not all legal readers are the same; we write to judges differently than we do to clients.

Coming from a different discipline or field of study, these various conventions may seem strange or unnecessary at first but trust your professor and the process. Whether it's learning how to state rules of law and state them concisely or how to cite sources properly according to the *ALWD Guide to Legal Citation* (*ALWD Guide*) or *The Bluebook: A Uniform System of Citation* (*Bluebook*), you're learning these things for a reason. If it's not clear why you should do something a certain way, ask.

Don't confuse legal writing conventions with "style" or "voice." There is a difference between what legal readers expect and writing with your own style and in your own voice. It can be tempting to dismiss legal writing conventions as rigid or formulaic and robbing you of your own style and voice. Legal writing can be as creative as the writer, but you must learn the basic tools of legal communication first and work within those parameters to be effective.

Commit to excellence. Despite the importance of this course, it can be difficult to juggle it with the demands of other courses and realities of life. Working through the Uniform Commercial Code in Contracts or straining to understand the Federal Rules of Civil Procedure can tempt you to relax your focus, particularly if interim assignments are not graded, but don't. You really do get out of this course what you are willing to put in.

Chapter 5

How Does This Course Differ from Other First-Year Courses?

Traditional first-year courses teach you about contracts, torts, civil procedure, property, criminal law, and constitutional law. These courses introduce you to basic subject areas of law in the United States and their general principles. Your books for these courses will be different from what you are used to reading. Most of them will be casebooks, which collect appellate decisions in a given area of law from federal and state courts across the country. The author of the casebook has chosen each case for a particular purpose and organized them according to the principles unique to that area of law. A contracts casebook, for example, is organized around the principles relating to contract formation, what makes a contract enforceable, when contracts can lawfully be broken (we call this "breaching"), and the sorts of remedies one can recover in the case of an unlawful breach.

These decisions have been edited by the book authors; they are not in the same form the courts issued or that lawyers read them. The casebook method you will use in these courses is designed to do more than teach you legal principles. It is also designed to teach you how to think analytically. You will be asked to reflect on the issues in these cases, how they were articulated by the parties and the court, the rules of law the courts used to resolve them, whether the rules of law the courts applied or created made sense, whether the law was applied in a way that was consistent with existing precedent, whether the outcome was fair, etc.

> **FYI**
>
> Decisions in casebooks look different from the way they look when they are published by the courts. See p. 19.

> **What's That?**
>
> Lawyers and law professors often use different words to mean the same thing.
>
> Appellate decisions are written by appellate judges. But your professors may also refer to decisions as "opinions," "cases," "case law," or "common law."

Throughout these courses, you will begin to get a sense of the range of issues that arise in that area of law and how courts analyze and resolve them. In so doing, you will form a schema, or mental map, of the law that will help you "spot" issues the professor wants you to discuss on an exam. Even more important, these courses build a knowledge base when the time comes to spot potential issues for real clients. Clients rarely know how to identify the legal issues involved. That's where you come in.

This course is not designed to teach you the legal principles that govern a particular area of law. Instead, it is designed to introduce you to thinking like a lawyer in the *practice* of law. Its goal is to introduce you to legal resources, legal research methods, and the conventions of legal writers and readers; to simulate the variety of situations in which lawyers are called upon to use these skills; and to further develop your analytical skills. In so doing, you will also become knowledgeable about the relevant law and how it affects your client.

All your courses work together to provide a solid foundation for your legal education and career. They will teach you to read and reason analytically, but they have different emphases. In your non-legal writing courses, the emphasis is on learning the bundle of issues, legal rules, and policies related to the subject matter of that class. In your legal research and writing course, the emphasis is on applied learning in the context of simulated law practice. You will also learn ways to organize written legal analysis; these same skills are likely to help you when it comes time to write exams in your non-legal writing courses.

Chapter 6

How Do I Read for Class?

Commit to do the reading for all your classes. Your professors have assigned it for a reason. You are not expected to memorize what you read, but you will need to engage with it. That will require active reading and note-taking. Your notes will help you participate in class discussion. Being exposed to new information just once and for the first time in class is not likely to be very effective in making that information stick (or more accurately, move it into long-term memory). In fact, the more prepared you are for class, the better off you are when it comes time to study for exams at the end of the semester.

Law professors tend to begin class where the reading leaves off. You may be asked to give the facts or **holding**[1] of a particular case, explain the court's reasoning, or apply the legal concepts from a case in a small group exercise. Don't assume that your professor will summarize the reading for you. To prepare well for class, you will need to develop a reading strategy.[2] Knowing how to read and think about the law is likely to be new to you, and you may find it harder than you anticipate. At first, it will take longer than you think it will to read just a few judicial decisions. Ten pages could take two hours.

Not all judicial decisions are "reported" or considered "published." That does not mean you will not find them during your research. What it means is that the deciding court did not want the decision to have precedential value or did not issue a supporting opinion for its decision.

Practice Pointer

It is not always easy to tell if a case is just new or should be considered unreported or unpublished.

For more information on how to tell the difference, see Ch. 19.

Decisions that do get published are organized by the deciding court and date. The volume number, case name, and page number on which the case first appears in a specific reporter is its **citation**. Legal citations tell you where to find the source. The official government version of a decision is usually the one you should cite. You will learn more about this when you study citation.[3]

---

1 *See infra*, at 28.

2 *See infra*, at 25.

3 *See infra* Part XIII.

You can usually identify the court that decided a case based on the name of the publication (we call these "**reporters**") in which the decision appears:

Federal decisions are published in the following reporters:

District (trial) courts:

- Federal Supplement

Appellate (circuit) courts:

- Federal Reporter

Supreme Court:

- U.S. Reports (official version)
- Supreme Court Reporter
- Lawyer's Edition

State decisions are often published by state governments (official version) and in one of West's regional reporters:

- Atlantic
- North Eastern
- North Western
- Pacific
- South Eastern
- South Western
- Southern

If you rented a car for a long journey to someplace new, would you just jump in the car and start driving? Would it be enough to know how to drive? Probably not. You might first familiarize yourself with that particular car and then get directions. You would probably also have some ideas about what you're going to do when you get there.

It's the same with reading judicial decisions. First, you need to know what they look like and how they are structured. Next, you will want to know what information they contain, so you know what to expect. It also helps to know how judicial decisions in specific cases can affect future, similar cases.[4] Finally, you're going to need a legal dictionary.

A. What does a typical decision look like?

The answer is that it depends on the source. Judicial decisions are published and available in print, online, and often in casebooks. Below is the first page of a 2010 decision titled *Copeland v. District of Columbia Department of Employment Services*, issued by the District of Columbia Court of Appeals (D.C.'s highest court). It is the version you see online in a legal database called Westlaw. Although the practitioner information up front may differ based on the source, the content of the decision itself is the same in each version. Knowing nothing yet about the subject matter of this case, you can glean a lot of information from the heading alone:

---

4 For more information on how decisions affect future cases, see *infra* ch. 19 on *stare decisis*.

Page Go

Original image of 3 A.3d 331 (PDF)

3 A.3d 331 (1)
District of Columbia Court of Appeals.

(2) Shirley A. COPELAND, Petitioner,
v.
DISTRICT OF COLUMBIA DEPARTMENT OF EMPLOYMENT SERVICES, Respondent.

No. 09-AA-240.
Submitted March 25, 2010. (3)
Decided Sept. 2, 2010.

(4)
Synopsis

Background: Appeal was taken from decision of the Compensation Review Board denying an award of attorney fees in a public sector disability compensation case.

(5)
Holding: The Court of Appeals, Glickman, J., held that Board erred as a matter of law in concluding that law students' work was not compensable in a reasonable attorney fee award under Comprehensive Merit Personnel Act.

(1) The **court** that issued the decision and its location in volume 3 of the Atlantic Reporter, third series, beginning on page 331.

(2) The **parties** to the lawsuit.

(3) The **docket number** assigned to the court (the first two digits usually refer to the year the case was filed), and the **date** of the decision.

(4) A **synopsis** or summary of what the case was about; these synopses are written by lawyers for West, not the court. The official decision begins after the judge's name in the text of the decision.

(5) The name of the **judge** who wrote the decision, the **holding** of the case (meaning how the judge ruled on the key legal issue), and the **disposition** of the case (meaning what happened procedurally in light of the appellate court's decision).

B. How is a typical decision organized?

Most judicial decisions have the same or similar organization. Often the author of the decision begins with an **introduction** that sets forth the legal issue(s) in the case, the decision of the court below, the holding of the court on appeal, the disposition of the case, or some combination of this information. Often the decision then sets out the **pertinent facts**, including the background facts necessary to understand the nature of the dispute and those facts the court considered significant in resolving the issues. The facts are often followed by a summary of the **procedural history** of the case, meaning what happened at the lower court level, who filed the appeal, and why. Here or perhaps later, the judge may describe the arguments the parties made with respect to the key legal issues. The bulk of the decision is usually then devoted to the

discussion of the legal issues, including the court's **holding** and **reasoning** with respect to each. The decision may conclude with a summary of the court's findings of fact, conclusions of law, or **disposition** of the case.

Below is the full *Copeland* decision as it appears in Westlaw's print Atlantic Reporter (this print version can also be downloaded as a pdf when viewing the case online). Skim the opinion now and notice where each section listed above appears. To learn how to read and brief the decision as if you were preparing for class, see *infra* p. 28.

COPELAND v. DEPT. OF EMPLOYMENT SERVICES D.C. 331

Cite as 3 A.3d 331 (D.C. 2010)

IV. Conclusion

Our *de novo* review of the trial court's ruling leads us to affirm its grant of summary judgment on the alternative ground [23] that the uncontroverted facts establish, as a matter of law, that Ms. Phillips's own negligence contributed to her death.

So ordered.

(1) **Shirley A. COPELAND, Petitioner,**

v.

DISTRICT OF COLUMBIA DEPARTMENT OF EMPLOYMENT SERVICES, Respondent.

No. 09–AA–240.

(2) District of Columbia Court of Appeals.

Submitted March 25, 2010.

Decided Sept. 2, 2010.

Background: Appeal was taken from decision of the Compensation Review Board denying an award of attorney fees in a public sector disability compensation case.

Holding: The Court of Appeals, Glickman, J., held that Board erred as a matter of law in concluding that law students' work was not compensable in a reasonable attorney fee award under Comprehensive Merit Personnel Act.

Reversed and remanded.

1. District of Columbia ⚷7 (3)

In public sector disability compensation case, appellate court will defer to the Compensation Review Board's (CRB) construction of statute if it is a reasonable one, i.e., not plainly wrong or inconsistent with the legislature's intent, but appellate court will not uphold a decision that reflects a misconception of the relevant law or a faulty application of the law.

2. District of Columbia ⚷7

In a public sector disability compensation case, claimant must utilize the services of an attorney-at-law in the successful prosecution of his or her claim in order to be entitled to statutory award of reasonable attorney fee, but when that threshold requirement is met, it is untenable to argue that a reasonable attorney fee cannot be based on the work of law students and other non-lawyers who assisted in the representation under the attorney's direction. D.C. Official Code, 2001 Ed. § 1–623.27(b)(2).

3. District of Columbia ⚷7

Fact that law students permissibly performed tasks in a public sector disabili-

alarm bell for 20 minutes with no response. *Id.* at 685, 555 N.Y.S.2d 669, 554 N.E.2d at 1259. The court concluded that, from the perspective of the perspiring, crying, and screaming plaintiff, *id.*, "the lapse of time did not necessarily permit [her] the opportunity for cautious deliberation because the precariousness of her situation continued unabated." *Id.* at 686–87, 555 N.Y.S.2d 669, 554 N.E.2d at 1260. In contrast, the record here does not permit an inference that Ms. Phillips did not have an opportunity to deliberate on her situation before she decided to leave the elevator. Significantly, this was not a situation where the plaintiff believes that no help is forthcoming or where the elevator cab appears to be unstable.

23. "[A]n appellate court can uphold a trial court decision for reasons other than those given by the trial court. This principle can be traced back for several decades, and is firmly established in the District of Columbia's case law." *Prince v. United States*, 825 A.2d 928, 931–32 (D.C.2003) (citations and quotation marks omitted).

(1) **Case caption**, with names of parties.

(2) The **court** that decided the case and the date the decision was issued.

(3) These numbered paragraphs are called "**headnotes.**" They contain principles of law that appear in the order listed throughout the decision. The numbers are called "**key numbers,**" which will be useful for research. See Chapters 23 and 25–26.

ty compensation case that otherwise would have fallen to full-fledged attorneys was not enough to exclude their work from the purview of the attorney fee statute in Comprehensive Merit Personnel Act, which provided that District of Columbia government employee who utilized services of attorney-at-law in successful prosecution of her claim was entitled to reasonable attorney fee award; critical point was that claimant was not represented before Department of Employment Services by the law students alone, and instead, she was represented by the law students together with a licensed attorney-at-law under whose direction the students did their work. D.C. Official Code, 2001 Ed. § 1–623.27(b)(2).

4. Attorney and Client ⚯64, 115

Under the Rules of Professional Conduct, a lawyer, who supervises law students, has an attorney-client relationship with the law students' client and is personally responsible for her representation. Rules of Prof.Conduct, Rule 5.3(b, c).

5. District of Columbia ⚯7

Claimant utilized the services of an attorney-at-law in the successful prosecution of her public sector disability compensation claim, and the law students who assisted her did so under direction and control of claimant's attorney, and therefore, Compensation Review Board (CRB) erred as a matter of law in concluding that the students' work was not compensable in a reasonable attorney fee award under Comprehensive Merit Personnel Act, which provided that District of Columbia government employee who utilized services of attorney-at-law in successful prosecution of her claim was entitled to reasonable attorney fee award. D.C. Official Code, 2001 Ed. § 1–623.27(b)(2).

Jeffrey S. Gutman for petitioner.

Peter J. Nickles, Attorney General for the District of Columbia, Todd S. Kim, Solicitor General, Donna M. Murasky, Deputy Solicitor General, and David A. Hyden, Assistant Attorney General, for appellee.

Before RUIZ, REID, and GLICKMAN, Associate Judges. (4)

GLICKMAN, Associate Judge:

This is an appeal of a Compensation Review Board ("CRB") order denying an award of attorney's fees in a public sector disability compensation case. D.C.Code § 1–623.27(b)(2) (Supp. 2010), a part of the Comprehensive Merit Personnel Act, provides that a District Government employee (5) who utilizes the services of an attorney-at-law in the successful prosecution of her claim is entitled to a reasonable attorney's fee award. The CRB interpreted this provision to bar a fee award where the claimant was represented by law students participating in a clinical program under a lawyer's supervision. We conclude that the CRB erred in its application of the statute.

I. (6)

In 1994, petitioner Shirley Copeland, an employee of the District of Columbia Department of Human Services, suffered a work-related injury to her back. She applied for, and received, disability compensation benefits. In June 2007, however, the Office of Risk Management in the Department of Employment Services terminated her benefits on the ground that her medical condition was not causally related to her workplace injury. Seeking to have her benefits reinstated, Ms. Copeland filed a request for an administrative hearing. To represent her in the administrative pro-

(4) The court's **official decision** begins here. Westlaw compiles the information up to this point for research purposes.

(5) The decision begins by introducing the reader to the nature of the case, including a **statement of the legal issue** on appeal.

(6) The court then summarizes the **legally significant facts.**

ceedings, Ms. Copeland retained the Public Justice Advocacy Clinic (the "Clinic") of the George Washington University Law School. The Clinic is directed by Professor Jeffrey Gutman, who is a member of the District of Columbia Bar. Under Professor Gutman's tutelage and supervision, two third-year law students, Daniel Greenspahn and Kiva Feldman, prepared Ms. Copeland's case. With Professor Gutman in attendance, the students represented her at her hearing.

(7) Ms. Copeland prevailed at the hearing, and on November 23, 2007, the administrative law judge entered a compensation order reinstating her benefits. The order identifies Professor Gutman as Ms. Copeland's counsel in the proceeding. Following their victory, Professor Gutman and the two law students applied pursuant to D.C.Code § 1–623.27(b)(2) for an award of reasonable attorney's fees for their work on Ms. Copeland's behalf. They sought fees for only half of the students' 170 hours (an exercise of "billing judgment," they explained, because some of the students' time was "pedagogical in nature, rather than directly focused on direct client service"), and no fees for Professor Gutman's time. The fee application stated that the fee award would be used for client services provided by the Clinic.

On September 8, 2008, Chief Administrative Law Judge Linda Jory entered an order denying the fee application on the ground that "[t]he plain language of the statute [D.C.Code § 1–623.27(b)(2)] provides for payments to 'attorney-at-law' and does not specify any other class of person eligible to receive such payments." The CRB agreed with this rationale, stating that law students "do not qualify as attorneys-at-law." The CRB rejected the argument that, for purposes of compensation in an attorney's fee award, the law students' work for Ms. Copeland was comparable to paralegal work:

> [It] is important to note that [paralegal] work is performed in support of, pursuant to, and under the direction of, an attorney-at-law. Work performed by a paralegal constitutes the work-product of the attorney of record ... in a case. Such a circumstance is distinguishable from the instant case as [ ] the two students directly represented Petitioner in court and engaged in the limited practice of law. Paralegals have no authority to do so.

II.

D.C.Code § 1–623.27(b)(2) provides that "[i]f a person utilizes the services of an attorney-at-law in the successful prosecution of his or her claim ..., there shall be awarded ... a reasonable attorney's fee, not to exceed 20% of the actual benefit secured, which fee award shall be paid directly ... to the attorney for the claimant...." Ms. Copeland argues that the (8)
CRB erred as a legal matter by construing this statute to preclude recovery as part of a "reasonable attorney's fee" award for any time devoted to the representation by law students and other para-professionals working with the claimant's attorney. The Department of Employment Services responds that the CRB did not interpret the statute as barring fee awards for paraprofessional work in all circumstances; rather, it distinguished between work performed by non-attorneys "in support of, pursuant to, and at the direction of" an attorney who represents a claimant, and work performed by non-attorneys who represent claimants themselves, even if they do so under the supervision of an attorney. The Department argues that the CRB reasonably construed D.C.Code § 1–623.27(b)(2) to preclude an award of attorney's fees only under the second set

(7) The court summarizes the **procedural history of the case** (i.e., how the case got to that court).

(8) The court then discusses the legal issue, setting forth its **analysis.** As you see here, courts often recount the parties' specific arguments.

334 D.C. **3 ATLANTIC REPORTER, 3d SERIES**

of circumstances, and that it reasonably applied that construction to the facts of this case.

(9) [1] The material facts of this case are not in dispute, and the CRB's interpretation and application of § 1–623.27(b)(2) are subject to *de novo* review in this court. We will defer to the CRB's construction if it is a reasonable one—i.e., "not plainly wrong or inconsistent with the legislature's intent" [1]—but we will not uphold a decision that "reflects a misconception of the relevant law or a faulty application of the law." [2]

[2] There is no question that a claimant must "utilize[ ] the services of an attorney-at-law in the successful prosecution of his or her claim" in order to be entitled to the award of "a reasonable attorney's fee" under § 1–623.27(b)(2). But when that threshold requirement is met, it would be untenable to argue that "a reasonable attorney's fee" cannot be based on the work of law students and other non-lawyers who assisted in the representation under the attorney's direction. The Council of the (10)
District of Columbia patterned § 1–623.27(b)(2) on the virtually identical attorney's fee provision of the District of Columbia Workers' Compensation Act, D.C.Code § 32–1530(a) (2001),[3] which the Department of Employment Services long has construed to cover the services of para-professionals assisting the claimant's attorney.[4] The presumption, absent good (11)
reason to think otherwise, is that when a legislature imports language from a statute of settled meaning to a new statute "with an identical stated purpose," it means for the imported language in the new law to be interpreted in the same way

1. *Howard Univ. Hosp. v. District of Columbia Dep't of Employment Servs.*, 952 A.2d 168, 173 (D.C.2008) (internal quotation marks omitted).

2. *Georgetown Univ. v. District of Columbia Dep't of Employment Servs.*, 971 A.2d 909, 915 (D.C.2009) (internal quotation marks omitted).

3. In pertinent part, D.C.Code § 32–1530(a) provides that "[i]f . . . the person seeking benefits . . . utilizes the services of an attorney-at-law in the successful prosecution of his claim, there shall be awarded . . . a reasonable attorney's fee . . ., which shall be paid directly . . . to the attorney for the claimant. . . ." The legislative history of § 1–623.27(b)(2) refers to this provision of the private sector workers' compensation law. *See* COUNCIL OF THE DISTRICT OF COLUMBIA, COMMITTEE ON GOVERNMENT OPERATIONS, REPORT ON BILL 16–238, *the District Government Injured Employee Protection Act of 2006* (2006), page 2. The purpose of each statutory provision is the same, to enable injured employees to obtain "legal services" to assist them with their claims. *Id.* ("Many employees[ ] who are injured on the job[ ] and are forced to seek legal representation find it extremely difficult to obtain legal services.").

4. Since 1986, the Department's regulations have required applications for attorney's fees under the Workers' Compensation Act to specify "the professional status (*e.g.*, attorney, paralegal, law clerk, or other person assisting an attorney) of each person performing the work" for which compensation is sought. 7 DCMR § 224.3(a) (2010). The Director of the Department of Employment Services issued a Policy Directive in 2005 confirming that "a reasonable paralegal fee . . . shall be afforded where appropriate" as part of the award under § 32–1530(a), "in recognition of the increasingly important role of paralegals to the practice of law in the D.C. area, including the practice of workers' compensation law before DOES." *Policy Directive Clarifying the Award of Attorney Fees in the District of Columbia Workers' Compensation Cases* (May 12, 2005). The Policy Directive is available on the Department's web site, at http://www.does.dc.gov/does/frames.asp?doc=/does/lib/does/services/Award_of_Attorney_Fees_OWC_011905.pdf. (last visited Aug. 3, 2010). In accordance with that directive, the CRB has upheld fee awards for para-professional work. *See, e.g., Steadman v. United Parcel Serv.*, CRB No. 05–262, 2005 DC Wrk. Comp. LEXIS 381 (Dec. 14, 2005).

(9) This is the first of the five **headnotes** previewed at the beginning.

(10) Here, the court **examines the language of the statute** to determine its meaning.

(11) The court also uses **canons of construction** and **legislative history** to determine its meaning. For information on methods of statutory interpretation, see Chapter 17.

as it is in the old one.[5]

In addition to finding no support in the statute's text or legislative history, an in-
(12) terpretation of § 1–623.27(b)(2) precluding the recognition of para-professional services in attorney's fee awards would render the statute an anomaly among fee-shifting statutes. As the Supreme Court has observed in a case construing one such statute (42 U.S.C. § 1988), the collaborative nature of legal representation implies that "a 'reasonable attorney's fee' cannot have been meant to compensate only work performed personally by members of the bar. Rather, the term must refer to a reasonable fee for the *work product* of an attorney ... [taking] into account the work not only of attorneys, but also of ... others whose labor contributes to the work product for which the attorney bills her client." [6] And "reasonable attorney's fee" awards historically have encompassed the work of law students; this court perceived nothing unusual or inappropriate, for example, in approving such an award under the Truth in Lending Act almost three decades ago.[7] An especially noteworthy
(13) case for present purposes, because it involved a fee application (under the Freedom of Information Act) for supervised student work in a law school clinic, is *Jordan v. United States Department of Justice.*[8] Rejecting the government's several objections, the D.C. Circuit Court of Appeals stated:

> The argument that law student services cannot possibly form the basis for an attorneys' fee award merely because law students are not lawyers has only superficial vitality. It loses force drastically when one notes the commonplace use of law students by law firms—usually full-time during summer months, and part-time during the academic year—to perform tasks that otherwise would fall to full-fledged attorneys. And the argument founders completely in the tide of state statutes and court rules authorizing law students, under appropriate circumstances, to undertake functions of licensed attorneys, including actual representation of clients before a court.... [W]e cannot condone a concept of attorneys' fees so narrow as to exclude the work of law students simply because they are not yet members of the bar.[9]

The Department of Employment Services does not take issue with these principles; it acknowledges that an application for an award of reasonable attorney's fees under § 1–623.27(b)(2) properly may seek compensation for the work of non-attorneys, including law students, who assisted an attorney in the successful prosecution of a claim. The Department disputes only that the law students rendered that type of assistance here. They did not do so, the Department argues, because as the CRB stated, "the two students directly represented [Ms. Copeland] in court and engaged in the limited practice of law" themselves.

[3, 4] This analysis is faulty. The fact that, as in *Jordan*, the law students permissibly "perform[ed] tasks that otherwise would [have] fall[en] to full-fledged attorneys" is not enough to exclude their work from the purview of the attorney's fee statute. The critical point is that Ms.

5. *Cannon v. Univ. of Chicago*, 441 U.S. 677, 696–98, 99 S.Ct. 1946, 60 L.Ed.2d 560 (1979).

6. *Missouri v. Jenkins*, 491 U.S. 274, 285, 109 S.Ct. 2463, 105 L.Ed.2d 229 (1989).

7. *See Frazier v. Franklin Inv. Co., Inc.*, 468 A.2d 1338, 1342 (D.C.1983).

8. 223 U.S.App.D.C. 325, 691 F.2d 514 (1982).

9. *Id.*, 223 U.S.App.D.C. at 332–33, 691 F.2d at 522–23.

(12) The court further infers legislative intent by looking at **similar statutes.**

(13) Finally, the court **analogizes to a similar case** to help resolve the issue.

336 D.C. **3 ATLANTIC REPORTER, 3d SERIES**

Copeland was not represented before the Department by the law students alone; she was represented by the law students together with Professor Gutman, a licensed attorney-at-law under whose direction the students did their work. This was in accordance with the Rules of this Court. Rule 48 permits eligible law students to engage in "the limited practice of law" and appear before the District's courts and administrative tribunals on behalf of indigent clients, provided they do so as part of a law school clinical program and work under the direction of a "supervising lawyer."[10] The "supervising lawyer" must be an "active" member of the District of Columbia Bar;[11] must "[a]ssume full responsibility for guiding the student's work . . . and for supervising the quality" of that work;[12] must do everything "necessary in [his or her] professional judgment to insure that the student's participation is effective on behalf of the indigent person represented";[13] and must sign all pleadings and other documents to be filed in the matter.[14] Under the Rules of Professional Conduct, a lawyer having such "direct supervisory authority" over a non-lawyer in the practice of law is obliged to make "reasonable efforts to ensure" that the non-lawyer's conduct is "compatible with" the lawyer's own professional obligations and may be held "responsible for conduct of such a person that would be a violation of the Rules . . . if engaged in by a lawyer."[15] Given these requirements, the "supervising lawyer" clearly has an attorney-client relationship with the law students' client and is personally responsible for her representation.

In this case, the "supervising lawyer" was Professor Gutman. The detailed time records submitted in support of the fee application confirm his assiduous supervision of the law students who handled Ms. Copeland's case.[16] As the administrative law judge recognized in the order reinstating Ms. Copeland's disability benefits, Professor Gutman was her legal counsel.

[5] Thus, contrary to the Department's characterization, this was not a case of lay representation before the Department. Ms. Copeland "utilized the services of an attorney-at-law in the successful prosecution" of her claim, and the law students who assisted her pursuant to Rule 48 did (14) so under that attorney's direction and control. The CRB therefore erred as a matter of law in concluding that the students' work was not compensable in a reasonable attorney's fee award under D.C.Code § 1-623.27(b)(2).

Accordingly, we reverse the decision of (15) the CRB and remand this case for an administrative law judge to consider the fee application on its merits and award a reasonable attorney's fee.[17]

10. D.C.App. R. 48(a)(1).

11. *Id.*, R. 48(e)(4).

12. *Id.*, R. 48(e)(2).

13. *Id.*, R. 48(e)(3).

14. *Id.*, R. 48(d)(1)(i).

15. D.C. Rules of Prof'l Conduct R. 5.3(b), (c).

16. According to the time records, Professor Gutman devoted considerable time providing his students with guidance and reviewing and correcting their work product. In preparing for Ms. Copeland's hearing, the students had weekly meetings with Gutman to discuss the case. Among other things, Gutman helped them with discovery and pleadings; advised them with respect to legal issues; and prepared them to conduct the hearing.

17. We note that the fee application asks for payment to be made to the George Washington University Legal Clinics ("GWULC"), not to Professor Gutman. The Department has

(14) The court states its **holding** or decision in this case.

(15) The court explains what happens next in terms of procedure.

C. How do I read decisions?

Most experts recommend that you get an overall sense of the decision before you read it slowly in detail. Skim the first page to see the parties involved, the deciding court, date of decision, whether it is considered reported or published, etc.

Then, get a sense of the nature of the decision (as in "figure out where you are going before you leave the house"). Ask yourself these questions:

Is the decision a majority or plurality decision? Is it followed by a concurrence or dissent? How long is it? How complicated are the facts? How many legal issues appear to have been decided? Which issues are of most interest for your purposes?

Answering these questions will help you gauge how long it will take to read the decision and how detailed your notes should be. As a practitioner, there may be parts of the decision you do not really need to rely on, but you should read carefully the entirety of decisions as they appear in your casebooks since the author has already excluded those portions considered unnecessary for purposes of that class.

FYI

The nature of the decision affects its weight and influence:

A majority decision represents the majority decision among the judges.

A plurality decision means no single decision received the support of a majority of the court.

A concurring decision represents those who agree with the decision of the court but for different or additional reasons.

A dissenting decision disagrees with the decision of the court.

Having assessed the context and scope of the decision, go back and read it closely. You may find it easier to take notes as you read or after you have read the entire decision. Do what works best for you: underline, highlight, write notes in the margins, type information in a new document, etc.

As you read, look for language that signals a transition from one part of the decision to another (e.g., from introduction to procedural history, from discussion of one issue to the next, and from the court's reasoning to the holding). Judges often say things like "The plaintiff filed her complaint," "The second issue in this case is whether," and "Therefore, we hold that . . . ," which can help orient you. Be sure to look up and write down the meaning of words you do not know. Begin to build your own glossary of legal terms.

For More Information

Here are just a few resources on learning how to read the law (if you do not know how to find them yet, ask your law school librarian):

Orin S. Kerr, *How to Read a Legal Opinion: A Guide for New Law Students*, 11 Green Bag 2d 51 (2007).

Ruth Ann McKinney, *Reading Like a Lawyer* (2d ed. 2012).

Laurel Currie Oates, *Leveling the Playing Field: Helping Students Succeed by Helping Them Learn to Read as Expert Lawyers*, 80 St. John's L. Rev. 227 (2006).

Ann Sinsheimer & David J. Herring, *Lawyers at Work: A Study of the Reading, Writing, and Communication Practices Of Legal Professionals*, 21 J. Legal Writing 63, 82–99 (2016) (describing in depth how lawyers read in practice).

D. Does it matter whether I read in print or online?

Many of your course books will be available in print, online, or both. Which should you choose? Is one better than the other? The classic answer to the classic law school question (in any class) is "it depends." That answer is just as apt here because it depends on what you mean by "better."

There may be differences in the way we understand and retain new information based on the form in which we read it. Studies show that our eyes track differently when reading online texts.[5] In the absence of headings, bullets, or other visual cues, we tend to focus on the words toward the beginning of lines and toward the top of the page in a pattern that resembles the capital letter F (as opposed to reading every line left to right as we move down a print page).[6] Studies also show that we use different parts of our brains to comprehend online versus print texts.[7]

See It

See the F pattern explained and depicted: https://www.nngroup.com/articles/f-shaped-pattern-reading-web-content-discovered/ (https://perma.cc/39D6-722F).

Below are some advantages and disadvantages to reading texts in print and online:

---

5 *See, e.g.*, Ellie Margolis, *Is the Medium the Message?* 12 Legal Commc'n. & Rhetoric: JALWD 1, 13 (2015) (citing Jakob Nielsen, F-Shaped Pattern for Reading Web Content, NIELSEN NORMAN GROUP (Apr. 17, 2006), https://perma.cc/39D6-722F).

6 Nielsen, *supra* note 5.

7 *See, e.g.*, Margolis, *supra* note 5, at 13 (citing Nicholas Carr, THE SHALLOWS: WHAT THE INTERNET IS DOING TO OUR BRAINS 168 (2010)).

Print

- Reading comprehension and retention may be better;
- The physical act of holding the book, turning the pages, and seeing the entire page at once makes it easier to navigate the content;
- Reading in print may lead to less cognitive overload and disruption by incoming email or other notifications;

but print texts may also be

- more expensive;
- harder to annotate or write in the margins (particularly if the book is rented or used);
- heavy to carry around.

Online

- may allow for easier annotation, highlighting, or note-taking;
- allows for access to hyperlinks (i.e., instant access to additional sources);
- may be searchable or have jump links;
- may be less expensive;
- less heavy to carry around;

but online texts may also

- lead to cognitive overload as you jump back and forth between different sources;
- not display an entire page at once;
- provide fewer contextual cues;
- distract you with incoming email or other notifications.

Just as you will need to determine what study method works best for you, you will need to figure out what form of text you prefer to read. Try both and see if you prefer one over the other. Regardless of the form you choose, it is going to take time to get used to juggling a textbook (print or online), your case briefs, your class notes, and whatever other materials you want handy in class.

For More Information

Here are just a few more resources on the differences between reading in print and online:

Rakefet Ackerman & Morris Goldsmith, *Metacognitive Regulation of Text Learning: On Screen Versus on Paper*, 17:1 J. Experimental Psychol.: Applied 18 (Mar. 2011).

Mary Beth Beazley, *Writing (and Reading) Appellate Briefs in The Digital Age*, 15 J. App. Prac. & Process 47–61 (2014).

Anne Mangen, Bente R. Walgermo & Kolbjørn Brønnick, *Reading Linear Texts on Paper versus Computer Screen: Effects on Reading Comprehension*, 58 Intl. J. of Educ. Research 61 (2013).

E. How do I brief decisions for class?

Case briefs are shortened versions of the major decisions you read for class.[8] Case briefs help you remember the significant aspects of the case, answer questions, and participate in discussion. The typical format of a **case brief** is similar to that of a judicial decision, and many professors, at least at the beginning of the semester, will ask questions in class that follow this typical format.

Bottom Line

A typical case brief includes:

- Facts
- Procedural History
- Legal Issues(s)
- Holding
- Court's Reasoning
- Disposition or Result
- Impact (optional)

Include only those **facts** necessary for you to remember what happened in the case and those the court considered important to its decision. The **procedural history** may be complicated and confusing; it's probably enough (except in a Civil Procedure class) to understand who the parties are, what happened at the lower court(s), and who has brought the appeal and why. The procedural history will become easier to understand once you have had a course in Civil Procedure. The **legal issue** is usually easy to identify. In a Torts class, focus on those issues that relate to Torts and not, for example, procedure. It's likely that your professor is less concerned about the procedural issues in a Torts class.

The **holding** of the case is the court's answer to the legal question or issue on appeal. In *Copeland*, the legal issue was whether the plaintiff could recover attorney's fees where the attorneys were law students representing her in their capacity as law

---

8 At the end of a section or chapter in a casebook, following the excerpted decisions, you may find short summaries or blurbs of additional noteworthy decisions. These are often called "case notes." These are included to show variations or additional considerations pertaining to the rule(s) of law explored in that chapter. You are not likely to have enough information to "brief them" in the sense used here.

students. The literal holding was "yes," but that is not helpful in understanding the case and its effect on D.C. law. That's why the **reasoning** of the court is important too. Try to understand the different reasons the court gives for its decision on each issue. They may be based on the language of a statute, prior case law, public policy, or other reasons. Finally, record the **disposition** or **result** in this case, meaning what happened next? Did the case end? Did it go back to the trial court? Who won? And what remedy, if any, was awarded?

Once you have identified the court's reasoning, reflect on the **overall impact** of the case. Did it change the law in some way? Represent a new or unique approach to the legal issue? Did you anticipate the outcome? Was it logical? Did it seem fair? These may be the questions your professor is most interested in discussing during class.

Try It: Case Briefing

(the online version of *Copeland* and sample case briefs can be found at App. A, at p. 497)

Re-read the *Copeland* case in Appendix A, then write a case brief as if it had been assigned in one of your classes.

- How did your understanding of the case differ before and after you briefed it?
- How long did it take you to write it? That will help you figure out how much time you will need to complete your reading (but you will also get faster with experience).
- Will the format you've chosen make it easy to answer questions?

Take Note

You can find a lot of online and print sources that will give you similar information on how to brief cases. Some of these will even brief the cases for you. Although they are popular, these "canned briefs" defeat the purpose of learning how to read, sort, and analyze case law, so use them sparingly.

Chapter 7

What Do My Professors Expect from Me?

Your professors will generally expect you to be prepared for class, ready to participate, and professional in your demeanor. They may even want to set some classroom guidelines for discussion of sensitive topics so that all viewpoints feel welcome and heard.

The leap from college to graduate school is a big one. You will have reading or other work assigned for each class, even the first time you meet. Most professors will give you a syllabus (increasingly only online), which you should check regularly. Some professors do not permit students to use laptops to take notes in class, so be sure to know what the class rules are. Many professors will also give you a written set of class rules or policies that explain the goals of the course, how it will be graded, exam dates, etc. Read these carefully.

Come to class having completed your assignments and with your notes, briefs, or other materials ready and available in case you are called on in class. Your professor may randomly call on students each week (often referred to as "cold-calling") or notify you in advance when to sign up or expect to be called on. If you were unable to prepare for class, it may help to notify your professor in advance. It is awkward for everyone in the room for you to have to "pass" when called on, but sometimes you just need to do it.[1] When you are asked a question in class, answer to the best of your ability. Don't be embarrassed to think out loud (your professors do it all the time) and don't pretend to know something you don't. Your classmates are likely to be just as nervous and confused as you.

> **Classroom Pointer**
>
> Assuming your professor allows laptops, use a note-taking application on your laptop, have the internet ready to check for external sources, and have your casebook open in front of you.
>
> If you are using an online casebook, fill half your screen with your notes and the other half with your casebook to easily reference assigned material.
>
> Have your briefs ready and open in case you are called on.

1 *See supra* ch. 2, at 6.

Law school is the place to begin developing your professional identity. How do you want to behave and have others perceive you? Is there a way for you to get a sense of the diversity of expertise and experience among your classmates? Open your mind to new ideas and the impact of your classmates' experience and point of view on your own. Be honest but always respectful.

Acting like a professional in law school begins with being prepared and participating in your classes. Here are few suggestions for do's and don'ts:

Do's

- Figure out when you will do the reading for each class period (use a written or online calendar to keep you on track).
- Complete the reading assignment first, then consult study guides if you have time.
- Notify your professor, in advance if possible, if you cannot attend class due to illness or other emergency.
- Read the material due for that class period (get as far as you can and skim what you did not finish so the reading does not pile up on you); remember that paper and pens can be useful at times.
- Ask questions in class.
- Volunteer to answer questions.
- Go to office hours.
- Take responsibility for your own education.

Don'ts

- Don't bring fragrant food to class.
- Don't ask the professor what the assignment is when you can find it in the syllabus.
- Don't email your professor with questions you can answer with a little effort (check the class syllabus or policies).
- Don't expect the professor to summarize the reading.
- Don't expect all professors to explain how a legal concept or rule of law fits into the overall subject of the class (they want you to do that for yourselves).
- Don't use your laptop in class to check your Facebook page, read the newspaper, play games, or shop.
- Don't multi-task to the point you can't absorb what's going on in class at the same time.

- Don't be disrespectful to classmates if they answer questions incorrectly.
- Don't ask questions that can better be answered during your professor's office hours.
- Don't lead the class down a rabbit hole.
- Don't write emails to your professors that are informal, sarcastic, or disrespectful in tone.
- Don't call a professor by their first name unless they invite that level of familiarity.
- If you miss class, don't ask the professor what you missed; ask a classmate instead or review posted class recordings, PowerPoints, etc.

Finally, remember that your professors went to law school too. It may have been a long time ago, but they know what it's like. We expect you to act like graduate students, but we want you to have fun too. We look forward every year to your enthusiasm, energy, insights, and innovations. We learn as much from you as you do from us.

Test Your Knowledge: Part I

To assess your understanding of the material in this part, click here to take a quiz.

PART II

Law and Rhetoric

Chapter 8

What Is Rhetoric?

"To use a technology metaphor, rhetoric isn't just an app that enhances instruction in argumentation; rhetoric is the operating system."[1]

—Jennifer Fletcher

Rhetoric is one of those words that has many different meanings. What do you think of when you hear that word? Flowery language? Language designed to distort or manipulate? Form over substance? Lawyers? Politics? Spin? If any of that came to mind, it would not be surprising. "Rhetoric" is commonly used in popular culture with a distinctly negative connotation.

But rhetoric started out in the fifth century BCE as the study of persuasion. The root word comes from the Greek words *rhema*, which means *that which is said* and *rhetor*, which means *one who speaks*. The English word comes from the Greek phrase *rhetorike techne* (rhetorical art) and the French noun *rhetorique*.[2] Some of the greatest philosophers of the ancient world wanted to understand what people find convincing. Put another way, they wanted to know how **persuasion** works.

> **FYI**
>
> Aristotle's *Rhetoric* addresses three kinds of speech: **political**, **judicial**, and **ceremonial**.

Aristotle, a Greek philosopher, studied three kinds of speech and is credited with having first articulated the principles of persuasion in the fourth century BCE. His book, *Rhetoric*, is still considered the greatest work on the subject.[3] The ancient Romans embraced the art of rhetoric and refined its principles. Unlike the Greeks, who were primarily interested in political speech, Roman rhetoricians like Cicero and Quintilian focused on judicial speech (legal argument).

---

1 Jennifer Fletcher, Teaching Arguments: Rhetorical Comprehension, Critique, and Response 16 (2015).

2 Edward P.J. Corbett & Robert J. Connors, Classical Rhetoric for the Modern Student 15 (4th ed. 1999).

3 *See* Aristotle, Rhetoric (c. 333 BCE), *reprinted in* The Rhetoric of Aristotle (Lane Cooper, trans., 1932), also available at http://www.perseus.tufts.edu/hopper/text.jsp?doc=Perseus:-text:1999.01.0060 (https://perma.cc/EK7U-MJ6U).

Rhetoric was taught to young men in the ancient world to prepare them for a civic life, which included participating in law courts and public debate, acting as jurors, and engaging in military service. Students typically started out learning grammar, then moved on to logic and rhetoric.[4] After mastering this "trivium," students moved on to the "quadrivium": arithmetic, astronomy, geometry, and music. Together, these seven subjects came to comprise the liberal arts.[5] This educational tradition continued in varying forms for years, until roughly the end of the nineteenth century, when rhetoric ceased to be taught as a separate subject in much of the Western world.

Despite its current absence in traditional education, rhetoric has flourished as a subject of academic interest. Contemporary scholars of rhetoric study all kinds of speech—oral and written, how speech is created, and its impact on the intended audience. James Kinneavy, a leading twentieth-century rhetorician, described it as "the whole field of the uses of language."[6] He described speech as having three components: a speaker (the encoder of a message), language (the signal that carries the message), and a receiver (the decoder of the message).[7]

Lloyd Bitzer, another well-known scholar of rhetoric, defined it as the result of a situation where language is used to bring about desired change.[8] Although rhetorical situations may be unique or recurring, each is comprised of

- an exigence,
- an audience that can help bring about change,
- and a set of constraints that limits the possibility of change.[9]

In law, for example, a person charged with a crime creates an exigence that requires a lawyer to convince a jury to acquit them. In such a situation, the constraints that limit the lawyer's ability to succeed might include unfavorable facts, legal rules, rules of evidence, and jurors' attitudes. Since lawyers tend to specialize in specific areas of law, such as tax or family law, they represent clients with comparable legal needs. In Bitzer's terms, these comparable situations prompt comparable responses. As a result, "rhetorical forms are born and a special vocabulary, grammar, and style are established."[10]

---

4 Logic was considered the art of thinking, rhetoric the art of communicating, and grammar the art of inventing and combining symbols. SISTER MIRIAM JOSEPH, THE TRIVIUM: THE LIBERAL ARTS OF LOGIC, GRAMMAR, AND RHETORIC 3 (Marguerite McGlinn ed., Paul Dry Books 2002 (1937).

5 The trivium and quadrivium became known as the liberal arts during the Middle Ages. *See liberal arts, in* OED ONLINE (June 2020), www.oxfordreference.com.

6 JAMES L. KINNEAVY, A THEORY OF DISCOURSE 3 (1971).

7 *See id.* at 19. Kinneavy explored the fields of study associated with each component of speech, known collectively as semiotics.

8 Lloyd F. Bitzer, *The Rhetorical Situation*, 1 PHILOSOPHY & RHETORIC 1, 3–4 (1968).

9 *Id.* at 6–8.

10 *Id.* at 13.

Typical rhetorical forms in law practice—the kinds of texts lawyers actually write—include legal memoranda, emails, opinion letters, contracts, and briefs. Any course in legal research and writing will familiarize you with some of these rhetorical forms and the language of the law. But that's not all. It's not enough to simply know and imitate these forms.

To become a good legal writer, you must learn how to think about the legal questions you are asked, how to gather relevant sources of law, how to develop rules of law, how to reason logically to a conclusion, how to organize your analysis, how to anticipate the needs of your intended audience, and how to sound (or, to be more precise, not sound) like a lawyer. Rhetorical theory provides us with many answers. As you will see, it helps us understand what makes legal analyses and arguments effective and why.

The rest of Part II discusses in detail the history of rhetoric (Chapter 9), why rhetoric is not taught in law school (Chapter 10), the intersection of law and rhetoric (Chapter 11), and whether rhetoric is a subset of law or the other way around (Chapter 12).

Chapter 9

A Brief History of Rhetoric

"From Rome rhetoric, in education, in public activity, and in all forms of writing, spread through the world, its influence waning only in the nineteenth century."[1]

—Brian Vickers

A. Ancient Greece and Rome (c. 466 BCE–50 CE)

The study of rhetoric began on the island of Sicily in 466 BCE following a massive legal dispute. The citizens of Syracuse had revolted against the tyrant Thrasybulus and established a democracy. Many citizens filed suit claiming title to the land stolen by Thrasybulus. There was no direct evidence to support their claims, so they had to rely on circumstantial evidence. Corax of Syracuse recognized that the citizens needed help to persuade the jury.

Inspired by the works of great orators and poets like Homer, Corax created a system of rules to help the citizens argue their cases—he and his pupil Tisias may even have written a handbook on the subject.[2] Corax's greatest contribution to rhetoric is thought to be his outline for legal argument, which remains the basic pattern for all forms of legal analysis and argument today.[3]

FYI

Corax's Outline of Legal Argument

- introduction
- statement of facts
- argument
- counterargument
- conclusion

---

1 Brian Vickers, In Defence Of Rhetoric 12 (1988).

2 *See rhetoric, Greek, in* The Oxford Classical Dictionary (Simon Hornblower, Antony Spawforth & Esther Eidinow, eds., 4th ed. 2012); George Kennedy, The Art of Persuasion in Greece 59 (1963); *see also* Daniel Fogarty, Roots For A New Rhetoric 9–10 (1959); Vickers, *supra* note 1, at 6.

3 *See Corax, of Syracuse, in* The Oxford Classical Dictionary, *supra* note 2; Corbett & Connors, *supra* ch. 8, note 2, at 490.

Around the same time, there were also philosopher-teachers, known as sophists, who traveled among the Greek city-states. "Sophos" translates into wisdom or knowledge, and a "sophist" was considered a wise man and teacher.[4]

FYI

The early Greek Sophists

- Protagoras
- Gorgias
- Hippias
- Isocrates

The sophists taught rhetoric and other subjects to the sons of wealthy families and those who could afford their services. Greek society revolved around the spoken word and direct participation in civic affairs. For that reason, sophists were thought to prepare their students to participate in politics and serve the common good.

In contrast, some philosophers like Plato criticized the sophists for their ability to argue either side of a dispute seemingly without regard to its truth or rectitude.[5] In theory, the sophists were not troubled by a jury finding inconsistent with the facts because they believed the jury defined what was true and right. In combination with some sophists' questionable ethics, calling someone a sophist changed from being a compliment to an insult.

The *Oxford English Dictionary* now defines a "sophist" as a person "engaged in the pursuit or communication of knowledge" and also as "[o]ne who makes use of fallacious arguments; a specious reasoner."[6] Due in part to the reputation of the sophists, rhetoric was criticized from the outset. Nevertheless, rhetoric grew quickly and became a required subject of study, a tool to enhance the general welfare of Greek society through political involvement, and a stepping stone to a leisurely life.

1. The Greeks

Plato (427–347 BCE) was one of the first to argue that rhetoric is inferior to philosophy because it does not produce truth. He was born in Athens and studied with Socrates. In c. 387, Plato opened his famous school, Plato's Academy, which survived for several centuries. Plato used the teaching method—dialogue or "dialectic"—he had learned from Socrates. Both believed that truth was achieved only by the exchange of ideas between scholars.

Plato dedicated his life to discovering the truth and rejecting what he considered to be the false rhetoric of his day, which he found embodied in the teachings of the sophists. Born to wealthy and influential parents, Plato was no fan of democracy. He believed the public was ignorant and lacked self-control. He attributed the corruption

---

4 Women were neither educated nor allowed to participate in public life.

5 Certain sophists may have contributed to the ultimate condemnation and death of Plato's teacher, Socrates. *See sophists*, *in* THE OXFORD CLASSICAL DICTIONARY, *supra* note 2.

6 *See sophist*, *in* OED ONLINE, *supra* ch. 8, note 5.

of Greek society to the ability of politicians and lawyers to distort the truth and dupe the unsuspecting public.

Ancient Greece and Rome

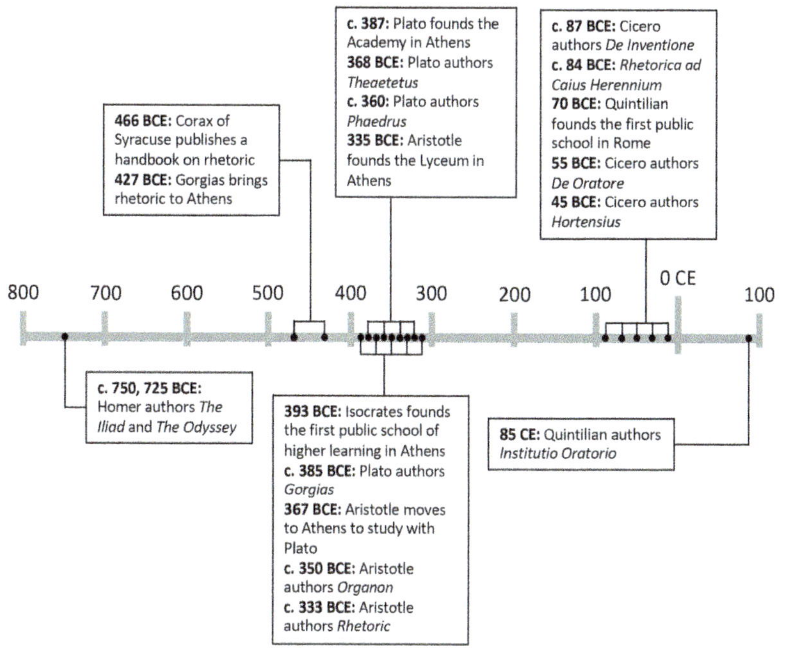

Plato's criticisms of rhetoric are well-documented in several of his dialogues.[7] In *Gorgias*, for example, Plato developed the idea that rhetoric is merely a form of flattery—like something sweet to eat—and not a subject of substance.[8] In the dialogue, Socrates asks Gorgias, a famous orator and teacher of rhetoric, to explain rhetoric, and Gorgias tells him it is the art of persuasive discourse. Socrates replies that all subjects—even arithmetic and astronomy—influence their audience through speech, implying that rhetoric is not unique in that sense.[9]

---

7 *See, e.g.*, PLATO, *Gorgias*, *Phaedrus*, and *Theaetetus*, *in* COMPLETE WORKS, (John M. Cooper & D.S. Hutchinson eds., Hackett Publ'g Co. 1997). Plato's dialogues often feature his teacher, Socrates, and address major philosophical issues such as morality, ethics, and virtue.

8 Socrates states, "You've now heard what I say oratory is. It's the counterpart in the soul to pastry baking, its counterpart in the body." PLATO, *Gorgias*, *in* COMPLETE WORKS, *id.* at 465e.

NOTE: Citations in works by Plato are to Stephanus numbers. They denote the page (number) and paragraph (letter) where the cited text appears in a famous 1578 translation by Henri Estienne, also known as Henricus Stephanus (1528–1598). The text can thus be found in any translation. Similar systems for citation are used for many classical texts.

9 *Id.* at 449d–450d.

Pressed to explain what distinguishes rhetoric as a subject in its own right, Gorgias tells Socrates that rhetoric is the speech found in law courts and concerns justice.[10] Socrates disagrees, claiming rhetoric is the false art of justice because a skilled orator can convince an audience to believe things that are not true and to act unjustly. For example, Socrates claims an orator can convince a jury to spare the life of a man whose crime might warrant the death penalty.[11] Socrates, and perhaps Plato, believed rhetoric yields only the appearance of truth or justice.[12] Given Plato's influence on Western thought, is it any wonder that modern society is predisposed to dislike lawyers?[13]

Bottom Line

Aristotle studied political, judicial, and ceremonial speech. He concluded that all forms of persuasion include arguments that appeal to logic, sympathy, and the speaker's own credibility (see Chapter 13).

Aristotle (384–322 BCE) was Plato's student. He devoted his life to studying, teaching, and writing about logic, rhetoric, philosophy, ethics, astronomy, physics, biology, politics, and psychology. Some of his most famous works include *The Organon* (c. 350 BCE) and *Rhetoric* (c. 333 BCE). *The Organon* is a collection of works that surveys the process of logical thinking and inventing argument.[14] Of interest here, it explores the nature of the syllogism, a form of deductive reasoning that proceeds from general rules to specific conclusions.[15] *Rhetoric* is a collection of lectures and teaching notes that assumes the reader is familiar with *The Organon* and examines the force and value of rhetoric, the types of rhetoric, and how best to persuade the audience while engaged in judicial, political, or ceremonial speech.

Unlike Plato, Aristotle believed that rhetoric serves a valuable function in human affairs. For example, in a lawsuit, advocates marshal and present their client's best arguments to a judge or jury. In the face of conflicting evidence and competing arguments, truth at the level of mathematical certainty does not exist. But rhetoric makes it possible for the judge or jury to determine the best truth and outcome under the circumstances. Aristotle wrote:

> [T]he art of Rhetoric has its value. It is valuable, first, because truth and justice are by nature more powerful than their opposites; . . . Thirdly, in Rhetoric, as in Dialectic, we should be able to argue on either side of a

---

10 *Id.* at 454b.

11 *Id.* at 481a–b.

12 *Id.* at 464b–465d.

13 *See supra* notes 7–12 and accompanying text.

14 1–2 ARISTOTLE, THE ORGANON (Harold P. Cooke & Hugh Tredennick eds., 1960). THE ORGANON includes Aristotle's *Categories, On Interpretation, Prior Analytics, Posterior Analytics, Topics*, and *On Sophistical Refutations.*

15 The syllogism and its comparable use in legal argument are discussed in detail in Chapter 31.

> question; not with a view to putting both sides into practice—we must not advocate evil—but in order that no aspect of the case may escape us, and that if our opponent makes unfair use of the arguments, we may be able in turn to refute them.[16]

Echoing *Gorgias*, Aristotle said rhetoric is "the counterpart of Dialectic,"[17] giving it an importance and status equal to logic. His *Rhetoric* is, in part, an attempt to theorize the art of persuasion in response to his teacher's legitimate criticisms.

2. The Romans

The Romans were heavily influenced by the Greeks, and, as is often said, they refined the Greek theory and put it into practice. Unlike the Greeks, who were interested primarily in political speech, the Romans were more interested in legal argument. Many of the great Roman orators were trained in law and rhetoric. Roman teachers of rhetoric were also different from their Greek predecessors in their practical approach to rhetoric and its benefit to society. Becoming an orator was a great achievement; it combined a mastery of philosophy, rhetoric, and the law with civic virtue.

Marcus Tullius Cicero (106–43 BCE) was considered the greatest Roman orator of the Republic. He began his career in law and was later elected to each major public office. He was a prolific writer of books, essays, poetry, and letters on philosophy, politics, rhetoric, and more. Roughly sixty of his courtroom and political speeches survive today.

As an orator, Cicero had a grand, eloquent style that served for hundreds of years as a model for students of rhetoric.[18] As late as the nineteenth century, American lawyers and legislators continued to emulate his style.

> **FYI**
>
> Cicero (pronounced *KIH-keh-roh*) means "chickpea" in Latin. Plutarch said he was named after an ancestor who had a "faint dent in the end of his nose like the cleft of a chick-pea."
>
> VII Plutarch, *The Life of Cicero, in Lives* 83, at ¶ 1:4 (Loeb Classical Library 1919) (c. 75 CE), https://penelope.uchicago.edu/Thayer/E/Roman/Texts/Plutarch/Lives/Cicero*.html (https://perma.cc/XHC9-ESSW).

---

16 ARISTOTLE, RHETORIC, *supra* ch. 8, note 3, at I.1, 1355a.

17 *Id.* at 1354a.

18 One of Cicero's most famous cases was the prosecution of Lucius Sirgius Catiline, a senator and political rival Cicero defeated in a consul election in 63 BCE. Cataline had conspired to assassinate several elected officials, including Cicero. His speech in that case began:

> When, O Catiline, do you mean to cease abusing our patience? How long is that madness of yours still to mock us? When is there to be an end of that unbridled audacity of yours, swaggering about as it does now?

M. TULLIUS CICERO, *Against Catiline, in* THE ORATIONS OF MARCUS TULLIUS CICERO (C.D. Yonge, trans. 1856) (c. 63 BCE). To read more of Cicero's speech, see http://data.perseus.org/citations/urn:cts:latinLit:phi0474.phi013.perseus-eng1:1.1 (https://perma.cc/D5MA-DDBH).

As the elegance of his speeches suggests, Cicero believed rhetoric could be both persuasive and pleasing. He also defended rhetoric, which he called eloquence, against criticisms such as Plato's:

> I find that many cities have been founded, that the flames of a multitude of wars have been extinguished, and that the strongest alliances and most sacred friendships have been formed not only by the use of reason but also more easily by the help of eloquence. . . . I have been led by reason itself to hold this opinion . . . that wisdom without eloquence does too little for the good of states, but that eloquence without wisdom is generally highly disadvantageous and is never helpful.[19]

His wrote several books on rhetoric, including *De Inventione*, *De Oratore*, and *Orator*.[20] In Cicero's opinion, orators were the most qualified to lead because they could guide both the Senate and the public. Cicero's major contribution to rhetoric is considered his status theory: the "question . . . from which the whole case arises."[21] As you will learn, lawyers today think of legal issues in similar terms.

> **FYI**
>
> **Cicero's types of issues in a legal dispute:**
>
> - Questions of fact
> - Questions of definition
> - Questions of quality
> - Questions of procedure

Questions of fact involve the details—who, what, when, where, why, and how—of a given dispute. Disputed facts are usually resolved by a jury who hears and observes all the evidence. Questions of law, on the other hand, involve questions of definition (e.g., do these facts constitute theft?) and quality (e.g., was the defendant's action justified?). These questions are usually reserved for the judge, who instructs the jury on the law and explains how to apply it to the facts.[22] Questions of procedure involve the rules adopted by courts to provide for fair and efficient processes (e.g., was this case filed within the appropriate time limit?).[23]

---

19 2 CICERO, DE INVENTIONE III.1.1 (H.M. Hubbell trans., 1968) (c. 87 BCE), available at https://archive.org/details/in.ernet.dli.2015.189092 (https://perma.cc/9J4H-ETFA). Cites to Cicero's works are to the volume or "book" number, chapter, and paragraph.

NOTE: Throughout this book, if the link to the original source does not work, use the permalink in parentheses and click on "view the live page." Both cites have been included to display the original source.

20 *Id.*; 3–4 CICERO, DE ORATORE, (E.W. Sutton trans., 1967) (c. 55 BCE); available at https://archive.org/details/cicerodeoratore01ciceuoft/page/n5/mode/2up (https://perma.cc/D9T7-LEUD); 5 CICERO, ORATOR (H.M. Hubbell trans., 1971) (c. 46 BCE), available at https://archive.org/details/orator00aubegoog (https://perma.cc/4VQ2-XRVL). Another popular handbook on rhetoric, RHETORICA AD CAIUS HERENNIUM (c. 84 BCE), available at https://archive.org/stream/adcherenniumdera00capluoft?ref=ol#page/n15/mode/2up (https://perma.cc/92S6-RNWN) was written during Cicero's time and believed to be his work until the seventeenth century. Most scholars now think the author is unknown. DE INVENTIONE and RHETORICA were the two most popular books on rhetoric in the ancient world.

21 2 CICERO, DE INVENTIONE, *supra* note 19, I.8.10.

22 *See infra* ch. 20.A, at 130.

23 *See* CICERO, DE INVENTIONE, *supra* note 19, at I.8.10–12.

To be effective, an orator had to be well educated. For this reason, Cicero conceived of rhetoric as the study of a number of subjects that would later be known as the liberal arts.[24] In De Oratore (c. 55 CE), a dialogue between Crassus, a leading politician, and Antonius, a well-known public official, Crassus states that an orator must be familiar with all important subjects and arts:

> For it is from knowledge that oratory must derive its beauty and fullness, and unless there is such knowledge, well-grasped and comprehended by the speaker, there must be something empty and almost childish in the utterance.[25]

Armed with such knowledge, one could become a great orator and citizen.

Marcus Fabius Quintilianus (Quintilian) (35–95 CE) practiced law and was a teacher of rhetoric. Though born more than one hundred years after Cicero died, Quintilian was heavily influenced by his work. At the age of fifty, Quintilian wrote *Institutio Oratorio*, a twelve-volume work on studying rhetoric throughout one's life. He wrote more than any other Roman about courtroom technique, and *Oratorio* is a veritable encyclopedia of the Roman legal system.[26]

In *Book Twelve*,[27] Quintilian developed the concept of the perfect orator as a "good man, skilled in speaking."[28] Embedded in that concept was a broader view of *ethos*: the need for the speaker's character, not just his speech, to appeal to the audience. Unlike Aristotle and Cicero, Quintilian thought of *ethos* as more than the speaker's appeal at the time the speech was delivered. According to Quintilian, only a good man—free from vice, a lover of wisdom, a sincere believer in his cause, and a servant of the people—could appeal to *ethos*.[29]

The fact that orators must be able to argue both sides of the same question did not detract from their goodness. "After all," Quintilian said, "the Academics argue both sides of a question, but live according to one side only."[30] As long as an orator believed in his cause, the audience would believe in him. An orator might even "cheat the judge of the truth" where necessary. Suppose "a good general, someone without whom the state cannot defeat its enemies, is labouring under a manifestly true charge: will not the common good call our orator to his side?"[31]

---

24 *See supra* ch. 8, note 5, and accompanying text.

25 CICERO, DE ORATORE, *supra* note 20, at I.6.20.

26 VICKERS, *supra* note 1, at 38.

27 *See* QUINTILIAN, INSTITUTIO ORATORIO (Donald A. Russell trans. & ed., 2001), *also at* http://www.perseus.tufts.edu/hopper/text?doc=Perseus%3Atext%3A2007.01.0069%3Abook%3D12 (https://perma.cc/YT44-EE54). Citations to this work are to book, chapter, and paragraph.

28 *Id.* at XII.1.1.

29 *Id.*at ¶¶ 3–10.

30 *Id.* ¶ 35.

31 *Id.* ¶ 43.

B. The Second Sophists and early Christianity (c. 50–400 CE)

As the Roman Empire replaced the Republic,[32] the need to train orators to participate in civic life declined. The Roman government had become an autocracy, and citizens were no longer free to speak their minds. Only trained lawyers were permitted to argue in the courtroom, further diminishing the need to train legal advocates.[33] And much of the Roman law in this period developed as edicts from the Emperor(s).

The Second Sophists (c. 60–230 CE) were orators and teachers of rhetoric with a renewed interest in the early Greek sophists like Gorgias.[34] Some were career speechmakers, entertaining Roman audiences on political and cultural matters while demonstrating their rhetorical prowess. They even helped stabilize Rome, which was defending itself against attacks from the outside and within (i.e., the growth of Christianity).[35] Despite this renewed interest, rhetoric could no longer play the vital role it once did in Roman politics.

Despite the persecution of early Christians (c. 150–400 CE), Christianity grew steadily in Rome. In 313 CE, once the Roman Empire lost its ability to slow its growth, Emperor Constantine issued an edict proclaiming that Christianity would be tolerated. Many pagan temples were turned into churches, and the Church gained a stronghold in civic affairs.

Although the "Latin Fathers of the Church" were trained in classical rhetoric,[36] they were conflicted about its pagan roots. That conflict led to a new kind of rhetoric called preaching. Two popular but very different kinds of preaching developed: homilies and sermons. Homilies were plain, unadorned teachings used to reinforce Christian beliefs as much as to educate. Sermons, on the other hand, were ornate speeches akin to those of the Second Sophists.[37]

Then, in the fourth century, **St. Augustine of Hippo** (354–430 CE) successfully argued that rhetoric could be used to persuade people to lead a holy life. Augustine's conversion to Christianity had convinced him that rhetoric could be used to enhance

---

32 Julius Caesar was named dictator for life in 46 BCE; the first emperor, Augustus Caesar, who ruled from 31 BCE to 14 CE, was his great-nephew. *See Augustus, Caesar* and *Caesar (Gaius) Julius, in* BRITANNICA CONCISE ENCYCLOPEDIA 131, 309 (2006).

33 JAMES J. MURPHY & RICHARD A. KATULA, A SYNOPTIC HISTORY OF CLASSICAL RHETORIC 230–31 (3d ed. 2003).

34 GEORGE A. KENNEDY, CLASSICAL RHETORIC & ITS CHRISTIAN & SECULAR TRADITION FROM ANCIENT TO MODERN TIMES 47 (2d ed. 1999).

35 *Id.* at 48.

36 The *Latin Fathers* were influential theologians and writers of the early Roman Church. KENNEDY, *supra* note 34, at 167.

37 *See* JAMES L. GOLDEN, GOODWIN F. BERQUIST, WILLIAM E. COLEMAN & J. MICHAEL SPROULE, THE RHETORIC OF WESTERN THOUGHT: FROM THE MEDITERRANEAN WORLD TO THE GLOBAL SETTING 99–100, 103 (9th ed. 2009).

the word of God.[38] In 396 CE, Augustine began writing a four-volume treatise on preaching that was heavily influenced by Cicero. Although Augustine believed truth was derived from the Bible, he concluded that classical rhetoric was necessary to "sway the mind" and "subdue the will."[39]

By 410 CE, the Visigoths—nomads from Germany—had invaded Rome. Various northern cultures invaded Italy repeatedly for the next forty-five years. As the western part of the Roman Empire fell, its culture crumbled. Many of the invading kings in the western part wanted to learn Latin, but a working knowledge of Greek was lost. In the eastern part of the Empire, much of Roman culture survived. Spoken Greek survived in Byzantium until 1453 CE, when the Turkish Ottomans conquered it. Until that time, rhetoric continued to be useful both in government and church-related matters. Despite the existence of a senate and law courts, ceremonial rhetoric was the predominant form of rhetoric. It was used to strengthen loyalty to the government and the Christian Church.[40]

Early Christianity and the Early Middle Ages

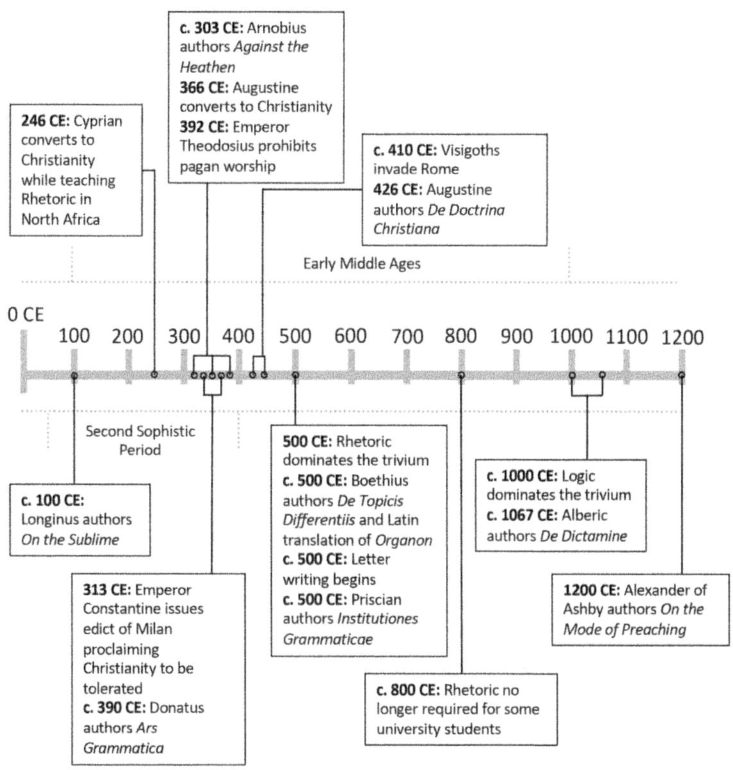

38 *See id.* at 103–05; SAINT AUGUSTINE, CONFESSIONS (Henry Chadwick trans., 1998).

39 A SELECT LIBRARY OF THE NICENE AND POST-NICENE FATHERS OF THE CHRISTIAN CHURCH: ST. AUGUSTINE'S CITY OF GOD AND CHRISTIAN DOCTRINE 584 (Phillip Schaff, ed. 1956).

40 KENNEDY, *supra* note 34, at 193–95.

C. The Middle Ages (c. 500–1400 CE)

After the fall of the Roman Empire, rhetoric was used primarily to spread Christianity. As people turned to Christian teachings to answer questions about politics and morality, the word of God became the only credible source of truth.

FYI

The parts of a thematic sermon:

- an opening prayer
- a statement of theme(s)
- the development of each theme and sub-theme
- conclusion

Scholars of rhetoric shifted their attention from content to expression, ultimately focusing on matters of style, literary composition, and the management of day-to-day affairs. Although Augustine had pushed to develop a rhetorical theory of preaching, the early Christians believed the message of Christ would speak for itself. According to Bitzer (see p. 38), a rhetorical form of preaching—the "thematic" sermon—did not appear until 1200 CE.[41] It is strikingly similar to Corax's outline of legal argument (see p. 41).

As populations grew and moved out from urban centers, writing became the primary mode of communication. Medieval scholars studied distinct areas of interest, including **logic**, **grammar**, and **letter writing**. Logic soon dominated the trivium (logic, rhetoric, and grammar), in part, because Aristotle's *Rhetoric* would not be translated into Latin until 1270 CE.[42] Aristotle's essays on logic in *The Organon* (translated into Latin by Boethius in the early 500s)[43] became popular, and scholars like Cassiodorus (c. 490–585 CE)[44] devoted more space to logic than rhetoric in their catalogs of classical works.[45] By the ninth and tenth centuries, some university students were no longer required to take a course in rhetoric.

Medieval scholars also explored parts of speech (e.g., nouns, verbs, and adjectives), sentence structure, and figures of speech (e.g., metaphor, simile, and alliteration).[46] After 1200 CE, the study of grammar expanded to include what we now

---

41 *See* JAMES J. MURPHY, RHETORIC IN THE MIDDLE AGES: A HISTORY OF RHETORICAL THEORY FROM SAINT AUGUSTINE TO THE RENAISSANCE 317–25 (2001) [hereinafter RHETORIC IN THE MIDDLE AGES].

42 Aristotle's RHETORIC had been lost. It came back to the West via Al-Farabi, a ninth century Arabic scholar. Hermannus Allemanus (Herman the German) translated Al-Farabi's commentary on Aristotle into Latin in 1240. Two Latin translations of RHETORIC were then made from the original: the first may have been by Bartholomew of Messina before 1250 CE. William of Moerbeke wrote the second translation in 1270 CE. KENNEDY, *supra* note 34, at 218–19.

43 *See supra* note 14.

44 Cassiodorus was a historian, statesman, and monk. He founded a monastery in Southern Italy to perpetuate the culture of Rome, collecting Pagan and Christian manuscripts for the monks to copy. *See Cassiodorus*, *in* BRITANNICA CONCISE ENCYCLOPEDIA, *supra* note 32, at 347.

45 MURPHY, RHETORIC IN THE MIDDLE AGES, *supra* note 41, at 64, 66.

46 *Id.* at 138–40.

think of as linguistics, literary criticism, and composition. Boethius (c. 480–524 CE), a historian, translated Greek works on logic and mathematics into Latin.[47] He was also one of many grammarians interested in using logic to explain the structure of language.[48]

In the ancient world, messages were communicated orally. By the Middle Ages, messages were being written.[49] As the medieval feudal system developed and populations spread out from the cities, secular and church offices hired letter writers to handle important correspondence. At first, form letters were drafted to cover typical situations. They were similar to the forms that lawyers use today as models for simple wills, contracts, and deeds.[50]

By the eleventh century, forms could no longer address the growing need for other kinds of communication. Around 1087 CE, Alberic, an Italian monk, used Cicero's work to develop an approach for letter writing;[51] he added a greeting to acknowledge the purpose of the letter and the social relationship between the writer and the recipient.[52]

FYI

Alberic's parts of a letter:

- greeting
- introduction
- narration of facts
- argument (or body)
- conclusion

D. The Renaissance (c. 1400–1600 CE)

In the early fifteenth century, an explosion of creativity in both the arts and sciences occurred in Europe that distinguished it from the "dark" Middle Ages. The Renaissance, as it is often called, signaled a return to the subjects of antiquity. Spurred on by classical scholars, writing, painting, sculpting, architecture, science, and rhetoric experienced a rebirth. As Aristotle's *Rhetoric* and the works of Cicero and Quintilian were re-discovered,[53] Europeans renewed their interest in these ancient texts.[54] As

47 *Boethius Anicius Manlius Severinus*, *in* BRITANNICA CONCISE ENCYCLOPEDIA, *supra* note 32, at 240–41.

48 MURPHY, RHETORIC IN THE MIDDLE AGES, *supra* note 41, at 152–53.

49 *Id.* at 194–95.

50 *See, e.g.*, AMERICAN JURISPRUDENCE LEGAL FORMS 2D; WEST'S LEGAL FORMS.

51 MURPHY, RHETORIC IN THE MIDDLE AGES, *supra* note 41, at 205.

52 LES PERELMAN, *The Medieval Art of Letter Writing: Rhetoric as Institutional Expression*, *in* TEXTUAL DYNAMICS OF THE PROFESSIONS: HISTORICAL AND CONTEMPORARY STUDIES OF WRITING IN PROFESSIONAL COMMUNITIES 103 (Charles Bazerman and James Paradis, eds., 1991).

53 In 1416, the secretary to Pope John XXIII discovered a complete copy of Quintilian's INSTITUTIO ORATORIO in the dungeon of a monastery in Switzerland. Quintilian had not been widely read with any real interest for nearly 600 years. In 1422, copies of Cicero's DE INVENTIONE, BRUTUS, ORATOR, and DE ORATORE, as well as RHETORICA AD HERENNIUM were found in a cathedral in Italy. The invention of the printing press in 1436 soon made it possible to reproduce and distribute these works throughout Europe.

54 *See* KENNEDY, *supra* note 34, at 227.

Renaissance writers sought to emulate Aristotle, Cicero, and Quintilian, judicial and other forms of rhetoric improved. For a relatively brief period—about two hundred years—the study and practice of rhetoric (by then referred to as eloquence) were as valued as they had been by the Second Sophists.

The High Middle Ages and the Renaissance

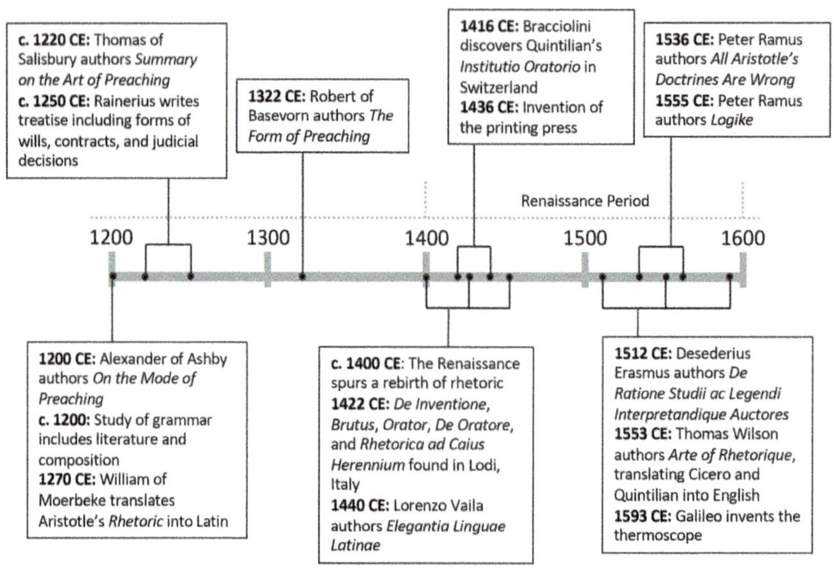

Lorenzo Valla (1407–1457 CE), an Italian humanist,[55] was opposed to the "scholasticism" of medieval universities that combined Aristotelian logic—which now dominated the trivium—with the doctrine of the Catholic church.[56] Although rhetoric was viewed primarily as a subset of logic, Valla argued that logic was a subset of rhetoric: the function of logic is to teach, but the duties of an orator are to teach, please, and persuade.[57] Valla also defended the use of eloquence against criticisms carried over from the early Christian Church and the Middle Ages:

> One should not condemn the language of the pagans, nor grammar, nor rhetoric, nor dialectic, nor any of the other arts—note that the Apostles

---

55 The humanists were scholars interested in subjects relating to human culture as opposed to science. "The humanities" refers to academic subjects such as history, literature, ancient and modern languages, law, philosophy, art, and music. *See the humanities*, *in* OED ONLINE, *supra* ch. 8, note 5. *But see* the study of law as a science in legal education, *infra* ch. 10.

56 Scholasticism dominated medieval university education in Europe and was criticized for using reason as a basis for faith and for ignoring empirical methods of understanding the world. *See generally* JOSEPH RICKABY, S.J., SCHOLASTICISM (1908).

57 *See* KENNEDY, *supra* note 34, at 242.

> wrote in the Greek language—but rather, only dogmas, religions, and false opinions concerning the performance of virtuous actions by means of which we are supposed to ascend to heaven.[58]

In 1512 CE, **Desederius Erasmus** (1466–1536 CE), a classical scholar and Christian priest, wrote two textbooks on rhetoric that set the standard for rhetorical studies in English grammar schools.[59] Then, in 1553, Thomas Wilson (1525–1581 CE), an English humanist, wrote *The Arte of Rhetorique*, translating much of the rhetoric of Cicero and Quintilian into English for the first time. His goals were to teach classical rhetoric and impart Christian values.

Peter Ramus (1515–1572 CE), a French humanist and logician, had a dramatic and negative impact on rhetoric as its own discipline. Unlike the Italian humanists, he was not interested in revitalizing rhetoric for judicial and political speech.[60] Instead, he was interested in using rhetoric to teach students to write in a clear and simple style.

Like Plato, Ramus believed that knowledge was the sole product of logic or reason. Although Aristotle had taught rhetoric as a counterpart to logic (including invention arrangement, style, memory, and delivery),[61] Ramus thought the process of creating argument was different from the expression of argument; essentially, rhetoric expressed what logic discovered. For that reason, he believed rhetoric should be taught only as the canons of style and delivery.[62]

"Ramism" heavily influenced the study of rhetoric in England, France, and Spain. The English Puritans brought Ramism to America, because it advocated a plain style consistent with their religious beliefs; thereafter, Harvard College modeled its curriculum on it. Ramus' influence can still be seen today. Logic is usually taught today as part of philosophy or math. Style and delivery have been divided among a number of subjects, including Composition, Communication, English, and Speech (see Chapter 10).

---

58 WAYNE A. REBHORN, RENAISSANCE DEBATES ON RHETORIC 40 (2000).

59 *See* DE RATIONE STUDII AC LEGENDI INTERPRETANDIQUE AUCTORES (ON THE METHOD OF STUDY) (1513) & DE DUPLICI COPIA VERBORUM AC RERUM (COPIA: FOUNDATIONS OF THE ABUNDANT STYLE) (1528), in 24 COLLECTED WORKS OF ERASMUS (Craig R. Thompson, ed. 1978). DE RATIONE STUDII is also at https://college.holycross.edu/faculty/wziobro/ClassicalAmerica/ErasmusdeRatione-HP.html (https://perma.cc/BH2R-K7GR).

60 *See* KENNEDY, *supra* note 34, at 251.

61 *See infra* ch. 13.

62 *See* PETER RAMUS, LOGIKE 17 (1574).

E. The Seventeenth and Eighteenth Centuries (c. 1600–1800 CE)

Art and science continued to flourish during this period. Shakespeare's great tragedies—*Hamlet*, *Macbeth*, and *Othello*—were first performed in England between 1600 and 1613 CE, while Galileo built the first telescope to observe the solar system from Italy.

Most important to rhetoric was the emergence of modern science. A group of philosophers—known as epistemologists—believed that logic or reason could not lead to the discovery of knowledge. They worked to develop a new method—what we now think of as the scientific method—for learning based on sensory perceptions and personal experience. Many criticized rhetoric, as Plato did, because it could not produce knowledge with any level of certainty. Others, like Francis Bacon and Giambattista Vico, continued to believe that rhetoric serves an important purpose in society.

FYI

Epistemology is the study of knowledge: how to distinguish justified belief from opinion.

As this new science began to alter views on the teachings of the ancient philosophers, a group of artists and architects in Western Europe struggled to preserve interest in the classics. By the mid-eighteenth century, rhetoric had been permanently reduced to the study of style and delivery. Some scholars studied legal argument as a way to defend Christianity, while others started the Belle Lettres Movement, which sought to define taste, beauty, and the sublime in poetry, prose, oratory, history, and philosophy. By studying all types of literature, the belletristic scholars expanded rhetoric to include the interpretation of texts or literary criticism.

1. The early epistemologists

The early epistemologists struggled to understand what knowledge is and how to define it. Most of them were **empiricists**, like Francis Bacon, who believed that knowledge is acquired primarily through collecting and interpreting data. Some were **rationalists**, like Rene Descartes, who believed that reason was the main source of knowledge.

FYI

The **empiricists** include:

- Francis Bacon
- Giambattista Vico
- Thomas Hobbes
- John Locke
- David Hume

The **rationalists** include:

- Rene Descartes
- Baruch Spinoza
- Gottfried Leibniz

Francis Bacon (1561–1626 CE), an Englishman, lawyer, and politician, was the first empiricist to reject logic as the source of knowledge. In 1605, he formed a plan, his so-called "Great Instauration," to develop a new philosophy of knowledge acquisition in all aspects of life. Bacon thought that scientists relied too much on the logic of ancient philosophers:

> [M]en have withdrawn themselves too much from the contemplation of nature and the observations of experience, and have tumbled up and down in their own reason and conceits.[63]

Although he did not complete this ambitious plan, he published the first of his intended works, *The New Organon*, in 1620 CE. Its title signaled his departure from Aristotelian philosophy,[64] and in it, he detailed his method for a new kind of learning.

Bacon argued that logic cannot produce new knowledge; it can only demonstrate the relationship between things already known. Formal logic consists of

> propositions, propositions consist of words, and words are counters for notions. Hence if the notions themselves . . . are confused and abstracted from things without care, there is nothing sound in what is built on them.[65]

Instead, Bacon argued that knowledge is acquired by **induction**, a systematic method that leads from particular observations to more general conclusions about the nature of things. But because human perception is flawed,[66] Bacon believed these conclusions had to be tested.

Bacon threatened established beliefs about rhetoric as well. Having practiced law, he knew the value of rhetorical skill, particularly in cases where reason alone was not persuasive. Bacon said, "The duty and office of Rhetoric is to apply Reason to Imagination for the better moving of the will."[67]

Bacon thought argument is derived from the memory of knowledge already acquired, including what he called "commonplaces": notions of what is good and evil; typical arguments for and against a particular position; stock phrases; and pithy statements. Because knowledge comes, in part, from our experience of the world,

---

63 FRANCIS BACON, *Book 1 of the Advancement and Proficiency of Learning*, *in* SELECTED WRITINGS OF FRANCIS BACON 191 (Hugh C. Dick ed., 1955) [hereinafter SELECTED WRITINGS], also available online, in SIR FRANCIS BACON, THE ADVANCEMENT OF LEARNING (Joseph Devey, ed. 2015) (1901), at https://oll.libertyfund.org/titles/bacon-the-advancement-of-learning (https://perma.cc/8VXL-QPCH).

64 *See supra* note 14.

65 FRANCIS BACON, *Book 1 of the New Organon, Aphorisms* XII and XIV, *in* SELECTED WRITINGS, *supra* note 63, at 463–64.

66 Bacon described four aspects of faulty perception as four idols: the idol of the tribe (the inherent limitations of man, such as excessive emotion and inadequate sensory perception), the idol of the cave (the negative impact that personality and experience have on one's ability to interpret perception), the idol of the marketplace (the inadequacy of language among people), and the idol of the theater (the perpetuation of faulty thinking from generation to generation). *See id.* at 469–81.

67 BACON, SELECTED WRITINGS, *supra* note 63, at 309.

Bacon even recommended that one keep a journal of "commonplaces" observed in daily life.[68]

> **FYI**
>
> Descartes' famous statement, "I think, therefore I am," was originally written in French, not Latin:
>
> *"Je pense, donc je suis."*

Rene Descartes (1596–1650 CE), a French philosopher, mathematician, and physicist, also had a law degree, though he did not practice law. Like Bacon, Descartes rejected logic as the source of new knowledge because its "precepts are of avail rather in the communication of what we already know . . . than in the investigation of the unknown."[69] But because Descartes also believed our senses deceive us,[70] he set out to develop a method for distinguishing "the true from the false, in order that [he] might be able clearly to discriminate the right path in life, and proceed in it with confidence."[71]

In 1635 CE, he published *Discourse on Method*, which laid out his method for acquiring knowledge: 1) accept as true only those propositions that are absolutely free from doubt, 2) divide each inquiry into as many parts as possible, 3) move from simple to complex concepts, and 4) be thorough.[72] Although he could doubt all that his mind perceived, Descartes' method led him first to the realization that the one thing he could not doubt was his own existence: "I think, therefore I am."[73]
This led him to believe that the nature of reality is derived from innate ideas, not the external senses, and his views on the source of knowledge became known as rationalism.

Although Descartes said he "esteemed Eloquence highly," he viewed it, like poetry, more of a gift than a real subject of study.[74] He observed,

> Those in whom the faculty of Reason is predominant and who most skillfully dispose their thoughts with a view to render them clear and intelligible, are always the best able to persuade others of the truth of what they lay down, though they . . . be wholly ignorant of the rules of Rhetoric.[75]

---

68 GOLDEN, ET AL., *supra* note 37, at 149.

69 RENE DESCARTES, DISCOURSE ON METHOD, *in* DISCOURSE ON METHOD AND THE MEDITATIONS pt. II, at 121 (John Veitch trans., 1901) (1637 CE) [hereinafter DISCOURSE ON METHOD], also available online at https://oll.libertyfund.org/titles/descartes-the-method-meditations-and-philosophy-of-descartes (https://perma.cc/U7BW-SRAY).

70 *See, e.g.*, DESCARTES, DISCOURSE ON METHOD, *supra* note 69, pt. IV, at 129.

71 *Id.* pt. I, at 118.

72 *Id.* pt. II, at 122.

73 *Id.* pt. IV, at 129 (translated as "I think, hence I am"); RENE DESCARTES, PRINCIPLES OF PHILOSOPHY, *in* DISCOURSE ON METHOD AND THE MEDITATIONS, *supra*, note 69, pt. VII, at 214 (translated as "I think, therefore I am").

74 DESCARTES, DISCOURSE ON METHOD, *supra* note 69, pt. I, at 116.

75 *Id.*

French philosophers Arnaud and Nicole later expanded on Descartes' views, focusing on the pursuit of truth to a mathematical certainty and eschewing old-fashioned logic, appeals to emotion, and even Bacon's commonplaces. By declaring that the function of rhetoric is to communicate knowledge acquired by philosophers, Arnaud and Nicole further cemented the division between logic and rhetoric.[76]

The Seventeenth, Eighteenth, and Early Nineteenth Centuries

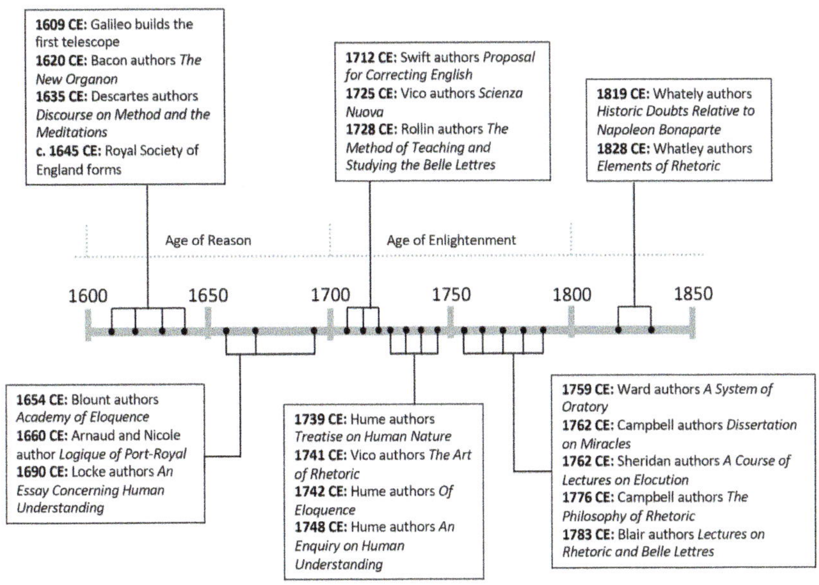

Giambattista Vico (1668–1744 CE), a professor of Rhetoric at the University of Naples, stands in sharp contrast to Descartes. Although Vico shared Descartes' interest in epistemology, he disagreed with Descartes about the importance of knowledge to a mathematical certainty. Vico argued that the overemphasis on logic in education stifled students' imagination by ignoring equally important yet non-quantifiable subjects such as rhetoric, history, and poetry.[77] "Since the invention of arguments is by nature prior to the judgment of their validity," he believed that students should learn rhetoric before logic.[78] He argued that rhetoric is the key to understanding past cultures, including their ideas, customs, and modes of communication.[79] He also

---

76 ANTOINE ARNAUD AND PIERRE NICOLE, LOGIC, OR THE ART OF THINKING 16, 181–82 (Jill Vance Buroker ed., 1996); *see* Ramus, *supra* note 62.

77 *See* GIAMBATTISTA VICO, ON THE STUDY METHODS OF OUR TIME 12–15 (Elio Gianturco, ed., Cornell Univ. Press 1990).

78 *See id.* at 14; KENNEDY, *supra* note 34, at 272.

79 THE NEW SCIENCE OF GIAMBATTISTA VICO (SCIENZA NUOVA) 65, 75–76 (Thomas Goddard Bergin & Max Harold Fisch trans., 3d ed. 1984).

argued that all cultures start with a form of mythology and develop an advanced philosophical system.[80]

2. The eighteenth-century epistemologists

By the eighteenth century, several leading epistemologists were also ordained ministers who sought to use rhetoric to prove the existence of God and defend the beliefs of the Christian church. But the growing interest in secular knowledge weakened Christianity's hold. Bacon's empiricism grew most in England, while Descartes' rationalism took hold in Western Europe.

David Hume (1711–1776 CE) was a Scottish philosopher with a skeptical point of view. Although heavily influenced by Descartes, Hume was an empiricist. He questioned both Descartes' reliance on reason and his belief in the existence of innate ideas. Hume believed that knowledge was acquired through experience and observation. He also doubted the reliability of human perception, particularly with regard to religion.[81]

These doubts led him to question the certainty of inductive reasoning. For example, if one billiard ball is moving toward another, and you want to predict what the balls will do, there is no way to prove your prediction is right. Although each time you observe the balls hit you begin to form an idea of what will happen the next time, you can never be certain. Although we assume there is a connection between an observed pattern of behavior and future behavior, that connection cannot be proved with certainty.[82]

George Campbell (1719–1796 CE) was a Scottish minister. He started his career as a law student in Edinburgh but quickly became interested in theology and philosophy. He became a professor of divinity at Marischal College in Aberdeen and used his observations of human nature to explain argument, poetry, and preaching. In doing so, he articulated general principles of rhetoric that could be used to teach it.

Campbell's *The Philosophy of Rhetoric*,[83] combined the best theories of the classical and eighteenth-century philosophers, rhetoricians, and scientists. According to Campbell, a speaker must engage the audience's imagination in order to stir its passions.[84] Although Campbell's theory can be applied to all forms of rhetoric, he

---

80 *See id.* at 104–06.

81 Hume was particularly skeptical about Christians' claims of having witnessed miracles: "[N]o testimony is sufficient to establish a miracle, unless the testimony be of such a kind, that its falsehood would be more miraculous, than the fact, which it endeavors to establish." DAVID HUME, AN ENQUIRY CONCERNING HUMAN UNDERSTANDING § 4, pt. 1, ¶ 25, p. 29 (Tom L. Beauchamp ed., 2000).

82 *Id.* at § 4, pt. 1, ¶ 25, p. 29.

83 GEORGE CAMPBELL, PHILOSOPHY OF RHETORIC (Charles Ewer ed., 1823), also at https://books.google.ht/books?id=CGqsjgEACAAJ&printsec=frontcover&hl=fr&source=gbs_ge_summary_r&cad=0#v=onepage&q&f=false (https://perma.cc/72CC-SRG8).

84 *Id.* at 95–97, 99–103.

intended it to prepare Christians to defend their beliefs against attacks, such as Hume's attack on miracles.

Campbell said that rhetoric had one of four goals: to enlighten understanding, to please the imagination, to move the passions, or to influence the will.[85] According to Campbell, truth could only be achieved through logic, but rhetoric was needed to spark the imagination and passions and motivate the will:

> If the orator would prove successful, it is necessary that he engage in his service all these different powers of the mind, the imagination, the memory, and the passions. These are not the supplanters of reason, or even rivals in her sway; they are her handmaids, by whose ministry she is enabled to usher truth into the heart, and procure it there a favourable reception.[86]

In Campbell's view, the best way to persuade was to combine strong appeals to reason with powerful appeals to emotion.

With respect to being credible, Campbell recognized that the audience must trust the speaker, a particular problem for lawyers because the audience knows "that he must defend his client, and argue on the side on which he is retained."[87] Campbell also observed that lawyers' explanations of the law could be so complicated that they "hath come to be distinguished by the name *chicane*, a species of reasoning too abstruse to command attention of any continuance even from the studious, and, consequently, not very favourable to the powers of rhetoric."[88] Thus, he advised speakers to make their arguments clear, lively, memorable, and stirring.

Richard Whately (1787–1863) was also an ordained minister. Like Campbell, he studied law and theology and explored rhetoric's ability to defend Christianity. In 1819, he published *Historic Doubts Relative to Napoleon Bonaparte*, a satire intended to show that Hume's skeptical response to the testimony of miracles could be used to doubt even the existence of Napoleon, who was known to be alive and living on the Italian isle of Elba.

Whately's *Elements of Rhetoric*,[89] was the precursor to modern argumentation theory, and its core concepts are still relevant today. Campbell had argued that logic was a separate "art of thinking and reasoning,"[90] but Whately disagreed: "The *finding*

---

85 *Id.* at 1.

86 *Id.* at 94.

87 *Id.* at 123.

88 *Id.* at 127. Chicane comes from French and means "to quibble"; Chaucer, who also studied law, associated the legal profession with trickery as early as the fourteenth century. *See supra* ch. 1, note 1.

89 RICHARD WHATELY, ELEMENTS OF RHETORIC (Douglas Ehninger, ed. 1963) (1828) also available online at https://archive.org/details/elementsofrheto00what (https://perma.cc/JT3C-ABKG).

90 CAMPBELL, *supra* note 83, at 56.

of suitable arguments to prove a given point, and the skilful *arrangement* of them, may be considered as the immediate and proper province of Rhetoric, and that alone."[91]

Whately is best known for his work on presumptions and burdens of proof. He defined a presumption as "such a *pre-occupation* of the ground, as implies that it must stand good till some sufficient reason is adduced against it; in short, that the *Burden of proof* lies on the side of him who would dispute it."[92] Stated in modern terms, a presumption is the advantage given by the factfinder to an alleged fact. If there is a presumption in favor of that fact, then the burden usually shifts to the opposing party to disprove it.

3. The Neo-Classicists

Writers like Jonathan Swift, Alexander Pope, John Lawson, John Ward, and John Dryden worried that empirical science would replace literary principles grounded in the classics. They advocated studying and imitating the works of Aristotle, Cicero, and Quintilian. Their books on rhetoric reiterated the principles of classical rhetoric in English, and their main interest was in the canon of style. The intensity of the struggle between the neoclassicists and the epistemologists is captured by Jonathan Swift in a wonderful story, *The Battle of the Books*.[93] In it, ancient and modern philosophers, each of whom is represented by a book in the stacks of a London library, engage in a battle that leaves Bacon wounded and Descartes dead.

4. The Belletristic Scholars

In the middle of the eighteenth century, the *Belle Lettres Movement* emerged. Belletristic scholars were well acquainted with the classics, but they were more interested in literature and style. They explored the concepts of taste, beauty, and the power to amaze. Scholars like Joseph Addison, John Baillie, Edmund Burke, and Charles Rollin analyzed whether good taste is innate or learned and what makes a work of art beautiful or sublime.

The *Belle Lettres Movement* expanded the focus of rhetoric from persuasive speech to all forms of literature (e.g., poetry, drama, oratory, history, and philosophy) and their aesthetic effect. The most influential belletristic scholar was **Hugh Blair** (1718–1800 CE), a minister and Professor of Rhetoric at the University of Edinburgh in Scotland. Blair's published lectures focus on style; they were taught in English and American schools until the end of the nineteenth century.[94]

---

91 WHATELY, *supra* note 89, at 39.

92 *Id.* at 112.

93 JONATHAN SWIFT, THE BATTLE OF THE BOOKS (Sir Henry Craik ed., 1912) also available online at https://www.gutenberg.org/files/623/623-h/623-h.htm (https://perma.cc/32R7-YRTQ).

94 HUGH BLAIR, LECTURES ON RHETORIC AND BELLE LETTRES (1833) also available online at https://quod.lib.umich.edu/e/ecco/004786433.0001.001?view=toc (https://perma.cc/E6H6-B9BL).

F. The Nineteenth Century

While the *Belle Lettres Movement* expanded rhetoric to include the study of all literature, the *Elocutionary Movement* of the late 1800s narrowed it to the study of delivery. Scholars like Thomas Sheridan, John Rice, John Walker, James Burgh, and Gilbert Austin believed the quality of speech had deteriorated in general society and attempted to establish a universal pronunciation and punctuation for the English language. They also studied the relationship between facial expressions, gestures, and persuasion. Walker, for example, stated that every emotion has "a particular attitude of the body, cast of the eye, and tone of the voice that particularly belongs to that passion."[95] Austin's book on public speaking included drawings of appropriate gestures and movements.[96]

---

95 2 JOHN WALKER, ELEMENTS OF ELOCUTION 266 (R.C. Alston, ed., 1969) (1781).

96 GILBERT AUSTIN, CHIRONOMIA, OR A TREATISE ON RHETORICAL DELIVERY (Mary Margaret Robb and Lester Thonssen, eds., 1806). "Chironomia" translates roughly into the study of hand gestures. The term dates back to a theatrical code of hand gestures used by Roman actors as far back as the first century CE. Both Cicero and Quintilian acknowledged this practice in their discussions of an orator's delivery, and Walker was an actor. *See also* THOMAS SHERIDAN, A COURSE OF LECTURES ON ELOCUTION (1762, reissued 1968).

Chapter 10

Why Don't Law Schools Teach Rhetoric?

"For most lawyers there is simply more going on in the creation of sound and convincing arguments than they can intuit in the pressure-filled context of law school and legal practice."[1]

—George D. Gopen

As you have just read, rhetoric was an integral part of Western education (one-third of the trivium) until the Renaissance. By the 1900s, it had basically disappeared from all schools in the United States and the Western world. The disappearance of rhetoric was due largely to the influence of Peter Ramus, who believed the creation of arguments was "logic" and the expression of argument was "rhetoric."[2]

Rhetoric was thus reduced to the study of speaking and writing style, contributing to its historic reputation as a subject of little substance. By the turn of the twentieth century, what was left of rhetoric had been divided among various subjects: English (reading and writing), Speech (oral speaking), and Communication Studies (the study of all forms of communication).

Rhetoric's focus on judicial speech—particularly the work of Roman scholars—and the three modes of persuasion seem to make it an obvious fit for training lawyers in the twenty-first century. If the study of rhetoric worked so well to train advocates back in ancient times, you might wonder why it isn't taught in law school today.

The answer is more complicated than you might think. Current law faculties tend to be composed primarily of scholars, not practitioners. However, most teachers in the nineteenth century were practicing lawyers. That changed after a momentous decision by Harvard Law School's Dean, Christopher Columbus Langdell.

Influenced by the dominance of the scientific method that had begun with Bacon (induction as opposed to deduction as the source of knowledge),[3] Langdell

1 George D. Gopen, *The State of Legal Writing: Res Ipsa Loquitur*, 86 Mich. L. Rev. 333, 353 (1987).

2 *See supra* ch. 9, note 62, and accompanying text.

3 *See supra* ch. 9, notes 63–66, and accompanying text.

believed that law should and could be taught like a science.[4] In turn, Langdell developed the case method "to inductively discover objective legal principles or doctrines" from which all rules of law could be deduced.[5] Conceived of this way, law was considered best taught by scholars who dedicated their careers to the study of law.[6]

In addition to treating law as a science with principles to be "discovered," Langdell introduced the Socratic teaching method. Instead of having students recite the law found in treatises (as was traditional then), he had them read judicial decisions, which they discussed in class, exploring the courts' reasoning.[7] Though students initially resisted Langdell's methods because they were not learning black letter law, but they gradually accepted it. Without really questioning the assumption that "true" principles of law actually exist or that they are derived solely from case law,[8] several law schools, including Columbia, Northwestern, Cornell, and Stanford, had switched to Langdell's case method by the mid-1890s.[9]

The case method and Socratic approach to teaching law shifted its focus from the practice of law to the theories of law. Although we no longer believe that law is comprised of absolutes or should be considered a "science," (see Chapter 12), this theoretical approach has endured. Traditional law classes are still taught as though the professor and students are engaged in a truth-finding process: What is the rule of law? Did the court make the right decision? Is it consistent with precedent? Is the reasoning flawed? Under Langdell's influence, legal education became focused on law to the exclusion of the humanities—including the study of rhetoric.

In the mid-twentieth century, law schools began to bring practical training back to legal education. Law clinics (where law students represent clients under faculty supervision) were introduced in the 1960s, and in the mid-1970s, formal legal writing courses for were introduced for the first time. Because law faculties were reluctant to teach writing courses, they began as student-taught courses and have since evolved into professional programs taught by full-time law professors with practice experience.

---

4 *See* Christopher C. Langdell, *Teaching Law as a Science*, 21 AM. L. REV. 123 (1887) ("Law is a science, ... If law not be a science, a university will consult its own dignity in declining to teach it. If it be not a science, it is a species of handicraft [recall Plato's analogy to cookery], and may best be learned by serving an apprenticeship to one who practices it.").

5 STEPHEN M. FELDMAN, AMERICAN LEGAL THOUGHT FROM PREMODERNISM TO POSTMODERNISM: AN INTELLECTUAL VOYAGE 93 (2000).

6 *See Langdell, supra* note 4, at 123–24; WILLIAM P. LAPIANA, LOGIC & EXPERIENCE: THE ORIGIN OF MODERN AMERICAN LEGAL EDUCATION 7 (Oxford U. Press 1994).

7 *See* Bruce A. Kimball, *Christopher Langdell: The Case of an 'Abomination' in Teaching Practice*, 20 NEA HIGHER EDUC. J. 23, 28 (Summer 2004); Charles R. McManis, *The History of First Century American Legal Education: A Revisionist Perspective*, 59 Wash. U. L.Q. 597, 630 (1981).

8 This assumption was not seriously questioned until the 1920s and 1930s. *See infra* ch. 12.A

9 Kimball, *supra* note 7, at 31.

Over the years, legal educators, bar associations, and employers urged law schools to provide even more and better practical training.[10]

It took the media, though, to get law schools to take serious notice of this advice. The financial crisis of 2008 seriously depressed the job market for law school graduates. Soon thereafter, the news media began to focus on the high cost of legal education, the shrinking legal market, and law schools' focus on theory and research, as opposed to training students to practice law.[11] Due, in part, to decreasing applicant pools, law schools have since gotten serious about improving skills training, including "on the job" training in the form of internships, externships, and practicum courses. The American Bar Association has since revised its accreditation standards to require that all students take at least six credits of experiential learning, including "a simulation course, a law clinic, or a field placement."[12]

The balance between theory and practice in legal education has gotten much better. But do not conclude from this section that learning the theory behind law or practice is unimportant. Just as law schools were rightly criticized for teaching contracts without teaching students how to draft them, skills faculty have been criticized for teaching lawyering skills without teaching the theory behind them (e.g., how are they acquired and why they are effective or ineffective).

To this point, Cicero said, "[W]isdom without eloquence does too little for the states, but . . . eloquence without wisdom is generally highly disadvantageous and is never helpful."[13] In a similar vein, Immanuel Kant, the German philosopher, said, "Thoughts without contents are empty, intuitions without concepts are blind."[14]

In sum, as had been recognized for centuries, both theory and practice are necessary for a well-rounded legal education. One without the other is insupportable. That is the primary motivation for this book: to expose law students to both the theory and practice of research, analysis, and persuasion; in short, to the study of

---

10 *See, e.g.*, AM. BAR ASS'N, TASK FORCE ON LAW SCHOOLS AND THE PROFESSION: NARROWING THE GAP (1992) [also known as THE MACCRATE REPORT]; ROY STUCKEY AND OTHERS, BEST PRACTICES FOR LEGAL EDUCATION: A VISION AND A ROAD MAP (2007); WILLIAM M. SULLIVAN, EDUCATING LAWYERS: PREPARATION FOR THE PRACTICE OF LAW 13 (2007) [also known as The Carnegie Report].

11 *See, e.g.*, David Segal, *Is Law School A Losing Game?*, N.Y. TIMES, Jan. 9, 2011, at BU1; David Segal, *What They Don't Teach Law Students: Lawyering*, N.Y. TIMES, Nov. 20, 2011, at A1; BRIAN Z. TAMANAHA, FAILING LAW SCHOOLS (2011); Charles Lane, *Book review: 'Failing Law Schools' by Brian Z. Tamanaha*, WASH. POST, (Aug. 3, 2012), https://www.washingtonpost.com/opinions/book-review-failing-law-schools-by-brian-z-tamanaha/2012/08/03/e7054c9c-c6df-11e1-916d-a4bc61efcad8_story.html (https://perma.cc/3WQE-CBL8).

12 *See* AM. BAR ASS'N, 2020–2021 STANDARDS AND RULES OF PROCEDURE FOR APPROVAL OF LAW SCHOOLS 18 (2020), https://www.americanbar.org/content/dam/aba/administrative/legal_education_and_admissions_to_the_bar/standards/2020-2021/2020-21-aba-standards-and-rules-chapter3.pdf (https://perma.cc/HZJ3-MNU4).

13 CICERO, DE INVENTIONE, *supra* ch. 9, note 19, at I.1.1.

14 IMMANUEL KANT, CRITIQUE OF PURE REASON 45 (F. Max Müller trans., Anchor Books 1966) (1781).

rhetoric. In recent years, scholars have begun to examine traditional teaching in the humanities, including literature, philosophy, history, law, politics, and rhetoric, for the role they play in perpetuating racial, gender, and other inequalities and silencing voices.[15] My goal is to hasten student learning by reintegrating the best of rhetoric with legal education: the theory of human persuasion as it relates to the practice of law. As lawyers, we must work within the constraints imposed by our governmental institutions, the rule of law, and our profession's ethical guidelines. The challenge is to ensure that our legal system operates justly, without bias, and with a willingness to find new ways to solve old problems. Rhetorical theory, grounded in reason, empathy, and ethics, provides some of the tools necessary to meet that challenge.

---

15 *See, e.g.*, (RE)CONSIDERING WHAT WE KNOW: LEARNING THRESHOLDS IN WRITING, COMPOSITION, RHETORIC, AND LITERACY 19 (Linda Adler-Kassner & Elizabeth Wardle, eds., 2019) (questioning the extent to which threshold concepts of writing studies "could be seen as attempting to impose a particular kind of stability and order that privileges the past."); Simon During, *What Were the Humanities, Anyway?*, CHRONICLE OF HIGHER EDUCATION: THE REVIEW (Aug. 31, 2020) (acknowledging that the humanities produce more interpretation than truth), https://www.chronicle.com/article/what-were-the-humanities-anyway (https://perma.cc/Q9GN-466D); Dan-el Padilla Peralta, *Why "Why Classics?"* (explaining that Classics involves studying "dead white guys" but exists to question ancient Greek and Roman history, culture, and literature, and even itself), https://classics.stanford.edu/dan-el-padilla-peralta-why-why-classics (https://perma.cc/U4T7-CBTD).

Chapter 11

Law as Rhetoric

"As soon as a communication tries to influence one or more persons, to orient their thinking, to excite or calm their emotions, to guide their actions, it belongs to the realm of rhetoric."[1]

—Chaim Perelman

Does the existence of law give rise to rhetoric (legal argument), or does rhetoric (legal argument) give rise to law? That is the essential to the debate between Plato and Aristotle, Valla and Ramus, and Descartes and Vico, each of whom explored the interrelationship between logic and rhetoric. On the one hand, knowledge is the result of logic (whether by deduction or induction), and rhetoric is merely the expression of knowledge. From that perspective, rhetoric has no real subject matter of its own. Remember Plato's *Gorgias*?[2]

On the other hand, logic and rhetoric can be seen as parallel processes, where logic produces knowledge that is certain, and rhetoric produces knowledge that is probable yet useful. From that perspective, logic and rhetoric both involve invention and arrangement.[3] This is closer to Aristotle's view.

Who was right? Does it matter?

There is a third option. Valla and Vico conceived of logic as a subset of rhetoric, not the other way around. Vico, in particular, argued that knowledge is a construct, and invention is as much a part of rhetoric as style and delivery.[4] Thus, knowledge is acquired as part of, not prior to, the rhetorical process. From this perspective, all knowledge is the product of rhetoric and thus probable.

Modern rhetoricians and philosophers tend to agree with Vico. For example, in the 1930s, Sister Miriam Joseph, an English professor at St. Mary's College in Indiana, stated, "Rhetoric is the master art of the trivium, for it presupposes and makes use of grammar and logic; it is the art of communicating through symbols ideas of reality."[5]

---

1 Chaim Perelman, The Realm of Rhetoric 162 (1982).

2 *See supra* ch. 9, note 8, and accompanying text.

3 *See supra* ch. 9.A.1, at 44.

4 *See supra* ch. 9.E.1, at 57. For example, laws are passed as the result of a legislative process that includes debate, and cases are decided and decisions written after argument by counsel.

5 Sister Miriam Joseph, *supra* ch. 8, note 4, at 9.

Chaim Perelman, a philosopher of law from Belgium, and his associate, Lucie Olbrechts-Tyteca, concluded in 1958 that even philosophers use rhetoric to convince their audience. Perelman stated:

> After having sought, for centuries, to model philosophy on the sciences, and having considered each of its particularities as a sign of inferiority [i.e., unable to prove truth with certainty], perhaps the moment has come to consider that philosophy has many traits in common with law.[6]

According to Perelman, lawyers and philosophers use rhetoric—appeals to *logos, pathos,* and *ethos*—to convince their audience; for that reason, law and philosophy are part of the same process.[7]

James Boyd White, a retired professor of law and English at the University of Michigan,[8] conceives of law as a rhetorical activity in which the meaning of law—which is in constant flux—is created. In White's view, rhetoric is neither a failed science nor shameful manipulation; rather, it is "the central art by which community and culture are established.[9] Just as Perelman questioned the dichotomy of philosophy and rhetoric, White questions the juxtaposition of law and science because neither produces absolute truth.[10] Lawyers, according to White, respond to the indeterminacy of law by creating arguments about what the law means in a given context, engaging not only in a creative process, but also one that reflects the lawyers' view of the world and what kind of society the law can or should create.[11]

In the late 1990s, rhetoric professors Andrea Lunsford and John J. Ruszkiewicz published *Everything's An Argument*.[12] They define rhetoric, at its best, as "the art, theory and practice of ethical communication," hoping to "inspire student writers to think of themselves as rhetors, as Quintilian's 'good person, speaking well.' "[13] As Lunsford and Ruszkiewicz see it, "an argument can be any text—written, spoken, aural, or visual—that expresses a point of view."[14] Even a question as simple as "Hi, how's it going?" can be viewed as an argument that the question deserves an answer.[15]

---

6 CHAIM PERELMAN, JUSTICE, LAW, AND ARGUMENT 174 (1980).

7 CHAIM PERELMAN, THE REALM OF RHETORIC 162 (1982); CHAIM PERELMAN & LUCIE OLBRECHTS-TYTECA, THE NEW RHETORIC: A TREATISE ON ARGUMENTATION 32 (1958); *see also* James Boyd White, *Law as Rhetoric, Rhetoric as Law: The Arts of Cultural and Communal Life*, 52:3 UNIV. CHICAGO L. REV. 684, 695 (1985) (even dialectic, "in which the speaker is himself willing, even eager, to be refuted, is in this sense a form of rhetoric").

8 White is often credited with founding the Law and Literature movement. *See* ch. 12, at 78.

9 James Boyd White, *supra* note 7, at 684.

10 *Id.* at 688.

11 *Id.* at 688–90.

12 ANDREA A. LUNSFORD & JOHN J. RUSZKIEWICZ, EVERYTHING'S AN ARGUMENT (8th ed. 2018).

13 *Id.* at vii.

14 *Id.* at 5.

15 *See id.*

If everything is an argument, then law does not give rise to rhetoric. Law *is* rhetoric. If that's right, the notion of law as rhetoric should affect how we think about the nature of law and the lawyers' role in the legal process. If, as Plato believed, truth or knowledge (here, the law) is discovered by philosophers (here, perhaps, legal scholars, lawmakers, and judges) then lawyers function solely as mouthpieces (communicators) of knowledge to influence their audience. Much criticism of lawyers and the legal profession stems from this implicit view. However, if all knowledge is created in the process of human communication and interaction, scholars and lawyers alike participate in its creation. We all engage in invention.

Chapter 12

Do Neutral Rules of Law Exist out There Somewhere?

"Rhetoric can never be innocent, can never be a disinterested arbiter of the ideological claims of others because it is always already serving certain ideological claims."[1]

—James Berlin

If we understand law as rhetoric, can law be said to be objective, neutral, true, or right with absolute certainty? Is there ever one right result in a court case? Do judges properly decide cases based only on the rule of law? Would that be fair? Would that be desirable?

Many twentieth-century legal scholars rejected the idea of natural law, as well as Langdell's view that law is objective truth and can be taught as a science. The theory of natural law is that law is universal and eternal. It is derived from an external source, such as God or the laws of nature, and endows us with certain rights and obligations.[2] Any human law that conflicts with this "higher order" is not binding.

Natural law had a significant impact on the American Revolution. Its influence can be seen in the framing of the Declaration of Independence: "We hold these truths to be self-evident, that all men are created equal, that they are endowed by their Creator with certain unalienable rights, that among these are the pursuit of Life, Liberty, and the pursuit of Happiness."

In the late 1800s, after the Civil War in the United States, the concept of natural law gave way to a more secular view of law. Science, not God, became the objective source of knowledge—this greatly influenced nineteenth century legal scholars like Langdell.[3] Langdell's case method was designed to discover legal principles through careful reading of judicial decisions. Although Langdell recognized that the law changes over time (i.e., it is not eternal), he sought to articulate the enduring principles that guide judges in making their decisions.[4]

---

1 James Berlin, *Rhetoric and Ideology in the Writing Class*, 50 Coll. Eng. 477, 477 (1988).

2 *See, e.g.*, Feldman, *supra* ch. 10, note 5, at 49–50.

3 *Id.* at 91.

4 *See supra* ch. 10, note 4, and accompanying text.

Langdell concluded that there were fewer general principles of law than he had supposed and that all legal rules could be deduced from these principles. Any decision in conflict with these rules was theoretically wrong. Over time, good legal reasoning became synonymous with logical thinking. However, to the extent logic alone excludes fairness and policy considerations, it can lead to absurd results.[5]

A. American Legal Realism

As early as 1897, Justice **Oliver Wendell Holmes** questioned Langdell's views: "You will find some text writers telling you that [the law] is . . . a system of reason, that it is a deduction from principles of ethics or admitted axioms or what not, which may or may not coincide with the decisions."[6] In Holmes' view, the point of studying law was to predict outcomes in judicial decisions, and knowledge of the law was not enough.

Karl Llewellyn, a Columbia law professor, followed Holmes' lead. In 1930, he published *The Bramble Bush*, a series of lectures explaining that judges say one thing but often do another:

> It will be [the judges'] *action* and the available means of influencing their action or of arranging your affairs with reference to their action which make up the 'law' you have to study. And *rules*, in all of this, are important to you so far as they help you see or predict what judges will do or so far as they help you get judges to do something. That is their importance. That is all their importance, except as pretty playthings.[7]

As this comment suggests, Llewellyn thought that judicial decisions were indeterminate; because judges can read cases narrowly or broadly, any decision could lead to a number of possible outcomes.[8]

Jerome Frank, another famous realist and federal circuit judge, believed that personality was the critical factor in judicial decision-making. He rejected the idea that sociological factors explain case outcomes. Frank saw the legal system as chaotic, driven primarily by the biases of juries and judicial hunch.[9] Witnesses often have

---

5 FELDMAN, *supra* ch. 10, note 5, at 94.

6 Oliver Wendell Holmes, *The Path Of The Law*, 10 HARV. L. REV. 457, 460 (1897), also at http://moglen.law.columbia.edu/LCS/palaw.pdf (https://perma.cc/Q3M8-9EYR).

7 KARL N. LLEWELLYN, THE BRAMBLE BUSH: ON OUR LAW AND ITS STUDY 5 (1960).

8 *See, e.g.*, Karl N. Llewellyn, *Remarks on the Theory of Appellate Decision and the Rules or Canons About How Statutes Are to Be Construed*, 3 VAND. L. REV. 395 (1950) (describing twenty-eight canons and counter-canons of statutory interpretation found in reported opinions and treatises), also at https://scholarship.law.vanderbilt.edu/cgi/viewcontent.cgi?article=2432&context=vlr (https://perma.cc/A4QJ-76LA).

9 *See* JEROME FRANK, LAW AND THE MODERN MIND (1949).

imperfect recollections, and juries credit false testimony or act out of bias.[10] The myth that law has certainty, Frank wrote, stems in part from a deep-rooted childish desire for a world of stability, where the law plays the father-figure.[11]

B. Some postmodern theories of law

In the second half of the twentieth century, realism (also known as modernism) gave rise to a number of theories about the nature of law. While realists had argued that truth in law is relative, proponents of **critical legal studies (CLS)** argued that truth in law is non-existent.[12] They also opposed traditional teaching methods in law school. CLS is known for three major critiques of the United States legal system.

First, the idea that rules of law are objective or neutral is a myth: one rule of law cannot possibly be fair to a multiplicity of people with differing political and moral views.[13] Duncan Kennedy stated:

> Teachers teach nonsense when they persuade students that legal reasoning is distinct, as a method for reaching correct results, from ethical or political discourse in general . . . There is never a 'correct legal solution' that is other than the correct ethical or political solution to that legal problem.[14]

Second, the law is internally inconsistent in providing multiple solutions to a single problem and striving to serve both individuals and society as a whole.[15] Kennedy argued the chief contradiction in law is the tension between rules and standards. While rules benefit individuals (i.e., they give advance notice of prohibited conduct), standards benefit society (i.e., a "reasonable" standard allows for flexibility to achieve society's goals).[16]

---

10 "[I]n most cases in the trial courts the parties do dispute about the facts, and the testimony concerning the facts is oral and conflicting. In any such case, what does it mean to say that the facts of a case are substantially similar to those of an earlier case? It means, at most, merely that the trial court regards the facts of the two cases as about the same. Since, however, no one knows what the trial court will find as the facts, no one can guess what precedent ought to be or will be followed. *Id.* at xiv.

11 *See id.* at 19–21. Here, Frank used "childish" in a Freudian sense: the law and judges act as a father figure who makes everything right.

12 "In the postmodern view, knowledge can never be certain or empirically established since, as Peter Schanck explains, '[W]hat we think is knowledge is always belief'—and '[b]ecause language is socially and culturally constituted, it is inherently incapable of representing or corresponding to reality.' " NANCY LEVIT AND ROBERT R. M. VERCHICK, FEMINIST LEGAL THEORY: A PRIMER 36 (2d ed., 2016) (quoting Peter C. Schanck, *Understanding Postmodern Thought and Its Implications for Statutory Interpretation*, 65 S. CAL. L. REV. 2505, 2508 (1992)).

13 *See, e.g.*, ANDREW ALTMAN, CRITICAL LEGAL STUDIES: A LIBERAL CRITIQUE 13 (1990).

14 Duncan Kennedy, *Legal Education as Training for Hierarchy*, *in* POLITICS OF LAW 47 (D. Kairys ed., 1982).

15 *See* ALTMAN, *supra* note 13, at 14–15.

16 *See id.* at 109; Duncan Kennedy, *Form and Substance in Private Law Adjudication*, 89 HARV. L. REV. 1685 (1976).

Third, CLS scholars argued that the law keeps the political majority in power and oppresses minority groups.[17] Because law and politics are synonymous, legal institutions operate to keep the political majority in power: "Law is an instrument of social, economic and political domination, both in the sense of furthering the concrete interests of the dominators *and* in that of legitimizing the existing order."[18]

Critical race theory (CRT) scholars picked up where CLS scholars left off, exploring racial inequality under law. They argue that racial identity is the "deciding factor in determining social standing and access to society's resources" in the United States.[19] Although CLS scholars acknowledged that the law perpetuates the power of the political majority, they did not identify themselves as members of that majority. Most CLS scholars were white men who attended Ivy League schools, had tenured positions at top-ranking law schools, and published in the most prestigious American law journals.

Just as CLS scholars criticize the legal system for its corruptness, CRT scholars criticize the legal system for its racism. According to Charles Lawrence, III, unconscious racism is taught and perpetuated by our culture through parents, peers, and authority figures: "Even if a child is not told that blacks are inferior, he learns that lesson by observing the behavior of others."[20] This unconscious racism necessarily influences judges.

Central to CRT is the idea that the law's "color-blind" approach may actually perpetuate racism. By eliminating race-based classifications, it became impossible to create "race-based remedies for discrimination while leaving untouched discriminatory action conducted through means that do not mention race."[21] What's more, CRT scholars argue, the idea of an objective form of merit is problematic. Since the majority defines and interprets "merit" from its own perspective, it can perpetuate its own privilege. Notions of merit that are ostensibly neutral act instead as "repositories of racial power."[22]

Focusing on gender discrimination, **feminist legal theory (FLT)** proponents argue that the legal system fails women and those who do not identify with cisgender, heterosexual norms. In the 1960s and 70s, **liberal feminists** advocated to eliminate gender-based classifications in law because men and women should be treated alike.[23]

---

17 *See* ALTMAN, *supra* note 13, at 15–16.

18 Louis B. Schwartz, *With Gun and Camera Through Darkest CLS-Land*, 36 STAN. L. REV. 413, 417 (1984) (*quoting* Invitation to First Conference on Critical Legal Studies, Jan. 17, 1977).

19 DERRICK BELL, RACE, RACISM AND AMERICAN LAW 1 (4th ed. 2000).

20 Charles Lawrence III, *The Id, the Ego, and Equal Protection Reckoning with Unconscious Racism*, in CRITICAL RACE THEORY: THE KEY WRITINGS THAT FORMED THE MOVEMENT 235, 238 (Kimberlé Crenshaw et al. eds., 1995) [hereinafter CRITICAL RACE THEORY: THE KEY WRITINGS].

21 BELL, *supra* note 19, at 132.

22 CRITICAL RACE THEORY: THE KEY WRITINGS, *supra* note 20, at xxvi.

23 This was the same theory used by the suffragists to gain women's right to vote.

The principle of equal treatment under law had been used successfully by the suffragists to gain women's right to vote some forty years earlier. The result of their efforts was a "system of 'formal' equality,"[24] and women began to gain access to traditionally male professions and Ivy League schools.

FYI

The late Supreme Court Justice Ruth Bader Ginsburg co-founded the Women's Rights Project for the American Civil Liberties Union and argued six (and won five) gender discrimination cases in the 1970s before the U.S. Supreme Court.

In the 1980s, however, feminist scholars took issue with the equal treatment theory, arguing women were still being discriminated against primarily in the areas of sexuality and reproduction. FLT proponents then had to decide "whether to continue to urge equality, or instead to concede difference."[25] Wendy Williams, a leading liberal feminist, disagreed with laws giving women special treatment: "If we can't have it both ways, we need to think carefully about which way we want to have it."[26]

Cultural feminists argued that the law should accommodate cultural and biological differences between men and women. For example, since only women get pregnant, they need to be treated differently in the workplace (e.g., receive maternity leave).[27] However, not all feminists in the 1980s believed that the difference debate was the proper focus of FLT. **Dominance** or **radical feminists** rejected the sameness/difference debate because it measured women against a male standard and argued that the inequalities women experience are due to patterns of male domination.[28]

Catharine MacKinnon, for example, argued that the problem was not whether women are treated differently, but whether their interests are subordinated to those of men. She argued that the legal system is "fundamentally opposed to women's interests and designed principally to perpetuate male dominance."[29] In contrast, Janet Halley criticized McKinnon's premise that society subordinates women, arguing that perceived injuries—such as sexual harassment in the workplace—inflict little, if any,

---

24 MARTHA CHAMALLAS, INTRODUCTION TO FEMINIST LEGAL THEORY 35 (1999).

25 Clare Dalton, *Where We Stand: Observations on the Situation of Feminist Legal Thought*, 3 BERKELEY WOMEN'S L.J. 1, 5 (1988); *see also* Lucinda M. Finley, *Transcending Equality Theory: A Way Out of the Maternity and the Workplace Debate*, 86 COLUM. L. REV. 1118 (1986); Ann C. Scales, *The Emergence of Feminist Jurisprudence: An Essay*, 95 YALE L.J. 1373 (1986).

26 Wendy W. Williams, *The Equality Crisis: Some Reflections on Culture, Courts, and Feminism*, 7 WOMEN'S RTS. L. REP. 175, 196 (1981–82).

27 *See, e.g.*, Jenny Morgan, *Feminist Theory as Legal Theory*, 16 MELB. U. L. REV. 743, 745 (1988), *reprinted in* 1 FEMINIST LEGAL THEORY (Frances E. Olsen ed., 1995); *see also* CAROL GILLIGAN, IN A DIFFERENT VOICE: PSYCHOLOGICAL THEORY AND WOMEN'S DEVELOPMENT (1982).

28 LEVIT & VERCHICK, *supra* note 12, at 20.

29 CHAMALLAS, *supra* note 24 at 53; *see also* CATHARINE A. MACKINNON, FEMINISM UNMODIFIED: DISCOURSES ON LIFE AND LAW (1987).

real harm.[30] Some women might actually enjoy being dominated,[31] so to characterize women as victims is a self-fulfilling prophecy.

In the late 1980s, **diversity** or **critical race feminists** argued that the predominantly white voices of 1970s and 80s feminists did not speak for all women, especially those who were lesbians or of color. When it comes to discrimination under the law, differences in race, ethnicity, sexual orientation, and socio-economic status among women are as important as gender.[32] Mari Matsuda, for example, articulated the notion of "multiple consciousness," alluding to an experience of the world from several perspectives at once—including gender and race.[33] Although all women experience a form of gender discrimination, "it is the *intersection* of characteristics like sex, race, wealth, and sexual orientation that really suggests how people will treat you."[34] The goal of critical race feminism is to break down assumptions about difference based on race and other minority attributes. The concept of intersectionality is now integral in understanding the lived experience of those with multiple characteristics that affect how society treats them.

Postmodern feminists emerged in the early 1990s. Like critical race feminists, postmodern FLT scholars rejected the idea that all women (or men, for that matter) are the same. Representing a variety of viewpoints, these FLT scholars generally agree that to identify women as "women" for the purpose of achieving equality is counterproductive. Put another way, there is no correct way to define the "female experience." Gender differences between men and women are socially constructed and perpetuated through language, including the law. The goal of postmodern feminists is to deconstruct the language of the law and find its motivating power and hidden biases. Mary Jo Frug, for example, rejected the idea that gender is an essential part of human nature and explored the extent to which "legal rules and discourse constitute a system that 'constructs,' or engenders the female body."[35]

Building on the work of critical race feminists, **queer theorists** battle discrimination against LGBTQ+ individuals. Like Frug and postmodern feminists,

---

30 *See* Janet Halley, *The Politics of Injury: A Review of Robin West's Caring for Justice*, 1 UNBOUND: HARV. J. LEGAL LEFT 65, 83–84 (2005), https://legalleft.org/wp-content/uploads/sites/11/2015/09/1UNB065-Halley.pdf (https://perma.cc/E2FJ-HQEM); JANET HALLEY, *Sexuality Harassment*, *in* DIRECTIONS IN SEXUAL HARASSMENT LAW 197–98 (Catharine A. MacKinnon & Reva B. Siegel, eds., 2003).

31 *See* Halley, *supra* note 30, at 88–91.

32 CHAMALLAS, *supra* note 24, at 85; LEVIT & VERCHICK, *supra* note 12, at 24.

33 Mari J. Matsuda, *When the First Quail Calls: Multiple Consciousness as Jurisprudential Method*, 14 WOMEN'S RTS. L. REP. 297, 299 (1992).

34 LEVIT & VERCHICK, *supra* note 12, at 24; *see generally Kimberlé Crenshaw, Demarginalizing the Intersection of Race and Sex: A Black Feminist Critique of Antidiscrimination Doctrine, Feminist Theory, and Antiracist Politics*, 1989:1 U. CHI. LEGAL F. 139 (1989).

35 MARY JO FRUG, POSTMODERN LEGAL FEMINISM 130 (1992); *see also* Mary Jo Frug, *A Postmodern Feminist Legal Manifesto* (An Unfinished Draft), 105 HARV. L. REV. 1045 (1992).

these scholars argue that gender is a construct, and the law incorrectly presumes that everyone experiences sex, gender, and sexual orientation the same way. Judith Butler argues that gender is performative, meaning it is constructed through a set of acts that may or may not comply with dominant societal norms.[36] In questioning the concept of "identity," Queer Theory focuses "on the manner in which heterosexuality has, silently but saliently, maintained itself as a hidden yet powerfully privileged norm" and questions the goals of formal equality that "reify the very categories that have generated heterosexual privilege and [Q]ueer oppression."[37]

Though more a methodology for problem solving than a distinct legal theory, **the law and economics (L&E) movement** views law as a social tool for maximizing wealth.[38] The fundamental principle of L&E is that legal rules are or should be efficient. Here, "efficiency" refers to the distribution of legal entitlements such that the benefit to society as a whole is maximized with as little waste—or sunk costs—as possible. Many L&E scholars explicitly reject the idea that law should be used to redistribute income and entitlements so that specific sub-groups of society receive their "fair share."

Descriptive or positive L&E theorists use cost-benefit analysis to explain and predict individual responses to legal rules and the impact of those decisions on society as a whole.[39] Prescriptive or normative L&E theorists use economics to assist lawmakers in fashioning legal rules.[40] L&E theory has been used to study virtually every area of law, including torts, contracts, property, criminal, family, and equal protection.[41] Judge Richard Posner brought economic analysis into the mainstream of legal academics and helped found what is known as the *Chicago School* of thought. Posner is particularly well-known for his work on judicial decision-making, concluding that just as individuals make rational choices to maximize their utility, judges should make do the same in resolving legal disputes.[42] Despite the enormous success

---

36 *See* JUDITH BUTLER, GENDER TROUBLE: FEMINISM AND THE SUBVERSION OF IDENTITY (1990).

37 Laurie Rose Kepros, *Queer Theory: Weed or Seed in the Garden of Legal Theory?*, 9 L. & SEXUALITY 279, 284 (2008).

38 Two foundational articles include Ronald H. Coase, *The Problem of Social Cost*, 3 J. L. & ECON. 1 (1960) and Guido Calabresi, *Some Thoughts on Risk Distribution and the Law of Torts*, 70 YALE L.J. 499 (1961).

39 *See, e.g.*, Robert C. Ellickson, *Property in Land*, 102 YALE L.J. 1315 (1993); Henry Hansmann, *Condominium and Cooperative Housing: Transactional Efficiency, Tax Subsidies, and Tenure Choice*, 20 J. LEGAL STUD. 25 (1991).

40 Gillian K. Hadfield, *Judicial Competence and the Interpretation of Incomplete Contracts*, 23 J. LEGAL STUD. 159 (1994); Richard L. Hasen, *The Efficient Duty To Rescue*, 15 INT'L REV. L. & ECON. 141 (1995).

41 *See, e.g.*, Guido Calabresi & Jon T. Hirschoff, *Toward a Test for Strict Liability in Torts*, 81 YALE L.J. 1055 (1972); Charles J. Goetz & Robert E. Scott, *Enforcing Promises: An Examination of the Basis of Contract*, 89 YALE L.J. 1261 (1980); Harold Demsetz, *Toward a Theory of Property Rights*, 57 AM. ECON. ASS'N 347 (1967); Steven Shavell, *Criminal Law and the Optimal Use of Nonmonetary Sanctions as a Deterrent*, 85 COLUM. L. REV. 1232 (1985); RICHARD A. POSNER, ECONOMIC ANALYSIS OF LAW (7th ed. 2007).

42 *See, e.g.*, Richard A. Posner, *What Do Judges and Justices Maximize? (The Same Thing Everybody*

of these and other related theories, using economic analysis to shape law and policy has been criticized on several grounds.[43]

Finally, the **law and literature (L&L) movement** focuses on the relationship between law and literature, standing somewhat in contrast to the cost-benefit approach of L&E theorists. One strand of L&L seeks to understand legal issues as explored in great literature, one uses literary techniques to interpret the meaning of legal texts, and another explores the role of narrative or storytelling in law.[44] James Boyd White, with his view of law as constitutive rhetoric, falls into the second strand.[45] In White's view, lawyers act like literary critics, reading legal texts "not so much . . . for a single meaning as reading for a range of possible meanings."[46] According to White, to ask whether law has a fixed or objective meaning is beside the point—the act of reading, writing, and speaking about law (or literature) is a creative process; the meaning of the text depends on the social context and changes over time.[47]

Part II of this book opened with a definition of rhetoric as the study of persuasion (at its narrowest), and as the study of all human communication (at its broadest). As Chapter 9 explains, rhetoric began in the ancient world as a method for preparing young men to engage in a life of public service. But from the beginning, rhetoric has had a complicated relationship with the law, viewed at various times throughout history as either the manipulation of truth or as a failed science.[48]

In contrast, scholars like Aristotle, Cicero, Quintilian, Bacon, Valla, Vico, and Lunsford have celebrated the role rhetoric plays in public affairs, using logic and emotion within ethical limits to inform and persuade audiences.[49] During the Middle Ages, rhetoric as a subject of study was fractured into distinct areas of interest, such as letter writing and preaching.[50] Although it enjoyed renewed interest during the Renaissance, it was ultimately reduced to the study of style and delivery, reinforcing

---

Else Does), 3 SUP. CT. ECON. REV. 1 (1993).

43 *See, e.g.*, Christine Jolls, Cass R. Sunstein & Richard Thaler, *A Behavioral Approach to Law and Economics*, 50 STAN. L. REV. 1471, 1545 (1998) (arguing that people make irrational choices); Duncan Kennedy, *Cost Benefit Analysis of Entitlement Problems*, 33 STAN. L. R. 387 (1981) (arguing that the notion of efficiency leads to more than one potential outcome).

44 *See, e.g.*, Jane B. Baron, *Law, Literature, and The Problems of Interdisciplinarity*, 108 YALE L. J. 1059, 1064 (1999).

45 *See, e.g.*, *supra* ch. 11, note 7.

46 JAMES B. WHITE, HERACLES' BOW: ESSAYS ON THE RHETORIC AND POETICS OF THE LAW 78 (1985).

47 *See id.* at 79–88 *see also* RICHARD H. WEISBERG, POETHICS AND OTHER STRATEGIES OF LAW AND LITERATURE (1992); Robin West, *Communities, Texts, and Law: Reflections on the Law and Literature Movement*, 1 YALE J. L & HUMANITIES 129, 155 (1989) (arguing for the need "to understand our laws not only as 'texts' that embody our traditions and our cultural ideals, but also as interactive instruments of violence, violation, compassion or respect").

48 *See supra* ch. 10, note 4, and accompanying text.

49 *See supra* ch. 9.A–9.F.

50 *See supra* ch. 9.C.

its ancient reputation as more form than substance.[51] By the end of the nineteenth century, it had disappeared in Western education.

Although rhetoric has enjoyed renewed scholarly interest outside the law in the twentieth and twenty-first centuries, it has not been a subject of much interest in legal education. Law school curricula are still largely influenced by the Langdellian approach to studying law as science,[52] despite the work of legal theorists demonstrating that law is neither objective nor true in any meaningful sense. Indeed, scholars like Perelman, Olbrechts-Tyteca, and White argue that rhetoric is the process by which all knowledge is acquired, making all knowledge probable at best.[53]

As a student of law, your challenge will be to reconcile the indeterminacy of law with your role as an advocate and the ethical duties that role imposes. If there is no truth in law, how will you know what the law "is"? How will you articulate the rules of law to your client or a decision-maker with any level of certainty? So as to argue for results warranted by existing law or by a non-frivolous argument for changing the law?[54] How can you be both creative and ethical without manipulating or distorting the truth?

Perhaps, as White and other L&L theorists might argue, these are not the right questions for the practitioner to ask. Perhaps, by viewing law as rhetoric, you can view your role differently—as advocate versus oracle and interpreter versus soothsayer. In representing clients, your role is to interpret the language of the law while remaining mindful of the implications of your interpretation. As White might say, what does your legal advice or argument say about you, your creative process, and the audience you envision? As White did say,

> What kind of response does it invite, or allow? What place is there for me, and for others, in the universe defined by this discourse, in the community created by this text? What world does it assume? What world does it create?[55]

Finally, as Aristotle would advise, your job as an advocate is to marshal all available means of persuasion to help the judge, jury, adjudicator, or opposing party achieve just results.

Test Your Knowledge: Part II

To assess your understanding of the material in this part, click here to take a quiz.

---

51 *See supra* ch. 9.A.1.

52 This refers generally to the tendency to still teach traditional law school subjects using casebooks and little additional non-legal material, with the exception of courses like Law and Literature or Law and Economics that are explicitly interdisciplinary.

53 *See supra* ch. 11.

54 See FED. R. CIV. P. 11, https://www.law.cornell.edu/rules/frcp/rule_11 (https://perma.cc/J9KP-J4XH).

55 White, *supra* ch. 11, note 7, at 702.

PART III

The Rhetorical Process

Chapter 13

Aristotle's Canons of Rhetoric

"So let Rhetoric be defined as the faculty [ability] of discovering in the particular case what are the available means of persuasion. This is the function of no other art."[1]

—Aristotle

Aristotle first observed and theorized the art of persuasion in *Rhetoric*, c. 333 BCE. For teaching purposes, he divided the rhetorical process into parts, now known as the **canons** of rhetoric. As you read this chapter, bear in mind that these canons give us a process for deconstructing and inventing arguments. They are intended to promote, not inhibit, creativity.

Aristotle divided persuasive speech into three types, based on the nature of the audience: **political**, **judicial**, and **ceremonial** (e.g., a presidential address such as the State of the Union).[2] Whereas politicians strive to influence legislatures with regard to future conduct (e.g., to pass a law restricting gun sales), lawyers tend to attempt to influence judges and juries about past conduct (e.g., to find a defendant guilty or not guilty for attempting to purchase a gun illegally). Ceremonial speech inspires and amazes.[3]

All types of speakers naturally use **artistic** and **inartistic appeals** to persuade their audience.[4] Artistic appeals are created. Aristotle divided artistic appeals into three types: ***logos***, ***pathos***, and ***ethos***. Appeals to *logos* rely on logic or reason, appeals to *pathos* engage the audience's emotion and motivate them to decide in the speaker's favor,[5] and appeals to *ethos* give the audience reason to believe in the speaker's credibility.[6] In contrast, inartistic appeals are pre-existing forms of proof

> **Bottom Line**
>
> Lawyers must use reason, put their audience in the right frame of mind, and be credible in order to persuade their audience.

1 Aristotle, Rhetoric, *supra* ch. 8, note 3, I.2, ¶ 1355b.

2 *Id.* at I.3, 1358b.

3 *See id.*

4 *See id.* at I.2, 1355b.

5 For more on emotional appeals, see *infra* ch. 44.A.

6 Aristotle, Rhetoric, *supra* ch. 8, note 3, at I.2, 1356a.

used to support arguments, such as the law, eyewitness testimony, contracts, and physical evidence.[7]

The Five Canons of Classical Rhetoric

English	Greek	Latin
invention	*heuresis*	*inventio*
arrangement	*taxis*	*dispositio*
style	*lexis*	*elocutio*
memory	*mnemea*	*memoria*
delivery	*hypokrisis*	*pronuntiatio*

A. Invention

The creative process is the same, regardless of the type of speech. **Invention** (*heuresis*), the most complex and time-consuming of the stages, happens when speakers develop their artistic appeals to reason, emotion, and credibility:

> Such being the instruments of persuasion, to master all three obviously calls for a [person] who can reason logically, can analyze the types of human character, along with the virtues, and, thirdly, can analyze the emotions.[8]

For inventing appeals to reason, the speaker consults the general and special topics.[9] Aristotle thought of the topics as potential sources or lines of argument.[10] General topics are those common to all argument, such as matters of quantity or quality and the possible and impossible. For example, with regard to past facts, Aristotle said:

> [Y]ou may argue that a man has done a thing, if he wished to do it, and if there was no external hindrance; or, if he could have done it, and was in a state of anger; or if he was in a position to do it, and was spurred on by desire.[11]

Special topics are those specific to a particular subject. Aristotle said the special topics of judicial speech involve motive, states of mind, and wrongdoing.[12]

---

7 *Id.* at 1355b.

8 *Id.* at 1356a.

9 *See id.* at 1358a.

10 *See id.* at II.23, 1397a.

11 *Id.* at II.19, 1392b. These concepts—motive, means, and opportunity—are still used to prove guilt where the evidence is circumstantial. *See* ch. 33.A, at 228.

12 *See* ARISTOTLE, RHETORIC, *supra* ch. 8, note 3, at I.3, 1358a & I.10 (all).

According to Aristotle, appeals to reason are either inductive or deductive.[13] He called induction in rhetoric "example" and deduction the "rhetorical syllogism" or "enthymeme."[14] By **example**, he meant "deriving a general law from a number of like instances."[15] By **rhetorical syllogism** or **enthymeme**, he meant the process of "concluding from certain assumptions that something else follows from those assumptions."[16] These two forms of reasoning, along with appeals to emotion and credibility, are discussed fully in Part VII.

B. Arrangement

Arrangement (*Taxis*) of Speech

English	Greek	Latin
introduction	*prooimion*	*exordium*
statement of facts	*diegesis*	*narratio*
statement of issues in dispute and outline of argument		*divisio or partitio*
argument (proofs)	*pisteis*	*confirmatio*
counterarguments		*refutatio or confutatio*
conclusion	*epilogos*	*peroratio*

Once speakers know their arguments, they must arrange them by deciding which points to put first, emphasize, or leave out. Cicero said the orator must "arrange his matter, not only in a certain order, but according to the weight of the matter and the judgment of the speaker."[17] The **arrangement** (*taxis*) of a classical speech is set forth in the text box above. The elements of a traditional legal memorandum or brief in the twenty-first century are strikingly similar.[18]

Aristotle said, "A speech has two parts. Necessarily, you state your case [the subject to be proved], and you prove it [make your arguments]."[19] However, he recognized that in real life, speakers add an introduction and a conclusion to benefit

13 *Id.* at I.2, 1356b; *see also infra* ch. 29.

14 *See* ARISTOTLE, RHETORIC, *supra* ch. 8, note 3, at I.2, 1356b.

15 *Id.; see also infra* chs. 30, at 195 and 32, at 219.

16 ARISTOTLE, *supra* ch. 8, note 3, at I.2, 1356b; *see also infra* ch. 31, at 205.

17 CICERO, DE ORATORE, *supra* ch. 9, note 20, at I.31.142.

18 *See infra* chs. 37 and 45.

19 ARISTOTLE, *supra* ch. 8, note 3, at III.13, 1414a.

the audience.[20] The **introduction** (*prooimion*) to a speech "pave[s] the way for what follows"[21] and secures the audience's good will and attention.[22]

Contemporary oral argument and written legal analysis and argument all begin with an introduction. Oral argument usually opens with an introduction of the speaker and the legal issue before the court, and written memoranda and briefs usually begin with a "question presented" or the "issue presented for review."[23] By framing the issue at the outset, the writer prepares readers for the analysis or argument to follow and puts them in the right frame of mind to understand it.

Bottom Line

Fact statements should be brief, clear, and plausible, yet complete and engaging.

Aristotle thought the only form of speech that needed a **statement of the facts** was judicial speech since it concerns past events.[24] Aristotle instructed plaintiffs to "narrate whatever tends to your own credit, or to the discredit of the other side."[25] Defendants, he said, "need less narration. Here you have to contend that the act did not occur, or that it did no harm, or that it was unjust, or that it had not the importance alleged."[26]

Cicero, Quintilian, and the author of *Rhetorica ad Herennium* further specified that statements of fact should be brief, clear, and plausible.[27] Quintilian said the statement of facts should begin at the point where the facts "first concern the judge," avoid stating irrelevant facts, and leave out everything that "can be removed without in any way damaging either the process of judgement or our own interest."[28]

Whether imparting legal advice to clients or drafting briefs, lawyers always include some version of a fact statement to put the legal issue in context and specify the facts on which their analysis is based. Today we give the same advice the ancient Greeks and Romans gave for creating effective statements of fact: include significant

---

20 *See id.* at 1414b.

21 *Id.*

22 *Id.* at 1415a. Quintilian said the purpose of the introduction is "to prepare the hearer to be more favorably inclined towards us for the rest of the proceedings." QUINTILIAN, INSTITUTIO ORATORIO, *supra* ch. 9, note 27, at IV.1.24; *see also* CICERO, DE INVENTIONE, *supra* ch. 9, note 19, at I.15.20.

23 *See infra* chs. 37.A and 45.A.

24 *See* ARISTOTLE, RHETORIC, *supra* ch. 8, note 3, at III.13, 1414b.

25 *Id.* at III.16, 1417a.

26 *Id.*

27 CICERO, DE INVENTIONE, *supra* ch. 9, note 19, at I.20.28; QUINTILIAN, *supra* ch. 9, note 27, IV.2.31; RHETORICA AD HERENNIUM, *supra* ch. 9. note 20, at I.9.14. Citations to this work are to book, chapter, and paragraph. Aristotle was not convinced that the statement of facts had to be brief. He said, "[T]he right thing is never rapidity nor brevity, but the proper mean. And the mean consists in saying just so much as will make matters plain." ARISTOTLE, *supra* ch. 8, note 3, at III.16, 1416b.

28 QUINTILIAN, *supra* ch. 9, note 27, IV.2.40.

legal facts and those background facts necessary for the context to be understood, state the facts succinctly so as not to confuse the reader or lose her interest, and tell an interesting and believable story.[29]

To Aristotle's basic outline of argument, the Romans added a **statement of the issue** by type[30] and an **outline or preview of the argument** (collectively, *divisio* or *partitio*). These sections identified the disputed issues to be resolved and enumerated for the audience (who was listening to, not reading) the arguments to follow.[31] The author of *Rhetorica Ad Herennium* explained the statement of the issues as follows:

Bottom Line

Effective legal argument identifies the issues in dispute and previews the argument to prepare the audience for what's to come.

> When the Statement of Facts comes to an end, we ought first to make clear what we and our opponents agree upon, . . . and what remains contested, as follows: 'Orestes killed his mother; on that I agree with my opponents. But did he have the right to commit the deed, and was he justified in committing it? That is in dispute.'[32]

Cicero said that by enumerating the disputed issues, the speaker indicated to the listener that "on which he ought to have his attention fixed."[33] Quintilian said it also indicates to the audience "that the Narrative is over and the Proof is beginning."[34]

Once the issues in dispute are identified, the speaker outlines the arguments to follow. Cicero said that in the outline

> the matters which we intend to discuss are briefly set forth in a methodical way. This leads the [listener] to hold definite points in his mind, and to understand that when these have been discussed the [speech] will be over.[35]

Rhetorica Ad Herennium instructed speakers not to list more than three arguments because one might forget to make one of them and a long list "instills in the hearer the suspicion of premeditation and artifice."[36] Quintilian disagreed; he thought it made no sense to limit the number of arguments to three since "a Cause may well

---

29 For a more detailed discussion on drafting statements of the case (facts) in written advocacy, see *infra* ch. 47.

30 *See* CICERO, DE INVENTIONE, *supra* ch. 9, note 19 and accompanying text.

31 *See id.* at I.22.31; RHETORICA AD HERENNIUM, *supra* ch. 9, note 20, at I.3.4.

32 RHETORICA AD HERENNIUM, *supra* ch. 9, note 20, at I.10.17.

33 CICERO, DE INVENTIONE, *supra* ch. 9, note 19, at I.22.31.

34 QUINTILIAN, *supra* ch. 9, note 27, at IV.5.1.

35 CICERO, DE INVENTIONE, *supra* ch. 9, note 19, at I.22.31.

36 RHETORICA AD HERENNIUM, *supra* ch. 9, note 20, at I.10.17.

need more."[37] He advised that the outline be brief, however, because the goal was just to highlight the arguments, not make them.[38]

In oral and written argument, lawyers today tend to put the statement of the issue first (*before* the facts).[39] However, after the statement of the facts and before the argument itself, we often include a summary of the argument to follow. It serves to foreshadow each argument and the order in which the reader should expect them. Even though legal audiences tend to read as opposed to listen to arguments, articulating the document's structure in advance aids comprehension. Having heard the argument stated briefly in advance, the reader recognizes and is better ready to receive the argument when it appears later, fully developed in the argument section.

The **argument** section is the focal point of oral and written argument. Aristotle said rhetorical syllogisms typify judicial argument but should be combined with appeals to pathos and ethos.[40] Quintilian defined argument as "a process of reasoning affording a proof, by which one thing is gathered from another, and which establishes what is doubtful by reference to what is certain."[41]

Deciding what arguments to make and how to arrange them is perhaps the most difficult part of the process. Aristotle said simply that arguments should function like proofs, either inductive or deductive, and the choice of arguments depends on the nature of the issues involved.[42] Aristotle advised against stringing too many proofs together at once or "your arguments will damage each other's effect."[43] He thus recommended that speakers weave appeals to *pathos* and *ethos* throughout appeals to *logos* for maximum effect.[44]

Neither the Greeks nor the Romans explored in much detail what we consider to be large-scale organization, offering little advice on how to choose one argument over another or in what order to present them. Yet the *Rhetorica Ad Herrenium* advised that the

> strongest arguments should be placed at the beginning and at the end . . . those of medium force, and also those that are neither useless to the discourse nor essential to the proof, which are weak if presented separately and individually, but become strong and plausible when conjoined with the others, should be placed in the middle.[45]

---

37 QUINTILIAN, *supra* ch. 9, note 27, at IV.5.3.

38 *Id.* at ¶ 26.

39 *See supra*, at 323.

40 ARISTOTLE, RHETORIC, *supra* ch. 8, note 3, at III.17, 1418a.

41 QUINTILIAN, *supra* ch. 9, note 27, at V.10.11.

42 ARISTOTLE, RHETORIC, *supra* ch. 8, note 3, at III.17, 1417b.

43 *Id.* at ¶ 1418a.

44 *Id.*

45 RHETORICA AD HERENNIUM, *supra* ch. 9, note 20, at III.10.18.

Cicero agreed that "the strongest point should come first, . . . while collecting into a general medley in the middle any points of moderate importance."[46]

Quintilian acknowledged that "just as much care should be taken in deciding what to put forward as in working out how what you have put forward should be proved."[47] He concluded, however, that because the selection of arguments depends so heavily on the specifics of each case and personal preference, "this is something that cannot be covered by textbooks."[48] He advised only to avoid making every conceivable argument because that approach will bore the audience and damage one's credibility.[49] As for the ordering of arguments, Quintilian disagreed; he said a speech should "never descend from the strongest argument to the weakest."[50]

Bottom Line

Arguments should be selected and organized intentionally, with restraint and an awareness of the relative strength of each.

Much conventional wisdom in legal writing today is rooted in these ancient concepts. Try to make conscious choices about which arguments to advance and in what order. With regard to which arguments to make, time and space constraints may help you choose, but the strongest and most relevant arguments should be advanced. The question, of course, is which arguments are strongest? Most relevant? These questions seem unanswerable at first, due in part to an expectation that there are "right" answers to these questions. As you gain experience and confidence, you will begin to have a sense of which arguments are most likely to persuade.[51]

As for how to order arguments, a survey I conducted in 2002 revealed that 74 percent of the federal judiciary considers it either essential or very important for advocates to put their strongest arguments first.[52] Although this is only one (and fairly old) survey, it suggests that modern legal audiences agree with Cicero and the *Rhetorica*. Most lawyers will likely recommend that your strongest arguments come first or, at a minimum, not last. If giving an oral argument, you may never get a chance to make that last argument, and if the argument is written, the judge may not finish reading the argument if overall it appears weak. As for interweaving appeals to logos with appeals to pathos and ethos, most experienced legal writers would agree that they should not stand apart.

---

46 CICERO, DE ORATORE, *supra* ch. 9, note 20, at II.77.314.

47 QUINTILIAN, *supra* ch. 9, note 27, at V.10.109.

48 *Id.* at ¶¶ 109–10.

49 *Id.* at V.12.8.

50 *Id.* at V.12.14.

51 For more on argument and organization, see *infra* ch. 48.

52 Kristen K. Robbins (Tiscione), *The Inside Scoop: What Federal Judges Really Think About the Way Lawyers Write*, 8 J. LEGAL WRITING 257, 273 (2002).

Aristotle considered counterarguments (refutation) part of the speaker's affirmative argument,[53] saying there were two ways to refute an argument: either by a counter-syllogism or by bringing an objection.[54] By counter-syllogism, he meant refuting an opposing argument by using a different argument altogether, such as relying on a different decision or posing an affirmative defense (e.g., even if the light was red when my client drove through the intersection, he was justified in doing so).[55] By objection, he meant refuting the party's argument by questioning their premises (e.g., the light was green, not red) or the relevance of prior, similar authority.[56] The Roman rhetoricians thought of counterarguments as separate from the argument.[57] Quintilian said that opposing parties use counterarguments "to rebut what is said by the other,"[58] and it is always harder to rebut than to make an argument because "wounding is easier than curing the wound."[59]

Bottom Line

Counterarguments rebut opposing arguments either by characterizing the same law differently, citing additional law relevant to the decision, or by challenging the premises of the opposing arguments themselves.

Today, we still think of counterarguments as being of two types: Aristotle's "counter-syllogisms" make the opposite argument on the same issue, often based on a different reading of the same law or on additional law not cited by the opponent that affects the decision. The second type, Aristotle's "objections," takes issue with the premises of the opposing argument, challenging the alleged facts or characterization of the law or both. The challenge of selecting the best counterarguments to make and when to make them is similar to that of selecting and arranging affirmative arguments.[60]

The **conclusion** signals the end of the speech in classical rhetoric. Aristotle said the conclusion should make the audience "well-disposed to yourself, and ill-disposed to your opponent," emphasize those points favorable to your case, put the audience in the right frame of mind, and refresh their memories.[61] To make the audience well-disposed, Aristotle said to "commend yourself, censure [your opponent], and

53 ARISTOTLE, RHETORIC, *supra* ch. 8, note 3, at III.13, 1414b.

54 *Id.* at II.25, 1402a.

55 *See id.*

56 *See id. at* ¶ 1402b.

57 *See* MICHAEL H. FROST, INTRODUCTION TO CLASSICAL LEGAL RHETORIC 44–45 (2005).

58 QUINTILIAN, *supra* ch. 9, note 27, at V.13.1.

59 *Id.* at V.13.3.

60 For a more complete discussion of the nature of counterarguments and their arrangement in legal writing, see *infra* chs. 38.C and 48.F.

61 ARISTOTLE, RHETORIC, *supra* ch. 8, note 3, at III.19, 1419b.

drive the difference home."[62] He said to refresh the audience's memory as to your arguments so they "learn them well."[63]

Cicero said speakers should summarize their arguments in a conclusion when "owing to the lapse of time or the length of your speech you distrust the memory of your audience, and when your case will be strengthened by recapitulating and briefly setting forth the main points of your argument."[64]

Classical advice on conclusions is as apt now for trial lawyers making closing arguments as it was to the ancients. In contrast, although lawyers used to include formal conclusions in written legal advice, they may be used less frequently. Email often substitutes for traditional legal memoranda, due in large part to time and expense.[65] Unlike classical rhetoric, conclusions in written legal argument are far more concise. Traditionally, they are comprised of one or two sentences that state clearly the desired relief sought.[66]

Bottom Line

Conclusions in legal argument are short statements of the relief sought by the parties from the court or other decision-maker.

C. Style

After deciding how to arrange the speech, a speaker must choose the right words or **style** to use. As Aristotle put it, "it is not enough to know *what* to say—one must also know how to say it."[67] Aristotle's view on style was straightforward. He said a speaker's words should be clear and appropriate to the circumstances:

> Thus we see the necessity of disguising the means we employ, so that we may seem to be speaking, not with artifice, but naturally. Naturalness is persuasive, artifice just the reverse.[68]

---

62 *Id.*

63 *Id.*

64 CICERO, DIVISIONS OF ORATORY, 17.59, at 355–56 (H. Rackham trans., Harv. Univ. Press 2004) (citation to chapter, paragraph, and page numbers), https://archive.org/details/in.ernet.dli.2015.186497/page/n357/mode/2up (https://perma.cc/LC35-A7J7); *see also* QUINTILIAN, *supra* ch. 9, note 27, at VI.1.1–2; RHETORICA AD HERENNIUM, *supra* ch. 9, note 20, at II.30.47.

65 *See infra* ch. 40.

66 *See* KENNEDY, *supra* ch. 9, note 34, at 54. For more discussion of the conclusion in legal memoranda and briefs, see *infra* chs. 37.A and 45.A.

67 ARISTOTLE, *supra* ch. 8, note 3, at III.1, 1403b.

68 *Id.* at III.2, 1404b.

He advised orators to construct sentences that are easy to follow, be as specific as possible, avoid ambiguous language, and follow rules of grammar and punctuation.[69]

The Romans divided style into at least three types: **low**, **middle**, and **high**.[70] A simple or low style was most effective for teaching or proving, the middle style was appropriate for delighting or moving an audience, and the grand or high style was reserved for persuasion.[71] Cicero, both an orator and statesman, was well known (and either idolized or criticized) for his ornate speech. A speaker's style was considered low, middle, or high depending on the complexity of the sentence structure and the use of figures of speech.

There are two categories of figures: schemes and tropes. A scheme is a "deviation from the ordinary pattern or arrangement of words."[72] An example of a scheme is alliteration, which is the repetition of a leading consonant sound in two or more adjacent words (*e.g.*, "Peter Piper picked a peck of pickled peppers.").[73] A trope is a "deviation from the ordinary and principal signification of a word."[74] The most common examples of tropes are metaphors and similes, which compare two things of unlike nature that seem to have something in common (*e.g.*, "He was a bear this morning when he got up" and "He acted like a bear this morning.")

Bottom Line

Speaking styles were divided into three basic types:

Low—*for teaching or proving*

Short sentences and plain language

Example: "My client didn't do it."

Middle—*for delighting*

Between Low and High

Example: "Members of the jury, my client is a respectable man. He had no motive, means, or opportunity to commit this crime. There is simply no evidence to support the charge."

High—*for persuading*

Complex sentence structures, ornate language, and use of figures

Example: "I ask you, most respected ladies and gentlemen of the jury, to consider whether, my client—a respectable, righteous, and religious man—would be capable of such a heinous act in the absence of any corroborating evidence."

A low style was characterized by short sentences, plain language, and little use of figures of speech; a high style was characterized by complex sentence structures,

---

69 *See id.* at III.5, 1407a-b.

70 *See, e.g.*, RHETORICA AD HERENNIUM, *supra* ch. 9, note 20, at IV.8.11 through IV.11.16; CICERO, ORATOR, *supra* ch. 9, note 20, at V.20; QUINTILIAN, INSTITUTIO ORATORIO, *supra* ch. 9, note 27, at XII.10.1–19.

71 CORBETT & CONNORS, *supra* ch. 8, note 2, at 21; RHETORICA AD HERENNIUM, *supra* ch. 9, note 20, at IV.8.11 n.c.

72 CORBETT & CONNORS, *supra* ch. 8, note 2, at 379.

73 *Id.* at 388–89.

74 *Id.* at 379.

ornate language, and the use of various figures; and the middle style was somewhere in-between.[75] The Attic orators, like Isocrates, used a low style, whereas the Asiatic orators, like Cicero, used a high style.[76] As the focus of rhetoric shifted from invention to style in the nineteenth century, scholars became interested in identifying and cataloging the figures of speech.[77]

Although Cicero advocated the use of a high style for persuasion, good legal writing in the twenty-first century is characterized more by an elegant, middle style.[78] As a result of the plain English movement of the mid-twentieth century,[79] the goal is to write in a way that readers not trained in the law can understand. We do that by avoiding legalese and long-windedness in favor of plain and simple terms and conciseness. Used sparingly, schemes and tropes have great effect. Finally, legal readers are exacting: they expect legal writing to be proofed, polished, and professional. In a word, perfect.[80]

D. Memory and delivery

Although Aristotle did not study **memory** or **delivery** in great detail, delivery was a critical part of an orator's education in ancient Greece and Rome.[81] Beginning in the Middle Ages and certainly by the time the printing press was invented in 1436, most communications were written, and the need to teach memory and delivery diminished greatly.

As you read in Chapter 9, rhetoricians did not focus on delivery in great detail until the eighteenth century, when the elocutionists first explored the impact of body language on audience. Today, these canons are the subject of speech and communication classes. As law schools have re-introduced performative skills training in clinical and experiential courses, more attention is now paid to these canons. Interacting with clients, reporting to supervisors, and speaking before a judge or jury are stressful—all the more so when you are speaking about topics that are new to you. Commit to taking a course in law school that requires you to engage in memory and delivery (e.g., Trial Advocacy, Negotiations, etc.) even if you do not plan to be a trial lawyer or litigator. Speaking with confidence in public settings is a requisite part of all legal careers. Part XIV provides information on preparing for client interviews,

---

75 RHETORICA AD HERENNIUM, *supra* ch. 9, note 20, at IV.8.11 through IV.11.16.

76 *See supra* at 92.

77 CORBETT & CONNORS, *supra* ch. 8, note 2, at 396.

78 *See infra* ch. 53.

79 *See id.* at 400.

80 For a more detailed discussion of style in legal writing, see *infra* ch. 53.

81 CORBETT & CONNORS, *supra* ch. 8, note 2, at 22.

meeting with supervisors, delivering an appellate oral argument, and public speaking in general.

Go Online

Read or watch these speeches as inspiring examples of **political/ceremonial speech**:

Amanda Gorman, *The Hill We Climb* (Presidential Inauguration, January 20, 2021), https://www.youtube.com/watch?v=Jp9pyMqnBzk (https://perma.cc/26G7-PLBQ).

Abraham Lincoln, *The Gettysburg Address* (November 19, 1863), http://showcase.netins.net/web/creative/lincoln/speeches/gettysburg.htm (https://perma.cc/KV7H-8Z52).

Martin Luther King, Jr., *I Have a Dream* (Aug. 28, 1963), http://freedomsring.stanford.edu/?view=Speech (https://perma.cc/A9PM-W4DP).

Barack Obama, *DNC Keynote Address* (July 27, 2004), http://www.csun.edu/~jg618373/classes-taught/american_history/speeches/obama_keynote.html (https://perma.cc/J6S6-JGPZ).

General Mattis, *Acceptance Speech for the Semper Fidelis Award* (Feb. 22, 2014), http://battlerattle.marinecorpstimes.com/2014/03/03/mad-dog-mattis-just-gave-what-may-be-the-most-motivating-speech-of-all-time/ (https://perma.cc/C2AV-3UJR).

Read or watch these speeches as excellent examples of **judicial speech:**

Closing Argument of Atticus Finch, To Kill a Mockingbird, https://www.americanrhetoric.com/MovieSpeeches/moviespeechtokillamockingbird.html (https://perma.cc/JVD5-VM7J).

Summation for the Prosecution by Justice Robert Jackson, The Nuremburg Trials (July 26, 1946), https://famous-trials.com/nuremberg/1933-jacksonsummation (https://perma.cc/3QTU-LESS).

Oral Argument of Petitioner, *in Obergefell v. Hodges* (Mary L. Bonauto, April 28, 2015), https://www.oyez.org/cases/2014/14-556 (https://perma.cc/K5DS-BL7U).

Chapter 14

What Is Writing, or How Were You Taught to Write?

What is writing? Is it the act of writing down pre-formed ideas? Or does the act of writing itself generate ideas? Does the act of reading and writing create shared knowledge between writer and reader? The answers to these questions are complicated, subject to debate, and evolving. They also affect how writing is taught. Understanding the nature of writing, how you were taught to write, and your own writing process will help you become a good legal writer.

FYI

Theories of writing

- Writing as the expression of thought (**Neo-Aristotelianism** and **current-traditional rhetoric**)
- Writing as the expression of the individual (**expressivism**)
- Writing as a generative process (**cognitive rhetoric**)
- Writing as the creation of knowledge in a community of readers (**social-epistemic rhetoric**)

As you know, by the late nineteenth century, classical rhetoric in the Western world was narrowed to the study of style, ultimately with an emphasis on reading as opposed to writing. However, as universities began to teach texts written in English, as opposed to Latin, and grow in size and number, it became necessary to develop ways to teach writing. That need increased substantially once children were required to attend primary and secondary school.

Under the influence of Ramism,[1] English departments in the United States taught literature (the study of ideas) and composition (the expression of ideas) separately. Even today, "[o]ne set of teachers is appointed to teach us how to read, while a second set tries to teach us how to write."[2] Theories on writing and how best to teach it have changed a great deal since the nineteenth century, but as you will read, each has had an effect on our development as writers.

---

1 *See supra* ch. 9, note 62, and accompanying text.

2 James J. Murphy, *Rhetorical History as a Guide to the Salvation of American Reading and Writing: A Plea for Curricular Courage, in* The Rhetorical Tradition And Modern Writing 3 (James J. Murphy ed., 1982).

Although these theories differ in terms of the writer's role in the creation of knowledge, they all address the same four elements of the writing process: a writer, the ideas expressed, a reader, and language.[3]

A. Theories of writing

1. Writing as the expression of knowledge or external reality (c. late nineteenth through mid-twentieth centuries)

To the extent Ramus believed that writing is not inventive,[4] Aristotle would probably have agreed with him. Aristotle assumed that invention occurs prior to writing. The critical feature of **neo-Aristotelianism**,[5] one early theory of writing, was the assumption that reality is "known and communicated, with language serving as the unproblematic medium of discourse."[6] The idea was that once you invent your arguments, the task of writing them down is relatively simple.

Current-traditional rhetoric (sometimes referred to as formalism or positivism) influenced writing classes from the latter nineteenth century through the 1960s. Like neo-Aristotelianism, it paid little attention to the writer's process, assuming invention occurs beforehand. It focused on arrangement and style: the "correctness" of the writing itself, in terms of format, grammar, and usage.

The current-traditionalists in the late nineteenth century were heavily influenced by the work of Bacon, Locke, Campbell, Blair, and Whately, who rejected logic (deduction) as the source of knowledge in favor of the scientific method (induction). If reality is objective and empirical, the writing teacher's job is to make sure the student's writing correctly reflects that reality.[7] The fact that pens, ink, and paper were neither readily available nor convenient to use must have contributed to treating thinking and writing as separate acts.[8]

---

3 James A. Berlin, *Contemporary Composition: The Major Pedagogical Theories*, 44 COLL. ENG. 765, 765–66 (1982), *reprinted in* THE WRITING TEACHER'S SOURCEBOOK 9–10 (Gary Tate, Edward P.J. Corbett & Nancy Myers eds., 3d ed. 1994). Note the similarity to Kinneavy's components of communication: encoder of a message, the reality to which the message refers, the decoder or receiver of the message, and the signal that actually carries the message. *See supra* ch. 8, note 6, and accompanying text.

4 *See supra* ch. 9, note 62, and accompanying text.

5 Sample textbooks include EDWARD P.J. CORBETT, CLASSICAL RHETORIC FOR THE MODERN STUDENT (1971) and RICHARD HUGHES AND ALBERT DUHAMEL, PRINCIPLES OF RHETORIC (1967).

6 Berlin, *Contemporary Composition*, *supra* note 3, at 11.

7 *See id.* at 13–14.

8 JAMES J. MURPHY, A SHORT HISTORY OF WRITING INSTRUCTION: FROM ANCIENT GREECE TO TWENTIETH CENTURY AMERICA 170 (1990).

You are likely to recognize several aspects of current-traditionalism that influenced your own writing classes: the division of writing into four basic types (description, narration, exposition, and argument);[9] a focus on large-scale organization, topic sentences, paragraph structure, and sentence construction;[10] and the five-paragraph essay.[11] Current-traditionalism is often criticized for emphasizing form over substance, misleading writers into thinking that writing is a mechanical process, with little or no attention to the reader.[12] Taught as "mechanics," writing was boiled down to transcribing ideas and checking for errors. As most of us have experienced, it is not quite that simple.

2. Writing as the expression of knowledge or reality from within the writer (c. 1960s)

Expressivism developed in the 1960s in response to current-traditionalism, focusing on the writing process as opposed to the final product. It is based on the idea that knowledge comes from within the individual writer.[13] Since knowledge resides within the writer, traditional writing teachers were theoretically unnecessary: "The teacherless writing class is a place where there is learning but no teaching. It is possible to learn something and not be taught."[14] Expressivist teachers tried to provide environments that would help students discover their inner vision. Composition students were often required to keep journals and engage in peer editing to help their classmates understand how successfully they had conveyed their vision.[15] If your writing teachers asked you to keep journals, record your reflections on reading assignments, or free write in class, they were influenced in part by expressivism.

3. Writing as a process that creates knowledge or constructs reality (c. early 1970s through early 1980s)

Cognitive rhetoricians disagreed with the idea that writing is simply the mirror of pre-existing knowledge, thought, or reality. They were interested in how

---

9 For a sample textbook, see ALEXANDER BAIN, ENGLISH COMPOSITION AND RHETORIC (Scholars' Facsimiles & Reprints 1996) (1871).

10 *See, e.g., id.*

11 A traditional five-paragraph essay is comprised of an introduction and thesis statement, three supporting examples in three separate paragraphs, and a conclusion. Far from extinct, this form of writing is still taught today in elementary and secondary education.

12 *See, e.g.,* Robert J. Connors, *The Rise and Fall of the Modes of Discourse*, 32 C. COMPOSITION & COMM. 444, 453–55 (1981), *reprinted in* THE WRITING TEACHER'S SOURCEBOOK 24, 32–34 (Gary Tate & Edward P.J. Corbett eds., 2d ed. 1988); KINNEAVY, *supra* ch. 8, note 6, at 28–30.

13 Berlin, *Contemporary Composition*, *supra* note 3, at 15. For a sample textbook, see PETER ELBOW, WRITING WITHOUT TEACHERS (2d ed. 1998).

14 ELBOW, *supra* note 13, at vii.

15 Berlin, *Contemporary Composition*, *supra* note 3, at 16.

people acquire knowledge, particularly language, and how that process affects the way people reason and write.[16] Knowledge resides neither in the external nor the internal world; instead, it is generated by the interaction of speaker, audience, message, and the reality the message represents.[17]

Cognitive rhetoricians focused primarily on the recursive nature of the writing process, as opposed to the writing itself, and studied the habits of expert writers.[18] The writing teacher's job was to intervene during the stages of the student's process—pre-writing, writing, and rewriting—to develop a better process and, in turn, better writing. Your writing teachers were probably heavily influenced by cognitive rhetoric. Brainstorming ideas, submitting a series of drafts, responding to written feedback, and attending writing conferences all come from cognitive rhetoric. Certainly, the advent of personal computers and word processing programs, which enable easy revision, contributed to the rise of cognitive rhetoric (e.g., no more typewriters and white-out).

Reminiscent of Valla and Vico,[19] **social-epistemic rhetoric** went one step farther in arguing that writing is a social act that produces knowledge. Reality is the result of the interaction between writer and reader or groups of similar readers, known as discourse communities.[20] Since knowledge is acquired neither by reason nor science, it is probable and relative, differing among communities and changing over time.[21] Social-epistemic knowledge is the opposite of Plato's absolute or universal truth, but it is no less valuable because it provides a way "to understand and change the world."[22]

Philip Kissam, a University of Kansas law professor, argues that law students "develop new connections or new ideas about what the law is and how it should be applied in particular situations" and that these ideas are knowledge in the social-epis-

---

16 *See* James Berlin, *Rhetoric and Ideology in the Writing Class*, 50 COLL. ENGLISH 477, 480–84 (1988), *reprinted in* THE WRITING TEACHER'S SOURCEBOOK 11–15 (Edward P.J. Corbett, Nancy Myers & Gary Tate eds., 4th ed. 2000).

17 *See* Berlin, *Contemporary Composition*; *supra* note 3, at 19.

18 *See, e.g.*, JANET EMIG, THE COMPOSING PROCESS OF TWELFTH GRADERS (1971); Linda Flower & John R. Hayes, *The Cognition of Discovery: Defining a Rhetorical Problem*, 31 C. COMPOSITION & COMM. 21–32 (1980), *reprinted in* THE WRITING TEACHERS' SOURCEBOOK 92–102 (Gary Tate & Edward P.J. Corbett eds., 2d ed. 1988).

19 *See supra* ch. 9.D.

20 *See, e.g.*, Ann E. Berthoff, *From Problem-Solving to a Theory of Imagination*, 33 COLL. ENGLISH 636, 646 (1972) (stating that reality is not something "out there" but the product of an interaction between observer and observed); Patricia Bizzell, *Cognition, Convention, and Certainty: What We Need to Know About Writing*, 3 PRE/TEXT 213, 230–31 (1982) (arguing that writing should be taught in its social context); Richard E. Young & Alton L. Becker, *Toward a Modern Theory of Rhetoric*, *reprinted in* CONTEMPORARY RHETORIC: A CONCEPTUAL BACKGROUND WITH READINGS 123, 140 (W. Ross Winterowd ed., 1975) (arguing that writers function within specific discourse communities and all writing choices, from content to style contribute to meaning).

21 Berlin, *Contemporary Composition*, *supra* note 3, at 19.

22 JAMES A. BERLIN, RHETORIC AND REALITY: WRITING INSTRUCTION IN AMERICAN COLLEGES, 1900–1985, 177 (1987).

temic sense.[23] Linda Berger, an emeritus law professor at the University of Nevada, Las Vegas, describes the creative process as the ebb and flow of writer and reader in the writer's mind.[24] The net effect of this internal dialogue is to construct meaning and create knowledge. The writing teacher's job is to explain the social function of a certain discourse community and the expectations of its readers. Although writing is rarely taught as the creation of knowledge, any time your teachers ask you to adopt a certain role, write for a specific purpose, and tailor your writing to a particular audience's needs, they were influenced by social-epistemic rhetoric.

B. The effect of writing theories on legal research and writing courses

Knowing a bit about these theories will help you understand why your professor is teaching legal writing a certain way. First, your professor is likely to focus on the "correctness" of your writing as a current traditionalist might: Did you follow the rules of the assignment? Did you turn it in on time? Is your paper over the word count? Is it in the correct font? Did you check for grammar, punctuation, and spelling errors? Are your citations in proper format?

Compliance with these requirements matters. Poor mechanics and a failure to follow instructions can obscure your intended meaning and draw your credibility into question. The legal profession, in particular, demands precise attention to detail: courts and agencies have complicated rules and procedures, and documents often have to be filed by a certain date, in a prescribed format, and under a given word count. To overlook a rule or a deadline can forfeit your client's rights. And you can expect legal readers to be both critical and impatient when it comes to errors.

Throughout the year, you may also be asked to free write in class, keep a journal of your research and writing process, or meet in peer groups to discuss your classmates' writing. These activities are inspired by expressivism, but you will not see much expressivism when it comes to your professor's expectations for the credibility of the information you rely on. Legal writing must be supported by external forms of proof (inartistic appeals) as well as artistic appeals that rely on constitutions, statutes, case law, administrative law, and agency decisions.

Perhaps for the first time, as a consequence of cognitive rhetoric, you will be asked to write multiple drafts of each assignment, respond to written feedback, and meet with your professor to discuss how to approach the next draft or assignment. The days of writing your one and final draft the night before an assignment is due are over. The first draft is never as good as the second, or third, or fourth . . . Finally,

---

23 Philip C. Kissam, *Thinking (By Writing) About Legal Writing*, 40 VAND. L. REV. 135, 140 (1987).

24 Linda L. Berger, *Applying New Rhetoric to Legal Discourse: The Ebb and Flow of Reader and Writer, Text and Context*, 49 J. LEGAL EDUC. 155, 168–69 (1999).

your legal writing course will draw on social-epistemic rhetoric in teaching you to construct rules of law in the context of your client's situation and the expectations of the legal discourse community.

C. Take time to assess your research and writing persona

Lawyers research and write for a living. Any real exception to this statement only proves the rule. Start thinking now about the kinds of research and writing you have done in the past. What subjects did you write about? To whom were you writing and for what purpose? What are your research and writing strengths and weaknesses? Where could your process improve?

Pam Jenoff, a novelist and clinical professor at Rutgers Law, encourages law students to use some of the tools fiction writers use to improve their writing process.[25] For example, take time early on to assess yourself as a writer to boost your productivity.[26] The following questions, several of which are inspired by Professor Jenoff, are designed to help you assess your research and writing persona. Some will help you understand your own habits and preferences, while others will help you understand the depth and breadth of legal research and writing. You will find that some of your writing habits work well for you in law school, but others will need to be adjusted to the nature and demands of legal writing.

1. Research

- Have you done much original research?
- Does research excite you or overwhelm you? Do you know why?
- Are you primarily familiar with print or electronic sources? What kind?
- Do you have a good sense of the costs or benefits of using one type of source over the other?
- Do you know how to evaluate the credibility of a print or online source?
- Do you know what a Boolean search is? A terms and connectors search? A keyword search?
- How do you know if a source is likely to help you? Do you evaluate it as a whole? Or do you tend to pick out good quotes?

---

25 Pam Jenoff, *The Self-Assessed Writer: Harnessing Fiction-Writing Processes to Understand Ourselves as Legal Writers and Maximize Legal Writing Productivity*, 10 LEGAL COMMC'N & RHETORIC: JALWD 187 (2013).

26 *See id.* at 191–95.

- Do you have a system for keeping track of your research?
- How do you know when you are done with your research?
- Do you have trouble stopping your research process and moving on to the writing stage?

2. Writing

- Have you done a lot of writing?
- Does writing excite you or overwhelm you? Do you know why?
- Do you make a schedule of interim deadlines, or do you tend to write the entire assignment the night before it is due?
- Do you have trouble turning assignments in on time?
- How do you prepare to write?
- How do you organize your thoughts?
- Are you in the practice of thinking first about what your audience needs and expects?
- Do you like to outline? Do you include just your ideas? Or do you include the sources you intend to rely on too?
- Do you like to talk your ideas over with a classmate first?
- Do you tend to write too soon, meaning before you have completed your research, or do you put off writing?
- Does writing make you feel stressed?
- Where do you like to write?[27]
- When do you like to write? Early in the morning? Late at night? Do you like being alone when you write?
- Do you like to listen to music while you write? Or do you like it quiet?
- Do you get writer's block?
- Do you have trouble meeting deadlines?
- Do you tend to write short and direct sentences or long convoluted ones?
- Are you the kind of writer who has trouble not having enough to say or having too much to say?
- Are you used to citing sources?

---

27 For more questions on your preferred writing environment, see *id.* at 192.

- What's the first thing you do once you finish your first draft?
- Do you review it?
- If so, what do you do?
- Do you look at the big picture? paragraphs? sentences? words?
- Do you usually have time left to polish your draft?
- How strong are your grammar and punctuation skills?
- Do you routinely spellcheck?
- Do you make sure your paper conforms to the rules of the assignment?

With some awareness of where your experience and strengths lie, you can begin to work on areas of weakness. When you get lost, stuck, or confused, reach out to your professor. Use this course as a way to improve your process and become a disciplined, healthy, and productive legal writer.

Test Your Knowledge: Part III

To assess your understanding of the material in this part, click here to take a quiz.

Part IV

Discovering Arguments

Chapter 15

Sources of Law

As Aristotle described it, the rhetorical process begins with discovery or invention. As lawyers, we begin this initial phase of the process by consulting "the topics"[1] or relevant sources of law. When we talk about "the law," we are talking about a relatively short list:

- **Constitutions**
- **Statutes** (enacted by the legislative branch of government)
- **Administrative rules and regulations** (enacted by the executive branch of government)
- **Judicial decisions** (issued by the judicial branch of government)
- **Agency decisions** (issued by the executive branch of government)

These are often called **primary** sources of law, and they can be issued by federal or state governments.

Secondary sources of law are publications that discuss or describe the law. They are commonly used in practice as a starting point for research because they explain the law in a variety of contexts and give citations to helpful, primary sources. Because they are not "the law," they are rarely cited to support statements about what the law "is." Some of the most useful secondary sources include:

- Legal dictionaries (e.g., *Black's Law Dictionary*)
- Legal encyclopedias (e.g., *American Jurisprudence* or *Corpus Juris Secundum*)
- Legal treatises (e.g., *American Law Reports* or Wright & Miller, *Federal Practice and Procedure*)
- Restatements (an American Law Institute publication that "restates" the majority common law rule on a variety of legal subjects)
- Legal periodicals, known as law reviews or journals (e.g., *Georgetown Law Journal*)

---

1 *See supra* ch. 13.A, at 84.

- Practice-specific reporting services, newsletters, or listservs (e.g., *Food, Drug and Cosmetic Law Reporter*)
- Law Blogs (e.g., SCOTUSblog or EvidenceProf Blog)

There is also a third and very different category of sources published exclusively for law students. These are study aids designed to help you prepare for class or study for exams. These include:

- Hornbooks (treatises that explain the law, such as *Nutshells*)
- Briefed cases and explanatory videos (e.g., Quimbee)
- Commercial outlines (to help prepare for class or exams, such as *Gilbert*, *Emanuel's*, and *Examples and Explanations*)
- Computer exercises (such as LexisNexis' Interactive Citation Workstation)

Law professors and lawyers will likely discourage you from relying too heavily on these study aids. Although they may save time or help you review for exams, they can also prevent you from doing the hard work required to develop your legal analytical skills. Before you invest heavily in any of these materials, get advice from librarians, faculty, and law students.

Bottom Line

Primary	***Secondary***	***Study Aids for Law Students***
Constitutions	Dictionaries	Hornbooks
Statutes	Encyclopedias	Case briefs
Administrative rules and regulations	Restatements of the Law	Commercial outlines
Judicial decisions	Law reviews or journals	Computer exercises
Agency decisions	Practice-specific reporting services/newsletters/listservs	
	Law blogs	

Chapter 16

Constitutions

A. Federal

> **FYI**
>
> The U.S. Constitution is the oldest written national constitution in use today.

The United States Constitution was written in 1787 and took effect in March 1789. It is the founding document of our federal government, and it establishes the Nation's fundamental laws, the three separate branches (legislative, executive, and judicial), and the roles and powers of each branch. Article I vests legislative power in Congress, Article II vests executive power in the presidency, and Article III vests judicial power in the courts.

The original constitution contained few civil rights guarantees for American citizens, and many states agreed to **ratify** (consent to) the Constitution contingent on the passage of a Bill of Rights. Twelve amendments were proposed in September 1789, ten of which the states had ratified by 1791. The rest of the amendments (eleven through twenty-seven) were adopted later. The most recent—prohibiting Congress from voting itself a pay raise before the next election in the House of Representatives—was adopted in 1992.

The federal government is one of limited power. Congress can exercise its authority only in furtherance of the powers enumerated in Article I. Examples of Congressional power include the power to levy taxes, borrow money, regulate interstate commerce, provide for military forces, and declare war. It can also pass laws "necessary and proper for carrying into Execution" the various powers vested in the national government (known as Congress' implied powers). The House may initiate impeachment proceedings, and the Senate adjudicates them. Under the Tenth Amendment, any powers not delegated to the federal government are reserved for the states.

Apply It: Exercise 16.1

The Constitution provides for "checks and balances" so that no one branch has more power than the other.

Can you name the ways in which each branch can "check and balance" the others? If not, check out the answers at App. B, at p. 511.

B. State

Each state's government is created by its own constitution. State constitutions are often modeled after the federal constitution, establishing its fundamental laws, a bill of rights, a state legislature, an executive branch headed by a governor, and a judicial branch or state court system. By 1780, each of the original thirteen colonies had a state constitution. Unlike the federal government, some states have had more than one constitution. Louisiana has had the most versions of any state. Its first constitution was written in 1812, and the eleventh iteration was written in 1974.

By creating a limited federal government, the founders of our **democratic republic** achieved a certain balance of power between federal and state governments. The idea is that Congress regulates those matters that affect the nation as a whole, and the states retain the power to govern local matters. For example, Congress has the power to regulate *interstate* commerce (i.e., commerce that crosses state lines, such as Amazon shipping products from one or more locations to destinations nationwide), but each state has the right to regulate *intrastate* commerce (i.e., commercial activity confined to its borders). This balance of power is also known as **federalism**.

States must grant their citizens the rights guaranteed by the U.S. Constitution. However, those federal rights act as a floor, not a ceiling. That means states can interpret their constitutional provisions to grant greater protections to their citizens than those guaranteed by similar provisions in the federal constitution.

C. Methods of interpretation

When parties disagree about the meaning or application of a particular law, they may also challenge its validity or constitutionality. Determining the constitutionality of the law (also known as **judicial review**),[1] either as it is written or applied in a given case, requires a method for interpreting the language of the constitution and what it either permits or requires.

---

1 The Supreme Court's authority to determine whether statutes violate the Constitution was first established in *Marbury v. Madison*, 5 U.S. 137, 177 (1803) ("It is emphatically the province and duty of the judicial department to say what the law is.").

Judges use a variety of different methods for interpreting constitutions. These different methods reflect their personal views about the nature of the constitution and their role as members of the judiciary (i.e., whether or not judges can or should "create law"). Similarly, lawyers use these methods to advance their clients' arguments. For example, if a judge feels strongly that constitutional language should be interpreted based on its meaning at the time it was written, you may be able to make an effective argument that the language meant then what your client argues it means now.

Some common methods of constitutional interpretation—textualism, originalism and living constitutionalism—are explained below.[2] Most often used at the appellate level, they guide both judges and lawyers in answering new or complicated questions of interpretation.

What's That?

Novel legal questions are often referred to as "questions of first impression."

1. Textualism

Textualism is a method of interpretation that focuses on the plain meaning of the text. It is used to interpret constitutional and statutory language[3] and looks only "within the four corners" of the document. In the textualist's view, the framers' intent should not be considered.[4] Instead, textualists often try to ascertain what the words in the text would have meant at the time of ratification. They may also infer meaning from the text's position in the structure of the document as a whole.[5] In short, a textualist asks, "What does the text alone say?"

FYI

The late Justice Antonin Scalia was an ardent textualist:

> *The text is the law, and it is the text that must be observed.*

Antonin Scalia, A Matter of Interpretation: Federal Courts and the Law 22 (Amy Gutmann ed., 1997) (https://perma.cc/JG2X-4RNX).

Textualism is often considered in conjunction with another method of interpretation.[6] When the text alone fails

---

2 *See* Brandon J. Murrill, Cong. Research Serv., R45129, *Modes of Constitutional Interpretation* (2018), https://fas.org/sgp/crs/misc/R45129.pdf; *see also* William A. Kaplin, *The Process of Constitutional Interpretation: A Synthesis of the Present and a Guide to the Future*, 42 RUTGERS L. REV. (1990) (discussing constitutional interpretation at the time but using different terminology for the major interpretive categories).

3 For more on statutory interpretation, see *infra* ch. 17.

4 Murrill, *supra* note 2, at 5.

5 *See generally* HON. ANTONIN SCALIA, *Common-Law Courts in a Civil-Law System: The Role of United States Federal Courts in Interpreting the Constitution and Laws*, *in* A MATTER OF INTERPRETATION: FEDERAL COURTS AND THE LAW 3 (Amy Gutmann ed., 1997).

6 Murrill, *supra* note 2, at 5.

to provide an objective meaning, textualists will consider other methods of constitutional interpretation, such as originalism.[7]

Critics argue that textualism, while attempting to limit the ability of judges to "legislate from the bench," actually gives judges too much power.[8] Allowing judges to have the final word on the objective meaning of the text gives them license to say whatever they think about the meaning of a constitutional provision that is inherently ambiguous.[9]

2. Originalism

Originalism is a method of interpretation that focuses on the original understanding of the text at the time the constitution was written. As Judge Robert Bork,[10] an early originalist, explained:

> All that counts is how the words used in the Constitution would have been understood at the time. The original understanding is thus manifested in the words used and in secondary materials, such as debates at conventions, public discussion, newspaper articles, dictionaries in use at the time, and the like.[11]

Food for Thought

Which justices on the Supreme Court are thought to be originalist (at least in part) in their approach to judicial review?

If you don't know, Google it!

Different forms of originalism focus on different individuals' understanding of what the text meant when the Constitution was written. For example, public meaning originalism attempts to identify the meaning of the text as it would have been understood by the general populace, not just by the framers.[12] Originalists contend that there is an objectively identifiable meaning of any constitutional provision and that it is the judiciary's job to discover that meaning.[13] In short, originalists ask, "What did this mean to the people when it was passed?"

Critics argue that originalists stifle progress by focusing only on the original meaning of constitutional provisions.[14] They also argue that the language of a con-

---

7 *Id.*

8 *See, e.g.*, Johnathan T. Molot, *The Rise and Fall of Textualism*, 106 COLUM. L. REV. 1 (2006).

9 *See id.* at 49–50.

10 Judge Bork was nominated to the Supreme Court by President Reagan in 1987 but rejected by the Senate, in part, because his views on constitutional interpretation were perceived by Senate Democrats as an attempt to roll back civil rights decisions of prior Courts.

11 ROBERT H. BORK, THE TEMPTING OF AMERICA: THE POLITICAL SEDUCTION OF THE LAW 144 (1990).

12 Murrill, *supra* note 2, at 7.

13 *Id.*

14 *See, e.g.*, Mitchell N. Berman, *Originalism is Bunk*, 84 N.Y.U. L. REV. 1 (2009).

stitutional provision does not necessarily match its intended outcome. For instance, the reason for adopting a provision in the Constitution might be different from the plain meaning of the text. In that sense, the text cannot reflect its original meaning.[15]

3. Living constitutionalism

Living constitutionalism is a method of interpretation that focuses on the current needs of society. As Lawrence Solum explains, proponents of this theory take "the view that the legal content of constitutional doctrine does and should change in response to changing circumstances and values."[16] Unlike textualists and originalists, living constitutionalists believe much of the constitution is yet unwritten, and it should be treated as a living, changing document.[17]

Proponents of living constitutionalism disagree on how it should be accomplished.[18] Some focus on pragmatic concerns, such as the effect of the judicial decision on the real world, morality, or which interpretation yields the most equitable outcome.[19] Others focus on structural or institutional concerns, such as deferring to the legislature, the superiority of international law to national law, or the superiority of treaties to the federal constitution.[20] In short, living constitutionalists ask, "How does this document need to change to fit current needs?" Critics argue that it encourages the judiciary to change—as opposed to interpret—laws, simply because the legislative and executive branches haven't.[21] They argue that it is not the judiciary's job to make laws, but rather to "call balls and strikes."[22]

Hear It

Listen to the late Justice Ruth Bader Ginsburg talk about her approach to interpreting the Constitution in an interview with Lesley Stahl on CBS' 60 Minutes in 2008.

https://www.youtube.com/watch?v=QxZlreaXX8Y (https://perma.cc/F5Z3-2T4R)

You can also hear what Justice Sonia Sotomayor had to say about theories of constitutional interpretation in a 2013 interview with Scott Pelley.

https://www.youtube.com/watch?v=kHvgiEWH6A4 (https://perma.cc/HMQ9-XJXZ)

---

15 *Id.* at 43–47.

16 *See, e.g.*, Lawrence B. Solum, *Legal Theory Lexicon 077: Living Constitutionalism*, LEGAL THEORY LEXICON (Nov. 25, 2018), https://lsolum.typepad.com/legal_theory_lexicon/2017/05/legal-theory-lexicon-077-living-constitutionalism.html (https://perma.cc/3ETQ-M6L3).

17 Lawrence B. Solum, *Originalism versus Living Constitutionalism: The Conceptual Structure of the Great Debate*, 113 NW. U. L. REV. 1243, 1271 (2019).

18 *Id.*

19 *Id.* at 1271–76.

20 *Id.*

21 *See e.g.*, SCALIA, *supra* note 5, at 41–47 (on the notion of a living constitution). William H. Rehnquist, *The Notion of a Living Constitution*, 54 TEX. L. REV. 693, 699 (1976).

22 *Roberts: "My Job is to Call Balls and Not to Pitch or Bat,"* CNN (Sept. 12, 2005), https://www.cnn.com/2005/POLITICS/09/12/roberts.statement/ (https://perma.cc/EJ3M-8ZY2).

For More Information

Resources related to Textualism:

Akhil Reed Amar, *The Supreme Court, 1999 Term—Foreword: The Document and the Doctrine*, 114 Harv. L. Rev. 26 (2000).

Oliver Wendell Holmes, Jr., *The Theory of Legal Interpretation*, 12 Harv. L. Rev. 417 (1889).

Vicki Jackson, *Holistic Interpretation:* Fitzpatrick v. Bitzer *and Our Bifurcated Constitution*, 53 Stan. L. Rev. 1259 (2001).

Resources related to Originalism:

Georgetown Center for the Constitution, Originalism Seminar Podcast (series), https://www.law.georgetown.edu/constitution-center/originalism-resources/.

John O. McGinnis, *Which Justices are Originalists?*, Law and Liberty (Nov. 9, 2018), https://lawliberty.org/which-justices-are-originalists/ (https://perma.cc/9AU4-BWLC).

H. Jefferson Powell, *The Original Understanding of Original Intent*, 98 Harv. L. Rev. 885 (1985).

Jack Rakove, *Original Meanings: Politics and Ideas in the Making of the Constitution* (1996).

Ronald Rotunda, *Original Intent, the View of the Framers, and the Role of the Ratifiers*, 41 Vand. L. Rev. 507 (1988).

Resources related to Living Constitutionalism:

Mari Matsuda, *When the First Quail Calls: Multiple Consciousness as Jurisprudential Method*, 11 Women's Rts. L. Rep. 7 (1989).

Charles Reich, *Mr. Justice Black and the Living Constitution*, 76 Harv. L. Rev. 673, 733 (1963).

David A. Strauss, *The Living Constitution* (2010).

Apply It: Exercise 16.2

(see suggested answers at App. B, at p. 511)

The Seventh Amendment to the United States Constitution states:

> In Suits at common law, where the value in controversy shall exceed twenty dollars, the right of trial by jury shall be preserved, and no fact tried by a jury, shall be otherwise re-examined in any Court of the United States, than according to the rules of the common law.
>
> The Coinage of 1792 defined dollar to mean "the value of a Spanish milled dollar as the same is now current, and to contain three hundred and twenty-one grains and four sixteenth parts of a grain of pure, or four hundred and sixteen grains of standard silver."

Assume your client wants a jury trial for a disputed amount of $42. Drawing on the text of the Seventh Amendment and the three methods of interpretation described above, what arguments could be made in support of and against your client's position? What types of arguments are they?

Chapter 17

Statutes

Statutes are laws enacted by a legislative body, either the United States Congress or a state legislature. The process for enacting federal and state statutes is similar. Statutes may prohibit certain acts (e.g., employers may not discriminate), require certain acts (e.g., you must wear a seat belt), make a declaration (e.g., failure to exercise a duty of care shall constitute negligence), or set forth governmental mechanisms for the good of society (e.g., the federal statute creating the Consumer Financial Protection Bureau).

Go Online

Just for fun, watch this vintage 1975 cartoon on the legislative process from the Schoolhouse Rock series, which used to air during Saturday morning cartoons: https://www.youtube.com/watch?v=FBpdxEMelR0 (https://perma.cc/DD6Q-AJC3).

For a more serious outline of the process legislatures use to pass bills, see https://www.usa.gov/how-laws-are-made (https://perma.cc/C758-XGZW).

Practice Pointer

Citations to federal and state codes include:

- the title number that corresponds to the subject matter of the statute,
- the name of the official code,
- the section(s) relied on, and
- a year (either the year the code was published or the date it was accessed online).

For example, 5 U.S.C. § 554 refers to Title 5, Section 554 of the United States Code. For more information, see Chapter 56.F.

Once a bill becomes law, it is usually **codified**. That means it becomes part of the federal or state government's official "code," which contains all statutes in force, arranged in alphabetical order by subject matter (e.g., banking, taxation, zoning, etc.). Statutes are also published in the order in which a particular Congress or legislative assembly passes them (these publications are commonly referred to as "statutes at large"). However, practitioners use codes to conduct research because they are arranged topically, not chronologically. Federal statutes are arranged topically in the United States Code.[1]

[1] *See* https://www.law.cornell.edu/uscode/text (https://perma.cc/45ZC-QE72). For more information on researching federal and state codes and how to cite them, see *infra* chs. 25–26 and 56.F.

Although no two statutes are identical, they are generally constructed in similar ways. Just as it helps to understand how judicial decisions are constructed, it helps to know the parts of a typical statute. Lawyers tend to call these parts "sections." Knowing the typical sections of a statute helps your research, too. When you find a section of a statute online, you will have a sense of whether there might be related sections before or after it. Because it is easier to see the entirety of a statute in print, some lawyers advise new legal researchers to double-check their online results in the corresponding print code.

Practice Pointer

To type the section sign (§) in Word, click on Insert, then Symbol, then Special Characters. You can also create a "shortcut key" or set up an "auto correct" command to insert that symbol. For more information, consult the help function in Word.

When parties disagree about the meaning or application of a particular statute, they rely on a variety of methods for interpreting the text. As with constitutional interpretation, there is disagreement about which methods are best. You will continue to learn about statutory interpretation throughout law school, but you will need some background at this point to help you read and interpret statutes for this course.

A. The sections of a typical statute

If the legislature decides to include a statement of the statute's purpose as part of the statute itself, that statement usually comes first. Next, the key terms used throughout the statute may be defined in a **definitions** section.

The most important parts of the statute tend to appear in the middle. In most statutes, one or more sections set out **the requirements to prove or avoid liability or guilt**: the elements of a crime, the elements of a cause of action, or the applicable standard of conduct.

If the legislature envisions a situation that would fall under the statute but does not want the statute to apply to that situation, it may list **exceptions** in a separate section. Finally, if the legislature wants to assign specific penalties in a criminal case, such as imprisonment or fines, or damages in civil cases, these usually appear in the last section of the statute.

Bottom Line

A typical statute may contain

- a stated purpose
- definitions
- the elements of a crime or cause of action, a rule, or a flexible standard that leads to guilt (in a criminal statute) or liability (in a civil statute)
- exceptions
- penalties or damages or both

Take a look at the statute on the next page. It is a Texas statute that prohibits making false statements about perishable food products knowing those statements to be false. It contains all the typical parts of a statute except a stated purpose, but the purpose to protect plant and fish farmers can be inferred.

Food for Thought

Why would the Texas legislature prohibit false statements about perishable but not all food products?

CIVIL PRACTICE AND REMEDIES CODE
TITLE 4. LIABILITY IN TORT

CHAPTER 96. FALSE DISPARAGEMENT OF PERISHABLE FOOD PRODUCTS[2]

(1) **Sec. 96.001. DEFINITION.** In this chapter, "perishable food product" (2) means a food product of agriculture or aquaculture that is sold or distributed in a form that will perish or decay beyond marketability within a limited period of time.

Added by Acts 1995, 74th Leg., ch. 80, Sec. 1, eff. Sept. 1, 1995. (3)

Sec. 96.002. LIABILITY. (a) A person is liable as provided by Subsection (b) if:

(1) the person disseminates in any manner information (4) relating to a perishable food product to the public;

(2) the person knows the information is false; and

(3) the information states or implies that the perishable food product is not safe for consumption by the public.

(b) A person who is liable under Subsection (a) is liable to the producer of the perishable food product for damages and any other appropriate relief arising (5) from the person's dissemination of the information.

Added by Acts 1995, 74th Leg., ch. 80, Sec. 1, eff. Sept. 1, 1995.

Sec. 96.003. PROOF. In determining if information is false, the trier of fact shall consider whether the information was based on reasonable and reliable scientific inquiry, facts, or data.

Added by Acts 1995, 74th Leg., ch. 80, Sec. 1, eff. Sept. 1, 1995.

Sec. 96.004. CERTAIN MARKETING OR LABELING EXCLUDED. A person is not liable under this chapter for marketing or labeling any agricultural product in a manner that indicates that the product:

(1) was grown or produced by using or not using a chemical (6) or drug;

(2) was organically grown; or

(3) was grown without the use of any synthetic additive.

Added by Acts 1995, 74th Leg., ch. 80, Sec. 1, eff. Sept. 1, 1995.

---

2 *See* https://statutes.capitol.texas.gov/Docs/CP/htm/CP.96.htm (https://perma.cc/2T4J-2C94). This is how the statute looks on the Texas government website. The formatting may differ somewhat in other sources, but the text will be exactly the same.

(1) "Sec." here stands for "**section**." The symbol for section looks like this: §.

(2) The key phrase in this statute, "perishable food product," is **defined** here.

(3) The dates each section was passed are indicated.

(4) The three **elements** of a claim for food disparagement are listed here.

(5) **Damages** under this statute are explained here.

(6) These **exceptions** to liability are situations the legislature anticipates the statute applying but does not want there to be liability in those situations.

B. Methods of interpretation

The goal of statutory interpretation is to carry out the intent of the legislature, as evidenced by the text or other information. When the text of a statute is arguably ambiguous, lawyers and judges may use several different methods to infer the legislative intent. Just as judges and scholars disagree on the appropriate methods for interpreting the constitution, they can disagree on the proper method for interpreting statutes.

> **Bottom Line**
>
> Methods of statutory interpretation (in general order of preference) include:
>
> - plain meaning
> - context
> - definitions
> - case law
> - canons of construction
> - legislative history
> - public policy

The starting point for interpreting statutes is often **plain meaning**. The presumption is that a legislature intends for words to have their plain and ordinary meaning in everyday use. If a court can resolve ambiguous terms by giving them their plain meaning, it will. As Justice White stated, "[W]e assume "that the legislative purpose is expressed by the ordinary meaning of the words used." *Am. Tobacco Co. v. Patterson*, 456 U.S. 63, 68 (1982).

As a practitioner, when plain meaning fails to resolve ambiguity, look next to the **context** of the statute to determine intent: can the ambiguity be resolved by looking at how similar statutes are interpreted? By understanding where and why the statute is located where it is within the code as a whole? Do the **definitions** help in any way?

These tools may help resolve the problem. When they don't, look next to **case law**, which may be **mandatory** (i.e., **binding**) on the court.[3] How have courts interpreted this statute in the past? How have courts interpreted similar statutes in the past? Is there a good argument that the statute at issue should be interpreted the same way?

Over the years, federal and state courts have developed guidelines for interpreting statutes, called **canons of construction**. These canons are like default rules for resolving ambiguity. For example, one canon of construction is that a statute that changes the common law should be interpreted as narrowly as possible. Yet another canon is that if a statute that changes the common law is **remedial**, it should be liberally construed.[4] Because there "are two opposing canons on almost every point,"[5] the canons of construction rarely resolve ambiguity on their own. However, they can provide additional reasons for choosing one interpretation over another.

Like canons of construction, the **legislative history** of a statute (also referred to as legislative evidence) may also be helpful.[6] The documents generated during the legislative process are often the best evidence of legislative intent. Conference committee reports are often considered the most persuasive because they are written by members of both the House of Representatives and the Senate. Conversely, statements made on the floor of one house by a single member are considered the least persuasive (as the view of just one legislator).

Finally, **public policy** may be used to help decide what a statute means. Public policy refers to that which furthers society's collective goals. For example, the federal tax code permits homeowners to deduct some or all of the interest they pay on their mortgage loans. The interest is deductible to make owning homes more affordable, demonstrating that our society values home ownership. Thus, one might argue that any ambiguity in the code related to the deductibility of mortgage interest should be interpreted in a way that furthers that goal.

---

3 For more information on mandatory or binding authority, see *infra* ch. 22.

4 Llewellyn, *supra* ch. 12, note 8, at 401; *see also* SCALIA, *supra* ch. 16, note 5, at 25–29 (on the use of canons of construction).

5 Llewellyn, *supra* ch. 12, note 8, at 401.

6 As with constitutional interpretation, some judges will consider outside resources such as legislative history, whereas others will focus mainly on the text itself. *See, e.g.*, SCALIA, *supra* ch. 16, note 5, at 29–37 (on the use of legislative history).

Chapter 18

Administrative Regulations

Federal and state legislatures delegate some of their authority to **administrative agencies** to carry out specific goals, usually related to establishing and regulating certain commercial activities, such as banking, aviation, and securities trading. Typically, agencies promulgate rules or **administrative regulations** to implement congressional statutes. Agencies are in a better position to promulgate these regulations because they have scientific, economic, and industry expertise that Congress does not.

For example, the Securities & Exchange Commission (SEC)[1] was created by The Securities Exchange Act of 1934.[2] Its purpose is to protect investors, provide fair and efficient markets, and facilitate economic growth. The SEC implements several statutes referred to as "federal securities laws" (including the 1934 Act) and promulgates regulations. Section 78j(b) of the 1934 Act[3] prohibits the use of manipulative or deceptive practices in the purchase or sale of **securities.**[4] In turn, the SEC promulgated several regulations to implement this broad prohibition. Rule 10b5–1 is a well-known regulation that prohibits insider trading. It defines manipulative or deceptive practices to include the purchase or sale of securities based on information not generally known to the public.

In addition to promulgating rules or regulations, agencies have the power to enforce their own rules. Agencies may investigate rules violations and hold admin-

---

1 You can view the SEC's website at https://www.sec.gov/.

2 FindLaw provides free access to the U.S. Code and other legal sources. *See* 15 U.S.C. § 78d, https://codes.findlaw.com/us/title-15-commerce-and-trade/15-usc-sect-78d-1.html (https://perma.cc/H9TH-7ZQC).

3 Cornell Law School also provides free access to the U.S. Code and other legal sources. *See* https://www.law.cornell.edu/uscode/text/15/78j (https://perma.cc/W2GT-VF2B).

4 Securities are certificates or other financial instruments that have monetary value and can be traded.

istrative hearings, which lead to **agency decisions**. Depending on the agency, its decisions may be reviewable by Congress or the courts.

Most agencies are governed by the executive branch.[5] The President of the United States has the power to appoint and remove the heads of federal agencies, including Cabinet members who advise the President. Federal agencies with Presidential appointees include the Federal Communications Commission, the Federal Trade Commission, and the Securities & Exchange Commission.[6]

The Cabinet is composed of the Vice President and the heads of the executive departments—the Secretaries of Agriculture, Commerce, Defense, Education, Energy, Health and Human Services, Homeland Security, Housing and Urban Development, Interior, Labor, State, Transportation, Treasury, and Veterans Affairs, as well as the Attorney General.

Some agencies, such as the Securities and Exchange Commission, are considered part of the executive branch but operate independently so as to be less vulnerable to political influence.

A. Rulemaking process

Agency regulations are often referred to as "rules." The federal rulemaking process is governed by Section 553 of the Administrative Procedure Act (APA), 5 U.S.C. § 553.[7] Typically, an agency publishes proposed regulations in the *Federal Register*.[8] The *Federal Register* is published daily and contains final rules, proposed rules, and notices of federal agencies and organizations, as well as executive orders and other presidential documents. Once a proposed rule is published in the *Federal Register*, a public comment period begins, during which the public is invited to submit written comments to the agency. Most agencies are required to respond to the comments either in the final rule or as an addendum to the final rule. Depending on the complexity of the rule, comment periods may last for thirty to one-hundred and eighty days.

Unless the agency publishes a second draft of the proposed rule for further comment, the final rule is published with explanations in the Federal Register. Once final, the rule is then codified in the *Code of Federal Regulations*,[9] commonly referred

---

5 There are some legislative agencies, too, that serve Congress. The Library of Congress and the Government Printing Office are two examples.

6 *See* https://www.whitehouse.gov/about-the-white-house/the-executive-branch/.

7 *See* https://www.law.cornell.edu/uscode/text/5/553 (https://perma.cc/3X6Y-5MJL)

8 *See* https://www.federalregister.gov/.

9 The U.S. government provides free access to its regulations, known as the e-cfr. *See* https://www.ecfr.gov/.

to by practitioners as "the CFR." The rule usually does not take effect for at least thirty days to give all interested parties time to come into compliance with the new rule(s).

B. Methods of interpretation

Methods for interpreting statutes, such as plain meaning, canons of construction, and the regulation's procedural (i.e., "legislative") history are also used for interpreting administrative regulations.[10] Kevin Stack, an administrative law scholar at Vanderbilt Law School, recommends adopting a purposive approach. To begin, consider the text of the regulation in light of its "statement of basis and purpose" (often referred to as the regulation's "preamble").[11] Then consider whether the regulation implements the statute that authorizes it. Thus, the regulation should also be interpreted in light of the goals of the statute that authorized it.[12]

C. Agency decisions

Under the APA, agencies may enforce the federal statutes they implement as well as their own regulations. The procedure for enforcement is outlined in 5 U.S.C. § 554.[13] Adjudications may be formal or informal, depending on the agency and the nature of the alleged violation. Formal adjudications resemble trials and are presided over by administrative law judges. Informal adjudications may or may not require a hearing; they are usually carried out through inspections, conferences and negotiations.

For example, the SEC may investigate suspected securities law violations, recommend that the agency bring civil actions in federal court or before an administrative law judge, and prosecute cases on behalf of the agency.

Go Online

To see agency decisions issued by the SEC, go to its website at https://www.sec.gov/litigation/opinions.htm (https://perma.cc/4NX4-2JJ3).

---

10 *See supra* ch. 17B.

11 Kevin M. Stack, *First Principles for Interpreting Regulation*, THE REGULATORY REVIEW (Feb 11, 2013) [hereinafter *First Principles*], https://www.theregreview.org/2013/02/11/11-stack-regulation-interpretation (https://perma.cc/4TJM-ZT6K); *see also* Kevin M. Stack, *Interpreting Regulations*, 111 Mich. L. Rev. 355, 361 (2012), https://repository.law.umich.edu/mlr/vol111/iss3/2 (https://perma.cc/6FDG-DLD8).

12 Stack, *First Principles*, *supra* note 11; Stack, *Interpreting Regulations*, *supra* note 11, at 363. If you take an Administrative Law class, you will learn much more about interpreting regulations and how courts review them for validity.

13 *See* https://www.law.cornell.edu/uscode/text/5/554 (https://perma.cc/5XP8-PK7P).

Chapter 19

Case Law

Judicial decisions are also referred to as case law, common law, or judicial opinions. As discussed in Chapter 6, a court typically issues a decision to explain its holding on a particular legal issue or bundle of issues.[1] The decision may represent the **majority** or **plurality** of the court, or it could be a **concurrence** or **dissent**. Often, the decision summarizes the parties' arguments before explaining the court's analysis or reasoning. The court then relies on and cites primary and, sometimes, secondary sources of law in explaining its reasoning.

A. *Stare decisis* and precedent

Courts rely on a variety of primary sources of law to support their decisions, but which ones and why?

As you will learn more about in Chapter 22, a court is bound to follow the sources of primary law in its **jurisdiction** that apply to a given legal situation. Everything else, including primary sources of law outside its jurisdiction and secondary sources of law, may be helpful—we call this **persuasive**—but is not binding on the court's decision.

> **It's Latin to Me**
>
> *Stare decisis* translates from Latin to "to stand by things."

In our common law system, primary law includes decisions or case law.[2] Common law systems are premised on the principle of ***stare decisis***. It means that like cases should be treated alike. Generally speaking, if a court is presented with a case where the facts and the legal issue(s) are sufficiently similar to a prior decided case from that jurisdiction, the prior case controls the outcome in the present case. We call this kind of case **mandatory** or **binding** on the court. The body of published case law that may apply in a given case is often referred to as **precedent**, which may be binding or persuasive. Some cases are reported but not published,

---

1 *See supra* ch. 6, at 15.

2 To understand which cases bind which courts, see *infra* ch. 22.B.

either because they are too new or will never be published. This latter category of cases is considered "unpublished" and not intended by the issuing courts to have precedential value.[3]

Due to *stare decisis*, there may be one or more prior decisions in the relevant jurisdiction that are similar enough to the client's case to be potentially mandatory (binding). On the one hand, if the case suggests a favorable outcome, a lawyer may be able to argue that the case is sufficiently similar or **analogous** to their client's case to mandate the same outcome. On the other hand, if the case suggests an unfavorable outcome, they may be able to argue that the case is sufficiently dissimilar or **distinguishable** so as to treat the client's case differently.

B. Holdings and dicta

When briefing a judicial decision to prepare for class discussion, you include the court's **holding** or ultimate decision in that case.[4] In this context, the holding is the answer to the legal question before the court. Once you identify the holding, you can evaluate the reasoning the court used to support it and the fairness of the result in that case. In the *Copeland* case,[5] for example, the legal issue was whether the plaintiff could recover attorney's fees under a D.C. statute, where "the attorneys" were law students representing her in their capacity as law students. The literal holding was "yes."

The holding of a case has another meaning as well. It's the case's main "takeaway" or the principle for which it stands. The holding guides courts in deciding future cases under *stare decisis*. The holding of a case is subject to interpretation and may be read narrowly or broadly, which can affect the outcome in future cases. For example, the narrow reading of a case might be one that limits the holding to its **legally salient facts**. In *Copeland*, the holding might be that law students acting as lawyers are entitled to attorney's fees under D.C. Code § 1–623.27(b)(2). This reading of the case—in terms of its most significant facts—might bind future courts only in cases where attorney's fees were being sought for legal work performed by law students in a law clinic under supervision.

Alternatively, the holding may be expressed in terms of the reasoning the court used to support its ultimate decision. Also known as the ***ratio decidendi*** ("the reason for deciding"), this approach tends to produce a broader reading or rule.[6] For example, in *Copeland*, the *ratio decidendi* might be that "precluding the recognition of para-professional services in attorney's fee awards would render the statute an

---

3 For more information on unpublished cases, see *infra* chs. 22.B and 56.E.7.

4 *See supra* ch. 6, at 28.

5 *See supra* ch. 6.B, at 19.

6 *See also holding* and *ratio decidendi*, *in* BLACK'S LAW DICTIONARY (11th ed. 2019).

anomaly among fee-shifting statutes."[7] This broader rule—expressed in terms of the underlying purpose of the statute—would be binding on a wider range of cases involving analogous facts and circumstances (even if unanticipated by the court) as long as the same underlying purpose(s) would be served.

In keeping with ethical constraints,[8] lawyers can use the fluidity of holdings to their clients' advantage. For instance, assume your opposition has articulated a broad holding from a case that is arguably binding and would produce an unfavorable outcome for your client. First, look for ways to argue that the holding should be limited to the legally salient facts of that case and distinguish yours. In contrast, if your opponent has articulated a narrow holding that will exclude your client to their detriment, look for ways to argue that the case should be read in terms of its reasoning and demonstrate how that same reasoning applies to your client's situation.

In contrast to holdings, **dicta** are never binding. Dicta, short for *obiter dictum* (singular) or *dicta* (plural), translates to statements "said in passing."[9] These are statements the court makes in decisions that may relate to but were not necessary to the court's holding or the result in the case.

C. Case reporters

Federal judicial decisions are published in official and unofficial versions:

- Supreme Court decisions are published in *U.S. Reports* (U.S.) (official), the *Supreme Court Reporter* (S. Ct.), and the *United States Supreme Court Reports, Lawyer's Edition* (L.Ed.).
- Courts of appeals decisions are published in the *Federal Reporter* (F., F.2d, F.3d) (official). Unpublished decisions are reported in the *Federal Appendix* (Fed. App'x) (official).
- District court opinions are published in the *Federal Supplement* (F. Supp., F. Supp. 2d, and F. Supp. 3d), *Federal Rules Decisions* (F.R.D.) (official), and *West's Bankruptcy Reporter* (B.R.) (official). Unpublished decisions are usually available online but not published in print form.

---

7 Copeland v. D.C. Dep't of Emp. Servs., 3 A.3d 331, 335 (D.C. 2010).

8 For example, a lawyer has a duty to "represent a client zealously and diligently [but] within the bounds of the law." D.C. Rules of Pro. Conduct r. 1.3(a) (last accessed Nov. 14, 2020), https://www.dcbar.org/For-Lawyers/Legal-Ethics/Rules-of-Professional-Conduct/Client-Lawyer-Relationship/Diligence-and-Zeal (https://perma.cc/G5HJ-LXZM). This rule recognizes that "the bounds of the law in a given case are often difficult to ascertain. The language of legislative enactments and judicial opinions may be uncertain as applied to varying factual situations. The limits and specific meaning of apparently relevant law may be made doubtful by changing or developing constitutional interpretations, ambiguous statutes, or judicial opinions, and changing public and judicial attitudes." *Id.* at cmt. [3].

9 *Dicta*, *in* BLACK'S LAW DICTIONARY (11th ed. 2019).

The judicial decisions of state courts are also reported in official and unofficial reporters. For the names of individual state reporters and which to cite as the official source, see *The ALWD Guide* Appendix 1 and the *Bluebook* Table 1.[10]

Apply It: Exercise 19.1

(suggested answers in App. B, at p. 512)

1. What is the purpose of *stare decisis*? Put another way, why do we treat like cases alike?

2. In *Wigham v. Richter*, a train conductor fell asleep, and the train collided with a car stopped on the train tracks. The court's opinion, in relevant part, read:

> Because the conductor should have been awake and alert while working, we hold that a person operating a vehicle who falls asleep and hits another vehicle is automatically at fault.

Assume you represent a client who fell asleep at the wheel of a car and rear-ended another car. The other driver's insurance company claims that this case is binding on your client's case, and your client is automatically at fault.

a. What is the holding the insurance company might articulate for *Wigham*? What is the holding based on? Is it broad or narrow?

b. How could you articulate the holding to distinguish this case from your client's? What is the holding based on? Is it broad or narrow?

Test Your Knowledge: Part IV

To assess your understanding of the material in this part, click here to take a quiz.

10 ALWD GUIDE, *infra* ch. 56, note 1, at App. 1; BLUEBOOK, *infra* ch. 56, note 1, at tbl. T.1.

Part V

Hierarchy of Authority

Chapter 20

The Federal and State Courts

In every case, some legal authority may be mandatory, while other legal authority is potentially useful but only persuasive.[1] When conducting legal research, you will find relevant authorities that seem useful because they involve your client's legal issue and seem to resemble your client's circumstances.

What's That?

Lawyers often refer to legal authority that speaks directly to the question at hand as being "on point."

The question is, how do you know which authorities are binding and which are not?

To answer this question, you need to know a few things: 1) you need to know what court or agency you are likely to be in if a dispute arises and the matter needs to be adjudicated; 2) you need to understand the basic structure of the federal and state courts, how these courts operate, and how they work together; and 3) you need to know a bit about the subject matter jurisdiction of each court—meaning the types of legal questions they have the power to hear.

This chapter introduces you to the structure of the federal and state courts and the functions of each. Chapter 21 explains a bit about the subject matter jurisdiction of each court in the federal and state systems, and Chapter 22 brings all this information together to help you identify potentially binding authority.

A. The federal court system

All federal courts at the same level have the same name, and each level of court has a specific function.

1 *See infra* ch. 22, at 140.

1. District courts

A lawsuit is usually filed first with a trial-level court.[2] Federal trial courts are called **district courts**. There are ninety-four district courts in the federal government, and each district may have more than one courthouse. The states with the highest populations have more than one district (e.g., California, New York, and Texas have four).

In each case, the function of the district court is to resolve **questions of fact** and **questions of law**.[3] In a jury trial,[4] the jury listens to the evidence and resolves questions of fact—what happened to whom. In addition to presiding over the trial, the district judge typically decides—with input from the parties—what law applies to the case and what that law requires. The judge then instructs the jury on how to apply the law to the facts they find. In federal civil cases, the jury is comprised of at least six people; in federal criminal cases, the jury has twelve. The right to a jury trial may be waived, in which case the judge also finds the facts. This is known as a **bench trial**.

For Example:

Assume the **plaintiff** in a civil case has filed suit in thet United States District Court for the Northern District of Texas for personal injuries. The plaintiff, a pedestrian, claims that the **defendant** ran a red light while driving his vehicle and struck her in the crosswalk. The defendant claims that the light was green when he

---

2 There may be other trial-level courts that handle disputes over relatively small amounts of damages or specific types of disputes. Often, these courts are not "of record," which means there is no court reporter or transcript of the proceedings. If an agency charges an individual or organization with violating its regulations, the charges are likely to be filed first with an adjudicative body within the agency.

3 *See also infra* ch. 46 (on the standard of review relating to questions of fact or law on appeal).

4 The Seventh Amendment of the United States Constitution preserves the right of a jury trial in suits at common law where the value in controversy exceeds twenty dollars. U.S. Const. amend. VII.

entered the intersection. He also claims that his wife was in the car, in labor with their first child, and as a precaution, he honked and flashed his lights as he entered the intersection. The plaintiff is a Texas resident and the accident occurred in Texas, but the defendant is a resident of the District of Columbia.

In this case, there are several questions of fact and law. The questions of fact might include when the accident occurred, whether the light was red or green, whether the defendant's wife was in the car and in labor, whether and how the defendant made an effort to warn pedestrians he was entering the intersection, and whether the plaintiff heard the warning.

The questions of law might include whether, when, and to what extent a party is liable under Texas law[5] for causing injuries as a result of running a red light. Was the driver negligent? Reckless? Does it matter if the driver was in distress? What if the defendant attempted to warn pedestrians and other drivers that he was approaching the intersection? Does the plaintiff bear any responsibility for her injuries?

If the case went to trial, the jury (or judge in a bench trial) would listen to the conflicting evidence and decide the answers to these questions. The plaintiff would have to prove certain facts necessary to win her case by a preponderance of the evidence, meaning the facts as she alleged them were more likely than not to have occurred.[6] The parties might also make arguments about the answers to the questions of law, but the judge ultimately decides. The judge in turn explains the law to the jury and how to apply it to the facts. Together, the judge and jury would have input on any damages awarded if the plaintiff prevails.

2. Courts of appeals

The party who loses in district court may appeal that decision without being given permission (this is known as an "appeal as of right").[7] There are thirteen circuits or **courts of appeals** in the federal government.[8] Each circuit is made up of several states and the District of Columbia. Each hears appeals from the district courts within its borders, or in some instances from other designated federal courts

---

5 If you are wondering if D.C. law might apply because the defendant lives there, that is a conflicts of law question. In most states, the law of the state where the accident occurred would apply. You will learn more about conflicts of laws in a civil procedure course.

6 The plaintiff's burden here includes the burden of proof—to put on sufficient evidence—and the burden of persuasion—to convince the fact-finder. These concepts are treated in depth in a civil procedure course.

7 There is an exception to this rule: In general, the government cannot appeal in a criminal case.

8 There are eleven numbered courts of appeals that include district courts from multiple states. There is also a court of appeals for the District of Columbia circuit and a court of appeals for the Federal Circuit, which hears special appeals. A map of the federal circuits is available at www.uscourts.gov/file/document/us-federal-courts-circuit-map (https://perma.cc/B3P2-ZS9S). To see a list of the states in each circuit, see ch. 22.B.1, at 142.

and administrative agencies. The Federal Circuit, located in Washington, D.C., has exclusive subject matter jurisdiction over certain appeals, including those involving patent and trademark law.[9]

Appeals are usually heard by a panel of three judges. The parties may petition for an ***en banc*** hearing (as the initial decision) or re-hearing (once the initial appeal is decided). *En banc* hearings are held before all the appellate judges in that circuit and are granted only if 1) a panel's decision arguably conflicts with a decision of the United States Supreme Court or of the court to which the petition is addressed, or 2) the case involves one or more questions of exceptional importance.[10]

On appeal, the function of the circuit court is to review the district court's decision for claimed error. These errors raise **questions of law**, not fact, even if the appellant claims the jury made a mistake in its fact-finding.

For Example:

Assume the defendant in our personal injury suit lost in the United States District Court for the Northern District of Texas and filed an appeal in the United States Court of Appeals for the Fourth Circuit. He claims that

1) the jury erred in finding the light was red, and

2) even if it was red, the court should have instructed the jury that he was excused (at least to some extent) because his wife was in labor and he tried to warn people that he was entering the intersection.

As to the first claim that the jury erred in its factual finding, the court of appeals will not substitute its judgment for that of the jury, who heard the evidence first-hand. Instead, the court will review the evidence to determine whether the finding was **clearly erroneous.**[11] Only if the answer to this question is yes (and even if the judges might have found differently) will the court reverse the district court's finding of fact.

As to the second set of claims that the court erred on questions of law, the court may substitute its judgment for that of the district court. This is known as **de novo** review, meaning to reconsider the legal question anew. If the court finds the lower court erred in answering any of the legal questions (and the error was not harmless), it may reverse the district court's decision. If the court of appeals finds no factual or legal error, it will affirm the lower court.[12]

---

9 28 U.S.C. § 1295.

10 *See* Fed. R. App. P. 35, https://www.law.cornell.edu/rules/frap/rule_35 (https://perma.cc/79QQ-VF92).

11 Different courts articulate this standard differently.

12 For more information on the standards of review courts use on appeal, see *infra* ch. 46.

3. The United States Supreme Court

Of course there is only one **Supreme Court** in the federal government, popularly referred to as either "the Court" or "SCOTUS." Nine justices—appointed for life—preside over the Supreme Court. Appeals from the courts of appeals to the Supreme Court are by permission only, known as **writs of certiorari**. The Supreme Court hears only a fraction of the cases it is called upon to review (roughly 100–150 out of more than 7,000 petitions).[13]

Like the courts of appeals, the Supreme Court does not revisit the evidence presented at trial to re-find facts. Instead, it deals solely with questions of law, including whether the lower courts erred in their assessment of the jury's fact-finding. Most often, the Supreme Court deals with questions of law relating to the constitutionality of statutes (either as written or applied) and lower court decisions.[14]

B. The state court system

Unlike federal courts, state courts at the same level in different states have different names.[15] Each state has its own court system, with courts at the trial and appellate level (although some states have only one court of appeal).[16]

In Texas, for example, trial courts are called district courts, but in New York, they are called supreme courts. In 2019, there were 472 trial courts in Texas. Appeals from Texas district courts are filed in one of fourteen courts of appeals. For example, in Fort Worth, a lawsuit would be filed first in a Tarrant County District Court, and appeals would be filed in the Second Court of Appeals in Fort Worth and heard

---

[13] *See* http://www.uscourts.gov/about-federal-courts/educational-resources/about-educational-outreach/activity-resources/about (https://perma.cc/6F8W-K83E).

[14] *See supra* ch. 16.

[15] The proper names of the state courts can be found in Appendix 1 of the ALWD Guide, *infra* ch. 56, note 1, at 421, and Table 1 of the Bluebook, *infra* ch. 56, note 1, at 227.

[16] *See id.*

by a three-judge panel.[17] With permission, appeals from there go either to the Texas Supreme Court (civil cases) or the Court of Criminal Appeals (criminal cases).[18]

Unlike most federal judges, who are appointed for life, state judges may be appointed or elected depending on the state.[19] The function of the state trial and appellate courts is the same as in federal court, with appellate courts addressing only questions of law. The number of jurors in civil cases varies by state, but twelve people are generally required in criminal cases.

17 This information is available on state court websites, which are listed in Appendix 1 of the ALWD GUIDE and Table 1 of the BLUEBOOK.

18 In contrast, state trial courts in New York are called supreme courts. *See* ALWD GUIDE, *infra* ch. 56, note 1, at App. 1, at 454; BLUEBOOK, *infra* ch. 56, note 1, at 272.

19 *See* https://litigation.findlaw.com/legal-system/how-are-judges-selected.html (https://perma.cc/DM6H-46UY).

CHAPTER 21

Subject Matter Jurisdiction

Subject matter jurisdiction relates to the court's power to hear certain types of cases. This power comes from the constitution that created the court. If a court issues a decision in a case where it lacked subject matter jurisdiction, the decision is invalid.

Although courts generally do not grant relief that has not been requested by the parties, a court will raise on its own—*sua sponte*—a lack of subject matter jurisdiction and dismiss a case it has no power to hear.[1]

A. Federal courts

Recall that the federal government has limited powers—only those granted to it by the United States Constitution.[2] Federal statutes enacted by Congress must be consistent with those enumerated powers, such as the power to regulate only interstate commerce.

Just as Congress has limited legislative power, the federal courts have **limited jurisdiction:** they are generally limited to hearing cases that involve questions of constitutional interpretation and federal law.[3]

1. United States Supreme Court

Under 28 U.S.C. § 1251,[4] the Supreme Court has **original** and **exclusive jurisdiction** over all controversies

> **Bottom Line**
>
> **Original jurisdiction** is a court's power to hear a particular type of case first—before any appellate review.
>
> **Exclusive jurisdiction** is a court's power to be the only court to hear certain cases.

1 *See, e.g.*, Fed. R. Civ. P 12(h)(3), https://www.law.cornell.edu/rules/frcp/rule_12 (https://perma.cc/KEL8-XCGF).

2 *See supra* ch. 16.A, at 107.

3 *See, e.g.*, 28 U.S.C. § 1331, https://www.law.cornell.edu/uscode/text/28/1331 (https://perma.cc/Z6GK-796R).

4 28 U.S.C. § 1251, https://www.law.cornell.edu/uscode/text/28/1251 (https://perma.cc/Q892-TWS3).

between states.[5] The Court has original but not exclusive jurisdiction over actions or proceedings to which ambassadors, other public ministers, consuls, or vice consuls of foreign states are parties; all controversies between the United States and a state; and all actions or proceedings by a State against the citizens of another State or non-U.S. citizens.[6]

The bulk of the Supreme Court's work is as an appellate court, granting petitions for review of courts of appeals decisions under 28 U.S.C. § 1254.[7]

2. United States Courts of Appeals

The United States Courts of Appeals have no original jurisdiction. Under 28 U.S.C. § 1291,[8] they have "jurisdiction of appeals from all final decisions of the district courts of the United States" in their circuit. They can also review certain interlocutory orders (interim decisions made prior to the conclusion of the proceedings).[9] Because the Supreme Court grants review of so few cases, these courts effectively have the last word on most questions of federal law and are thus quite powerful.

3. Federal district courts

> **FYI**
>
> The jurisdiction of the United States District Court for the Northern District of Texas over the hypothetical car accident case in Chapter 20 would be based on diversity of citizenship under 28 U.S.C. § 1332.

Under 28 U.S.C. § 1331,[10] federal district courts have original (but not exclusive) jurisdiction over all civil actions arising under federal law: the Constitution, laws, or treaties of the United States. A major exception to this rule is when the parties to the suit are citizens of different states (and similar situations). Under those circumstances, claims based on state law may be heard in federal court as long as the disputed amount exceeds $75,000. This kind of jurisdiction is known as diversity of citizenship.[11]

---

5 *See also* U.S. CONST. art. III, § 2, https://www.law.cornell.edu/constitution/articleiii#section2 (https://perma.cc/Q53S-SRX6).

6 *See* 28 U.S.C. § 1251, *supra* note 4.

7 *See* 28 U.S.C. § 1254, https://www.law.cornell.edu/uscode/text/28/1254 (https://perma.cc/9M3G-TY-CM).

8 *See* 28 U.S.C. §§ 1291–92, https://www.law.cornell.edu/uscode/text/28/1291 (https://perma.cc/J4DD-GJV9) and https://www.law.cornell.edu/uscode/text/28/1292 (https://perma.cc/JV8X-PUEC).

9 *See* 28 U.S.C. § 1292, https://www.law.cornell.edu/uscode/text/28/1292 (https://perma.cc/JV8X-PUEC).

10 *See* 28 U.S.C. § 1331, https://www.law.cornell.edu/uscode/text/28/1331 (https://perma.cc/RVQ5-ZM59).

11 28 U.S.C. § 1332, https://www.law.cornell.edu/uscode/text/28/1332 (https://perma.cc/N6W7-QCQ3). You will learn more about federal court subject matter jurisdiction in your civil procedure course.

In general, federal courts have original and exclusive jurisdiction of criminal actions arising under federal law and certain areas regulated by federal law, such as admiralty, bankruptcy, and copyright law.

B. State courts

Unlike federal courts, state courts are courts of **general jurisdiction:** they have original (but not exclusive) jurisdiction to hear all civil actions arising under federal and state law. This is because the Tenth Amendment reserves the bulk of governmental power for the states.[12] States may enact statutes on almost any subject matter as long as they are constitutional (both under the federal and their state constitution) and not **pre-empted** by federal law. Similarly, state courts may hear federal and state civil claims, but they have jurisdiction to hear criminal cases based on state law only.

Bottom Line

General jurisdiction refers to a state court's power to hear civil cases arising under federal or state law.

12 *See supra* ch. 16, at 107.

Chapter 22

Mandatory and Persuasive Authority

A. Order of authorities

Sources of law are also known as legal authorities, and some legal authorities have more influence than others. Generally speaking, primary authority supersedes secondary authority, and within primary sources of law, there is a distinct hierarchy.

1. Primary sources of law

In general, primary sources of law can be ranked in this order:

- constitutions
- statutes (including court procedural rules)[1]
- administrative regulations
- cases
- agency decisions

Assume that there is primary authority in each of the above categories relevant to and binding on a federal court hearing a federal law claim. If the federal statute conflicts with the federal constitution, the constitution controls. If the federal regulation conflicts with the federal statute, the statute controls, and so on. The order of authorities is the same with state law.

Federal courts are generally bound by the federal constitution, and any statutes, regulations, cases, or agency decisions—in that order of preference—that apply to the case before them. States courts, which hear federal and state law claims, are bound in the same way—by applicable federal or state law—in the order of preference

1 *See, e.g.*, Fed. R. Civ. P. 8 on general rules of pleading, https://www.law.cornell.edu/rules/frcp/rule_8 (https://perma.cc/D6YH-LKDD).

described above. Where federal law conflicts with state law, federal law prevails under the Supremacy Clause.[2]

2. Secondary sources of law

Although secondary sources of law are not "law" in the technical sense, secondary authority can be persuasive, particularly where the court has no law "on point" in its own jurisdiction.

It's not possible to rank secondary authority with any level of certainty. However, the following statements seem generally true (although check with your professors to get their view as well):

Restatements,[3] as well **model codes, model acts,** and **uniform laws**[4] can be highly persuasive, particularly in the absence of binding law. Often, these sources are authored collaboratively by judges, scholars, and practitioners, so they carry a great deal of weight. **Law review articles** can also be persuasive to courts, especially in **cases of first impression** or where different courts have treated substantially similar legal questions differently, and the scholar has offered useful ways to resolve the issue.

Treatises on specific legal subjects can also be useful, but again, some are more useful or respected than others. When you become familiar with the law in a particular jurisdiction, you can usually get a sense of the secondary sources, including treatises, that the court is likely to find persuasive. Finally, **encyclopedias, annotations,**[5] and **dictionaries** may be useful but are likely to be the least persuasive. The more specific the treatise or encyclopedia to the jurisdiction or law at issue, the better.

B. Who binds whom?

The following summarizes when and how each court is bound by the published decisions of other courts.

---

2 *See* U.S. CONST., art. VI, ¶ 2 (the laws of the United States "shall be the supreme law of the land"), https://www.law.cornell.edu/constitution/articlevi (https://perma.cc/XCW8-UHR6).

3 *See infra* ch. 25.

4 The Uniform Law Commission of the National Commissioners on Uniform State Law proposes uniform laws to increase uniformity of laws across state lines. Model acts are proposed to legislatures with the aim of reforming existing laws rather than ensuring uniformity.

5 "Annotations" here refers to collections or articles that address federal or state legal issues in greater depth than encyclopedias. Often, they focus on rapidly developing or controversial areas of law, not all areas of law.

1. Federal courts

The United States Supreme Court is bound only by its prior decisions.[6] In turn, it binds all federal and state courts on all questions of federal law.

The Court does not generally hear matters relating solely to state law. If the Court agrees to hear a case that involves state law, it does so because the state law allegedly involves or violates federal law.[7]

The Courts of Appeals are bound by the Supreme Court on questions of federal law.

In general, on questions of state law only, the courts of appeals are bound by state court decisions. This is known as the *Erie* doctrine,[8] which can be more complicated than it sounds. The theory is that federal courts "sitting in diversity" are bound by state court decisions because states have the power to interpret what their law means. In this context, decisions by a state's highest court would certainly be considered binding, but it's less clear if decisions from intermediate or trial-level courts should be considered binding, persuasive, or something in between.

In turn, courts of appeals bind all federal district courts in their circuit (and

FYI

United States Supreme Court

(binds all federal and state courts on questions of federal law)

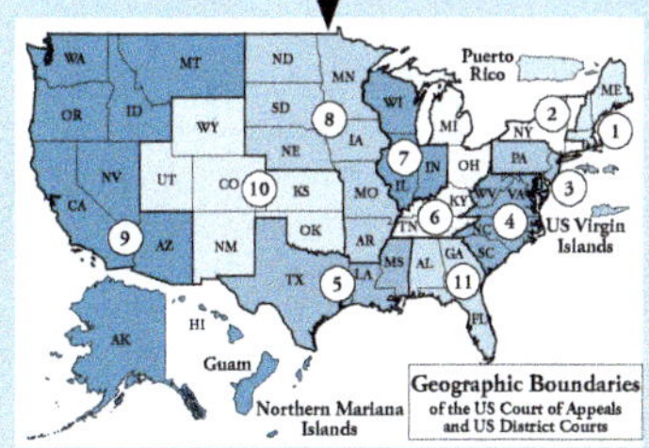

Federal Courts of Appeals

(bind lower district courts in their circuit only on questions of federal law; bound by state courts on questions of state law)

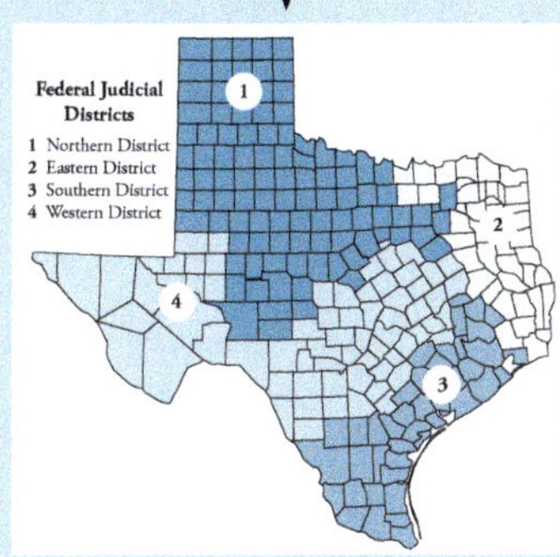

Federal District Courts

(bound by decisions of their circuit only on questions of federal law; bound by state courts on questions of state law)

---

6 Although the Court is reluctant to overturn its own decisions, it has done so over 200 times. *See, e.g.*, Trump v. Hawaii, 585 U.S. ___, 138 S. Ct. 2392 (2018) (repudiating Korematsu v. United States, 323 U.S. 214 (1944) on the grounds of racial prejudice); Obergefell v. Hodges, 576 U.S. 644 (2015) (overruling Baker v. Nelson, 409 U.S. 810 (1972), which denied same-sex couples the right to marry under state law); and Brown v. Bd. of Education, 347 U.S. 483 (1954) (overruling Plessy v. Ferguson, 63 U.S. 537 (1896) and the doctrine of "separate but equal").

7 The circuit courts are most likely to make decisions on state law when hearing appeals of diversity of citizenship cases or cases alleging that state law violates the U.S. Constitution.

8 *See* Erie R.R. Co. v. Tompkins, 304 U.S. 64 (1938) (holding that state law is binding in federal cases based on diversity of citizenship); *Comparing Federal and State Courts*, http://www.uscourts.gov/about-federal-courts/court-role-and-structure/comparing-federal-state-courts (https://perma.cc/6K-DK-WCNT); *supra* ch. 21.A.3.

Bottom Line

States in Each Circuit

First	*Maine, Massachusetts, New Hampshire, Puerto Rico, Rhode Island*
Second	*Connecticut, New York, Vermont*
Third	*Delaware, New Jersey, Pennsylvania, Virgin Islands*
Fourth	*Maryland, North Carolina, South Carolina, Virginia, West Virginia*
Fifth	*District of the Canal Zone, Louisiana, Mississippi, Texas*
Sixth	*Kentucky, Michigan, Ohio, Tennessee*
Seventh	*Illinois, Indiana, Wisconsin*
Eighth	*Arkansas, Iowa, Minnesota, Missouri, Nebraska, North Dakota, South Dakota*
Ninth	*Idaho, Montana, Nevada, Oregon, Washington, Guam, Hawaii*
Tenth	*Colorado, Kansas, New Mexico, Oklahoma, Utah, Wyoming*
Eleventh	*Alabama, Florida, Georgia*
D.C.	*District of Columbia*
Federal	*All federal judicial districts*

only their circuit) on questions of federal law. This is sometimes referred to as *vertical stare decisis*. Courts of appeals' decisions on state law would likely be treated as nearly binding or highly persuasive to district courts in the same circuit.[9]

Traditionally, federal courts of appeals do not bind each other; there is no *horizontal stare decisis*. This is how we get "circuit splits," meaning two different federal courts of appeals can issue conflicting decisions in substantially similar cases. However, most circuits have developed some version of a "law of the circuit" rule, which requires panels *in the same circuit* to follow prior decisions.[10]

District courts are bound by the Supreme Court and their court of appeals on questions of federal law. They are not bound by courts of appeals decisions outside their own circuit.

Just like courts of appeals, district courts sitting in diversity are bound by state court decisions (meaning, at a minimum, decisions of the state's highest court). There is no *horizontal stare decisis* among district courts (even in the same district), but their decisions are considered very persuasive.

2. State courts

- State courts are similar to federal courts in terms of *vertical stare decisis* within their own jurisdiction.

---

9 *See* Colin E. Wrabley, *Applying Federal Court of Appeals' Precedent: Contrasting Approaches to Applying Court of Appeals' Federal Law Holdings and Erie State Law Predictions*, 3 SETON HALL CIR. REV. 1, 4 (2006).

10 *See, e.g.*, Joseph W. Mead, Stare Decisis *in the Inferior Courts of the United States*, 12 NEV. L. J. 787, 794–95 (2012).

In general, the **state's highest court** is bound only by the United States Supreme Court on questions of federal law. Again, the Supreme Court might hear a case involving state law but only to the extent that the case implicates federal law. The Court's decision would be limited to the constitutionality of the state law under the federal constitution. Like the United States Supreme Court, a state's highest court can overturn its own decisions.

> FYI
>
> **state supreme court**
>
> (binds all lower state courts)
>
> ↓
>
> **state appellate court**
>
> (depending on the state, binds all state trial courts or only those in its geographical region)
>
> ↓
>
> **state trial court**

A state's highest court is *not* bound by decisions of federal courts of appeals (even in their circuit) or federal district courts on questions of federal or state law.

In turn, the state's highest court binds intermediate appellate courts (if the state has them) and trial courts in that state on questions of federal and state law.

Intermediate appellate state courts (if the state has them) are bound by their state's highest court on questions of federal and state law.

A state's intermediate appellate courts are *not* bound by decisions of federal courts of appeals (even in their circuit) or federal district courts on questions of federal or state law.

There is no horizontal *stare decisis* among intermediate appellate state courts. In some states, the appellate courts have limited vertical *stare decisis*, meaning they bind only those trial courts in their districts (e.g., Ohio).[11] In others, the intermediate appellate courts bind all trial courts in the state (e.g., Illinois).[12]

State trial courts are bound by their state's highest court and some (if not all) decisions of their state's intermediate appellate courts (if they exist) on issues of federal and state law.

State trial courts are *not* bound by decisions of federal courts of appeals (even in their circuit) or federal district courts on questions of federal law. As with federal district courts, there is no *horizontal stare decisis* among state trial courts.[13]

---

11 Hudson Distributors, Inc. v. Eli Lilly & Co., 209 N.E.2d 234, 240 (C.P. 1965).

12 J & J Ventures Gaming, LLC v. Wild, Inc., 38 N.E. 194, 201 (Ill. App. Ct. 2015), *aff'd*, 67 N.E.3d 243 (2016).

13 For more information on mandatory and persuasive authority, *see, e.g.*, Robyn Painter, Kate Mayer & Kate Mathews, *Which Court Is Binding?: Binding vs. Persuasive Cases*, Georgetown Law Writing Center (2d ed. 2017), https://www.law.georgetown.edu/wp-content/uploads/2018/07/Which-Court-is-Binding-HandoutFinal.pdf (https://perma.cc/65H2-T88A).

Apply It: Exercise 22.1

(suggested answers at App. B, at p. 513)

Your clients live in Pennsylvania and own a vacation home in Maine. They started using it like an Airbnb (but not through Airbnb) a few months ago, and the neighbors are beginning to complain about increased traffic on their road and noisy parties.

You have done some preliminary research for your clients to get a feel for the law on short term rentals of private property in Maine. Your research has produced the following results:

a) A Maine treatise on zoning law that discusses using private property as a bed and breakfast or inn

b) A 2020 decision by the United States Court of Appeals for the First Circuit on Maine law

c) A 2018 regulation from the Code of Maine Rules

d) A 2000 decision by Maine's Supreme Judicial Court

e) A Restatement of Property on short term rentals discussing a variety of different state approaches

f) A 2016 decision by the United States District Court for the District of Maine

g) A zoning statute in West's Maine statutes

h) An excellent law review article on Maine law encouraging creative land use

i) A federal rule of civil procedure

1. Assuming each of these authorities is relevant, how would you rank them from most to least binding or persuasive if a suit were filed in a Maine state court?

2. Under these circumstances, would a federal court in Maine have jurisdiction to hear a claim based on this state law?

3. If a lawsuit were filed in federal court based on state law, which of these authorities would be binding and in what order?

4. If a lawsuit were filed in state court based on state law, which of these authorities would be binding and in what order?

Test Your Knowledge: Part V

To assess your understanding of the material in this part, click here to take a quiz.

PART VI

Finding the Law

CHAPTER 23

The Tools of Legal Research

Legal research is like mining for gold. Sometimes it feels like you'll never find anything. For the most part, though, with a bit of preparation and patience, you will find the vein that leads to the motherlode. The key is to understand that you rarely find "the answer" to your client's legal question in one place. What you will find are the raw materials—the gold nuggets—you need to construct the answer.

Before you set out to mine for that gold, you need to know a bit more about the tools available to you. Almost all legal research can be conducted online, but many, if not most, legal sources are still published in their official print form. Many online sources are digital versions of the print sources, so it helps to know how online and print sources have evolved, complement, and differ. You might even find that some sources are easier to use in print, such as statutes or rules of procedure.

Most online and print resources will be free to you as a law student. When you start working in a law office of any kind, be sure to ask about the cost difference to your employer or client associated with using one type of resource over another. Some offices rely more heavily on print resources, particularly for sources of local law, while others will have more online resources and limited print resources. Among online resources, your office may have a preference based on custom or cost.

A. From print to online tools

1. Pre-1980s

Before the mid-1980s, lawyers researched exclusively in print, using indexes to search volumes of primary and secondary authority (e.g., statutory compilations, judicial decisions, legal encyclopedias, law review journals, etc.) and citators (e.g., Shepard's)[1] to update their results. For example, to find a federal or state statute, a law student went to the library, consulted the index to the relevant code, and found citations to relevant statutes. The citation was (and still is) the shorthand for the

---

1 A citator tracks all legal authorities that have cited a particular source of law. *See infra* ch. 27, at 183.

statute's physical location within the code.[2] The student then took the appropriate volume of the code off the shelf and read the statute.

Researching for cases was always a bit different. Cases were—and for the most part still are—published in printed, chronologically ordered official (government) and unofficial (commercial) reporters. The unofficial reporters were—and still are—published by a private company formerly known as West Publishing ("West"). The text of the decision is the same in official and unofficial reporters.

> FYI
>
> West developed the **Key Number System** over 100 years ago that is still in use today.

Because there was no way to search for specific content of cases in print reporters, West developed the **Key Number System**, which organizes federal and state case law using the same 400+ topics (e.g., Civil Procedure, Contracts, Torts, etc.). Each topic is divided into subtopics or specific points of law and assigned a **Key Number**.

West (and now other online providers) analyzes new judicial decisions to identify the topics and subtopics discussed and assigns each a Key Number. The headnotes of a case represent the order in which these Key Numbers appear in the decision.[3] At the beginning of an unofficial decision, you will find the headnotes, which 1) summarize the law applied in that case, and 2) indicate its location in the decision. Each headnote includes the Key Number.

West also publishes print volumes called **digests**, which are published in conjunction with reporters to search for judicial decisions by jurisdiction, topic, and Key Number. Today, we can do the same type of search online.[4]

2. The first online research platforms

In the late 1970s and early 1980s, LexisNexis ("Lexis") and West launched the first electronic databases for legal research. In some ways, the electronic research process mirrored the print research process because you could still search within separate resources, such as codes, encyclopedias, annotations, law journals, etc. The

---

2 For example, the citation, "28 U.S.C. § 1332 (2018)," refers to the statute giving federal courts subject matter jurisdiction over disputes in excess of $75,000 between citizens of different states. "28" refers to the subject or title (Judiciary and Judicial Procedure) of the code, "U.S.C." is short for United States Code, the official source for federal statutes, and "§ 1332" is the section number of that statute. "2018" refers to the date of the print publication. The titles of the print code are arranged by volume in numerical order. The print version of the United States Code is available online at https://uscode.house.gov/download/annualhistoricalarchives/downloadPDF.shtml (https://perma.cc/4KT9-BXV4). For more information, see *supra* ch. 15; *infra* ch. 56.F.

3 *See supra* ch. 6, at 19.

4 *See infra* ch. 26, at 175.

big change to the process was being able to search 1) within multiple publications for different types of authority at the same time, and 2) for specific words both in text and by subject matter.[5]

Being able to find every page where a particular word or combination of words appeared among countless pages and types of documents at the same time was completely new. In conjunction with subject matter searches,[6] these "full text searches" made research exponentially more efficient. To conduct these new searches, lawyers had to learn to construct **Boolean searches** (also known as **terms and connectors searches**) that combine keywords and connectors.[7]

Practice Pointer

Terms and connectors searches should be supplemented by Key Number searches (or their equivalent on another database) because you can't always anticipate the words a court will use to describe a particular issue. See Chapter 26, at p. 177.

3. The next generation of online research platforms

In 2009, Bloomberg Law ("Bloomberg") launched its first online research platform. In 2010 and 2011, West (now Thomson Reuters) and Lexis introduced significantly improved versions of their platforms: WestlawNext (now known as Westlaw Edge and hereinafter referred to as "Westlaw") and LexisAdvance (also known now as Lexis+ and hereinafter referred to as "Lexis").

These three platforms have revolutionized legal research. For the most part, you can now

- conduct natural language (Google-type) searches,
- conduct terms and connectors searches to find content within one or more types of authority at the same time,
- conduct subject matter searches, and
- select the types of authority to search and/or filter your results afterwards to display specific authorities or content.[8]

Based on your search input, these systems also predict what you might be looking for and provide additional sources. Each platform has now added advanced artificial intelligence (AI) tools to improve research results, provide practical guidance, and develop litigation strategies.[9]

---

5 *See infra* ch. 26, at 170.

6 *See supra* ch. 26, at 175.

7 *See id.*

8 Lexis and Bloomberg Law have similar subject matter search capability. *See infra* ch. 26.

9 Be sure to ask your professor about using any of the advanced artificial intelligence tools, such as Quick Check (Westlaw) or Brief Analysis (Lexis), for class assignments.

B. Online databases

The research platforms described above are available only by subscription, but there are also a host of websites that provide either low-cost or free access to different legal sources. The following section describes better-known sites, their advantages, and disadvantages.

1. Major legal research platforms

Westlaw[10] Lexis,[11] and Bloomberg,[12] are the most comprehensive and expensive legal research systems available in the United States. These platforms allow for full-text and subject matter searches of federal, state, and some international primary and secondary sources of law.

You are likely to have access to one or more of these during law school. If so, take time to experiment with all three systems to see which you like best or whether you like certain aspects of each. As you will learn in Chapter 26, the same search on all three platforms—which vary by features, appearance, function, and feel—may yield different results.

The advantages of these systems include the breadth and depth of their content; the ability to organize and update your research results; cross-references to additional, helpful information and sources; and the ability to set alerts and notifications for changes in the law. The disadvantages include the time it takes to learn how to use these systems efficiently and their cost.

2. Low-cost legal research[13]

In practice, you may find your office using less expensive databases to access primary authority such as statutes and cases. Low-cost databases include Casetext, Fastcase, FindLaw, and VersusLaw. Some bar associations provide these databases to their members for free.

Casetext[14] has federal and state statutes, case law, and regulations annotated by members of the legal community. Fastcase[15] is a good resource for federal and state

10 *See* www.westlaw.com.

11 *See* www.lexis.com.

12 *See* www.bloomberglaw.com.

13 These services and their locations may have changed since this edition was published; consult your law librarian if you have trouble locating them.

14 *See* https://casetext.com/coverage (https://perma.cc/WUG2-KN29).

15 *See* https://www.fastcase.com/coverage/ (https://perma.cc/8JVE-BTEZ).

statutes and federal court decisions.[16] It has a relationship with HeinOnline[17] that gives users access to their law review materials and has acquired LoisLaw, a resource with an extensive treatise collection. FindLaw[18] is a Thomson-Reuters product that's more geared towards finding an attorney but has some rudimentary research tools. VersusLaw[19] has federal and state statutes, regulations, and case law, plus some specialty and foreign court materials. Though case law in this resource has varying dates of coverage, the Supreme Court jurisprudence is comprehensive.

The advantage to using these services is their lower cost. However, they may not have comprehensive coverage, and they do not have comparable methods for searching and updating primary authorities. Moreover, they are unlikely to have the same AI tools as larger commercial databases.

3. Free legal research[20]

There are a number of very good, free online sources for accessing federal and state law texts. These include Congress.gov (federal bills and legislative history)[21]; Google Scholar (federal and state cases and scholarly articles);[22] GovInfo (replacing FDsys, with selected federal court of appeals and district court cases, federal statutes, legislative histories, federal regulations, and other administrative law materials);[23] Justia (federal and state cases and statutes);[24] Cornell Law Library's Legal Information Institute;[25] Library of Congress (federal cases and statutes, with some state coverage);[26] and federal and state government websites.

The advantage of such resources is that their services are free, but note that the coverage is not comprehensive, the search functions may be limited to citation and keyword searching, and there are no annotations or advanced finding tools.[27]

---

16 As of 2020, state court decisions went back to 1950.

17 *See* https://www.fastcase.com/blog/fastcase-law-reviews-with-heinonline/ (https://perma.cc/V7XX-2R8H).

18 *See* https://caselaw.findlaw.com/.

19 *See* http://www.versuslaw.com/products/all.aspx.

20 These services and their locations may have changed since this edition was published; consult your law librarian if you have trouble locating them.

21 *See* www.congress.gov.

22 *See* http://scholar.google.com/.

23 *See* https://www.govinfo.gov/.

24 *See* http://law.justia.com.

25 *See* https://www.law.cornell.edu/.

26 *See* https://www.congress.gov/.

27 For more information on low cost and free resources, see https://guides.ll.georgetown.edu/free-lowcost (https://perma.cc/M6R7-QCPH).

C. When to use print versus online sources

As a new legal researcher, take the time to visit the library and get a feel for primary and secondary sources in print. Though you will need to develop efficient online research strategies, it will likely come in handy to be familiar with print resources as well.

For one thing, some print resources are just easier to use than their online analogs. For example, you can search online for statutes and find a section in the middle of a long and complicated statute without having a good sense of where it fits within the statute as a whole. Using the print version helps you understand that context better. Additionally, you may better understand how online databases work if you experience the print resources from which they were derived. Lastly, some valuable finding aids like indexes now available online may be easier to use once you have experienced working with them in print.

Finally, many students find that their internship or externship employers do not have access to the same online resources they have at law school (e.g., the resources are too expensive or their employers are not subscribers), and they must learn to use print resources with the added stress of being on the job. This is all the more reason to develop diverse skills now that you can fall back on later.

CHAPTER 24

Assessing Your Client's Situation

In classical rhetoric, invention is a two-step process. First, you identify the issue to be resolved,[1] and then you consult the topics (a range of ideas) to create your best arguments.[2] The same is true for lawyers: first, we identify the issue by assessing the client's situation and making a research plan (this chapter and the next). Then we consult the topics—primary and secondary sources of law—to discover our best arguments (Chapter 15).

Sometimes, the client knows or already understands the legal questions and options for consideration. More often, though, the client presents you with a problem—a set of facts and circumstances—and requests your help. They do not have the legal training to know what law is involved. You will likely need to identify the legal questions and options yourself. And that takes good listening, communication, planning, and research skills.

A. Meet your first clients[3]

Your new clients—Ramon and Christina Velas, a husband and wife team—own and operate a Starbucks in Dallas, Texas. They are very health conscious and have permission from Starbucks to sell only organic coffee beans, which they also use to make all their coffee beverages. Although Starbucks has its own organic coffee beans, your clients source the beans for their location themselves. They used to purchase them from local suppliers, but since October 2018, they have gotten them directly from sources in Central and South America. The Velases claim these beans are fresher, they taste less bitter, and their customers prefer them.

There is a nationwide consumer advocacy group called Citizens for Safe Products (CSP). The local chapter in Dallas publishes a monthly newsletter. The March 2019 newsletter contained an article stating that one of its reporters had conducted an undercover investigation and discovered that the coffee beans and coffee beverages

---

1 *See* CICERO, DE INVENTIONE, *supra* ch. 9, note 19, at I.8.10.

2 *See* ARISTOTLE, *Topics*, THE ORGANON, *supra* ch. 9, note 14.

3 For information on conducting client meetings, see *infra* ch. 59.

sold at your clients' Starbucks location are not organic. The newsletter went on to suggest some of the beans might even be dangerous due to the particular pesticides used in the growing process.[4]

The effect of the newsletter has been disastrous. The Velases have lost customers, and their sales have dropped significantly. They want to know if they can do something about the newsletter.[5]

B. Gather and evaluate the facts[6]

The first step in assessing the situation is to examine the facts for what you do and don't know. Play the role of a news reporter here. Be sure to ask for as much information as possible and identify any relevant documents for review.

Bottom Line

- **Evaluate the facts**

  Who, What, When, Where, Why, and How?

  What does the client want?
- **Identify the controlling jurisdiction(s)**
- **Determine the case law likely to be most binding and persuasive**
- **Draft a question to guide your research**

1. Who all is involved?

Who was the CSP reporter? Who were the local suppliers? Who are their bean suppliers now? Where do all the beans come from? How long have the Velases known their current suppliers? Have any of their suppliers changed recently?

2. What happened?

How long have the Velases run this Starbucks? Have there been any disputes at the shop with customers or suppliers? Any sick customers? Do they have a copy of the newsletter? Did the Velases contact anyone at CSP? Did CSP contact them before it published the newsletter? How many members does CSP have? How many newsletters were sent? Are they publicly available? Is CSP generally accepted as a reliable source of information?

---

4 See the CSP newsletter in Appendix C, at 527.

5 Mr. and Mrs. Velas will be your clients throughout the book, so be sure to read these facts carefully.

6 Much of the research advice in this section is indebted to and derived from the work of early experts in the field of legal research. *See, e.g.*, MARJORIE DICK ROMBAUER, LEGAL PROBLEM SOLVING: ANALYSIS, RESEARCH, AND WRITING chs. 5–9 (1991); AMY E. SLOAN, BASIC LEGAL RESEARCH: TOOLS AND STRATEGIES (7th ed. 2018); AMY E. SLOAN, RESEARCHING THE LAW: FINDING WHAT YOU NEED WHEN YOU NEED IT (2d ed. 2017); CHRISTOPHER G. WREN & JILL R. WREN, THE LEGAL RESEARCH MANUAL: A GAME PLAN FOR LEGAL RESEARCH AND ANALYSIS chs. 3–8 (2d ed. 1986).

3. When did these events occur?

When did the Velases find out about the article in the newsletter? When did they start losing customers? When did their sales start to drop significantly?

4. Where did all the relevant activity occur?

Where are their suppliers located? Where are the beans grown and shipped from? Have any other of the suppliers' customers encountered similar issues?

5. Why did these events occur?

Have the Velases had disputes with CSP before? Do they have any reason to think the beans are not organic? What kind of proof do they have? Do they know anything about the reporter? Why would CSP want to target them?

6. How did this happen?

Did the Velases hire anyone new before the newsletter article came out? Have they noticed any suspicious activity in the shop? Have they experienced any vandalism or threats?

7. What are your client's goals? What do they want to happen now?

Do they want an opportunity to prove their beans are organic and safe? Do they want CSP to print a retraction or apologize? Do they want to recover their lost profits?

The answers to questions like these will help you identify the facts you know as well as those you don't know but may need to find out. The best way to gather facts is to ask the client directly, ask the client who else might know, read all available files and documentation, and speak with colleagues who are familiar with the client's situation or the nature of the client's situation.

C. Identify the controlling jurisdiction(s)

For purposes of legal research, you will need to know which jurisdiction's law likely applies to the situation, even if you do not know what area of law is involved. The controlling jurisdiction may or may not be obvious.

If federal and state law might apply, you will need to determine whether federal law pre-empts state law.[7] If you think two states' laws might apply, as in our car

---

7 *See supra* ch. 21.B, at 137.

accident case between a District of Columbia driver and a Texas pedestrian, search the jurisdiction(s) where an action might be filed for its rules on choice or conflicts of law. You may need to research the underlying law of the states whose law might apply.

In transactional cases, such as breach of contract cases, the parties often identify in advance the law that governs in the event of a dispute. If your clients are involved in a situation where no advance choice was made, you will need to consult your jurisdiction's choice of law rules. In multi-party, multi-issue situations, the law of several jurisdictions (federal and state) could apply.

Example: In the Velas matter, the controlling jurisdiction is probably Texas. State (as opposed to federal) law is likely to apply because the dispute involves an alleged harm (a civil wrong, not a crime) between private citizens in Texas. For now, let's assume that's correct.

D. Determine the case law likely to be the most binding and persuasive

> **FYI**
>
> Whether authority is **binding** depends on
>
> - where the case is filed
> - what level court you would be in, and
> - the nature of the legal issues
>
> See Chapter 22, at p. 143.
>
> Once you identify the most binding and persuasive authority, you know what you're looking for.

Assuming you were to file suit against CSP in a Texas state court, what case law would be binding on a trial (district) court in Dallas? Look back at Chapter 22.B before you answer.

If you said the Texas Supreme Court (for civil cases only), and the court of appeals that presides over the relevant state court district, you got it right. Between the Texas Supreme Court and the Court of Appeals, which cases would be the most binding?

Once you've considered the case law likely to be the most binding and persuasive, you know what cases to look for.

Think of the case law likely to be the most binding and persuasive as an archery target, with the cases from the most binding court in the middle (the bullseye) of the target. Each ring represents the body of case law from a particular court. As the rings move out and away from the bulls-eye, the courts become less binding but still likely to be persuasive. For every new research project, ask yourself, what's in the bullseye? What cases come next, etc.?

Example: In the Velas matter, case law from the Texas Supreme Court is likely in the bullseye. The next best cases would be from the court of appeals to which cases from the Dallas trial courts are appealed, and then any other Texas Court of

Appeals case. Any reported Texas district court decision (reported state trial court decisions are less common) would be next best.

Although it is unlikely to exist, a relevant United States Supreme Court case could be important but only in addressing the constitutionality of the relevant Texas law under the federal constitution.

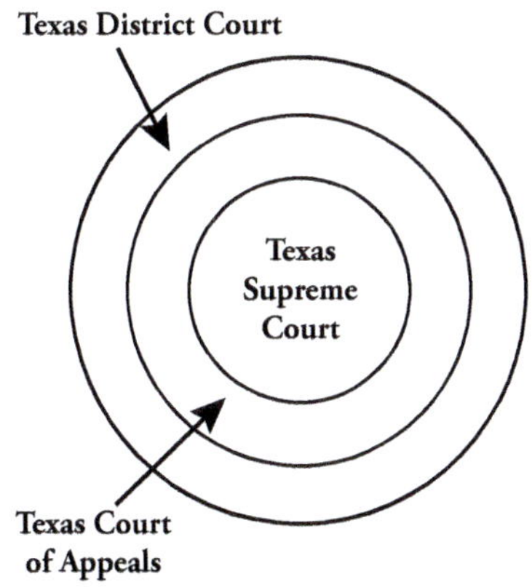

Apply It: Exercise 24.1

(see suggested answers at App. B, at p. 513)

1. Assuming state law applies to the Velases' situation, could a suit be filed against CSP in federal court? Under what circumstances?
2. If a suit could be and were filed in a Dallas federal district court in the Northern District of Texas and Texas law applies, what cases would be binding on that court?

E. Draft a question to guide your research

The last step in planning your research is to put this information together and draft a question to crystalize your thinking and guide your research.

The goal is to include the **controlling jurisdiction**, the **legal question** you identified, and some **significant facts** (although your understanding of the question and which facts are significant may change the more you learn about the applicable law). The following template should help get you started. You can move the parts around if it makes sense to do so:

> Under [the **controlling jurisdiction's**] law, can the client [this is the **legal question**, depending on what the client wants] when [these **significant facts** occurred]?

At this stage, you may not know what types of legal claims, if any, are available to your client, but you can use this question to begin your research (see the next chapter).

Example: In the Velas matter, you might write something like this:

> Under Texas law, can the Velases sue CSP for publishing a false statement about their coffee beans not being organic?

Or this:

> Does Texas law permit the recovery of damages against CSP for making inaccurate statements about the Velases' products?

Or this:

> Can the Velases sue CSP under Texas law for publishing false statements in a newsletter?

Apply It: Exercise 24.2

(see suggested answers at App. B, at p. 514)

Your Pennsylvania clients, Troy Bean and Liam Hawke, with the vacation home in Maine, need more advice (see Chapter 22, at p. 144). The neighbors' complaints have become more frequent about increased traffic on the public road that leads to the neighbor's and your clients' home. Last week, one neighbor called to say the guests had a large party on a weeknight with a live band that played loudly and late into the night. The neighbor said it has affected his family's quality of life and is threatening to sue.

Using the methods described in this chapter, assess the clients' situation:

1. gather and evaluate the facts
2. identify the controlling jurisdiction(s)
3. determine the law likely to be most binding and persuasive
4. draft a research question to guide you

Chapter 25

Planning Your Research

Plan your research carefully. A well-designed plan will make you more efficient, reduce frustration, and cost your client less. You need to decide how much, if any, background information you need to get started; where you will start; where all you need to search; and how you will keep track of where you've been.

To devise a good research plan, follow these basic steps:

- brainstorm search terms to help you find relevant authority,
- decide whether to use print or online resources or both,
- decide whether to start with secondary or primary sources of law, and
- for online searches, decide what type(s) of authority to search and in what combination (you can also filter your results later).

A. Brainstorm search terms

The first step in planning your research process is to brainstorm **keywords** or **search terms** you will use in full text and subject matter searches. The specific facts of your client's situation may be too specific or narrow to yield relevant results, so you will need to convert those facts into more generic words likely to be used by legislators and judges in similar circumstances. When searching for case law, do not expect to find a case just like yours; it doesn't typically work that way.

Example: In the Velas matter, if you search primary or secondary authority for the words "Starbucks" or "CSP," you are unlikely to retrieve any useful results. Similarly, if you search for "newsletter" or "coffee," your results may

> **Food for Thought**
>
> **Sample questions to guide research in the Velas matter (from Ch. 24, at p. 153):**
>
> - Under Texas law, can the Velases sue CSP for publishing a false statement about their coffee not being organic?
> - Does Texas law permit the recovery of damages against CSP for making inaccurate statements about their products?
> - Is CSP liable under Texas law for publishing false statements in a newsletter?
>
> *See* Chapter 24.E, at p. 157.

be quite limited. If you search just for "lost sales," you might miss cases that use "economic harm" to mean the same thing or cases that discuss other kinds of harm to Starbucks caused by CSP's newsletter. To find a broad range of relevant and useful authority, you will need to generate search terms likely to retrieve it.

The chart below is adapted from Amy Sloan's *Researching the Law: Finding What You Need When You Need It.*[1] It is based on the categories that the major research databases use to analyze cases and assign topics, Key Numbers, or subtopics. The object is to sort the known facts into categories of information: parties, places and things, potential claims and defenses, and relief sought.

List these facts under the "Facts" column as shown in the chart below. In the next column, "increased breadth," generate terms that are synonymous or related to your facts. Finally, in the third "increased depth" column, express these concepts both more concretely and more broadly. If the words in the "increased breadth" column are not working, you may get better results using those in the "increased depth" column. You may need to try many combinations of these words to find what you need.

Example: The chart below contains the facts of the Velas matter. Be aware that there are many ways to do this; use this chart to broaden your thinking and improve your search results.

Categories of information	Facts	Increased breadth (synonyms or related terms)	Increased depth (concepts expressed more concretely and more broadly)
Parties involved Describe according to relationships to each other	Mr. and Mrs. Velas, Starbucks, CSP, reporter	Manager, owner, coffee shop, store, advocacy group	Business, seller, organization, news provider, public
Places and things For example: Geographic location Type of location (School? Office?) Tangible objects (automobile) Intangible concepts (vacation)	Organic coffee beans and coffee drinks Newsletter, article Investigation Texas, out-of-state bean suppliers	Beverages, organic produce News article, report	Plant, groceries, fruits and vegetables, product

1 *See* SLOAN, *supra* ch. 24, note 6, at 26.

Categories of information	Facts	Increased breadth (synonyms or related terms)	Increased depth (concepts expressed more concretely and more broadly)
Potential claims and defenses If not obvious, consider: Parties' conduct (acts done/undone) Parties' mental state Injury suffered	Statements Published Decreased sales	Lies Distributed, disseminated Lost profits	False statements, misrepresentations, claims, allegations Damage, economic harm
Relief sought by the complaining or Injured party	Lost sales, apology, retraction	Money, correction	Compensation, injunction, damages

B. Decide how to use print and online resources strategically

As mentioned earlier, you will likely have access to a full range of online resources in law school, but these are expensive. If your law office maintains print copies of local law you frequently consult, you may be expected to use print. You may also find you prefer print for certain types of research. For as long as print versions last, don't forget about print as an easy and affordable option.

FYI

The Recursive Nature of Research

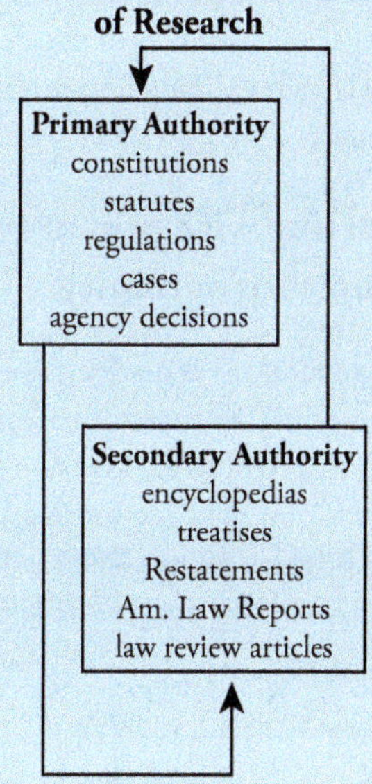

C. Decide whether to start with primary or secondary sources

When conducting research online, you can search all available sources at once. However, you are likely to find that overwhelming. Most experts advise that you take a more intentional approach and decide to start with either **primary** or **secondary sources**.

Under both strategies, your goal is to end up in the same place: having found any and all binding or persuasive law applicable and useful to your client. The discussion below should help you decide where to start.

1. Starting with secondary sources of authority[2]

> **Bottom Line**
>
> Secondary sources **give you an overview** of the relevant area of law, and **lead you to binding primary authority.**

If you don't know much about the area of law you are researching or how to think about the legal question involved, it's a good idea to start with secondary sources, including legal encyclopedias, treatises, American Law Reports, and law review articles.

Starting with secondary sources can save you a lot of time. At a minimum, they give you background information or an overview of the law (in easily readable prose); no single case is likely to do that.

Additionally, and equally important, secondary sources often cite binding primary authority (i.e., quickly lead you to nuggets of gold). Finally, secondary sources also cite other helpful secondary sources, which may in turn cite more binding authority (i.e., more nuggets).

Remember, the more specific to your jurisdiction, the more the secondary source is likely to help.[3] When you feel you know enough or have some good leads on binding authority, switch over to searching primary sources of law. See the example below.

Example: In the Velas matter, you might have a sense that CSP has engaged in some form of libel, slander, or defamation, but you are not really sure what each of these terms means (and they can mean different things in different states). For that reason alone, you might well decide to start with secondary authority and read up on those terms before diving into primary sources. To learn how to search these sources, see Chapter 26.

2. Starting with primary sources of authority

> **Practice Pointer**
>
> Although we cite official legal sources, we also use unofficial sources to conduct research. In addition to the official text, unofficial sources (like Westlaw, Lexis, and Bloomberg) add research tools and cross-references to additional authority both in print and online.

In general, as a novice researcher, take the time to consult secondary sources first. It will likely save you time. However, if you have a good reason to start with primary sources, such as 1) you are familiar with the area of law or **cause**

---

2 *See supra* ch. 22.A.2, at 140.

3 *See id.*

of action (legal claim) to research, or 2) you have the controlling statute or a good case to start with, begin here.

a. Start by looking first for binding constitutional provisions, statutes, and regulations. These sources of law will take precedence—in this order of authority[4]—over case law or agency decisions that pre-date them.

If you do find a binding constitutional provision, statute, or regulation, be sure you are searching an unofficial source, which may cite cases or agency decisions that have interpreted that authority in your jurisdiction. These are called annotations.[5]

If you skip this step, it is possible to "back into" these sources of law by reading about them in case law, but do not rely on that as your go-to method.

b. The next step is to search for cases or agency decisions that interpret the authority you found in step 2(a) above. If the question involves state law, be sure to check whether any federal courts have interpreted that state's law in a diversity of citizenship case under similar circumstances. If the question involves federal law, remember that state courts can also construe federal law.[6]

c. If there is no constitutional provision, statute, or regulation on point, focus on case law. In this situation, the question is likely to be a question of common law and you should focus your research on relevant, binding cases.

FYI

Where to Look

For federal court cases: use an online database but cite the court's official reporter.

For federal agency decisions: use online databases, agency websites, and loose-leaf services but cite the agency's official reporter (if therein) or the online source.

For state court cases: use an online database but cite the court's official reporter.

For state agency decisions: use an online database or state government or agency website.

For information on citation format, see Chapter 56.

d. If there is no case law in your jurisdiction, expand your search to other jurisdictions, starting with jurisdictions geographically closest to yours. Where courts have no law on point in their own jurisdiction, they tend to look at neighboring states or courts for guidance. For example, the District of Columbia courts often look to Maryland law for guidance (more so than Virginia).

e. If you still find nothing, continue to research secondary sources to figure out why you are having trouble finding what you need. It may be that you are not using the right words to tap into the relevant area of law. Don't be afraid to ask your professor or law librarian for help.

To learn how to search these sources, see Chapter 26.

---

4 *See supra* ch. 22.A, at 139.

5 *See infra* ch. 22, note 5, and accompanying text.

6 Of course these would be persuasive, not binding. *See supra* ch. 21.B, at 141.

D. For online searches, decide what type(s) of authority to search and in what combination (or filter your results later).

> **Practice Pointer**
>
> **Select type(s) of authority to search** based on the controlling jurisdiction and binding authority:
>
> **To search by content type:**
>
> Select among statutes, court rules, cases, secondary sources, regulations, administrative decisions, briefs, forms, Key Numbers, topics, proposed legislation and regulations, etc.
>
> **To search for federal or state law:**
>
> Select among annotated codes, regulations, administrative decisions, cases (by court), proposed legislation and regulations, secondary sources, etc.
>
> **To search by practice area:**
>
> Select a subject matter, such as antitrust, data privacy, government contracts, etc.

Once you make the decision to start with primary or secondary sources, the next step is to decide what type(s) of authority to search and in what order or combination to search them. This is a critical step in narrowing your results and researching more efficiently.

1. Decide what type(s) of authority to search.

In Westlaw, Lexis, and Bloomberg, the default content for searches is expansive: including cases, statutes, court rules, regulations, administrative decisions and guidance, trial court orders, secondary sources, briefs, pleadings, motions, and memoranda, expert witness testimony, jury verdicts and settlements, pending and proposed legislation, and pending and proposed regulations. The list alone is overwhelming. Thus, you will find it easier to evaluate your results if you narrow the possibilities in advance.

Westlaw divides all its legal content into four major categories: Content types, Federal materials, State materials, and Practice areas.[7] Within each of these categories, you can select one or more types of authority. For example, under "Content," you can choose to search statutes, regulations, cases, secondary sources, etc. Under "Federal or State Materials," you can choose to search for any type of federal or state law. Searching in "Practice areas" allows you to limit the content by subject matter, such as Antitrust, Data Privacy, or Government Contracts.

Example: In the Velas matter, you might limit your initial search to secondary sources in Texas to learn about potential claims for publishing false statements. From there, you might decide to conduct a systematic search of primary authorities, such as Texas statutes, regulations, and cases.

---

7 Lexis' categories are similar: Content, Federal, State, Practice Area, and International. Bloomberg's home page is set up a bit differently, but its comparable categories are Content Type, Sources by Global Jurisdiction, and Sources by U.S. jurisdiction.

2. Filter your results.

By default, the results of your search will be listed in the order that the platform's algorithm considers **most to least relevant**. You can change the default to sort results by date, court level, most cited, etc., depending on the platform.

> **Practice Pointer**
>
> Online search results are listed in order of relevance, **not by date or hierarchy of authority**. That means a law review article might be first and a binding statute last, based on your search terms.
>
> Filter your results to find them in the order that you need.

You can also **filter** your results after your search to narrow them, using the same categories listed above in section D.1. When using terms and connectors searches, you can filter further by searching for specific words within those results.[8]

Example: In the Velas matter, you could search all content types (statutes, regulations, cases, etc.) in Texas and then filter your results first by secondary authority, then by statutes, cases, etc.

Apply It: Exercise 25.1

(see suggested answers at App. B, at p. 514)

Having assessed the situation for Troy and Liam (see Chapter 24, at p. 158), you are ready to plan your research. Using the methods described in this chapter, plan your research:

1. brainstorm search terms
2. determine whether to use print or online resources or both
3. decide whether to start with primary or secondary sources, and
4. decide what type(s) of authorities to search

---

8 *See infra* ch. 26, at 170.

Chapter 26

Conducting Your Research

Having assessed the clients' situation and planned your research, you are now ready to mine for gold. To begin the research process, you will want to

- conduct multiple full text and subject matter searches, and
- keep track of, analyze, and organize research results as you go.

In an effort to teach legal research, law professors and librarians tend to characterize it as a linear process. It's not. It's a messy, often confusing, and recursive process that can feel maddeningly circular at times.

Think of it this way: you may start out thinking you're searching for gold, but you don't know yet if you want it to be in the form of nuggets or bars. At the very least, you know you want something valuable. So you start your research, assess what you have found, research some more, assess again, etc.

Before long, you realize you don't want gold after all. What you really want is silver. Or you discover you need both gold nuggets and silver in any form. The point is to keep your mind open to what you find and adapt your thinking and strategy accordingly. If you have not done complicated online research before, be patient with yourself. This is not easy. It takes time to get good at it; you'll get there.

A. Conduct multiple full text and subject matter searches[1]

For the most part, full-text and subject matter searches are used to search both primary and secondary sources. **Full-text searches** use natural language (i.e., Google-type searches) or terms and connectors (i.e., Boolean searches) to find words as they appear in the text of the authority. Your research results will depend largely on the words you choose, how you construct your searches, and the nature of the algorithm your database uses to retrieve results.

---

1 This section introduces you to the myriad forms of legal research. It does not address the nuances or possibilities with respect to all types of searches. To gain a deeper understanding of the complexities of legal research, particularly as you gain experience, consult your professor, law librarian, and the many helpful research guides published by law libraries nationwide and the database providers themselves. You can find them just by Googling. Westlaw, Lexis, and Bloomberg also provide excellent research support.

Subject matter searches are very different. They use tables of contents, indexes, or other "finding tools" to sort information by subject matter (you are already very used to these tools). Your research results will depend largely on knowing the subject matter to research. In case research, for example, your results will depend on becoming familiar with the Key Number or equivalent system on one of the three platforms (Westlaw, Lexis, or Bloomberg) and the expertise of those who index, sort, and summarize the authority.

1. Natural language searches

Natural language searches are available on Lexis,[2] Westlaw,[3] and most searchable online databases. This type of search most resembles what we think of as a Google search. You can enter search terms, phrases, or a question and retrieve documents that seem most relevant (based on the platform's algorithm)[4] to your search terms.

Basically, the software identifies legal words or phrases in your search (such as *injury*, *adverse possession*, *offer* and *acceptance*, or *state of mind*), removes common terms (such as *is*, *for*, and *the*), and generates variations of those terms (such as *possess*, *possesses*, *possessing*, and *possessed*).

Natural language searches are a good way to find a few relevant documents that can help you conduct more informed terms and connectors searches. Because natural language searches are not sophisticated searches, they can often yield too many or too few results. Additionally, the results are neither ranked by date nor order of authority.

Use this type of search primarily to get started in an area of law with which you are unfamiliar. Note that the same search in different databases will yield similar but not identical results in part because the algorithms of the databases differ. Also, when searching full text, you are also searching that database's editorial annotations, which will use different terms and phrases. In the case of secondary sources, different databases will have completely different offerings.

> **Go Online**
>
> Recreate this search yourself. What do you see? Have the results changed at all?

Example of natural language searching: As indicated above, assume you decide to start out using secondary sources to research the Velas matter. You select either Westlaw or Lexis and limit your search first to Secondary Sources and then to Texas.

---

2 *See* LexisNexis, *Natural Language Searching*, https://www.lexisnexis.com/communities/academic/w/wiki/94.natural-language-searching.aspx (https://perma.cc/4ZQM-G42F).

3 *See* Westlaw, *Searching with Natural Language: Retrieving Documents on Westlaw*, (2009), http://info.legalsolutions.thomsonreuters.com/documentation/westlaw/wlawdoc/wlres/wlnatlan.pdf (https://perma.cc/989T-UCQN).

4 *See supra* at 165.

You type a natural language search based on the question you framed to guide your research and the search terms you brainstormed earlier:

Is a person liable for making false statements about products?

As shown below, the same search yields somewhat different results on Westlaw and Lexis. The searches retrieve law review articles that discuss different topics. Yet both retrieve articles at the top of the relevance list that look promising because they refer to a Texas statute called "False Disparagement of Perishable Food Products."

Westlaw

Secondary Sources - Texas (10,000)

1-20 > Sort: Relevance

Select all items · No items selected

1. LET THEM EAT BEEF: THE CONSTITUTIONALITY OF THE TEXAS FALSE DISPARAGEMENT OF PERISHABLE FOOD PRODUCTS ACT
Texas Tech Law Review · 1998

2. PUBLISHER LIABILITY FOR MATERIAL THAT INVITES RELIANCE
Texas Law Review · May, 1988

3. WHERE'S THE BEEF? A RECONCILIATION OF COMMERCIAL SPEECH AND DEFAMATION CASES IN THE CONTEXT OF TEXAS'S AGRICULTURAL DISPARAGEMENT LAW
Review of Litigation · Spring 2000

Lexis

ARTICLE: First Amendment Imperialism and the Constitutionalization of Tort Liability
Texas Law Review | Apr 01, 2020 | 98 Tex. L. Rev. 813 | 50677 words | Kenneth S. Abraham and G. Edward White*

ARTICLE: Falsity and the First Amendment
SMU Law Review | Jul 01, 2019 | 72 SMU L. Rev. 513 | 21144 words | G. Edward White*

COMMENT: LET THEM EAT BEEF: THE CONSTITUTIONALITY OF THE TEXAS FALSE DISPARAGEMENT OF PERISHABLE FOOD PRODUCTS ACT *Special thanks to Prof. Alison Myhra, J.D., L.L.M., Mr. Marvin Sprouse, J.D., Texas Tech University School of Law, 1998, and Mr. Charles Miller, J.D., Texas Tech University School of Law, 1998 for their help in preparing this comment, and to Ms. Ali R. McLane-Hagy for her patience while this comment was being prepared.
Texas Tech Law Review | Jan 01, 1998 | 29 Tex. Tech L. Rev. 851 | 21902 words

A close read of these articles reveals that Texas and several other states have passed statutes to protect producers of perishable food products against false statements. The reason for protecting the producers appears to be that the damage caused by the false statements cannot be corrected before the producers' products have perished and can no longer be sold.

In addition, the articles cite the disparagement statute, Tex. Civ. Prac. & Rem. Code Ann. §§ 96.001–.004 (Vernon 1996) and an interesting case involving that statute, *Texas Beef Group v. Winfrey*, 11 F. Supp. 2d 858 (N.D. Tex. 1998). Have you struck gold? Perhaps. If coffee beans or beverages are considered perishable, this may be worth pursuing.

2. Terms and connectors (Boolean) searches

Terms and connectors searches are constructed using (1) the search terms you brainstormed earlier (see Ch. 25.A, at p. 159), and (2) "connectors" that specify the relationship between those terms.

For example, you can require that your terms appear in the same sentence or in the same paragraph. If you require the words to be in the same sentence, you are likely to get fewer results; if you require only that they be in the same paragraph or the same document, you will get more results.

Well-constructed terms and connectors searches are more efficient than natural language searches because you are providing better and more specific guidance on the documents you want retrieved.

FYI

The word "Boolean" comes from the man who invented Boolean Logic in the 19th century—George Boole (1815–1864). Boolean Logic is the basis of modern computer logic.

Image by Gordon Johnson from Pixabay, www.pixabay.com.

You can conduct terms and connectors searches on each of the three major research platforms, but the process varies a bit.

Practice Pointer

You will not always be successful with your first attempts, but don't get discouraged.

If you do not find anything useful at first, expand the number of sources you are searching, change your search terms, add connectors, or use a combination of terms and connectors. Change elements one at a time, methodically, for best results.

a. Search terms

You can modify search terms for more precise results. For example, to search for words with multiple endings, use a punctuation mark as a root expander. For example, "object!" will retrieve object, objected, objection, and objecting. It will also retrieve objectify and objectification, so be careful how far back you truncate your root term. Described below are the basic modifiers for search terms used by Westlaw (W), Lexis (L), and Bloomberg (B):

To search for	Example
Words with multiple endings, use **!** as a root expander	object! will also retrieve objected, objection, objecting, objectify, and objectification
Words with variable characters, use * as a universal character	withdr*w will retrieve withdraw and withdrew
Words as a phrase, use **quotation marks** around words	"false disparagement" will retrieve those two words together in this order
One word but not another, use ***but not*** (WL), ***and not*** (L), ***not*** (B)	Puerto but not Rico Puerto and not Rico Puerto not Rico will retrieve documents only with Puerto
A word exactly as typed, without plurals or equivalents, use #	#objected will retrieve only objected
Groups of similar words or to create an order of operations, use ( ). Terms within parentheses are processed first.	(coat or jacket or duster or poncho) /p leather will search first for any of the four synonyms and then for any of those words in the same paragraph as leather

b. Connectors

Once you choose your search terms, you will need to choose proximity connectors to specify the relationship between those terms. For example, you could require that "disparagement" and "product" appear in the same sentence, paragraph, or document as shown below:

disparagement /s product (same sentence)

disparagement /p product (same paragraph)

disparagement and product (same document)

Set forth below are the basic connectors used by Westlaw (W), Lexis (L), and Bloomberg (B):[5]

Connector	Example
and means you require both terms	disparagement and product
or means you require at least one of those terms	disparagement or product
/p (W and B) or ***w/p*** (L) means the search terms must appear in the same paragraph	disparagement /p product disparagement w/p product
/s (W and B) or ***w/s*** (L) means the search terms must appear in the same sentence	disparagement /s product disparagement w/s product
/n (W), ***w/n*** (L), ***N/x*** (B) means the search terms must appear within n or x terms of each other	disparagement /3 product disparagement w/3 product disparagement n/3 product (within three words)
but not (WL), ***and not*** (L), ***not*** (B) as a connector will retrieve one term but not the other	disparagement but not product disparagement and not product disparagement not product

c. Fields/segments

Most documents of the same type (e.g., statutes, cases, secondary sources) are divided into parts that can be searched independently. Westlaw and Bloomberg call these "fields"; Lexis calls them "segments."

Searching by field or segment can help you find what you need more quickly, because the platform limits searches to only those fields. For example, fields make it easy to find cases written by a specific judge, involving particular parties, or decided before or after a certain date. Assume you want to find a famous Supreme Court case about campaign finance, but the only thing you remember is that one party's name is *Citizens United.*

To conduct a field search in Westlaw or Lexis, you would select the content type (cases) first, then click on "advanced" next to the search bar. A list of the avail-

5 *See* Bloomberg Law, *Legal Search Operators* (2020), https://help.bloomberglaw.com/docs/blh-010-search-and-browse.html#search-browse-basics (https://perma.cc/CK6K-MVFH); LexisNexis, *Search Commands and Connectors* (2019), https://www.lexisnexis.com/pdf/lexis-advance/terms-and-connectors.pdf (https://perma.cc/KX7R-QBAV); Westlaw, *Searching with Boolean Terms and Connectors*, https://static.legalsolutions.thomsonreuters.com/product_files//westlaw/wlawdoc/web/wlnterms.pdf (https://perma.cc/6ESF-AEX7).

able fields is displayed on a template or fillable form. Type "Citizens United" under "Party Name." The platform automatically converts the form to "ti(Citizens United)" in the search bar (see below). Click "search" and voila! Here's the case you wanted.

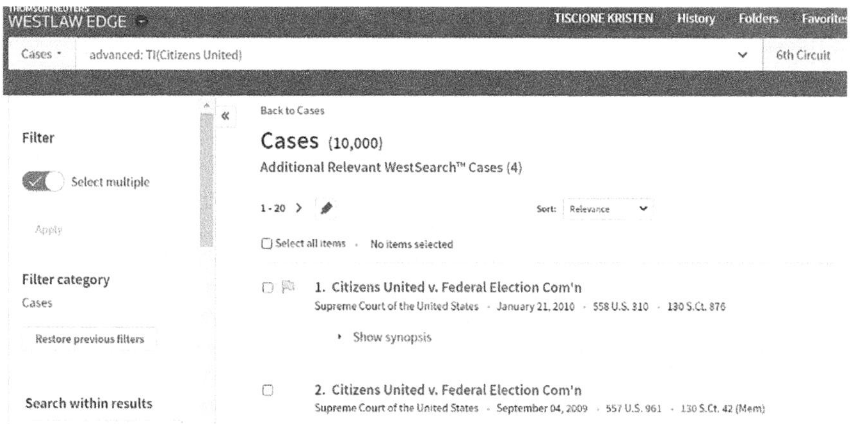

Note that each field has its own abbreviation. Once you get familiar with the abbreviations, you can skip the fillable form and enter the search in the search bar yourself: type the abbreviation followed immediately by parentheses (no space) with the term(s) required.

Example of terms and connectors searching: In the Velas matter, assume you begin your research by searching primary sources. In search of any statutes, regulations, or cases that might be relevant, you decide to use a database that will search all three types of content at the same time. In Westlaw, you select "State Materials," then "Texas," and include case law (state and federal in Texas), statutes, and regulations in the search.

You conduct the following terms and connectors searches, based on the search terms you brainstormed:

- False w/2 statement or misrepresentation /p article newsletter /p product coffee beverage

This seems like a reasonable search, but it retrieves results that are all over the place, and nothing even remotely related to what you're interested in is at the top of the list. So, it's time to narrow the search.

Since statutes supersede cases in legal authority, you decide to narrow the database to statutes and enter the following simplified search:

- False /s statement /s (plant or beverage or product)

These results look a bit better, closer to the mark. The tenth result is "§ 96.002 Liability." You click on that and see a statute that relates to liability for disseminating false information about food products. This is the same statute found in the law review articles when starting with secondary sources (and it was easier to find that way). Eureka!

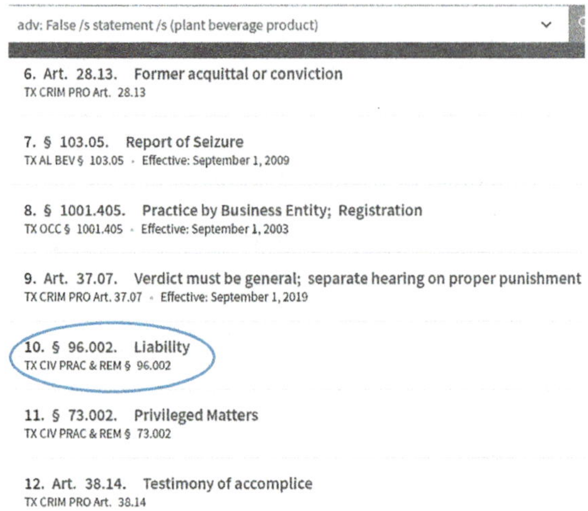

Go Online

Recreate this search yourself. Can you find the statute using another method?

You also notice that the statute is numbered 96.002, indicating that there might be a related section 96.001 or 96.003, etc. If you click on § 96.002 and use the forward and backward arrows in the Texas code, you find all four sections of the statute, 96.001–.004. Or you can use the table of contents to quickly gain insight into the surrounding sections.

Annotated codes are particularly useful because they include citations to cases (some, but not all) that interpret the statute.

Scrolling down from section 96.002, you see the summary of the Oprah Winfrey case that was discussed in the law review articles found using secondary sources.

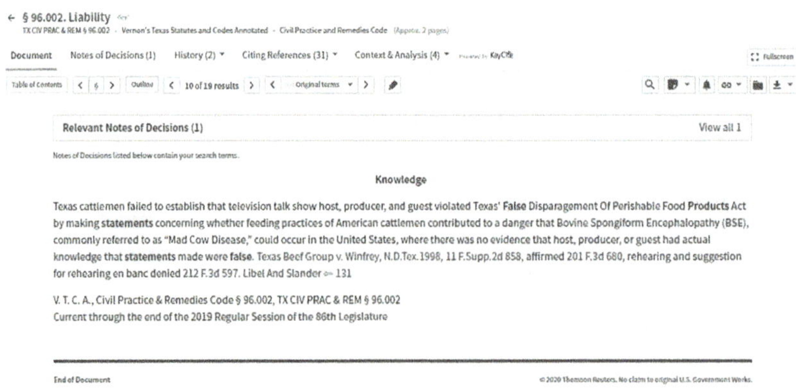

Terms and connectors searches such as these can be used to find all types of content. From here, you might decide to read the Oprah Winfrey case and learn more about the Texas statute you found and whether it might help you advise the Velases.

3. Subject matter searches

Develop a habit of conducting subject matter searches in addition to full text searches. Particularly with areas of law that are new to you or industries that are heavily regulated, you may not be able to anticipate the words used in the authorities most relevant to your search. Using tables of contents, indexes, the Key Number (or an equivalent) system, and other organizational tools gives you another point of entry into that authority. Let the experts who organize and analyze these sources do some of that work for you.

a. Constitutions, statutes, regulations, and secondary sources

You can search these sources by subject matter in print or online (using Westlaw, Lexis, or Bloomberg) by consulting their tables of contents and indexes (if they have them). Most topical (not chronological) compilations of these sources will have detailed tables of contents that you can skim to get a feel for what's there and then home in on particular subjects of interest.

For example, you can browse or search the index to the United States Code in print or online, which refers you to relevant sections of the Code. You can also use the Popular Name Table in print or online if you know the name of the federal statute you want to find. Westlaw has popular name tables for state codes as well.

b. Case law

The West Key Number System[6] categorizes federal and state law using more than 400 topics (e.g., Civil Procedure, Contracts, Torts, etc.).[7] Each topic is divided into individual subtopics that represent specific points of law.[8] Each subtopic or point of law has a specific number, known as a **Key Number.**[9]

---

6 *See, e.g.*, https://legal.thomsonreuters.com/en/insights/articles/using-the-west-key-numbers-system (https://perma.cc/KUU3-BVN6).

7 Lexis has its own "topics," and Bloomberg Law identifies "points of law" within each decision.

8 In Lexis, the topics are broken down into subtopics that can be searched separately.

9 Neither Lexis's subtopics nor Bloomberg Law's points of law have corresponding numbers.

The headnotes that appear before the text of the official decision in a West reporter are numbered (see right).[10] They summarize the specific points of law as applied in that case. They are arranged in the order that they appear in the decision. Each point of law is assigned a topic and a Key Number, which appear next to the headnote. At present, there are roughly 100,000 Key Numbers.

> 558 (N.D.Tex. 1998)
>
> **6. Libel and Slander ⇨68**
>
> Under Texas law, action for defamation is to protect the personal reputation of the injured party as distinguished from an action for disparagement which is to protect the economic interest of the injured party against pecuniary loss.
>
> **7. Libel and Slander ⇨21**
>
> Texas cattlemen failed, as matter of law, to establish that statements made on television show concerning whether feeding practices of American cattlemen contributed to a danger that Bovine Spongiform Encephalopathy (BSE), commonly referred to as "Mad Cow Disease," could occur in the United States were "of and concerning" the Texas cattlemen, such that cattlemen failed to make defamation claim under Texas law, where there was evidence that there are "about a million" cattlemen in United States. V.T.C.A., Civil Practice & Remedies Code § 73.001.

The **headnote** numbers also appear in the text of the decision (see below, right).

Key Numbers make it possible to search for content by subject matter without knowing the specific words courts use to discuss your issue. Before online research was possible, lawyers used print volumes called **digests** to search for cases discussing relevant Key Numbers. Today, we do the same type of searching online.

> **[7]** Even if a statement on the program could be construed to meet the statutory definition of defamation, it cannot meet the "of and concerning" requirement. None of the Plaintiffs were mentioned by name on the April 16, 1996 *Oprah Winfrey Show*, and it is stipulated that this program did not mention by name the State of Texas, the Texas Panhandle, or West Texas. Plaintiff Paul Engler testified that the statements made were about him "as well as the rest of the cattle

When searching for Key Numbers online, combine the number assigned to the topic, the letter "k," and the Key Number. In Headnote 7 above, the Key Number is "Libel and Slander 21." Libel and slander has the numerical equivalent of 237, which you can see in the online version of the case or in the index to the Key Number System. To search for other cases containing this Key Number, you would enter "237k21" in the search bar. Key Number searches can also be combined with other terms and connectors.

You can use Key Numbers in several ways: (1) when you find a case with relevant Key Numbers, you can search for more cases with those Key Numbers; (2) you can combine Key Number searches with terms and connectors searches to narrow your results; and (3) you can use the Key Number System to help you determine the area of law you are interested in or find more Key Numbers related to the ones you already have.

Example of using Key Numbers to find more cases: In the Velas matter, having read the *Winfrey* case, you decide you are particularly interested in the discussion in Headnote 2, which has been assigned Key Number 237k130. The *Winfrey* case involved statements made about beef, which the court decided did not fall

---

10 These are headnotes to the Winfrey case, *see supra* ch. 6, at 19. Lexis Advance has headnotes; Bloomberg Law does not.

within the statutory protection because live cattle are not perishable as defined by the statute.[11]

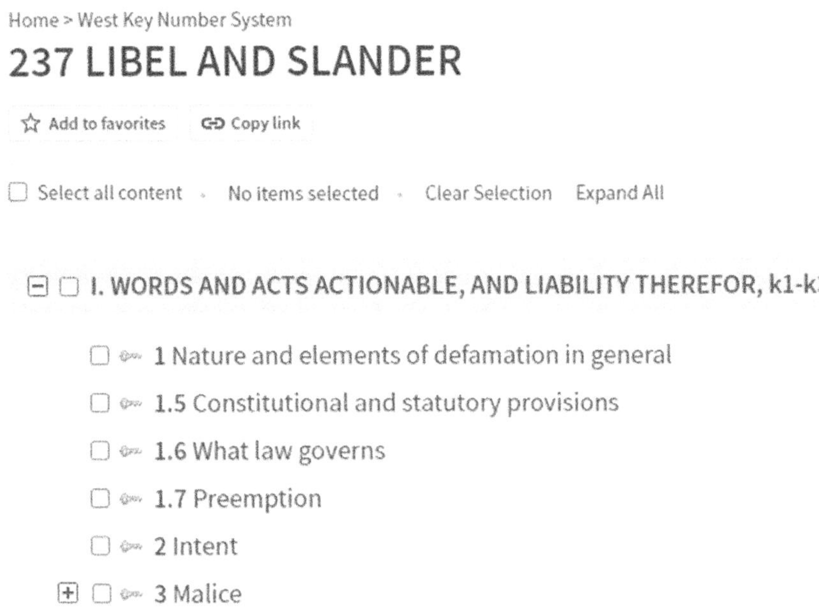

You realize that this statute will only apply if the coffee beans or beverages are perishable and want to see if there are any other Texas cases that discuss this definition. In the Texas cases database, you search for any other Texas case in state or federal court that discusses that point of law by entering "237k130."

Example of using Key Numbers with other terms and connectors to narrow results: Once you find a relevant Key Number, you can use that in conjunction with other terms and connectors to narrow your search. For example, if you wanted only cases that discuss 237k130 after a certain date and written by a Judge Jones, you would enter: 237k130 & DA(aft 12-31-2000) & WB(Jones). The "advanced" templates in the major research platforms will help you build these searches.

Example of using Key Numbers to determine the area of law you are interested in or find more Key Numbers: Finally, you can go directly to the Key Number System to find potentially relevant areas of law. Knowing that CSP has made a false statement and not much else about this area of law, you skim the table of contents to the Key Number System[12] and see a topic called "Libel and Slander" that looks promising.

---

11 11 F. Supp. 2d at 863.

12 You can find the number assigned to each topic in Westlaw by clicking on "Key Numbers" under "All Content."

When you look at the points of law listed under this topic, you find one called "Nature and elements of defamation in general." The topic "Libel and Slander" has been assigned number 237, and the specific subtopic or point of law has been assigned number 1. Together, the key number is 237k1.

To get a feel for how your jurisdiction treats false statements, and without knowing how to describe any potential claim, you can search for all cases in your jurisdiction by entering "237k1." Once you find a Key Number you are interested in, such as 237k1 or 237k130, look at the table of contents for neighboring Key Numbers that look potentially relevant as well.

B. Keep track, analyze, and organize your research as you go

If I've done it once, I've done it a thousand times. In the course of my research (usually early on), I find a case that looks pretty good, but I decide there must be something better out there, so I don't save it. Hours later, I decide it was the best case *ever*, and I spend hours looking for it and never find it again.

On this subject, one of my research assistants, Molly, told me years ago, "I did not always do this first semester. I did not always do this second semester. In fact, I did not always do this when I started doing research this summer. I regretted it EVERY TIME." So, be overly inclusive. And read and analyze the law as you find it. If you don't, you may think you're collecting cookies, when in fact, you're collecting cupcakes.

There are lots of good ways to keep track of your research. Here are just a few ideas:

Practice Pointer

Be sure to include citations when you cut and paste so you 1) know where the information came from, and 2) don't forget to attribute the source.

- Create a chart with space for each type of authority you plan to search. As you retrieve results, save them in a folder and transfer citations and specific notes to the chart. Sort within the chart by date, deciding court, etc. An example in the Velas matter is below.

Sample Chart for Keeping Track of Research Results

Secondary Source	**Citation**	**Date Found/ Updated**	**Title**	**Notes**		
Law review	29 Texas Tech. 851 (1998)		Where's the Beef?	Discusses the Texas statute		
Statute	**Citation**	**Date Found/ Updated**	**Elements**	**Result**	**Exceptions**	
Food disparage-ment	Tex. Code §§ 96.001 –004		1.dissem info re pfp 2. known to be false 3. states or implies unsafe for public	Liable to producer for D and equitable relief	Labeler or marketer as organic or no use of chemicals	
Cases	**Citation**	**Date Found/ Updated**	**Facts**	**Issue or Element Discussed**	**Holding**	**Reasoning**
Tex. Beef Grp.	11 F S 2d 858 (N.D. Tex. 1998)		Oprah—mad cow segment Cattle ranchers sued for dispar-agement	96.001 and .002 on perishabil-ity Knowledge of falsity (dicta)	Cattle not perishable No evidence of known falsity	Assumes cattle is a FP, but not perishable since not sold in a form that perishes or decays

- Create a document or chart for each legal question, element, factor, etc. relevant to your analysis and include citations, case names, etc. and how they contribute to that concept. When the time comes to put the law all together, you can select the authority relevant to each concept—and save time re-reviewing your research.
- Create an electronic folder in one of the major research platforms for separate jurisdictions, legal issues, sources of law, etc. Every time you find something potentially helpful, save it to the appropriate folder. Then review each folder in turn and update.
- Print potentially helpful sources and organize them in physical folders.

- If you need to find a case or another authority that you did not write down, you may be able to find it by consulting your research history (not your browser history, but the search history feature in the platform).
- Do not create a "kitchen sink" document, where you cut and paste everything potentially helpful into one document in the order that you find it. For one thing, it puts off the analytical work you should be doing throughout the process. For another, it is not going to be easy to work with when it comes time to write.

C. How do I know when to stop?

One of the hardest things about legal research is knowing when to stop. Sometimes you need to stop because you run out of time, making efficient research methods critical to successful results. In a perfect world, as you search primary and secondary sources, use two or more types of searches (natural language, full text, and subject matter) to access that material. Keep track of the searches you've done and take good notes on what you have found.

If you approach your research from different angles, using a variety of sources and search methods, you should begin to see the same authorities in your research results. At some point, you will begin to feel you have come full circle. When that happens, you can feel fairly confident that you have conducted a thorough and comprehensive search. When in doubt, consult the checklist in Chapter 28.

In short, all roads should eventually lead to Rome.[13] If you start getting completely different authorities or cases, make sure you are not going down a rabbit hole. We've all been there. After an hour or so, re-read your assignment or go back to your research question.[14] That first hour is full of potential rabbit holes and byways. Rereading your assignment will help you stay on course and perhaps identify additional significant details you ignored because you did not have enough context at the outset to realize they matter.

---

13 The roads of the Roman Empire radiated out from the capital, like the spokes on a wheel, so all roads did literally lead to Rome.

14 *See supra* ch. 24.E, at 157.

Apply It: Exercise 26.1

(see suggested answers at App. B, at p. 516)

Conduct research for Troy and Liam (see Chapter 22, at p. 144, and Chapter 24, at p. 158). Then create a chart like the one on page 179 with any helpful secondary sources and binding statutes or cases (up to five) you found.

Chapter 27

Updating and Evaluating Your Results

When you are satisfied that you have conducted a thorough search, you are ready for the final steps: updating and evaluating your results.

During the course of or at the end of your research, you will need to update the law you have found to make sure it is still valid. At the same time, you can determine if other authorities, potentially more recent ones, have cited your results. You will also need to evaluate your results to be sure you are not missing anything you will need later.

A. Updating research results

1. Are my sources still good law?

The major research platforms have **citators** that will check the current validity of almost all primary authority.

a. Constitutions, statutes, and regulations[1]

In Westlaw and Lexis, you can check for validity in the text of the constitutional provision, statute or regulation. Both services will tell you whether the statute is current and through what date.

---

1 Bloomberg Law does not have a citator for statutes or regulations.

Example: Assume you want to verify that the Texas false disparagement statute is still valid. In Westlaw, click on "currentness" or scroll down to the bottom of the statute, which indicates the section is valid through the 2019 legislative session.

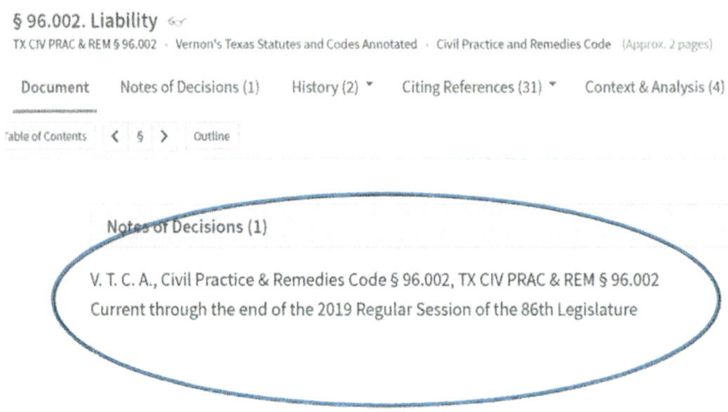

b. Case law

All three platforms can verify the validity of case law. Westlaw's case citator is known as Key Cite, Lexis' is known as Shepard's, and Bloomberg calls its BCite. You can access the case citator directly from the case itself.

You need to check the validity of the cases you have found because you don't want to rely on a case that has been reversed, overruled, or seriously questioned by another court. If the case has been reversed or overruled on some point of law, you will see a red warning signal, such as a red flag or stop sign.[2] This does not necessarily mean you cannot rely on this case; the point of law you want to cite may still be valid.

If the case has been seriously questioned or distinguished by a court in a different case, you will see a different warning, usually in yellow or orange, such as a yellow flag or yellow triangle.

You can also access the case's **direct history**, which cites each decision that has been made in your case. For the most part, when relying on a case with subsequent history, you will need to include that history in the citation to your case.[3]

---

2 You will need to familiarize yourself with the specific signals used by the platform you used for your search.

3 *See infra* ch. 56.E.6, at 454.

Example: Assume you want to verify that the *Winfrey* case is still good law. In Westlaw, at the top of the screen, you see a reference to "History (3)." When you click on that tab, you will see the three decisions in this case. The citator indicates that the case was affirmed by the Fifth Circuit in February 2000, and that court denied a request for rehearing two months later.

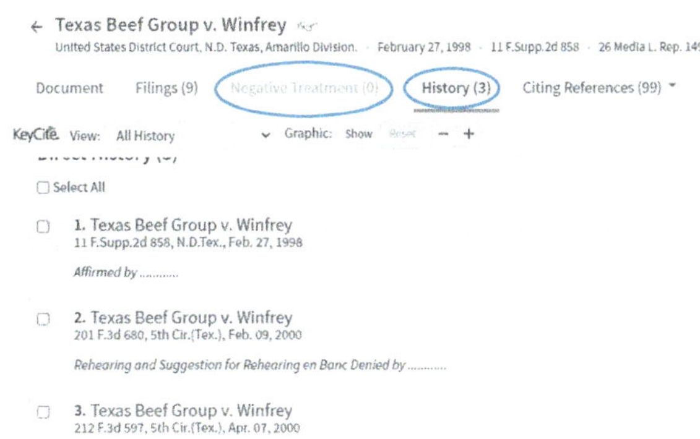

You can also see "Negative Treatment (0)." This indicates there are no cases that have distinguished or called the *Winfrey* case into question.

2. Are there better, perhaps more recent, authorities that discuss the same law in the cases I have found that I might want to rely on?

As a supplement to your research, you will want to know whether there are other, perhaps more recent, cases or authorities that discuss the same points of law in the cases you've already found. The same citators discussed above provide this information, which is also referred to as the case's **indirect history** or **citing references**.

> **Practice Pointer**
>
> You will likely get different results for citing references on different platforms.

From the case itself, you will see links to Citing References (Westlaw), Shepard's (Lexis), or BCite (Bloomberg). You will be able to see the number and types of authorities that have cited your case and in what manner they relied on it. You can also see to what extent they discussed your case (known as "depth of treatment") and for what point of law (sorted by headnote).

Example: Assume you want to know whether there are any cases citing the *Winfrey* case that might help you interpret the Texas statute. In Westlaw, you can see below that there are 99 citing references (4 cases, 56 secondary sources, 16 appellate court documents, and 23 trial court documents) as of 2020.

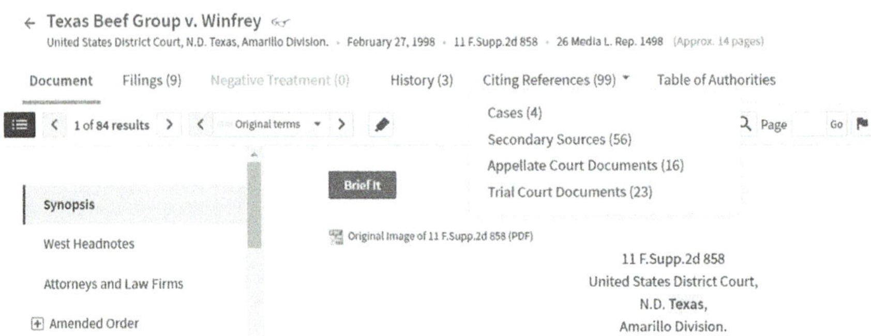

You can select each of these entries for more information. Under cases, you can see the name of the case, its citation, a brief summary, the date of decision, the depth of treatment, and whether the case addressed a specific point of law in a headnote from your case.

You can see below that the fourth case, *Cummins v. Suntrust Capital Markets, Inc.*, cites the *Winfrey* case relating to Headnote 5. The two (out of four possible) green blocks indicate there may a sentence or two of discussion. One block indicates a citation only; three or four blocks signal more in-depth discussion.[4]

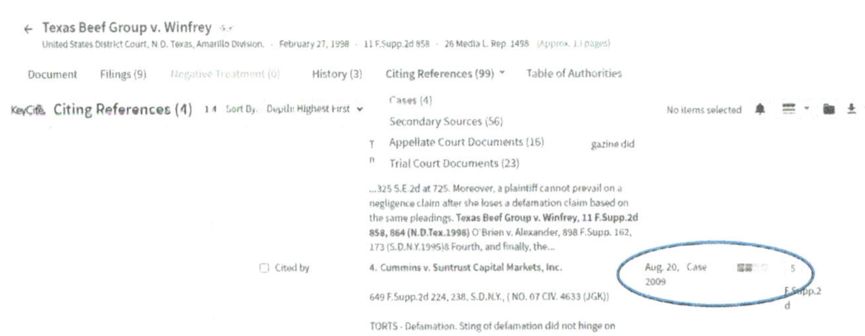

B. Evaluating your results

It is now time to take stock and be sure you have everything you need—all the raw materials available—to begin to analyze your client's situation. Before you take that next step, remind yourself what jurisdiction's law is likely to be most binding and

4 Lexis uses a very similar system; Bloomberg includes references to topics but does not have headnotes or depth of treatment.

persuasive. Then ask yourself these questions. If the answer to any of these questions is no, go back and fill in any gaps in your research.

- Do I have a statute or regulation that might apply to this situation? If not, am I satisfied that there is none?
- Do I have any cases interpreting the statute or regulation? If not, am I satisfied that there aren't any?
- If there is no statute or regulation, do I have the relevant case law?
- Do I have enough law to be confident it represents the law in this jurisdiction on this legal question?
- Do the cases I have adequately explain the law (e.g., if there are three elements to a cause of action, do I have at least one case explaining each element)?
- Are the cases I have from binding courts? If not, am I satisfied there aren't any?
- Have I checked to see if a federal court has construed the relevant state's law (e.g., in a diversity case) or that a state court has construed the relevant federal law?
- Are the cases I have the most recent cases available?
- Are there factually similar cases in my jurisdiction? If there are none, have I looked for factually similar cases from neighboring jurisdictions with similar law?
- Did I check my results for validity?

Apply It: Exercise 27.1

(see suggested answers at App. B, at p. 516)

Using the methods described above, update and evaluate your research results for Troy and Liam regarding neighbors' complaints about their guests' use of the Maine vacation house.

Chapter 28

Research Checklist

Use this checklist to plan, conduct, and evaluate your research. As you gain experience, you will discover the resources you prefer to use, what approaches work best for you, and how best to keep track of your results. Use this checklist as a starting point to develop your own best practices.

☐ **1.** **Gather and evaluate the facts** (Ch. 24.B, at p. 154).

Who, what, when, where, why, and how? Are there facts missing that I need to answer the question(s)? How will I get them?

What is the client's ultimate goal?

☐ **2.** **Brainstorm search terms** (Ch. 25.A, at p. 159).

Convert specific facts into generic search terms. Think in terms of parties, places and objects, claims, defenses, and remedies.

☐ **3.** Decide whether to search in **print or online** resources or both (Ch. 25.B, at p. 161).

☐ **4.** Decide whether to **start with secondary or primary sources** (Ch. 25.C, at p. 161).

☐ **5.** **Select type(s) of authority to search** and/or filter results afterwards (Ch. 25.D, at p. 164).

☐ **6.** Conduct **multiple searches of all types**: natural language, full text, and subject matter (Ch. 26.A, at p. 167).

☐ **7.** **Update** research to make sure results are still valid (not repealed, overturned, reversed, or criticized) (Ch. 27.A.1, at p. 183).

☐ **8.** **Update** research to find recent, relevant authority (Ch. 27.A.2, at p. 185).

☐ **9.** **Evaluate** your results (Ch. 27.B, at p. 186).

Do I have everything I need? Any statute, regulation, case law? Cases from highest, binding courts? Most recent cases? Enough to explain the law? Any factually similar cases?

Test Your Knowledge: Part VI

To assess your understanding of the material in this part, click here to take a quiz.

Part VII

Appeals to Reason

Chapter 29

The Analytical Paradigm

"Argument is proof-giving, by which one thing is inferred from another, and which confirms what is doubtful by means of what is not doubtful."[1]

—Quintilian

"Logic is the lifeblood of American law."[2] Appeals to *logos* (reason) are the first of Aristotle's three forms of artistic proof. According to Aristotle, appeals to *logos* are either **inductive** or **deductive**.[3]

Both forms of reasoning are used in logic or philosophy as well, but the results are theoretically different. Whereas logic produces absolute truth (as in mathematics or the hard sciences), rhetoric produces only probable truth (as in "more likely than not" or "beyond a reasonable doubt").

For example, we cannot know for certain if a defendant committed a crime unless there is a credible confession, but the jury process leads us to the best possible answer under the circumstances. As Aristotle would say, legal argument is not capable of certainty because who would bother to debate matters "which admit of no alternative?"[4]

Induction refers generally to the process of accumulating adequate bits of information or evidence to form a reasonable generalization or rule.[5] In some ways, this process mirrors the scientific method. In law, we use inductive reasoning to create or **synthesize** rules from statutes, judicial decisions, and other sources of law.[6]

Deduction refers generally to the process of applying a general rule to a specific set of facts to reach a specific outcome that is either certain or probable.[7] In law,

---

1 Quintilian, *supra* ch. 9, note 27, at V.10.11.

2 Ruggero J. Aldisert, Stephen Clowney & Jeremy D. Peterson, *Logic for Law Students: How to Think Like a Lawyer*, 69 Univ. Pitt. L. Rev. 1, 1 (2007).

3 *See* Aristotle, Rhetoric, *supra* ch. 8, note 3, at I.2, 1356b.

4 *See id.* at ¶ 1357a.

5 Aristotle also called this reasoning by *example*. *See supra* ch. 13, note 15, and accompanying text.

6 *See, e.g.*, Linda H. Edwards, Legal Writing and Analysis 36 (4th ed. 2015); Jane Kent Gionfriddo, *Thinking Like A Lawyer: The Heuristics of Case Synthesis*, 40 Tex. Tech L. Rev. 1, 3; *see also infra* ch. 30.

7 *See infra* ch. 31.

Bottom Line

Induction is a series of observations that lead to a general rule.

Deduction is the application of a general rule to specific facts to reach a conclusion.

we use deductive reasoning to apply rules of law to specific facts and circumstances to predict or argue for a particular outcome that is arguably (not undoubtedly) correct. This form of reasoning is also referred to as a **legal** or **rhetorical syllogism.**[8]

Stare decisis requires that like cases be treated alike in a common law system like ours.[9] Thus, in the course of applying rules of law, we often need to compare our client's facts and circumstances to similar cases to argue for the same (or different) outcome in our client's case. This too is a form of induction, also known as **analogical reasoning.**[10]

In sum, this combination of reasoning—creating **rules** of law, **applying** rules to specific facts (often relying on similar or different cases), and predicting or arguing for a particular **conclusion**—constitutes the analytical paradigm of legal reasoning.

FYI

The Analytical Paradigm

General rule

Application to specific facts and circumstances

(may involve analogical reasoning as required by *stare decisis*)

Conclusion

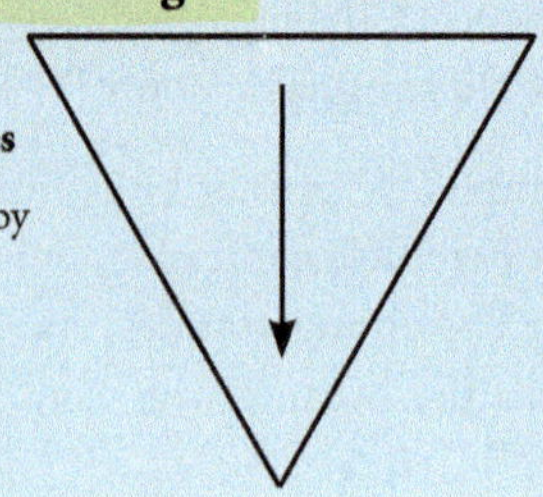

Today, we focus less on whether the forms of reasoning used in law produce truth or are inductive or deductive processes. We now recognize that a myriad of forms of reasoning (that may include both processes) are at work in legal analysis and argument, several of which are briefly explained in this part of the book.

Remember that appeals to reason (*logos*) are just one of the three modes of persuasion.[11] Appeals to emotion (*pathos*) and credibility (*ethos*) are discussed in Chapter 44.A–B.

---

8 Aristotle sometimes referred to logical appeals in persuasion as rhetorical syllogisms or enthymemes. These forms of proof yield only probable knowledge, and speakers often omit assumed premises. *See* ARISTOTLE, RHETORIC, *supra* ch. 8, note 3, at I.2, 1356b. The term legal syllogism is used from here on because it is more commonly recognized and understood.

9 *See supra* ch. 19.A.

10 *See supra* ch. 32.

11 *See supra* ch. 13.

Chapter 30

Rule Synthesis

"Inductive generalization is a form of logic in which big, general principles are divined from observing the outcomes of many small events."[1]

—Judge Ruggero J. Aldisert et al.

Inductive reasoning serves as the model for the scientific method: a series of observations leads to a hypothesis or general rule. For example, because every person born has also died, we can hypothesize that all people will die, but we cannot prove this hypothesis with absolute certainty (since not everyone ever born has died yet). As Hume argued, despite the number of times a particular outcome is observed, one cannot be sure that future outcomes will always be the same.[2]

Lawyers use a form of induction to hypothesize or **synthesize** rules of law from a series of binding judicial decisions.[3] Although these rules cannot be proven with certainty, they play a major role in our common law system. In a common law system, the rules of law change over time. Even if there is a statute that applies to a given situation, our understanding of the meaning of that statute evolves and changes as it is applied in different cases.[4]

Rule synthesis can require that you piece together a number of judicial decisions from the same or several binding courts; a statute and cases that interpret the statute; or a combination of binding primary sources, such as constitutional provisions, statutes, regulations, and judicial decisions. It all depends on what you find during your research.

Bottom Line

Rule synthesis is like putting pieces of authority together to complete a puzzle.

---

1 Aldisert at al., *supra* ch. 29, note 2, at 12.

2 Hume, *supra* ch. 9, note 81, at ch. 4, pt. 1, § 25.

3 *Id.* A logician would likely distinguish between the scientific method and rule synthesis on the ground that the scientific method hypothesizes a rule about future, as opposed to past, outcomes. *See, e.g.*, Wayne A. Davis (with the Georgetown Logic Group), An Introduction to Logic 94, 138 (2011). Despite this difference, the similarity between the two processes is helpful in understanding how induction works in legal reasoning.

4 *See supra* ch. 17.B.

Rule synthesis is like putting together a jigsaw puzzle. The picture on the box does not tell you how to complete it. In law, there is no "picture" of the finished product. You have to find and examine the pieces and put them where you think they belong. Once the puzzle is finished, you have a complete picture of the law that you can express in terms of a legal rule.

A. How rule synthesis works

Assume a classmate has just transferred to your law school and asks whether it is permissible to bring cell phones to class. There is no explicit policy, so the rule is unclear. Here's what you know:

1. On the first day of school, Emily Green answered a phone call in Torts, and your Torts professor said, "Please don't bring cell phones to class."
2. A week later, the guy who sits in the back row in Property answered a call on his cell phone in class, and the professor was upset. When the student told the professor he was waiting to hear whether his mother had survived heart surgery, your Property professor said it was all right.
3. Last week, in Civil Procedure, Ben Oggi had his cell phone on his desk. Ben asked your Civil Procedure professor if that was okay, and she said as long as the phone was turned off, it was not a problem.
4. Then, yesterday, in Contracts, that same guy from the back row in Property answered his phone again. When he told your Contracts professor he was waiting to hear if his sister had gotten into law school, your Contracts professor said, "Put your phone away."

So, what's the rule on cell phones in class? How do the pieces of this puzzle fit together? Put another way, what do incidents 1 + 2 + 3 + 4 equal?

Think of each particular incident in class as a judicial decision. Based on the facts and outcome in each new case, you can infer the current rule. Start with the first incident in Torts. After Torts, the rule seemed to be "no cell phones in class." But did the rule change after the incident in Property? How so?

Perhaps at that point, the rule was something like "no cell phones in class unless you have an emergency." Or perhaps the rule was "no cell phones in class unless you have a good reason to bring one." You might be able to think of different ways to express the rule, and your rule might be different based on your reason for synthesizing one.

For example, in arguing on a student's behalf, you might say the rule is "no cell phones without a good reason." On behalf of a professor, you might say the rule is "no cell phones unless there is a medical emergency in your immediate family." The broad statement of the rule benefits the student, whereas the narrower statement of the rule benefits the professor.

Apply It: Exercise 30.1

(see suggested answers at App. B, at p. 518)

How did the rule change after the incident in Civil Procedure? Perhaps the rule became something like "no cell phones in class unless you have an emergency or your phone is turned off." How else might you characterize the rule?

What about after the incident in Contracts? What is the rule now? What will you tell the new transfer student?

B. Rule synthesis in law

Once in a great while, the rule of law applicable to your client's situation is stated comprehensively by the court in a recent binding case, but this is rare. More often than not, in order to know what the current rule of law is in a given jurisdiction, you will need to synthesize a rule from one or more sources of law (those nuggets of gold you found while researching). Here's one way to do that.

FYI

The **elements** of a statute or common law claim are those items that a plaintiff must prove to win her case.

1. List the component parts of a legal rule or the elements of a cause of action.

Start out by listing the **component parts** of the binding legal rule or the **elements** of a **cause of action**. Often, there is no one right way to do this. For example, if your client were to be charged with "driving recklessly while intoxicated," you might break this phrase down into three component parts: "driving," "recklessly," and "intoxicated." Sometimes the words or concepts are so interdependent that they cannot be understood separately. That's okay. The goal is to identify all critical aspects of the legal language and not overlook anything significant.

For causes of action, it is often easiest to begin by laying out the **elements** from the statute, regulation, or case law. As we know from the Texas false disparagement statute, there are three elements a plaintiff must prove to prevail. See the chart on page 179.

2. Add any relevant definitions from statutes or regulations.

Recall the methods of statutory interpretation from Chapter 17. The starting point for interpreting statutes is plain meaning, and sometimes the legislature or agency defines terms for you. Be sure to add any relevant definitions (including citations) where they belong to your growing puzzle.

3. Add any interpretations of each part of the rule or elements using binding case law or agency decisions.

Add case law interpretations (including citations) of words, definitions, and elements as applied to specific facts and circumstances to continue building your puzzle. As you do so, you will begin to get a feel for where your case fits into the puzzle.

4. Write out the rule in a complete sentence or two.

When you're done, your task is to put this information together and, for each component part or element, write out a **synthesized rule**. The more complicated the rule, the longer it may take to articulate. If you can do it in one sentence, great. If not, take the space you need.

Bottom Line

- Lay out the component parts of rules or each element
- Add definitions
- Add case law or agency interpretations

At first, you may feel uncomfortable articulating rules not stated directly in the statute or by a binding court, particularly if you need to resolve inconsistencies in the law. However, not only should you do this, you will be expected to do so.

5. Example in the Velas matter

Assume your research uncovered the Texas false disparagement statute, the *Winfrey* case, and three additional cases that interpret the Texas statute.[5] The relevant portions of these authorities are set forth below:

---

5 Very few courts have construed the Texas statute, and none of the decisions is helpful in resolving this hypothetical. The three additional cases here are fictitious. They have been invented for purposes of illustrating rule synthesis and application in this part of the book as well as conventions of legal analysis and argument throughout.

Research Results Velas

- **The Texas statute.** The Texas statute (see Chapter 17, at 116) prohibits a person from making false statements about perishable food products. A person found liable must compensate the producer of the food product for damages and any other appropriate relief.

  96.001 defines "perishable food product" as a food product of agriculture or aquaculture that is sold or distributed in a form that will perish or decay beyond marketability within a limited period of time.

  96.002 requires plaintiffs to prove the following elements:

  (a) the person disseminates in any manner information relating to a perishable food product to the public;

  (b) the person knows the information is false; and

  (c) the information states or implies that the perishable food product is not safe for consumption by the public.

- ***Texas Beef Group v. Winfrey*, 11 F. Supp. 2d 858 (N.D. Tex. 1998).** Cattlemen sued the Oprah Winfrey show claiming that false statements were made suggesting that beef in the U.S. was dangerous due to "mad cow disease." The court assumed that live cattle qualified as a "food product" but granted the defendant's motion for judgment on the grounds that cattle do not perish or decay as that term is defined in the statute.

  - **Additional** case law (fictitious)

    - ***Pet Barn, Inc. v. Holmes*, 224 S.W.2d 99 (Tex. 2016).** This case was brought by the owner of a pet food store against a disgruntled employee who suggested the store's most popular product was unsafe. The product was baked from all-natural ingredients including flour, beef stock, and salt. Even though the ingredients were harvested from the ground or derived from livestock and the plaintiff did not need to have grown the products itself, the court held the product was not a food product of agriculture or aquaculture. It stated, "The product sold is a combination of products of agriculture, not a sole product of agriculture, as the statute contemplates." (p. 102) "Moreover, the snack does not perish or decay beyond marketability in a limited period of time." (p. 103) The label on the box indicates it "remains fresh for six months after opening." (p. 103)

    - ***Thomas Meats, Inc. v. Safeway, Inc.*, 3 S.W.3d 45 (Tex. 2018).** The plaintiff meat distributor sued Safeway for posting a sign in its window stating that the ground beef Safeway purchased from the plaintiff the week before was unsafe and advising customers to throw it away. Safeway had heard rumors that the beef was tainted but did not investigate them before posting the sign. The court held that posting the sign, which Safeway estimated was seen by at least 100 customers, was dissemination to the public. (p. 46) It further held that although Safeway employees did not have actual knowledge that the statements were false, their "reckless indifference to the truth was tantamount to knowledge of falsity" (p. 47) and ruled for the plaintiff.

- ***Green's Grocer & Co. v. Janus*, 4 S.W.3d 94 (Tex. App. 2019).** This case was brought by a farm stand owner against a local TV newscaster who said during a broadcast that his wife choked on an apple he bought from the plaintiff. The court held that making the statement on television reached "a large enough audience" to constitute "dissemination to the public in the sense we normally mean that word." (p. 95) However, even if the statement had been false, it did not state or imply that the product was unsafe. The court concluded, "The statute intends to protect producers from false accusations that the produce is tainted in some way. People choke on all sorts of foods. We have no authority to interpret the statute so broadly." (p. 96)

---

(1) List the component parts of a legal rule or the elements of a cause of action.

Section 96.002 of the statute contains three elements, which serve as a good starting point. As discussed above, the elements are further broken down into component parts (at least for now). Remember, there is no one right way to do this; this is just an example:

(1) The person disseminates in any manner information

to the public that

relates to a perishable food product

(2) The person knows

the information is false, and

(3) The information states or implies that the perishable food product
is not safe for consumption
by the public

(2) Add any relevant definitions from statutes or regulations.

Re-read the definition of perishable food product. Where should that go in the chart above? "Perishable food product" is part of the first element, so we can add the definition there:

(1) The person disseminates in any manner information
to the public that
relates to a perishable food product **[defined as a product of agriculture or aquaculture that is sold or distributed in a form that will perish or decay beyond marketability within a limited period of time (§ 96.001)]**

(2) The person knows
the information is false, and

(3) The information states or implies that the perishable food product
is not safe for consumption
by the public

(3) Add any interpretations of each part of the rule or elements using binding case law or agency decisions.

Re-read the three additional cases. Do they help flesh out the meaning of the first element? How so?

First, the *Winfrey* case indicates that live cattle do not perish or decay in the sense that harvested fruits and vegetables do.

Second, *Pet Barn* seems to have narrowed the meaning of "a product of agriculture or aquaculture" to a sole product, not a combination of products. It also indicates that six months is not a limited period of time.

Third, *Green's Grocer* used plain meaning to interpret "public," concluding that "a large enough audience" is equivalent to the public, although how many is large enough is not clear.

Fourth, *Thomas Meats* held that a sign seen by 100 customers constituted the public.

All of this information can be added to the first element:

(1) The person disseminates in any manner information

to the public **[interpreted to mean a large enough audience to constitute the public in the normal sense of the word (from *Green's Grocer*)][and 100 people is likely enough to constitute the public (from *Thomas Meats*)]**, that

relates to a perishable food product [a product of agriculture or aquaculture that is sold or distributed in a form **[as a sole product (from *Pet Barn*)]** that will perish or decay beyond marketability within a limited period of time (§ 96.001)] **[six months was too long (from *Pet Barn*)]. [Food products cannot be "living" (from *Winfrey*)].**

(2) The person knows

the information is false, and

(3) The information states or implies that the perishable food product

is not safe for consumption

by the public

(4) Write out the rule(s) in a complete sentence or two.

The rule(s) relating to the first element might be stated as follows:

The first element requires the plaintiff to prove that the defendant disseminated in any manner information to the public that related to a perishable food product [cite statute here]. The public refers generally to a large enough audience to constitute the public in the plain meaning of that word [cite *Pet Barn*], and 100 people is likely large enough to constitute the public [cite *Thomas Meats*]. A perishable food product is likely a sole product of agriculture or aquaculture that has been harvested and perishes or decays beyond marketability in a limited period of time [cite the statutory definition; *Pet Barn*]. In one case, a Texas court held that six months was too long to be considered a limited period of time [cite *Pet Barn*].

Apply It: Exercise 30.2

(see suggested answers at App. B, at p. 518)

Use the same process illustrated above to synthesize a rule for the second and third elements of the statute.

6. Avoid hasty generalizations or rules

Before you synthesize rules of law, be sure your research is thorough, or you may make **hasty generalizations.**[6] A generalization is hasty when you "jump to a conclusion" from inadequate evidence.[7] For example, if you rely on too few cases, you may not have a complete enough picture of the law (i.e., you're missing a significant piece of the puzzle).

Similarly, if you do not find all the binding law, such as the definitions section of the Texas statute, your rule will be incomplete and inaccurate. You may be creative with your synthesized rules, but they will be vulnerable to criticism if they don't provide the best overall explanation for the outcomes in the prior cases or don't include important information relevant to those outcomes.[8]

For example, it would be hasty to state that any period greater than six months is too long *per se* for plaintiffs to qualify for protection under the Texas statute. Only the *Pet Barn* court has considered that phrase and in a particular context. Thus, if the product were such that it had to cure for at least six months, a defendant might be liable for making a false statement about it seven months after its manufacture and before it perished or decayed beyond marketability.

For More Information

Here are just a few more resources that address inductive reasoning in legal analysis and argument:

Ruggero J. Aldisert, *Logic For Lawyers: A Guide To Clear Legal Thinking* (3d ed. 2001).

James A. Gardner, *Legal Argument: The Structure and Language of Effective Advocacy* (2d ed. 2007).

Dan Hunter, *No Wilderness of Single Instances: Inductive Inference in Law*, 48 J. Leg. Educ. 365 (1998).

6 The hasty generalization is one of many fallacies Aristotle describes as spurious enthymemes. *See* ARISTOTLE, RHETORIC, *supra* ch. 8, note 3, at II.24, 1401a-1402a; *see generally* ARISTOTLE, ON SOPHISTICAL REFUTATIONS (E. S. Forster, trans. 1955).

7 CORBETT & CONNORS, *supra* ch. 8, note 2, at 68.

8 *See* DAVIS, *supra* note 3, at 139–40.

Chapter 31

Legal Syllogisms

"When presented with the properly framed major and minor premises of a syllogism, the human mind seems to produce the conclusion without any additional prompting."[1]

—James Gardner

In law, we use deductive reasoning when we apply rules of law to specific facts and circumstances to predict or argue for a specific outcome.[2] Deduction is often described as being comprised of a major premise (the rule), a minor premise (the specific facts and circumstances), and a conclusion:

> [W]hen you present an argument in the form of a syllogism, if your listeners accept your premises, then they must accept your conclusion.[3]

Syllogisms can also be expressed in mathematical terms as the principle of transitivity: If a = b and b = c, then a = c.

In logic, if the premises are indisputably true and the reasoning is valid, the conclusion is indisputable. Although we use a form of syllogistic reasoning in law, the premises are rarely indisputably true. For that reason, **legal syllogisms** do not prove truth with certainty. However, they can have a similarly powerful impact on the reader. The acronym IRAC is often taught in law school as a shorthand for deductive reasoning—issue, rule, application, conclusion.

A. The categorical syllogism in logic

The most well-known example of a categorical syllogism is the following:

Major premise: All people are mortal.

Minor premise: Socrates is a person.

Conclusion: Socrates is mortal.

---

1 James A. Gardner, Legal Argument: The Structure and Language of Effective Advocacy 5 (2d ed. 2007).

2 *See supra* ch. 29.

3 Corbett & Connors, *supra* ch. 8, note 2, at 43.

FYI

For a categorical syllogism to be sound:

- the premises must be indisputably true, and
- the reasoning must be valid.

Instinctively, we accept the conclusion as indisputable, but there *is* a way to determine whether the syllogism is sound. First, the premises themselves must be indisputably true. Second, the reasoning involved—the application of the major premise to the minor premise—must be valid or make sense. As for the truth of the two premises, they appear to be true beyond question (notwithstanding Hume's objections, p. 58).

As for the validity of the reasoning, there are two ways to check it. One is to draw the syllogism using a Venn diagram. The second is to apply the rules Aristotle devised for this purpose. The first is sometimes easier than the second.

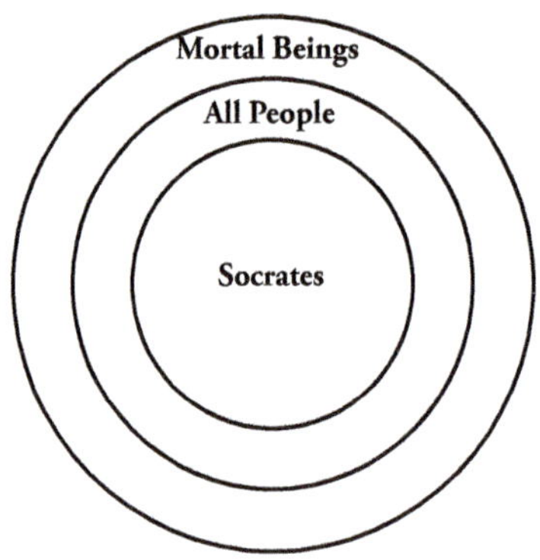

In the diagram on the right, the large circle contains all mortal beings. The medium circle contains all people. Because all people are mortal, the circle that contains people fits entirely within the large circle. The small circle contains Socrates.

Because Socrates is a person and no other creature (like a minotaur), the circle that contains him fits entirely within the people circle. Since the Socrates circle fits within the people circle, and the people circle fits within the mortal beings circle, Socrates fits within both, and therefore, he must be mortal.

B. Rules for testing the validity of a categorical syllogism

Aristotle also devised a set of rules to test the validity of a syllogism. These rules are explained and applied to the sample syllogism below to demonstrate its validity.

Sample syllogism:

Major premise: All people are mortal. Minor premise: Socrates is a person. Conclusion: Socrates is mortal.

Testing its validity:

Rule 1. There must be only three terms or ideas being compared.

Here, only three terms of comparison are used:

- People/person
- mortal
- Socrates

Rule 2. The following rules of distribution must be followed:

a. The middle term must be distributed once.

The **middle term** is the term that appears in the major and minor premise but not the conclusion. Here, the middle term is "people" or "person."

Distributed means the extent to which a term encompasses all or some of the named objects or individuals. "All people" is a distributed term, because it refers to all of the named individuals. "Some people" is an undistributed term—something less than the total number of people.

When the middle term is the subject of the premise, it's fairly easy to tell if the term is distributed ("all people"). When the subject is a proper noun, it is also distributed.

When the term appears in the predicate of the sentence (the part of the sentence containing the verb and stating something about the subject), you can assume that predicate terms of affirmative propositions (even proper nouns) are undistributed, and predicate terms of negative propositions are distributed.[4]

In the sample syllogism, the middle term (people/person) is distributed at least once (in the major premise).

b. No term can be distributed in the conclusion that was not distributed in at least one of the premises.

In the conclusion, the subject term "Socrates" is distributed (as a proper noun). "Socrates" is also distributed in the minor premise. The predicate term "mortal" is undistributed in the minor premise as the predicate of an affirmative proposition.

c. No conclusion can be drawn from two premises where the subject terms of the premises are undistributed.

The subject terms of the premises are distributed, so this rule does not apply.

---

4 CORBETT & CONNORS, *supra* ch. 8, note 2, at 44.

d. Valid conclusions are rarely drawn from two negative premises.

Neither premise is negative, so this rule does not apply.

e. If one premise is negative, the conclusion usually needs to be negative too.

Neither premise is negative, so this rule does not apply.

C. Syllogistic reasoning in law

Legal syllogisms are the *sine qua non*[5] of legal analysis. Yet they differ from categorical syllogisms in two significant ways. First, the premises are rarely indisputably true. As for the major premise—usually the rule of law—opposing parties often synthesize different, yet reasonable rules of law from the same statute, case, or group of cases. In that sense, neither rule can be said to be absolutely or undeniably true. In some cases, the parties may reasonably argue that two *different* rules of law should apply. As for the minor premise—the facts and circumstances of the situation—the parties are even less likely to agree on how to characterize those.

> **It's Latin to Me**
>
> *Sine qua non* translates to "without which it does not exist."

Second, although legal analysis and argument must be logical, it rarely sounds like a mathematical proof because other considerations, such as fairness, consistency, and extenuating circumstances, are also important to the ultimate conclusion.

D. Example in the Velas matter

The first element of the Texas statute requires that several things be proved: that CSP disseminated information in any manner to the public and that the information was about a perishable food product.[6] When an element has discrete sub-issues like these, it is often easiest for you and your reader to analyze them separately.

Let's work with the first part:

Did CSP disseminate information in any manner to the public?

---

5 *Sine qua non* was a phrase Aristotle used to mean that which is essential or an integral part of something. *See, e.g.*, 3 ARISTOTLE, *On Memory and Reminiscence*, *in* THE WORKS OF ARISTOTLE 452a (W.D. Ross ed., 1952) (remembering is the "*sine qua non* of recollecting.").

6 *See supra* ch. 30, at 199.

Test Yourself: Exercise 31.1

Draw this syllogism using a Venn diagram and check App. B, at p. 518 to see a suggested answer.

Assume CSP's monthly newsletter is distributed by email to 150 subscribers. Is that dissemination to the public? We don't know how many people saw the local news broadcast in *Green's Grocer*, but the court in *Thomas Meats* (the highest Texas court) held that a sign visible to 100 Safeway customers was disseminated "to the public."

If you wanted to argue that by emailing its newsletter to 150 subscribers, CSP disseminated information to the public, is that sound reasoning? It certainly seems to make sense. When in doubt though, try to draw the syllogism using a Venn diagram or use the rules explained above for testing its validity.

First, let's frame the legal syllogism. The numbers in parentheses refer to each of its three terms:

The major premise in the legal syllogism is the synthesized rule of law:

Major premise: Disseminating information to at least 100 people (1) equals dissemination to the public (2).

The minor premise consists of those facts regarding CSP's newsletter:

Minor premise: CSP (3) disseminated its newsletter to at least 100 people (1).

Conclusion: CSP (3) disseminated information to the public. (2)

Unlike the categorical syllogism above, both premises of this syllogism are not indisputably true. With regard to the major premise, it is possible that dissemination to at least 100 or even 150 people under certain circumstances might not equal dissemination to the public. For example, a court might rule that 100 people was sufficient to constitute the public in *Thomas Meats* because the sign was visible to all who walked by without having to take any affirmative action to read it. In that case, dissemination to the public might depend both on the nature of the dissemination and the number of people who receive the information. Although the major premise here is reasonable, it is not indisputable.

Now let's apply the validity rules (reprinted below):

FYI

Testing the Validity of a Syllogism

1. There must be only three terms (or ideas) of comparison, and
2. The following rules of distribution must be followed:
   a. The middle term must be distributed at least once.
   b. No term can be distributed in the conclusion that was not distributed in at least one of the premises.
   c. No conclusion can be drawn from two premises where the subject terms of the premises are undistributed.
   d. Valid conclusions are rarely drawn from two negative premises.
   e. If one premise is negative, the conclusion usually needs to be negative too.

Rule 1. There are only three terms (here, ideas) of comparison:

- CSP
- disseminating to at least 100 people
- dissemination to the public

Rule 2(a). The middle term (the one not in the conclusion) is disseminating to at least 100 people. It is distributed in the major premise because all (not some part) of the information at issue was disseminated to each recipient. In contrast, the middle term is undistributed in the minor premise because it is the predicate term of an affirmative proposition (see p. 207). This makes sense because dissemination in the minor premise refers not to all forms of dissemination by all people, just that which CSP engaged in. Thus, the middle term is distributed at least once (in the major premise).

Rule 2(b). No term is distributed in the conclusion that is not also distributed in at least one of the premises. The only term in the conclusion that is distributed is CSP. It is distributed because it operates as the subject of this affirmative conclusion, and, as a proper noun, it refers to the entire organization, not some fraction of it. In the same way that Socrates was distributed, CSP is distributed (as a proper noun).

"Disseminated to the public," is undistributed as the predicate term of an affirmative proposition. Thus, Rule 2(b) does not apply to this term.

Rule 2(c). Neither subject term in the major or minor premise is undistributed. Disseminating to at least 100 people is distributed (see Rule 2(a) applied above) as is CSP (see Rule 2(b) applied above).

Rule 2(d). The premises are positive, not negative.

Rule 2(e). Neither premise is negative.

Legal writers do not typically use these rules to engage in deductive reasoning. Formulating and applying rules comes fairly easily with experience. In more complicated situations, if you suspect your reasoning does not make sense, or it feels wrong somehow, use these techniques to determine if it is sound. Try to draw it using a Venn diagram or use these validity rules. When in doubt, use a Venn diagram or the validity rules to double-check it.

For More Information

Here are just a few more resources on deductive reasoning in legal analysis and argument:

Ruggero J. Aldisert, *Logic For Lawyers: A Guide To Clear Legal Thinking* (3d ed. 2001).

Steven J. Burton, *An Introduction To Law And Legal Reasoning* Ch. 3 (3d ed. 2007).

James A. Gardner, *Legal Argument: The Structure and Language of Effective Advocacy* (2d ed. 2007).

Test Yourself: Exercise 31.2

(suggested answers at App. B, at p. 519)

1. Which terms in these premises are distributed?
   - A. All roads lead to Rome.
   - B. Fifth Avenue is not a road.
   - C. Fifth Avenue does not lead to Rome.
   - D. No roads lead to Rome.
   - E. Fifth Avenue leads to Rome.
   - F. To tell information to one person is not dissemination in any manner to the public.
   - G. CSP did not tell just one person.
   - H. CSP disseminated information in any manner to the public.

2. Assume the following premises in these syllogisms are reasonably true. Apply the validity test on page 210 to determine whether the logic is sound.
   - A. All roads lead to Rome.

     Fifth Avenue is not a road.

     Therefore, Fifth Avenue does not lead to Rome.
   - B. No roads lead to Rome.

     Fifth Avenue is not a road.

     Therefore, Fifth Avenue leads to Rome.

C. To tell information to one person is not dissemination in any manner to the public.

CSP did not tell just one person.

CSP disseminated information in any manner to the public.

E. A modern take on the legal syllogism

FYI

Toulmin's informal logic

- **Data** (facts) leads to a **claim** (the legal conclusion)
- Claims are backed up by **warrants** (legal rules)
- Warrants may be **qualified** and **backed** (legal rules are rarely indisputable)
- **Counterclaims** are anticipated and resolved

Stephen Toulmin, a twentieth-century philosopher, recognized that Aristotelian logic does not mirror the way people reason and resolve disputes in everyday life. He set out to articulate a workable theory of argumentation. In 1958, he published *Uses of Argument*, a series of essays, in which he described his attempt to "reject as confused a conception of 'deductive inference' . . . as impeccable."[7]

You may find Toulmin's informal logic easier to understand than categorical syllogisms. According to Toulmin, an argument "is like an organism. It has both a gross, anatomical structure and a finer, as-it-were physiological one."[8]

According to Toulmin, an argument generally begins with evidence or **data** that lead to a **claim**. Toulmin might describe the argument that Socrates is mortal as follows:

Socrates is mortal **(claim)** because Socrates is a person **(datum)**, and all people are mortal **(warrant).**

Informal logic can be used to help you construct arguments too. For example, the "dissemination to the public" analysis discussed above might be framed as follows:

> CSP disseminated information to the public **(claim)** because it emailed its newsletter to 150 subscribers **(datum)**.

The datum appears to support the claim, but to prove the claim, we often include **warrants** (i.e., justifications) to explain why the claim makes sense:

> CSP disseminated information to the public because it emailed its newsletter to more than 150 subscribers. **Disseminating information to at least 100 people constitutes the public [warrant].**

---

7 STEPHEN E. TOULMIN, THE USES OF ARGUMENT xiii (updated ed. 2003).

8 *Id.* at 87.

In legal argument, the data often correspond to the facts (like the minor premise in a syllogism). Here, the relevant fact is that CSP emailed the newsletter to 150 subscribers. Warrants correspond to the rules of law (like the major premise in a syllogism). A warrant that is not absolute carries less force.

Where the warrant is not absolute, one can include a **qualifier** that recognizes the claim is only probably correct. Here, there is only one case that defines how many people constitute the public:

> CSP **likely [qualifier]** disseminated information to the public because it emailed its newsletter to 150 subscribers. Disseminating information to at least 100 people constitutes the public.

An argument is even more persuasive where it anticipates reasonable **counterclaims** that might defeat the claim:

> CSP likely disseminated information to the public because it emailed its newsletter to 150 subscribers. Disseminating information to at least 100 people constitutes the public. **The Texas statute does not require proof of how many people actually read the newsletter [potential counterclaim].**

Finally, if the warrant is not convincing on its face, we can include a **backing** for it:

> CSP likely disseminated information to the public because it emailed its newsletter to 150 subscribers. Disseminating information to at least 100 people constitutes the public. The Texas statute does not require proof of how many people actually read the newsletter. **If posting a sign to 100 customers constitutes the public, emailing 150 subscribers is more than sufficient [backing].**

As in this example, the rule of law that forms the major premise of a syllogism is usually the warrant in Toulmin's model. The facts that form the minor premise of a syllogism are usually the data that lead to the conclusion (Toulmin's claim). Both tools for learning deductive reasoning may help you develop a systematic, logical, and effective method for engaging in deductive reasoning.

Apply It: Exercise 31.3

(suggested answers at App. B, at p. 520)

Analyze the following information using Toulmin's informal logic and identify the parts of the analysis using Toulmin's terminology:

Maine law holds landowners liable for common law nuisance when they act or fail to act in such a way that causes neighbors discomfort that is unreasonable under the circumstances. Discomfort can include loud noise. Your clients have been sued because of the music coming from parties held by guests staying in their vacation home over the summer. Parties are held approximately two times a week, usually on Friday or Saturday and again on Sunday. With rare exception, the parties shut down around midnight. Music played at the parties can be heard inside neighbors' homes if their windows are open. Closing the windows is usually enough to eliminate the noise. You wish to argue that your clients, Troy Bean and Liam Hawke, have not caused a nuisance.

F. Fallacies in deductive reasoning

Lawyers are usually quite careful in articulating their premises (i.e., their rules of law and characterizations of the facts), but they do not routinely test the validity of their logic using the test described above. With experience, you will develop a sort of "sixth sense" for constructing logical appeals. However, intuition is not always foolproof. To help you identify fallacies in your logic, this section describes typical mistakes beginning legal writers make that can easily be fixed.

1. The book report (both premises missing)

This fallacy looks like a legal syllogism, but it is missing too much information. The analysis is like a book report in the sense that it just summarizes the story of the cited case. It does not include a major premise (rule or synthesized rule) from the cited authority and, as a consequence, it does not include a minor premise either. It is simply a description of the authority perceived by the writer to support the stated conclusion. Without the necessary premises, there is no syllogism (and no datum or warrant) and no real analysis. The result is that the reader is forced to infer the premises and the writer's reasoning.

Example:

> For CSP to be liable, it must have disseminated information in any manner to the public. Tex. Civ. Prac. & Rem. Code Ann. § 96.002(a). In *Green's Grocer*, the defendant stated on a local TV news broadcast that a woman choked on an apple she had bought from the plaintiff's farm stand. In *Thomas Meats*, the defendant grocery store posted a sign in its window. The Velases are thus likely to prove CSP disseminated information by email to the public **[conclusion only].**

As you can see, the writer states what the statute requires but does not explain what it means to disseminate information to the public. Although the writer refers to the facts of *Green's Grocer* and *Thomas Meats*, there is no explanation of the court's holding or reasoning in those cases to flesh out the rule. The reader could infer a broad rule that making a statement to lots of people constitutes dissemination to the public, but they might also infer a narrower rule such as dissemination to the public requires a TV broadcast or a live audience. The reasoning is ineffective because it leaves too many holes for the reader to fill in and does not convey the writer's reasoning.

Revised example:

> For CSP to be liable, it must have disseminated information in any manner to the public. Tex. Civ. Prac. & Rem. Code Ann. § 96.002(a). Distributing information to a large enough audience to constitute the public in the normal sense of the word is dissemination to the public [cite *Green's Grocer*] **[major premise]**. In *Green's Grocer*, the defendant stated on a local TV news broadcast that a woman choked on an apple she had bought from the plaintiff's farm stand. The court held that information disseminated via a newscast was disseminated to the public [cite *Green's Grocer*]. In *Thomas Meats*, the defendant grocery store posted a sign in its window that was viewed by 100 customers, and the court held that was sufficient to constitute the public [cite *Thomas Meats*]. In this case, CSP disseminated information by email to 150 subscribers, which is large enough to constitute "public" in the normal sense of the word and more than the 100 customers in *Thomas Meats* **[minor premise]**. Therefore, the Velases are likely to prove CSP disseminated information in any manner to the public **[conclusion]**.

2. Fear of commitment (missing a conclusion)

This fallacy has the opposite problem—although the reasoning includes a major and minor premise, there is no conclusion. With the conclusion missing, the reader may miss the writer's point or forget it. Although the reader might supply the missing conclusion herself, it may not be what the writer intended. What might seem redundant or obvious is necessary to clarify meaning, be correctly understood, and reinforce the writer's conclusion.

Example:

> For CSP to be liable, it must have disseminated information in any manner to the public. Tex. Civ. Prac. & Rem. Code Ann. § 96.002(a). Distributing information to a large enough audience to constitute the public in the normal sense of the word is dissemination to the public [cite *Green's Grocer*] **[major premise]**. In *Green's Grocer*, the defendant stated on a local TV news broadcast that a woman choked on an apple she had bought from the plaintiff's farm stand. The court held that information disseminated via a newscast was disseminated to the public. [cite *Green's Grocer*]. In *Thomas Meats*, the defendant grocery store posted a sign in its

> window that was viewed by 100 customers, and the court held that was sufficient to constitute the public [cite *Thomas Meats*]. In this case, CSP disseminated information by email to 150 subscribers, which is more than the 100 customers in *Thomas Meats* **[minor premise]**. We do not know if all 150 subscribers received or read the newsletter.

Here, the writer does not feel comfortable concluding that 150 subscribers is adequate to constitute the public. They are uncomfortable because so little information is available about how many people saw the broadcast in *Green's Grocer* and there are potentially significant differences between emailing subscribers and posting a sign to a live audience. Nevertheless, the writer must predict an outcome based on the information they have available, qualifying their conclusion as necessary. Only then can the reader assess the strength of the analysis and decide how best to deal with the uncertainty. In this example, the writer must act as the factfinder and predict the ultimate outcome.

Revised example:

> For CSP to be liable, it must have disseminated information in any manner to the public. Tex. Civ. Prac. & Rem. Code Ann. § 96.002(a). Distributing information to a large enough audience to constitute the public in the normal sense of the word is dissemination to the public [cite *Green's Grocer*] **[major premise]**. In *Green's Grocer*, the defendant stated on a local TV news broadcast that a woman choked on an apple she had bought from the plaintiff's farm stand. The court held that information disseminated via a newscast was disseminated to the public [cite *Green's Grocer*]. In *Thomas Meats*, the defendant grocery store posted a sign in its window that was viewed by 100 customers, and the court held that was sufficient to constitute the public [cite *Thomas Meats*]. In this case, CSP disseminated information by email to 150 subscribers, which is more than the 100 customers in *Thomas Meats* **[minor premise]**. Since there is no indication that the statute requires proof that all 150 subscribers read the newsletter, and it can easily be forwarded to even more people, it was likely disseminated to the public **[conclusion]**.

3. The deceptive hypothetical (denying the antecedent)

This fallacy occurs with the use of "if, then" propositions, where the writer assumes that if the required cause does not occur (the "if"), the effect (the "then") cannot occur either. This may occur when a broader reading of the case law and a more general synthesized rule (or major premise) is required.

Example:

> For CSP to be liable, it must have disseminated information in any manner to the public. Tex. Civ. Prac. & Rem. Code Ann. § 96.002(a). Distributing information via a television newscast or a sign posted in the shop window constitutes dissemination to the public [cite *Green's Grocer*; *Thomas Meats*]. CSP sent its statement about the Velases' coffee beans in a newsletter, not on a local TV news broadcast or by posting a sign. Therefore, CSP probably did not disseminate its information to the public.

Here, the writer assumes that the only way to disseminate information to the public is to broadcast information on local TV news or via a sign in a shop window. However, there may be several different ways to do that. See the revised examples above.

4. The double negative proof (two noes don't make a yes)

This fallacy occurs when a prior case in which a condition is not met is used to claim that the condition is met in the client's factually different case. It is as if to say, "I need to prove x. In the prior case, the court found not-x, but my case is not like that case. My case is not not-x" (thus the double negative), so it must be x.

A legal writer makes this mistake most often when there are no factually similar cases with a favorable outcome for their client, and their only recourse is to distinguish the unfavorable case on the basis of its facts. This is common and a perfectly legitimate way to deal with unfavorable precedent, but it does not conclusively prove the condition is met, and the writer will need to find additional ways to support their analysis or argument.

In this example, assume that the court in *Thomas Meats* held that posting a sign that 100 customers saw did not constitute dissemination to the public.

For CSP to be liable, it must have disseminated information in any manner to the public. Disseminating information to a large enough audience to constitute "public" in the normal sense of the word is dissemination to the public [cite *Green's Grocer*]. Recently, the Supreme Court of Texas held that posting a sign in a window that 100 customers saw did not constitute dissemination to the public [cite *Thomas Meats*]. **[Not X]** Here, CSP emailed its newsletter to 150 subscribers. **[Not (Not-X)]** The number of people who received the newsletter is thus large enough to constitute the public under the Texas statute. **[Not (Not-X) = X]**

The faulty reasoning here stems from assuming that having more than 100 recipients is a "large enough audience." However, the court might not consider an audience large enough to be the "public" unless it is more than 200 viewers/readers. This does not mean *Green's Grocer* and *Thomas Meats* cannot be used to support "dissemination to the public"; it just does not conclusively prove it.

Revised Example:

> For CSP to be liable, it must have disseminated information in any manner to the public. Disseminating information to a large enough audience to constitute "public" in the normal sense of the word is dissemination to the public [cite *Green's Grocer*]. Although no cases define what size audience is large enough to constitute "the public," the Supreme Court of Texas recently held that posting a sign in a window that 100 customers viewed did not constitute dissemination to the public [cite *Thomas Meats*]. Here, CSP emailed its newsletter to 150 subscribers, which is fifty percent more than the 100 customers in *Thomas Meats* and may be sufficiently large to constitute the public.

5. Begging the question

You are probably already familiar with this one. To beg the question is to assume the conclusion you are trying to prove, which leaves the initial question unanswered. Typically, the minor premise and the conclusion are the same proposition but phrased in different words.

Example:

> For CSP to be liable, it must have disseminated information in any manner to the public. Tex. Civ. Prac. & Rem. Code Ann. § 96.002(a). In *Green's Grocer*, the defendant disseminated information to the public via a local TV broadcast [cite]. Since CSP sent its newsletter to its subscribers, it disseminated information in any manner to the public.

This is also known as circular reasoning. It is akin to saying that CSP disseminated information to the public because it disseminated information. We still need to know if the information was disseminated to the public.

Revised example:

> For CSP to be liable, it must have disseminated information in any manner to the public. Tex. Civ. Prac. & Rem. Code Ann. § 96.002(a). In *Green's Grocer*, the defendant disseminated information to the public via a local TV broadcast, and the court held that the audience was large enough to constitute "the public" in the normal sense of the word [cite]. Since CSP sent its newsletter to 150 members who subscribed to its newsletter, it likely disseminated information in any manner to the public as that word is commonly understood.

Chapter 32

Analogical Reasoning

"In the language of logicians, analogy is a process of reasoning from the particular to the particular."[1]

—Judge Ruggero J. Aldisert et al.

Analogical reasoning is a form of induction. It operates on the principle that "two things that resemble one another in a number of respects resemble one another in a further, unconfirmable respect."[2] Like rule synthesis, it proceeds from one or more particular instances to reach a general conclusion. The power of an analogy depends on the nature and number of the similarities and differences between the two things being compared.

Which of the four objects here does not belong? Put another way, which of these objects are most similar and why?

To answer that question, you begin to think in categories. You might notice first that all of these objects keep time, except the compass, so you conclude that the compass does not belong. But what if that is not the similarity among the objects that matters? What if shape is the determining feature? Then perhaps the hourglass does not belong. Can you think of other ways to categorize these objects?[3] How do you know which similarities matter, and which don't?

---

1 Aldisert et al., *supra* ch. 29, note 2, at 17.

2 *See* Corbett & Connors, *supra* ch. 8 note 2, at 94.

3 You might say that the clock and watch belong together because they are both round, keep time, and drawn with thin lines. In contrast, the hourglass and compass belong together because neither keeps time in the way that a clock or watch does, and both are drawn with thick lines.

A. Analogical reasoning in law

In law, we rely heavily on analogical reasoning—examining similarities and differences—because *stare decisis* requires that like cases be treated alike. By comparing our client's situation to similar situations in binding cases, we can predict or argue for the same outcome.

If the case is similar enough to dictate the outcome in our client's case, we say it is **analogous**; if the case is different enough not to dictate outcome, we say it is **distinguishable**. A case may be analogous in some but not all respects and still be used to support your client's position. Although analogies do not provide conclusive proof of similarity or difference for purposes of *stare decisis*, they are a requisite part of legal analysis in a common law system.

In the Velas matter, the Velases must prove CSP disseminated information in any manner to the public. Tex. Civ. Prac. & Rem. Code Ann. § 96.002(c). Recall that in *Green's Grocer*, the Texas Court of Appeals held that a live news show was broadcast to a large enough audience to constitute the "public" in the normal sense of the word, but we do not know how many people watched the news show. In *Thomas Meats*, the Supreme Court of Texas held that 100 customers who viewed a sign in the defendant grocery store's window constituted the public.

To determine whether CSP disseminated its newsletter to the public, we need to think about the similarities and differences among these three situations. If dissemination "to the public" depends on the number of people involved, we can analogize our case to *Green's Grocer* on the basis of a large audience in general and to *Thomas Meats* on the ground that CSP sent its newsletter to 150 subscribers, which is 50 more people than the customers in *Thomas Meats*. In that sense, *Green's Grocer* and *Thomas Meats* can be used to predict or argue for a finding in our case that CSP disseminated information "to the public."

Example:

> For CSP to be liable, it must have disseminated information in any manner to the public. Tex. Civ. Prac. & Rem. Code Ann. § 96.002(a). Disseminating information to a large enough audience to constitute "public" in the normal sense of the word is dissemination to the public [cite *Green's Grocer*]. The Texas Supreme Court recently held that 100 customers who viewed a sign in the window of a grocery store constituted the public [cite *Thomas Meats*].
>
> In *Green's Grocer*, the defendant made an allegedly false statement on a local TV news broadcast, which the court held was large enough to constitute the public, presumably because a large number of viewers would have seen the broadcast [cite]. In *Thomas Meats*, the defendant posted a

> sign in its window with allegedly false information about the plaintiff's products. The court held the defendant had disseminated information to the public because at least 100 customers had seen the sign. Similarly, CSP disseminated false information by emailing it to 150 subscribers. This large number of people was fifty more than the court deemed the "public" in *Thomas Meats*. For these reasons, CSP likely disseminated information to the public.

Do you find the analogy persuasive? If you represented CSP, how would you try to distinguish *Green's Grocer* and *Thomas Meats*?

B. How do I know which similarities matter and which ones do not?

Deciding what facts and circumstances make one case similar to or different from another can be difficult. Assume the facts and circumstances of a relevant, binding case (Case 1) and your case (Case 2) are similar in some ways and different in others. They are represented visually as follows:

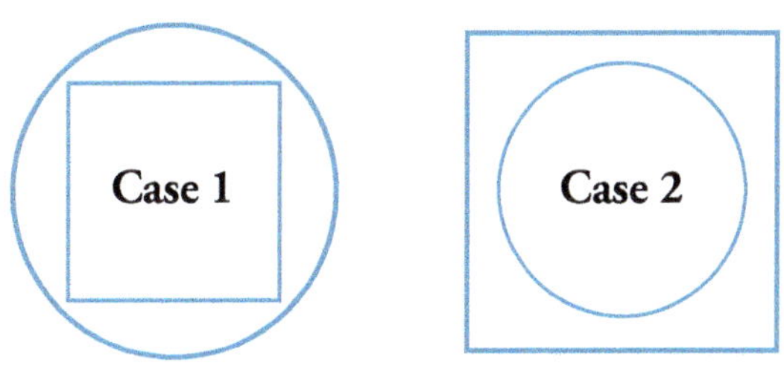

For purposes of *stare decisis*, are these cases similar or different?[4]

Similar v. Different

Similar	Different
Both have a circle and a square.	The primary feature in Case 1 is a square and the primary feature in Case 2 is a circle.
Both cases have the same two defining features and no more.	The sizes of the circles and squares are different.
Their overall size is roughly the same.	

The truth is that there is no definitive way to decide which features are more important—the similarities, the differences, or which ones. In our legal system, these decisions are generally left to the discretion of the lawyers and judges involved in the case.

---

4 Remember that the cases need not be identical; if they were, there would be no need for an analogy. They only need to be sufficiently "alike" to be treated the same way.

Steven Burton, a law professor at the University of Iowa College of Law, has said that resolving these competing factors requires a "judgment of importance."[5] Although analogical reasoning arguably "leave[s] the crucial judgment of importance . . . unconstrained by the law and open to abuse,"[6] Burton argues that judicial bias is kept in check by "allowing and disallowing *reasons* to count in judicial and other deliberations."[7] While reasons grounded in the law are allowed to count, those "stemming from a judge's personal interests, prejudices, and religious or moral views" are not.[8]

Joseph Hutcheson, a federal judge from Texas, has said that the problem of importance is harder for a judge to solve since a lawyer knows what his goal is and "regards only those hunches which keep him in the path that he has chosen."[9] As a legal writer, you too will be challenged to identify the similarities and differences between cases and exercise that judgment of importance. On what will you rely? To a large extent, those decisions will be guided by your client's goals, your ethical duty to represent your client zealously, and your ethical duty to represent the law accurately.

For More Information

Ruggero J. Aldisert, *Logic For Lawyers: A Guide To Clear Legal Thinking* (3d ed. 2001).

Steven J. Burton, *An Introduction To Law And Legal Reasoning* (3d ed. 2007).

James A. Gardner, *Legal Argument: The Structure and Language of Effective Advocacy* (2d ed. 2007).

C. Fallacies in analogical reasoning

A good analogy supports your characterization of the facts (the minor premise in your legal syllogism) by illustrating its similarity to a decided case. If the two cases are similar, the rule (your major premise) must be applied the same way. Analogies can be ineffective where they do not include enough information, rely on insignificant similarities, or "overlook pertinent, significant dissimilarities."[10] To help you identify

---

5 Steven J. Burton, An Introduction To Law And Legal Reasoning 27 (3d ed. 2007).

6 *Id.* at 27–28.; *see also* Cass R. Sunstein, Commentary, *On Analogical Reasoning*, 106 Harv. L. Rev. 741, 773 (1993).

7 Burton, *supra* note 5, at 90.

8 *Id.*

9 Joseph H. Hutcheson, Jr., *The Judgment Intuitive: The Function of the "Hunch" in Judicial Decision*, 39 S. Tex. L. Rev. 889, 894 (1998) *reprinted from* 14 Cornell L. Q. 274 (1929).

10 Corbett & Connors, *supra* ch. 8 note 2, at 69.

fallacies in your own analogical reasoning, this section describes typical mistakes beginning legal writers make.

1. The missing link (too much information missing)

When too much detail is left out, either about the decided case or your case, the reader is unable to make the leap to overall similarity or difference. In addition to including these details, be sure to explain in explicit terms how the two cases compare to each other.

Example:

> For CSP to be liable, it must have disseminated information in any manner to the public. Tex. Civ. Prac. & Rem. Code Ann. § 96.002(a). Disseminating information to a large enough audience to constitute "public" in the normal sense of the word is dissemination to the public [cite *Green's Grocer*]. The Texas Supreme Court recently held that 100 customers who viewed a sign in the window of a grocery store constituted the public [cite *Thomas Meats*]. Similarly, CSP disseminated information about the coffee beans to the public.

In this example, the writer attempts to analogize to *Green's Grocer* and *Thomas Meats* to argue that CSP disseminated information to the public. However, without any specific information about the facts of *Green's Grocer* or *Thomas Meats*, the reader cannot draw any comfortable conclusion about the similarity of the Velases' situation to these cases. The factual and circumstantial link between them is missing. What did the defendants in *Green's Grocer* and *Thomas Meats* do or say? How did they say it? To whom did they say it and to how many people? Specifically, how did CSP act like the defendant in these cases such that the same outcome is compelled on the question of dissemination to the public? See the sample analysis in Chapter 37.B.

2. The house of cards (relying on a case with an adverse outcome)

When the case law seems to favor your client's opponent, you may have no choice but to rely on it (when the law is bad, argue the facts and vice versa). Even though the outcomes of the cases are unfavorable, the court's statements about the law may still be binding. In this situation, you need to acknowledge the adverse outcome(s), explain why those cases are distinguishable, and demonstrate how the law should be applied differently in your case.

Example:

> For CSP to be liable, it must have stated or implied that the coffee beans are unsafe for public consumption. *See* Tex. Civ. Prac. & Rem.

> Code Ann. § 96.002(c). In *Green's Grocer*, the court held that a statement implying that a product is inherently dangerous in some way is sufficient to satisfy this element. [cite *Green's Grocer*]. Similarly, CSP implied that the Velases' coffee beans are inherently dangerous by claiming they are grown using pesticides. Therefore, CSP stated or implied that the beans are unsafe for public consumption.

Here, the writer appropriately relies on *Green's Grocer* for a synthesized rule of law but does not mention that the defendant in *Green's Grocer* won that case. This undercuts the writer's analysis because it does not explain why there should be a different outcome in the Velas case. Here, the best option is to rely on *Green's Grocer* for the rule of law and then distinguish it by explaining the differences between the two cases (i.e., CSP did imply the beans are inherently dangerous and how).

Revised example:

> For CSP to be liable, it must have stated or implied that the coffee beans are unsafe for public consumption. *See* Tex. Civ. Prac. & Rem. Code Ann. § 96.002(c). Statements implying that a product is inherently dangerous are equivalent to saying the product is unsafe for public consumption. In *Green's Grocer*, the court held the plaintiff had not proved this element because a statement that someone had choked on the plaintiff's apple did not suggest anything inherently dangerous about the apple, and people choke on all sorts of food [cite *Green's Grocer*]. In contrast, CSP suggested there is something inherently dangerous about the Velases' coffee beans because they are grown using pesticides. Therefore, CSP stated or implied that the beans are unsafe for public consumption.

3. The problem with analogies in totality of circumstances tests

Certain rules of law are fluid. They allow the parties, judge, and jury to measure prior acts against a flexible **standard** as opposed to a rigid rule. Standards in tort law, for example, include "the reasonable person" and "what a person knew or should have known." To determine whether these flexible standards are met, courts often examine a number of **factors** that make up **the totality of circumstances**.

The court then engages in a balancing test, examining each factor and weighing them against each other to determine, on balance, whether the standard has been met. Put another way, they determine which party the factors favor. Sometimes courts articulate a list of relevant factors. When they don't, you may infer them based on the court's analysis.[11]

---

11 The choice as to which factors to rely on is another example of a "judgment of importance." *See* BURTON, *supra* note 5.

In factor-based analysis, analogical reasoning is critical because the analysis is heavily factual. The challenge is not to ignore relevant or unfavorable facts and factors that will weaken your analogies. To demonstrate, assume that in *Green's Grocer*, the court held that dissemination to the public depends on the following factors:

- the nature of the message,
- the way in which it is disseminated,
- the number of potential recipients,
- the actual number of recipients, and
- whether the message is heard or read

These factors make up the totality of circumstances the court will use to determine whether the defendant disseminated information "to the public."

Assume that the *Green's Grocer* court applied these factors and held, on balance, that they favored the plaintiff because the broadcast message allegedly concerned a potential health risk to a significant portion of the community, television news is available to virtually everyone, and the broadcast was viewed live by roughly 50,000 homes in that station's viewing area. Subsequently, *Thomas Meats* held that the sign in the grocery store window was disseminated to the public and knew that at least 100 customers had seen it.

Example:

> For CSP to be liable, it must have disseminated information to the public. See Tex. Civ. Prac. & Rem. Code Ann. § 96.002(c). Whether information is disseminated to the public depends on the totality of the circumstances. Relevant factors include the nature of the message, the way in which it is disseminated, the number of potential recipients, the actual number of recipients, and whether the message is heard or read [cite *Green's Grocer*]. In that case, the court held the defendant disseminated information to the public when he broadcast a statement about the plaintiff's apples on local television news [cite]. Recently, the *Thomas Meats* court held that posting a sign in a shop window to at least 100 customers is dissemination to the public [cite *Thomas Meats*]. Like the defendant in *Green's Grocer* and *Thomas Meats*, CSP disseminated information to the public about a health risk to the community when it sent its newsletter to 150 subscribers.

How persuasive is this analysis? Which factors does it emphasize, and which does it ignore? Although the writer examines the first and fourth factors, they ignore the second, the third, and the fifth factors. In response, one might counter that CSP's message does not imply the same level of immediate danger that choking does, that the manner of distribution here matters (the audiences in the two cases were live audiences), and it is unclear how many of CSP's subscribers actually read the newsletter.

Revised example:

For CSP to be liable, it must have disseminated information to the public. See Tex. Civ. Prac. & Rem. Code Ann. § 96.002(c). Whether information is disseminated to the public depends on the totality of the circumstances. Relevant factors include the nature of the message, the way in which it is disseminated, the number of potential recipients, the actual number of recipients, and whether the message is heard or read [cite *Green's Grocer*]. In that case, the court held the defendant disseminated information to the public when he broadcast a statement about the plaintiff's apples on local television news. Recently, the *Thomas Meats* court held that posting a sign in a shop window to at least 100 customers is dissemination to the public [cite *Thomas Meats*].

Like the defendant in *Green's Grocer* and *Thomas Meats*, CSP disseminated information about a health risk to the community. Although CSP's information was disseminated by email, the statute covers dissemination *in any manner*. Although it is unknown how many members CSP's local chapter has, the newsletter was sent to 150 subscribers, which is fifty more than those who viewed the sign in *Thomas Meats*. Assuming the majority of email addresses were current, there is no reason to believe the newsletter was not received. Although we cannot know whether each recipient read the newsletter, this is just one factor in determining whether there is public dissemination. In addition, the rumors spreading about the potential danger of the beans has affected sales, which tends to prove that a sufficient number of recipients read the newsletter to qualify as "the public."

Chapter 33

Inferences of Fact

"An inference is not itself evidence; it is the result of reasoning from evidence."[1]

—Janet Gusdorff

All reasoning is inferential. **Inferential reasoning** refers generally to the process of moving from rules or observations to conclusions.[2] When we induce a rule from several cases, we infer the rule. When we apply a legal rule to facts to deduce a conclusion, we infer the conclusion. When we use analogical reasoning, we are encouraging our audience to make an inference of similarity or difference. The forms of reasoning described so far in this part of the book—rule synthesis, legal syllogisms, analogical reasoning—largely involve inferences relating to questions of law and the application of law to specific facts. This chapter discusses **inferences of fact:** the process of inferring one fact from the existence of another.

> **Bottom Line**
>
> Inferential reasoning is equivalent to "if x, then y."

A. Facts can be inferred from direct and indirect evidence

In a civil or criminal proceeding, the parties submit evidence to prove or disprove the facts central to their case, also known as **ultimate facts**. Put another way, the evidence is submitted for the factfinder[3] to infer that a disputed fact does or does not exist. Evidence can take many forms—testimony, documents, tangible objects—and be either **direct** or **indirect**. **Direct evidence** is evidence based on personal knowledge or observation and tends to prove the existence or non-existence

1 Janet Gusdorff, *Inferences explained: Using and rebutting inferences* (Dec. 2019), https://www.advocatemagazine.com/images/issues/2019/12-december/reprints/Gusdorff_article.pdf (https://perma.cc/3PSK-62PG).

2 *See inference*, *in* Black's Law Dictionary (11th ed. 2019).

3 The factfinder in a legal dispute can be either the judge or jury. *See supra* ch. 20.A.1, at 130.

of a fact without the need for any additional inference or **presumption**.[4] **Indirect or circumstantial evidence** is evidence that proves the existence or non-existence of a fact using an *additional* inference.[5]

When evidence is direct, the factfinder makes a one-step inference—from the evidence (x) to the ultimate fact (y). For example, assume your client's grandfather, James Henry, left all his property in his will to a distant nephew, Robert. Your client, Lucy, expected to inherit her grandfather's property because until recently, she was the named beneficiary. She wishes to contest the validity of the new will on the grounds that her grandfather changed his will as a result of Robert's undue influence.[6]

> FYI
> **Direct inference: x → y**
> Ex: conversation between Robert and James → undue influence

Now assume that James' brother, Tom, was in the room when Robert insisted that James owed him money and told him he better leave his property to Robert "or else." If Tom testifies about that conversation (x), it leads to an inference about the ultimate fact to be proved: that James changed the will as a result of Robert's undue influence (y).

Where the evidence is indirect or circumstantial, the factfinder makes a two-step inference—from the direct evidence of one fact (w), to the inference of a second fact (x), to an inference about the ultimate fact to be proved (y). In the example above, assume instead that on several occasions, Lucy heard Robert argue with James about money James allegedly owed him, which debt James repeatedly denied. Lucy did not hear or see Robert pressure James to change his will, but she is convinced that Robert must have done so. Otherwise, James would not have changed his will the day after Robert's last visit.

> FYI
> **Indirect inference: w → x → y**
> Ex: conversations between Robert and James → Robert pressured James to change the will → undue influence

In this case, to prove the will was changed as a result of Robert's undue influence, there would need to be two inferences instead of one: If Lucy testifies to the arguments between Robert and James about money (w), it could lead to

---

4 A presumption is a deduction required by law. For example, the law requires the factfinder to presume the innocence of a criminal defendant in the absence of any evidence. *See* Coffin v. United States, 156 U.S. 432, 453 (1895) ("The principle that there is a presumption of innocence in favor of the accused is the undoubted law, axiomatic and elementary, and its enforcement lies at the foundation of the administration of our criminal law."). You will learn more about presumptions in civil procedure and evidence classes.

5 *See evidence*, *in* Black's Law Dictionary (11th ed. 2019).

6 Undue influence "may take the form of force, intimidation, duress, excessive importunity or deception used in an effort to overcome or subvert the will of the maker of the testament and induce the execution thereof contrary to his will." In re Estate of Scott, 601 S.W.3d 77, 89 (Tex. App. 2020).

an inference that Robert pressured James to change his will (x), which could lead to an inference about the ultimate fact to be proved: that James changed the will as a result of Robert's undue influence (y).

B. Fact inferences must be reasonable, logical, and not based on speculation or conjecture

Drawing inferences from the facts in evidence is the sole duty of the factfinder. A factfinder can rely on direct or indirect evidence (or both) to find the existence of a particular fact.[7] Circumstantial evidence can be used to infer knowledge and intent, which are rarely proved directly (e.g., a person accused of an intent crime rarely admits to that intent).[8] Even in a criminal trial, the factfinder may find the facts necessary to convict on the basis of circumstantial evidence alone.[9] As long as the factfinder's inferences are logical and reasonable, based on probabilities as opposed to possibilities, and not based on speculation or conjecture, its ultimate findings of fact will be upheld.[10]

In representing your client, you will often need to describe to the decision-maker the relevant facts that are known or agreed to by the parties, as well as those that are in dispute or unknown. This process will necessarily involve making the same types of inferences a factfinder is called upon to make when presented with evidence at trial. Put another way, you will want to state something as a fact that you have inferred from the existence of another fact (i.e., the *x* in w → x → y). Thus, you need to be mindful of the facts you have inferred from the existence of other facts and are stating as known facts. The inference should be based on "substantial evidence, not conjecture. . . . It must be such that a rational, well-constructed mind can reasonably draw from it the conclusion that the fact exists[.]"[11] Even slight evidence may be enough to support the inference.[12] The factfinder, not the court, ultimately decides how much weight to give the evidence. If you make an inference that is not logical or reasonable and based more on speculation or conjecture, your opponent will be sure to take issue with it.

---

7 *See, e.g.*, Etheridge v. Opitz, 580 S.W.3d 167, 177 (Tex. App. 2019).

8 *See, e.g.*, Clementson v. State, 492 S.W.3d 802, 806 (Tex. App. 2016).

9 *See, e.g.*, Jenkins v. State, 493 S.W.3d 583, 599 (Tex. Crim. App. 2016).

10 *See, e.g.*, Dixie Carpet Installations, Inc. v. Residences at Riverdale, S.W.3d 618, 625 (Tex. App. 2020); Etheridge v. Opitz, 580 S.W.3d 167, 178 (Tex. App. 2019); Aguimatang v. California State Lottery, 286 Cal. Rptr. 57, 74 (Cal. Ct. App. 1991); Gusdorff, *supra* note 1, at 1–2.

11 Kubbernus v. ECAL Partners, 574 S.W.3d 444, 479 (Tex. App. 2018); Fashion 21 v. Coalition for Humane Immigr. Rts. of L.A., 12 Cal. Rptr. 3d 493, 501 (Cal. Ct. App. 2004).

12 *E.g.*, Fashion 21, *supra* note 11, at 501.

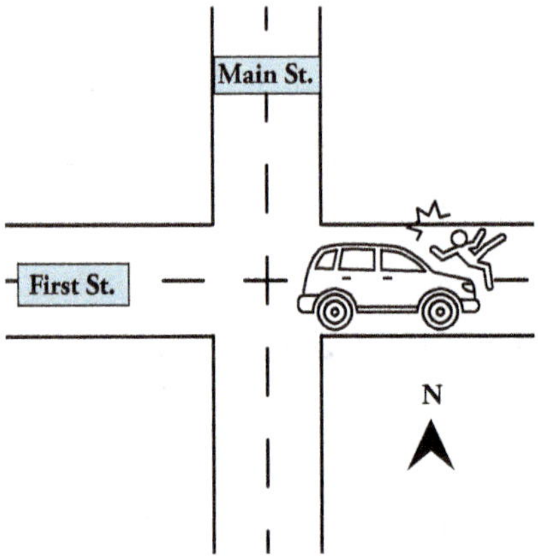

For another example, let's go back to the car accident case in Chapter 20 on page 130. In that case, the plaintiff, a pedestrian, claims that the defendant ran a red light while driving his vehicle and struck her in the crosswalk. The defendant claims that the light was green when he entered the intersection. He also claims that his wife was in the car, in labor with their first child, and as a precaution, he honked and flashed his lights as he entered the intersection. The plaintiff has now sued the defendant in a Texas state court for negligence.

The ultimate facts (here, the elements) to be proved in a negligence case are a duty to the plaintiff, the defendant's breach of that duty, and damages proximately caused by the breach of that duty.[13] The only issue in this case is whether the defendant breached his duty to the plaintiff. In describing the facts of the accident, the plaintiff alleges that she saw the light for the cars on First Street change from green to yellow and then to red before she entered the crosswalk. If she testified to that fact, that would be direct evidence (x) leading to the inference of the ultimate fact: that the driver breached a duty by running the red light (y).

What if the plaintiff did not have direct evidence that the light was red? Instead, she has a witness who will testify that she was walking south on Main Street toward the intersection. She remembers noticing the light for cars on Main Street had turned from red to green because the red light had been bothering her eyes. She then heard screeching brakes and a thud, which was the sound of the car hitting the plaintiff. In this case, the plaintiff can submit the witness' testimony of the light turning green for cars on Main Street as evidence of the light having turned red for cars on First Street. Since that is how alternating traffic lights work and assuming the witness is credible, it is logical and reasonable to assume that if the light for one direction of traffic was green (w), the light for the oncoming traffic was red (x), and the defendant breached a duty by running the red light (y).

Based on either the direct or circumstantial evidence described above, which of the following inferences could the plaintiff further make?

1. That because red lights are more noticeable than green lights, the defendant must have seen that the light was red?

The inference may sound logical because red lights are red because they are more noticeable, but it is probably speculative to say for certain that this defendant

13 *See, e.g.*, Van Horn v. Chambers, 970 S.W.2d 542, 544 (Tex. 1998).

saw the red light that night solely because red lights are more noticeable than green. He may have been distracted by his wife or something else, there may have been a tree branch blocking his view, etc.

2. That if the defendant had his wife and unborn child in the car, he must have been driving extra carefully and noticed the light was red?

Again, this inference has some element of reason to it because the defendant was probably driving differently that night due to the circumstances. However, it is speculative to say that the stress of the evening necessarily made it certain that he was focused on the red light and not on other things.

3. That because the plaintiff saw the light on First Street turn red, the crosswalk sign was lit for pedestrians to cross First Street?

This inference seems reasonable because that's how crossing signs work. As long as the testimony is credible, a jury could infer that the light turning red for First Street would trigger the First Street pedestrian crossing light.

4. That the plaintiff would never have entered the intersection if the light on First Street had not turned red?

This is not a logical inference. We know that people frequently cross streets against the light and are often hurt. Without more evidence, the fact that the plaintiff crossed the street does not make it more likely than not that the light had turned red. The plaintiff could just as easily have noticed the defendant's car coming and tried to cross anyway. In fact, the defendant claims he honked and flashed his lights to avoid any accident.

Apply It: Exercise 33.1

(see suggested answers at App. B, at p. 520)

In the Velas matter, which of the following facts can reasonably be inferred from the known fact?

- Since CSP disseminated its newsletter to its subscribers, it disseminated information "in any manner."
- Since CSP disseminated its newsletter to 150 subscribers, it disseminated it "to the public."
- Assuming the statement that the coffee is grown using pesticides is false, CSP knew it was false.
- Since the newsletter states that the Velases' coffee is grown using pesticides, it states or implies that it is not safe for consumption.

CHAPTER 34

Narrative Reasoning

"Tell me an argument and I might consider it. Tell me a story and I am yours."

—David Ball

Narrative reasoning is the use of storytelling techniques to persuade your audience to take specific action. Stories are a primary mode of communication among people across all cultures. We use them to share experiences, teach, and entertain. We respond instinctively to stories, particularly those with evocative images and recurring themes. Lawyers use stories to explain their client's circumstances and as an integral part of induction, deduction, and analogy. While the more "logical" forms of reasoning help persuade the audience that a lawyer's legal analysis is correct, narrative reasoning can bring that analysis to life.[1] As you will read, narrative reasoning thus combines appeals to logic, emotion, and credibility.

All forms of legal representation begin and end with a client's story. Brian Foley and Ruth Anne Robbins explain that to develop a powerful story for your client, consider the key elements of fiction: character, setting, conflict, resolution, and a good plot.[2] Your client should always be the hero of the story in some sense, and the story should be told from the client's perspective in a way that is both plausible and responsible.[3]

Practice Pointer

Compelling client stories often incorporate the key elements of fiction:

- character
- setting
- conflict
- resolution
- a good plot

For example, in the Velas matter, if you described your client as a multi-billion dollar corporation with over 30,000 stores in 70 countries, that would tell one kind of story. However, if you described

---

1 *See, e.g.*, Linda Berger, *How Embedded Knowledge Structures Affect Judicial Decision Making: An Analysis of Metaphor, Narrative, and Imagination in Child Custody Disputes*, 18 S. CAL. INTERDISC. L.J. 259, 264 (2009) (quoting JEROME BRUNER, ACTUAL MINDS, POSSIBLE WORLDS 11 (1986)).

2 *See, e.g.*, Brian J. Foley & Ruth Anne Robbins, *Fiction 101: A Primer for Lawyers on How to Use Fiction Writing Techniques to Write Persuasive Facts Sections*, 32 RUTGERS L. J. 459, 466 (2001).

3 *See also* Ruth Anne Robbins, *Harry Potter, Ruby Slippers, and Merlin: Telling the Client's Story Using the Characters and Paradigms of the Archetypal Hero's Journey*, 29 SEATTLE U. L. REV. 767, 772 (2006).

your client as an independent licensee of the Starbucks brand, struggling to make his one coffee shop succeed in the face of multiple setbacks, then that would tell a quite different story. CSP is likely to develop a competing story, perhaps that this megastore is deceiving unwitting consumers and putting them at risk.

Your client's story should help the factfinder understand the situation from your client's perspective and affect the way they interpret the facts in evidence. The more your story resonates with the ultimate decision-maker, the more persuasive it will be. For additional discussion on telling your client's story in advocacy and argument, including ethical constraints, see Chapter 47.

Lawyers also use narrative reasoning to frame legal rules and make legal arguments. Where the rule of law does not favor the client, they look for ways to reframe the law to fit the client's story.[4] For example, if the law requires the client to prove an element that likely cannot be proved, a lawyer might be able to reframe a synthesized rule that includes an exception that fits the client's situation.[5] For example, we might argue that even if 150 subscribers does not constitute the "public" in the normal sense of the word, it is sufficient if the information is such that it is likely to become public.

More often, though, lawyers use narrative reasoning as part of the analytical paradigm. When lawyers explain the rule of law in a given case, including the context in which it was applied and why, they tell the story of the client in the cited case. When they compare the facts and circumstances of their client's case to those of the cited case, they compare the clients' stories.[6]

Judges use stories in a variety of ways too: to create or modify legal rules, to help them decide what similarities and differences matter for purposes of *stare decisis*, and to explain their decisions in judicial opinions. Common law rules evolve over time as a direct result of client stories. In each new case, "the narratives of future litigants bump up against the rule created from the narratives of the first set of litigants, with the result that the rule becomes more and more refined."[7]

Consider the *Pet Barn* case in the Velas matter.[8] In *Pet Barn*, the plaintiff argued that its food product was a product of agriculture even though it was comprised of multiple agricultural products. In effect, that story "bumped up against" the rule created by the Texas legislature, and the court had to further refine the definition of a "food product of agriculture."

---

4 Linda H. Edwards, *The Convergence of Analogical and Dialectic Imaginations in Legal Discourse*, 20 LEG. STUD. FORUM 7, 32–34 (1996).

5 *See id.*

6 *Id.* at 23–24; *see also* Christy DeSanctis, *Narrative Reasoning and Analogy: The Untold Story*, 9 LEGAL COMM. & RHETORIC: JALWD 149, 167–68 (2012).

7 Edwards, *supra* note 4, at 21.

8 *See supra* ch. 30, at 199.

Stories may even help judges make better "judgments of importance" (see Chapter 32, at 222). Judges use these when they decide which similarities and differences matter in analogical reasoning or whether a factor-based test weighs in the plaintiff's favor. To the extent your client's story prompts a judge to see your client's story as similar to one in a decided case with a favorable outcome, you may help the judge make a better decision that also favors your client.[9]

For More Information

Kenneth D. Chestek, *Competing Stories: A Case Study of the Role of Narrative Reasoning in Judicial Decisions*, 9 Legal Commc'n & Rhetoric: JALWD 99 (2012).

Linda H. Edwards, *Speaking of Stories and Law*, 13 Legal Commc'n & Rhetoric 157 (2016) (discussing the role of narrative in law and distinguishing between rules and stories).

Todd E. Pettys, *The Emotional Juror*, 76 Fordham L. Rev. 1609, 1629–36 (2007) (discussing the power of narrative in jury decision-making).

---

9 Linda L. Berger, *A Revised View of the Judicial Hunch*, 10 LEGAL COMMC'N & RHETORIC: JALWD 1, 25 (2013).

Chapter 35

Policy-Based Reasoning

The task of good public policy making is not to reason what is good for others but to envision imaginatively, from diverse standpoints, the present reality and the desirable future.[1]

—D. Don Welch

Lawyers use **policy-based reasoning** or **public policy** arguments that consider how a particular decision will benefit parties in future, similar disputes or society as a whole.[2] Lawyers use policy-based reasoning in a number of ways: to argue for legislative change, to interpret the law, and to argue for a particular decision in a given case. Policy arguments often require the decision-maker to choose between competing values.[3]

As Wilson Huhn explains, policy-based arguments typically begin by predicting the "consequences that will flow from giving the law one interpretation over another"[4] and end with arguments on "which set of consequences is more consistent with the underlying values of the law."[5] Policy-based arguments tend to rely on non-legal authority for support, such as the work of sociologists, economists, psychologists and political scientists[6] and are presented in the form of scientific models, economic analysis, empirical studies, statistics, and expert opinion.

Some of the most famous policy-based arguments based on non-legal support were presented by Justice Louis Brandeis, then acting as **amicus curiae** (friend of the court) for the State of Oregon, in *Muller v. State of Oregon*, 208 U.S. 412 (1908). Oregon had enacted a statute limiting the number of hours women could work to ten per day, which the plaintiff laundry owner claimed was unconstitutional.

---

1 D. Don Welch, *Ruling with the Heart: Emotion-Based Public Policy*, 6 S. Cal. Interdisc. L. J. 55, 85 (1997).

2 Edwards, *supra* ch. 34, note 4, at 10.

3 *See* Michael R. Smith, *The Sociological And Cognitive Dimensions Of Policy-Based Persuasion*, 22 J.L. & Pol'y 35, 44 (2013).

4 Wilson Huhn, Five Types of Argument 63 (2d ed. 2014).

5 *Id.*

6 Edwards, *supra* ch. 34, note 4, at 10 (citing Benjamin N. Cardozo, The Nature of the Judicial Process (1921)).

In support of the legislation, Brandeis submitted an argument (now known as the "Brandeis brief,"[7]) consisting of two pages of legal argument and over 100 pages of social science data supporting the reasonableness of the restriction, such as the adverse effects of long-term exposure to excessive heat and steam and standing for more than eight to ten hours at a time.[8]

> **FYI**
>
> 
>
> Justice Brandeis' sister-in-law, Josephine Goldmark (1877–1950), advocated for labor law reform on behalf of the National Consumers League. She helped him compile the data for the brief from medical and social science journals.
>
> *https://jwa.org/encyclopedia/article/goldmark-josephine-clara (https://perma.cc/7VWJ-QF3L).*
>
> *(image in the public domain)*

Judges—particularly appellate judges—are often receptive to policy-based arguments when they are being asked to adopt a legal rule in a situation they have not confronted before.[9] Because appellate courts bind all lower courts in their jurisdiction, those judges are also concerned about the impact their decisions will have on lower courts.

Like stories, policy-based reasoning may even help judges make better "judgments of importance" (see Chapter 32, p. 222). In the cases you read for your courses, take notice of the kinds of situations where judges rely heavily on policy-based arguments to reach their decisions.

> **Bottom Line**
>
> Policy arguments are based on
>
> - improving judicial administration
> - the good of society
> - institutional competence
> - economic efficiency

Ellie Margolis, a professor at Temple Law, divides policy-based reasoning into four broad categories: the administration of the judicial system, the overall good of society, institutional competence, and economic efficiency.[10]

The first category refers to promoting a fair and efficient judicial system.

---

7 *See* http://louisville.edu/law/library/special-collections/the-louis-d.-brandeis-collection/the-brandeis-brief-in-its-entirety (https://perma.cc/LT9C-AFUN).

8 Although the Brandeis brief has been criticized for reinforcing stereotypes about the superiority of men over women, it educated the Court about real world problems the statute was attempting to address. *See* Ruth Bader Ginsburg, Assoc. Justice of the United States Supreme Court, *Lessons learned from Louis D. Brandeis*, Brandeis Now (Jan. 28, 2016), https://www.brandeis.edu/now/2016/january/ginsburg-remarks.html (https://perma.cc/65FL-33J8).

9 Ellie Margolis, *Closing the Floodgates: Making Persuasive Policy Arguments in Appellate Briefs*, 62 MONT. L. REV. 59, 60 (2001).

10 *See id.* at 71–79; *see also* Elizabeth Fajans, *Legal Writing in the Time Of Recession: Developing Cognitive Skills for Complex Legal Tasks*, 49 DUQ. L. REV. 613, 626 (2011); HELENE S. SHAPO ET AL., WRITING AND ANALYSIS IN THE LAW 264–70 (5th ed. 2008).

An argument that a court should apply a definitive rule of law serves the goal of efficiency because people will know in advance what the rule is and how to behave. In contrast, an argument that a court should apply a more flexible rule, where a host of factors can be applied to each unique set of circumstances, serves the goal of fairness to individuals.

This category also includes arguments based on a "slippery slope" and the "floodgates of litigation."[11] To argue that a proposed rule of law creates a slippery slope is to argue that it will be difficult to limit the application of the rule to a prescribed set of circumstances. In turn, this may open up a "floodgate of litigation," which the courts will not be able to manage.

The second category refers to furthering the overall good of society. It leads to arguments based on what people should or should not be able to do, how society should function, and how we should punish wrongdoers. These are often called **normative** arguments. The abortion debate, which is rooted in moral or religious beliefs, often relies on these sorts of policy arguments.

The third category refers to ensuring that governmental tasks are delegated to the branches best suited to handle them. For example, an argument against a court creating a new rule that is better left to the legislature is a policy argument based on institutional competence.

The final category refers to economic efficiency and promoting the economy. It leads to arguments that a rule of law should or should not be applied based on economic theory, such as cost-benefit analysis or the effect on competition.

In addition to rule-based, analogical, and narrative reasoning, policy-based reasoning can make your analysis or arguments more convincing. Start by considering the goals of the controlling law, the goals of your client, and the goals of anyone opposed to your client. Then determine the policy goals best served by your client's position. Margolis suggests that you cite binding legal authority in support of the importance of the goal itself (e.g., promoting efficiency or fairness in the judicial system).[12] Then explain how your client's position will help achieve that goal. Here is where non-legal support (e.g., scientific evidence or theory) comes in. Finally, be sure to anticipate and refute the goals potentially served by any opponent's position.

Bottom Line

To make a **policy argument,** consider:

- the underlying goals of the applicable law
- the goal that is served by your client's position, and
- how your proposed rule or outcome will achieve that goal

11 *See, e.g.*, Toby J. Stern, *Federal Judges and Fearing The "Floodgates Of Litigation,"* 6 UNIV. PA. J. CONST. LAW 377 (2003).

12 Margolis, *supra* note 9, at 79–81.

For example, in the Velas matter, assume our client would want the Texas court to find that emailing a newsletter to 150 subscribers is equivalent to disseminating information in any manner to the public (see Chapter 30, at 199). *Thomas Meats* seems to establish that 100 people constitute the public, but this case is different from *Thomas Meats* and *Green's Grocer* in the sense that the audience in those cases was "live" and sure to have received the false information.

To enhance the analogy to *Thomas Meats*, you might make the "public" analysis stronger by including a policy-based argument. Let's start by considering the underlying goals of the Texas statute. Texas, like several other states with large agricultural economies, passed this statute in response to an apple scare in the late 1980s. The national news media reported that apples were unsafe because they were sprayed with Alar, a chemical designed to prevent them from falling off trees. The public panicked and stopped buying apples, which caused the apple industry to lose millions of dollars. The resulting "food disparagement" statutes, including the Texas statute, were designed to protect farmers against false claims about crops, which can perish before the public has a chance to learn the truth.

You might argue that the primary goals of the statute are to promote the economy and ensure economic efficiency (the second and fourth categories of goals). False statements about the safety of crops can destroy farmers, hurt the economy, and hinder competition. Despite the importance of keeping the public informed about the safety of its food supply, the Texas legislature decided that the benefit of imposing liability in these situations outweighs the costs to freedom of speech.

Then, you might argue, interpreting "the public" broadly in this case, particularly where news about the safety of the food supply is likely to travel quickly, serves those interests by expanding the scope of protection for plaintiffs. Support for this argument might come from non-legal evidence indicating that even minor disruptions to local agricultural economies can adversely affect our national economy.

For More Information

Paul T. Wangerin, *Skills Training in "Legal Analysis": A Systematic Approach*, 40 Univ. Miami L. Rev. 409, 455–59 (1986) (explaining the key to making good policy arguments).

D. Don Welch, *Ruling with The Heart: Emotion-Based Public Policy*, 6 S. Cal. Interdisc. L. J. 55 (1997) (arguing for the appropriateness of emotional appeals in public policy arguments and decision-making).

You might also be interested in reading the following landmark cases where the parties made effective policy arguments relying on non-legal support:

Lake River Corp. v. Carborundum Co., 769 F.2d 1284 (7th Cir. 1985) (using theory of economic efficiency to support efficient breach of contract).

Roe v. Wade, 410 U.S. 113 (1973) (using medical-legal history and medical evidence to legalize abortion).

Brown v. Board of Education, 347 U.S. 686 (1954) (using empirical data to support integration in schools).

Apply It: Exercise 35.1

(see suggested answers at App. B, at p. 521)

1. What might CSP argue is the primary goal of the Texas statute?
2. What policy arguments would CSP make in response to our client's policy argument for interpreting "public" broadly?
3. How would interpreting "the public" narrowly here serve those interests?
4. How could we refute those arguments?

Test Your Knowledge: Part VII

To assess your understanding of the material in this part, click here to take a quiz.

Part VIII

Predictive Writing and the Legal Memorandum

Chapter 36

What Is Predictive Writing?

Most clients seek legal advice when they have a problem to solve or a specific goal in mind. They may know what they want but not how to achieve it. Whether the client is accused of a crime, has been injured in some way, or wants to form a small business, your job will be to research the law and advise the client with various options and likely outcomes. Although you give the advice, the client makes the final decision on how to proceed.

When lawyers give written advice, we often describe it as predictive or objective writing. Both terms refer to the same thing: giving advice based on known facts and applicable rules of law. Because this form of analysis is usually written to the client or in anticipation of litigation, it is also privileged, meaning it need not be disclosed to third parties.

> **Practice Pointer**
>
> **Learn These Concepts Now:**
>
> The **attorney-client privilege** is an evidence rule that protects communications from disclosure.
>
> The **duty of confidentiality** is a lawyer's ethical duty to keep client information confidential.
>
> **Work product** is material prepared by or for a lawyer in anticipation of litigation and is also privileged against disclosure to third parties.

The goal of giving advice is to be as objective as possible in terms of assessing options and predicting outcomes, while at the same time trying to help your clients achieve their ultimate goals. There is often a tension between what the law permits and what the client hopes to achieve, which can make giving legal advice difficult. Because of this tension, giving legal advice rarely feels objective, which is why the phrase "predictive writing" is used from here on out.

> **FYI**
>
> **Forms of predictive writing include**
>
> - memoranda
> - email
> - opinion letters
> - bench memoranda

Effective predictive writing clearly and concisely explains the legal issue(s), informs the client about the relevant law, predicts outcome, and suggests a strategy for going forward. It can come in a variety of written and oral forms, including memoranda (memos), email, opinion letters, PowerPoint presentations,[1] texts, client meetings, telephone calls, and voicemail. The form of the advice usually depends on the nature, complexity, and sensitivity of the issues; the client's wishes; cost constraints; and the urgency of the matter. Bench memos (Chapter 42) are another form of advice used by judicial clerks to help judges make their decisions. The next chapter discusses the most traditional form of written legal advice, the legal memorandum. Chapters 40 through 41 describe other forms of predictive writing you are likely to encounter. Chapter 43 addresses how to handle a situation where you need to draft a document but have no sample to use.

But before we move on to legal memos, let's circle back to the notion that all communication has a persuasive component.[2] Although memos and other forms of legal advice are not arguments in the traditional sense, they must persuade the reader—your client, your supervisor, even you—that the advice is sound. Moreover, they are often written in anticipation of a formal legal dispute or proceeding and function as a rehearsal for arguments that may need to be made later. For these reasons, legal advice relies on Aristotle's three modes of persuasion as much as legal argument does.[3]

The building blocks of legal reasoning are the same, whether it takes the form of advice or argument. Appeals to *logos* in predictive writing include all the appeals to reason detailed in Part VII. Rules of law are induced or synthesized, the law is applied to facts in a deductive manner, and analogies to precedent are made, all to demonstrate the logic of your analysis.

With regard to *pathos* (appeals to emotion), Quintilian said that whoever can put his audience in the right frame of mind "reigns supreme."[4] In this context, putting the audience in the right frame of mind means preparing the client to understand and accept your advice and to decide what to do next. Try to propose various options in a straightforward way, remaining as neutral as possible, and be careful to identify the advantages and disadvantages of each option. Because clients are often in some form of distress, such as anxiety, fear, or worry, choose your words and tone carefully. Clients rely on us to be understanding and sensitive. Most important, always be honest about your clients' ability to achieve their goals.

With regard to being credible, Aristotle said that "character [*ethos*] is the most potent of all the means to persuasion."[5] In other words, you will not be persuasive unless your clients like and respect you. Your clients must believe you are well-informed, competent, and focused; they must also believe you are being sincere and sensitive to their needs. Mistakes as well as insincerity will cause clients to doubt your

---

1 *See* Jonah Perlin, *Making Your Power(Point): An Introductory Guide to Digital Presentation Design for Lawyers*, 18 LEGAL COMMC'N & RHETORIC: JALWD ___ (forthcoming 2021).

2 *See supra* ch. 11.

3 *See supra* ch. 13.

4 QUINTILIAN, *supra* ch. 9, note 27, at VI.2.3–4.

5 ARISTOTLE, RHETORIC, *supra* ch. 8, note 3, at I.2, 1356a.

advice. For that reason, do not make assumptions or speculate about or exaggerate facts. And always assume they are telling the truth.

Finally, your first chance to make a good impression is often the physical appearance of the written communication you send your supervisors and clients. It's like the icing on a cake because it is the first thing they see. If your writing looks sloppy, is full of errors, or does not follow procedural or customary rules, your client will suspect there is something wrong with the cake too. For more on professionalism in legal writing, see Chapters 44.B.3 and 48.G.

Practice Pointer

Credibility in legal writing depends on:

- an accurate and fair characterization of the facts
- thorough legal research
- citation to adequate supporting authority
- reasonable, synthesized rules of law
- disclosure of binding negative authority
- a professional-looking product

Chapter 37

Legal Memoranda

Before fax machines, the internet, or PDFs, the legal memorandum (memo) was a typical form of communication between lawyers and clients. Legal memoranda (memos) inform the client about the law, predict outcome, and determine next steps. They can be written for clients (especially when the client is another lawyer), other lawyers working for the same client, or even "the client file" to preserve the lawyer's thought process.

Today, the legal profession moves at a much faster pace, and clients often prefer getting some or all of their advice via email (see Chapter 40), which may be less expensive too. Nevertheless, there will be many occasions when a traditional, comprehensive memo is necessary or appropriate.[1] Your professor may ask you first to write a memo to learn how to analyze legal issues and engage in analogical reasoning. Once you know how to draft a legal memo, you can use that as a basis for designing almost any predictive document you need.[2]

Recall your clients Ramon and Christina Velas, the owners of the Dallas Starbucks.[3] Citizens for Safe Products (CSP), a consumer advocacy group, published a newsletter suggesting that the beans they use are not organic as claimed and might even be dangerous.[4] Having met with your clients, you now know more about the newsletter's disastrous effects on their coffee bean and beverage sales.

In the course of your research, you discovered that at common law, defamation actions (libel and slander)[5] protect the reputation of people, not things. The Texas statute alters the common law and provides a potential avenue for relief against CSP for publishing false statements about the coffee beans.[6] As a threshold matter, the

---

1 For example, memos are commonly used in large litigation matters with complicated issues, in-house counsel for a corporation may request a memo from outside counsel to make strategic decisions, and summer associates often write legal memos to hone their analytical skills and preserve their findings for later use by their employers.

2 *See infra* ch. 43.

3 *See supra* ch. 24.A, at 153.

4 *See infra* App. C, at 527.

5 Libel is written defamation; slander is oral.

6 *See supra* ch. 26, at 179.

question is whether the beans or beverages are "perishable food products" as defined by the statute.[7]

In light of this information, you and your clients begin to discuss possible options for responding to CSP's newsletter. The first step is to determine the strength of a claim under the Texas statute. In addition to the legal research discussed in Chapter 26, you have done some fact investigation on what constitutes food, whether coffee can be considered a food, how long it can be stored, and whether it spoils.

If your preliminary research has led you to believe there is a good chance of success, you might first outline your findings in an email (see Chapter 40). If your client wanted formal advice for Starbucks' in-house counsel on which of many potential options to pursue, you might write a client or opinion letter (see Chapter 41). At the moment, let's assume that based on your sense of the strength of this claim, your clients have requested a memo to help them decide next steps.

Arrangement (*Taxis*) of Speech

English	Greek	Latin
introduction	*prooimion*	*exordium*
statement of facts	*diegesis*	*narratio*
statement of issues in dispute and outline of argument		*divisio or partitio*
argument (proofs)	*pisteis*	*confirmatio*
counterarguments		*refutatio or confutatio*
conclusion	*epilogos*	*peroratio*

A. Format of a typical memo

Legal memos are typically organized a lot like classical judicial speech. They begin by introducing the speaker, the intended audience, and the subject matter; state the legal issue to be analyzed; proceed to state the facts; summarize the analysis (including potential arguments and anticipating or refuting counterarguments); and conclude.[8] A sample memorandum in the Velas matter appears on pp. 254–261.

7 *See supra* ch. 30, at 198.

8 *See supra* ch. 13, at 85.

Heading (p. 254)

The heading indicates to whom the memo is written, by whom, for what purpose, and when.

Question Presented (p. 254)

The question presented (can also be called Statement of the Issue or something similar) is a precise statement of the legal issue or question(s) to be resolved.[9] It should include the controlling (binding) jurisdiction or law, the specific legal question, and a pithy statement of the legally significant facts.

There is no one format for drafting Questions Presented as long as they contain this information.

Typical forms include:

> "Under [applicable federal or state law], can the client recover for [cause of action], given [these particular facts]?"
>
> "Whether the client can recover for [cause of action] under [applicable federal or state law] given [these particular facts]."

A question presented that begins with "whether" usually ends with a period, rather than a question mark.

Brief Answer (p. 254)

A brief answer summarizes the lawyer's predicted answer to the legal question. Typically, it begins with a one or two-word answer like "probably not," "unlikely," or "no."[10] It then proceeds in a paragraph or two to summarize the legal analysis. The Romans called this the outline of the arguments.[11] As Cicero explained, it helps the reader "hold definite points in his mind, and to understand that when these have been discussed the [analysis] will be over."[12]

An effective Brief Answer includes the legal framework for answering the question presented (e.g., the elements of the false disparagement claim), a high-level summary of the analysis (e.g., a discussion of each element of the claim), and the writer's reasoning. In this section, legal writers typically speak in their own voice,

---

9 *See supra* ch. 13, at 87.

10 For an excellent discussion on the need for these probabilities to accurately reflect the writer's assessment, see Joe Fore, *"A Court Would Likely (60–75%) Find . . .": Defining Verbal Probability Expressions in Predictive Legal Analysis*, 16 LEGAL COMMC'N & RHETORIC: JAWLD 49 (2019).

11 *See supra* ch. 13, at 87.

12 CICERO, DE INVENTIONE, *supra* ch. 9, note 19, at I.22.31.

without using citations. Even the doubting legal reader will wait for proof (i.e., citations) until the discussion section.

Statement of Facts (p. 255)

Take Note

Statement of Facts should include

- Background facts for context
- Legally significant facts
- The client's goals
- Any pertinent procedural history

The statement of facts includes the facts known to you, any missing facts, the client's goals, and any pertinent procedural history. The statement should include all legally significant facts and any other background facts necessary to understand what has happened and what the clients would like to have happen in the future. Typically, the facts are organized chronologically. The procedural history typically is placed at the end of the statement.

Because it is not always easy to identify the legally significant facts, some legal writers prefer to write the facts section after they write the Discussion (see below). Any facts used in the discussion should appear in the statement of facts so as not to confuse or surprise the reader. Once you present the client's full story in this section, it can easily be referred to in other parts of the memo without having to restate them. For example, once the publication of CSP's newsletter is described in this section, you could later refer to it in the Discussion as just "the newsletter" or the "statements about the beans," without having to repeat all the details.

Discussion (p. 255)

Take Note

The Discussion:

- Begins with an introduction (also known as a roadmap or umbrella paragraph(s) that lays out the legal framework for analysis and indicates how the Discussion is organized overall
- Proceeds to analyze each issue in the order listed in the introduction
- Examines each issue fully and concludes before moving on to the next one

The discussion is the heart of the memo. It explains the detailed answer to the question presented, including citations to supporting authority.[13] In some ways, it acts as a speech within a speech because it typically begins with an introductory paragraph or two (often referred to as a **roadmap** or **umbrella paragraph**) that lays out the legal frame-

13 Legal readers expect you to prove your assertions. Any time you state a rule of law from any legal authority, state the holding of a case, or discuss the reasoning of a court, you will need to cite your source(s). The citation is the source's address; it tells the reader where to find it. Signals (e.g., *see*, *see also*, *cf.*) indicate how directly or indirectly the cited source supports the writer's assertion. For more information on citation and signals, see *infra* chs. 56–57.

work for analyzing the issue(s) and indicates the **large-scale organization**[14] of the analysis.

Although the writer provided a summary or outline of the arguments in the Brief Answer, it is customary to include this introduction at the outset to remind the reader how the analysis will proceed. That way, the reader doesn't have to go back to the Brief Answer. It also has the advantage of making the Discussion severable from the rest of the memo. Even if all your client read was the Discussion, the analysis would be complete.

Once the legal framework is laid, the discussion then proceeds to analyze each issue in turn in a systematic and logical way. Your analysis should be organized according to the rules of law in the order you refer to them in the roadmap (see the detailed discussion on organization below).[15] Both large and small-scale organization are discussed at Chapter 38.

Conclusion (p. 261)

The conclusion summarizes the writer's analysis in more detail than the brief answer. It recaps the discussion section and reinforces it in the reader's mind.[16] The length of the conclusion varies depending on the complexity of the analysis but one to two pages is common. Again, if all your reader had time to review was the Conclusion, it would be a complete but less-detailed analysis. As with brief answers, conclusions rarely include citations.

---

14 *See infra* ch. 38.A, at 263.

15 *See also supra* ch. 13, at 87.

16 *See id.* at 90.

B. Sample memo in the Velas matter

To:	Supervising Attorney
From:	Junior associate
Date:	August 1, 2019
Re:	Potential False Disparagement Claim

Question Presented

Under Texas law, can the Velases recover against Citizens for Safe Products (CSP) for false disparagement of a perishable food product when CSP published statements in its monthly newsletter claiming that Starbucks' coffee beans are not organic and grown using pesticides?

> The **Question Presented** identifies the controlling law, legal issue, and the writer's view of the legally significant facts. Would you add or subtract any facts here?

Brief Answer

Probably yes, as to coffee beans but not coffee beverages. In order to succeed in a claim for false disparagement under the Texas statute, the Velases must prove three elements and that they qualify as a *producer*. First, they can likely prove that CSP disseminated information in any manner to the public about a *perishable food product*. Although CSP likely disseminated information about a perishable food product to the public through its newsletter, the product is likely limited to coffee beans. Perishable food products are sole, not combined, products of agriculture or aquaculture, disqualifying prepared coffee beverages for protection.

> The **Brief Answer** succinctly states the legal framework for answering the question above (i.e., the three elements of the statutory claim), the ultimate answer, and a concise summary of the writer's reasoning (without citation). The summary thus prepares the reader for the analysis to come later.

Second, CSP likely knew its information was false. Because there is no evidence to date that CSP contacted Starbucks or the Velases to verify the truth of its statements, CSP likely demonstrated a reckless indifference to the truth that equates to actual knowledge under the statute. Third, the newsletter implied that the coffee beans are unsafe for consumption by associating them with pesticides.

> Notice the use of transition words to help the reader anticipate the organization of the analysis (i.e., First, Second, Third). The writer separated the elements into two paragraphs to make the Brief Answer easier to read.

To recover damages, the Velases must also prove that they are *producers* of the coffee beans. Although neither Starbucks nor the Velases grow or roast the beans, the statute would appear to protect those who sell unprocessed and processed perishable food products regardless of where they are grown.

Here, the writer starts a new paragraph on the issue of "producer" and damages.

Statement of Facts

Our clients, Mr. and Mrs. Velas own and operate a Starbucks in Dallas under a licensing agreement. They attribute much of their success to selling and using only organically grown coffee beans from fair trade sources. CSP is a California non-profit corporation, with a local Dallas chapter composed of 150–200 members. It publishes a monthly newsletter about products sold in the Dallas area. In March 2019, CSP published and emailed a newsletter to roughly 150 subscribers stating that the Velases' beans are not organic and grown using pesticides.

The **Statement of Facts** identifies the parties, sets forth the background as well as legally significant facts, and states the client's goal.

Within days after the newsletter was distributed, the Velases' coffee bean and beverage sales dropped significantly, which our clients attribute to the statements in the newsletter. They have had to dispose of a significant number of packages of whole and ground beans that did not sell by their "best before" dates, which range from six to eight weeks from the time of packaging. To our clients' knowledge, CSP made no effort to contact them or otherwise verify the statements in its newsletter before it was sent. At a minimum, the Velases are interested in CSP publishing a retraction of its allegations and recovering lost sales from CSP. This memo is limited to addressing the likelihood of success under Texas' false disparagement statute.

Discussion

The Velases are likely to succeed in an action against CSP for false disparagement with respect to coffee bean sales but not coffee beverages. Section 96.002 of the Texas false disparagement statute makes

The **introduction** reiterates the legal framework for analysis, acting as a roadmap of the analysis to follow or an umbrella that encompasses all the relevant issues.

a person liable to the producer of a perishable food product if

> (a) the person disseminates in any manner information relating to a perishable food product to the public;
>
> (b) the person knows the information is false; and
>
> (c) the information states or implies that the perishable food product is not safe for consumption by the public.

Tex. Civ. Prac. & Rem. Code Ann. § 96.002 (Vernon 2020).

The organizing principle for the introductory paragraph is the rule of law laid out in the statute, consisting of three elements.

Notice that citations are included in the Discussion.

A. CSP likely disseminated information to the public about a perishable food product.

This element consists of two distinct parts: whether emailing the newsletter constituted dissemination to the public, and if so, whether the information in the newsletter concerned a perishable food product as defined by the statute.

The first **heading** (A.) visually indicates where the discussion of the first element begins and states the writer's overall prediction on this element. The first paragraph acts as a mini-introduction to Section A., which is divided into two parts. The first **sub-heading** (1.) indicates that the first part of this element is discussed here.

1. The newsletter was disseminated to the public.

The Velases are likely to prove this part of the first element. Since information can be disseminated in any manner, the only real issue is whether it was sent to the public. *Public* refers generally to a large enough audience to constitute the public in the normal meaning of that word, and dissemination to at least 100 people is likely large enough to constitute the public. *See Green's Grocer & Co. v. Janus*, 4 S.W.3d 94, 95 (Tex. App. 2019) (holding that a statement made during a television news broadcast was public); *Thomas Meats, Inc. v. Safeway, Inc.*, 3 S.W.3d 45 (Tex. 2018). In *Thomas Meats*, the defendant grocery store posted a sign in its window seen by at least 100 customers, which the court held constituted the public. 3 S.W.3d at 46.

The first sentence here acts as a topic sentence and indicates the writer's **predicted outcome** on this part of the element. The third sentence states a **synthesized rule** on what "public" means. The fourth sentence **explains** how the rule was applied in *Thomas Meats*. The key facts, holding, and implicit reasoning, are included to prepare to make a favorable analogy.

Because CSP emailed its newsletter to 150 subscribers, which is fifty percent more readers than the 100 customers in *Thomas Meats*, it likely disseminated information to the public. Although we cannot confirm that all the emails were read, the court has focused in the past more on the number of potential recipients as opposed to the number who actually heard or read the information. *See Green's Grocer*, 4 S.W.3d at 94 (assuming the television audience was large but saying nothing about the number of actual viewers); *Thomas Meats*, 3 S.W.3d at 46 (describing the number of customers who saw the posted sign but saying nothing about how many responded to the information). Thus, CSP likely disseminated the newsletter to the public.

In the first sentence of the second paragraph, the writer applies the rule to the facts (the **minor premise**) and **analogizes** to *Thomas Meats*. The second sentence anticipates a **counterargument** that *Thomas Meats* is distinguishable and refutes it, citing two cases in support. The third sentence **concludes** the legal syllogism.

2. Coffee beans are likely perishable food products.

This second **sub-heading** (2.) indicates that the discussion of the second part of the first element begins here.

The Velases can likely prove only that their coffee beans are perishable food products. The statute does not define food product, but *food* is generally understood to mean a nutritious substance ingested in solid or liquid form to maintain health and life. *See, e.g.*, *Food, OED Online*, www.oed.com (last visited July 29, 2019). Even though we do not think of coffee as food, coffee beans contain nutrients such as potassium and magnesium as well as antioxidants. *See Coffee is number one source of antioxidants*, EurekAlert! (August 28, 2005), https://www.eurekalert.org/pub_releases/2005-08/acs-cin081905.php#:~:text=WASHINGTON%2C%20Aug.,of%20Scranton%20(Pa.) (https://perma.cc/5GV4-EWV2) (last visited July 20, 2019).

Some studies even show that drinking coffee has health benefits. *See, e.g.*, Robert van Dam, *Ask the Expert: Coffee and Health*, The Harvard School of Public Health Nutrition Source (Feb. 23, 2015), https://www.hsph.harvard.edu/nutritionsource/2015/02/23/ask-the-expert-coffee-and-health-2/ (https://perma.cc/R7KS-3D4X) (last visited July 20, 2019). In addition, coffee and tea have their own category as food under federal food and drug law. *See* 21 C.F.R. § 170.3(n)(7) (2019); Nat'l Coffee Ass'n, *The Coffee Industry Guide to*

Here—without subheadings—the writer addresses whether coffee is a perishable food product by addressing first "food," then "food products of agriculture," and last, perishability. Sometimes headings overcomplicate your organization and cause you to repeat yourself unnecessarily. Do what you think works best under the circumstances. There is no one right way to organize most legal issues.

Notice the writer uses 1) **plain meaning** to define "food" because neither the statute nor the case law defines it, and 2) the fact that coffee is regulated as food in another **context to** conclude that coffee is food. Do you agree?

Note: Perma Links have been added to citations for ease of access to online book users.

Labeling, https://www.ncausa.org/Industry-Resources/Coffee-Labeling (https://perma.cc/MB4L-A7PE) (last visited July 29, 2019); 21 C.F.R. § . Thus, coffee is likely to qualify as a food product.

The discussion of whether coffee is a "product of agriculture" is divided into two paragraphs for the reader's benefit. Here, the analysis is separated between the explanation and application of the rule.

The statute defines a perishable food product as "a food product of agriculture or aquaculture that is sold or distributed in a form that will perish or decay beyond marketability within a limited period of time." § 96.001. To qualify, the product must be a sole food product, not a combination of food products, and "a limited period of time" may mean no longer than six months. *See Pet Barn, Inc. v. Holmes*, 224 S.W.2d 99, 102 (Tex. 2016). In that case, the court held that a baked pet snack was not a product of agriculture even though it contained several products of agriculture: "The result is a *combination* of products of agriculture, not a sole product of agriculture as the statute contemplates." *Id.*

Under this definition, coffee beans could qualify as perishable food products but not coffee beverages. Like baked pet snacks, most Starbucks coffee beverages are a combination of products of agriculture such as sugar and milk. They also contain water. *Pet Barn* might be distinguishable on the ground that coffee beverages are different because the agricultural ingredients are not chemically altered by baking as they were in that case. However, this argument seems weak; it would likely extend protection under the statute to more plaintiffs and products than the legislature intended. For that reason, only the coffee beans could likely qualify as perishable food products.

The beans must also "perish or decay" beyond marketability within a limited period of time. The statute does not define "limited period of time," but since the statute is intended to protect sellers of meat, fish, and produce, it likely refers to days or weeks as opposed to several months. *The Pet Barn* court indicated that the six month period in that case was not a limited period. *The Pet Barn*, 224 S.W.2d at 102. Although coffee beans do not perish or decay in days or even a week, they are labeled as *best before* six to eight weeks after production because they begin to lose flavor. Once the best before date passes, the Velases remove these beans from their shelves. For that reason, the beans arguably perish or decay beyond marketability within a limited period of time.

B. CSP likely knew the information was false.

The heading (B.) indicates the writer has moved on to discuss the second element.

The Velases are likely to prove knowledge of falsity because this element includes actual knowledge of falsity as well as a reckless indifference to truth. *Thomas Meats v. Safeway*, 3 S.W.3d 45 (Tex. 2018). Reckless indifference or disregard for truth occurs when the defendant made his statements with a "high degree of awareness of their probable falsity." *Garrison v. Louisiana*, 379 U.S. 64, 74 (1964) (holding that states may not impose criminal sanctions for defamation of public figures without proving actual knowledge of falsity or reckless disregard for truth). In *Thomas Meats*, the defendant grocery store posted a sign in its windows saying that the plaintiff's meats were unsafe. Because the defendant had relied solely on rumors and failed to investigate the truth of those rumors, the court held the defendant's "reckless indifference to the truth was tantamount to knowledge of falsity." *Id.* at 46.

The analysis begins with a sentence that combines the **C**onclusion on the second element and a statement of the **R**ule. The second sentence states a synthesized rule on what reckless indifference or disregard for truth means, which is not obvious. The rest of this paragraph **E**xplains the rule (how has the court applied the knowledge requirement in a similar situation) using *Thomas Meats*. The writer also sets up an analogy to *Thomas Meats* by including the key facts, holding, and reasoning of the court.

Although we have no information indicating that CSP had actual had knowledge of falsity, it failed to contact Starbucks or the Velases, much like the defendant in *Thomas Meats* failed to investigate rumors about the meat the plaintiff was selling. To date, there is no evidence that CSP made an effort to contact them before the newsletter was published. Thus, a court is likely to find CSP's reckless indifference to the truth amounted to knowledge of falsity.

In the second paragraph, the writer **A**pplies the rule on knowledge to the clients' facts by analogizing to *Thomas Meats*. Anticipating no valid counterargument, the writer **C**oncludes on this issue.

C. The newsletter likely implied the beans are unsafe for consumption.

The Velases are also likely to prove the third element requiring that CSP stated or implied that coffee beverages are not safe for consumption by the public. To state or imply that a perishable food product is unsafe, the defendant must indicate that the product is inherently dangerous in some way. *Green's Grocer*,

Deconstruct the analysis:

In the discussion of the third element, identify the major premise, the synthesized rule, an explanation of the rule as applied by the court, the minor premise, any analogical reasoning, anticipated counterarguments, and the writer's conclusion.

4 S.W.3d at 95. There, the court held that a statement that a customer had choked on one of the plaintiff's apples did not imply that it was inherently dangerous because people choke on all sorts of food. *Id.* at 96.

Unlike in Green's Grocer, CSP implied that the Velases' product is inherently dangerous. By saying the beans are grown using pesticides, CSP raised serious concern among consumers about the beans' safety. For years, the public has associated pesticides and other chemicals used to grow crops as carcinogenic or otherwise harmful. CSP might argue it stated only that the beans are not as advertised, but given the fears associated with chemicals in our food supply, the Velases have the better argument.

D. The Velases are likely producers and can recover damages.

Notice the writer uses a variety of statutory interpretation tools to determine the meaning of "producer": context (comparing the statute to other state statutes), legislative history, and case law.

Finally, either the Velases or Starbucks must be a producer of the perishable food product to recover under the statute. § 96.002(b). Unlike other states, Texas does not limit the definition of producer to those who actually grow the crops. *See, e.g.*, Fla. Stat. § 865.065 (2014) (limiting recovery to "the person who actually grows or produces" the food products). The legislative history also indicates that "unprocessed" was deleted from the definition of perishable food product "so the statute would apply to both processed and unprocessed food." H. Bill Analysis, 74–722, Reg. Sess., at 4 (Tex. 1995). Finally, the *Pet Barn* court stated in dicta that plaintiffs need not have grown the product to be protected under the statute. 224 S.W.2d at 102.

Here, the writer divides the paragraphs into the potential arguments for the Velases and then CSP's likely counterargument on this issue.

CSP is likely to argue that the dicta in *Pet Barn* is not controlling and that the statute was not intended to protect sellers of food products that they neither grew nor sourced in Texas. However, CSP's false statements about the Velases' coffee beans have affected our clients and the economy in Texas, and failing to treat the Velases as producers in this case would leave them without a remedy under the Texas statute. Given that the Velases import roasted coffee beans for sale in Texas as a sole product of agriculture, they likely qualify as "producers" and would be entitled to damages and other appropriate relief arising from the statements in the newsletter.

Conclusion

The Conclusion summarizes the Discussion in more detail than the Brief Answer, presuming the reader's familiarity with the preceding Discussion.

The Velases may succeed in a false disparagement action against CSP with respect to its coffee beans but not its coffee beverages. By sending its newsletter to 150 subscribers, CSP likely disseminated information to the public. The information was likely about a perishable food product, since coffee beans are a sole agricultural product with some nutritious value that perishes or decays beyond marketability within six to eight weeks.

By summarizing the writer's reasoning on the three elements and the Velases' standing as a producer, the conclusion serves to make the audience "well-disposed to yourself, and ill-disposed to your opponent," emphasize those points favorable to your case, put the audience in the right frame of mind, and refresh their memories. (Chapter 13, at p. 90)

Assuming that CSP did not contact Starbucks, the Velases, or their suppliers about the truth of the statements in its newsletter, CSP likely knew the information was false. This failure demonstrates a reckless indifference to truth that is equivalent to actual knowledge of falsity. Finally, CSP's newsletter implied that its beans are unsafe for consumption by the public. Most consumers associate pesticides with a health risk and would infer that the beans are inherently dangerous in some way.

Finally, the Velases are likely producers under the statute. The statute does not require that they actually grew the beans, and it protects both processed and unprocessed foods.

Chapter 38

Organizing Written Legal Analysis

It may be easiest to think about organizing legal analysis in terms of two stages, large-scale and small-scale. If you were going to paint a picture, you might begin by sketching the overall composition and placement of objects. Only then would you be prepared to paint and refine the details of the objects themselves. So too with legal writing.

A. Large-scale organization

Start by assessing what all needs to be included. Even with just one question presented, there may be several legal issues to discuss.

One set of facts might give rise to several **causes of action** or claims, based on different theories of recovery and different legal rules. Some issues might be procedural and some substantive (e.g., the statute of limitations for filing a tort claim and the merits of the claim itself).

In general, each of these discrete issues should be set out and discussed separately. Use headings to separate these sections visually (e.g., I., II., III., etc. or A., B., C.).

In the Velas memo, the writer addresses just the one issue—the likelihood of success under the Texas false disparagement statute. The statute has

> FYI
>
> **Large-Scale Organization**
>
> - Begin the Discussion with an introduction that lays out the legal framework for your analysis
> - Organize the Discussion by each discrete issue (e.g., I., II., III., . . . or A., B., C., . . .)
> - Use the applicable rules of law to organize the analysis within each issue by sub-issue (e.g., by elements, factors, tests, etc.) and discuss each of those sub-issues separately (e.g., as A., B., C., or 1., 2., 3.)
> - For each sub-issue, move from general rules to specific conclusions, using deductive and analogical reasoning, anticipating counterarguments, and concluding
> - Use headings to divide the analysis visually and guide your reader
> - Place citations in text
> - Avoid footnotes

three elements and a requirement that the plaintiff be a producer in order to recover. Each of these discrete sub-issues is thus analyzed separately as A., B., C., and D. (there is no need for a Roman numeral I. without a second issue (II.) The introduction in the Discussion lays out this legal framework so the reader knows what to expect.

In general, each time you further subdivide your analysis (e.g., **A. to 1. and 2.** or **1. to a. and b.**), consider providing a **mini-introduction** (a.k.a. mini-roadmap or mini-umbrella) that explains why. These mini-introductions will not always be necessary, but where you think the reader might be confused as to why your analysis is being further divided, these explanations can be helpful.

FYI

Large-Scale Organization of the Discussion Section of the Sample Memo

Discussion

[Introduction]

A. [Element one]

[mini-introduction]

1.

2.

B. [Element two]

C. [Element three]

D. [Potential Damages for Producers]

Notice in the sample memo that the first element is analyzed in two parts.[1] An example of a mini-introduction appears in the sample memo on page 256, where the writer explains the division of the first element (A.) into 1. and 2.

Part 2 analyzes "perishable food product" in three stages: whether coffee is food, a food product of agriculture, and perishable (pp. 257–259). Notice that here, the writer did not—but could—further subdivide that analysis into a., b., and c. Sometimes further subdivisions and the consequent need for additional introductions feel too cumbersome or repetitive. Again, do what you think makes sense and let your readers' response inform you. There is no one right way to organize most legal issues.

Common Questions on Large-Scale Organization

- *Does it matter in what order I arrange discrete issues?*

  The order in which to present discrete issues is likely more important when writing an argument than when predicting outcomes (see Chapter 48.B). That said, if you are analyzing two or more different theories of

---

1 Recall the discussion of separating statutory or common law requirements into discrete, component parts. *See supra* ch. 30.B.1.

recovery based on the same set of facts, putting them in order from strongest to weakest likely makes sense.

If you have two or more issues to discuss, one of which is dispositive (e.g., if the complaint was filed too late, the merits of the claim might be less critical), it likely makes sense to put the dispositive issue first (here, e.g., the timing issue).

You can always explain your organizational choices in the introduction to your Discussion, which is likely what your reader will expect. Be sure to get your professor's advice too.

- *Within each issue, how do I know in what order to arrange sub-issues (e.g., the elements or factors or parts of a test) for analysis?*

For the most part, let the law be your guide. Follow the same order for your analysis as the order of the elements in a statute or case law. If the elements, factors, etc. are from a common law cause of action, courts usually cite and analyze them in the same order.

- *Does each issue get the same amount of analysis?*

Not necessarily. Less complicated issues typically require less analysis. As part of plotting your large-scale organization, consider proportionality: with a given page limit or word count, how many pages should likely be devoted to the Discussion and how much space should be devoted to each issue based on its complexity? In the sample memo, the most space is devoted to the first element, which has two discrete issues, one of which (the second) has three subparts.

- *Do I need to include an analysis of "obvious" issues? If they're "obvious" do I even mention them?*

Not usually, and yes. For example, if a criminal statute requires that the defendant be eighteen-years-old to convict, and there is no dispute that the defendant is twenty-five years old, there would be no need to analyze whether that requirement is met. It likely makes sense to note the requirement, explain why it's met, and then quickly move on.

- *Do I always need to use headings?*

No. Short memoranda with few issues or sub-issues likely do not require this sort of visual separation, but they are very helpful to keep you on track and guide the reader.

- *Do I always need to include mini-introductions?*

No. There are few hard and fast rules when it comes to legal writing because each situation is different and requires judgment. These mini-introductions can really become burdensome but are often helpful so the reader understands why the analysis is being further divided. If the reason for the division is obvious, and the headings make your organization clear, you may not need them.

B. Small-scale organization

Small-scale organization refers to the way in which you organize the discussion of each individual issue (referred to above as sub-issues in terms of large-scale organization), like an element of a cause of action or a factor in a totality of the circumstances test. Some issues, like the first element in the sample memorandum, contain distinct issues that must be analyzed separately as more fully described here. Remember breaking the Texas statute into its component parts?[2]

This is where the **analytical paradigm** from Chapter 29 comes into play.[3] In general, for each issue, a rule of law is stated and applied to specific facts to reach a conclusion. This legal syllogism is comprised of a major premise (the rule of law), the minor premise (your client's facts and circumstances), and your prediction.[4]

FYI

The Analytical Paradigm

General rule

Application to specific facts and circumstances

(may involve analogical reasoning where mandatory or persuasive cases are available that interpret the rule)

Conclusion

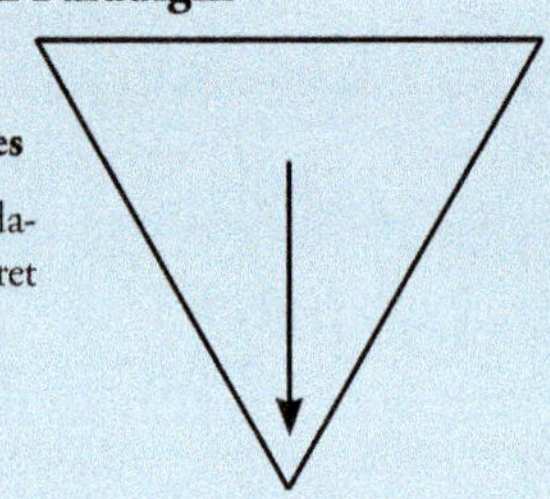

But legal analysis consists of more than two premises and a conclusion. To this deductive schema, we often need to add an induced or synthesized rule that explains further what the rule (an element, factor, requirement, standard, etc.) has been interpreted to mean an explanation of how the rule has been applied by the binding court(s), analogical reasoning because of *stare decisis*, and ways to refute any valid potential counterarguments before concluding. More specifically, this process is often taught as beginning with a **topic sentence** that either 1) identifies the **issue** to be analyzed, or 2) identifies the issue and states the writer's predicted outcome or **conclusion** at the same time. The sample memorandum uses the latter type; the headings

2 *See supra* ch. 30.B.1, at 200.

3 *See supra* ch. 29, at 197.

4 *See supra* ch. 31.A, at 205.

contain the predictions as well. Ask your professor or work colleagues if they have a preference or custom for one over the other.

Then, the requirement or **rule of law** is usually stated next (the major premise). In the Velas matter, these were the three elements and the "producer" requirement to recover for false disparagement. Citation(s) is usually required.

Where the rule is not self-explanatory and its complexity cannot be understood well without further detail, the writer states a **synthesized rule** that explains what the rule means in that jurisdiction at that moment in time. A friend once described knowing when to provide a synthesized rule as "every time you can imagine your reader wanting to click on a term or phrase for more information." Citation(s) should be included here as well. Often, synthesized rules are composed of two or more authorities.[5]

> FYI
>
> **Small-Scale Organization (I/CREAC)***
>
> As you develop your analytical writing skills, practice using this process to analyze distinct issues:
>
> - Begin with a **topic sentence** that identifies the issue (and perhaps states your conclusion on that issue) **(I) or (C)**
> - Then state the general requirement or **rule of law** [the major premise] **(R)**
> - Where needed, explain what that rule means with a **synthesized rule** from the case law
> - **Explain** how the rule has been applied in a similar case, including key facts, holding, and the court's reasoning to set up analogical reasoning **(E)**
> - **Apply the rule** to the client's facts, analogizing to cases to compare to or distinguish [the minor premise] **(A)**
> - Anticipate and refute potentially legitimate **counterarguments**
> - State prediction on that issue [conclusion] **(C)**
>
> ***Note:** Your professor may use a different acronym, such as IRAC, CRAC, or TREAT. These are all designed to teach you the same process.

To further illustrate the rule, **explain** how the rule was applied under similar circumstances (if they exist in a prior case). Remember to rely first on binding and then persuasive authority.[6] Try to rely on the most current authority for what the law *is*; you may rely on older authority for factually similar situations as long as the law has not changed.[7] When explaining the law, include the key facts, holding, and the court's reasoning in any cited case.[8] Without this information, the reader will not be able to tell whether it is good or bad to be similar to the cited authority.[9]

Next comes the minor premise. Apply the rule, which you've now identified, supported by citation, and explained, to your client's facts and circumstances. In so

---

5 *See supra* chs. 56.E.5, at 453 and 57.B, at 468 on how to create explanatory parentheticals and string citations.

6 *See supra* ch. 22, at 140.

7 *See supra* ch. 24.D, at 156.

8 You may explain these cases in text or in explanatory parentheticals. For when to use which, see *infra* at 273.

9 *See* House of Cards, *supra* ch. 32.C.2, at 223.

doing, analogize to existing cases with favorable outcomes (whenever possible).[10] If there are no binding cases, look for persuasive authority that is similar in terms of the law and facts of your client's situation. If the analysis is constitutional or statutory, and you cannot find binding or persuasive case law, use your jurisdiction's interpretation tools.[11] Where possible, use the same case(s) to explain the rule as you do for one of your analogies. That will help make your writing more concise.

Practice Pointers

Make your analogies as specific as possible, explaining to the reader *how* the situations are similar or different, both factually and situationally.

In abstract terms, "The orange (your client's case) is like the lemon (the cited case) because both are citrus fruit."

Where possible, use the same terms and phrases the courts use to describe your client's facts.

The most effective analogies make the comparison between the cited case and the client's case explicit. In the sample memo, for example, the writer says, "Because CSP emailed its newsletter to 150 subscribers, which is fifty percent more readers than the 100 customers in *Thomas Meats*, it likely disseminated information to the public." The writer also says that "much like the defendant in *Thomas Meats*," CSP failed to investigate the truth of its statements. In distinguishing *Green's Grocer*, the writer says, "Unlike in *Green's Grocer*, CSP implied that Velases' product is inherently dangerous."

Before concluding, you should consider and refute any valid counterarguments. Put another way, if you represented the opposing party, what holes might you point out in your own analysis? For a fuller discussion of counterarguments, see the next section of this chapter.

In the annotations to the sample Velas memo, the small-scale organization of the third element is identified. Attached as Appendix D is another sample memo, written by a student on an issue of tort law that is similarly annotated.

C. Anticipating and refuting counterarguments

As you know, you have an interest in your client succeeding, but your predictive analysis must assess the situation as honestly as possible. In the event of litigation, you will also have a duty to disclose to a decision-maker any authority contrary to your position.[12] In both legal analysis and argument, you should anticipate what your client's opponent will argue: in order to predict outcome, you need to assess the

10 *See* The Double Negative, *supra* ch. 31.F.4, at 217.

11 *See supra* ch. 17.B.

12 *See infra* ch. 44.B.2, at 317.

strength of the opponent's position, and in order to persuade, you need to convince the decision-maker why your arguments are better.

There are several types of counterarguments. One is the simple **denial of a party's allegations**. In the car accident case,[13] where the plaintiff alleges that the light was red when the defendant drove through the intersection, she might anticipate the defendant claiming the light was green. Denials of allegations can involve questions of fact, questions of law, or mixed questions of law and fact.

> **Practice Pointer**
>
> **Counterarguments** include:
>
> - denials of a party's allegations (usually a factual dispute)
> - disagreement with the party's characterization of the binding law
> - a superseding law or circumstance that affects the outcome despite the party's arguments (usually an affirmative defense)

In the Velas matter, we can anticipate CSP denying many potential allegations, such as the information was not false, it was not disseminated to the public, CSP had no knowledge of falsity, the information did not involve a "perishable food product," and the information did not state or imply the coffee was unsafe for consumption by the public.

A second type of counterargument is a disagreement with **the party's characterization of the binding law**. An opponent may argue that your interpretation of the law is incorrect, overbroad, too narrow, inapplicable, etc. For example, you might interpret the terms of a statute to mean one thing and anticipate your opponent will argue the terms mean something else. You might interpret a case to stand for a certain proposition of law and then anticipate your opponent to claim you have read the case too narrowly. Or your opponent may claim the holding of the case you rely on has been modified by the holding of a later case from the same jurisdiction.

For example, in the sample memo in the Velas matter (Chapter 37.B, p. 256), the writer relies on *Thomas Meats* to argue that CSP disseminated information to the public. In that case, the court held that a sign posted in the storefront of a grocery and viewed by at least 100 customers was disseminated to the public. We might anticipate CSP trying to distinguish that case on the grounds that it did not create a bright-line rule, and there is a difference between viewing a sign live and sending a newsletter that might or might not be read. In effect, CSP would be arguing that we are reading *Thomas Meats* too broadly. Can you think of other grounds?

A third type of counterargument is a **superseding argument**. It is the argument that even if your allegations are true, or your interpretation of the law is correct, there is another law that supersedes yours. For example, assume the defendant in the car accident case claimed that even if the light was red as he approached the intersection,

---

13 *See supra* ch. 20, at 130.

he attempted to stop and avoid hitting the plaintiff, but his brakes failed. If he had no knowledge that the brakes were faulty, his liability may be negated, at least in part. Here, the fact that the defendant had no knowledge that his brakes were about to fail might supersede (in part) the fact that the light was red, and he was required to stop.

As in the example above, superseding arguments are often **affirmative defenses** that excuse or limit the defendant's liability in a civil or criminal context. Typical affirmative defenses in a civil context include contributory negligence, assumption of the risk, consent, and even statutes of limitation, which prevent liability if the plaintiff fails to assert its rights after a certain period of time has elapsed. Insanity, necessity, and self-defense are a few examples of affirmative defenses in a criminal context.

In predictive writing, the strength of your ultimate predictions will rest heavily on your ability to anticipate the best arguments your client's opponent will make. To do that, put yourself in the shoes of the opponent. How would *you* respond to your analysis? What factual allegations would you deny? Which interpretations of the law would you challenge? Would you rely on different law? Are there any rules of law or cases that might act to negate your legal arguments?

D. How deep do I need to dig into my analysis of each issue?

Not all issues require the same level of analysis. Some may not need any (e.g., the defendant is twenty-five years old and need only be eighteen). Some are relatively straightforward: once the rule is stated, synthesized, and explained, it can be applied without much discussion or analogical reasoning, as in the sample memo in the Velas matter, where there was not much law interpreting the statute.

That said, as the issue becomes more complicated, the deeper your analysis will likely need to be. For example, expand your analysis where

- the rule is a synthesis of more than one authority or type of authority;
- the rule is composed of several component parts or sub-issues;
- there is a lot of differing case law on the same issue;
- the trend of the law is changing;
- there are several cases or categories of cases that need to be distinguished;
- you have several counterarguments to anticipate and refute; or
- you anticipate the issue being highly controversial.

As a result, it will take longer to explain your analysis, and you will need to provide more detail. For example, it might take several sentences to explain the synthesized rule. You might cite several authorities in support of your rule, some of which you choose to discuss in text for the reader to fully understand the scope of the issue and for some of which you include only explanatory parentheticals.[14] You might want to explain the nuances of a rule by explaining how it has been applied by the binding court(s) under different circumstances in more than one case so as to place your client's situation somewhere between. Similarly, your application of the rule may also require you to cite and analogize to several cases and then distinguish one or two cases or even one or two categories of cases. You might also need to dispense with several valid yet surmountable counterarguments.

A note on role and audience: One of the hardest parts about becoming a good legal writer is recognizing that you are no longer writing for yourself or to meet your professor's expectations. You're writing on behalf of another, your client, who has retained you to exercise your informed judgment. Typically, when writing a memo or other form of predictive analysis, you know the law better than anyone else at that moment, and only you can really decide how much needs to be said under the circumstances.

As a law student and young lawyer, you should always ask your professor or work colleagues for advice on the appropriate scope or depth of your analysis if you are unsure. You may have word counts or cost limits that need to be factored into your decision-making. For more information on depth of analysis, see the answers to common questions below.

Common Questions on Small-Scale Organization

- *How many cases should I cite in my memo or other predictive analysis?*

  This is a fair but unanswerable question in the abstract. It's like asking, "How much water do I need to fill a swimming pool?" The answer depends on the size of the pool. Here too, there is no magic formula. The honest answer is that it depends. Further complicating matters is your need to be as concise as possible while at the same time being comprehensive. For each distinct issue (e.g., element, factor, requirement, etc.), start by considering the factors listed above on page 270.

  Your goal is to fairly and concisely represent the current state of the law without sacrificing significant nuances. For tips on conciseness, see Chapter 53.B. If there is a large volume of case law, you may be able to group them into categories, which can be illustrated using one case for each category. Or, you might explain one case in text and cite additional cases in a string cite and include explanatory parentheticals. If the issue is likely to be controversial and you anticipate litigation, you may need more in-depth discussion. Think of it this way: If you leave something

14 *See infra* at 273.

out, is it the very thing your client's opponent is likely to rely on? If so, include it.

- *How many cases do I need to cite in support of each of my synthesized rules?*

  Again, this is a fair question, and the answer is still that it depends. That said, here are some guidelines: First, assess whether the rule comes from the constitution, a statute, common law, or some combination thereof. The more complicated or synthesized the rule, the more authority you will likely need to cite. Put another way, how many authorities and cases does it take to adequately support each part of your synthesized rule?

  Second, consider the nature of the relevant case law. Are the cases very different or largely duplicative? Your rule should account for all the results in the cases on that issue in your jurisdiction. If the case law is all over the place, you may need to cite more cases to support your rule. On the other hand, if the cases are largely duplicative, you may need to cite only one. Here is where signals can really help. For example, if there are several cases that state the rule, you can cite just one using the *E.g.*, signal. See Chapter 57.

  Third, consider whether there are strategic reasons for citing more or less case law. For example, if you anticipate your opponent taking issue with your rule, you may want to cite several cases that have been decided over a period of time to demonstrate the longevity of the rule. This also preserves those cases for a later argument.

  In general—and check with your professor on this one—my advice is to cite from one to four cases in support of a rule, with four being reserved for the most complicated. More than that, and you are likely being duplicative, or you may need to break your issue down into further parts.

- *How do I decide which cases to cite in support of my rule?*

  To prove what the law *is* at a given moment in time, focus on the most recent, binding cases from the highest court in your jurisdiction. Remember the bull's eye (ch. 24.D, at 156–157)? If there are no recent cases, you will need to cite older ones. That's okay.

  Sometimes, you can cite an older case from the jurisdiction's highest court in conjunction with a recent case from its intermediate appellate court. This gives you support that is both from the highest court and recent. If there are only cases from the intermediate appellate court, cite those. In a diversity case in federal court, look for state cases on your issue; in state cases, look for federal cases construing that state's law.

Choose cases that best help you support your synthesized rule, regardless of their facts. If you have cases that support the rule and are factually similar, use those.

- *How many cases do I need to explain in support of my rule?*

  In general—and again, check with your professor on this one—my advice is to use one to three cases to explain how courts have applied your rule, with three being reserved for the most complicated. Where the cases are fairly similar, you can discuss one in text and cite additional cases using explanatory parentheticals.

- *How do I decide which cases to use in text versus explanatory parentheticals?*

  For the textual discussion, choose the case that best illustrates the rule as you have synthesized it and as you predict it will apply to your client's situation. Ideally, the same case you explain can be used to analogize to your facts for a similar result under *stare decisis*. Recall that analogizing to favorable cases is more effective than distinguishing cases. Sometimes, you have no choice but to rely on cases you must distinguish.

- *Is it okay if my analysis takes longer than a paragraph?*

  Absolutely! The length of your written analysis will vary, depending on its depth. The acronyms used to teach the organization of written analysis (e.g., CREAC) represent a thinking process; they are not a template for paragraphs. One good place to start a new paragraph is between your explanation and application of a rule.

- *Do I need to refute every counterargument I can think of?*

  No. It would be a waste of time challenging your ultimate prediction with arguments that have no chance of succeeding. Put another way, do not make up counterarguments just to refute them. Refute only those counterarguments you think make your prediction vulnerable, that you might yourself raise, and that you think are necessary to persuade the reader that your prediction is sound.

- *How do I know if I am generally in keeping with the analytical paradigm?*

  Create a reader-based outline of your analysis. Where is your statement of the issue/prediction on the issue? It should come first and serve as a topic sentence. Label or highlight each sentence as supporting part of your rule, your explanation, or your application (including analogies). What pattern do you see? If you see something other than C-R-E-A-C, you are jumping back and forth in a way that will be hard for your reader to follow or be convinced.

- *How do I know if my professor expects me to use this paradigm, regardless of what it might be called?*

  When in doubt, ask!

- *Why is it so important to follow the recommended way to organize analysis?*

  Think back to Chapters 9 and 13, which detail the history of rhetoric and centuries of thinking on inductive, deductive, and analogical reasoning in legal argument. These recommendations or acronyms serve as a shorthand for learning these forms of reasoning, which dominate Western thinking. Even if you want to disrupt a system, you need to learn first how it operates.

- *Do all issues get analyzed in this way? With all these rules for organizing analysis, is there any room left for me to be creative?*

  Lots and lots. Think of it this way: Even Rembrandt had to learn how to create effective compositions, blend colors, and achieve texture and depth to his paintings. Once he mastered those skills, his talent was boundless. In the case of a Cassatt, Picasso, or Klimt, their success was based in part on their noticeable departure from traditions they had practiced and understood.

  The creativity or art of legal writing comes in many forms: the choice of cases to rely on, the way in which you state a synthesized rule, the analogies you create, the way in which you "see" and organize legal issues, the emotional response you create from your reader, the sense of credibility you convey, etc. This creativity will become even more apparent when you practice writing legal argument. See Chapter 48.

- *Why didn't my professor explain a lot of this before I turned in my first draft?*

  As you learn legal writing, it is common to feel like your professor did not tell you everything you needed to know before you started writing. My guess is that they did. If it didn't sink in, perhaps you weren't yet able to hear it. Typically, we limit the information to what you can be expected to assimilate in order to complete an assignment. We don't want you to feel like you are drinking from a fire hose.

  Once you have written an assignment and gained some concrete experience, you are often in a better position to understand the information you had in advance or incorporate new information in light of that experience.

CHAPTER 39

Legal Memorandum Checklist

Use this checklist to plan, write, and assess your draft memos. As you gain experience writing memos or similar forms of predictive analysis, the purpose of each section and the analytical paradigm used to organize legal writing will start to become second nature. Use this checklist to guide you as you write your first assignments. You should not begin writing until your research is essentially complete and you have analyzed it. See Chapter 26 and the checklist at page 189. If you cannot seem to get started writing, it may be that you are trying to write too soon or need to make some sort of preliminary outline.

☐ **1.** **Question Presented** (Ch. 37, at p. 251)

Do I include the controlling jurisdiction? Legal question? A concise summary of two to three legally significant facts?

Do I use "Under, can/did, when," "Whether," or a complete sentence to state the question at issue?

Is my Question Presented longer than three lines of text or so long that I cannot read it out loud without taking a breath? (If so, condense it.)

☐ **2.** **Brief Answer** (Ch. 37, at p. 251)

Have I summarized the applicable legal rules and analysis in my own words (no cites), including why or how I reached my conclusions on each issue or sub-issue?

Where helpful, have I combined legal rules and application for conciseness (e.g., The Velases will be able to prove x because y . . .)?[1]

Does the Brief Answer outline the analysis that follows in my Discussion section?

☐ **3.** **Statement of Facts** (Ch. 37, at p. 252)

Does it contain a complete account of the known facts?

Does it indicate significant facts that are missing?

---

[1] This is an example of the type of enthymeme Aristotle described that argues by omitting a premise (here, the major premise is omitted). *See supra* ch. 29, note 8, and accompanying text.

Are enough background facts as well as the legally significant facts included?

Are all the facts in the Discussion section included here?

☐ 4. **Discussion: Content** (Ch. 37, at p. 252)

Is this section complete? Have I addressed all issues necessary to answer the question? Is anything missing?

Have I remembered to look for and include all potentially binding law (constitutions, statutes, regulations, cases)?

Have I cited cases to support my rules of law that are binding, recent, and from the highest court possible?

Have I remembered to look for factually similar cases or other courts construing this law (e.g., federal courts sitting in diversity construing state law)?

Have I remembered to anticipate and refute reasonable counterarguments?

Have I reached a conclusion on each disputed issue that is consistent with the Brief Answer?

☐ 5. **Discussion: Large Scale Organization** (Ch. 38, at p. 263)

If I have more than one issue, have I considered in what order to discuss them and why?

Does my Discussion open with an introduction (roadmap or umbrella) that outlines the legal framework used to answer the question presented?

Have I used headings where helpful to visually divide my analysis?)

Have I organized the Discussion of each issue (e.g., disparagement) using the legal rules (e.g., elements) as my guide and not the cases I discuss?

Is each issue (e.g., disparagement) or sub-issue (e.g., each of the three elements) analyzed separately?

Have I analyzed fully each element, factor, requirement, etc. in a deductive manner using analogical reasoning where helpful or necessary?

☐ 6. **Discussion: Small Scale Organization** (Ch. 38, at p. 266)

Are my paragraphs a reasonable length? Or are they too long for my reader to digest (more than one page or screen may be difficult to follow and signal an organizational problem or conciseness issue)?

Does each new issue begin with a new paragraph and topic sentence that identifies and/or predicts the outcome on that issue?

Do I then state the rule of law, including a synthesized rule where necessary to explain its meaning?

Do I explain how the court(s) has applied the rule of law in similar cases (either in your text or explanatory parentheticals)?

Have I applied the rule to my client's facts and circumstances, using analogical reasoning where helpful, available, or necessary?

Do my analogies include adequate information about the facts, the holding, and an explicit comparison (as opposed to a simple description of the case that forces the reader to make the comparison herself)?

Do I anticipate and refute potentially legitimate counterarguments based on problematic law or cases?

Do I definitively conclude on each issue?

Do I incorporate more than one case per issue, where available and helpful to fully explain the law?

☐ 7. **Conclusion** (Ch. 37, at p. 253)

Do I summarize my Discussion, touching on each sub-issue with the gist of my reasoning?

Did I remember not to include citations to authority?

☐ 8. **Style** (Ch. 53, at pp. 402–421)

Have I maintained a neutral tone (i.e., even-handed as opposed to argumentative)?

Have I written in plain English?

Have I avoided long or complicated sentence structures?

Is my writing concise without sacrificing important content?

Does the memo conform to the expectations of a typical legal reader?

☐ 9. **Professionalism**

Have I re-read the assignment to be sure I know when and where it is due?

Have I followed all formatting instructions, including font type and size, word or character count, page limit, margin settings, and page numbers?

Have I proofed for grammar and punctuation errors? (Ch. 54, at p. 423)

Are my citations and string citations formatted properly? (Ch. 56, at p. 445)

Have I used signals appropriately? (Ch. 57, at p. 465)

Have I spellchecked?

Test Your Knowledge: Part VIII

To assess your understanding of the material in this part, click here to take a quiz.

PART IX

Other Forms of Predictive Writing

Chapter 40

Predictive Email[1]

In today's fast-paced, global economy and with high-tech options readily available, lawyers often use email (and even texts) to communicate with other lawyers and clients. Of course email may contain legal advice just as legal memoranda do. And communicating via email can be less expensive for the client.

Unlike legal memoranda, email as a vehicle for predictive legal writing is relatively new. Before the mid-1990s, it was common to send legal memoranda to clients in print through the U.S. mail. Once internet service providers became commercially available, that process quickly evolved from sending memos as attachments to email to communicating advice directly in the body of the email itself. As it has evolved, **predictive email** tends to look like a stripped down legal memorandum designed for efficiency. If a legal memorandum is a luxury sedan—large, fully equipped, and expensive—then legal email is a hybrid—the product of new technology designed for the same purpose but compact and fuel efficient.

Unlike legal memoranda, the audience for email is never "the file." Email always represents part of a larger, ongoing conversation with a specific recipient in mind. For that reason, it is more immediate, more personal, and sometimes more stressful to write because email senders often expect quick replies. It also carries a greater risk of being disclosed to the wrong people.

A. Format of predictive email

The format and tone of predictive email depends on a number of factors, including whether the recipient is the client, another lawyer representing the same client, opposing counsel, or some other interested party. This section addresses the kind of email you might send to a supervising lawyer who asks you to "look into something" (i.e., conduct research on a specific legal issue and send them an email). Formal advice written directly to clients is addressed in more detail in Chapter 41.

1 In earlier work, I referred to legal advice via email as substantive email. That was intended to distinguish it from the transitional practice of attaching memos as documents to email, which functioned like a cover letter. This new phrase is intended to convey the sort of email that substitutes for legal memos in that it engages in predictive analysis as opposed to email sent for other purposes.

Predictive email rarely looks exactly like a legal memorandum on a computer screen. Nor is it just a summary of the analysis like a brief answer or conclusion.

As it has currently evolved, this type of email usually begins with a **greeting**, followed by a **short introduction** that restates the legal issue the writer was asked to research, the overall findings or conclusions, and the most legally significant facts. There is rarely a separate section or paragraph that restates the facts; the relevant or key facts are often known to the intended recipient.

The writer's **predictive analysis** usually follows in a separate paragraph or paragraphs. Because email is more conversational, the analysis is often less formal and complete, in terms of spelling out each step in the analysis. You may find yourself assuming or combining parts of your analysis because you know your specific reader will not be confused. Depending on the complexity and number of issues, you may or may not need to begin with a detailed roadmap. If your reader already has enough context for the analysis to dispense with it, do so.

Take Note

Predictive email often includes:

- a greeting
- a short introduction restating the issue, conclusion, and legally significant facts
- detailed legal analysis with citations, with headings where helpful
- a short conclusion that makes a recommendation or asks for next steps
- closing
- a confidentiality statement

As with all legal analysis, organize first by the issues and put them in a logical order (e.g., does the court have jurisdiction? What causes of action might the plaintiff pursue? What damages might be recoverable?). For each issue, organize based on the controlling rules of law relevant to each issue (e.g., the controlling test, elements, standard, factors, etc.). You may include headings, lists, and bullets to visually guide your reader, who will often be busy or rushed.

Your small-scale organization should generally follow the analytical paradigm: issue→ rule→ application→ conclusion (Chapter 29). You should include citations, but depending on your office, you may not be expected to use a traditional format (when in doubt, use it). To the extent the email leaves out any portion of the analysis for the sake of expediency, be sure to specify what is being left out. The email should end with a **summary of your conclusion**, if necessary, or **any requested or recommended next steps**.

The tone of legal advice via email tends to be more casual and conversational than that of a memorandum. For example, although legal writers traditionally avoid using personal pronouns and contractions in formal legal writing, they are more likely to use them in email because they are writing in the context of a conversation.

It's also easier not to indent paragraphs. Despite the informality, your email should still look professional and be well-written and proofed.

Your email should also contain a **confidentiality statement**. Because it can easily be forwarded to third parties, email presents a challenge in keeping client communications confidential and protecting the attorney-client privilege.[2] As a practicing lawyer, you have an ethical obligation to keep your client's communications confidential.[3] Anything your client discloses to you in confidence is also protected by the attorney-client privilege (a matter of state law). That means you cannot be required to testify about the content of those communications. However, if those communications are intentionally disclosed to third parties, they are no longer protected. If you accidentally send an email to a third party, you could put the privilege in jeopardy. Before sending or forwarding email, be sure to make sure that the recipient falls within the scope of the attorney-client privilege and would not be considered a third party.

Practice Pointer

Don't send email to third parties (anyone who is not representing the client) without authorization. You might inadvertently waive the attorney-client privilege.

Finally, email is an easy and quick way to communicate, but it should not be sent in haste or anger. Just like personal email, once you send it, you cannot get it back. Avoid sending email accidently. Leave the addressee section blank until the email message is complete and proofed. If you write an email while angry or frustrated, save it. Once you've calmed down and gained perspective, delete it. Find a better way to respond or not at all.

Below is an example of an email that a lawyer might send to her supervisor having been asked to conduct legal research on false disparagement in the Velas matter.

---

2 *See supra* ch. 36, at 245.

3 *See id.*

B. Sample predictive email

From: Sara Jan Sent: Fr 7/12/19 4:18 p.m.
To: jelkins@elkinsfirm.com
CC:
Subject: Velas and false disparagement
Attachments:

Jim:

You asked me to research the likelihood that the Velases would succeed in a claim for false disparagement under the Texas statute. Assuming that their coffee beans "perish or decay in a limited period of time," they could probably succeed with respect to lost bean but not beverage sales. Since the beverages are not a product of agriculture, they do not qualify for protection under the statute. It would help to know the extent to which the sales losses can be attributed to beans as opposed to beverages.

> Short introduction that restates the issue researched and the writer's ultimate conclusion. It also raises a factual question as to the nature of the coffee beans and the extent to which sales losses are attributable to bean sales.

To succeed under the statute, the Velases would have to prove three elements:

(1) CSP disseminated the information to the public about a "perishable food product";

(2) CSP knew its information was false; and

(3) the newsletter stated or implied that the beans are unsafe for consumption.

> Legal analysis begins here with a short roadmap outlining the elements of a claim for false disparagement in Texas and the statutory remedy.

Tex. Civ. Prac. & Rem. Code Ann. § 96.002 (a)–(c) (Vernon 2020). A person is liable only to the producer of the perishable food product for damages and any other appropriate relief. § 96.002(b).

Dissemination to the public

> The headings quickly signal to the reader the organization of the analysis to follow.

Dissemination "to the public" refers generally to a large enough audience to constitute the public in the normal meaning of that word, and dissemination to at least 100 people probably qualifies. *See Green's Grocer & Co. v. Janus*, 4 S.W.3d 94, 95 (Tex. App. 2019) (holding that a statement made during a television news broadcast was public); *Thomas Meats, Inc. v. Safeway, Inc.*, 3 S.W.3d 45 (Tex. 2018) (holding that a sign posted in the defendant's window and seen by at least 100 customers constituted the public). Since the newsletter was sent to 150 subscribers, it was likely disseminated to the public.

Notice the more conversational tone but the same deductive form of reasoning with respect to each issue: rule→ application→ conclusion.

A "perishable food product" is "a food product of agriculture or aquaculture that is sold or distributed in a form that will perish or decay beyond marketability within a limited period of time." § 96.001. Like coffee beans, the product must be a sole food product, not a combination of products. *See Pet Barn, Inc. v. Holmes*, 224 S.W.2d 99, 102 (Tex. 2016) (holding that a baked pet snack was not a product of agriculture even though it contained products of agriculture). The beans are probably products of agriculture, but prepared coffee beverages are not. Like the pet snacks, most coffee beverages are a combination of products of agriculture, such as sugar and milk. They also contain water. Extending protection to coffee beverages would likely be inconsistent with *Pet Barn* and impermissibly expand liability.

Separate paragraphs visually divide the analysis of the first element into its sub-issues. These first two sentences state the synthesized rule on perishable food products. Each part of the rule is discussed in turn.

Although we do not think of coffee as food, it likely qualifies as "a nutritious substance ingested in solid or liquid form to maintain health and life. *See, e.g., Food, in OED Online*, www.oed.com (last visited July 29, 2019). Coffee contains nutrients such as potassium and magnesium, as well as antioxidants, and may even have health benefits. *See* Coffee is number one source of antioxidants, EurekAlert! (August 28, 2005), https://www.eurekalert.org/pub_releases/2005-08/acs-cin081905.php#:~:text=WASHINGTON%2C%20Aug.,of%20Scranton%20(Pa.) (https://perma.cc/5GV4-EWV2) (last visited July 20, 2019); Robert van Dam, *Ask the Expert: Coffee and Health*, The Harvard School of Public Health Nutrition Source (Feb. 23, 2015), https://www.hsph.harvard.edu/nutrition-source/2015/02/23/ask-the-expert-coffee-and-health-2/ (https://perma.cc/R7KS-3D4X) (last visited July 20, 2019). Finally, coffee and tea have their own category as food under federal food and drug law. See 21 C.F.R. § 170.3(n)(7) (2019). Thus, coffee is likely to qualify as a food product.

Finally, the coffee beans must perish or decay within a limited period of time. § 96.001. Six months is likely too long to be considered a limited period of time, *id.* at 103, but since the "best before" date is six to eight weeks, and the Velases do not sell them past that date, we have a good argument that this portion of the element is satisfied. CSP could argue that coffee beans do not spoil like fresh produce or meat, but if the beans are no longer salable within six to eight weeks, they likely perish beyond marketability in a limited period of time.

Rule on perishable food product.

Application of rule.

Anticipation and resolution of counterargument.

Knowledge of falsity

Knowledge of falsity can include actual knowledge as well as a reckless indifference to truth. *Thomas Meats*, 3 S.W.3d at 46. There the defendant grocery store posted a sign in its window saying that the plaintiff's meats were unsafe. Because the defendant failed to investigate the truth before posting the signs, the court held the store's "reckless indifference to the truth was tantamount to knowledge of falsity." *Id.* Given that CSP failed to investigate the nature of the beans much as the store in *Thomas Meats* failed to investigate rumors about the meat it was selling, we should be able to prove CSP was recklessly indifferent to the truth.

Synthesized rule on knowledge of falsity.

The writer explains the rule from *Thomas Meats* in text because it would be difficult to capture in an explanatory parenthetical.

Conclusion.

Implies unsafe for public consumption

To state or imply that a PFP is unsafe, the defendant must indicate that the product is inherently dangerous in some way. *Green's Grocer*, 4 S.W.3d at 95. In that case, the court held that a statement that a customer had choked on the plaintiff's apple did not state or imply the apple was unsafe because the statement did not indicate there was anything wrong with the apple *per se*. *Id.* at 96. However, CSP implied that the coffee beans are dangerous by associating them with pesticide use. Although CSP might argue it stated only that the beans are not organic as they are advertised, the popularity of organic produce is due to public concern about the safety of ingesting pesticides. In addition, the fact that sales dropped precipitously is evidence of the perceived danger.

Synthesized rule on what "states or implies" means.

Explanation of rule from *Green's Grocer*.

Application, including analogical reasoning to distinguish the Velases' case.

Producer of a perishable food product

Although several states limit "producer" to those who actually grow agricultural crops, *see, e.g.*, Fla. Stat. § 865.065 (2014) (limiting recovery to "the person who actually grows or produces" the food products), Texas does not. *See Pet Barn*, 224 S.W.2d at 102 (stating in dicta that plaintiffs need not grow the product themselves to be protected under the statute). The legislative history also indicates that "unprocessed" was deleted from the definition of PFP "so the statute would apply to both processed and unprocessed food." H. Bill Analysis, 74–722, Reg. Sess., at 4 (Tex. 1995). Thus, the Velases did not have to grow or roast the beans, and the statute protects both processed and unprocessed food products.

Use of legislative history to interpret ambiguous term.

Conclusion.

As I say, there is a good chance of the Velases succeeding but only if coffee beans "perish or decay" in a limited period of time and they are "producers." When you meet with the Velases, it would help to get a better idea of the reason and need for the "best before" dates and how much of their sales losses are attributable to bean sales.

This paragraph reminds the reader of the writer's overall conclusion and the information still needed from the client.

It also makes reference to a prior conversation, with which both reader and writer are familiar, about other ongoing work related to this client.

Let me know if there is anything else you need from me before the meeting. I will continue research on the other options we discussed last week.

Sara
SARA JAN
THE ELKINS FIRM
874 MAIN STREET, SUITE 130
DALLAS, TEXAS 75034
214-993-9012
sjan@elkinsfirm.com

This email is confidential, protected by the attorney-client privilege, and intended only for the recipients listed above. If you receive it in error, please contact me at the above address and then destroy it.

Confidentiality statement.

For More Information

Here are some additional resources on writing predictive email:

Brad Desnoyer, *E-Memos 2.0: An Empirical Study of How Attorneys Write*, J. Legal Writing (forthcoming 2021).

Katrina June Lee, *Process Over Product: A Pedagogical Focus on Email as a Means of Refining Legal Analysis*, 44 Cap. Univ. L. Rev. 655 (2016).

Kristen K. Robbins-Tiscione, *From Snail Mail to E-Mail: Traditional Legal Memoranda in the Twenty-First Century*, 58 J. Legal Educ. 32 (March 2008).

Kristen K. Tiscione, *The Rhetoric of Email*, 92 Or. L. Rev. 575 (2013).

Jennifer Will, *Call It an E-Convo: When an E-Memo Isn't Really a Memo at All*, 24 J. Leg. Writing 269 (2020).

Chapter 41

Client or Opinion Letters

Client letters (also called **opinion letters**) are formal letters stating the legal opinion (both research findings and conclusions) of a lawyer, law firm, governmental agency, or other organization with respect to work done on behalf of a client. For example, a cosmetics manufacturer might want advice on whether certain claims about its products comply with federal law. Before its legal department will approve proposed advertising for its new products, the manufacturer gets advice from an expert on food and drug law. So it retains outside counsel to provide that advice.

A. Format of a client letter

Client letters can be written for a variety of clients, including private individuals, government officials, lawyers, lawyers in private practice, and in-house counsel. They can advise clients on how to comply with administrative law, such as securities regulation, tax, education, immigration, or food and drug law. They can be written for other reasons as well, including how to structure a new business venture, how to respond to a criminal investigation, and whether to proceed with litigation or seek a different remedy. Any time a client wishes a formal opinion and the lawyer is willing to give one, it is likely to be in writing. Putting the opinion in writing protects both the lawyer and client by specifying the nature and scope of the opinion and the information on which it is based.

Take Note

A **client letter** should include:

- a greeting
- a short restatement of the issue and conclusion
- the facts on which the opinion is based
- any unknown facts
- an explanation of the opinion with or without legal citations, depending on the client
- a summary of the opinion
- next steps
- closing

Like predictive email, client letters have no universal format. The format used is likely to be specific to a particular area of practice or a particular law office. Because client letters make a law office vulnerable in the event the advice turns out to be "wrong," young lawyers are not often asked to write them. However, in the event you are asked to draft a client letter, first ask if there is a desired format or sample for you to use. In the absence of guidance, structure the letter loosely like a legal memorandum: state the **issue**, your **conclusion**, **the facts** on which the opinion is based, and any **unknown facts** that might alter the opinion.

Proceed to **explain your opinion** based on the law. This should resemble the discussion section of a memo in the sense that it is organized first by issue and then by the controlling rules of law. The tone and level of detail here will depend on the nature of the client. For example, if the client is a lawyer, you might write the letter in as much detail as you would in the discussion section of a memorandum, including signals, citations to authority, and full explanations of your analysis. If the client is not a lawyer, you might explain the law in a more cursory manner and use fewer citations to authority. If the client is not a lawyer but an executive of a large corporation used to reading legal analysis, you might do something in between. When in doubt, include citations to authority and let your supervisor take them out if necessary. At the end, **summarize** your opinion and make sure the client understands **what to do or expect next**.

Below is an example of a client letter that a senior lawyer might send to the Velases stating the firm's opinion on whether to file suit against CSP under the Texas false disparagement statute. Given the uncertainty that roasted coffee beans perish or decay beyond marketability in a limited period of time, the firm has chosen to recommend caution in filing suit as a first step. Notice that the writer includes some citations that preserve their thinking, communicate the support for the opinion, and add to the *ethos* of the opinion, but they have chosen not to overwhelm the clients with too much detail. The writer also avoids using legal jargon, which can be both off-putting and confusing to non-lawyers.

B. Sample client letter

The Elkins Firm
874 Main Street
Suite 130
Dallas, Texas 75034
214-993-9000

September 19, 2019

Ramon and Christina Velas
Starbucks Coffee Company
6223 Commerce St.
Suite #100
Dallas, TX 75034

Dear Mr. and Mrs. Velas:

I enjoyed meeting you last month and am pleased to advise you in this matter. In particular, you have asked for our opinion with respect to financial and other losses due to statements made by Citizens for Safe Products (CSP) about your coffee products in its newsletter. Based on our research, we believe that your claim under the Texas false disparagement statute has some merit but is not without risk. As we discussed, litigation of this case is likely to be expensive. For these reasons, we recommend sending CSP a demand letter first about compensating you for your losses before we make a decision about filing suit.

> This paragraph restates the issue and the firm's overall conclusion.

This conclusion is based on the facts set forth below. If I have misunderstood or failed to include any facts you think significant, please let me know as soon as possible. Any change in these circumstances could alter this opinion. CSP is a national non-profit corporation with a local chapter in Dallas. The chapter has roughly one hundred and fifty members to whom it distributes its newsletter. The March 2019 newsletter claimed that the beans (ground and whole) and prepared coffee beverages you sell are not organic. To the best of your knowledge and belief, the beans are not grown using pesticides, contrary to CSP's claims, and they are organic in all other respects. Also to the best of your knowledge, CSP made no effort to contact you,

> The second paragraph states the facts on which the opinion is based and asks for clarification about an unknown fact.

your suppliers, or Starbucks' headquarters about the nature of the beans. Since this newsletter was published, coffee bean and beverage sales have dramatically declined, and customers have been asking questions related to the newsletter and the nature of the beans. You have also been required to remove bagged beans from your shelves because they were not sold by the "best before" date, which is roughly six to eight weeks after production. We understand that the beans do not spoil in the sense that that they will make customers ill, but they lose freshness and flavor. Please correct us if that is wrong.

The Texas statute we discussed is designed primarily to protect Texas farmers. The law provides a remedy for false statements about the safety of their products because fruits, vegetables, meat, and fish often spoil before a farmer has a chance to reassure the public that the product is safe.

This paragraph begins the legal analysis and support for the conclusion. It starts by explaining the purpose behind the statute, which supports the ultimate conclusion that the claim here may be viable but is not ironclad.

In order to succeed in a claim against CSP, we would have to prove three things we call "the elements" of a claim: First, we would need to establish that your products are food products of agriculture that "perish or decay beyond marketability within a limited period of time." Second, we would need to prove that CSP had knowledge that its statements were false, and third, that CSP stated or implied that your products are unsafe for consumption by the public. *See* Tex. Civ. Prac. & Rem. Code Ann. § 96.002 (a)–(c) (Vernon 2020).

This paragraph sets out a roadmap for the reader and explains what "elements" are because the client may be unfamiliar with that term.

As for the first element, coffee beans probably qualify as food products of agriculture. CSP might claim they are not food, since they carry little nutritional value, but they are grown, harvested, and ingested, in some form, like other agricultural crops, and they do contain minerals and antioxidants. The real issue is whether they "perish or decay" in a limited period of time. I understand that you do not sell your beans past the six to eight-week "best before" date, but a court might conclude that they do not spoil beyond marketability in the same way that heads of lettuce or cuts of meat

In this paragraph, the writer explains the law and the potential trouble they will have proving the first element.

do, and therefore, they are not intended to be protected under this statute.

Coffee beverages, on the other hand, are almost certainly not protected under the statute. First, there is a Texas Supreme Court case indicating that the product must be a sole product of agriculture, not a combination of agricultural products. *Pet Barn, Inc. v. Holmes*, 224 S.W.2d 99, 102 (Tex. 2016) (holding that a baked pet snack made of several agricultural products was not a food product of agriculture). Since the coffee beverages you sell usually contain milk, sugar, and syrups, they are not sole products of agriculture. Second, they cannot really be said to "perish or decay" because you do not prepare them ahead of time; you make them to order.

This paragraph explains that at best, only the beans are protected under the statute.

As for the second element, we could likely prove that CSP had knowledge that its statements were false. We cannot know what CSP members were thinking when they published the newsletter, but we do know they did not check with you or anyone else to verify their information. The Texas court has held that recklessness is equivalent to knowledge, *Thomas Meats, Inc. v. Safeway, Inc.*, 3 S.W.3d 45 (Tex. 2018), and CSP appears to have been reckless in failing to contact you, demonstrating recklessness as to the truth or falsity of its statements.

The writer continues to translate the law and explains in the next two paragraphs that they can likely prove the second and third elements as to lost bean sales.

As to the third element, we could likely prove that CSP implied that your products are unsafe for consumption by the public. As your lost sales demonstrate, people tend to think that chemicals make food "inherently dangerous in some way." *Green's Grocer & Co. v. Janus*, 4 S.W.3d 94, 95 (Tex. 2019). The Texas statute (and others like it) was enacted in response to a public scare in the late 1980s relating to the use of Alar, a chemical used to keep apples from falling off trees before they were ripe.

If these elements can be proved, the defendant is liable to the "producer of the perishable food product for damages and any other appropriate relief." § 96.002(b). The statute does not require that you grew or roasted the beans yourselves. *See Pet Barn*, 224 S.W.2d at 102

Here, the writer sums up the basis for the firm's ultimate conclusion.

(stating in dicta that plaintiffs need not grow the product themselves to be protected under the statute). Still, CSP is likely to argue that it protects only Texas farmers, not those who resell food products purchased outside of Texas. The legislative history indicates that the statute is intended to include processed as well as unprocessed food products, which may help refute CSP's claim.

In sum, although we would likely be able to prove the second and third elements of the claim, we anticipate having difficulty proving that coffee beans are "food products of agriculture," that they "perish or decay beyond marketability within a limited period of time," and you are "producers" of the beans.

For these reasons, we recommend sending CSP a demand letter outlining the nature of your loss and the grounds on which a future claim might be based. As we discussed, I hope you have already posted signs in your store and published advertisements in the local paper explaining the confirmed organic nature of the beans. Please contact me at your earliest convenience to schedule a meeting to discuss our recommendation.

The writer recommends next steps and invites the client to schedule a meeting to discuss them.

Sincerely,

James U. Elkins

James U. Elkins, J.D.

214-993-9025

jelkins@elkinsfirm.com

CHAPTER 42

Bench Memoranda

Bench memoranda are written by law clerks to trial and appellate court judges to help them make decisions. In accordance with each court's procedural rules, parties may make **motions** (requests to the judge to make a certain decision) before, during, or after trial. For example, if a defendant in a criminal case believes the evidence against her was obtained in violation of her rights, she could file a motion to exclude the evidence at trial. To help the judge rule on the motion, a law clerk might research the legal issues, evaluate the parties' arguments, and write her conclusions in the form of a bench memo.

At the appellate level, a law clerk reviews the entire record on appeal, conducts original research on the legal issues, evaluates the parties' arguments, and may write a bench memorandum to prepare the judge for oral argument. As a law student, you might write a bench memorandum in an upper-level writing course or as part of a moot court competition. If you decide to clerk for a state or federal court judge, you will most certainly write bench memos.

Practice Pointer

A **bench memorandum** should include:

- The case caption, docket number, judge(s) involved, and the name of any lower court (if the case is now on appeal)
- statement of the case, including the procedural history and current status
- a brief statement of the facts of the case
- a statement of the issues raised by the parties
- standard of review for the appeal in that case
- brief overview of the law (if necessary) and a summary of the arguments raised by the parties
- any matters to be addressed in court or during oral argument, and
- if requested by the judge, a discussion of your views on the merits of the case, supported by analysis and explanation, and recommendations on the disposition of the case

A. Format of a bench memo

There is no universal format for bench memoranda; each court or judge tends to have specific requirements. In general, they can be structured like legal memoranda with additional information helpful to the judge. In the absence of a prescribed format, use the following guidelines:[1]

In the heading, include the caption of the case, the **docket number** (the number assigned to the case by a court clerk), the judge(s) involved, and the name of the lower court (if the case is now on appeal).

The body of the memo should begin with a **statement of the case** that includes the procedural history, the current status of the case, and, if on appeal, the name of the lower court, the disposition below, and the party that filed the appeal. Next, give a brief and objective **statement of the facts**.

In an appeal, you should not take the facts as stated by the parties for granted. You will need to verify the facts by checking them in the **record**. The record consists of all the documents and evidence that the appellate court receives from the lower court. Usually it is all collected and paginated as one document for easy reference. You will need to cite the record to support your statement of the facts. Also, it is easier for the judge if you refer to the parties by name. "Appellant" and "appellee" can be confusing.

Following the facts, describe the issues as raised by the parties. If necessary, give a **brief overview of the law** and then **summarize the parties' arguments** with respect to each issue. Your judge may want you to summarize only what the parties have actually argued. Some judges will also want you to give the parties' best arguments (i.e., the arguments they should have made).

This is also a good place to verify the **standard of review** if the case is on appeal. Some judges will also want you to inform them of issues that the parties failed to address, matters that need to be clarified, or questions the judges might ask the parties.

Finally, if requested, discuss **your views on the merits of the case**. Again, you cannot rely on the parties' statements of the law. They may be incomplete, inaccurate, or biased. The parties' arguments will provide a good starting point, but you should verify that their characterizations of the law are accurate. You may then state your recommended ruling here or directly after the statement of the issues.

Like client letters and legal memoranda, the tone of a bench memorandum is formal, and it should include proper citations to the record and legal authority. Unless your judge asks you to write as though you are the court speaking, you should write a bench memorandum from your own perspective.

Assume that the Velases attempted to negotiate with CSP but were forced to file suit. They filed their claim against CSP for false disparagement in a federal district

---

1 *See, e.g.*, FEDERAL JUDICIAL CENTER, LAW CLERK HANDBOOK: A HANDBOOK FOR LAW CLERKS TO FEDERAL JUDGES § 5.2.E.2, at 87–88 (4th ed. 2020), https://www.fjc.gov/sites/default/files/materials/43/Law_Clerk_Handbook_Fourth_Edition.pdf (https://perma.cc/XF49-GKHS); *see also* MARY L. DUNNEWOLD, BETH A. HONETSCHLAGER, & BRENDA L. TOFTE, JUDICIAL CLERKSHIPS: A PRACTICAL GUIDE (8th ed. 2010).

court in Texas (see the sample complaint, Chapter 51.B). (To review the facts of the Velases' case, see Chapter 24.A, at 153.) CSP then filed a motion to dismiss for failure to state a claim under Fed. R. Civ. P. 12(b)(6), which the district court denied (see the sample motion and supporting memorandum, Chapter 52). The case went to trial, and at the close of the plaintiff's case, CSP filed a motion for judgment as a matter of law under Federal Rule of Civil Procedure 50,[2] which the court granted on the grounds that coffee beans are not perishable food products under the Texas statute. Below is a sample bench memorandum that might be written on appeal for the appellate judges prior to oral argument.

B. Sample bench memo

To:	The Honorable Judge Amelia Spoke
From:	Law Clerk
Date:	December 15, 2021
Re:	*Velas v. CSP*, Docket No. 21–422CIV, on appeal from the Northern District of Texas, The Honorable S. Samson

---

Statement of the Case

In January 2020, Ramon and Christina Velas, doing business as Starbucks, filed suit against Citizens for Safe Products (CSP) under the Texas false disparagement statute, Tex. Civ. Prac. & Rem. Code Ann. § 96.002 (Vernon 2020). They sought to recover losses allegedly due to statements CSP made in its March 2019 monthly newsletter. The case was filed in the United States District Court for the Northern District of Texas on January 13, 2020. At the close of the trial, the defendant moved for judgment as a matter of law, which the court granted on June 2, 2020. Judge Samson held that the Velases are not producers of a perishable food product: coffee is not a food prod-

---

2 FED R. CIV. P. 50(a)(1) states, "If a party has been fully heard on an issue during a jury trial and the court finds that a reasonable jury would not have a legally sufficient evidentiary basis to find for the party on that issue, the court may: (A) resolve the issue against the party; and (B) grant a motion for judgment as a matter of law against the party on a claim or defense that, under the controlling law, can be maintained or defeated only with a favorable finding on that issue."

uct, coffee beans do not perish or decay "beyond marketability" in a limited period of time, and the Velases resell the beans; they do not produce them. Thus, they were not entitled to protection under the statute. R. at 1. The Velases now appeal.

This is a typical format for citing the compiled record. Here, the citation is to page 1. Always check a court's local rules for their citing customs and requirements.

Statement of Facts

Each of these facts is verified by checking and citing the record.

The appellants own and operate a Starbucks in Dallas, Texas under a licensing agreement. They attribute much of their success to their exclusive use of organically grown coffee beans from fair trade sources. R. at 12. The Velases import their roasted beans primarily from Central and South America. None of the beans they sell or use to make coffee beverages is grown in Texas. R. at 13.

CSP is a Dallas-based consumer rights group that publishes a monthly newsletter about products sold in the Dallas area. In March 2019, CSP published its newsletter stating that the Velases' beans are grown using pesticides. R. at 22. They put on uncontroverted evidence that CSP did not contact anyone to verify the information before it published the newsletter. R. at 24.

The Velases also put on evidence that almost immediately after the newsletter was distributed, their coffee bean and beverage sales decreased significantly. Customers began to ask questions about the source of the beans. R. at 16. This Starbucks location has disposed of hundreds of packages of whole and ground beans that did not sell by their "best before" dates, which range from six to eight weeks from the time of production. R. at 18. These dates are set in consultation with bean suppliers. R. at 19.

Statement of the Issue

The issue is whether coffee beans qualify for protection under the Texas false disparagement statute, which protects producers of perishable food products from false statements (made either knowingly or recklessly) about their products. The parties have stipulated that CSP disseminated information to the public with reckless disregard to the truth that stated or implied the Velases' beans were unsafe for consumption. The remaining issues are whether the coffee beans are perishable food products and the Velases qualify as producers.

Standard of Review

This Court reviews the decision to grant judgment as a matter of law de novo, applying the same legal standard as the district court. *Texas Beef Grp. v. Winfrey*, 201 F.3d 680, 686 (5th Cir. 2000).

Standard of review is a term of art that refers to the level of deference the reviewing court must give to the lower court's decision. For more information on standard of review, see Chapter 46.

Summary of the Parties' Arguments

A. Overview of the law

Section 96.002 of the Texas false disparagement statute makes a person liable if

> (a) the person disseminates in any manner information relating to a perishable food product to the public;
>
> (b) the person knows the information is false; and
>
> (c) the information states or implies that the perishable food product is not safe for consumption by the public.

Here, the clerk provides an overview of the false disparagement statute, including its elements, the relevant definition, and the overall intent of the legislature.

Tex. Civ. Prac. & Rem. Code Ann. § 96.002 (a)–(c) (Vernon 2020). A perishable food product is defined as a "food product of agriculture or aquaculture that is sold or distributed in a form that will perish or decay beyond marketability within a limited period of time." § 96.001. A person liable under this statute is liable to the producer of the perishable food product for damages and any other appropriate relief arising from the person's dissemination of the information. § 96.002(b).

Several states like Texas passed these so-called "veggie libel" statutes in response to the Washington apple scare in the 1980s. The goal was to protect their local food economies. *See, e.g.*, Sara Lunsford Kohen, *What Ever Happened to Veggie Libel?: Why Plaintiffs Are*

Not Using Agricultural Product Disparagement Statutes, 16 Drake J. Agric. L. 261, 267–68 (2011).

B. Appellant Velases' Argument

The appellants argue that they are producers of a perishable food product and their coffee beans are entitled to protection under the Texas false disparagement statute. The statute does not define "food product," but a perishable food product is defined as one that perishes or decays "beyond marketability" within a limited period of time. § 96.001.

Since the Velases are the appellants, their arguments are presented first.

Appellants argue that coffee is "food," which is generally understood to mean a nutritious substance ingested to maintain health and life. *See, e.g.*, *Food, OED Online*, (last visited April 12, 2021). Like wheat, coffee is ground and used to make a variety of food products. Coffee beans contain nutrients such as potassium and magnesium, as well as antioxidants, and coffee even has some health benefits. Thus, they argue, coffee qualifies as a food product under the statute.

The Velases also argue that coffee beans perish or decay beyond marketability within a limited period of time. The statute does not define a limited period of time, but the Texas Supreme Court has indicated in dicta that six months is not a limited period of time. *Pet Barn, Inc. v. Holmes*, 224 S.W.2d 99, 103 (Tex. 2016). In contrast, the beans lose flavor and cannot be sold after their "best before" dates, about six to eight weeks after they are shipped. These dates are recommended by the bean suppliers, not Starbucks. The Velases put on evidence that customers generally will not purchase bagged beans after their "best before" dates.

Finally, as coffee bean sellers, the Velases argue that they are "the producer[s] of a perishable food product." § 96.002(b). Unlike most states with false disparagement statutes, Texas does not restrict the meaning of "producer" to those who actually grow the products being sold. *See, e.g.*, Fla. Stat. § 865.065 (2014) (limiting recovery to "the person who actually grows or produces" the food products); *see also Pet Barn*, 224 S.W.2d at 102 (stating in dicta that plaintiffs need not grow the product themselves to be protected under the statute).

The legislative history indicates that "unprocessed" was deleted from the definition of a perishable food product so the bill would apply to both processed and unprocessed food. Since the meaning of "producer" is not limited either to growers or unprocessed food, the legislature intended to include a larger group of defendants, like appellants, who purchase and resell perishable food products in Texas. *See also Johnson v. GlobalSantaFe Offshore Servs.*, 799 F.3d 317, 325 (5th Cir. 2015 (holding that remedial legislation should be liberally construed).

C. Appellee CSP's Argument

CSP disputes that the Velases produce a perishable food product. First, CSP argues that coffee is not a food product. Food consists of protein, carbohydrate, and fat used by the body to sustain growth, repair, and vital processes and to furnish energy. *Merriam-Webster Dictionary* 324 (8th ed. 2020). Neither coffee beans nor brewed coffee meets this definition. The fact that coffee must be labeled for sale under federal labeling requirements does not make it a "food product" under the Texas statute.

Although coffee beans may contain some minerals, they are not food in the normal sense of the word. *See United States v. Kaluza*, 780 F.3d 647, 658–59 (5th Cir. 2015) (stating where the language of a statute is unambiguous, its terms should be given their plain and ordinary meaning). CSP also argues that calories convert into energy, and coffee has very few calories. Although the caffeine in coffee has a stimulant effect, it does not convert to energy in the sense that calories do.

CSP also argues that coffee beans do not "perish or decay" beyond marketability within a limited period of time. The statute protects producers of meat, fish, and produce, which spoil in days or weeks. *See* H. Bill Analysis, 74–722, Reg. Sess., at 1 (Tex. 1995). In *Pet Barn*, the court held that the product at issue was not a product of agriculture because it was a combination of agricultural products. 224 S.W.2d at 102. It went on to suggest that six months is too long to be "a limited period of time." *Id.* at 103. As *Pet Barn* indicates, several months do not constitute a "limited" period of time. One-and-a-half to two months here was more than adequate time for the Velases to correct any false statements about its coffee. Finally, the beans do not spoil in the sense that they become inedible or dangerous. As the "best before" phrase suggests, the beans simply lose flavor after that date.

Finally, CSP argues that the Velases are not producers as required by the statute. *See* § 96.002(b). Despite the dicta in *Pet Barn*, the false disparagement statute is intended to protect local farmers and the local economy. The Velases do not grow anything. They purchase beans from outside the United States and resell them. Even if they were considered producers, the product is not grown in Texas, and thus the beans are not covered by the statute.

Questions for Oral Argument

1. What did the Texas legislature intend to accomplish here? To protect Texas farmers or the Texas economy more generally?

2. Why is (or is not) coffee a food product?

3. Must the product be spoiled or inedible to perish or decay beyond marketability?

4. Why is (or is not) six to eight weeks a limited period of time?

5. Is "producer" an ambiguous term? Why?

6. Why should (or should not) "producer" include a merchant one step removed from the actual grower?

7. Must the food product be grown in Texas to qualify for protection? Why?

Merits of the Case (if requested)

This Court should affirm the judgment granted below. Even if coffee beans can be considered as food, they do not likely perish or decay beyond marketability in a limited period of time. Although the coffee beans lose flavor in six to eight weeks, they do not spoil. As CSP argues, the statute is intended to protect products such as fresh produce, meat, and fish, which spoil quickly, in a matter of days, before false statements can be corrected. Six to eight weeks seems to fall outside the legislature's concern. In addition, although the *Pet Barn* court indicated in dicta that producers need not grow the beans themselves, the plaintiff imports the beans from outside Texas and resells them. It does not seem likely that the legislature intended to protect coffee bean producers outside of Texas. To extend liability here would include a host of plaintiffs the Texas legislature likely did not intend to protect.

Here, the clerk discusses the merits of the case. The clerk's memo, along with the parties' briefs, can serve as the basis for the appellate courts' written decision.

Recommended Ruling

I recommend that Your Honors affirm the judgment of the United States District Court for the Northern District of Texas.

Chapter 43

What If I Need to Draft a Document I've Never Heard of?

Early in your career, you may be asked to conduct research and report your findings, state your predictions, or advocate your client's position in a document you have never seen or heard of. The person requesting the document might not have a specific format in mind, but they will expect you to bring your creativity to the task. Fortunately, the basic format of a legal memo (Chapter 37), along with any of the documents in Chapters 40 and 41, can be adapted to suit your needs. The legal research and analytical skills required to put together a predictive memo, email, client letter, demand memo, brief, etc. are easily transferable to something new.

To begin, ask if there are any samples of the kind of document you have been asked to write. If not, do a bit of research: ask other colleagues for advice, Google around a bit, and check out Westlaw and Lexis' Forms database. You can search by jurisdiction or practice area. Bloomberg Law has forms too, particularly for transactional documents. If you find samples, study them. Which do you consider most effective? As Katie Rose Guest Pryal suggests, look for similarities and differences among the samples. "[W]hat patterns emerge across the documents[?] These patterns are the generic conventions that [you] should adhere to when writing" your own document.[1]

Practice Pointer

- Ask for any samples of similar documents
- Do some research
- Assess the rhetorical situation:
  - Purpose
  - Audience
  - Context
  - Stance
  - Constraints
- Adapt a familiar format to suit your needs
- Ask for feedback before you write

If you cannot find any samples, you will need to design the document—a new rhetorical form—yourself. Recall Lloyd Bitzer's concept of the rhetorical situation,

1 Katie Rose Guest Pryal, *The Genre Discovery Approach: Preparing Law Students to Write Any Legal Document*, 59 Wayne L. Rev. 351, 380 (2013).

where language is used to bring about desired change. According to Bitzer, each situation is comprised of an exigence, an audience that can help bring about change, and a set of constraints that limits the possibility of change.[2]

You can use the rhetorical situation to help you construct your document. You may even have had reading and writing teachers refer to these rhetorical concepts as a way to write or interpret a particular text. To assess the rhetorical situation, consider the following:

- What is the **purpose** of the document (there may be more than one)?
- Who is the **audience** for the document (both intended and potential)?
- In what **larger context** is the document being written? What external factors should you take into consideration?
- What is your **stance** as the writer (are you predicting or arguing or something in between)?
- What **constraints** are you operating under (e.g., the law, cost, time, etc.)?

Answering these questions will help you decide how much information to include, what to omit, how to anticipate counterarguments, how to organize the document on a large and small scale, the nature of your word choice, tone, length, etc. Since legal readers are familiar with memos and briefs, you can be confident that they will have little trouble adjusting to a variation on one of those genres. Once you have adopted a plan for your document, try to check with your supervisor in advance for feedback. Together, you may come up with a better plan and save yourself some time and the client money.

For example, a former student contacted me while working during the summer after her first year. She had been asked to research the legislative history of a statute and write a memo. She knew that the memos she had written for class were not quite right for this project because she did not have specific facts to which she needed to apply the law and predict an outcome. As she said it, "I just got a grip on what the research looks like but have no clue how to write this kind of memorandum, since it doesn't seem like the CREAC format applies." She was understandably unsure what to do instead and reached out to me for advice. That's when I realized I needed to include this chapter in the book.

I suggested first that she consider the purpose of and the audience for the memo. Why was she asked to write it? Who would be reading it? Would it be shared or kept private? And was she asked to write it with a particular goal in mind or just for information purposes? Was it supposed to be written as a separate document or

---

2 *See supra* ch. 8, note 8, and accompanying text.

in an email? I also suggested that if she did not know the answers to these questions, she should feel free to ask.

Second, I suggested she modify the basic format of a traditional memo:

- State the **question for research**, such as "did Congress intend this provision to apply to x?" Or "what did Congress think [a particular phrase in the statute] meant?"
- **Summarize your findings** (kind of like a Brief Answer in a memo)

  Provide the **context** for the research (kind of like a Statement of Facts) to put it in perspective for the reader
- **Discuss your findings**

  Use the basic analytical paradigm (rule-application-conclusion) and your research findings to organize your discussion. In this context, the "rules" might be the various purposes of the statute or the different ways in which it has been interpreted. Examples in case law might also be helpful.
- **Conclude (if necessary)**

This was enough to get her started. I doubt she followed this format exactly, especially since she knew much more about the project than I did. My hope was that it was enough for her to know that she could trust her instincts, she had the skills necessary to complete the assignment, and she could adapt what she already knew to fit her particular purpose. By the end of your first year of law school, you will too.

Test Your Knowledge: Part IX

To assess your understanding of the material in this part, click here to take a quiz.

Part X

Persuasive Writing and the Appellate Brief

Chapter 44

What Is Legal Argument?

Legal argument is persuasion in its quintessential form.[1] It can be oral or written, and its goal is to change the status quo. Whereas the purpose of legal advice is to inform and predict, the **purpose** of legal advocacy is to inform and persuade.[2] Here, appeals to logic, emotion, and credibility[3] combine in an effort to convince a decision-maker to rule in your client's favor. The **audience** differs as well. Predictive advice is usually kept confidential, but legal argument often takes place in the presence of third parties or even the public.

The nature of legal argument will differ based on the type of law you practice. As described in Chapter 41,[4] a lawyer specializing in food and drug law might advise her clients how to comply with the law and argue against proposed changes to the law as part of the rulemaking process.[5] A transactional lawyer advocates for her client when negotiating a deal. Litigators[6] and trial lawyers advocate in anticipation of or in the midst of legal disputes.

> **Take Note**
>
> **Written legal advocacy** includes:
> - complaints
> - motions
> - memoranda of points and authorities, and
> - various trial and appellate briefs ("brief" is also a generic term for written legal argument in any form)

As you will learn, most civil lawsuits begin with a **complaint**, followed by an answer. Criminal prosecutions begin with a complaint, information, or indictment. Prior to and after trial, the parties may file **motions** that ask the court to do something: dismiss the complaint or charges, exclude evidence, enter judgment in their favor, etc. These motions can be supported by written legal argument in **memoranda of points**

1 *See supra* ch. 8.

2 *See supra* ch. 36, at 245.

3 *See supra* ch. 13, at 84.

4 *See supra* ch. 41, at 289.

5 *See supra* ch. 18, at 120.

6 "Litigator" generally refers to a lawyer who represents plaintiffs or defendants in civil suits involving large corporations or other entities, where the bulk of the advocacy occurs prior to trial in "motions practice." Most litigators do not consider themselves trial lawyers.

and authorities (these sound predictive, but they aren't). A court's rules of criminal and civil procedure state when, how, and whether a party can file a particular motion.

If a case goes to trial, the court may request a **trial brief** that sets out the facts still in dispute, the evidence to be presented, and the parties' legal arguments. On appeal, an **appellate brief** tries to convince the court that the lower court erred in its ruling. Almost all written argument in whatever form that is filed with a court is commonly referred to as a brief.

Appeals to *logos* (reason) are the same, whether they occur in the context of giving advice or making an argument. But appeals to *pathos* (emotion) and *ethos* (credibility) play a more vital role in the context of legal argument. To convince your reader, you must put them in the right frame of mind[7] and be credible.[8]

A. Appeals to emotion

> **Practice Pointer**
>
> ***Pathos*** in legal writing helps develop the audience's empathy for your client's circumstances.

If a child breaks a vase, it matters to their parents whether they broke it by accident or on purpose. Knowing the break was an accident affects the parents' response and any punishment the child receives. Similarly, in legal argument, the circumstances of your client's situation will affect an audience's emotional response. Putting the audience in the right frame of mind—as Aristotle described it—means helping the audience identify with your client's situation, feel what your client is feeling, and be open to deciding in your client's favor (as long as your reasoning is sound and your authority credible).

Aristotle devoted more space in his *Rhetoric* to emotional than logical appeals. In Book II, he examined fourteen emotions, often in pairs.[9] He considered their cause, the state of mind of those who experience them, and those to whom we direct each type of emotion.[10] He defined anger as "desire, accompanied by distress, for apparent retaliation because of an apparent slight that was directed, without justification, against oneself or those near to one."[11] By defining anger as the result of thinking that

---

7 *See* ARISTOTLE, RHETORIC, *supra* ch. 8, note 3, at II.1, 1377b.

8 *See id.* at I.2, 1356a.

9 *See id.* at II.2–11.

10 *See, e.g., id.* at II.5, 1382a–83b (defining fear as a sort of pain and agitation in *anticipation* of a future evil and confidence as the opposite).

11 *Id.* at II.2, 1378b.

one has been slighted, Aristotle recognized that emotion has a cognitive component.[12] Put another way, emotion can be the product of thought.[13]

Because thought can lead to emotion, emotion is open to reason or persuasion: "The emotions [pathé]," Aristotle said, "are those things through which, by undergoing change, people come to differ in their judgments and which are accompanied by pain and pleasure."[14] If a jury (mistakenly) perceives a slight against another and seeks to retaliate (i.e., experiences anger), a skillful rhetor can change the jury's mind about the nature of the slight and the need for punishment (i.e., produce calmness, the opposite of anger).[15] For these reasons, Aristotle thought legal advocates should be familiar with the range and complexity of human emotion to arouse the appropriate emotion in others. That said, he criticized the sophists for teaching students "to warp the jury by leading them into anger or envy or pity: that is the same as if someone made a straight-edge ruler crooked before using it."[16]

Today, we know more about the inextricable link between reason and emotion. We experience emotion in one of two ways: either first as a change in body state and then a feeling (the cognitive component), or we experience a feeling (the cognitive emotion) and a subsequent change in body state.[17] Since the time of Plato, we have been conditioned to think that reason is good and emotion is bad. Remember *Gorgias*?[18] In that dialogue, Socrates argued that rhetoric was akin to cookery because it feeds the base pleasures of the body and not the needs of the soul.[19]

Yet we have learned that emotion is an integral part of decision-making.[20] Few complex decisions are made on the basis of reason alone. Emotion helps us choose among options based on the feeling we associate with each outcome. If we attempted to make decisions using a lengthy cost-benefit analysis, we might never make a decision.[21]

---

12 *See* W.W. FORTENBAUGH, ARISTOTLE ON EMOTION 12 (2d ed. 2002).

13 *See* Terry A. Maroney, *Judicial Emotion as Vice or Virtue: Perspectives Both Ancient and New*, *in* ARISTOTLE ON EMOTIONS IN LAW AND POLITICS 11, 14 (Liesbeth Huppes-Cluysenaer & Nuno M.M.S. Coelho eds., 2018) (noting that Martha Nussbaum was the first to recognize Aristotle's cognitive theory of emotion in MARTHA NUSSBAUM, UPHEAVALS OF THOUGHT: THE INTELLIGENCE OF EMOTIONS (2001)).

14 ARISTOTLE, RHETORIC, *supra* ch. 8, note 3, at II.1, 1378a8.

15 *See id.* at II.3, 1380a.

16 *See id.* at I.1, 1354a.

17 *See* ANTONIO DAMASIO, SELF COMES TO MIND: CONSTRUCTING THE CONSCIOUS BRAIN 101–02 (2010); ANTONIO R. DAMASIO, DESCARTES' ERROR: EMOTION, REASON, AND THE HUMAN BRAIN 155–56 (1994) [hereinafter DESCARTES' ERROR].

18 *See supra* ch. 9, note 7, and accompanying text.

19 *See id.*

20 DAMASIO, DESCARTES' ERROR, *supra* note 17, at 170–75.

21 *See, e.g.*, Jonathan Haidt, *The Emotional Dog and Its Rational Tail: A Social Intuitionist Approach to Moral Judgment*, 108 PSYCHOL. REV. 814, 824 (2001) (explaining that patients with damage to the decision-making centers in the brain often have trouble making decisions: "[T]hey perform disastrously, showing poor judgment, indecisiveness, and what appears to be irrational behavior.").

Knowing that emotion plays a role in decision-making helps explain why advocates must take emotion into account. And that emotion may be based on conscious or unconscious bias. By acknowledging the role that bias plays in decision-making, we can begin to address it. Justice Brennan once said, "Sensitivity to one's intuitive and passionate responses, and awareness of the range of human experience, is . . . not only an inevitable but a desirable part of the judicial process, an aspect more to be nurtured than feared."[22] As psychologist Jonathan Haidt has suggested, we can use emotion to trigger empathy and combat bias.[23] In fact, bringing your audience's attention to those instances where they are likely to employ bias can cause them to question their assumptions and engage in slower, more effortful, and deliberative thinking.[24]

As you learn to craft emotional appeals, you may begin to feel uncomfortable, particularly in a political climate where facts are manipulated to gain audience adherence. But lawyers have an ethical duty to represent their clients with zeal in advocacy.[25] Our judicial system is based on the expectation that both sides to a dispute will make their best arguments, and the judge or jury will decide the best truth under the circumstances. Just like the child who broke the vase, your client's best arguments will include emotional appeals that put the audience in your client's shoes.

For More Information

Jamal Greene, *Pathetic Argument in Constitutional Law*, 113 Colum. L. Rev. 1389 (2013).

Harold Anthony Lloyd, *Cognitive Emotion and the Law*, 41 Law & Psychol. Rev. 53 (2016).

Eric A. Posner, *Law and the Emotions*, 89 Geo. L.J. 1977 (2001).

Kristen Konrad Tiscione, *Feelthinking Like A Lawyer: The Role of Emotion in Legal Reasoning and Decisionmaking*, 54 Wake Forest L. Rev. 1159 (2019).

B. Appeals to credibility

To be credible, you must not only be competent, you must also be reasonable and sincere. No decision-maker—judge, jury, or otherwise—wants to feel like they're being manipulated.

Practice Pointer

Ethos in legal writing requires

- a good character, and
- credibility

22 William J. Brennan, Jr., *Reason, Passion, and "the Progress of the Law,"* 10 CARDOZO L. REV. 3, 10 (1988).

23 *See* JONATHAN HAIDT, THE RIGHTEOUS MIND: WHY GOOD PEOPLE ARE DIVIDED BY POLITICS AND RELIGION 823 (2012); Haidt, *supra* note 21, at 829.

24 *See* DANIEL KAHNEMAN, THINKING, FAST AND SLOW 21 (2011); Daniel Kahneman & Gary Klein, *Conditions for Intuitive Expertise: A Failure to Disagree*, 64 AM. PSYCHOLOGIST 515, 519 (2009).

25 "As advocate, a lawyer zealously asserts the client's position under the rules of the adversary system." AM. BAR ASS'N, MODEL RULES OF PRO. CONDUCT (2020) [hereinafter MODEL RULES]; https://www.americanbar.org/groups/professional_responsibility/publications/model_rules_of_professional_conduct/model_rules_of_professional_conduct_table_of_contents/ (https://perma.cc/NEB3-2UNB).

Ethical appeals are even more important in legal argument. Aristotle said a speaker must have a good character and be credible: "He must give the right impression of himself, and get his judge into the right state of mind."[26] Cicero said a speaker must make his audience "well-disposed, attentive, and receptive."[27] As discussed in Chapter 9, Quintilian developed an even broader view of ethos than Aristotle or Cicero: *ethos* encompasses more than the speaker's appeal at the time a speech is delivered; "a good man skilled in speaking" is a person free from vice, a lover of wisdom, a sincere believer in his cause, and a servant of the people.[28]

Michael Smith, a professor at University of Wyoming School of Law, describes *ethos* in legal writing as intelligence, character, and good will.[29] Intelligence is demonstrated by being well-informed, competent, empathetic, articulate, and creative.[30] Character is demonstrated by truthfulness, candor, zeal, and professionalism.[31] Good will is the extent to which the reader respects the writer's motivation.[32]

1. Truthfulness

The need to demonstrate good character can involve conflicting goals and duties. On the one hand, lawyers have an ethical duty to "zealously assert[ ] the client's position under the rules of the adversary system."[33] On the other hand, lawyers also act as officers of the court and must be candid with the tribunal (a court or other decision-making body). Under the Model Rules of Professional Conduct, lawyers cannot make false statements "of fact or law," must disclose "legal authority in the controlling jurisdiction known to the lawyer to be directly adverse to the position of the client and not disclosed by opposing counsel," and "cannot offer evidence the lawyer knows to be false."[34]

At what point do these duties intersect? At what point does fulfilling the duty of zeal in advocacy conflict with the duty of candor to the tribunal? How far can you go in telling your client's story without beginning to mislead the court? How far can you go in framing rules of law from your client's perspective without misleading the court or violating your duty to be candid?

---

26 ARISTOTLE, RHETORIC, *supra* ch. 8, note 3, at II.1, 1377b.

27 CICERO, DE INVENTIONE, *supra* ch. 9, note 19, at I.15.20.

28 QUINTILIAN, *supra* ch. 9, note 27, at XII.1.1.

29 MICHAEL R. SMITH, ADVANCED LEGAL WRITING: THEORIES AND STRATEGIES IN PERSUASIVE WRITING 127 (3d ed. 2012).

30 *Id.* at 149–89.

31 *Id.* at 127–44.

32 *Id.* at 144–47.

33 MODEL RULES, *supra* note 25.

34 *Id.* at r. 3.3(a)(1)–(3).

To start, even if the story you tell is internally consistent, it cannot be fictitious.[35] Although told from your client's perspective, the facts must be accurate and complete. How you characterize those facts is important. Avoid assumptions, speculation, and exaggeration. Any inferences you make based on the facts should be reasonable.[36] Most of us have an internal alarm that sounds when we feel (here's emotion affecting our decision-making) we are beginning to distort the truth. Listen to that alarm. Think about the opposing party's likely characterization of the same facts. When in doubt, get a colleague's reaction to your version of the facts. Is it reasonable?

For example, in the Velas matter, we cannot state with certainty that 150 people read CSP's newsletter. We only know that it was sent to 150 people. Nor can we assume without investigation that CSP's newsletter caused the Velases' plummeting sales or that CSP did not investigate the nature of the coffee beans. These facts may all be true but need to be verified. The goal is to make only reasonable inferences from the known facts.[37]

With regard to rules of law, review Chapter 30 on rule synthesis. To be reasonable, your rules must be comprehensive, accurate, and fair. Your rule must account for all relevant binding authority and fairly represent the court's holding or reasoning in a cited case. For example, as to the second element of the disparagement statute, this rule likely goes too far: "Where the defendant fails to verify the truth of the statement with the producer of the perishable food product, it acts with knowledge of falsity." Under *Thomas Meats* (see p. 199), reckless disregard for the truth can amount to knowledge of falsity, but in that case, the defendant failed to conduct any investigation. It may be possible to obtain the truth from a variety of sources other than the producer.

For More Information

On ethical storytelling—

Steven J. Johansen, *Was Colonel Sanders a Terrorist? An Essay on the Ethical Limits of Applied Legal Storytelling*, 7 Legal Commc'n & Rhetoric: JALWD 63 (2010).

Jeanne M. Kaiser, *When the Truth and Story Collide: What Legal Writers Can Learn from the Experience of Non-Fiction Writers about the Limits of Storytelling*, 16 J. Legal Writing 163 (2010).

On the ethos of arrangement and style in legal writing—

Melissa H. *Weresh, Morality, Trust & Illusion: Ethos as Relationship*, 9 Legal Commc'n & Rhetoric: JALWD 229 (2012).

35 *See infra* ch. 47.

36 *See supra* ch. 33.

37 *See id.*

2. Duty of candor to the tribunal

To demonstrate good character and be credible, lawyers must cite legal authority to support their assertions. They must accurately represent the law of the controlling jurisdiction and may rely on persuasive authority that might help the court or decision-making authority resolve the dispute. As mentioned above, Model Rule of Professional Conduct 3.3 requires lawyers to disclose "legal authority in the controlling jurisdiction known to the lawyer to be directly adverse to the position of the client and not disclosed by opposing counsel."[38] A comment to Rule 3.3 states that a lawyer must present the client's case "with persuasive force," but that obligation is tempered by the duty of candor to the tribunal.[39] Thus, a lawyer may present the law from the client's perspective but may not "allow the tribunal to be misled by false statements of law."[40]

The Rule does not define adverse authority, but the comment explains the "underlying concept is that legal argument is a discussion seeking to determine the legal premises properly applicable to the case."[41] Lawyers generally understand this phrase to mean any case from a binding court with the same or strikingly similar facts where the holding on the same issue is opposite to the client's position.

Practice Pointer

Directly adverse authority:

- has arguably similar facts
- comes from the same or higher level binding court
- holds in favor of client's opponent on the same issue

What if there was also a more recent case from the Texas Court of Appeals, *Fresh Farms v. Oleander* (Tex. App. 2020), holding that the false disparagement statute requires that the information be heard simultaneously by a live audience to constitute the public? Would you need to disclose that case to the trial court as "directly adverse to the position of the client"? Yes. *Thomas Meats* is a Texas Supreme Court case, but *Fresh Farms* further articulates that rule and is binding on the trial court.

Instead, what if *Fresh Farms* was decided by the United States Court of Appeals for the Tenth Circuit (applying Texas law)? Would you need to disclose that case to the federal trial court as "directly adverse to the position of the client"? Probably not. The federal district Court in Texas is bound by decisions of the Fifth Circuit. *Fresh Farms* would only be persuasive authority, but it could be helpful in the absence of a Fifth Circuit decision. Under Rule 3.3, however, *Fresh Farms* is not "legal authority from the controlling jurisdiction."

---

38 MODEL RULES, *supra* note 25, at r. 3.3(a)(2).

39 *Id.* at r. 3.3(a)(2) cmt. [2].

40 MODEL RULES, *supra* note 25, at r. 3.3(a)(2) cmt. [2].

41 *Id.* at cmt.[4].

Even if you do not need to cite the Tenth Circuit decision, should you? Frances DeLaurentis, a professor at Georgetown Law, makes an excellent case that you should. First, both the American Bar Association and courts across the country have interpreted Rule 3.3 more broadly than the language seems to require.[42] In some courts, failure to disclose the Tenth Circuit case could lead to sanctions against the lawyer. Second, "ethical advocacy is a stronger, more effective advocacy."[43] If the case could be construed as reasonably helpful to the deciding court, it makes sense to disclose it. You can then argue to the court why the case is distinguishable (i.e., not analogous under principles of *stare decisis*), no longer valid, or wrongly decided.[44] If you do not disclose the Tenth Circuit case, you risk both your credibility with the court and damaging your reputation among colleagues.[45]

This does not mean that you must scour the earth for every adverse decision by any potentially helpful court. As a general matter, your research should be focused on finding binding cases on similar facts or analogous situations. Where the controlling jurisdiction has not construed its own law, it makes sense to look for persuasive authority construing the same or similar law under similar or analogous circumstances:

- Where the issue is one of state law in state court, look for federal court decisions construing that state's law in diversity jurisdiction cases.
- Where the issue is one of state law in federal court, you are obliged to look for controlling state court decisions. Even though only state supreme court decisions may bind that federal court, it would be prudent to cite any reported state court decision on the same issue.
- Where the issue is one of federal law in state court, look for decisions by federal courts in the state's federal circuit or beyond.
- Where the issue is one of federal law in federal court, look for decisions by other district and circuit courts.

3. Professionalism in legal advocacy

Two adages are particularly relevant to professionalism in advocacy. One is "it's hard to recover from a bad first impression." The second is "it takes years to build a good reputation and just minutes to destroy one." The same is true for lawyering and legal writing. Your credibility as an advocate will be based, in part, on how you behave

42 *See* Frances DeLaurentis, *When Ethical Worlds Collide: Teaching Novice Legal Writers to Balance the Duties of Zealous Advocacy and Candor to the Tribunal*, 7 DREXEL L. REV. 1, 9–19 (2014).

43 *Id.* at 37; *see also infra* ch. 48.F.

44 When you cite adverse authority, use one of the three signals that indicate contradiction. If the authority is directly adverse, use *contra*. If the authority clearly supports the opposing position, use *but see*. If the authority supports an analogous opposing position, use *but cf. See infra* ch. 57.

45 DeLaurentis, *supra* note 42, at 14.

first as a law student and then as a lawyer. For that reason, it is helpful to start thinking now about the kind of lawyer you want to be and how to become that lawyer.

As a law student and practitioner, everything you do reflects in some way on your professional identity. In exchange for the privilege of practicing law, lawyers are expected to conform to the ethical rules of the profession; represent their clients competently, diligently and promptly; act with integrity, and serve the public interest.[46]

Practice Pointer

A lawyer's **professional identity** is based on

- conformity to ethical rules
- competent, diligent, and prompt performance
- personal integrity, and
- commitment to public service

In addition to representing clients zealously and disclosing adverse authority, the Model Rules of Professional Conduct require that lawyers be competent, diligent, and prompt.[47] Competent lawyers have the "legal knowledge, skill, thoroughness and preparation reasonably necessary" to represent their clients.[48] Lawyers are reasonably diligent and prompt as long as they take appropriate and ethical measures on their client's behalf without delay.[49] In doing so, they are not obliged to use offensive tactics or treat people without courtesy or respect.[50]

Being competent, diligent, and prompt means mastering specialized reading, analytical, and writing skills, as well as conforming to the standards of the legal profession. The legal community has certain conventions that you will be expected to be familiar with and respect (e.g., how you address your supervisor, how to introduce testimony in court, how to treat opposing counsel, etc.). Your experiences in simulation courses, internships, externships, and summer employment will help you learn these. When in doubt, ask a lawyer you know, your classmates, or your professors. No question along these lines is ever a stupid question.

There are also a variety of procedural rules that must be followed in order to maintain efficiency and ensure fairness of our federal and state governments (e.g., bar admission rules, court procedural rules, and agency requirements). You will become familiar with some of these rules in legal research and writing, such as formatting requirements, deadlines, and word counts.

Competence in legal writing is the ability to produce quality writing. Legal writing should not only be credible; it should also *look* credible. It should conform to the formatting rules of any applicable court or other decision-making body, use proper grammar and punctuation, cite authority according to the prescribed or

---

46 *See, e.g.*, SULLIVAN, *supra* ch. 10, note 10, at 129–32.

47 MODEL RULES, *supra* note 25, at r. 1.1 and 1.3.

48 *Id.* at r. 1.1.

49 *See id.* at r. 1.3, cmt. [3].

50 *Id.* at cmt. [1].

conventional format, and contain no typographical errors. If the writing looks sloppy, the reader is likely to assume the content is sloppy too. If the reader questions the writer's credibility, it will be hard to gain the reader's trust.

Lawyers act with integrity when they treat everyone they encounter in the course of their profession with honesty, respect, and a conscious understanding of the difference between right and wrong. For example, the Model Rules require lawyers to keep their client's communications confidential, to bring or defend only meritorious claims, to communicate with third parties (including opposing counsel) truthfully and respectfully, and to report any known violation of the Rules committed by another lawyer to the appropriate authority.[51]

While in law school, practice framing facts and law without misrepresenting them. No one likes or hires the lawyer who was sanctioned for filing a frivolous claim or reprimanded by the court for filing motions just to cause delay. Your integrity is revealed in your actions as well as the tone of your writing. Sarcasm, accusations, and personal attacks are usually ineffective. They will serve more to diminish your integrity than accomplish the client's goals, and judges are critical of these tactics.

Finally, lawyers have a professional responsibility to provide free legal services to persons of limited means or charitable organizations. The Model Rules suggest that lawyers donate fifty hours of their time per year.[52] While in law school, take advantage of the opportunity to donate law-related services through your school or other organizations. You may find an area of the law you find particularly satisfying or decide to go into public service. At the very least, you will learn a lot along the way and end up feeling good about your efforts.

For More Information

Judith D. Fischer, *The Role of Ethics in Legal Writing: The Forensic Embroiderer, the Minimalist Wizard, and Other Stories*, 9 Scribes J. Legal Writing Inst., 77 (2003–2004).

Judith D. Fischer, *Bareheaded and Barefaced Counsel: Courts React to Unprofessionalism in Lawyers' Papers*, 31 Suffolk U. L. Rev. 1 (1997).

Margaret Z. Johns & Clayton S. Tanaka, *Professional Writing for Lawyers* (2d. ed. 2012).

Melissa H. Weresh, *Legal Writing: Ethical and Professional Considerations* (2d ed. 2009).

51 *Id.* at r. 1.6, 3.1, 3.4, 4.1, 4.4, and 8.3. Civil procedure rules also require that lawyers file claims grounded in fact and warranted by law. *See, e.g.*, FED. R. CIV. P. 11.

52 MODEL RULES, *supra* note 25, at r. 6.1.

Chapter 45

The Appellate Brief

Appellate briefs contain the parties' legal arguments at either the intermediate or highest appellate court in a given jurisdiction. The party who files the appeal is called the **appellant** or **petitioner**. The opposing party is called the **appellee** or **respondent**. The appellant claims that the lower court erred with respect to a particular issue or issues. The appellate court's job is to review the lower court's decision in light of the parties' arguments. In some cases, both parties have appealed (called cross appeals).

Appellate courts do not retry cases. The trial court hears and examines the evidence, including live witness testimony, and evaluates its credibility. Based on the evidence, the judge or jury determines or "finds" the facts and then applies the law to those facts to make a decision.[1] In jury trials, the jury makes the factual determinations, and the judge instructs the jury on the law to help them reach a verdict. On appeal, the reviewing court reviews the evidence submitted to it in the form of a written **record**, or **joint appendix**. Based on the written record and the parties' arguments, which may include oral argument, the appellate court determines whether the trial court erred.

For several reasons, many first-year courses introduce law students to persuasive writing through the appellate brief. First, the legal issues are often current, complex, and interesting. Second, students are used to reading appellate decisions, which provides a nice symmetry. Third, appellate briefs tend to be the most complicated in terms of format. Having written an appellate brief, you can adapt those skills to almost any brief-writing context.

A. Format of an appellate brief

Federal and state court rules of appellate procedure often detail the sections that briefs filed in their court must contain, and most courts also have local supplementary rules. The format for appellate briefs used here is adapted from Federal Rule of Appellate Procedure 28. It serves as a good model for all appellate briefs.

1 *See supra* ch. 20.

In a work setting, be sure to consult applicable appellate court rules as well as the local rules of the court where you intend to file.[2] These rules can be very specific. For example, Federal Rule 32 requires that print covers of an appellant's brief be blue and that covers of an appellee's brief be red.[3] It also sets a limit of thirty pages or 13,000 words for each party's initial brief and specifies that footnotes are included in the word count.[4] In the Fifth Circuit Court of Appeals, all briefs must be filed electronically.[5]

Assume that the Velases filed suit in September 2020 against CSP for false disparagement in a federal district court in Texas. To review the facts of the case, see the complaint, p. 381. Shortly thereafter, CSP filed a motion to dismiss for failure to state a claim under Fed. R. Civ. P. 12(b)(6), which the district court denied. To read the motion, see pp. 389, 391. The case proceeded to trial, and at the close of the plaintiff's case, CSP filed a motion for judgment as a matter of law under Federal Rule of Civil Procedure 50. The court granted the motion and entered judgment for CSP on February 26, 2021. As you read about appellate briefs, refer to the sample brief, beginning on page 326, that the Velases might file on appeal.

Cover Page (p. 326)

The cover page should include the caption of the case, the docket number, the title of the brief, the names of the attorneys filing the brief, and the date of filing.

Table of Contents (p. 327)

The table of contents lists each section of the brief and the page numbers where they begin. All headings (discussed below on p. 354) are reprinted in the table of contents. The headings summarize the client's arguments and act as a detailed outline for the reader. Page number one of the brief typically begins with the jurisdictional statement. All prior pages are numbered using small roman numerals (i, ii, iii, etc.).

---

2 You can usually find these on Westlaw, Lexis, and Bloomberg Law, as well as on the courts' own websites. To review the Fifth Circuit's local rules embedded in the Federal Rules of Appellate Procedure, see the Fifth Circuit's website at http://www.ca5.uscourts.gov/docs/default-source/forms-and-documents---clerks-office/rules/federalrulesofappellateprocedure (https://perma.cc/9G63-JQET).

3 FED. R. APP. P. 32(a)(2).

4 *Id.* at 32(a)(7) & (f).

5 To view sample rules for electronic filing, see the website of the United States Court of Appeals for the Fifth Circuit, at http://www.ca5.uscourts.gov/electronic-case-filing/electronic-case-filing/ecf-information-page (https://perma.cc/P96K-TF4J).

Table of Authorities (p. 328)

The table of authorities provides an alphabetical list of the statutes, cases, and other authorities cited in the brief. Separate the authorities by type and in hierarchical order (constitutions, then statutes, etc.). Cases should be separated by level of court and then put in alphabetical order. Do not include pin cites here. The table should include the page number(s) on which each of the cited sources appears. Some court rules require the parties to indicate in the table of authorities the sources they primarily rely on.

Jurisdictional Statement (p. 329)

The jurisdictional statement provides the statutory basis for the court's exercise of subject matter jurisdiction (subject matter jurisdiction refers to the court's authority to hear the subject matter of the claim). It should cite the applicable statute and/or regulation and the facts that establish the court's jurisdiction.

Statement of the Issue(s) Presented for Review (p. 329)

The statement of the issue(s) presented for review is akin to the question presented of a legal memo (see Chapter 37). It should identify the controlling rule of law or jurisdiction, the precise legal question, and the significant facts.

Unlike a question presented, though, the statement of the issue(s) should be stated from your client's perspective. To be persuasive, it should suggest that your client's desired outcome is the natural and most reasonable outcome. A good way to frame the statement of the issue(s) is to state it so that it suggests an affirmative answer, but that may not always make sense.

For example, from the Velases' point of view, the issue might be whether the court erred in granting judgment for CSP or whether they are entitled to protection under the Texas statute. If written persuasively, the reader will want to answer yes to either question. On the other hand, CSP might phrase the issue as whether the court should affirm the lower court's ruling or whether the Texas legislature intended to protect plaintiffs under the false disparagement statute who simply resell produce grown outside Texas. In this instance, the desired answer would be "no."

Statement of the Case (p. 329)

The statement of the case combines the procedural history and the relevant facts of your client's situation. It should contain enough background information for a reader unfamiliar with the case to understand the conflict and the facts relevant to the legal issues on appeal. All facts must include citations to the record so they can be verified. A typical citation to page four of an appellate record might be: R. at 4.[6]

The statement of the case is similar to the statement of facts in a legal memo, but it should stir the emotions and make the reader want to act in the client's favor. Generally speaking, the statement of the case includes the introduction and the rising action of the client's story (see Chapter 47.A on framing the client's story). The climax does not occur until you make the client's arguments. For more information on drafting the statement of the case, see Chapter 47.

Summary of Argument (p. 331)

Like the brief answer in a legal memorandum, the summary of argument previews the writer's legal conclusions and legal reasoning. Since this is the reader's first introduction to the client's argument, it should capture the reader's attention, evoke your theory of the case (see Chapter 48.A), and crystallize your arguments.[7] Federal Rule of Appellate Procedure 28 requires that the summary "contain a succinct, clear, and accurate statement of the arguments made in the body of the brief" and not "merely repeat the argument headings."[8] A summary that synthesizes the arguments (contains both your conclusions and your reasoning) prepares the reader for the detailed arguments to follow. Think of the summary as the section that allows you to paraphrase the essence of the arguments for maximum impact. As with brief answers in legal memos, you do not need to include citations.

Standard of Review (p. 331)

Federal Rule of Appellate Procedure 28(a)(8)(B) requires that the standard of review for each issue be stated concisely.[9] It may appear in the argument on each issue or under a separate heading (as shown here and in the sample brief) before the Argument. The standard of review is the level of deference the reviewing court must give to the lower court's decision. The standard of review can differ, even in the same case, depending on the issues before the reviewing court. See Chapter 46 for a more detailed explanation of the standard of review.

---

6 *See* ALWD GUIDE, *infra* ch. 56, note 1, at R. 25.6(a); BLUEBOOK, *infra* ch. 56, note 1, at R. B17.1.2.

7 Judith D. Fischer, *Summing It Up with Panache: Framing a Brief's Summary of the Argument*, 48 JOHN MARSHALL L. REV. 991 (2015).

8 FED. R. APP. P. 28(a)(7).

9 *Id.* at 28(a)(8)(B).

Argument (p. 331)

The argument is to the brief what the discussion is to the legal memorandum. As Federal Rule of Appellate Procedure 28(a)(8)(A) states, the argument should contain "the appellant's contentions and the reasons for them, with citations to the authorities and parts of the record on which the appellant relies."[10]

Just as with legal memos, your reader will expect an overview of the argument at the outset. For that reason, the argument should begin with an introductory section (often called a roadmap or umbrella paragraph) that previews the controlling rules of law applicable to the issue(s) on appeal. As with the Discussion in a memorandum, the argument proceeds deductively, moving issue by issue, from general rules of law to specific conclusions, anticipating and refuting legitimate counterarguments (see Chapter 38). Legal arguments usually contain point headings, which outline the party's arguments.[11]

Conclusion (p. 334)

Unlike in legal memos, conclusions in appellate briefs are short, usually just one sentence. A court will grant only the specific relief requested, so the relief sought should be stated precisely and succinctly.[12]

---

10 *Id.* at 28(a)(8)(A).

11 *See infra* ch. 48.C, at 354.

12 *See* FED. R. APP. P. 28(a)(9).

B. Sample appellate brief in the Velas matter

United States Court of Appeals
for the Fifth District

Christina Velas and Ramon Velas, d/b/a Starbucks, Appellants, vs. Citizens for Safe Products, Appellee.	Case No. CIV–21–33–112

Brief for Appellant

James U. Elkins, J.D.
Attorney for Appellant

The Elkins Firm
874 Main Street
Suite 130
Dallas, Texas 75034
jelkins@elkinsfirm.com
214-993-9000

September 11, 2020

Table of Contents

Table of Authorities

Statutes

Cases

Secondary Sources

Jurisdictional Statement

This diversity action was filed in the United States District Court for the Northern District of Texas pursuant to 28 U.S.C. § 1332(a). The District Court granted the Appellee's Motion for Judgment at the close of Appellant's case and entered final judgment on February 26, 2021. This Court has jurisdiction of the appeal pursuant to 28 U.S.C. § 1291.

Statement of the Issue Presented for Review

Under the Texas False Disparagement of Perishable Food Products Act, is the seller of coffee beans protected against false statements about the nature and safety of its products when the falsity of those statements cannot be communicated effectively to the public before the product can no longer be sold?

Statement of the Case

Christina and Ramon Velas, small business owners doing business as Starbucks, filed this diversity action against Appellee, Citizens for Safe Products (CSP), a nationwide consumer advocacy organization, in January 2020. CSP filed a motion to dismiss shortly thereafter, which the district court denied. The case went to trial, and at the close of the Appellant's case in chief, CSP moved for judgment on the pleadings claiming that the Texas statute prohibiting false disparagement of perishable food products did not protect the Appellant, who sells coffee beans and beverages. The district court granted the motion for judgment in June 2020 on the ground that the Appellant is not the producer of a perishable food product under Texas law. Starbucks now appeals.

This paragraph provides the procedural history of the case.

The Velases have owned and operated a successful Starbucks in Dallas, Texas since 2003. R. at 15. Most Starbucks locations are owned by Starbucks Coffee Company. However, the demand for specialty coffee in a variety of unique spaces and locations has led Starbucks to enter into license agreements with certain small business owners like appellants. The license agreement permits them to operate under the Starbucks name. The Velases entered into one of the first license agreements with Starbucks in Dallas. R. at 17.

Notice the citations indicate the source of the stated facts in the record.

Attuned to their community's interests and demands, the Velases are committed to serving and selling quality products, preferably from local sources. Since October 2018, they have used only organic ingredients to make coffee beverages and sold only organic snacks and pastries. R. at 24. When they switched to organic ingredients, their profits increased fifteen percent. R. at 24.[13] Although the Velases would like to sell locally grown coffee as well, coffee plants simply do not grow in the United States. At that time, they cancelled their bean contracts with local suppliers because the beans were not organic, and they were disappointed with the taste and slightly stale quality. R. at 30. With Starbucks' support, the Velases contracted directly with coffee bean suppliers in Central and South America. R. at 37. These fair trade sources supply them with a variety of fresh-roasted, organic beans their customers have come to love. R. at 44. Despite common belief, coffee beans do not stay fresh indefinitely, even in the freezer. For optimum quality, coffee beans should be used within six to eight weeks of packaging and no later than the "best before" dates determined by the grower. R. at 65.

In March 2019, the Dallas chapter of CSP published its monthly newsletter on the availability of organic products in and around the Dallas metropolitan area. One article falsely stated that the Velases do not use or sell organic coffee beans:

> [P]erk up reader! You know that Starbucks on Commerce Street? The supposedly "organic beans" are not so organic after all. A confidential source reports that the beans are grown using pesticides. We thought you'd want to know what you're drinking. Just another example of how we're working hard to protect our membership.

R. at 103. CSP did not contact Mr. or Mrs. Velas, their employees, anyone else at Starbucks, or their bean suppliers about the nature of the coffee beans either before or after it published its newsletter. R. at 40.

Almost immediately after CSP sent its newsletter, the Velases' bean and beverage sales plummeted. R. at 72. Some customers came to the store, asking whether the beans being sold at that location were actually organic but made no purchases. R. at 74–76. Due to the false allegations in CSP's newsletter, the Velases have incurred damages of at least $100,000 in lost sales, good will, and other consequential damages. R. at 92–97. They are now at risk of losing their business.

2

[13] The ALWD Guide and Bluebook discourage the use of *id.* in this context unless the title of the document is very long. *See* ALWD Guide, *infra* ch. 56, note 1, at R. 25.7; Bluebook, *infra* ch. 56, note 1, at R. B17.1.2.

Summary of Argument

The District Court erred in granting the Motion for Judgment. The Texas False Disparagement of Perishable Food Products Act protects all producers of perishable food products, regardless of where the products are grown. Under the Texas statute, coffee beans are a perishable food product because they are used to make a variety of coffee beverages, and the beans perish or decay beyond marketability in a limited period of time. CSP's false statements about the nature of the beans were disseminated to the public and could not be corrected effectively within six to eight weeks, before the beans could no longer be sold. The Velases are producers of the beans as sellers of a sole agricultural product. The Texas statute does not limit recovery to those who grow the beans. To hold otherwise would protect only those business owners whose products grew or can be grown in Texas. Coffee beans cannot.

The Summary contains the party's legal conclusions and reasoning.

Standard of Review

This Court reviews the district court's grant of judgment as a matter of law de novo,[14] applying the same legal standard that the district court used in deciding the motion. *Seibert v. Jackson Cnty., Miss.*, 851 F.3d 430, 436 (5th Cir. 2017).

Argument

The District Court's order granting CSP's Motion for Judgment should be reversed. The Texas legislature chose to protect producers of perishable food products from false statements. If the falsity of the statements cannot be corrected before the products can no longer be sold, they cause significant damage to the producer. *See* Tex. Civ. Prac. & Rem. Code Ann. § 96.001–.004 (Vernon 2020). To succeed in a claim for false disparagement, a plaintiff must prove that the defendant disseminated information about a perishable food product to the public, knew the information was false or acted recklessly with regard to the truth, and implied that the product was unsafe for consumption by the public. *Id.* § 96.002 (a)–(c).

This first paragraph acts as a roadmap to inform the reader of the controlling requirements or rules of law (i.e., the elements of the claim).

Although the Velases put on sufficient evidence of each element of the claim, the district court granted CSP's motion for judgment on the ground that they are not the producer of a perishable food product. As argued below, nothing in the statute or case law prohibits the appellants from being producers of a perishable food product to protect them as the legislature intended. Because they put on sufficient evidence for a jury to conclude that they are producers of a perishable food product, *see Seibert*, 851 F.3d at 176, and coffee beans qualify as perishable food products under Texas law, the lower court erred in granting judgment for CSP.

3

14 No italics here since de novo is commonly used in legal writing. *See* ALWD GUIDE, *infra* ch. 56, at R. 1.3(f); BLUEBOOK, *infra* ch. 56, at R. 7(b).

I. Coffee Beans Are a Perishable Food Product Under the Texas False Disparagement Statute Entitling the Velases to Relief.

Coffee beans are perishable food products. A perishable food product is "a food product of agriculture or aquaculture that is sold or distributed in a form that will perish or decay beyond marketability within a limited period of time." § 96.001. Under Texas law, coffee beans are "food products of agriculture," and they "perish or decay beyond marketability within a limited period of time." *Id.*

This paragraph acts as a mini-roadmap to inform the reader that this first argument is comprised of two sub-issues, which are identified in the sub-headings A. and B. below.

A. Because ingesting coffee helps maintain life and health, coffee beans are food products of agriculture under Texas law.

Coffee beans are food products under the Texas statute, which protects agricultural producers. **[conclusion on this issue]** Although the statute does not define "food products," food products are generally understood to mean nutritious substances ingested to maintain health and life. *See, e.g., Food, OED Online*, www.oed.com (last visited June 2, 2021). **[major premise based on definition of food]** Coffee beans contain nutrients such as potassium and magnesium, as well as antioxidants. *See, e.g., "Coffee is number one source of antioxidants,"* EurekAlert! (August 28, 2005), https://www.eurekalert.org/pub_releases/2005-08/acs-cin081905.php#:~:text=WASHINGTON%2C%20Aug.,of%20Scranton%20(Pa.) (https://perma.cc/5GV4-EWV2) (last visited June 2, 2021).

Coffee beans also contain caffeine, which provides a stimulant effect that people all over the world rely on to "maintain health and life." *Food, OED Online*, www.oed.com (last visited August 23, 2021). In fact, recent studies show that drinking coffee may be associated with a number of health benefits, including protecting against type 2 diabetes, Parkinson's disease, liver disease, liver cancer, and promoting a healthy heart. *See, e.g.*, Robert van Dam, *Ask the Expert: Coffee and Health*, The Harvard School of Public Health Nutrition Source (Feb. 23, 2015), https://www.hsph.harvard.edu/nutritionsource/2015/02/23/ask-the-expert-coffee-and-health-2/ (https://perma.cc/R7KS-3D4X) (last visited June 2, 2021). Finally, the FDA has a separate category for coffee and tea for purposes of labeling and other food safety requirements. *See* 21 C.F.R. § 107.3(n)(7). **[the rest of this paragraph states the minor premise about the nature of coffee beans]**

CSP argues that coffee beans are not food in the normal sense of the word, *see United States v. Kaluza*, 780 F.3d 647, 658–59 (5th Cir. 2015) (stating that when the language of a statute is unambiguous, its terms should be given their plain and ordinary meaning); *Lippincott v. Whisenhunt*, 462 S.W.3d 507, 509 (Tex. 2015), because people do not "eat coffee." But CSP's definition of food would disqualify wheat as a food product of agriculture because people do not "eat wheat." Wheat is harvested, processed, and ground into flour to make a variety of food products, such as bread, rolls, cake, etc. Similarly, coffee is harvested, processed, and ground to make a variety of beverages. CSP also argues that calories in food are what convert into energy to maintain life, and coffee has very few calories. However, like wheat products, most coffee beverages contain additional ingredients, such as milk, sugar, and syrup, which do contain calories. **[anticipation and resolution of anticipated counterargument]** Thus, coffee beans qualify as food under the statute. **[re-conclusion]**

B. Because coffee beans cannot be sold after six to eight weeks, they perish or decay beyond marketability in a limited period of time.

The coffee beans the Velases sell and use to make coffee beverages perish or decay beyond marketability within a limited period of time. *See* § 96.001. The statute does not define "limited period of time," but its purpose is to protect sellers of agricultural products, which become unsalable before false statements can be exposed to the public. The beans the Velases import have a "best before" date of six to eight weeks, past which they are no longer fresh and flavorful. At trial, Mr. Velas testified that customers will not purchase bagged beans after the "best before" dates. As the appellants' lost sales indicate, the falsity of CSP's statements could not be corrected before the beans became unsalable, causing significant damage to appellants' business.

> This is a potential situation where two noes don't necessarily make a "yes" (i.e., six to eight weeks being less than six months does not necessarily make that a "limited period."). *See* The Double Negative, Chapter 31.F. Thus, the writer also argues why six to eight weeks should qualify as limited.

CSP's reliance on *Pet Barn, Inc. v. Holmes*, 224 S.W.2d 99, 103 (Tex. 2016) is misplaced. In that case, the court held a baked pet snack was not a product of agriculture because it combined several different products of agriculture. *Id.* It explained that because the snack had a shelf life of at least six months, it was not perishable. *Id.* Although not binding on this Court, the dicta in *Pet Barn* suggests there is no bright line rule for a "limited period of time," which differs depending on the nature of the product and circumstances at issue. Even if the court's suggestion were not dicta, *Pet Barn* establishes only what a limited period of time is *not*, not what it *is*, particularly in this case.

CSP further argues that appellants have admitted that coffee stored in one of its unopened FlavorLockTM bags stays fresh for several months. However, they also indicated that the beans they import are not packaged using FlavorLock bags. The imported beans thus lose flavor within six to eight weeks, at which point they can no longer be sold. In this case, the beans "perished or decayed beyond marketability in a limited period of time" because the statements could not be corrected in time to prevent the Velases' loss. **[counterarguments anticipated and resolved]**

5

II. The Velases Are Producers of Coffee Beans Under Texas Law and Entitled to Recover Against CSP.

Finally, the Velases are "producer[s] of a perishable food product" and entitled to relief. *See* § 96.002(b). The majority of states that prohibit false disparagement of perishable food products restrict protection to those plaintiffs who actually grow or produce the crops. *See, e.g.*, Fla. Stat. Ann. § 865.065 (West 2014) (limiting recovery to "the person who actually grows or produces" the food products). In contrast, Texas does not restrict the meaning of "producer" to those who actually grow the agricultural or aquacultural products. Moreover, the legislative history indicates that "unprocessed" was deleted from the definition of a perishable food product so the statute would provide greater protection by applying both to processed and unprocessed food. H. Bill Analysis, 74–722, Reg. Sess., at 4 (Tex. 1995).

Since the statute does not limit "producer" to growers or "food" to unprocessed food, the Texas legislature intended to protect a larger group of plaintiffs, like the Velases, who purchase and resell perishable food products in Texas. *See also Johnson v. GlobalSantaFe Offshore Servs.*, 799 F.3d 317, 325 (5th Cir. 2015); *In re Certain Underwriters at Lloyd's of London*, 294 S.W.3d 891, 904–05 (Tex. Ct. App. 2009) (both holding that remedial legislation should be liberally construed). That the beans are roasted and imported from outside Texas does not disqualify appellants from recovering under the statute. To hold otherwise would be to grant protection only to producers of food products that grow in or are capable of being grown in Texas. Although false statements about both types of products would damage the local Texas economy, only producers of local products could recover under the statute.

Conclusion

For the reasons stated above, the Appellant respectfully requests that this Court reverse the District Court's order granting the Appellee's motion for judgment.

Respectfully submitted,

James U. Elkins

James U. Elkins, J.D.
Attorney for Ramon Velas

The Elkins Firm
874 Main Street
Suite 130
Dallas, Texas 75034
jelkins@elkinsfirm.com
214-993-9000

For More Information

Tessa L. Dysart, Leslie H. Southwick & Ruggero J. Aldisert, *Better Briefs and Oral Argument: Winning on Appeal* (3d ed. 2017).

Bryan A. Garner, *The Winning Brief: 100 Tips for Persuasive Briefing in Trial and Appellate Courts* (3d ed. 2014).

Ross Guberman, *Point Made: How to Write Like the Nation's Top Advocates* (2d ed. 2014).

Noah Messing, *The Art of Advocacy: Briefs, Motions, and Writing Strategies of America's Best Lawyers* (2013).

Antonin Scalia & Bryan Garner, *Making Your Case: The Art of Persuading Judges* (2009).

Chapter 46

What Is Standard of Review?

To understand the appellate process, you need to understand the concept of **standard of review.** The standard of review refers to the level of deference the reviewing court must give to the lower court's decision. The level of deference depends on the nature of the legal question on appeal. Although an appellate court decides only questions of law, the questions can relate to the lower court's factual findings or its legal conclusions or both. Depending on the nature and number of issues on appeal, there may be more than one applicable standard of review. Sometimes, different courts in the same jurisdiction disagree about the proper standard to use.

When the claimed error relates to factual findings, the appellate court affords *more* deference to the trial court. This is because the judge or jury was in the best position to evaluate the evidence and determine what happened. When the claimed error relates to legal conclusions, the appellate court affords *less* deference to the trial court. This is because the appellate court is in as good a position as the trial court to apply the law to the facts found below.

The most deferential standard is **"arbitrary and capricious."** Unless the appellate court concludes that the decision of the lower court was arbitrary and capricious, it cannot reverse. This standard is often used for appeals of agency decisions, where the agency's expertise in a particular area of the law is often greater than the court's. A mid-level standard of review is often phrased as **"clearly erroneous"** or **"against the weight of the evidence."** This standard is generally used for claimed error with regard to factual findings. The least deferential standard of review is **de novo**, which translates into "anew." With de novo review, the appellate court gives no deference to the lower court decision. It may substitute its judgment for that of the lower court. This standard is generally for claimed error with regard to conclusions of law.

> **Take Note**
>
> **Typical standards of review:**
>
> - arbitrary and capricious (most deference) → agency decisions
> - clearly erroneous or against the weight of the evidence (mid-level deference) → questions of fact
> - de novo (no deference) → questions of law

It may help to put these standards in context. For example, as in Chapter 20, assume a pedestrian (P) sues a driver (D) for striking her with his car as she crossed the street in front of him at an intersection. D claims the light was green as he entered the intersection, and even if it was not, his brakes failed when he tried to stop to avoid hitting her. Assume the jury found the light was green when D entered the intersection, and the court held D not liable because P improperly entered the intersection.

Questions on Appeal:

Was the light green?

Question of fact, entitled to deference

Was the defendant justified in entering the intersection even if the light was not green?

Question of law, entitled to less deference

P appeals. On appeal, P claims the court erred because the light was red and even if it was not, D should still be liable. The first question—was the light green—was a question of fact for the jury. Since the appellate court did not hear the evidence first-hand, it would grant the lower court decision deference. Unless the jury's finding was clearly erroneous or against the weight of the evidence, the jury's factual finding is likely to be affirmed. The second question—does brake failure relieve a defendant from liability for striking a pedestrian—is a legal question. The appellate court would likely review this question de novo and make its own decision about the law under these circumstances.

The standard of review can affect the parties' arguments. As stated above, if the appeal is based on a factual finding, the appellate court will treat the lower court decision with deference. This makes it harder for the appellant to succeed. In the example above, P will need to convince the appellate court that the evidence clearly pointed in the direction of the light being red or that the finding was against the weight of the evidence. If she cannot do that, she will lose the appeal on that issue. Who benefits when the standard of review is de novo?

The standard of review may be different for different issues in the same appeal. Sometimes, the appropriate standard of review is not clear. For example, different appellate judges from the same level court in the same jurisdiction may have applied a different standard of review for the same type of question on appeal. In that situation, the parties will have to argue for the standard of review they think applies in their case. Where the question on appeal is a mixed question of fact and law, different courts may treat these questions differently.

You will need to research the standard of review just like all other binding authority, but it can be difficult to find. The appellate court often recites the applicable standard of review in its decision, but that portion of the opinion is not always assigned a headnote. In Westlaw, that means it does not get incorporated in the Key Number System. If it is, you may find it under "Courts" or "Appeal and Error." As you research case law relating to the legal issue on appeal in procedural circumstances similar to that of your client, you may be lucky enough to stumble across the applicable standard of review. If there is a headnote or Key Number, use one of these to update the law on the applicable standard of review.

If not, search for cases in the controlling jurisdiction that discuss the standard of review in a similar context. For example, in the Starbucks case, you might select the Fifth Circuit in an online database and search for all cases that discuss standard of review in connection with a motion for judgment under Fed. R. Civ. P. 50: "standard of review" /s "motion for judgment" "Rule 50." This search would yield several cases that state the de novo standard and could easily be updated to find the most recent.

CHAPTER 47

Drafting a Persuasive Statement of the Case

The Statement of the Case combines the procedural history and the relevant facts of your client's situation. It should contain enough background information for the reader to understand the context and the legally significant facts. All facts must include citations to the record so they can be verified. A typical citation to page four of an appellate record would be: R. at 4.[1]

The Statement of the Case is similar to the Statement of Facts in a legal memo, but it should also help the reader (e.g., an opposing party or decision-maker) sympathize with your client and want to respond favorably.[2] To do that, express your client's predicament in the form of a compelling story. Storytelling can capture the audience's interest and imagination, tap into shared experience, and induce empathy.

According to Gary Klein, a psychologist with expertise in decision-making, storytelling helps us make decisions, but its source of power is not reason.[3] We make sense of the external world through patterns, and stories help us organize our internal world: ideas, concepts, objects, and relationships.[4] Jurors, for example, manage the evidence in a complex case by organizing it into a story; they then compare the lawyers' competing stories.[5]

The Statement of the Case is your first opportunity to tell the client's full story in an appellate brief. Once you state the procedural history of the case, tell the story that led to the parties' dispute. To write an effective story, you will need to be familiar with the record and the controlling law. Some lawyers find it easier to write the argument first. Once they have written the argument, they have a better sense of the legally significant facts, how the law applies to them, and, as a result, the parts of the story they need to tell and emphasize. Either way works.

---

1 *See* ALWD GUIDE, *infra* ch. 56, note 1, at R. 25.6(a); BLUEBOOK, *infra* ch. 56, note 1, at R. B17.1.2.

2 *See supra* ch. 44.A.

3 *See* GARY A. KLEIN, SOURCES OF POWER: HOW PEOPLE MAKE DECISIONS 3 (1999).

4 *Id.* at 177.

5 *Id.* at 184.

A. Framing the client's story

Generally speaking, a story is a series of events involving a central character and secondary characters. The central character usually faces some sort of conflict or dilemma that ultimately gets resolved. A good story can be understood in terms of its essential elements: character, conflict, resolution, and plot.

> **FYI**
>
> To **frame your client's story**, consider
>
> - how to cast your client as "hero"
> - what role the other parties play
> - the nature of the client's conflict
> - how to resolve the conflict
> - the storyline or plot

1. Character

Think of your client (not you) as the central character of the story. How can you best characterize your client? As an individual? An accused? Society? A corporation? An agency? The central character of your client's story could even be an inanimate object or an idea, like a piece of valuable property that both parties want to control.[6]

In the Velas matter, we could characterize the Velases in a number of ways: "just a hard-working couple," "regular people," "the victims of defamation," "small business owners," "successful entrepreneurs," "part of a multi-billion dollar corporation," etc. There is no right answer in the face of countless options. Disassociating the Velases, the hard-working couple, from Starbucks, a giant and wealthy corporation, is likely to convey the situation more accurately and induce more sympathy.

When determining the character your clients play in their story, consider the nature of their story as well. Certain stories are embedded deep in our psyche and resonate with all people (e.g., two people meet, fall in love, get married, live happily ever after). These familiar or "stock stories" often feature familiar central characters or hero types. The mythologist Joseph Campbell believed that all cultures develop stories about the same hero types: the warrior, creator, caregiver, every[person], and explorer.[7]

> **FYI**
>
> Who is the central **character** in your client's story?
>
> Consider whether your client plays the role of hero from a stock story:
>
> - warrior
> - creator
> - caregiver
> - every[person]
> - explorer

---

6 *See* Stephen Paskey, *The Law is Made of Stories Erasing the False Dichotomy Between Stories and Legal Rules*, 11 LEGAL COMMC'N & RHETORIC: JALWD 51, 66 (2014).

7 *See, e.g.*, JOSEPH CAMPBELL, THE HERO WITH A THOUSAND FACES, ch. 3 (Robert Walter & David Kudler, eds., 3d ed. 2008).

As Ruth Anne Robbins, a legal storytelling expert explains, these hero types are based on the work of psychologists, such as Carl Jung, and anthropologists, such as Andrew Bastian.[8]

Robbins and other experts recommend that lawyers consider whether these stock stories and hero types provide a starting point for framing your client's story.[9] Although people play many roles in life (e.g., student, teacher, parent, child, friend, etc.), one of those may help you frame a compelling story in the context of your client's legal goals. Being a hero does not mean your client cannot have flaws.[10] Flaws help us relate to heroes and their plight. Although it may be tempting, avoid casting your client's opponent as the villain of the story (you don't really need one). If you do, the opponent may then counter by casting your client in that role, which is almost always impossible to defend. You also run the risk of overstating your case and damaging your credibility. Better to treat the opponent as some sort of obstacle to be overcome.[11]

Assume that when you met with the Velases for the first time, you learned that since they opened their shop in 2003, they have faced a number of setbacks. In 2017, they had to take out a second mortgage on their home to keep the business going. When they decided to sell only organic products, they cancelled their contracts with local bean suppliers. One of those suppliers claimed the Velases owed it damages for improperly cancelling the contract. To avoid an expensive lawsuit, they settled with the supplier. More recently, the Velases discovered that a CSP member owns the supplier they paid to avoid a lawsuit. Although the Velases make every effort to sell locally sourced, organic ingredients, coffee does not grow in Texas and needs to be imported. They switched bean suppliers because they could not get quality organic beans from local suppliers.

Given these facts, what sort of hero might the Velases represent? Warriors? Creators? Caregivers? Ordinary people? Explorers? Given their struggle to keep their business going and dedication to using locally grown, organic ingredients to serve a unique, quality product, are they creators? Or do you identify with them more as a "regular, hard-working couple" who have been harmed for no good reason? Or do you see them as different kinds of heroes? Is there a familiar story in these facts that might resonate like a stock story?

---

8 *See* Robbins, *Harry Potter, Ruby Slippers, and Merlin*, *supra* ch. 34, note 3, at 773; 7 THE COLLECTED WORKS OF C. G. JUNG, ch. VII (Sir Herbert Read, Michael Fordham, & Gerhard Adler, eds. 1966).

9 *See, e.g.*, RUTH ANNE ROBBINS, STEVE JOHANSEN, & KEN CHESTEK, YOUR CLIENT'S STORY: PERSUASIVE LEGAL WRITING 89–90 (2d ed. 2018); Robbins, *Harry Potter, Ruby Slippers, and Merlin*, *supra* ch. 34, note 3, at 802, App. I. The full list of hero types includes the outlaw/destroyer, scholar/sage, magician, ruler, lover, jester/fool, and innocent.

10 ROBBINS, JOHANSEN, & CHESTEK, YOUR CLIENT'S STORY, *supra* note 9, at 92.

11 *See* Robbins, *Harry Potter, Ruby Slippers, and Merlin*, *supra* ch. 34, note 3, at 786–88.

2. Conflict and resolution

FYI

What is the nature of the **conflict**?

- person v. person
- person v. self
- person v. nature
- person v. society
- person v. machine
- something else?

Conflict is what makes a story interesting, suspenseful, and exciting. There are universally recognized types of conflicts too. They include person against person, person against self, person against nature, person against society, and person against machine.[12] Just as stock stories and hero types may help you define your client's role in his or her own story, the nature of the conflict may help you frame the story. The conflict that gives rise to the dispute should bring out, not conflict with, your client's character. Although the nature of the conflict is important, your client's response to the conflict is more important. That's what the reader will care about.[13]

What is the nature of your clients' conflict? CSP seems to have attacked the Velases for no apparent reason. Is the former bean supplier owned by a CSP member responsible for the disparaging newsletter? If so, this dispute could really be about revenge (i.e., person against person). Or is the conflict more akin to person against machine, where CSP is "the machine" working to protect consumers by safeguarding their food supply but without regard to the damage it causes the small business owners? Here, the machine's power is crushing your clients' business. But why wouldn't CSP check with the Velases first?

Once you cast your client as a sympathetic figure in the midst of a troubling conflict, the reader will want to **resolve** the conflict with a happy ending (i.e., work toward or decide in your favor). To do that, you must propose a resolution that is consistent with the story you tell.[14]

3. Plot

FYI

A **plot** usually contains:

- an introduction
- a complicating incident or rising action
- a climax
- a resolution or falling action, and
- a conclusion

Finally, your client's story will need a plot. The plot is the series of events that give rise to the conflict. Where does the story start? Which details matter? How should it end? Fiction writers describe a good plot as containing the following

---

12 *See, e.g.*, Kenneth D. Chestek, *The Plot Thickens: The Appellate Brief as Story*, 14 J. LEG. WRITING 127, 140–41 (2008); Foley & Robbins, *Fiction 101*, *supra* ch. 34, note 2, at 469.

13 Foley & Robbins, *Fiction 101*, *supra* ch. 34, note 2, at 469.

14 *Id.* at 472.

stages: an introduction, a complicating incident or rising action, a climax, a resolution or falling action, and a denouement.[15] Stories often begin in a state of calm. The characters and setting are introduced, and then a conflict arises. Or the story can start at the precise moment the conflict arises (e.g., when the police officers crash through the door without a warrant). The climax is the point at which it all comes together and the reader is anxious to know how the story will end. The resolution answers the question of how the story will end. The denouement is the conclusion of the story.

In the Velas matter, you would first need to decide where the story starts. When the couple opened the shop? When they decided to sell only organic products? When they cancelled their former suppliers' contracts? Or when CSP published its newsletter? As an example, if the story were to start in a state of relative calm, perhaps it could begin with the Velases having found quality organic beans that their customers like and have come to value **(introduction)**. Then, out of the blue (or not), a consumer safety group publishes a newsletter claiming that the beans are not organic as advertised. Their customers start asking questions and stop buying their products **(complicating incident or rising action)**. As the "best before" dates come and go, the Velases must pull coffee beans from the shelves. Soon thereafter, their business is in trouble **(approaching the climax)**. How will the story end? That's the question you want your reader to ask, but you cannot know the answer to that question until the dispute is resolved.

How else might you tell the same story? Put yourself in the role of lawyer for CSP. How would you cast CSP here? What kind of hero is CSP? What is the nature of CSP's conflict? And what series of events would CSP select to write the plot? What is the rising action? And what is the climax of its story?

In terms of the plot, your Statement of the Case contains the introduction and the rising action of the story. The climax and resolution of the story take place in the Argument, when the reader knows the characters, is familiar with the facts that led to the dispute, and is introduced to the controlling law.[16] This is where you use the law to solve the client's problem. As you explain how the law applies, the reader begins to feel less discomfort, knowing there is a fair and just way to resolve the dispute. The conclusion in the brief is the denouement of the story. Here, you explain how the story ends by stating the requested relief from the court. Once that relief is granted, the story ends happily, and peace and order can be restored.[17]

---

15 Chestek, *supra* note 12, at 147.

16 *Id.* at 149.

17 *Id.* at 149–50.

B. Specific techniques for drafting persuasive statements of the case

Lawyers have an ethical duty to represent their clients with reasonable diligence, including zeal in advocacy.[18] As an advocate, you may emphasize favorable facts and deemphasize unfavorable ones in your Statement of the Case, but the facts must be stated accurately, without intentionally misleading the reader or making unreasonable inferences.[19] Facts are often presented in chronological order to avoid confusing the reader, but that's not a hard and fast rule. Some lawyers also advise that you begin and end the story with favorable facts.

1. Characterize facts to your client's advantage

One of the Velases' potential problems is that the product they sell is not locally grown. Yet the brief describes them as "committed to serving and selling quality products, preferably from local sources." And, as the brief points out, "coffee plants simply do not grow in the United States." CSP would likely characterize these facts quite differently. For example, CSP might put it this way: "The appellants sell a product that they do not grow and that cannot be grown in Texas." Both approaches are factually accurate, but the facts are stated from each client's perspective.

2. Make effective and colorful word choices that bring the case to life

The sample brief for the Velases states that they own and operate a "successful Starbucks," that coffee beans should be used within six to eight weeks "for optimum quality," and that their "sales plummeted" after the March newsletter was disseminated to the public. In contrast, CSP might state that the Velases "are inseparable from Starbucks," that coffee beans "neither expire nor spoil," and that "the Velases allege to have incurred losses."

3. Begin and end with favorable facts

The Statement of the Case for your clients begins by introducing the Velases as small business owners who own and operate a successful Starbucks. The statement ends with their having incurred damages of at least $100,000 in lost sales, good will, and other consequential damages. CSP would undoubtedly begin and end its story differently. For example, it might begin by stating that the public relies on organizations like CSP to ensure the safety of the food supply. It might end with the

---

18 MODEL RULES, *supra* ch. 44, note 25, at r. 1.3.

19 *See id.* at r. 3.1.

fact that the Velases sell a product they claim is organic, but isn't. How else might the Velases or CSP begin and end their stories?

4. Sandwich unfavorable facts between favorable facts

Notice that in the Velases' brief, the fact that they do not grow the beans, which are actually grown outside of Texas, is sandwiched between the fact that they are committed to selling local organic produce and that the beans they import are not only organic but also better than what they could buy locally. CSP might want to "sandwich" the fact that it did not reach out to the Velases before publishing its newsletter or that one of its members owns one of the local companies that used to supply the Velases' beans. What other facts might it need to de-emphasize?

Chapter 48

Making a Persuasive Argument[1]

As you craft your client's arguments, there are a number of considerations that will significantly increase their persuasiveness. This chapter discusses the concept of "theory of the case," how to organize your argument on the large and small scale, framing the law from your client's perspective, how to minimize counterarguments, and how to make your brief visually appealing. These techniques will enhance your appeals to *logos*, *pathos*, and *ethos*.

A. Theory of the case

> **Take Note**
>
> The theory of the case captures the essence of the reasons why your client should prevail.

Although they might have a slightly different phrase for this concept, most lawyers are familiar with the need to develop a theory of the case. The **theory of the case** succinctly conveys the ultimate reason why the client should prevail in any context. Having a theory of the case means being able to complete the following sentence: "My client should win because . . ." All arguments, both oral and written, that support the client's position should be consistent with this theory. Typically, your theory will incorporate some or all three modes of appeal and may consider policy implications as well. When you start to feel lost or confused about whether you are arguing in the right direction, go back to your overarching theory of the case to keep you on course.

Your theory should inform all sections of the brief—the statement of the case, summary of the argument, headings, and argument—in terms of the images and emotion each section invokes. In combination with framing the facts and the law from your client's perspective, effective word choice primes the reader to respond more favorably to your arguments. As Kathy Stanchi explains:

> The early sections of a brief . . . can work as primes for the case as a whole. These sections can prime the reader to see the case in a particular way

1 This advice also applies to drafting other types of briefs.

> by pushing the the[ory] of the case and evoking particular emotions in the reader.[2]

A coherent theory will help the reader remember your client's story and even fill in any missing or ambiguous information consistent with the theory.[3]

The well-known case of *Clinton v. Jones*, 520 U.S. 681 (1997), provides a good example of two effective but competing theories of the same case. Paula Jones, a former Arkansas state employee, sued then-sitting President Clinton. She claimed that he had made sexual advances toward her while he was Governor of the State of Arkansas and that she was punished by her supervisors for rejecting him. Clinton claimed he was "immune from suit" while acting as President. Although the district court held that the trial could not go forward while Clinton was still in office, it held that discovery could proceed. 869 F. Supp. 690 (E.D. Ark. 1994).

Both parties appealed, and the United States Court of Appeals for the Eighth Circuit reversed. 72 F.3d 1354 (8th Cir. 1996). Clinton appealed to the United States Supreme Court. The parties' competing theories of the case were effectively woven throughout their written arguments. The Supreme Court ruled that President Clinton was not immune from suit for unofficial actions and that forcing him to defend himself while in office did not violate separation-of-powers principles. 520 U.S. at 695, 703.

Clinton's and Jones' theories were in direct opposition. Clinton's goal was to postpone the trial. He argued he was too busy to take time away from the presidency to defend his case. He also argued that it would be an unconstitutional violation of the separation of powers for the judiciary to tell the Chief Executive what to do. In sum, his theory was that he was immune from suit because the Presidency is a special office, and presidents should not be bothered with defending against civil suits while in office.[4]

Jones, on the other hand, said the President should not be permitted to use his official position to avoid trial when sued as a private citizen for sexual harassment. She argued that as a practical matter, Clinton would have no trouble carrying out the duties of his office and defending himself at the same time. In sum, her theory was that the trial should go forward because the president is no different from anyone else. Requiring him to answer for his actions did not interfere with his presidential duties in any way.[5]

---

2 *See, e.g.*, Kathryn M. Stanchi, *The Power of Priming in Legal Advocacy: Using the Science of First Impressions to Persuade the Reader*, 89 OR. L. REV. 305, 310 (2010).

3 *Id.* at 313.

4 *See* Brief of Petitioner, *Clinton v. Jones*, No. 95–1853, 520 U.S. 681 (1997) [hereinafter *Clinton v. Jones*].

5 *See* Brief of Respondent, *Clinton v. Jones.*

What images do these theories evoke? Which one do you find more convincing? Why?

In the Velas matter, your clients are seeking damages caused by CSP's statements about the nature of their coffee beans. As you know, the Velases may have trouble convincing a court that they are "producers" of a food product that perishes or decays quickly enough to warrant protection under the statute, particularly since they import the beans already roasted. Given this context, why should the Velases prevail in this matter? Is it their unique relationship with Starbucks that makes recovery emotionally appealing here? Or is it the service they provide their customers? What policy arguments support their interpretation of the Texas statute?

To craft a persuasive theory of the case, you will need to be thoroughly familiar with the facts and the controlling law and have made decisions—even if tentative—about the central character in your client's story, what role the client plays, and the nature of the conflict.[6] Assume you've decided to cast your clients as the central character in their story. They play the role of ordinary, hard-working people (everypersons) who have struggled with great success to keep a small business afloat amidst repeated setbacks. Since you cannot prove the newsletter was instigated by the former bean supplier, you decide to frame the conflict as person against machine, with CSP as the machine crushing the Velases' business. As an example, you might then adopt the following theory:

> The Velases should prevail because they are hard-working, small business owners who provide a valuable product and community service that should not be jeopardized by reckless and potentially dangerous consumer groups like CSP.

What image does this evoke? Is it persuasive? What other theories can you think of? What might CSP's theory of the case be?

B. Large-scale organization

Planning the organization of the Argument is similar to planning the Discussion in a memo, but here, your decisions should be strategic as well as intentional. To organize persuasively, consider the following:

Practice Pointer

To organize your argument on the large scale, consider

- the nature of the legal issues
- your theory of the case
- the standard of review

6 *See supra* ch. 47.A.

1. The nature of the legal issues

As explained in Chapter 38 (see p. 263), first consider the nature of the legal issues: How many **discrete** issues are there? Each discrete issue should be argued as a separate point with its own **major point heading** (e.g., two different theories of recovery based on the same set of facts, labeled as I., II., III., etc.).[7] If the issues are really sub-issues of the same discrete issue, they belong together under the same point but with their own **minor point headings** (e.g., the elements of the false disparagement statute, labeled as A., B., C., etc.).[8]

Also consider whether any of the issues is dispositive. A **dispositive issue**, also called a **threshold issue**, is one that has the potential to dispose of the case and eliminate the need to resolve the remaining issues. If you have two or more issues to discuss, one of which is dispositive, argue the dispositive issue first.[9] If the court agrees with you, it will not need to address the rest of the issues in its decision. Since courts are interested in acting efficiently, this choice serves the court's interest as well as your client's.

If the issues or sub-issues are on the same level (e.g., two different causes of action, the elements of the same cause of action, or the factors in a totality of the circumstances test),[10] you have several options. First, it might make sense to **argue them in the same order the court does** in its decisions. Sometimes, arguing the issues in a different order just to be creative doesn't make sense. The advantage to following the standard order is that the court will be familiar with it and may infer nothing about the strength of the arguments based on their order.

Alternatively, you might decide to order these issues from **strongest to weakest** or from **strongest to strong and then stronger**, ending on a relatively high note. When given the option, avoid arguing the weakest argument first.[11] Also consider whether issues on the same level can be **re-ordered**, **separated**, or **combined** to your client's advantage. For example, assume a court uses a variety of factors to determine whether a defendant acted reasonably under the circumstances, including the defendant's age, level of education, and experience. Where the argument on each factor is strong, you might choose to argue each factor separately, in order from strongest to weakest (or with weaker factors sandwiched in between). However, if the arguments on some of the factors are weak, you might argue them together under one heading (e.g., the defendant's "personal characteristics") to deemphasize the weakness of the individual arguments.

---

7 *See supra* ch. 38.A, at 263.

8 *See id.* at 264.

9 *See id.*

10 *See id.*

11 *See id.*

Finally, before you write, think about **proportionality**. Which issues deserve the most attention given their complexity or importance? Note that your reader will assume that you have devoted the most space to the issues that are most complicated or in dispute. Where the law is straightforward or the argument is strong, do not linger. Save precious space for the client's most difficult and important arguments. Then use your sense of proportionality to work backwards. For example, assume you have 3,000 words for your argument on four issues, but the first issue is the most critical and complicated. You might plan in advance to give yourself 1,500 words for the first issue and then split the remaining 1,500 words three ways.

In the sample brief for the Velases, their argument is separated into two discrete but related issues: whether the coffee beans are a perishable food product and whether the Velases are producers for purposes of the Texas statute. The perishable food product issue is further divided into two sub-issues: whether coffee beans are a food product and whether they perish or decay beyond marketability in a limited period of time. How else could the issues have been organized? How might CSP organize its brief?

2. Your theory of the case

Does your theory of the case suggest how to approach the brief? In the Velas appeal, the working theory is that they should prevail because the Velases' business provides a valuable product and community service that should not be jeopardized by consumer groups like CSP. It makes sense, then, to emphasize the Velas' efforts to provide a product the community values and the extent to which CSP has threatened their business. Notice, for example, the writer's description of the Velases as being "[a]ttuned to their community's interests and demands" and "committed to serving and selling quality products." The Statement of the Case ends with the prospect of them "losing their business." The Argument is consistent with the theory as well, emphasizing the need to extend the protection of the statute to the Velases.

3. The standard of review

In some cases, the standard of review may affect how you organize or frame your argument. Where the standard of review is actually in dispute, you may need a separate argument on whether the court owes the lower court deference. This argument should likely come first.

Where the standard of review is de novo, as in the Velas appeal, the appellate court owes no deference to the lower court in making its decision.[12] A de novo standard arguably benefits neither party because both are similarly situated, but the appellant can emphasize the appellate court's power to substitute its own judgment

12 *See supra* ch. 46, at 337.

for that of the lower court. Where the appellate court does owe deference to the lower court (e.g., the standard of review is clearly erroneous or against the weight of the evidence), the appellee has an advantage because the appellate court can only reverse under limited circumstances.

A case may involve two issues on an equal level but with a different standard of review (e.g., the appeal of a factual finding and a ruling of law). In that case, it may make sense to argue the issue with the more desirable standard of review first. In other words, the appellant might argue the issue of law first (with the desirable de novo standard) and the issue of fact second (with the less desirable standard).

C. Using point headings and roadmaps effectively

1. Headings

Point headings serve two purposes: they outline your argument for the reader and provide a summary of each individual argument at a glance. Your reader should be able to glean the thrust of your argument on each issue just by reading the headings in the table of contents of your brief. Unless instructed otherwise, resist the temptation to let your headings substitute for topic sentences in the text of your argument to follow. If the reader skips the heading, the point of your argument may be lost.

In general, you can use the word "Argument" or a heading tailored to your client's argument to indicate the beginning of the argument section in the brief (see suggested format below). Then, create a **major point heading** for each discrete issue you argue. These are usually numbered using Roman numerals (e.g., I., II., III.). They should do more than identify the legal issue: they should state your legal conclusion on each issue from the client's perspective.

The format of the major point headings will vary based on the custom and nature of your practice area. In the sample brief in the Velas appeal, major headings are capitalized according to *ALWD Guide* Rule 3 and *Bluebook* Rule 8: all words in the major point headings are capitalized except for articles and prepositions of less than five letters.[13]

Where a discrete issue is comprised of several sub-issues, indicate the sub-issues using **minor point headings** (e.g., A., B., C., etc.). As demonstrated in the sample brief, the minor point headings provide some factual detail and the gist of your reasoning on each issue. Try to include the word "since" or "because" in the minor point headings. This will remind you to articulate the reasoning for your conclusion on that sub-issue. Again, the formatting depends on the situation. Various options

---

13 ALWD GUIDE, *infra* ch. 56, at note 1, at R. 3.2(a); BLUEBOOK *infra* ch. 56, note 1, at R. 8(a).

include capitalizing only the first word and underlining or italicizing them, although underlining interferes with the letters and makes the heading harder to read.[14] In the sample brief and the suggested format (below), only the first word of the minor point headings is capitalized, and the subheadings are italicized. Italics slow down the reader as well but not as much as underlining.[15]

Regardless of the format you use, the minor point headings should be formatted differently than the major headings. This helps the reader keep track of where they are in the argument and how the section fits within the argument as a whole. If necessary, you can further divide minor point headings into **subheadings** (usually numbered 1., 2., 3., etc.). In the suggested format, they are italicized to distinguish them from the minor headings.

Suggested format:

Argument

[roadmap here that previews the two discrete issues on appeal]

I. First Major Heading (follow *ALWD Guide* Rule 3/*Bluebook* Rule 8 for capitalization)

[mini-roadmap here that previews the controlling rules of law and the two sub-issues]

A. First minor heading (capitalize first word only)

B. Second minor heading

II. Second Major Heading

[mini-roadmap here that previews the controlling rules of law and the three sub-issues]

A. First minor heading

B. Second minor heading

[may need a mini-mini-roadmap here]

1. *First subheading*

2. *Second subheading*

C. Third minor heading

14 *See infra* ch. 48.G, at 366.

15 *See id.*

2. Roadmaps

As indicated above,[16] your headings should make each point of your argument clear, but your reader will not always understand the reason you've subdivided the argument in the way you have or the transition from one argument to the next. Thus, each time you subdivide your argument, it may help to explain why. You can do that by including a **roadmap** or **umbrella** paragraph or two (whatever you need) before each new subdivision.

Where a sub-issue is further divided into minor headings, it helps to include a **mini-roadmap** or **mini-umbrella** paragraph directly after the major point heading to introduce the sub-issues under that heading (e.g., between I. and A. and between II. and A. in the suggested format for headings on page 355). Whether to use mini-roadmaps or umbrellas at lower levels of division (e.g., between a minor point heading and subheadings) is up to you. At this level of subdivision, you may feel you are spending too much time on roadmap paragraphs that make your argument feel repetitive and cumbersome. If you find that dividing the argument at the subheading level is more trouble than it's worth, you have at least two options: one is to introduce the points in the subheadings in the roadmap for the minor heading (e.g., between A. and 1., 2., 3., etc.). Another option is to dispense with the subheadings altogether and separately argue each point under A.

D. Small-scale organization

As with predictive writing, the argument on each issue in a brief typically follows the analytical paradigm by proceeding deductively: rule→ application→ conclusion (review small-scale organization in a legal memo, Chapter 38.B, pp. 266–268).

One major difference between memos and briefs is the framing of the issue and rules. Instead of identifying or predicting the outcome of each new issue, briefs argue the conclusion from the outset. Each new issue is thus introduced with a topic sentence that makes the party's affirmative argument on that issue **(conclusion)**. Then, the legal rule is framed from the client's perspective as opposed to a neutral one **(major premise)**. The legal rule is then explained, the writer explains how the rule should be applied in that case using analogical or other reasoning **(the minor premise)**, anticipates and rebuts any problematic counterarguments the opposing party is likely to make, and **re-concludes** on that issue.

In the sample Velas brief, the topic sentences that introduce each of the three issues state conclusions on that particular issue:

---

16 *See supra* at 355.

- Coffee beans are food products under the Texas statute, which protects agricultural producers.

  v. the topic sentence in the memorandum:

  The Velases can likely prove only that their coffee beans are "perishable food products."

- The coffee beans the Velases sell and use to make coffee beverages perish or decay beyond marketability within a limited period of time.

  v. the topic sentence in the memorandum:

  The beans must also "perish or decay" beyond marketability within a limited period of time.

- Finally, either the Velases or Starbucks must be a producer of the perishable food product to recover under the statute.

  v. the topic sentence in the memorandum:

  Finally, the Velases are "producer[s] of a perishable food product" and entitled to relief.

FYI

Small-Scale Organization (CREAC)*

As you develop your persuasive writing skills, practice using this process to organize your arguments on individual issues:

- Begin with a **topic sentence** that makes the party's affirmative argument on the issue (headings do not substitute for these) **(C)**
- Then state the general legal requirement or rule (usually accompanied by a **synthesized rule** that explains what the rule means or how it has been interpreted) from the client's perspective and include citation to authority **[major premise] (R)**
- **Explain** how the rule has been applied in a similar case, including key facts, holding, and court's reasoning to set up analogical reasoning **(E)**
- **Apply the rule** to the client's facts, analogizing if possible to cases to compare to or distinguish **[minor premise] (A)**
- Anticipate and refute potentially legitimate **counterarguments**
- Re-state the argument on that issue **[conclusion] (C)**

***Note:** Your professor may use a different acronym, but they are all designed to teach you the same process.

Each topic sentence is then followed by a synthesized rule framed from the client's perspective; an explanation of the rule, including the facts and holdings of cited case law; the application of the rule to the facts of the case, including analogical or other reasoning (where possible) to relevant case law; the rebuttal of potential valid counterarguments, and a conclusion on that issue.

E. Framing the law from your client's perspective

Even in framing rules of law, you can help put your audience in the right frame of mind. By stating rules of law and the policies behind them from your client's point of view, you can prime your audience to be more open to your argument. As Stanchi explains, "Priming can also be used to introduce rules or other legal material as a way of coloring the reader's perception of the meaning of those rules."[17]

To demonstrate, the Fourth Amendment to the United States Constitution prohibits unreasonable searches and seizures.[18] From the defendant's perspective in a criminal case, the Fourth Amendment *prohibits* police from searching their home unless they have a warrant issued by a judge based on probable cause that specifies with particularity the items to be seized. But from the prosecution's perspective, the Fourth Amendment *entitles* the police to search a home as long as they have probable cause to believe a crime has been committed, the items they seek are likely to be in the home, and a judge has issued a proper warrant.

It takes practice seeing the law from both sides, so don't be discouraged at first. You will need to have conducted thorough research and gained a full understanding of the law to do it well. Knowing how to frame the law from your client's perspective will help you tell your client's story, select the best cases to rely on in support of your legal rules, and make favorable analogies. Although you cannot distort or misrepresent rules of law,[19] you can state them in such a way as to make your client's position more favorable. Word choice is particularly important.

How might you frame the overall goals of the Texas false disparagement statute from Starbucks' perspective? Recall that the Texas statute does not explicitly limit "producers" to those who actually grow the perishable products. From the Velases' perspective then, the false disparagement statute prohibits a person from making false statements about the safety of a single, perishable food product of agriculture and holds that person liable to the seller of that product. How would CSP characterize the law?

A legal memorandum often serves as a starting point for litigation. The memo or another form of predictive writing can serve as a starting point for framing legal rules from the client's perspective. To give you an idea of how to rewrite legal rules from your client's perspective, read the chart below. Each neutral rule of law is rewritten from the Velases' point of view. This is where the art of advocacy truly comes into play. There are always many options. This is just one example. The reframed rule primes the reader for the argument to follow.

---

17 *See* Stanchi, *supra* ch. 48.A, note 2, at 311.

18 "The right of the people to be secure in their persons, houses, papers, and effects, against unreasonable searches and seizures, shall not be violated, and no Warrants shall issue, but upon probable cause, supported by Oath or affirmation, and particularly describing the place to be searched, and the persons or things to be seized." U.S. CONST. amend. IV.

19 Lawyers have an ethical obligation to state the law accurately. MODEL RULES, *supra* ch. 44, note 25, at r. 3.3.

Element of the Texas statute	**Neutral rule**	**Rule from the Velases' perspective**
First dissemination to the public	"Public" refers generally to a large enough audience to constitute the public in the plain meaning of that word, and dissemination to more than 100 people is likely large enough to constitute the public.	An audience of at least 100 people constitutes the "public" as that word is commonly understood.
food product	The statute does not define food product, but "food" is generally understood to mean a nutritious substance ingested in solid or liquid form to maintain health and life.	A food product is a nutritious substance ingested in liquid or solid form to maintain health and life.
perishable food product	The statute does not define "limited period of time," but since the statute is intended to protect sellers of meat, fish, and produce, it likely refers to days or weeks as opposed to several months.	A limited period of time is that period when an agricultural product becomes unsalable before false statements can be exposed to the public.
producer	Unlike other states, Texas does not limit the definition of producer to those who actually grow the crops.	Sellers of agricultural or aquacultural food products are producers, whether or not they have grown the products themselves.
Second	Reckless indifference or disregard for truth occurs when the defendant made his statements with a "high degree of awareness of their probable falsity."	Where a defendant makes a statement with actual knowledge or a "high degree of awareness of its probable falsity," the defendant knows the information is false.
Third	To state or imply that a perishable food product is unsafe, the defendant must indicate that the product is inherently dangerous in some way.	A defendant states or implies a food product is unsafe for consumption by the public when it suggests that a product is inherently dangerous.

What do you think about the reframed rules? Are they reasonable? Do any of them go too far? If so, why? Using the same neutral rules of law, try to frame them from CSP's perspective. Which rules seem more convincing?

F. Minimizing counterarguments

To persuade your audience, you will need to anticipate and explicitly rebut strong arguments the opposing party is likely to make for which you have an effective rebuttal.[20] Under these circumstances, it is best to "volunteer negative information and rebut it early," rather than give it "indirect and cursory treatment."[21] The goal is to persuade the decision-maker that you have already taken these arguments into account and demonstrate that they do not present a problem for your client's position.

> **Practice Pointer**
>
> **When and where to address counterarguments:**
>
> - Address only those that
>   - present a significant risk to your client's position
>   - you can be relatively sure the opposing party will raise, and
>   - you can effectively rebut.
> - In general, sandwich counterarguments between stronger arguments or between your arguments and your rebuttal of the counterargument on a particular issue.
> - Where the counterargument is central to the issue, raise it early and address it directly.

As discussed in Chapter 38, most counterarguments will take issue with your **characterization of the facts** or **the binding law.**[22] In brief writing, you can minimize these arguments either by directly refuting them or by exposing their implications for future cases. For example, in the Velas appeal, the argument is that the Velases are producers of coffee beans, which qualify as a perishable food product under the Texas statute. We can anticipate CSP arguing, among other things, that 1) the Velases are not producers because they resell beans grown outside of Texas, 2) coffee is not "food" in the traditional sense, and 3) when it is ingested, coffee is combined with other products and thus disqualifies under *Pet Barn* (see page 199).

In the sample brief, the writer argues that the statute is not limited to those who grow the product (even though this has been suggested in only one case in dicta) and that to exclude the Velases would be to set a precedent that the statute protects only those sellers of produce that can be grown in Texas. As for coffee being food, the sample brief anticipates the argument that coffee is not food by defining food as something ingested with nutritional value and arguing that coffee fits that definition. As for the third argument above, the writer of the sample brief chose not to address it. Because the Velases are arguing only that their sales of beans are protected, an

---

20 *See* Kathryn M. Stanchi, *Playing With Fire: The Science of Confronting Adverse Material in Legal Advocacy*, 60 RUTGERS L. REV. 381, 429 (2008) (suggesting it may not be effective to raise counterarguments that the opposing party does not raise or for which you have no good response).

21 *Id.* at 383.

22 *See supra* ch. 38, at 269.

argument based on the beans as prepared beverages is not strictly relevant and thus not necessarily worth rebutting.

Although you have an ethical duty to disclose adverse authority to the court, not all cases with unfavorable outcomes qualify as adverse authority and need be raised. Instead, they may stand for the same proposition of law but be distinguishable (i.e., the factual or situational differences are greater than the similarities) (see Chapter 32, p. 220). If distinguishable, these cases are not binding in your client's case. Where a case with an unfavorable outcome is arguably analogous and potentially binding, you should expect the opposing party to rely on it. In that case, it is wise to anticipate the counterargument the opposing party will make and explain to the court why that argument is not persuasive.[23]

There can be a fine line between needing to anticipate credible counterarguments and not wanting to make opposing parties' arguments for them. For that reason, choose the counterarguments you raise carefully: address only those you think present significant problems for your client. If the opposing party raises a counterargument you did not think of or chose not to address, you will likely have at least one opportunity to respond to it in writing (usually in the form of a reply brief).

Most lawyers agree it is best to sandwich counterarguments between your arguments and your rebuttal so as to de-emphasize them.[24] Ross Guberman recommends minimizing some counterarguments by putting them in footnotes.[25] But where the counterargument is particularly strong, you may want to address it earlier and head-on so the reader is not "unpleasantly surprised when they happen upon the information after already having been convinced by the primary argument."[26] Your reader may feel you have misled them, which can harm your credibility as well.

Stacy Rogers Sharp, an adjunct professor at the University of Texas School of Law, studied the Supreme Court's 5–4 opinions from the 2011–2012 Term for the ways in which the Justices handle counterarguments.[27] Based on her study, here are some of the techniques she describes for minimizing counterarguments:

---

23 For an article about gauging the strength of a potential counterargument, see Lisa T. McElroy & Christine N. Coughlin, *The Other Side of the Story: Using Graphic Organizers to Counter the Counter-Analysis Quandary*, 39 U. BALT. L. REV. 227, 230 (2010).

24 *See, e.g.*, WILLIAM H. PUTMAN, LEGAL ANALYSIS AND WRITING 362 (3d ed. 2009) ("When interpreting and applying a rule of law, always introduce your arguments first, address the counterarguments, then present your response."); Stacy Rogers Sharp, *Crafting Responses to Counterargument: Learning from the Swing-Vote Cases*, 10 LEGAL COMMC'N & RHETORIC: JALWD 201, 217 (2013) ("Explicit rebuttal of counterarguments should be buried in the middle, where they will receive less attention and so that the writer can make both a strong first impression and conclude with its best, offensive points.").

25 ROSS GUBERMAN, POINT MADE: HOW TO WRITE LIKE THE NATION'S TOP ADVOCATES 184 (2d ed. 2014).

26 Sharp, *supra* note 24, at 205.

27 *See generally* Sharp, *supra* note 24.

1. Recharacterize or "label" the counterargument to minimize its impact.

Practice Pointer

Just a few techniques for minimizing counterarguments:*

- re-characterize or label the counterargument to minimize its size, weight, or character
- recast the counterargument as a metaphor to expose its weakness
- announce the gist of the counterargument and then reject it
- Describe the counterargument using a critical adjective

*Adapted from Stacy Sharp's *Crafting Responses to Counterargument: Learning from the Swing Vote Cases*, note 24.

As Sharp explains, a counterargument can be minimized by recharacterizing or labelling it "so that the reader views it in a negative light before the rebuttal has even begun."[28] Recharacterizing the counterargument can minimize its size, weight, or character and prepare the reader for your rebuttal.[29] Sharp points out that counterarguments can be recharacterized concisely by using a critical adjective to describe them before giving your response.[30]

For example, CSP might argue that reading the Texas statute broadly so as to include the Velases as producers would unduly expand liability and impermissibly infringe on the critical First Amendment freedoms of entities like CSP. You might minimize this argument by labeling it as an unfounded concern without any basis in fact. Or you might argue that CSP's position favors false statements over protecting business owners in Texas. To use the concise method, you might describe the counterargument as CSP's "short-sighted attempt" to limit liability. How else might you re-characterize CSP's argument?

2. Recast the counterargument in the form of a metaphor.

Another way to minimize counterarguments is to recast them as a metaphor, which can be powerful because metaphors resonate subconsciously and are often memorable.[31] For example, you could describe CSP's concern about expanding liability under the statute as the fear of opening the floodgates of litigation without any basis for that fear. The "floodgates" argument is so overused that just referring to CSP's argument this way might diminish it. Or, you might characterize CSP's argument that coffee is not food as an attempt to cabin the court's ability to protect producers operating in Texas.

---

28 *Id.* at 206.

29 *Id.* at 209.

30 *Id.* at 208.

31 *See id.* at 209–10.

3. "Announce the rebuttal."

A particularly effective way to minimize counterarguments is to describe the counterargument first and then start a new sentence that signals the rebuttal is coming or summarizes its rejection.[32] As Sharp explains, the announcement sentence can begin with "but" or a phrase, such as "this concern is unfounded," or "the analogy is inapt."[33] The tone change is particularly powerful[34] and should likely be used sparingly. To demonstrate this technique, in response to CSP's floodgates argument, you might write: "CSP has expressed its concern that compensating the Velases in this case will open the floodgates of litigation. This concern is unfounded."

G. Designing the document for visual appeal

Last, but not least, don't forget to consider the visual impact of your argument. Imagine this scene: A judge sits down at her desk with her morning coffee. She didn't sleep well last night, and she has three sets of briefs to get through before her oral arguments begin at 1:00 p.m. that afternoon. She is still at home, reading on her laptop, not the big screen on her desk in chambers. She opens up the first brief to the Table of Contents and sees this:

TABLE OF CONTENTS

TABLE OF AUTHORITIES...iii
JURISDICTIONAL STATEMENT.. 1
STATEMENT OF THE ISSUE PRESENTED FOR REVIEW..........................1
STATEMENT OF THE CASE.. 1
SUMMARY OF ARGUMENT.. 2
STADARD OF REVIEW 3
ARGUMET 3
I. COFFEE BEANS ARE A PERISHABLE FOOD PRODUCT UNDER THE TEXAS FALSE DISPARAGEMENT STATUTE ENTITLING THE VELASES TO RELIEF... 4
A. BECAUSE INGESTING COFFEE HELPS MAINTAIN LIFE AND HEALTH, COFFEE BEANS ARE FOOD PRODUCTS OF AGRICULTURE UNDER TEXAS LAW...4
B. BECAUSE COFFEE BEANS CANNOT BE SOLD AFTER SIX TO EIGHT WEEKS, THEY PERISH OR DECAY BEYOND MARKETABILITY IN A LIMITED PERIOD OF TIME............................ 5
II. THE VELASES ARE PRODUCER S OF COFFEE BEANS UNDER TEXAS LAW AND ENTITLED TO RECOVER AGAINST CSP................................ 6
CONCLUSION...7

ii

[32] *See id.* at 213.

[33] *Id.* at 216.

[34] *Id.*

How likely is the judge to want to read this brief? Why? Putting aside the content of the text, what all do you see and what do you want to change? How could you make this easier to read? What assumptions will the judge make based on just the appearance of this page?

Although exaggerated for effect, this example makes the point. A picture is worth a thousand words, and the appearance of your brief matters. It matters because your reader will be affected by the look of the document. Visual effects can "set a persuasive and positive mood for the document itself: a form of *pathos* or emotional appeal."[35] In addition, a document that is difficult to read will be difficult to remember.[36] If you make the brief visually appealing, you will not only help put your audience in the right frame of mind, you can help them better understand and remember your arguments.

In some cases, the ability to design your document will be affected by a court's specific filing requirements, such as font type and size, how lines should be spaced, margin size, and word or character limits. These are easily found in the court's procedural and local rules (be sure to check both).[37] But where you have the freedom to choose, consider the following factors to maximize visual appeal and readability:

1. Font type and size

Some fonts are silly. Some fonts feel casual. SOME FONTS ARE HARD TO READ. And some are just right.

In order to choose the best font for your document, consider whether to use a serif or sans serif font and whether that font is monospaced or proportionally spaced.[38] **Serif fonts** have small decorative lines attached to the end of the letters. This book is in a serif font called Adobe Garamond Pro: you can see the lines clearly at the end of "T," "k," and "l." **Sans serif** fonts do not have the decorative lines: this sentence is in a sans serif font called Calibri. Which do you find easier to read?

Serif fonts are used in newspapers and books. Because they are more traditional, they create the impression of being serious and trustworthy. Sans serif fonts are simpler and cleaner, which creates the impression of being more modern and accessible. Sans serif fonts used to be considered best for digital text, but with improvements

---

35 Ruth Anne Robbins, *Painting with Print: Incorporating Concepts of Typographic and Layout Design into the Text of Legal Writing Documents*, 2 LEGAL COMMC'N & RHETORIC (formerly J. ALWD) 108, 110 (2004).

36 *See id.* at 111.

37 *See, e.g.*, Fed. R. App. P. 32 & 5th Cir. R. 32.1, http://www.ca5.uscourts.gov/docs/default-source/forms-and-documents---clerks-office/rules/federalrulesofappellateprocedure (https://perma.cc/XN4Z-JCFN); D.C. Ct. App. R. 32(a), https://www.dccourts.gov/sites/default/files/2017-07/DCCA%20Rules%20Complete%2011-30-2016_1.pdf (https://perma.cc/79AQ-538R).

38 *See* Robbins, *supra* note 35, at 119–21.

in screen resolution on digital devices, both types of fonts can be used in print and in digital formats.[39]

Fonts have different widths and point sizes as well. Each letter in a monospaced font is the same width, whereas the letters in proportionally spaced fonts have different widths. Proportionally spaced fonts are easier to read.[40] When you use a font in 12-point, the 12 refers to a measurement based on the height of that font. So different fonts in the same point will not necessarily be the same size. As a general rule, choose a point size between 11 and 13 for text and save 14-point or larger sizes for headings.[41] As indicated above, court rules may differ from the experts' advice. For example, the federal rules of appellate procedure permit the use of proportionally spaced or monospaced fonts, but if a proportionally spaced font is used, it must have serifs and be in 14-point.[42]

The chart below identifies these key characteristics of fonts commonly available on computers. They are all in 12-point font. Notice the difference in size and feel:

Serif/proportionally spaced fonts	**Sans serif/proportionally spaced fonts**
Cambria	Arial
Century Schoolbook	Calibri
Courier New	Geneva
Garamond	Gill Sans
Georgia	Helvetica
Palatino Linotype	Lucida Sans
Perpetua	Tahoma
Times New Roman	Verdana

Typography expert Matthew Butterick advises lawyers to choose fonts for print documents carefully. He strongly discourages using the common serif font, Times New Roman, and sans serif font, Arial, in part because they are overused.[43] Times New Roman can be difficult to read because it is designed to fit more text per line,

39 *See, e.g., id.* at 127; *Web Design Debate: Do I Really Need to Use Sans Serif Fonts?*, https://designshack.net/articles/typography/web-design-debate-do-i-really-need-to-use-sans-serif-fonts/ (https://perma.cc/QRJ5-K5D5).

40 Robbins, *supra* note 35, at 121; Kathleen Dillon Narko, *How Do I Look? Design Your Documents for Greater Legibility and Persuasion*, 33-DEC CBA Rec. 38, 38 (2019).

41 Robbins, *supra* note 35, at 122.

42 Fed. R. App. P. 32(a)(5)(A).

43 *See* MATTHEW BUTTERICK, TYPOGRAPHY FOR LAWYERS: ESSENTIAL TOOLS FOR POLISHED & PERSUASIVE DOCUMENTS 84 (2010); Narko, *supra* note 40, at 38.

and Arial, he claims, is a sloppy substitute for the more refined Helvetica.[44] He recommends using a professional font, but there are plenty of good, free choices available.

2. White space and margins

Graphics designers generally adhere to a fifty percent rule, meaning that the text of your document should take up no more than half the page.[45] The white space is pleasing, it emphasizes the text, and it gives the reader's eyes a rest.[46] To increase white space, use margins that are slightly wider than one inch on both sides.

3. Format of headings

The format of your headings is critical. As the sample above illustrates, the use of capital letters, especially all together in a Table of Contents, is not very pleasing. Strung together in a sentence, capital letters may make you feel like the writer is shouting at you. John Irving used this technique each time one of the main characters spoke in *A Prayer for Owen Meany.* Owen was a very small child and had something wrong with his vocal chords. To be heard, he had to shout through his nose in a "strangled, emphatic falsetto."[47] To denote the shouting, Irving used all capital letters every time Owen spoke.[48] Capital letters should also be avoided because they are hard to read.[49]

Instead, or in addition to some variation in capitalization, you can use font size, boldface, and italics to highlight headings and indicate to readers where each point fits within the overall argument. For example, in a document where the text is in 12-point, the major point headings might be 14 point, minor point headings might be 13-point, and the subheadings in 12-point and italicized. You can use underlining in headings, but it interferes with the bottom-half of some letters, making the text harder to read, and tends to look old-fashioned. Finally, you can even use one typeface for headings (e.g., a sans serif font) and a different one for text (a serif font).[50] The contrast will make the headings stand out as well.

---

44 BUTTERICK, *supra* note 43, at 84, 110.

45 *See, e.g.*, Narko, *supra* note 40, at 38; Robbins, *supra* note 35, at 124.

46 *See* Narko, *supra* note 40, at 38–39; Robbins, *supra* note 35, at 124.

47 JOHN IRVING, A PRAYER FOR OWEN MEANY 7 (1989).

48 When Owen's teacher walked into the classroom and saw the children holding him up in the air, she told Owen to get down and get back to his seat. Irving imagines Owen responding, "*THEY* DID IT! THEY *ALWAYS* DO IT! THEY PICK ME UP AND LOSE MY MONEY AND MESS UP MY BASEBALL CARDS—AND THEY *NEVER* PUT ME DOWN WHEN I ASK THEM TO! WHAT DO YOU THINK, THAT I *FLEW* UP HERE? *Id.*

49 Robbins, *supra* note 35, at 115–16.

50 *Id.* at 127–28.

4. Use one space after the period in a sentence.

Like many of my colleagues, I learned to type on a typewriter and was taught to add two spaces after a sentence as a visual cue for the reader. I have been reluctant to accept that two spaces after the period make text harder to read. It just feels wrong. That said, as Kathleen Narko explains:

> Two spaces were necessary to see the end of a sentence in the days of monospaced fonts and typewriters. With word processing and proportionally spaced fonts, however, use of two spaces creates a wide white space after each sentence. String a few of these together, and you have rivers of white space in your document—which 'interfere with the eyes moving from one word to the next.'[51]

So I defer to the science. When I typed this book, I automatically put two spaces after each period, but the publisher dutifully removed that extra space to improve the readability of the text.

Here is the same Table of Contents shown on page 363 but with design considerations in mind. The font has been increased a bit and changed to Palatino Linotype, a proportionally spaced serif font but with a more modern and distinctive look than Times New Roman. The major entries and point headings are in 11-point font, and the minor point headings are in 10.5-point to set them off and indicate their place in the organization of the argument.

Major point headings are capitalized according to Bluebook Rule 8(a), but only the first letter of the minor point headings is capitalized, again to set them apart. Only the Argument and point headings are in bold, which calms down the appearance of the page and draws the reader's attention to them. The side margins have been increased and the leaders (the little dots connecting the line entry to the page number) have been eliminated to streamline the page. With sufficient white space, the leaders are not necessary. Also notice how the page numbers and the major and minor point headings are aligned for a less confusing and cleaner look. Finally, the spelling errors are corrected so as not to slow down the reader and harm credibility.

---

51 Narko, *supra* note 40, at 39.

Table of Contents

ii

For More Information

Mary Beth Beazley, *Writing (and Reading) Appellate Briefs in the Digital Age*, 15 J. App. Prac. & Process 47 (2014).

Derek H. Kiernan-Johnson, *Telling Through Type: Typography and Narrative in Legal Briefs*, 7 Commc'n & Rhetoric: JALWD 87 (2010).

Mark Sableman, *Typographic Legibility: Delivering Your Message Effectively*, 17 Scribes J. Legal Writing 9 (2017).

Chapter 49

Checklist for Writing (Appellate) Briefs

Use this checklist to plan, write, and assess your draft appellate brief. Before you start writing, be sure you have a good idea of your theory of the case and the arguments you plan to make. Work backwards in terms of how many words or pages you can and should devote to certain sections and arguments of the brief. Remember that not all issues deserve the same level of attention. Finally, it may help to outline your argument in advance and draft tentative headings to guide you. You can adapt this checklist to write any kind of brief.

☐ **1.** **Cover Page** (Ch. 45, at p. 322)

Does it include the case caption, the docket number, title of the document, my name, and date?

☐ **2.** **Table of Contents** (Ch. 45, at p. 322)

Does it include all sections of the brief including the headings?

Does it include a page reference for all sections of the brief, including the headings?

Can the reader get the gist of the argument from reading the headings?

Does the design of the table make a good first impression?

☐ **3.** **Table of Authorities** (Ch. 45, at p. 323)

Are the cited sources organized by hierarchy and type of authority and then in a logical order, such as alphabetical order by case name, author, etc.?

Does the table list each page on which the sources appear?

Do the formatting rules require that the sources most heavily relied on be indicated in some way?

☐ **4.** **Jurisdictional Statement** (Ch. 45, at p. 323)

Does the statement explain the basis for the court's exercise of subject matter jurisdiction in this case? Is there citation to supporting authority?

☐ **5.** **Statement of the Issue(s) Presented for Review** (Ch. 45, at p. 323)

Does the statement convey the controlling jurisdiction or rule(s) of law, the precise legal question, and the legally significant facts?

At the same time, is it phrased in a way that suggests the client's desired outcome is the most natural or reasonable one?

☐ **6.** **Statement of the Case** (Ch. 45, at p. 323)

Does the statement include the procedural history of the case?

Does the statement explain the legally significant events leading up to the dispute from your client's perspective?

Does the statement tell a compelling story? Who is the central character? What is the nature of the conflict?

Will the story induce empathy in the reader?

Are all the facts relied on in the argument included here?

Is each fact supported by a citation to the record (e.g., R. at 4)?

☐ **7.** **Summary of Argument** (Ch. 45, at p. 324)

Does it contain a succinct, clear, and accurate summary of the argument on each issue?

Does the statement do more than just repeat the headings?

Does the theory of the case come through?

Are there citations to authority? (typically, citations are omitted in this section)

☐ **8.** **Standard of Review** (Ch. 45, at p. 324, and Ch. 46)

Does this section provide the level of deference the reviewing court must give to the lower court's decision? Is there citation to supporting authority?

Have you considered how that affects the strength of the client's position?

If the standard of review is unclear, does this section argue what the standard should be and why?

☐ **9.** **Argument** (Ch. 45, at p. 325)

Does the argument open with some context for the reader to understand the nature or significance of the dispute?

Does it begin with an introductory paragraph that sets forth the legal issues and outlines the major legal rules the brief will address (usually those identified in the major point headings)?

Does it reach an ultimate conclusion on all issues?

Are those conclusions consistent with the arguments made in the summary of argument?

Are the issues most in dispute given the greatest attention?

☐ **10.** **Organization** (Ch. 48)

☐ **Large scale: (p. 351)**

Do the **rules of law drive the organization** of the argument?

Are discrete issues argued in the **most persuasive order**?

Have you considered and rejected **alternative organizational options**?

☐ **Headings: (p. 354)**

Are the headings **consistent with the theory of the case** and the statement of the issue?

Do the headings **make an argument** about (as opposed to just identify) the legal issues they address?

Do they **capture the gist** of the argument on that issue?

Do they **convey your reasoning**?

Are they designed to help the reader **visually identify** where each individual argument fits within the argument as a whole?

☐ **Small scale: (p. 356)**

Do arguments on individual issues, such as elements, factors, etc., **proceed deductively**, from conclusion to general rule to explanation, application and then back to conclusion?

Does each individual argument begin with a **strong topic sentence** that states the client's argument?

Where necessary, is the legal rule **synthesized** for the reader?

Does the argument demonstrate how the legal rule has been **applied** in similar cases? Are those cases **explained**, **analogized**, or **distinguished**? Do analogies include the court's holding, the court's reasoning, and **direct comparisons** between the cited cases and the client's situation?

Do the arguments anticipate and rebut strong **counterarguments**?

Do citations make effective use of **parentheticals** where full textual comparisons are not used or parentheticals can provide additional support?

Are **signals** used properly and effectively?

Are paragraphs and sentences a **manageable length** for the reader?

☐ **Style (Ch. 53, at p. 399)**

Is the brief written in **plain English**?

Does the brief **argue** as opposed to discuss?

Do the arguments **advocate** with zeal but without crossing the line and becoming unreasonable?

Are the arguments **concise**?

Does the writing conform to the **legal reader's expectations**? (Ch. 53.C)

Have you double-checked for **grammar**, **usage**, and **punctuation** errors? (Ch. 54)

Are citations correct? (Ch. 56)

Are **signals** used appropriately? (Ch. 57)

Have you **spell-checked**?

☐ **Professionalism and Design (Ch. 48, at p. 363)**

Re-read the assignment. Does the brief **follow all formatting rules**, including font type and size, margin size, line spacing, and word or character count?

Have you inserted **page numbers**?

If you have choices to make, have you made them **intentionally**?

Is there **adequate white space** on each page?

Is the brief **pleasing** to look at?

☐ **11.** **Conclusion** (p. 325)

Does the conclusion state in one sentence the precise relief sought?

Have you signed the brief?

Test Your Knowledge: Part X

To assess your understanding of the material in this part, click here to take a quiz.

Part XI

Other Forms of Persuasive Writing Related to Lawsuits

Chapter 50

Demand Letters

A **demand letter** is a formal letter written on behalf of a client to a third party. These letters are usually sent after some effort has been made either by the client or the lawyer to resolve the matter more informally. The demand letter alleges in writing that the third party has wrongfully harmed the client in some way and demands compensation or some other remedy. Demand letters may invite the third party to enter into negotiations or indicate that failure to comply with the demand will result in the client taking further legal action, such as filing a lawsuit. The goal is to resolve the matter quickly without the need for litigation or at least to invite negotiations.

If you have ever received a final notice of overdue payment from a creditor, such as a credit card company or utility, that's a demand letter. Usually, these final notices state that unless payment is received by a certain date, the debt will be turned over to a collection company, which means a lawyer will get involved.

Like email, there is no one way to write demand letters, but they tend to share certain characteristics. If asked to write a demand letter, be sure to ask for samples before trying to re-invent the wheel. In the absence of a sample, you can follow these guidelines.

Begin with an **introduction** that identifies you, your client, and the subject of the letter. Next, describe the **facts and circumstances of the legal dispute** and your client's position with respect to the third party's obligations. The letter should then **argue the legal basis for the demand**, including the party's arguments, rebuttal of anticipated counterarguments, and citation to authority.

> **Practice Pointer**
>
> **Demand letters** should
>
> - identify you and your client
> - describe the circumstances of the legal dispute and the demand
> - argue the legal basis for the demand, including citation to authority
> - reiterate the demand, including specific details about the action demanded

The level of detail will depend on the circumstances, including the strength of your client's position. How much of the argument to reveal is a strategic decision. In some cases, you will not want to disclose too much detail so as not to expose the weaknesses of your client's position or help the third party prepare its defense.

Finally, the letter should conclude with the **specifics of the demand**, including the requested action, amount owed, deadlines, etc.

Set forth below is an example of a demand letter that might be sent to CSP. The Velases case is not ironclad, so the letter has been written in an effort to encourage CSP to compensate them for some of their loss and avoid litigation.

The Elkins Firm

874 Main Street
Suite 130
Dallas, Texas 75034
214-993-9000

October 10, 2019

Ms. Constance Pruitt
Executive Director
Citizens for Safe Products
P.O. Box 4332
Dallas, Texas 75034

Re: Citizens for Safe Products' March 2019 Newsletter

Dear Ms. Pruitt:

This firm represents Christina and Ramon Velas, doing business as Starbucks, 1635 Commerce Street, Suite 100, Dallas, Texas 75201. I write with regard to the newsletter your organization published in March 2019. If you are represented by counsel, please provide that information to me, and I will direct this letter to them.

> This paragraph identifies the sender as counsel for the Velases in connection with the March 2019 newsletter.

The purpose of this letter is to advise you that CSP has falsely disparaged a perishable food product in violation of Tex. Civ. Prac. & Rem. Code Ann. § 96.001-.004 (2020) and demand that CSP print a retraction and compensate the Velases for their financial losses. This demand supersedes any and all prior offers of compromise made by the Velases in connection with the March 2019 newsletter.

> This paragraph previews the nature of the dispute, the legal support for the demand, and the demand itself.

As you know, this particular newsletter discussed the availability of organic products in the Dallas metropolitan area. On page 1, the newsletter falsely states that the Velases do not sell or use organic coffee beans to prepare their coffee beverages. To the best of the Velases' knowledge, CSP made no effort to verify these statements with them or their suppliers before publishing the newsletter. Soon after the

> Here, the writer summarizes the facts and circumstances of the dispute from the clients' perspective, including their alleged damages.

newsletter was distributed to your membership, the Velases' sales plummeted. Customers were understandably shaken by this false report and reluctant to accept the Velases' assurances that the story was indeed false. Over the last several weeks, the Velases and I have left several messages on your voicemail, and I sent you an email last week, but you have ignored our efforts to communicate. As a result, the Velases continue to incur losses.

The Texas statute prohibits the public dissemination of false statements about perishable food products that are known to be false and that state or imply that the product is unsafe for public consumption. *See id.* § 96.002. By publishing its newsletter CSP disseminated information to the public, as evidenced by customer concerns and the Velases' financial loss. Knowledge of falsity includes the reckless indifference to truth. *Thomas Meats v. Safeway*, 3 S.W.3d 45, 45 (Tex. 2018). By failing to verify the information in the newsletter with the Velases, CSP demonstrated a reckless indifference to truth, thus satisfying the knowledge requirement. Finally, the newsletter stated or implied that the Velases' coffee was not safe for consumption. Pesticides are known carcinogens, which is precisely why their customers are keen to consume organic food products.

> The writer summarizes the legal argument, based on the false disparagement statute. The writer has chosen not to address here the argument on more vulnerable issues (i.e., whether coffee is a perishable food product, whether 150 people constitute the public, and whether his clients are producers under the statute). If CSP responds, those issues can be addressed later and provide some room for negotiation.

Thus, CSP is liable to the Velases "for damages and any other appropriate relief arising from [CSP's] dissemination of the information." § 96.002(b). To date, the Velases have incurred damages in excess of $100,000 in lost sales, good will, and other consequential damages. The Velases thus demand that CSP publish a retraction immediately to stop further loss and compensate the Velases for their damages to date. A failure to respond to this letter within two weeks will give our clients no choice but to proceed with formal legal action.

> The specifics of the demand are laid out so as to be perfectly clear.

I look forward to your prompt attention to this matter. I can be reached directly at 214-993-9221 or at jelkins@elkins.com.

Sincerely,

James U. Elkins

James U. Elkins

CHAPTER 51

Complaints

A **complaint** is a document filed with a trial court to initiate a civil lawsuit or criminal prosecution. In civil suits, a complaint is one of several **pleadings** or formal statements that set forth the parties' allegations. For example, once a civil complaint is filed, the defendant files an **answer** that admits or denies the allegations, asserts any defenses, or makes the defendant's own claim for relief. In advance of settlement or trial, the pleadings help narrow the subject of the lawsuit to the facts truly in dispute and the legal claims worthy of pursuit.

A. Format of a complaint

You will learn much more about this process in your courses on civil and criminal procedure, but it will help to give you some idea of what this process looks like here. The Federal Rules of Civil Procedure govern all civil actions in federal district courts (each district court also has its own local rules). The Federal Rules of Criminal Procedure govern all criminal actions in federal court.

> **Take Note**
>
> A **complaint** contains:
>
> - a statement of the court's jurisdiction
> - a statement of the claim showing the pleader is entitled to relief
> - a demand for relief

Each state has its own civil and criminal procedure rules (including local rules for each court), most of which are modeled after the federal rules. Under federal Rule 8, a civil complaint must contain a short and plain statement of the grounds for the court's jurisdiction, a short and plain statement of the claim showing the pleader is entitled to relief, and a demand for relief.[1]

This is known as **notice pleading**. Notice pleading requires that the plaintiff allege enough information to entitle him to relief under the law. The plaintiff need not disclose in detail the legal theories that justify that relief. Although **motions** (requests to the court to take specific action) can be filed throughout the process,

---

1 FED. R. CIV. P. 8(a)(1)–(3).

some of the most significant motions are made at the pleadings stage: to dismiss, for judgment on the pleadings, for summary judgment, etc.[2]

For example, if the defendant thinks the plaintiff has not stated a valid claim based on the alleged facts, the defendant may file a motion to dismiss it.[3] If the case is not dismissed and judgment is not entered for either party, or the parties don't agree to settle the case, it may then go to trial.

Although a civil complaint need not be detailed, it must conform to Rule 8 (or the applicable state procedural rule) and be reasonably grounded in fact and law.[4] It must also allege sufficient facts to state a claim upon which relief can be granted. For example, in the Velas matter, there are three elements of a claim for false disparagement under the Texas statute. If the Velases fail to allege facts in support of each element, the complaint could properly be dismissed for failure to state a claim.

The factual allegations in a complaint thus mirror the proof required for each claim. Below is a complaint that might be filed in federal court on behalf of the Velases. Try to identify those allegations that correspond to the three elements of the claim: dissemination of information to the public, knowledge of falsity, and a statement or implication that the product is unsafe for consumption.

With the filing of a civil complaint, the client also begins to tell his or her story for the first time. So even before the complaint is filed, the lawyer needs to be thinking about the theory of the case and the client's story. Recall that the working theory in the Velas matter is that they should prevail because their business provides a valuable product and community service that should not be jeopardized by the whims of uninformed and potentially dangerous consumer groups like CSP. The central characters of the story are the Velases, who have come in conflict with CSP, a sort of institutional machine that pursues its goals without regard to the effect it has on ordinary, hard-working people (see Chapter 47). Try to find where the complaint begins to hint at this story.

---

2 *See, e.g.*, FED. R. CIV. P. 12 and 56.

3 *See, e.g.*, FED. R. CIV. P. 12(b)(6).

4 *See, e.g.*, FED. R. CIV. P. 11. Rule 11 states that by signing any form of pleading or motion, a lawyer certifies that the information contained is true to the best of her belief, reasonably grounded in fact and law, and filed in good faith.

B. Sample complaint

United States District Court Northern District of Texas

The line below is left blank until the court clerk assigns the case a docket number.

Christina Velas and Ramon Velas, d/b/a Starbucks, Plaintiffs, vs. Citizens for Safe Products, Defendant.	Case No: ______ **Complaint** **Demand for Jury Trial**

Jurisdiction

1. This court has jurisdiction over this claim under 28 U.S.C. § 1332(a) because the matter in controversy exceeds $75,000 and the parties are citizens of different states.[5]

As used here, jurisdiction refers to the court's authority to hear the subject matter of the claim. Courts of general jurisdiction have broader **subject matter jurisdiction** than courts of limited jurisdiction (see Chapter 21). Here, subject matter jurisdiction is authorized by the diversity of citizenship statute.

There is another kind of jurisdiction, called **personal jurisdiction**, which refers to the court's authority to hear the claim with respect to the persons involved. It is the court's power over the particular defendant(s).

5 Extra spaces between paragraphs in the text of the complaint are to make room for the annotations at right.

Venue

2. Venue is proper pursuant to 28 U.S.C. § 1391 because the defendant resides in this district.

Venue is related to personal jurisdiction but refers to the location of the court. If the federal or state court has personal jurisdiction over the defendant, there may be several trial courts where a complaint can be filed. Most venue rules require that defendants be sued in the district (or other geographical region) where they reside, the district in which a substantial part of the events that gave rise to the claim occurred, or any court that has personal jurisdiction. Here, venue is proper under the cited federal statute.

Parties

3. Plaintiffs Christina and Ramon Velas, doing business as Starbucks pursuant to a license agreement with Starbucks Coffee Company, are residents of the State of Texas. They own and operate a coffee shop located at 1635 Commerce Street, Suite 100, Dallas, Texas 75201.

These paragraphs identify the plaintiffs and defendant in the case.

4. Defendant, Citizens for Safe Products (CSP), is a non-profit corporation, incorporated under the laws of the State of California, having its principal place of business in the State of California.

5. To the best of the plaintiffs' knowledge, information and belief, the Dallas chapter of CSP has roughly 150 members.

Statement of Facts

6. The Velases have owned and operated a coffee shop under a license agreement with Starbucks Coffee Company at the above address for seventeen years.

This section sets forth the relevant facts based on the law of a false disparagement claim.

7. The coffee shop sells coffee beverages, coffee beans in whole and ground form, snacks, pastries, and other popular beverages.

8. Since October 2018, all the beans that the Velases purchase, use to make beverages, and sell directly to customers are grown organically, without the use of pesticides. They are imported from various countries in Central and South America from fair trade sources.
9. Coffee beans do not grow in Texas.
10. Since the plaintiffs started using and selling only organic beans, their sales have increased fifteen percent.
11. The Velases (or one of their employees) grind coffee beans daily for making beverages or to bag for direct sale.
12. Within six to eight weeks after roasting and bagging, coffee beans begin to lose flavor and can no longer be sold.
13. The Velases must discard any bagged beans that do not sell before their "best before" date.
14. On or about March 11, 2019, the defendant distributed its monthly newsletter to all of its Dallas membership via email.
15. An article in the March 2019 newsletter discussed the availability of organic products in the Dallas metropolitan area. One paragraph stated:

    > Perk up reader! You know that Starbucks on Commerce Street? The supposedly "organic beans" are not so organic after all. A confidential source reports that the beans are grown using pesticides. We thought you'd want to know what you're drinking. Just another example of how we're working hard to protect our membership.

16. To the best of the plaintiffs' knowledge, no member of CSP has ever contacted

plaintiffs, their employees, suppliers, or anyone at Starbucks' headquarters with respect to the nature of the beans sold at the Commerce Street location.

17. CSP acted either with knowledge of the falsity of the statements made in its March 2019 newsletter regarding the Velases' coffee beans or reckless indifference to the truth of those statements.

Plaintiffs may plead in the alternative. Here, the Velases claim CSP acted either with actual knowledge or reckless indifference to the truth.

18. Within days of CSP disseminating its March 2019 newsletter by email, the plaintiffs began to lose customers. Some customers came to the shop and asked whether the beans being sold at that location were organic but did not make purchases.

19. Since March 2019 and as a direct result of CSP's statements, the plaintiffs have incurred damages in excess of $100,000 in lost sales, good will, and other consequential damages.

False Disparagement Claim

20. Plaintiffs incorporate here paragraphs 1 through 19.

21. The defendant's actions, as described above in Paragraphs 14–17, violated the Texas statute prohibiting false disparagement of perishable food products, Tex. Civ. Prac. & Rem. Code Ann. § 96.001–004 (Vernon 2020) and is liable to the plaintiffs "for damages and any other appropriate relief arising from the dissemination of the information." § 96.002(b).

This section describes the legal claim, also known as a "cause of action." A plaintiff may plead several claims based on the same set of facts. Here, there is just one cause of action pled.

Request for Relief

WHEREFORE, the plaintiff requests:

22. Compensatory damages, including lost sales, consequential damages, and good will; and
23. Any further relief the court deems appropriate.

Demand for Jury Trial

24. Plaintiffs hereby request a jury trial on all issues raised in this complaint.

Dated: January 13, 2020

James U. Elkins

James U. Elkins, J.D.
Attorney for Ramon Velas

The Elkins Firm
874 Main Street
Suite 130
Dallas, Texas 75034
jelkins@elkinsfirm.com
214-993-9000

Chapter 52

Motions and Supporting Memoranda

A **motion** is usually a short document that asks a court to take specific action in the course of a lawsuit. Motions are designed to help the court resolve disputes fairly and efficiently. In civil and criminal cases, motions can be filed before, during, or after trial. For example, before trial, a defendant can file a motion to dismiss the complaint for a variety of reasons, including failure to state a claim, improper service, lack of personal jurisdiction, and improper venue.[1] The parties to a civil action can file motions for summary judgment on the theory that no material facts are in dispute and the moving party should prevail on those facts as a matter of law.[2]

Criminal defendants can file motions to suppress evidence on the theory that the evidence was obtained in violation of their constitutional rights.[3] During trial, parties may move for judgment in their favor if their opponent has failed to prove their case, and motions can be filed after trial asking the court to enter judgment despite the jury's verdict or to order a new trial.[4]

A. Format of a motion

A typical motion contains the **caption** of the case, the **docket number** assigned to the case when it was filed, a **title** identifying the purpose of the motion, the party's **specific request**, and a **brief explanation** of the basis for the

Take Note

A typical **motion** contains:

- the case caption
- the docket number
- a title identifying the party's specific request
- a brief explanation
- the lawyer's signature

1 *See, e.g.*, Fed. R. Civ. P. 12(b) and Fed. R. Crim. P. 12(b).

2 *See, e.g.*, Fed. R. Civ. P. 56.

3 *See, e.g.*, Fed. R. Crim. P. 12(b)(3)(C).

4 *See, e.g.*, Fed. R. Civ. P. 50 and Fed R. Crim. P. 29 and 33.

motion. The lawyer's signature at the bottom certifies that the document is reasonably grounded in both fact and law.

Assume in the Velas case that soon after the complaint was filed (see Chapter 51.B), CSP filed a motion to dismiss under Federal Rule of Civil Procedure 12(b)(6) for failure to state a claim upon which relief can be granted. CSP's theory is that even if the facts alleged by the Velases are true, they cannot win because coffee beans are not perishable food products under Texas law. What follows is the motion CSP might file.

B. Sample motion

United States District Court
Northern District of Texas

Christina and Ramon Velas, d/b/a Starbucks, Plaintiffs, vs. Citizens for Safe Products, Defendant.	Case No. CIV–20–33

Motion to Dismiss Under Rule 12(B)(6)
for Failure to State a Claim

For the reasons set forth in the Memorandum in Support of the Defendant's Motion to Dismiss, the defendant, Citizens for Safe Products, moves to dismiss the action under Fed. R. Civ. P. 12(b)(6) because the complaint fails to state a claim upon which relief can be granted.

February 13, 2020

Respectfully submitted,

Kaitlyn White, J.D.

Kaitlyn White, J.D.
Attorney for the Defendant

White & Associates
640 Second Street
Suite 500
Dallas, Texas 75034
kwhite@whiteandassoc.com
214-932-3200

C. Format of a memo of points and authorities

Many motions, particularly in complex civil litigation, are supported by legal argument. When the supporting arguments are filed in a separate document that accompanies the motion, they're often referred to as **memoranda of points and authorities**. Although "memoranda" makes them sound like a form of predictive writing, they contain legal arguments for why the court should grant the motion. When the supporting legal arguments are not long or complicated, it may be possible to combine the motion and supporting argument.

When filing a separate memorandum in support of a motion, you will need to consult the local procedural rules of the court. You can find these on the court's website, in a local law library, or on a proprietary legal database. They often specify in detail the required content, formatting requirements, and the process for filing.

For example, the local rules of the United States District Court for the Northern District of Texas require that memoranda in support of motions contain "the moving party's contentions of fact and/or law, and argument and authorities," "typed, printed, or legibly handwritten on numbered pages," in "12-point or larger" font, and "not exceed 25 pages."[5]

All federal and most state courts also accept electronic filing of documents and have separate rules regulating electronic submissions. For example, motions and supporting memoranda in the Northern District of Texas must be filed electronically if the party is represented by a lawyer.[6]

In general, a supporting memorandum should contain the case **caption**, the **docket number**, a **title** indicating the purpose of the memorandum, an **introduction** that puts the motion in context for the court, a short **statement of the relevant facts**, the **legal argument**, and a **conclusion**. Below is a sample memorandum of points and authorities that CSP might file in conjunction with its motion to dismiss the Velases' claim. The legal argument on each issue follows the analytical paradigm: it identifies the issue and the party's position on that issue, states the rule, applies the rule, and concludes.

Take Note

A typical **memorandum of points and authorities** contains:

- the case caption and docket number
- a title indicating its purpose
- an introduction
- a short statement of the facts relevant to the motion
- legal argument (including the standards for granting the motion) organized first by issue and then by the controlling rules of law applicable to that issue
- a conclusion
- the lawyer's signature

---

5 N.D. Tex. Civ. R. 7.1(d), 7.2(c), and 10.1(d), http://www.txnd.uscourts.gov/civil-rules (https://perma.cc/W5ZA-TDJA).

6 *Id.* at R. 5.1(e).

D. Sample memo of points and authorities

United States District Court
Northern District of Texas

Christina and Ramon Velas, d/b/a Starbucks, Plaintiffs, vs. Citizens for Safe Products, Defendant.	Case No. CIV–20–33

Memorandum of Points and Authorities in Support of Defendant's Motion to Dismiss

The plaintiffs' complaint should be dismissed under Fed. R. Civ. P. 12(b)(6) because it fails to state a claim upon which relief can be granted. They seek damages and other relief for business losses allegedly due to statements the Defendant made about the Plaintiffs' coffee beans.

> The argument de-emphasizes the Velases as individuals by referring to them as the plaintiffs.

Even if the factual allegations in the complaint are true, they do not entitle the plaintiffs to relief under Texas false disparagement law. First, coffee beans are not a "perishable food product." Tex. Civ. Prac. & Rem. Code Ann. § 96.001 (Vernon 2020). Second, even if coffee beans are perishable food products, the Velases are not "producers" of the beans as required by Section 96.002(b). For these reasons, the complaint should be dismissed.

> The introduction puts the memorandum in context by explaining why the Defendant seeks to dismiss the complaint. Under 12(b)(6), the factual allegations are taken as true to determine if the plaintiff could recover on the alleged legal theory.

Factual Background

The defendant, Citizens for Safe Products (CSP), is a non-profit corporation dedicated to consumer education and advocacy. By encouraging the sale and use of safe, reliable products and services, CSP supports the healthy growth of the United States' and individual states' economies and protects consumers. CSP has local chapters all over the United States, including a relatively new chapter located in Dallas, Texas. The Dallas chapter was formed about eighteen months ago.

The factual background is stated from the defendant's point of view. You can begin to see the story CSP will tell if the case is not dismissed. A motion to dismiss is filed even before the defendant answers the complaint. Here, CSP provides very little information beyond that which is necessary to support its motion.

In January 2020, plaintiffs filed a claim against CSP under the Texas false disparagement statute, §§ 96.001–.004, alleging that certain statements in the Dallas chapter's March 2019 newsletter caused alleged business losses for which they now sue. CSP is organized under the laws of California, with its principal place of business in San Francisco, California. Since the plaintiffs are residents of Texas, they filed this state law claim in federal court under 28 U.S.C. § 1332. CSP now files its motion to dismiss the plaintiff's complaint under Fed. R. Civ. P. R. 12(b)(6) in conjunction with this memorandum of points and authorities.

Argument

Dismissal for failure to state a claim upon which relief can be granted is proper under Rule 12(b)(6) where it appears the plaintiff can prove no set of facts in support of the claim which would entitle him to relief. Under the 12(b)(6) standard, "the plaintiff must plead enough facts to state a claim that is plausible on its face." *Zastrow v. Houston Auto Imports Greenway, Ltd.*, 789 F.3d 553, 559 (5th Cir. 2015); *Fisher v. Dallas County*, 299 F.R.D. 527, 533 (N.D. Tex. 2014). Although the court must accept well-pleaded facts as true and view them in the light most favorable to the plaintiff, the plaintiff's claim here fails under Texas law. *See Zastrow*, 789 F.3d at 559; *Fisher*, 229 F.R.D. at 533.

This introductory paragraph explains the legal standard for granting motions to dismiss. The defendant cites binding Fifth Circuit law as well as a case from the same district court where the complaint has been filed. Notice how the law is framed from the defendant's perspective (e.g., "dismissal is proper" as opposed to "a court should not grant a motion to dismiss unless . . .").

The Texas false disparagement statute and others like it protect local producers of perishable food products from the harm caused by false statements about their products. These statutes protect farmers whose products, such as fruit, vegetables, or meat, perish or decay quickly. The short timeframe is critical. The statute protects only this kind of producer, who may not be able to inform the public that the statements are false before the entire crop is spoiled.

This and the next paragraph are a roadmap of the controlling legal rules the court should use to decide the motion. It begins to tell CSP's story as it sets up a natural outline for the legal argument so the reader knows what to expect in the next paragraphs.

Texas defines a perishable food product as "a food product of agriculture or aquaculture that is sold or distributed in a form that will perish or decay beyond marketability within a limited period of time." Tex. Civ. Prac. & Rem. Code Ann. § 96.001 (Vernon 2020). If a defendant disseminates information to the public it knows to be false about such products, it is liable "to the producer of the perishable food product for damages and any other appropriate relief." § 96.002(b).

The plaintiffs' complaint in this case should be dismissed for two reasons. First, the coffee beans the plaintiff sells are not "perishable food products" under the Texas statute. Second, even if the beans are perishable food products, the plaintiffs are not "the producers" of the beans.

1. The plaintiffs do not sell a perishable food product.

The heading and topic sentence indicate this paragraph will argue that the Velases do not sell perishable food products.

As indicated above, the Texas statute is intended to protect producers of food products that perish or decay quickly—within a limited period of time. § 96.001. To begin, coffee beans are not even food products. Food consists of protein, carbohydrate, and fat used by the body to sustain growth, repair, and vital processes and to furnish energy. *Merriam-Webster Dictionary* 324 (7th ed. 2019). Neither coffee beans nor brewed coffee meets this definition. Although coffee beans do contain some minerals, they are not food in the normal sense of the word. *See United States v. Kaluza,* 780 F.3d 647, 658–59 (2015); *Lippincott v. Whisenhunt,* 462 S.W.3d 507, 509 (Tex. 2015), (both stating where the language of a statute is unambiguous,

"Food consists of . . ." This sentence is the major premise (i.e., the applicable rule). Since there is no law to support it, the writer cites the dictionary definition of food.

its terms should be given their plain and ordinary meaning). People do not generally "eat coffee." Moreover, the caffeine in coffee may provide a stimulant effect, but coffee has very few calories of its own, and calories provide the energy associated with the consumption of food. Thus, coffee beans are not food.

These sentences state both the minor premise (coffee beans do not meet the definition of food) and apply the rule to the facts of this case.

"Thus, coffee beans are not food." Here is the writer's conclusion once again. In this case, the conclusion may be so obvious that re-stating it is not necessary.

Nor do coffee beans perish or decay beyond marketability in a limited period of time. The statute protects producers of meat, fish, and produce, all of which can spoil in days or weeks. *See, e.g., Green's Grocer v. Janus,* 4 S.W.3d 94 (Tex. App. 2019) (fresh apples); *Thomas Meats v. Safeway,* 3 S.W.3d 45 (Tex. 2018) (fresh meat); H. Bill Analysis, 74–722, Reg. Sess., at 1 (Tex. 1995). The Texas Supreme Court has indicated that several months is not a limited period of time. *See Pet Barn, Inc. v. Holmes,* 224 S.W.2d 99, 103 (Tex. 2016) (indicating that a baked pet snack with a shelf life of six months did not perish or decay in a limited period of time).

Even plaintiffs acknowledge that "[u]nopened, whole-bean coffee will last in [Starbucks'] FlavorLock™ sealed bags for 34 weeks." Starbucks Coffee Company, https://athome.starbucks.com/keeping-coffee-fresh/ (https://perma.cc/2GSN-J2H3) (last visited February 1, 2020). Thirty-four weeks is roughly eight and a half months, two months longer than the period in *Pet Barn,* 224 S.W.2d at 103. At that point, the beans cannot be said to spoil; they just lose some of their flavor. To use them to make coffee is not harmful. *See, e.g.,* Katherine Gillen, *Does Coffee Go Bad? The Answer Is Complicated* (Aug. 25, 2020) ("No, coffee doesn't really 'go bad.' "); Teah Teriele, *Does Coffee Go Bad?* (Feb. 18, 2016), https://www.deathwishcoffee.com/blogs/news/does-coffee-go-bad (https://perma.cc/JXX2-MW4U) ("Coffee doesn't necessarily go *bad.*") (last visited February 1, 2020).

Explanatory information may take the form of a present participial phrase, a quoted sentence, or a short statement that is appropriate in context.

The Texas legislature did not intend for liability under this statute to extend to products that take months to spoil or do not spoil at all.

2. Even if the plaintiffs sell a perishable food product, they are not the producers of that product.

Even if coffee beans are "perishable food products," the plaintiffs do not "produce" them. Although "producer" is not defined in the statute, it is understood to mean the farmer who actually grows the fruits, vegetables, or grains, or raises the beef, pork, poultry, or fish. *See* H. Bill Analysis, 74–722, Reg. Sess., at 1 (Tex. 1995); Fla. Stat. Ann. § 865.065 (West 2014) (explaining that producer is intended to mean "the person who actually grows or produces" the food products).

Only the actual farmer incurs the loss this statute seeks to redress. In contrast to traditional farmers, neither Starbucks nor the Velases are farmers. They do not grow the plants or harvest or roast the beans. All they do is import and resell them. Even if the Velases were to be considered producers, the beans are not grown locally and thus not protected by the statute. The false disparagement statute is designed to protect only Texas farmers and Texas' local economy.

Conclusion

The Texas false disparagement statute is designed to protect Texas farmers of perishable food products. Even if the allegations in Plaintiffs' complaint were true, they would not be entitled to relief: Coffee beans are not perishable food products under Texas law. Even if coffee beans were to be considered perishable food products, plaintiffs do not produce those beans. They simply resell them.

For the foregoing reasons, the Defendant respectfully requests that Plaintiffs' complaint be dismissed in its entirety.

February 13, 2020 Respectfully submitted,

Kaitlyn White, J.D.

Kaitlyn White, J.D.
Attorney for the Defendant

White & Associates
640 Second Street
Suite 500
Dallas, Texas 75034
kwhite@whiteandassoc.com
214-932-3200

Test Your Knowledge: Part XI

To assess your understanding of the material in this part, click here to take a quiz.

Part XII

Style

Chapter 53

Legal Writing Style

"With communication the object, the principle of simplicity would dictate that the language used by lawyers agree with the common speech, unless there are reasons for a difference."[1]

—David Mellinkoff

Aristotle said it is not enough to know what to say, one must know *how* to say it.[2] In this context, style refers to word choice, phrasing, sentence structure, figures of speech, pacing, and tone. Classical rhetoricians divided speaking style into three types: low, middle, and high. A **low or plain style** was considered suitable for teaching, the middle style for entertaining, and the high style for persuasion.[3] Cicero was known for his grandiloquent speeches in a high style.[4]

For example, if a friend were to say, "I got into law school," that sentence would be in a fairly low or plain style. It conveys the information directly with no ornamentation or fanfare. However, if the friend said, "Having worked like a dog to earn good grades in college and a high score on the LSAT, I have been admitted to law school," this sentence would be in more of a **middle style**. The word choice and phrasing are more interesting, there is more detail, and it includes a colorful simile, a specific figure of speech that compares one thing to another using "like" or "as" (I worked "like a dog").

The same statement from your friend in a **high style** might be: "Having struggled, as all highly motivated scholars of the law must, to achieve only the highest level of academic excellence in both my grade point average and my standardized tests, I have, it appears, been fortunate enough to have been welcomed into the legal academy as a member of the fold." It uses flowery language; a long, convoluted sentence, with several dependent clauses; figures of speech, and a dramatic or emotionally charged tone. Its emotional impact is completely different from the sentences in the low and

---

1 David Melinkoff, The Language of the Law vii (1963).

2 Aristotle, Rhetoric, *supra* ch. 8, note 3, at III.1, 1403b.

3 Cicero, Orator, *supra* ch. 9, note 20, at XXI.69.

4 *See supra* ch. 13.C, at 93.

middle styles. Cicero described the high or grand style as "magnificent, opulent, stately and ornate."[5]

Throughout history, lawyers have been accused, and in some cases rightly so, of speaking in a bombastic, high style to their clients' detriment. They have also been accused of using a sort of deliberate doublespeak, an overly complicated language to make them indispensable to clients and justify their expensive fees.[6] As early as the seventeenth century, Francis Bacon said that the Renaissance interest in cultivating a high writing style (emulating Cicero) had focused too much on form and not enough on substance:

[M]en began to hunt more after words than matter; and more after the choiceness of the phrase, and the round and clean composition of the sentence, . . . than after the weight of matter, worth of subject, soundness of argument, life of invention, or depth of judgment.[7]

Bacon's preference for simple prose mirrored the clarity of scientific certainty he sought to achieve (see Chapter 9). By the end of the nineteenth century, traditional legal writing was characterized as intentionally complicated and impenetrable.

In the twentieth century, the impenetrability of much legal writing gave rise to the **Plain English movement**. In 1953, Stuart Chase, an American economist, wrote a book entitled *The Power of Words*. In a chapter called "Gobbledygook," he observed that the practice of "squandering words" and "packing a message with excess baggage" had grown "wild and lush in the law."[8] Ten years later, David Mellinkoff, a professor of law at UCLA, published *The Language of the Law*,[9] which illustrated what Chase may have been referring to and what Mellinkoff considered absurd legal writing. For example, Mellinkoff criticized how lawyers tend to use commonly understood words to mean something entirely different:

> Nothing serves better to mark the gulf between the language of the law and the common speech than a listing of common words that mean one thing to the eye or ear of the non-lawyer, and may mean something completely different to the lawyer.[10]

---

5 CICERO, ORATOR, *supra* ch. 9, note 20, at XXVIII.97.

6 Jeremy Bentham, an English philosopher and legal scholar, believed that the language of lawyers had been "wrought up to the highest possible pitch of voluminousness, indistinctness, and unintelligibility." 6 JEREMY BENTHAM, WORKS bk. II, ch. VIII, at 332 (Bowring ed., 1839) https://babel.hathitrust.org/cgi/pt?id=mdp.39015070476315&view=1up&seq=12 (https://perma.cc/SF8Y-DK8S). He also described lawyers as "harpies of the law" who knew "the art of poisoning language in order to fleece their clients." 5 *id.* at 236–37, https://babel.hathitrust.org/cgi/pt?id=mdp.39015074712186&view=1up&seq=251&q1=fleece (https://perma.cc/7HQJ-4ARL). *Ouch.*

7 FRANCIS BACON, *Advancement and Proficiency of Learning, in* SELECTED WRITINGS, *supra* ch. 9, note 63, at 181.

8 STUART CHASE, THE POWER OF WORDS 251 (1953).

9 DAVID MELLINKOFF, *supra* note 1.

10 *Id.* at 11.

A few of the words he chose are listed below:

action	lawsuit
instrument	legal document
executed	signed and delivered
prayer	form of pleading to the court[11]

To this, Mellinkoff added that lawyers (as well as other poor writers) are wordy, unclear, pompous, and dull.[12] He was even more critical of form letters and contracts. In those, he said, "[a lawyer] could find anything—the good and the bad, with the accolade of precedent claimed for each."[13] A lawyer "surrounded by old boilerplate" can never feel alone.[14] Good examples of these form contracts today are the restrictions in leases, mortgages, and airplane tickets (see Chapter 9.C, p. 51).

The preference for simple language that Chase and Mellinkoff inspired is now commonplace. Richard Wydick's and Amy Sloan's *Plain English for Lawyers*[15] is a good example of a text that helps lawyers achieve a simple but elegant style. Outside the legal academy, several administrations have worked to improve the quality of writing in legal contexts. In 1972, President Nixon ordered that the Federal Register be written in lay terms.[16] In 1978, President Carter signed executive orders requiring that federal regulations be written "in a simple and straightforward fashion."[17] Although President Reagan rescinded these orders, some agencies, such as the Social Security Administration, have made clear, plain writing a priority.

By 1980, over half of the states had introduced legislation or administrative regulations designed to make legal documents readable. By 1991, eight states had enacted such legislation.[18] In 1998, President Clinton revived plain language as a major government initiative and issued a presidential memorandum requiring that federal employees write all new regulations in plain English.[19] In 2010, President Obama signed the Plain Writing Act, which requires federal agencies to use "clear Government communication that the public can understand and use."[20] In 2011, he

---

11 *Id.* at 12. In addition to using common words with uncommon meanings, Mellinkoff said that lawyers use rare Old and Middle English words, Latin words and phrases, terms of art, jargon, formal words, words and expressions chosen for their flexible meaning, and language designed to achieve [unduly] extreme precision of meaning. *See id.* at 11.

12 *Id.* at 24.

13 *Id.* at 278.

14 *Id.*

15 RICHARD C. WYDICK & AMY E. SLOAN, PLAIN ENGLISH FOR LAWYERS (6th ed. 2019).

16 William Lutz, *Notes Toward a Description of Doublespeak* (Revised), 13 Q. REV. DOUBLESPEAK 10 (1987).

17 Exec. Order No. 12,044, 3 C.F.R. 152 (1978); Exec. Order No. 12,174, 3 C.F.R. 462 (1980).

18 KAREN A. SCHRIVER, DYNAMICS IN DOCUMENT DESIGN 26 (1997).

19 MARTIN CUTTS, THE PLAIN ENGLISH GUIDE 6 (1995).

20 Plain Writing Act of 2010, Pub. L. No. 111–274, 124 Stat. 2861; *see also* https://www.plainlanguage.gov/ (https://perma.cc/4E8Q-63PY).

issued Executive Order 13,563, which requires that "[our regulatory system] must ensure that regulations are accessible, consistent, written in plain language, and easy to understand."[21]

Cicero said the grand style was best suited to persuasion. However, the plain English movement has transformed legal writing. Lawyers today strive to write in more of a middle style, using elegant but understated language that does not sound exaggerated or melodramatic. The reality is that lawyers and judges today do not have time to wade through ornate or verbose language. Nor do clients want to pay for the time it takes to create or decipher it.

At first, being immersed in appellate opinions dating back to the early nineteenth century may make the law seem as indecipherable as a foreign language. You will be surprised though how quickly you become familiar with and able to translate it into everyday language. Having struggled to learn this language, you may then be tempted to use legal jargon and Latin phrases (*i.e.*, legalese) in your writing. But don't. Remember that the goal is to write in a middle style: artful, elegant, and easy-to-understand.

The best way to achieve an **elegant middle style** is to write **clearly** and **concisely**. These terms are not easy to define, and it can be even harder to achieve them in legal writing.

A. What is clear legal writing?

Practice Pointer

To achieve **clarity**, avoid

- double negatives
- elegant variation
- Latin words and phrases
- old-fashioned phrases from Old and Middle English
- passive voice
- redundancy

A survey of federal judges indicates that the best legal writers "state clearly . . . what the case is about and why the court should affirm or reverse," "[m]ake things clear and interesting," "clearly and concisely identify and analyze the issues presented," and "state their positions clearly."[22]

Conversely, the worst briefs "read like a Joycean stream-of-consciousness and seem to have no theme or clear purpose," "are anything but" clear, "muddy

---

21 Exec. Order No. 13,563, 76 FED. REG. 3,821 (Jan. 18, 2011), *reprinted in* 5 U.S.C. § 601 (2012).

22 Kristen Robbins-Tiscione, *The Inside Scoop: What Federal Judges Really Think About the Way Lawyers Write*, 8 J. LEG. WRITING 257, 282 (2002).

up the water," "cloud the main issues with trivia," or contain "fuzzy, imprecise thinking and writing, leaving the reader to guess or assume as to the meaning."[23]

All legal readers demand clarity, but what does it mean to write clearly? The idea that writing can and should be "clear" probably comes from the assumption that writing is the mechanical act of recording pre-formed ideas.[24] Writing clearly, then, would mean using language that does not pose a barrier between the reader and the ideas the writer wants to convey. Today, we understand that the act of writing is far more complicated than putting fully formed thoughts on paper. Often, our ideas are not really clear to us until we write them.

Nevertheless, most of us still think of clear writing as writing that conveys intended meaning as unambiguously as possible. To help achieve clarity in legal writing, keep the following suggestions in mind.

1. Avoid double negatives.

You may be surprised to find yourself writing in double negatives for the first time, particularly as you analogize to or distinguish case law. Phrases such as "not unreasonable," "not unfair," and so on, can confuse the reader when they appear in a complicated sentence. It's easier to take out the negatives and just say "reasonable" and "fair."

2. Avoid elegant variation.

If you majored in the humanities in college, you may have been encouraged to vary your word choice to make your writing more interesting. Known as elegant variation, this practice should generally be avoided in legal writing. If you use two different words or phrases to mean the same thing, your reader will assume the words are different for a reason and likely be confused.

For example, read this passage from a real estate contract:

> . . . The <u>buyer</u> of the property agrees to apply for a mortgage loan within five days of today's date. Once the loan is approved, the <u>mortgagor</u> shall notify the <u>seller</u> in writing. . . .

Here, the writer uses two different words to describe the buyer ("buyer" and "mortgagor"), which is confusing. It sounds as if there are three parties to the contract: buyer, mortgagor, and seller. Since the buyer and mortgagor (one who gives a mortgage to the lender) are the same, it makes more sense to refer to the buyer as "buyer" throughout.

---

23 *Id.*

24 *See* ch. 14.A, at 96.

3. Avoid Latin words and phrases.

Many legal terms of art are taken from Latin words and phrases. Although lawyers often understand these terms, clients and non-lawyers do not. Whenever possible, translate these into English. Where there is no good substitute for the Latin phrase because it has become a part of the language (e.g., dicta and prima facie), you may use the Latin without italics.[25] Below are just a few Latin words and phrases that can be translated into English to improve clarity.

a fortiori—even more so, or with even stronger reason

ab initio—from the beginning

assuming arguendo—assuming for the sake of argument

bona fide—good faith

caveat emptor—buyer beware

de facto—in fact, even if not prescribed by law

de jure—prescribed by law

de minimus—minimal

et al.—and others

et seq.—and those that follow

in camera—in private

in toto—entirely

inter alia—among other things

ipso facto—because of that fact

nil—nothing

per se—by itself

prima facie—on its face, at the first instance

pro se—to represent oneself

quid pro quo—to exchange one thing for another

sua sponte—of its own accord

25 ALWD GUIDE, *infra* ch. 56, note 1, at R. 1.3(f); BLUEBOOK, *infra* ch. 56, note 1, at R. 7(b).

4. Avoid old-fashioned words and phrases.

As you read judicial opinions, you will encounter old-fashioned phrases and terms of art that are no longer used in everyday speech. Several of these come from Old and Middle English. Where there is a good modern substitute, use it.

aforementioned—mentioned above or before

aforesaid—stated above or already

aver—to claim

demur—to object

enclosed please find—enclosed

herein—in this place

hereinafter—from now on

heretofore—until now

instant case—the present or current case

one John Doe—refers to the party, usually the defendant, in the case

party of the first (or second) part—refers to one of the parties to a contract

purported—reputed or claimed

said individual—the named or previously mentioned

thence—from that source

thenceforth—from that time

therein—in that place

whereas—considering that

whereby—under the terms of which

wherefore—for that reason

5. Use passive voice intentionally and selectively.

Passive voice consists of some form of the verb "to be" (e.g., is, was, were, been) followed by the past participle of the form of a second verb. The past participle of regular verbs is formed by adding –d or –ed to the basic verb form (e.g., proved, used, explained). Passive voice expresses an action performed upon the subject of the sentence. Think of passive voice as sentences where the actor is often missing.

For example, to say "the decision *was explained* by the judge in her opinion" is in passive voice. The act of "explaining" is performed on the subject of the sentence, "the decision." To say "the decision *was explained* in the opinion" is also in passive voice. In the first example, the actor (the judge) appears after the verb. In the second sentence, the actor is missing, and the sentence becomes unclear. Who explained the decision?

In the active voice, these sentences would read: "The judge explained the decision in her (or the) opinion." Here, the actor is the subject of the sentence and "decision" is the direct object (The judge explained what? She explained the decision.). Using passive voice in legal writing is not wrong, but it can be confusing and less effective. Most lawyers use primarily active voice, which often leads to shorter sentences. They reserve passive voice for situations where the goal of the sentence is to soften the impact of action taken by their client.

For example, if a lawyer wanted to divert explicit attention from the mistakes her client, the FDA, made in approving a new drug, she might write: "Mistakes were made in calculating the data submitted with the pharmaceutical company's application for approval of a new drug." This is far less harsh than the same sentence in the active voice: "In reviewing the pharmaceutical company's application for approval of a new drug, the FDA made mistakes in calculating the data."

6. Avoid redundancy.

Over the years, in an effort to be precise, lawyers have developed the habit of saying the same thing several times in different ways, particularly in transactional and estate planning documents. Saying the same thing differently not only takes up valuable space, it can actually mislead the reader into believing that each word is supposed to mean something different. One strong word that conveys the intended meaning will suffice. Follow the same principle when explaining what the law means or how it applies to your facts. If you find yourself saying, "in other words" or adding additional information in parentheses, you may be repeating yourself unnecessarily.

first *and foremost*

fit *and proper*

force *and effect*

for all intents *and purposes*

give, *devise, and bequeath*

good *and sufficient*

if *and when*

knowledge, *information, and belief*

null, *void, and of no effect*

rest, *residue, and remainder*

totally *and completely*

tried *and true*

true *and correct*

7. Use transition words to indicate the relationship between sentences or paragraphs.

Single words and short phrases are concise ways to demonstrate clearly the relationship between ideas, sentences, and paragraphs. They act as primes or cues for your reader to better understand the text that follows. The following is a short list to get you started. As you develop your own legal writing persona, you will invent others and rely on some of the same ones again and again.

To make an additional point:

also
coupled with
finally
furthermore
in addition
moreover
not only . . . but also
plus
so too
together with

To show similarity:

as
here too
in like manner
in the same way
just as
like
likewise
similarly

To demonstrate:

especially
for example
for instance
first, second, third
in particular
particularly
specifically
such as
to clarify
to demonstrate

To demonstrate difference:

but

but here

conversely

in contrast

on the contrary

on the other hand

unlike

unlike in

whereas

whereas here

yet

To signal a counterargument:

although

but

[defendant] argues

despite

even if

nevertheless

nonetheless

notwithstanding

regardless

To conclude:

accordingly

as a result

consequently

for this reason

in effect

in sum

therefore

thus

hence

to conclude

B. Concise legal writing

Judges also complain that briefs are "almost invariably *too long* and frequently repetitious," "excessively long and incomprehensible," "too long, too repetitious and meandering," and "too long and do not focus on the critical issues in the case."[26] One judge wrote, "We are *drowning* in 50 page briefs that are poorly written when the case should have been presented in a 20 page brief."[27] In legal writing, conciseness is a virtue. It saves time and reduces the possibility that you will be misunderstood.

You may find it very challenging to write concisely. In high school and college, you may have used long, complicated sentences to sound sophisticated or to satisfy a minimum word count requirement. Just like elegant variation, complicated sentences with several dependent clauses and prepositional phrases can be confusing. Legal readers in a hurry may not take the time to untangle such sentences, and the point of your sentence may be lost. To that end, try not to separate the noun and verb of your sentence with lengthy, intrusive clauses.

Being concise is not just about cutting out words. Often, it means covering more ground in fewer words: address one issue at a time as opposed to combining or blurring them, be selective about the arguments you advance and the cases you rely on, summarize the legal rule or the case law at a higher level, or provide less detail when that detail is not critical. For example, review this discussion on the issue of CSP having knowledge that the story it published about the Velases' beans was false:

Practice Pointer

To be concise, cover more ground with fewer words:

- discuss one issue at a time
- be selective about the issues and arguments to address
- be selective about the authority to rely on
- summarize at a higher level
- provide less detail when detail is not critical

> The Velases can likely prove that CSP knew that the statements in the newsletter were false. In *Thomas Meats, Inc. v. Safeway, Inc.*, 3 S.W.3d 45 (Tex. 2018), the plaintiff was a meat distributor. It sued the defendant, Safeway, for posting a sign in its storefront window that stated that the ground beef Safeway had purchased from Thomas Meats was unsafe. The sign further advised customers to dispose of the meat immediately. Safeway had heard rumors about the meat being tainted, but it failed to investigate the truth of its statements. Safeway stipulated that the sign had been viewed by at least 100 customers before it was taken down. The plaintiff moved for summary judgment, and the court granted the motion.

26 Robbins-Tiscione, *supra* note 22, at 280.

27 *Id.* at 281.

> The court stated, "Posting the sign in the storefront window, without having bothered either to contact Thomas Meats first or conduct any investigation at all, clearly satisfies the knowledge requirement." *Id.* at 46. The court held that the manager's "reckless indifference to the truth was tantamount to knowledge of falsity" and ruled for the plaintiff. *Id.* at 47.
>
> In the Velases' case, the newsletter was sent to 150 subscribers and, to the best of their knowledge, CSP did not make any attempt to investigate the truth or falsity of its statements: it did not contact Mr. or Mrs. Velas or any of their current bean suppliers to verify its story. Just as the manager of the Safeway in *Thomas Meats* failed to investigate the truth of the allegations about the safety of the ground beef, CSP did not inquire about the organic nature of the beans. For this reason, even if CSP did not know for a fact that newsletter was false, it acted with reckless indifference to the truth, which was "tantamount to knowledge of falsity." *Id.* The court is likely to hold that CSP had knowledge of falsity under the Texas statute. **(315 words)**

As a friend of mine might say, "That was a long way to go for a short drink of water." Did you find yourself feeling impatient with this discussion? Were you confused at any point? Did it feel repetitive in any way? Although the analysis is sound, it could be written more concisely and effectively. It could be more concise for several reasons. First, the summary of *Thomas Meats* is longer than necessary; it uses more words and provides more detail than the reader needs. Second, it discusses the facts relating to "public dissemination" that are not relevant to the falsity issue. Third, it's missing a synthesized rule for knowledge of falsity, and the writer works up to the rule as the case is explained (see The Book Report, p. 214). Finally, the analogy could be pithier and more effective. The writer uses two different phrases—"failed to investigate" and "did not inquire about"—to describe similar situations. The analogy is stronger if you can describe your client's situation in the same terms. See the revision below.

> The Velases can likely prove that CSP knew that the statements in the newsletter were false. Knowledge of falsity includes the reckless indifference to truth. In *Thomas Meats,* the plaintiff sued Safeway for posting a sign in its storefront window stating that its ground beef was unsafe and advised customers to dispose of it. Although the defendant's manager had heard rumors about the beef being tainted, he made no effort to investigate them. The court held that the manager's "reckless indifference to the truth was tantamount to knowledge of falsity" and granted summary judgment for the plaintiff. *Id.* at 47. Just as Safeway failed to investigate whether the beef was safe, CSP failed to investigate whether the Velases' coffee beans are organic. Thus, the court is likely to hold that CSP had knowledge of falsity under the Texas statute. **(139 words)**

To further achieve conciseness in legal writing, keep the following suggestions in mind:

1. Combine topic sentences with predictions, argument, or rules of law.

You can sometimes save space by combining a topic sentence that identifies the subject of your paragraph with the law or part of your reasoning. Remember, the legal syllogism is a form of reasoning, not a template for each paragraph. As long as you adhere to the analytical paradigm (rule→ application→ conclusion), you may vary your paragraph structure as you feel necessary and the complexity of the issue requires.

For example, the analysis of "food product" in the sample Starbucks memorandum (p. 257) begins:

> The Velases can likely prove only that their coffee beans are perishable food products. The statute does not define food product, but "food" is generally understood to mean a nutritious substance ingested in solid or liquid form to maintain health and life. *See, e.g., Food, OED Online*, www.oed.com (last visited June 2, 2021).

For conciseness, you could combine your prediction of the outcome on this element, the rule of law, and your reasoning:

> The Velases are likely to prove that coffee beans are a "perishable food product" because they contain ingestible nutrients, such as potassium and magnesium, which help maintain health and life. *See, e.g., Food, OED Online*, www.oed.com (last visited June 2, 2021).

In the sample appellate brief (p. 198), the argument that coffee beans are perishable food products begins:

> Coffee beans are food products under the Texas statute, which protects agricultural producers. Although it does not define "food products," food products are generally understood to mean nutritious substances ingested to maintain health and life. *See, e.g., Food, OED Online*, www.oed.com (last visited June 2, 2021). Coffee beans contain nutrients such as potassium and magnesium, as well as antioxidants. *See, e.g.,* "*Coffee is number one source of antioxidants,*" EurekAlert! (Aug. 28, 2005), https://www.eurekalert.org/pub_releases/2005-08/acs-cin081905.php#:~:text=WASHINGTON%2C%20Aug.,of%20Scranton%20(Pa.) (https://perma.cc/5GV4-EWV2) (last visited June 2, 2021).

For conciseness, you could combine some of these sentences:

> Coffee beans are food products under the Texas statute because food is generally understood to mean nutritious substances ingested to maintain health and life. *See, e.g., Food, OED Online*, www.oed.com (last visited June 3, 2021). Coffee beans contain ingestible nutrients such as potassium and magnesium, as well as antioxidants. *See, e.g., "Coffee is number one source of antioxidants,"* EurekAlert! (Aug. 28, 2005), https://www.eurekalert.org/pub_releases/2005-08/acs-cin081905.php#:~:text=WASHINGTON%2C%20Aug.,of%20Scranton%20(Pa.) (https://perma.cc/5GV4-EWV2) (June 3, 2021).

2. Do not devote more space to an issue than it deserves.

Not all issues are equally important. As you plan any document, think about how much space you have and how much should be devoted to your analysis (e.g., in the discussion section of a memorandum or in the argument section of a brief). Then consider how much space should be devoted to each issue (e.g., those that are most important, in dispute, or particularly complicated).

3. Do not explain to the reader what you, as the writer, intend to do or what you will do next.

Writing often helps you learn the law you are analyzing. In early drafts, you may "think out loud" in your writing. For example, assume you have listed the elements of a statutory claim and cited the statute. Immediately afterward, you write: "Each of these elements needs to be applied to the facts of our case." This last sentence indicates what you, the writer, intend to do next in your analysis. Your reader already expects you to discuss these elements because you just listed them, so the explanatory sentence can be deleted without confusing your reader.

4. Avoid long sentences with strings of intrusive clauses and phrases.

To achieve conciseness, your sentences and paragraphs should be relatively short and to the point. Avoid using long, complicated sentence structures and intrusive dependent clauses and prepositional phrases. A reader can struggle to keep the subject of the sentence in mind when it is separated from the action (the verb) by long, intrusive clauses and phrases:

> The *plaintiffs*, having suffered considerable damage from the false statements about the coffee beans, which are imported from Central and South America, that were published in the March 2019 newsletter, *claim* that CSP is liable under the Texas false disparagement statute.

Short does not have to mean choppy:

> The *plaintiffs claim* CSP is liable for making false claims about its coffee beans. These statements have caused them considerable damage.

Saying no more than necessary helps you make intentional word choices. These, in turn, will lead to writing that has a more powerful impact. Both in litigation and transactional practice, less is often more.

5. Avoid nominalizations.

A nominalization is a word that is not a noun (e.g., a verb, an adjective or an adverb) used as a noun. Nominalizations sound more formal than the simpler verb form, but they make your sentences longer and harder to understand. You can use them but do so sparingly and only for effect.

Common nominalizations are listed below:

to reach agreement (to agree)

to take into consideration (to consider)

to make a decision (to decide)

to make an inquiry (to inquire)

to conduct an investigation (to investigate)

to give notice (to notify)

to make an objection (to object)

to make a recommendation (to recommend)

to bring suit (to sue)

to be in violation of (to violate)

6. Discuss only those issues relevant to your analysis.

Discuss or argue only those issues that relate directly to your analysis. When taking exams, students are often reminded to answer only the question asked. The same in law practice. If you are writing a memo on potential defenses to a tort claim, but only two out of five possible defenses apply to your case, you may choose to list all five but analyze only the two. Of course, if you are unsure about whether they apply, err on the side of over-inclusion.

On the other hand, if in the course of research, you discover legal issues that affect your analysis that no one has yet thought of or known about, be sure to raise those issues with your supervisor or colleagues for potential discussion in the memo.

7. Use explanatory parentheticals to add supporting authority without adding length.

Parentheticals allow you to provide additional supporting authority without taking up a great deal of space. You can use them to support statements about the law and to make analogies to additional cases. For example, assume you have one or more cases that support your statement of a rule of law, but you don't really need to discuss them in text because the rule is self-explanatory. In that situation, you can use a parenthetical to telegraph concisely how the case supports your statement:

> A limited period of time is significantly less than six months. *See Pet Barn, Inc. v. Holmes*, 224 S.W.2d 99, 103 (Tex. 2016) (holding that a baked pet snack that remained fresh for up to six months did not perish or decay in a limited period of time). Unlike in *Pet Barn*, the coffee beans Velas sells can no longer be sold within six to eight weeks. . . .

You can also use parentheticals to analogize to cases. Assume you have two cases that are similar to your client's situation and both help the court decide the issue in your client's favor. For conciseness, you might choose to discuss the best case fully in text and cite the other case using a parenthetical. For example:

> . . . A limited period of time is significantly less than six months. *See Pet Barn, Inc. v. Holmes*, 224 S.W.2d 99, 103 (Tex. 2016). In that case, the plaintiff sued for damages due to statements made about its product, a baked pet snack. The snack was made of products of agriculture that had been combined and baked, and it had a shelf life of about six months. The court held that the snack had to be a sole product of agriculture and went on to indicate that six months was not a limited period of time. *Id.* at 103. Unlike in *Pet Barn*, the coffee beans Velas sells can no longer be sold within six to eight weeks. *See also Thomas Meats v. Safeway*, 3 S.W.3d 45, 47 (Tex. 2018) (acknowledging that apples that begin to rot after ten to twelve days without refrigeration perish or decay in a limited period of time).

As these examples illustrate, parentheticals usually begin with a present participle such as "finding" or "holding." Both the *ALWD Guide* and the *Bluebook* discuss the use and formatting of explanatory parentheticals.

8. Provide only the facts, issues, and reasoning of the cited case(s) necessary to analogize or distinguish a case.

When you explain a cited case for purposes of analogizing it to your client's case or distinguishing it, you do not need to summarize all of the facts, holding, or reasoning in that case. Be selective and provide only those portions critical to your analysis.

For example, here the writer analyzes whether coffee beans are a perishable food product. She writes:

> The beans must also "perish or decay" beyond marketability within a limited period of time. § 96.001. The statute does not define "limited period of time," but since it is designed to protect sellers of meat, fish, and produce, it likely refers to days or weeks as opposed to several months. In *Pet Barn, Inc. v. Holmes*, 224 S.W.2d 99 (Tex. 2016), the owner of a pet food store sued a disgruntled former employee who suggested the store's most popular product was unsafe. The product was a dog treat, baked from all natural ingredients including flour, chicken stock, and salt. Even though the ingredients were harvested from the ground or derived from livestock, the court held the product was not a food product of agriculture or aquaculture because it was not a sole product of agriculture. *Id.* at 102. As for perishing or decaying in a limited period of time, the court held "the snacks do not perish or decay beyond marketability in a limited period of time because they remain fresh for six months after opening." *Id.* at 103. Unlike the product in *Pet Barn*, the coffee beans have a "best before" date of just six to eight weeks past which Velas can no longer sell them. For that reason, they likely perish or decay beyond marketability within a limited period of time.

Although the writer distinguishes *Pet Barn* on the grounds that the product at issue did not perish or decay for six months, the strength of the analysis is lost. The writer includes unnecessary information about the facts of the case and the court's holding and reasoning on a related but separate issue. A streamlined version appears below:

> The beans must also "perish or decay" beyond marketability within a limited period of time. § 96.001. The statute does not define "limited period of time," but since it is designed to protect sellers of meat, fish, and produce, it likely refers to days or weeks as opposed to several months. In *Pet Barn, Inc. v. Holmes*, 224 S.W.2d 99 (Tex. 2016), the court held that a baked food product that remained fresh for six months after opening did not perish or decay beyond marketability in a limited period of time. *Id.* at 103. Unlike the product in *Pet Barn*, the coffee beans have a "best before" date of just six to eight weeks past which Velas can no longer sell them. For that reason, they likely perish or decay beyond marketability within a limited period of time.

9. State rules of law just once.

If your analysis requires you to examine the elements of a cause of action or crime or the factors in a totality test, you can set them out in a roadmap paragraph just once. For example, you do not need to quote the elements from a statute or a case and then restate them in your own words.

10. Do not summarize the history of the controlling rules of law.

Although you may find the evolution of a particular area or rule of law interesting as a historical matter, your reader usually does not need to know what the law used to be or why or how it changed. Unless the law's history is directly relevant to your legal analysis, begin with the current rules of law and proceed to analyze the law from there. The history can be directly relevant where the law has recently changed or different judges have interpreted it differently over the years. But usually, it is not necessary to your analysis.

11. Omit unnecessary words and phrases that add no meaning.

Writers of all kinds tend to clog their sentences with unnecessary words and phrases, particularly in first drafts. Often referred to as surplus[28] or needless words,[29] they add little or no meaning to the sentence and take up valuable space. Or, they unnecessarily complicate a simple idea. As you revise your writing, keep these examples in mind.

- in spite of the fact that (just say *although*)
- owing to the fact that (just say *because*)
- due, in part, to the fact that (just say *because*)
- it is important that (delete this phrase and start the sentence with the noun "it" refers to)

  ~~It is important that~~ the defendant [must] investigate the truth of its statements.
- it is well-established that (delete this phrase and start the sentence with the next word)

  ~~It is well-established that~~ a television audience constitutes the public.
- the United States Supreme Court (or any court) has held that . . . (delete this phrase and just state the holding; the cite will give the reader the same information)
- in order to succeed, the plaintiff must prove that (just delete)
- it is beyond question that (just delete)

---

28 WYDICK & SLOAN, *supra* note 15, at 7–18.

29 BRYAN A. GARNER, LEGAL WRITING IN PLAIN ENGLISH 17 (2d ed. 2013).

For More Information

Terri LeClercq & Karin Mika, *Legal Writing with Style* (2016).

Joseph M. Williams & Joseph Bizup, *Style: Lessons in Clarity and Grace* (12th ed. 2016).

Anne Enquist, Laurel Currie Oates & Jeremy Francis, *Just Writing: Grammar, Punctuation, and Style for the Legal Writer* (5th ed. 2017).

Try It: Exercise 53.1

(see suggested answers at App. B, at p. 521)

Use the principles discussed above to rewrite these sentences and make them clearer and concise.

1. Assuming arguendo that the Velases, doing business as Starbucks, produce a perishable food product, it must be proved that CSP knew that its statements were false or untrue.

2. In its opinion, the United States Court of Appeals for the Ninth Circuit held that thenceforth, any contract to engage in illegal activity would be null, void, and of no effect whatsoever.

3. The agency cited the respondent for being in violation of the pertinent regulations set forth herein and determined sua sponte to assess a fine.

4. In no way did the defendant contribute or add to the confusing nature of the situation, making it highly unlikely that he had anything whatsoever to do with the cause of the accident.

5. The next section of this memo addresses the three major defenses that were discussed at the meeting.

C. Legal writing conventions

Like all professionals, lawyers have their own way of doing things. The following conventions may not be wholly unique to legal writing, but adopting them will go a long way toward enhancing your credibility as a legal writer.

1. Avoid use of first person in formal legal writing.

Lawyers generally write in the third person.[30] In formal legal writing, they tend not to refer to themselves or their clients in the first person unless it is necessary or does not otherwise make sense. For example, instead of saying, "I do not think that coffee is a perishable food product," a lawyer might write that "coffee is probably not a perishable food product," or "The Velases are unlikely to prove that coffee is a perishable food product." Instead of saying, "You asked me to determine whether," they'd say, "The issue is whether." The exception to this rule is likely in direct communications (e.g., emails, letters, etc.) between lawyer colleagues or with some clients, where the nature of the communication is informal.

2. Use contractions sparingly in persuasive legal writing.

Traditionally, lawyers consider contractions too informal for predictive legal writing, such as memos or opinion letters, and transactional documents, such as contracts (but probably not email). Until you have a sense of the practice in a specific job setting, err on the side of formality and spell out both words. However, contractions can be used sparingly in persuasive writing for effect.[31]

3. Start sentences with conjunctions in persuasive legal writing to signal a tone shift.

Most of us learned not to start sentences with conjunctions because conjunctions are used to join two sentences. Many lawyers may still expect you to follow this rule. The situation can be different in persuasive writing, where the tone shift in using a word like "and" or "but" to start a sentence can be very effective.[32] Use these sparingly for maximum impact.

4. Spell judgment with one "e."

"Judgement" with two "e's" is an older English version. Lawyers in the United States consistently omit the first "e."

---

30 *See, e.g.*, BRYAN A. GARNER, THE ELEMENTS OF STYLE 82–83 (2d ed. 2002).

31 *See, e.g.*, *id.* at 81–82 (quoting Denny v. Radar Industries, 184 N.W.2d 289, 289 (Mich. Ct. App. 1970): "The appellant has attempted to distinguish the factual situation in this case from that in Renfroe v. Higgins Rack Coating and Manufacturing Co., Inc. [citation omitted]. He didn't. We couldn't. Affirmed.").

32 *Id.* at 49–50; *see also supra* ch. 48.F, at 363.

5. Do not pose questions to the reader.

Unlike in this textbook, lawyers generally do not ask questions of their readers (e.g., "What does it mean to be a perishable food product?"). Instead, it is more common to state the issue as a declarative sentence: "The issue is whether coffee beans are perishable food products under the Texas statute."

6. Use adverbs sparingly.

The most persuasive writing uses a limited number of adverbs, such as "clearly," "obviously," "undoubtedly," and "certainly." These words tend to weaken your analysis or argument. If something truly is clear, for example, you need not say so. Excessive use of adverbs calls into mind the famous line from Hamlet: "The lady doth protest too much, methinks."[33]

7. Use few direct quotes.

Whenever possible, paraphrase or excerpt relevant text and then cite supporting legal authority. Long, direct quotes from statutes and cases are generally ineffective. Readers often skip over them or cannot identify that portion of the quote you think is most significant. It is more effective to highlight the significant language by quoting short passages directly in your text. As a general rule, quote the original source directly only when it articulates the matter better than you can paraphrase it or you need to ensure you do not alter its meaning (as with some statutes). Quotations of fifty or more words should be set off as block quotes.[34]

8. Use past tense to discuss cited cases and present tense to discuss your case.

When summarizing the facts or holding of a case, use the past tense. For example, "In *Pet Barn*, the owner of a pet food store sued [not sues] a former employee." But "the plaintiffs claim [not claimed] CSP made false statements about its coffee beans."

9. Use a comma to separate all items in a series.

Commas are used to separate three or more items listed in a series, and there is usually a conjunction before the last item. Legal writers always use a comma before each item in a list, including the last one (i.e., the Oxford comma). For example, "The plaintiff must prove duty, breach, causation, and damages." The comma before "and"

---

33 WILLIAM SHAKESPEARE, HAMLET act 3, sc. 2, line 230 (New Folger ed., Wash. Square Press 2003) (Gertrude, Hamlet's mother, to Hamlet about the fictitious queen in Hamlet's play, *The Murder of Gonzago*).

34 ALWD GUIDE, *infra* ch. 56, note 1, at R. 38.5(a); BLUEBOOK, *infra* ch. 56, note 1, R. B5.2 and 5.1.

makes the sentence clear. With it, there are four elements to prove, but without it there appear to be just three: duty, breach, and causation and damages.

10. Use first, not firstly, in a list of reasons.

When listing a number of reasons that support an assertion, use "first," "second," and so on, as opposed to "firstly," and "secondly."[35] Both are adverbs, but the shorter form is more modern. Similarly, use "more important," as opposed to "more importantly."

11. Refer to corporations and courts as "its."

Corporations, government bodies, and similar fictitious entities are referred to as "its," as opposed to "hes," "shes," or "theys." For example, "Starbucks must prove that CSP knew its statements were false," and "In its opinion, the court stated . . ."

12. Avoid proper names when describing case law.

When describing the facts of a cited case, avoid referring to the parties by using their proper names. They can confuse your reader because they do not identify the role the party plays in that case. For example, in *Pet Barn*, the owner of a pet food store "sued a former employee," not "the owner sued Holmes."

13. You may use em dashes to set off important phrases.

Em dashes can be used in legal writing to set off phrases both visually and for emphasis. Used sparingly, dashes can have a dramatic effect. For example, "The hearing committee—comprised solely of men—determined that the victim was partially responsible for the sexual assault."

14. Avoid colloquialisms and slang.

In formal legal writing, most lawyers avoid using informal colloquialisms and common slang. For example, instead of "the chance that the court will rule in the Velases' favor is slim to none," write "the court is unlikely to rule in the Velases' favor."

15. Use proper date form.

In text, indicate dates using one of the following formats:

September 19, 1959

September 1959

On the nineteenth of September, 1959

---

35 *See, e.g.*, GARNER, *supra* note 30, at 83–84.

16. If your heading is a sentence, put a period at the end of it.

A. The relevant factors

or

A. The factors relevant to reasonableness include [x].

Try It: Exercise 53.2

(see suggested answers at App. B, at p. 522)

Use the principles discussed above to rewrite these sentences in accord with legal writing conventions.

1. We believe that our opponent's position doesn't make the grade.

2. The question becomes, "Did the witness commit perjury?"

3. The judgement included damages for attorney's fees, out-of-pocket costs and consequential damages.

4. In that case, the FAA charges United Airlines with violating safety regulations; they said the mechanics weren't thoroughly checking the planes before each flight.

5. In so holding, the *Jones* court stated:

> In cases such as these, where the totality of the circumstances is the key to the validity of the stop, the court must look at each factor and then make a determination as to whether or not the officer's belief is reasonable.

Jones, 87 N.W.2d at 75.

Chapter 54

Grammar, Punctuation, and Usage

Although most legal readers will forgive the occasional dangling modifier or misplaced comma, your credibility as a writer will depend in part on proper grammar, usage, and punctuation. As Lillian Hardwick explains, "[N]one of Aristotle's persuasive means can reliably be achieved without proficiency in grammar and punctuation."[1]

Many lawyers were taught to adhere to traditional grammar and punctuation rules, and they criticize your writing if you repeatedly break them. Until you have a sense of the practice in a specific job setting, follow the traditional rules to the extent possible. At a minimum, your employers will expect you to have a basic understanding of them.[2]

A. The basics

In my experience, law students struggle most with these grammar, punctuation, and usage rules. Mastering these rules will go a long way toward improving your writing. As indicated below, some of these rules are in flux.

Commas:

1. Use commas after introductory phrases.

Commas should be used after introductory phrases that contain more than three or four words. The comma makes the sentence easier to read and sets off the main idea:

To prove self-defense, Mrs. Myers will need to prove two elements.

---

1 Lillian B. Hardwick, *Classical Persuasion Through Grammar and Punctuation*, 3 Legal Commc'n & Rhetoric: JALWD (formerly J. Ass'n Legal Writing Directors) 75, 77 (2006).

2 *See generally* Bryan A. Garner, *The Legal Writing Skills Test*, 5 Scribes J. Leg. Writing 107 (1995).

Having examined the fourth factor, the court concluded the defendant was innocent.

2. Use commas between independent clauses joined by coordinating conjunctions.

Commas should be used between two independent clauses (they contain a subject and verb) that are joined by a coordinating conjunction (for, and, nor, but, or, yet, or so, abbreviated as *fanboys*):

The plaintiff filed the complaint on time, but she failed to file in accordance with the local rules.

If you eliminate the subject "she" in the second clause, you would no longer need a comma because you would now have a single clause with a compound verb:

The plaintiff <u>filed</u> the complaint on time <u>but failed</u> to file in accordance with the local rules.

3. Use commas to set off most appositives.

An appositive is a noun or pronoun, often used in a phrase, that explains or identifies the noun or pronoun it modifies. Where the appositive is necessary to understand the sentence, do not set if off with commas:

Former Vice-President Joe Biden is now the President.

But where the appositive is not necessary to understand the sentence, meaning the appositive supplies additional information, set it off using commas:

Joe Biden, the former Vice-President, is now the President.

Hyphens:

4. Use hyphens to join compound adjectives.

Use hyphens to join compound adjectives when they come before a noun and act together as a single idea:

five-mile radius

twenty-year-old daughter

However, when one of the words is *very* or an adverb (a word that modifies a verb), no hyphen is necessary:

very bright student

fully formed idea

Modifiers:

5. Avoid dangling modifiers.

A dangling modifier does not clearly or sensibly refer to the word or phrase it is intended to modify (often the subject of the sentence):

> Taking all factors into consideration, the defendant is likely to prove Officer McFadden violated his Fourth Amendment rights.

In this example, "taking all factors into consideration" does not modify the subject, "defendant." Instead, it refers to what the writer or court might do to resolve the issue.

> *Revised:* Taking all factors into consideration, the court is likely to conclude that Officer McFadden violated the defendant's Fourth Amendment rights.

6. Place "only" as close as possible to the word or phrase it modifies.

"Only" can modify a word or a phrase. It should be placed as close as possible to the word or phrase it modifies to avoid confusion:

> "Only the defendant hit the plaintiff with his car."

The placement of "only" in this sentence indicates that just one person, the defendant, hit the plaintiff.

> "The defendant hit only the plaintiff with his car."

Here, the placement of "only" means the defendant hit the plaintiff but no other pedestrian.

> "The defendant only hit the plaintiff with his car."

Here, it is unclear what the placement of "only" means. Only the defendant hit her? That the defendant "hit" the plaintiff but did nothing else?

7. Use "hopefully" and "badly" properly.

"Hopefully" is an adverb. Just as one can run "quickly," one can think "hopefully." When you begin a sentence with the word "hopefully," it usually means something other than what you intend.

For example, "Hopefully, Starbucks has data regarding sales losses," means that the state of Starbucks' possession of the data is a hopeful one. What you really mean is that you hope Starbucks has the data in the first place.

"Badly" is another commonly misused word. When you say, "Nora feels badly," it means Nora's capacity to feel is impaired in some way. What you really mean is that Nora feels bad. In this example, "feels" is a linking verb used to express Nora's emotion and not an action verb (as in she "feels" the fabric). Adjectives are used to modify linking verbs, and adverbs are used to modify action verbs.

Grammar Girl Mignon Fogarty recommends that when in doubt, substitute a form of the verb "to be," such as "am," "is," "was," and "are," for the verb you are using. If you can do so, and the sentence sounds correct, use the adjective (i.e., bad). If not, use the adverb (i.e., badly).[3]

For example, "Nora [is] badly" sounds wrong. That's how you know to use the adjective, bad. What about "the fish I ate tastes badly?" Since "the fish I ate [is] badly," sounds wrong, you know it tastes "bad."

Pronouns:

8. Decide when and how to use or avoid gendered pronouns.

Many legal writers are increasingly uncomfortable with the use of gendered pronouns and in search of a satisfactory way to avoid using them without creating ambiguity.

Sometimes, you can write around a gender-based term or phrase, such as "reasonable man," by substituting "reasonable person." Similarly, "the men and women present" can become "all those present." But when you need or want to use gender-neutral pronouns to refer to people in general or to identify a person already named in your text, *they*, *their*, and *them* seem to be gaining the most acceptance.

> "A reasonable person 'checks [their] bias at the door.' " *Peck*, 224 F.2d at 17.
>
> When the defendant heard the police knock, they were afraid.

In some situations, the use of a plural pronoun to refer to a single person will make your writing ambiguous:

> Where the defendant notifies the plaintiff about the defect within thirty days, they are required to notify the relevant regulatory agency.

Here, it is not clear who must give the required notice. In this situation, you can easily change the sentence to make the requirement clear:

> Where the defendant notifies the plaintiff about the defect within thirty days, the defendant is required to notify the relevant regulatory agency.

---

3 *See* Mignon Fogarty, *Bad Versus Badly*, http://www.quickanddirtytips.com/education/grammar/bad-versus-badly?page=1 (https://perma.cc/3WCN-U4MA).

9. Avoid pronouns with ambiguous referents.

Excessive use of pronouns in compound sentences can be confusing to the reader, who may be unsure to whom the pronoun refers.

> At present, Susan has custody of the children; however, she has informed her daughter that she must do nothing to jeopardize the situation.

In this example, it is not clear whether the second "she" refers to Susan or the daughter. It is best simply to rename the intended person:

> At present, Susan has custody of the children; however, she has informed her daughter that *Susan* must do nothing to jeopardize the situation.

Noun/verb agreement:

10. Make sure nouns and pronouns agree with verbs.

In general, a singular noun requires a singular verb, and a plural noun requires a plural verb.

> Treat "either . . . or" as singular: Either the plaintiff or her guardian makes the decision.
>
> Treat a single period of time as singular: Six months is not a limited period of time.
>
> The relevant criteria are set forth below.
>
> The data are confusing.
>
> The court examined the evidence, and it concluded there was no reasonable articulable suspicion on these facts.

Quotations:

11. Place commas and periods inside quotation marks.

Commas and periods always go inside quotation marks, even when quoting short phrases that are not complete sentences:

> "Contributory negligence," the court said, "is no longer a complete bar to recovery."
>
> The plaintiff must prove it produces "perishable food products."

12. Place colons and semi-colons outside quotation marks.

Colons and semi-colons always go outside quotations marks:

She suffered from "battered women's syndrome": a form of temporary insanity that can excuse guilt.

The defendant claimed it was a "crime of passion"; however, he introduced no evidence to support that claim.

13. Place question and exclamation marks inside quotation marks only if they are part of the quotation.

The defendant then asked, "Did you see that the light was red?"

The victim screamed, "Help!"

Does it make sense to argue the beans "perish or decay"?

14. Introduce quotations properly.[4]

Quotations can be introduced into your text in several ways. A phrase can be taken from the quoted source and inserted directly into your text:

Reasonableness in this context refers to "what most people in the same situation would do." *Peck*, 224 F.2d at 17.

You can also introduce the quote using a comma or a colon. In general, use a colon only where the phrase introducing the quotation is a complete sentence.

The court held, "The defendants acted reasonably because they did what most people in the same situation would do."

When you alter the quote to fit smoothly within your text, indicate that alteration using brackets:

The defendant acted reasonably because "[she] did what most people in the same situation would do." *Peck*, 224 F.2d at 17.

15. Indicate omissions using ellipses.[5]

When you delete a portion of a quoted phrase, indicate the omission using an ellipsis, which is three periods separated by spaces and with spaces in between.

Here, the defendant acted reasonably because at that moment, he "did what most people . . . would do." *Peck*, 224 F.2d at 17.

---

4 *See also* ALWD GUIDE, *infra* ch. 56, note 1, at R. 38.4; BLUEBOOK *infra* ch. 56, note 1, at R. 5.3.

5 *See also* ALWD GUIDE, *infra* ch. 56, note 1, at R. 40; BLUEBOOK, *infra* ch. 56, note 1, at R. 5.3.

Do not use an ellipsis to begin a quotation. In that case, begin the sentence by capitalizing the first word and indicating the alteration using brackets.

> "[T]hey did what most people . . . would do." *Peck*, 224 F.2d at 17.

Semi-colons:

16. Use semi-colons to join short independent clauses that are related in some way.

Semi-colons join two short, independent clauses that have some relation to each other.

> Comparative negligence apportions liability among the parties; each party pays according to their share of the fault.

17. Use a semi-colon to separate independent clauses joined by a conjunctive adverb.

> Self-defense is comprised of two elements, both of which are measured by a reasonableness standard; however, for the first element, the question is whether that particular defendant acted reasonably.

18. Use semi-colons to separate items in a series, where any item of the series contains a comma.

Although items in a series are usually separated by commas, semi-colons should be used where any item in the series itself contains a comma:

> The court based its decision on the fact that Eleanor had a prestigious college degree; ample experience with high-paying, professional employment; and a stellar performance record.

Split Infinitives:

19. Avoid splitting infinitives.

The infinitive form of a verb is usually the word *to* plus the verb itself, such as "to state," "to decide," "to go." To split the infinitive is to place a word or phrase between them. The rule against splitting infinitives appeared in the nineteenth century. Instead of, "The tenant shall not be entitled <u>to</u> without prior permission <u>paint, remodel, or renovate</u> the apartment," write, "The tenant shall not be entitled to paint, remodel, or renovate the apartment without the landlord's permission."

Although some still adhere strictly to this rule, modern readers will not object to a split infinitive when it makes the sentence smoother and easier to read (e.g., to fully appreciate).

Words ending in *s*:

20. Use correct plural forms for singular words ending in *s*.

To form the plural of a singular noun ending in "s," simply add "es":

The house belongs to the Joneses.

21. Use correct possessive forms for words ending in *s*.

Add an apostrophe alone or an apostrophe and *s* to form the possessive of singular nouns already ending in "s." Add only an apostrophe to form the possessive of plural nouns already ending in *s*:

Mr. Jones' (or Mr. Jones's) claim cannot succeed.

The Newells' best hope for recovery lies in a cause of action for wrongful pregnancy.

The agencies' need for the data supports disclosure.

Prepositions:

22. Do not end sentences with prepositions.

Many legal writers were taught not to end sentences with prepositions. Prepositions are words that begin phrases that usually end in a noun or pronoun. These phrases demonstrate the relationship between a noun or pronoun and some other word in a sentence. For example, in the sentence "the keys are under the table," "under" is the preposition that begins the phrase "under the table." This phrase shows the relationship between the keys and the table.

Prepositional phrases can act as adverbs or adjectives. Common prepositions include *in*, *out*, *above*, *under*, *up*, *down*, *with*, *to*, *at*, *through*, *between*, and *by*. Although this rule has relaxed over time because the grammatically correct sentence often sounds awkward, you may want to check with your supervisor or colleagues before you break it:

Incorrect: The first issue is the one the court is concerned with.

Correct: The first issue is the one with which the court is concerned.

Even better: The court is concerned with the first issue.

That or *Which*?

23. When in doubt, use *that.*

"That" is used with restrictive clauses. A restrictive clause narrows or limits the meaning of its subject. In the sentence, "All cars that are parked in the lot will be towed," the word "that" restricts the meaning of cars to only those parked in the lot. Commas are not used to set off restrictive clauses.

"Which" is used with non-restrictive clauses. A non-restrictive clause provides additional information about the subject without restricting its meaning. In the sentence, "All cars, which are parked in the lot, will be towed," the word "which" explains where the cars to be towed are located, but it does not limit them in any way. Commas are used to set off non-restrictive clauses.

It can be hard sometimes to tell whether "that" or "which" should be used. In those cases, opt for "that"; it is usually less likely to be confusing:

> The issue *that* poses the greatest problem for the plaintiff is whether she gave the defendant adequate notice of the defect.

This sentence refers to one of many issues that pose a problem for the plaintiff; here, *that* limits the meaning of *issue.*

> The issue, which poses a great problem for the plaintiff, is whether she gave adequate notice of the defect.

The phrase set off by commas does not restrict the meaning of *issue*; it amplifies it.

24. Commonly confused words

affect v. effect

"Affect" is used most often as a verb, as in "her attitude did not affect me." Used as a noun, "affect" refers to a person's demeanor. "Effect" is most often used as a noun, as in "her attitude had no effect on me," and "the price increase had no effect on demand."

imply v. infer

"Imply" and "infer" are verbs, but "to imply" is to suggest meaning that is not explicitly stated. For example, "when she asked if I needed any assistance, she implied I could not manage on my own." "To infer," on the other hand, is to draw a conclusion from another's statement or action. For example, "she inferred that the speaker thought she was helpless," and "he inferred that he should remain silent." In general, "if I do the implying, you do the inferring."

it's v. its

"It's" is a contraction that stands for "it is." Contractions should generally be avoided in formal legal writing. On the other hand, "its" is the possessive form of "it." Since corporations, fictitious entities, and courts are referred to as "it," you will use "its" often.

their v. there v. they're

"Their" is a plural possessive pronoun, as in "their feelings" or "their property." "There" means "at that place," as in "put the couch over there." "They're" is a contraction of "they are."

who v. whom

"Whom" should be used to refer to the object of a verb or preposition. If the word can be replaced with "him" or "her," use "whom": "He gave the document to whom [to him]?" If the word can be replaced with "he" or "she," use "who": "Who [He] gave her the document?"

For More Information

Mary Barnard Ray & Jill J. Ramsfield, *Legal Writing: Getting It Right and Getting It Written* (5th ed. 2010).

Anne Enquist, Laurel Currie Oates & Jeremy Francis, *Just Writing: Grammar, Punctuation, and Style for the Legal Writer* (5th ed. 2017).

Ian Gallacher, *A Form and Style Manual For Lawyers* (2005).

Bryan A. Garner, *The Redbook: A Manual on Legal Style* (3d ed. 2013).

Ruth Ann McKinney & Katie Rose Guest Pryal, *Core Grammar for Lawyers*, https://coregrammarforlawyers.com (https://perma.cc/E7ME-QP7P).

Try It: Exercise 54.1

(see suggested answers at App. B, at p. 523)

Use the principles discussed above to rewrite these sentences with proper grammar, punctuation, and usage.

1. Looking at each element, the plaintiff will not meet it's burden of proof.

2. If the officer's belief is reasonable they are permitted to conduct a brief investigatory stop without a warrant.

3. The court must first terminate the parents rights and then it must determine what is in the child's best interest.

4. The frisk, that must be based on a reasonable belief that the suspect is armed and dangerous, must be confined to a weapons search.

5. An employer is not entitled to unilaterally terminate an employee for "blowing the whistle" on his illegal activities.

6. The parties' were unable to agree on contract terms and thus failed to form an enforceable contract.

7. An employee such as the plaintiff in this case can be fired for any reason and is considered "at will;" however, they cannot be fired for reporting illegal activities to the appropriate authorities.

8. CSP will argue that the Velases coffee beans are not "perishable food products".

9. The Jones primary complaint was that their neighbors were effecting there ability to enjoy their backyard.

10. Knowledge of falsity can be imputed, constructive, which means the defendant should have known, or actual.

B. Figures of speech

Figures of speech use words or phrases for effect in ways that depart from customary sentence construction, order, or meaning. They add color, light, and spice to your writing. Because they appeal to emotion, they can suggest powerful mental images and make your arguments more memorable. Be careful though. Excessive use can weigh down your analysis, detract from your credibility, and make your writing sound overly dramatic. Find just the right amount and transform your persuasive writing from dull or plain into bright and elegant.

Do not be afraid to experiment with figures of speech in advocating for your client. They can be particularly useful in conveying your client's character, your client's story, the nature of your client's conflict, the unfairness of your client's current situation, or the impact of the law on your client. Ask your colleagues whether your figures of speech are effective in achieving your goals. Below is a short list of figures you might consider incorporating into your legal arguments. You will recognize many of these from your English classes.

1. Alliteration

Alliteration is the use of words that begin with the same sound (usually consonants) near one another:

CSP's newsletter was premature and provocative.

The police officer neither knocked nor notified the residents of his presence.

2. Assonance

Assonance is the use of words that have the same or similar vowel sounds near one another. It can be used to produce a lyrical quality to your writing:

CSP made fallacious statements.

The plaintiff is in the business of improving the local food supply.

3. Irony

Irony expresses meaning through opposites. For example, if your friend arrived late for a party, and you said, "Glad you got here early," that would be irony. Although you said your friend was early, he was actually late. In this form, the irony is sarcastic. Sarcasm often requires context or inflection to be understood properly and can be interpreted as offensive or aggressive. For these reasons, sarcasm does not often work well in legal writing.

However, irony can be used to represent an inconsistency between the actual result of a sequence of events and the normal or expected result. You can use this type of irony to express the unintended or undesirable but inevitable consequences of a given statute or rule of law. In the sample appellate brief, the Velases argue:

> That the beans are roasted and imported from outside Texas does not disqualify appellants from recovering under the statute. To hold otherwise would be to grant protection only to producers of food products that grow in or are capable of being grown in Texas. Although false statements about both types of products would damage the local Texas economy, only producers of local products could recover under the statute.

4. Metaphor

A metaphor is a word or phrase for one thing that is used to refer to another thing in order to show or suggest that they are similar. Aristotle said that "metaphor is of the utmost value in poetry and prose."[6]

I.A. Richards, an English-born literary critic, poet, teacher, and rhetorician, observed that language often leads to misunderstanding. Since words have no intrinsic meaning, they only have the meaning the listener attributes to them. Assume you tell a friend that you are going on vacation with your family. Every family vacation she has ever been on has been a disaster, and the minute you say the word "vacation" she gets a stomachache. To you, "vacation" means relaxation, conversation, movies, and fun food. To your friend it means something entirely different: stress, arguments, lost tickets, and bad service. As this example illustrates, the meaning we attach to words

---

6 ARISTOTLE, RHETORIC, *supra* ch. 8, note 3, at III.2, 1405a.

comes from past experiences. In this way, words communicate our thoughts about things but not the things themselves.[7]

Because words mean different things to different people, we make comparisons to clarify meaning: "[T]hought is metaphoric, and proceeds by comparison, and the metaphors of language derive therefrom."[8] In *Romeo and Juliet,* for example, Romeo observes Juliet approach her bedroom window and cries, "But, soft! What light through yonder window breaks? It is the east, and Juliet is the sun."[9] Romeo compares Juliet (the tenor of the metaphor or the thing referred to) to the rising of the sun (the vehicle of the metaphor). In a powerful and elegant way, the metaphor communicates Romeo's joy in seeing Juliet and how he thinks about her.

Metaphor is a powerful tool in legal writing as well. As Michael Smith, Professor of Law and Director of Legal Writing at University of Wyoming College of Law, explains, metaphor is used in law in a variety of ways. Rules of law can be expressed as metaphors:

- Treating a corporation as a "person" under the law;
- The relationship between "parent corporations" and subsidiaries and "piercing the corporate veil" under corporations law;
- The "fruit of the poisonous tree" doctrine under criminal law and evidence law;
- "Long arm" statutes under personal jurisdiction law.[10]

Analogical reasoning is also a form of metaphor. *Stare decisis* requires that like cases be treated alike to ensure fairness and predictability. If the case before the court resembles a prior case in a number of significant ways, an advocate may convince the court to decide the case the same way. Because no two cases are identical, the analogy is used to persuade the court to treat the two cases as though they were the same.

As a figure of speech, metaphor can also be used to embody the theory of your client's case (Chapter 48.A, p. 349).[11] Recall that the theory of the case encapsulates the ultimate reason why your client should prevail. It is not a rule of law but the reason why a rule of law should or should not apply in a certain way. Recall the potential theory of the Velases' case being that their business should not be jeopardized by the whims of uninformed and potentially dangerous consumer groups like CSP. If you were to characterize CSP as a machine that pursues its goals without regard to

---

7 *See* I.A. RICHARDS & C.K. OGDEN, THE MEANING OF MEANING 9 (1923).

8 I.A. RICHARDS, THE PHILOSOPHY OF RHETORIC 94 (1936).

9 WILLIAM SHAKESPEARE, ROMEO AND JULIET, act II, sc. 2 (New Folger ed., Wash. Square Press 2004).

10 Michael R. Smith, *Levels of Metaphor in Persuasive Legal Writing*, 58 MERCER L. REV. 919, 922 (2007).

11 *See id.* at 933–35.

whatever it destroys in its path, the image of CSP as a machine is a powerful metaphor that embodies the theory of the case.

Metaphors can also be used to make specific legal arguments. They can span paragraphs or appear in the form of a single word.[12] For example, CSP might want to challenge the Velases' interpretation of the Texas false disparagement statute as too broad. In that case, it might argue that under their interpretation, the statute is a "strait jacket" inhibiting free speech and endangering the public. Or, CSP might use just a single word to convey this image: the statute "restrains" or "obstructs" free speech.

5. Onomatopoeia

Onomatopoeia refers to the use of words that imitate the sound of the action or object they describe, such as "buzz" and "hiss." Recall the hypothetical from Chapter 20, p. 130, where the plaintiff sued the defendant for hitting her with his car as she crossed the street in front of him. Instead of saying the defendant hit her, the plaintiff's lawyer might describe the impact as a "thud" or "thump."

6. Oxymoron

An oxymoron is the use of words with opposite or different meanings to create a dramatic effect. It is often comprised of an adjective and a noun that don't make sense together, such as "sweet sorrow" or "seriously funny." They can be used in persuasion as well. For example, the Velases might refer to CSP as a "harmful watchdog" or an "invading Samaritan." CSP, on the other hand, might refer to the court protecting the Velases under the Texas statute as an "unacceptable solution" or "the wrong answer even if for the right reasons."

7. Paradox

As a figure of speech, paradox refers to a statement that seems to contradict itself. It can be used to express astonishment or disbelief at something unusual or unexpected. Oxymorons are a form of paradox. In the Velas case, CSP might argue that the Velases are not producers under the Texas false disparagement statute because they do not grow the coffee beans in Texas. However, coffee cannot grow in Texas. Under CSP's interpretation of the statute, the Velases cannot be protected under the statute if they want to sell coffee beans. That's a paradox.

8. Personification

Personification is giving human-like attributes to a thing, an idea, or an animal: "the wind howled" or "the light danced." It can provide powerful imagery and help

---

12 *See id.* at 936.

bring your writing to life. For example, the Velases want to be considered producers even though they don't grow the agricultural product they sell. CSP might argue that extending protection to them would create an exception that "swallows" the rule.

9. Simile

A simile is used to compare two things using "like" or "as": "My life is like a song," or "she is as light as a feather." In legal writing, similes can be used to describe the effect of a party's actions, the parties' arguments, or the outcome if a rule of law is applied in a certain way. When metaphor is expressed as a simile, it can sound less dramatic or harsh. For example, to say CSP "is a machine" may seem worse than to say CSP is acting "like a machine."

For More Information

Linda L. Berger, *The Lady, or the Tiger? A Field Guide to Metaphor and Narrative*, 50 Washburn L. J. 275 (2011).

Encyclopedia of Rhetoric (Oxford Univ. Press 2001).

David T. Ritchie, *The Centrality of Metaphor in Legal Analysis and Communication: An Introduction*, 58 Mercer L. Rev. 839 (2007).

Michael R. Smith, *Advanced Legal Writing: Theories and Strategies in Persuasive Writing* (3d ed. 2012).

Chapter 55

Checklist for Style Issues

Use this checklist to keep track of problem areas and quickly find guidance on clarity; conciseness; legal writing conventions; grammar, punctuation, and usage; and figures of speech.

Ch. 53.A. Clear Legal Writing		**Page Number**
☐ 1.	Avoid double negatives	403
☐ 2.	Avoid elegant variation	403
☐ 3.	Avoid Latin words and phrases	404
☐ 4.	Avoid old-fashioned words and phrases	405
☐ 5.	Use passive voice intentionally and selectively	405
☐ 6.	Avoid redundancy	406
☐ 7.	Use transition words to indicate the relationship between sentences or paragraphs	406

Ch. 53.B. Concise Legal Writing		
☐ 1.	Combine topic sentences with predictions, argument, or rules of law	411
☐ 2.	Do not devote more space to an issue than it deserves	412
☐ 3.	Do not explain to the reader what you, as the writer, intend to do or what you will do next	412
☐ 4.	Avoid long sentences with strings of intrusive clauses and phrases	412
☐ 5.	Avoid nominalizations	413
☐ 6.	Discuss only those issues relevant to your analysis	413
☐ 7.	Use explanatory parentheticals to add supporting authority without adding much length	414
☐ 8.	Provide only the facts, issues, and reasoning of the cited case(s) necessary to analogize or distinguish a case	414

Ch. 53.C Legal Writing Conventions

Ch. 54.A Basic Grammar, Punctuation, and Usage

Ch. 54.B. Figures of Speech

Test Your Knowledge: Part XII

To assess your understanding of the material in this part, click here to take a quiz.

Part XIII

Citations and Signals

Chapter 56

Citations

A. What are citations?

Legal **citations** are a shared shorthand for referring to legal authority. As with other forms of citation, they tell the reader where to find the cited authority, but in conjunction with the use of signals (see *infra* Chapter 57), they also indicate how you are relying on that authority. Even the absence of a signal is a signal: it tells the legal reader that the cited authority directly supports your proposition.[1]

Both the *ALWD Guide to Legal Citation* (hereinafter *ALWD Guide* or ALWD)[2] and *The Bluebook: A Uniform System of Citation* (hereinafter *Bluebook* or BB)[3] are comprehensive guides to citation format for academic (legal scholarship) and non-academic (law practice) use. You or your professor may assign or prefer one guide over the other. The results should be the same regardless of which guide you use. There are also free guides to legal citation format, including *The Indigo Book*[4] and Dionne Anthon, *The Bluebook Uncovered: A Practical Guide to Mastering Legal Citation*.[5]

You may be surprised to learn that the format for citing the same authorities in legal scholarship and law practice differs somewhat. The main differences include the location of the citations and the formatting of statutes, case names, and other sources, such as books and law review articles. Citations in legal scholarship, such as law review articles and books, are placed in footnotes (and sometimes endnotes).[6] Citations in law practice documents are placed within the text.

---

1 *See* Carolyn V. Williams, ALWD, ALWD Guide to Legal Citation R. 35.2, at 370 (7th ed. 2021) [hereinafter ALWD Guide]; The Bluebook: A Uniform System of Citation R. 1.2(a), at 62–63 (Columbia L. Rev. Ass'n et al. eds., 21st ed. 2020) [hereinafter Bluebook].

2 ALWD Guide, *supra* note 1, https://www.alwd.org/about-guide (subscription only).

3 Bluebook, *supra* note 1, https://www.legalbluebook.com/ (subscription only).

4 *See* Sprigman et al., The Indigo Book: A Manual of Legal Citation, Public Resource (2016), https://law.resource.org/pub/us/code/blue/IndigoBook.html (https://perma.cc/95FH-PVEU).

5 *See* Dionne Anthon, The Bluebook Uncovered: A Practical Guide to Mastering Legal Citation (2020), http://dionneanthon.com/bbu/bbu21.html (https://perma.cc/W5G4-UGUH).

6 ALWD Guide, *supra* note 1, Part B.3, at l; Bluebook, *supra* note 1, R. 2, at 68.

Law reviews use two sets of typeface conventions. Ordinary roman type and italics are used in text; in footnotes, large and small caps are also used.[7] Ordinary roman type and italics are used in law practice; large and small caps are not used at all. Some of the major formatting differences between legal scholarship and practice are illustrated below.[8]

Sample Differences in Citation Format Based on Type of Legal Writing		
	Legal Scholarship	**Law Practice**
Case names (ALWD R. 12.2; BB R. 10.2)	**In text:** In *Copeland v. District of Columbia Department of Employment Services*, . . .	**In text:** *Copeland v. District of Columbia Department of Employment Services*, 3 A.3d 331 (D.C. 2010). **[ALWD R. 2.3; BB Rule 10.2.1]**
	As footnote: Copeland v. D.C. Dep't of Emp. Servs., 3 A.3d 331 (D.C. 2010).	**As citation sentence:** *Copeland v. D.C. Dep't of Emp. Servs.*, 3 A.3d 331 (D.C. 2010). **[ALWD R. 12.2 & App. 3(E); BB Rule 10.2.2 & T.6]**
Constitutions (ALWD R. 13; BB R. 11)	U.S. CONST. art. III, § 2.	U.S. Const. art. III, § 2.
Statutes (ALWD R. 14; BB R. 12)	TEX. CIV. PRAC. & REM. CODE ANN. § 96.003 (Vernon 2020).	Tex. Civ. Prac. & Rem. Code Ann. § 96.003 (Vernon 2020).
Books (ALWD R. 20; BB R. 15)	AMY E. SLOAN, BASIC LEGAL RESEARCH: TOOLS AND STRATEGIES (7th ed. 2018).	Amy E. Sloan, *Basic Legal Research: Tools and Strategies* (7th ed. 2018).
Law Review Articles (ALWD R. 21; BB R. 16)	Linda L. Berger, *Applying New Rhetoric to Legal Discourse: The Ebb and Flow of Reader and Writer, Text and Context*, 49 J. LEG. EDUC. 155 (1999).	Linda L. Berger, *Applying New Rhetoric to Legal Discourse: The Ebb and Flow of Reader and Writer, Text and Context*, 49 J. Leg. Educ. 155 (1999).

In the *Bluebook*, the examples in the Whitepages are formatted for legal scholarship. You should follow them, but be sure to convert them to practitioner format (as shown above). The Bluepages in the *Bluebook* are solely for practitioners. They were written long after the Whitepages and act as a supplement to the rules (i.e., Rule B1 supplements Rule 1 in the Whitepages, and they should be read together). Where the Bluepages do not have the information you need, go to the Whitepages. To cite properly, you will need to be familiar with both. The *ALWD Guide* explains formatting differences for citations in scholarship and practice under each rule.

Are you getting confused yet?

---

7 ALWD GUIDE, *supra* note 1, R. 1.1–.2, at 2; BLUEBOOK, *supra* note 1, R. 2.1–.2, at 69–72.

8 *See also* ALWD GUIDE, *supra* note 1, *Fast Formats, passim*; BLUEBOOK, *supra* note 1, R. B2, at 6.

To help you get started, both citation manuals have quick reference guides for common citations:

ALWD Guide

- There is a "Fast Formats" Locator on the inside front cover to sample formats throughout the book. The online version is the same as the print.

Bluebook

- Sample citations for law review footnotes are on the inside front cover, and sample citations for practitioner use in court documents and legal memoranda are on the inside back cover.

In the online version of the *Bluebook*, the quick reference guide for scholarly writing is found as the *Quick Guide*[9] on the left navigation pane. For practitioner examples, see the Bluepages. The index is also a great way to navigate both manuals.

Although you need to become increasingly familiar with at least one of these citation guides, this chapter does not attempt to recap all the information they contain. The goal here is to explain the basic citation process in simple terms and highlight the information most useful to beginning legal writers.

As a way of demonstrating the difference in citation formats, the citations in the text of this book (what scholars call "above the line") are in practitioner format; the citations in footnotes ("below the line") are in scholarship format.[10]

Take Note

If you are working with a print version of the *ALWD Guide* or the *Bluebook*, tab or highlight (or something) these rules to find them easily. You will be happy you did.

ALWD Rule	BB Rule	
35–37	1	Signals and string cites
2, 4	6	Abbreviations, numerals, and symbols
3	8	Capitalization
12	10	Cases
14	12	Statutes
App. 1, 4	T.1	U.S. Jurisdictions
App. 3(E)	T.6	Case name abbreviations
App. 3(B)	T.10	Geographical abbreviations
App. 5	T.13	Periodical abbreviations

9 *See* https://www.legalbluebook.com/bluebook/v21/quick-style-guide.

10 I say this with some trepidation: The twenty-first edition of the BLUEBOOK and the seventh edition of the ALWD GUIDE were new at the time this chapter was being written. All effort has been made to make the citation format correct throughout.

B. Why do I need to provide citations?

The reason is two-fold: First, legal readers demand proof that the law is as you've described it. Second, because they are doubting readers, they will want to know where to find the information if they want to read it and decide for themselves what it says.

C. When do I need to provide a citation?

As a general rule, you should cite legal authority every time you 1) quote or paraphrase a rule of law from any source, including your own synthesized rules, and 2) explain the holding of a case or the reasoning of a court.[11] Your professor might also require that you cite when you describe the facts of a case. My practice is to cite facts only where the case has not already been cited. Be sure to ask your professor what is expected in your class.

D. What are full and short citations?

In general, the first time you cite legal authority, you must provide a **full citation** according to citation rules. Thereafter, you may provide a **short citation**, again according to citation rules. Some writers will provide another full citation if the last one was several pages back so the reader need not struggle to find it. The rest of this chapter will describe how to create full and short citations to common legal authority.

E. Cases (ALWD R. 12; BB Rules B10 & 10)

Cases are cited according to Rule 12 of the *ALWD Guide* and Rule 10 of the *Bluebook*.[12] As the diagram below illustrates, the first full citation to a case is composed of the case name, reporter volume, reporter name, page where the case begins, the page number referenced or pincite (where applicable), the court and year in parentheses, and any subsequent history. Each rule explains in detail how to build the parts of a full and short case citation.

---

11 *See* ALWD GUIDE, *supra* note 1, R. 34.2, at 368.

12 Some courts have their own additional citation rules. *See* ALWD GUIDE, *supra* note 1, App. 2, at 479; BLUEBOOK, *supra* note 1, tbl.BT.2, at 30. Some states have also adopted simpler citation rules (sometimes called public domain cites) for citing cases in documents filed with their courts. These citation rules are listed in ALWD GUIDE, *supra* note 1, R. 12.11, at 94, & App. 1, at 421; BLUEBOOK, *supra* note 1, R.10.3.3, at 104, & tbl.T.1, at 227.

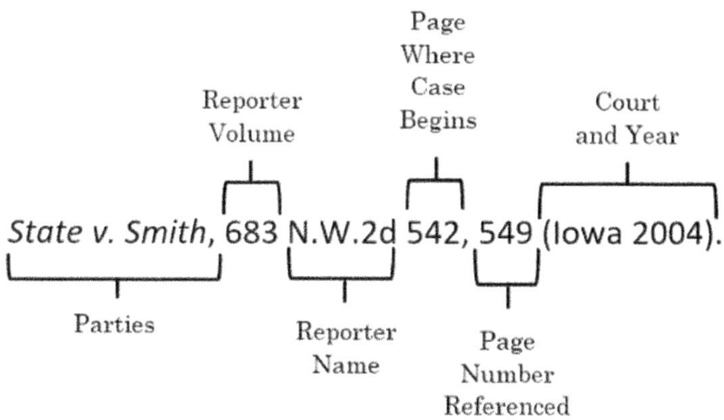

1. Case name (ALWD R. 12.2; BB R. 10.2)

The case name is composed of the two parties to the lawsuit (both sides of the "v."). In practice format, the cases are underlined *or* italicized (pick one and stick with it).[13] The parties' names can be seen at the beginning of the reported decision in the case caption or at the top of the page in a Westlaw, Lexis, or Bloomberg search. While the parties' names are generally easy to find, citing them correctly is the hardest part about building a case cite.

The format for the case name depends on where the citation appears: either as part of your text (embedded in a sentence) or standing alone as a citation sentence. If the citation appears as part of your text, follow *ALWD Guide* Rule 2.3 or *Bluebook* Rule 10.2.1. If it appears as a stand-alone or citation sentence, follow *ALWD Guide* Rule 12.2 or *Bluebook* Rules 10.2.1 and 10.2.2.

For **textual citations**, abbreviate the case name under limited circumstances (to maintain the flow of the writing for the reader.) For example, only the words *&*, *Ass'n*, *Bros.*, *Co.*, *Corp.*, *Inc.*, *Ltd.*, and *No.* are abbreviated, unless a party's name begins with one of these words.[14]

For **citation sentences**, further abbreviate words as shown in *ALWD Guide* Appendices 3(B) & 3(E) or *Bluebook* Tables 6 and 10.[15]

Thus, if a party's name is Maritime Production Company, it would appear in text as *Maritime Production Co.* and in a citation sentence as *Mar. Prod. Co.* Many legal readers and writers prefer citation sentences because textual citations can interrupt the flow of the text. Textual citations are not *wrong*, however, and both citation

---

13 *See, e.g.*, BLUEBOOK, *supra* note 1, *Introduction* to Bluepages, at 3.

14 ALWD GUIDE, *supra* note 1, R. 2.3, at 9–10; BLUEBOOK, *supra* note 1, R. 10.2.1(c), at 99.

15 ALWD GUIDE, *supra* note 1, App. 3(B), at 481, & App. 3(E), at 486; BLUEBOOK, *supra* note 1, tbl.T.6, at 304, & tbl.T.10, at 312.

guides have rules for formatting them. You may want to use them interchangeably to vary your writing.

Assume you want to cite the United States Supreme Court case on reckless disregard in the context of defamation (see p. 259) in a citation sentence (the most abbreviated form). The title of the case appears in Westlaw as:

Jim GARRISON, Appellant,
v.
STATE OF LOUISIANA.

The general rule is to use just the last name of individual parties.[16] Abbreviating names of corporate (and other fictitious entities) and governmental entities is a bit more complicated and requires a closer read of *ALWD Guide* Rule 12 and *Bluebook* Rule 10.

In this example, omit *State of* in this citation because it is not a decision of a Louisiana state court.[17] Geographical terms are abbreviated according to *ALWD Guide* Appendix 3(B) and *Bluebook* Table 10. Thus, the case name would be:

Garrison v. La.,

Note that this is **not** the name as it appears at the top of the page in Westlaw (see screenshot below).

2. Volume of the reporter, name of the reporter, and page where the case begins (ALWD R.12.3–.5; BB R. 10.3)

The next part of the citation contains information about the reporter where the case is published. The volume number of the reporter is followed by the appropriate abbreviation of the name of the reporter to be cited (there may be more than one, so when available, cite the official version). At the top of the page in a Westlaw, Lexis, or Bloomberg search, you will see one or more reporters in which the case appears.

For example, in *Garrison v. La.*, the top of the page in Westlaw indicates that the case appears in three reporters: *United States Reports*, the *Supreme Court Reporter*, and *Lawyers' Edition*, 2d. It also appears in the *Media Law Reporter*, a reporting service for lawyers interested in keeping up with developments in media law:

Garrison v. State of La.
Supreme Court of the United States · November 23, 1964 · 379 U.S. 64 · 85 S.Ct. 209 · 13 L.Ed.2d 125 · 1 Media L. Rep. 1548

---

16 ALWD Guide, *supra* note 1, R.12.2(d)(1), at 60; Bluebook, *supra* note 1, R. B10.1.1(ii), at 11–12.

17 If it were a state court decision cited to that state court, *La.* would be abbreviated as *State*. See ALWD Guide, *supra* note 1, R. 12.2(i), at 66–67; Bluebook, *supra* note 1, R. 10.2.1(f), at 99.

To know which reporter to cite, find the name of the official reporter for Supreme Court decisions and how to abbreviate it. The official reporter is *United States Reports*, and its abbreviation is U.S.[18] Where *United States Reports* is unavailable, in the listed order of preference: *Supreme Court Reporter* as S. Ct. and then *Lawyers' Edition* as L. Ed. You only need to cite one reporter. Notice that Westlaw has listed the reporters in the preferred order for citing them.

Since *Garrison* has been reported in *United States Reports*, this part of the case cite would be 379 U.S. 64, where 64 represents the page where the case begins.

Note: Although the reporter name is abbreviated correctly in this Westlaw example, that is not always the case. Always check your citation manual for the official reporter to cite and its abbreviation.

When formatting names of reporters, follow the abbreviations exactly as shown. The basic formatting rule is to close up adjacent single capitals (U.S.) but not single capitals with longer abbreviations (S. Ct.).[19] Every abbreviation should be followed by a period (Univ.), except those in which the last letter is set off by an apostrophe (Soc'y).[20] The easiest way to get the spacing right is to check *ALWD Guide* Appendix 1 and *Bluebook* Table 1.

Practice Pointer

In legal citations, the numbers indicating the edition of the reporter and a given federal circuit are called ordinals.

ALWD R. 4.3(b); BB R. 6.2(b). Ordinals are abbreviated using one number, one letter, and no superscript:

Example: second is 2d, not 2nd; the proper format would be:

F.2d

F. Supp. 2d

N.W.2d

(2d Cir. 1999)

Exception for documents filed in court: Because many court systems impose word limits for briefs and other documents submitted to the court, abbreviations in reporter names may be closed to count as one word, even if they would normally be separated under this rule.[21] For example, "S. Ct." could become "S.Ct." and "F. Supp. 2d" could become "F.Supp.2d.

3. Page number reference or pincite

Whenever possible, include the page number of the print reporter where the specific information you are citing is found (even if it is the first page of the case).

---

18 See ALWD GUIDE, *supra* note 1, App. 1, at 418; BLUEBOOK, *supra* note 1, tbl.T.1, at 227.

19 ALWD GUIDE, *supra* note 1, R. 2.2, at 7–8; BLUEBOOK, *supra* note 1, R. 6.1(a), at 88.

20 *See* ALWD GUIDE, *supra* note 1, R. 2.1(a), at 7; BLUEBOOK, *supra* note 1, R. B6, at 9.

21 *See* ALWD GUIDE, *supra* note 1, R. 2.2(e), at 8; BLUEBOOK, *supra* note 1, R. B6, at 9.

These are also known as **pincites** or **pinpoint citations.** In *Garrison*, if the first full citation were to page 78, this part of the citation would look like this:

379 U.S. 64, 78

How to find pincites online: When using an online version of a case, the page numbers in the print reporter are indicated. Recall that in *Garrison*, the official reporter is listed first at the top of the page, with the two unofficial reporters next, in order of preference. 85 S. Ct. 209 is the *Supreme Court Reporter* (a West publication), and 13 L. Ed. 2d is the *Lawyers' Edition* (a Lexis publication).

Garrison v. State of La.

Supreme Court of the United States · November 23, 1964 · 379 U.S. 64 · 85 S.Ct. 209 · 13 L.Ed.2d 125 · 1 Media L. Rep. 1548

If you scroll down in the case, somewhere between the headnotes and the beginning of the official opinion, you will see **210 *64:

Attorneys and Law Firms

**210 *64 Eberhard P. Deutsch, New Orleans, La., for appellant.

Jack P. F. Gremillion, Baton Rouge, La., for appellee.

Mr. Justice BRENNAN delivered the opinion of the Court.

The ****210** marks the end of page 209 and the beginning of page 210 in the *Supreme Court Reporter*. Everything up to this point was added by West; the official opinion begins here at ***64**. The number of asterisks corresponds to the order in which the reporters are listed at the top of the page. Did you notice that there is no page number for the Lexis publication? If you look up *Garrison* in Lexis, you can see page numbers for all of these reporters. Why do think that is?

How to cite multiple pages (ALWD R. 5.3; BB R. 3.2): When citing to more than one page, give the inclusive numbers separated by an en-dash or hyphen. Retain the last two digits but drop other repetitious digits:

369 U.S. 64, 78–79

43 A.3d at 298–99

43 A.3d at 298–301

4. Court name and date parenthetical (ALWD R. 12.6–.7; BB R. 10.4–.5)

The court that decided the case and the year of decision should be indicated in parentheses. Abbreviations for court names are found in *ALWD Guide* Appendices 1 (Primary Sources by Jurisdiction) and 4 (Court Abbreviations) and *Bluebook* Tables

1 (United States jurisdictions), 2 (foreign jurisdictions), and 7 (Court Names).[22] As of the twenty-first edition of the *Bluebook*, T.2 is now available only online.[23]

Supreme Court decisions should be abbreviated as "U.S."[24] However, since the name of the reporter indicates the court that decided the case, this abbreviation can be omitted,[25] but most citations will require the court abbreviation in the date parenthetical. This part of the *Garrison* citation would thus be:

(1964)

All put together, the proper cite for *Garrison* is:

Garrison v. La., 379 U.S. 64, 78 (1964).

Notice that there is a period at the end of the citation because it is a citation sentence.

5. Explanatory parentheticals

Explanatory parentheticals can serve several functions. They should be placed directly after the date parenthetical and before prior or subsequent history (see Chapter 56.E.6 below). Generally, they should begin with a present participle (a verb ending in –ing), such as *holding that, stating that, rejecting*, etc.

a. Relevance of authority (ALWD R. 37; BB R. 1.5)

Explanatory parentheticals are probably most commonly used to explain to the reader the relevance of the authority cited. They can be used alone or in conjunction with detailed case explanations in text to add depth and support to your analysis or argument without adding a lot of words.[26] A well-constructed explanatory parenthetical includes enough information for the reader to understand how and why it supports your proposition. That usually includes a reference to the legal issue if necessary, a key fact or two, and the holding or disposition of the case). Explanatory parentheticals are recommended for use with the following signals: *see also*, *cf.*, *compare . . . with*, *but see also*, *but cf.*, and *see generally*.

If you were citing *Garrison* and wanted to include a parenthetical explaining its relevance to the Velas matter, it might read something like this:

> *See also Garrison v. La.*, 379 U.S. 64, 78 (1964) (explaining that reckless disregard of the truth lies between actual knowledge of falsity and mere negligence).

---

22 ALWD GUIDE, *supra* note 1, App. 1, at 417 & App. 4, at 493; BLUEBOOK, *supra* note 1, tbl.T.1, at 227 & tbl.T.7, at 307.

23 BLUEBOOK, *supra* note 1, tbl.T.2, https://www.legalbluebook.com/bluebook/v21/tables/t2-foreign-jurisdictions.

24 ALWD GUIDE, *supra* note 1, App. 1, at 418; BLUEBOOK, *supra* note 1, tbl.T.1, at 227.

25 ALWD GUIDE, *supra* note 1, R. 12.6(c)(5), at 85; BLUEBOOK, *supra* note 1, R. 10.4(a), at 105–06, and B10.1.3, at 13–14.

26 *See supra* ch. 38.D, at 271, and 53.B.7, at 414.

b. Weight of authority (ALWD. R. 12.10; BB R. 10.6.1)

Parentheticals can also explain the weight of a decision, such as whether it was unpublished, whether you are citing a concurring or dissenting opinion, and whether the decision was *per curiam*, among other things.[27] For example, if you were citing a dissenting opinion, a weight of authority parenthetical would look like this:

(Appel, J., dissenting).

c. Quoting/citing parentheticals (ALWD R. 37.4(a); BB R. 10.6.3)

Parentheticals can also be used to let your reader know when the proposition you are citing quotes or cites another source.[28] The *Bluebook* indicates that you need only cite back to one case, even if that case cited an earlier one, and so on. A citing parenthetical would look like this:

> *State v. Smith*, 683 N.W.2d 542, 549 (Iowa 2004) (Appel, J. dissenting) (citing *Brainerd v. Cummings*, 499 N.W.2d 123, 134 (Iowa 1998)).

6. Prior and subsequent history (ALWD R. 12.8–.9; BB R. 10.7)

Prior and subsequent history refer to decisions made in the same case either before or after the case you are citing. With the exception of certain denials of certiorari or similar discretionary appeals (read the relevant rule in full), you should include the entire subsequent history of a case, but the prior history should be included only if it is relevant to the point you are making.[29] Subsequent history includes reversals, affirmations, and decisions vacated by higher courts. It also includes cases that have been overruled, abrogated, or superseded by statute.[30] A list of abbreviations for explanatory phrases can be found in *ALWD Guide* Chart 12.3 and Table 8 of the *Bluebook*.[31] For examples of how to cite prior and subsequent history, see *ALWD Guide*, *Fast Formats*, at 54, and *Bluebook* Rule 10.7.

7. Pending and unreported cases available on electronic media (ALWD R. 12.14; BB R. 10.8.1)

Some cases are so new they are not yet published in print reporters, while others have been designated by the court as not for publication. When citing one of these cases, you may cite the electronic database as follows: provide the case name, docket number, database identifier, court name, and full date of the most recent major disposition of the case.[32] One example in the *Bluebook* is:

---

27 ALWD GUIDE, *supra* note 1, R. 12.10, at 91–92; BLUEBOOK, *supra* note 1, R. 10.6.1(a), at 108.

28 ALWD GUIDE, *supra* note 1, R. 37.4(a), at 388; BLUEBOOK, *supra* note 1, R. 10.6.3, at 109.

29 *See* ALWD GUIDE, *supra* note 1, R. 12.8, at 85 & 12.9, at 91; BLUEBOOK, *supra* note 1, R. 10.7, at 109.

30 ALWD GUIDE, *supra* note 1, R. 12.8(a), at 85; BLUEBOOK, *supra* note 1, R. 10.7.1, at 111.

31 ALWD GUIDE, *supra* note 1, Chart 12.3, at 87; BLUEBOOK, *supra* note 1, tbl.T.8, at 310.

32 *See* ALWD GUIDE, *supra* note 1, R. 12.14, at 97; BLUEBOOK, *supra* note 1, R. 10.8.1, at 112.

Gibbs v. Frank, No. 02-3924, 2004 U.S. App. LEXIS 21357, at *18–19 (3d Cir. Oct. 14, 2004).

For more information on citing electronic sources, see *ALWD Guide* Rules 30–33 and *Bluebook* Rule 18.

8. Short citations (ALWD R. 12.16; BB R. 10.9)

Short citations may be used in memos and briefs instead of full citations once you have provided a full citation to that case.[33] If the immediately preceding cite is to that first full citation, you may use *id.* (see below). In general, the short cite includes the name of the first party,[34] the volume and name of the reporter, and a pincite. For example, if several citations back, you cited *Garrison* in full and now want to cite it again but to page 69, the short cite would be:

Garrison, 379 U.S. at 69.

Notice that the second party's name, the first page of the case, and the date parenthetical are removed. Where the first name of the party is a common litigant, such as a state or other governmental entity, use the second party's name for easier identification. For example, a short cite to *State v. Smith* would be:

Smith, 683 N.W.2d at 549.

Practice Pointer

For even more concise citations, you may omit a case name from your full or short citation sentence if you provide it in text. For example:

Smith held the defendant was not "seized" when asked for his ID and checked for outstanding warrants during a traffic stop. 683 N.W.2d at 549.

9. Use of *id.*

When writing legal memoranda and briefs, you may use *id.* (short for *ibid*) instead of a full or short citation if you are citing the immediately preceding authority.[35] You may not use *id.* if your previous citation has more than one authority because the reader may be confused about which authority you are citing.[36]

Practice Pointer

The period at the end of *id.* is *always* italicized or underlined.

For example, if you just cited *State v. Smith*, either as a full or short citation and want to cite it again—with no cite intervening—to the same page, the cite would be: *Id.* If you wanted to cite Smith again but to page 547, which is a different page, the citation would be: *Id.* at 547.

---

33 *See* BLUEBOOK, *supra* note 1, R. B10.2, at 16–18.

34 *See* ALWD GUIDE, *supra* note 1, R. 12.16(b), at 103; BLUEBOOK, *supra* note 1, R. 10.9(a)(i), at 116.

35 ALWD GUIDE, *supra* note 1, R. 12.16(a), at 103; BLUEBOOK, *supra* note 1, R. 4.1 at 79.

36 *See* ALWD GUIDE, *supra* note 1, R. 12.16(a), at 103; BLUEBOOK, *supra* note 1, at 80.

Try It: Exercise 56.1

(answers at App. B, at p. 525)

For use in a legal memorandum, create the requested citations based on the following information:

Appellant: Smith Industries, Incorporated

Appellee: United States Department of Agriculture

Reporter: Volume 890 of the third edition of the Pacific reporter, starting at page 300

The quote you are referencing is on page 342.

The case was decided by the Oregon Supreme Court in 2017.

1. Create a first full citation to the case.
2. Create a short citation to page 344 with intervening citations.
3. Create a short citation with no intervening citations, but you want to cite only page 350.

F. Statutes (ALWD R. 14; BB Rules B12 & 12)

Statutes are cited according to Rule 14 of the *ALWD Guide* and Rule 12 of the *Bluebook*.[37] As the diagram below illustrates, the first full citation to a statute is composed of the name of the act (in limited circumstances) when passed, the title number and name of the code cited, the section(s) cited, and the year of the print code (according to the seventh edition of the *ALWD Guide* and the twenty-first edition of the *Bluebook*, the year of the code is required only for state statutes).[38] Each rule explains in detail how to build each part of a full and short citation to statutes.

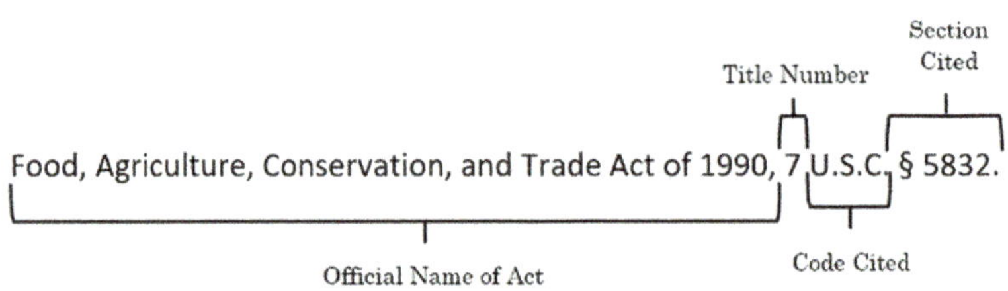

37 ALWD GUIDE, *supra* note 1, R. 14, at 112; BLUEBOOK, *supra* note 1,R. 12, at 120.

38 *See* ALWD GUIDE, *supra* note 1, R. 14.2(f), at 118–19. BLUEBOOK, *supra* note 1, R. 12.3.2, at 125. The year of publication is not readily available online. You may need to consult the print code in your law library.

1. Name of statute (ALWD R. 14.2(a); BB R. 12.3.1(a))

Unlike cases, the names of statutes are included in the citation only if the name is commonly included in the citation or it would help the reader identify it. If so, you can use either the official or popular name of the statute.[39] As shown above, the name comes first and is capitalized according to *ALWD Guide* Rule 3 and *Bluebook* Rule 8,[40] followed by a comma.

2. Title number and name of code (ALWD R. 14.2–.4; BB 12.3)

Most statutory codes are organized by subject matter and divided into titles or chapters. For federal statutes, the preferred source is the official code, the *United States Code* (abbreviated as U.S.C.), but you can also cite U.S.C.A or U.S.C.S.[41] As shown in the example above, the name of the statute is followed by the title number and the abbreviation to the official code.

> **Practice Pointer**
>
> Remember not to use large and small caps for practitioner citations:
>
> D.C. Code, NOT D.C. CODE

For state statutes, consult *ALWD Guide* Appendix 1(B) and *Bluebook* Table 1. Each provides the official and unofficial codes for each state and explains how to cite them.

3. Sections cited (ALWD R. 6; BB R. 3.3)

> FYI
>
> **How do I make the § symbol?**
>
> To make the section symbol in Word, click on *Insert*, *Symbol*, and *Special Characters*.
>
> From that last screen, you can insert a section symbol. You can also create an auto-correct rule or shortcut key to make it easier next time. I have an auto-correct rule: when I type sec, it auto-corrects to §.
>
> Always add a space after your section symbol.

The next part of the citation is to the specific section(s) you want to cite. First, you insert the section symbol (§), a space, and the number from the code, including any original punctuation, such as dashes or periods.[42] If you are citing multiple sections, use two section symbols (§§), and give inclusive numbers (do not use *et seq.*).[43]

---

[39] Recall that you can search for federal statutes in print or online based on their popular name (*e.g.*, Affordable Care Act). *See supra* ch. 26.A.3(a), at 175.

[40] Capitalize the initial word, any word that follows a colon, and all words except articles (e.g., a, the), conjunctions, (*e.g.*, and, but, or) and prepositions of four or fewer letters (*e.g.*, in, of, on). ALWD GUIDE, *supra* note 1, R. 3.2(a), at 11; BLUEBOOK, *supra* note 1, R. 8(a), at 91.

[41] *See id.* ALWD GUIDE, *supra* note 1, App. 1(A), at 418; BLUEBOOK, *supra* note 1, tbl.T.1, at 227.

[42] ALWD GUIDE, *supra* note 1, R. 6.1(b), at 29; BLUEBOOK, *supra* note 1, R. 3.3(a), at 76.

[43] ALWD GUIDE, *supra* note 1, R. 6.2(a)–(b), at 31; BLUEBOOK, *supra* note 1, R. 3.3(b), at 76–77.

4. Year of code (state statutes only) (ALWD Rules 14.2(f) & 14.4; BB R. 12.3.2)

As of the *Bluebook*'s twenty-first edition, the year of the federal code is no longer required as part of the citation. If you are using the *ALWD Guide*, check with your professor on this point. For state statutes, provide parenthetically the year that appears on the spine of the volume, the year that appears on the title page, or the latest copyright year—in that order of preference.

5. Short citations (ALWD R. 14.5; BB R. 12.10)

There are several ways to short-cite statutes. The most common (in a situation where you have not included the statute's name) is to include the title and section number or just the section number (as long as the reader will not be confused) and a period:

28 U.S.C. § 1332. *or*

§ 1332.

Note: Do not begin sentences with a section symbol (*e.g.*, Section 15-2 defines "driving" as . . .).[44]

6. Use of *id.*

You may use *id.* to cite a statute if the preceding cite is to the same statute:

same statute and section: *Id.*

same statute, different section: *Id.* § 1331.

Do **not** use *at.* This would be wrong: *Id.* at § 1331.

Try It: Exercise 56.2

(answers at App. B, at p. 525)

For use in a legal memorandum:

1. Create a full citation to title 5, section 552 of the United States Code.
2. Create a citation to chapter 562.9 and 562.10 of the Iowa Code published in 2018.

---

44 ALWD GUIDE, *supra* note 1, R. 6.6, at 33; BLUEBOOK, *supra* note 1, R. 6.2(c), at 90.

3. Create a short citation to the statute in question 1. Assume there are intervening citations.

4. Create a short citation to section 562.10 of the statute described in question 2. Assume there are no intervening citations.

G. Constitutions (ALWD R. 13; BB Rules B11 & 11)

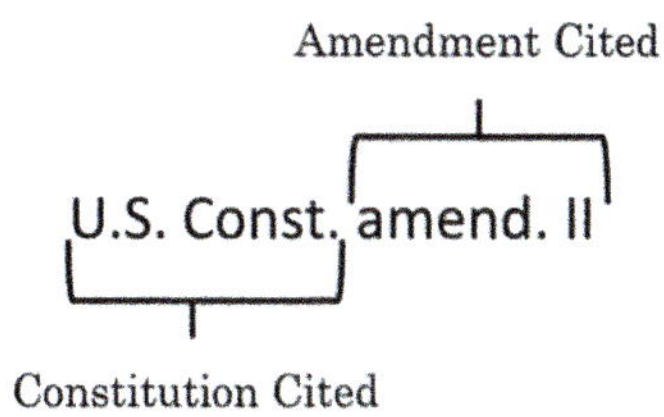

Constitutions are cited according to Rule 13 of the *ALWD Guide* and Rule 11 of the *Bluebook*.[45] As shown above, the citation begins with the correct abbreviation of the jurisdiction (see ALWD App. 3(B); BB T.10), followed by "Const.," and then the correct abbreviation of the subdivision you are citing, such as the article, clause or amendment (see ALWD App. 3(C); BB T.16).[46] A full citation to a particular article of the U.S. Constitution would look like this:

> **Practice Pointer**
>
> Remember not to use large and small caps for practitioner citations:
>
> Const, NOT CONST.

U.S. Const. art. I, § 9, cl. 1.

Try It: Exercise 56.3

(answers at App. B, at p. 525)

Create a citation to article II, section 1 of the Iowa Constitution for use in an appellate brief.

---

45 ALWD GUIDE, *supra* note 1, R. 13, at 108; BLUEBOOK, *supra* note 1, R. 11, at 119.

46 ALWD GUIDE, *supra* note 1, App. 3(C), at 485; BLUEBOOK, *supra* note 1, tbl.T.16, at 327.

H. Law review articles (and other secondary sources) (ALWD Rules 20 & 21; BB Rules B15, 15, B16, & 16)

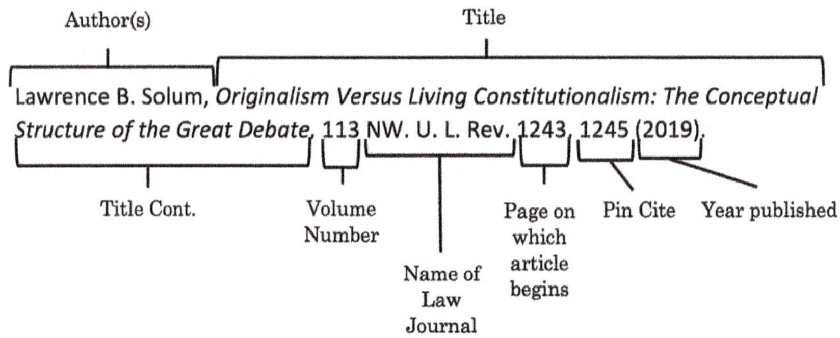

Each citation manual devotes two rules to citing secondary sources, and the citations follow a general pattern. *ALWD Guide* Rule 20 and *Bluebook* Rule 15 govern citations to books and other nonperiodic materials, such as treatises and encyclopedias.[47] *ALWD Guide* Rule 21 and *Bluebook* Rule 16 govern citations to periodical materials, such as law journals or reviews, newspapers, and magazines.[48] The example discussed below is a law review article, which you will likely need to know how to cite at some point soon.

1. Author name (ALWD R. 21.2(a); BB R.16.2)

Insert the author's name as it appears in the article, first name first.[49]

2. Title of Article (ALWD R. 21.2(c); BB R.16.3)

The title of the article should appear in italics or underlining. If a word or phrase in the title would usually be italicized, it should be in ordinary font.[50] For example, an article titled, The Legacy of Roe v. Wade: Recent Supreme Court Decisions on Abortion Rights, would be cited as:

> *The Legacy of* Roe v. Wade*: Recent Supreme Court Decisions on Abortion Rights*

Practice Pointer

When citing multiple articles, list them in a logical order. See BB R. 1.4.

The BB used to have strict rules on the correct order. Some of your co-workers will not know the rule has changed. The old rule was to cite by the author's last name in alphabetical order.

---

47 ALWD GUIDE, *supra* note 1, R. 20, at 214; BLUEBOOK, *supra* note 1, R.15, at 147.

48 ALWD GUIDE, *supra* note 1, R. 21, at 235; BLUEBOOK, *supra* note 1, R.16, at 157.

49 ALWD GUIDE, *supra* note 1, R. 21.2(a), at 237; BLUEBOOK, *supra* note 1, R.16.2, at 159.

50 ALWD GUIDE, *supra* note 1, R. 21.2(c), at 238; BLUEBOOK, *supra* note 1, R.16.3 at 159.

3. Journal volume, title, page where article begins (ALWD R. 21.2(d)–(f); BB R. 16.4–.5)

Next comes the volume number (the "113" in the example above) and the correct abbreviation of the journal name (see *ALWD Guide* Appendices 3 & 5; *Bluebook* Tables 6, 10, and 13). In this example, the article appeared in the Northwestern University Law Review, abbreviated as NW. U. L. Rev. Then add the page the article begins on.

4. Pincite(s)

Following the abbreviated journal name and the page where the article begins, add a comma and the pages you rely on.

5. Publication date (ALWD R. 21.2(g); BB R. 16.4–.5)

The last part of the citation is the year of publication in parentheses.

6. Short citations and *id.* (ALWD R. 21.7; BB R. B15.2)

Use *id.* to cite an immediately preceding citation. Otherwise, once you have cited an article in full, you may refer to it as having already been or going to be cited in full later (perhaps where the fuller discussion appears). Example adapted from the *Bluebook*:

Full cite: Deborah L. Rhode, *Justice and Gender* 56, 67 (1989).

Short cites: *Id.* at 69.

Rhode, *supra*, at 60–61.

Rhode, *infra*, at 60–61.

Try It: Exercise 56.4

(answers at App. B, at p. 526)

Create a citation for a law review article for use in an appellate brief using the following information:

1. Author: F.H. Buckley.
2. Title: "The Fall and Rise of Crown Government."
3. The article was published in the sixty-eighth volume of the Drake Law Review in 2020.
4. The article begins on page 252. You intend to cite page 265.

I. Citation tips

1. When to capitalize "court" (ALWD R. 3.4; BB R. 8(c)(ii))

When referring to "the court," capitalize it when you refer to the United States Supreme Court, name a court by its full name, or refer to the same court in which you are filing an argument. In all other cases, use a lower case "c":

The United States District Court for the Southern District of New York

The Court declared separate but equal laws unconstitutional. *See Brown v. Bd. of Educ.*, 347 U.S. 483 (1954).

(in a memo): The court took several factors into account, including time, place, and location. *James v. Juniper*, 99 S.E.2d 676, 681 (Ga. 1999).

(in a brief to the Georgia Supreme Court): This Court took several factors into account, including time, place and location. *James v. Juniper*, 99 S.E.2d 676, 681 (Ga. 1999).

2. Numerals (ALWD R. 4.2(a); BB R. 6.2(a))

The general rule is to spell out numbers zero to ninety-nine in text; for larger numbers, use numerals. One major exception to using numerals is where the number begins a sentence:[51]

The safe-harbor test has four requirements.

The defendant had 1,250 customers.

Three hundred residents were affected.

3. Do not abbreviate *United States* to *U.S.* in case names (ALWD R. 12.2; BB Rules 6.1(b) & 15.1)

United States may be abbreviated to "U.S." only when used as an adjective. Do not omit the periods: U.S. history.[52]

4. Block quotations (ALWD R. 38.5; BB Rules B5.2 & 5.1)

Quotations of fifty or more words should be single spaced, indented on both sides, justified, and without quotation marks.[53] The citation appears on the next line on the left margin:

---

51 ALWD GUIDE, *supra* note 1, R. 4.2(a), at 17; BLUEBOOK, *supra* note 1, R. 6.2(a), at 89.

52 ALWD GUIDE, *supra* note 1, R. 12.2(h), at 66 & App. 3(B)(3), at 482; BLUEBOOK, *supra* note 1, R. 6.1(b), at 89, & 15.1, at 148.

53 ALWD GUIDE, *supra* note 1, R. 38.5(a), at 397; BLUEBOOK, *supra* note 1, R. 5.2, at 84, & 5.1, at 83.

> . . . The plain meaning of driving encompasses the following actions:
>
> [fifty or more quoted words indented and single spaced]
>
> *Klink v. Clack*, 64 F. Supp. 2d 32, 40 (S.D.N.Y 2009).

Use block quotations sparingly. Your reader may skip over them, and you can often paraphrase without sacrificing content.

5. Use ellipses to indicate omissions in text (ALWD R. 40; BB R. 5.3(b))

Indicate omissions in any quoted text "using three periods separated by a space as shown . . . here."

Where the beginning of a quoted sentence is omitted, capitalize the first letter of the quoted language and place it in brackets if it is not already capitalized: "[T]his is how the sentence appears as a result."

Where the end of a quoted sentence is omitted, insert an ellipsis between the last word being quoted and the final punctuation of the sentence being quoted: "This is how the sentence appears . . . ."[54]

---

[54] *See* ALWD GUIDE, *supra* note 1, R. 40.1–.2, at 407–08; BLUEBOOK, *supra* note 1, R. 5.3(b), at 86.

Chapter 57

Signals and String Citations

A. What are signals? (ALWD R. 35; BB Rules B1 & 1)

The authorities you cite rarely function in exactly the same way. **Signals** are like a universal code in legal writing that indicate how the cited authority supports or contradicts your proposition.

Practice Pointer

Capitalize signals only when used to begin a citation sentence.

1. Signals indicating support

No signal → No signal is itself a signal. It indicates that the authority directly supports the proposition, identifies the source of a quotation, or identifies an authority referred to in the text.[1]

E.g., → This signal indicates there are other authorities that state the proposition, but citing them is not beneficial or necessary.[2]

Accord → This signal indicates that two or more sources stand for the same proposition, but you are citing only one. The law of one jurisdiction can also be cited as being in accord with the law of another.[3]

See → This signal indicates that the authority clearly supports but does not directly state the proposition. There is an inferential step required between the cited authority and the stated proposition.[4]

---

1 ALWD Guide, *supra* ch. 56, note 1, R.35.2, at 370; Bluebook, *supra* ch. 56, note 1, R. 1.2(a), at 62.

2 ALWD Guide, *supra* ch. 56, note 1, Chart 35.1, at 371; Bluebook, supra ch. 56, note 1, R. 1.2(a) at 62.

3 ALWD Guide, *supra* ch. 56, note 1, Chart 35.1, at 371; Bluebook, *supra* ch. 56, note 1, R. 1.2(a) at 62.

4 ALWD Guide, *supra* ch. 56, note 1, Chart 35.1, at 371; Bluebook, *supra* ch. 56, note 1, R. 1.2(a) at 62.

See also → Use this signal when you have an authority that supports a proposition, and you have already cited another.[5] This signal often follows citation to authority that does not require a signal. Explanatory parentheticals are strongly encouraged.

Cf. → This signal indicates the cited authority supports an analogous proposition close enough to lend support.[6] Explanatory parentheticals are strongly encouraged.

2. Signals indicating contradiction

Contra → This signal indicates the cited authority is directly contrary to your proposition.[7]

But see → This signal indicates that the cited authority clearly supports a contrary proposition but only by inference.[8]

But cf. → Use this signal when the authority supports a proposition close enough to the contrary of yours that it detracts from your argument.[9] Explanatory parentheticals are strongly encouraged.

3. Other signals

Compare . . . with → Use this signal when you wish to compare two or more authorities, often to show differing treatment.[10] Explanatory parentheticals are strongly encouraged.

See generally→This signal indicates the cited authority is useful as background information related to the proposition. This signal is used primarily for **secondary authority**. Explanatory parentheticals are strongly encouraged.

Supra and *infra*→ These signals refer to material that has already been or will be cited later in your document. These signals should be used in legal memos and court documents only when referring to periodical materials.[11] Do **not** use these signals to refer to primary authority.

---

5 ALWD Guide, *supra* ch. 56, note 1, Chart 35.1, at 371; Bluebook, *supra* ch. 56, note 1, R. 1.2(a) at 63.

6 ALWD Guide, *supra* ch. 56, note 1, Chart 35.1, at 371; Bluebook, *supra* ch. 56, note 1, R. 1.2(a) at 63.

7 ALWD Guide, *supra* ch. 56, note 1, Chart 35.1, at 372; Bluebook, *supra* ch. 56, note 1, R. 1.2(c), at 63.

8 ALWD Guide, *supra* ch. 56, note 1, Chart 35.1, at 372; Bluebook, *supra* ch. 56, note 1, R. 1.2(c), at 63.

9 ALWD Guide, *supra* ch. 56, note 1, Chart 35.1, at 372; Bluebook, *supra* ch. 56, note 1, R. 1.2(c), at 63.

10 ALWD Guide, *supra* ch. 56, note 1, Chart 35.1, at 372; Bluebook, *supra* ch. 56, note 1, R. 1.2(b), at 63.

11 *See* ALWD Guide, *supra* ch. 56, note 1, R. 10.2(a), at 42; Bluebook, *supra* ch. 56, note 1, R. B4, at 8; *see also* ALWD Guide, *supra* ch. 56, note 1, R. 11.4, at 49; Bluebook, *supra* ch. 56, note 1, R. 3.5, at 78 (explaining use of these signals as cross-references to portions of text in law review articles).

4. Combining signals

When it makes sense to do so, signals can be combined. For example, if there are several cases that support your proposition by inference, one of those cases could be cited and introduced by combining see and e.g.,: *See, e.g.,*

Practice Pointer

Only the first comma in *see, e.g.*, is italicized.

Try It: Exercise 57.1

(answers at App. B, at p. 526)

Assume you want to make this proposition in a case governed by Florida law:

"All fresh fruit perishes within a limited period of time."

What signal would you use to introduce the following cited authority?

1. A Florida District Court of Appeal case stating that bananas perish in a limited period of time.

2. A treatise on food disparagement law and its underlying policy.

3. A Florida case stating that not all fresh fruit perishes within a limited period of time.

4. A Florida statute stating that all fresh fruit perishes within a limited period of time.

5. One of many Florida cases stating that all fresh fruit perishes within a limited period of time.

6. A case from the Florida Supreme Court stating that all produce perishes within a limited period of time.

7. A Florida case holding that all fresh fruit perishes in a limited period of time, and an Alabama case holding that only some fresh fruit perishes within a limited period of time. You wish to cite these authorities to show that Florida is more protective of fresh fruit growers.

8. A Florida case stating that fresh green beans perish in a limited period of time.

9. One of many Florida cases stating that bananas, apples, and pears perish in a limited period of time.

10. A Florida case stating that fresh green beans do not perish in a limited period of time.

11. Two authorities each of which stands for the proposition that all fresh fruit perishes within a limited period of time. One is a Florida case and the other is a California case.

12. One of many Florida cases holding that watermelon does not perish within a limited period of time.

13. A Florida case stating, "All fresh fruit perishes or decays beyond marketability in a limited period of time."

B. String citations (ALWD R. 36; BB R. 1.4)

Practice Pointer

When citing multiple authorities in a citation sentence, separate them using semi-colons.

A citation to more than one authority at a time is called a **string citation**. According to the *ALWD Guide* and the *Bluebook*, authorities within the same signal should be ordered in a logical manner. "If one authority or several authorities together are considerably more helpful or authoritative than the other authorities cited within a signal, they should precede the others. Authorities cited in short form are ordered as though cited in full."[12]

Note: This is a significant deviation from the old rules, which specified the order of authorities in a string citation. The old rule required that authorities be listed in hierarchical order (meaning primary then secondary authority, and within primary authority, constitutions came first, then statutes, etc.). Then there was an order for stringing together the same type of authority. For example, the highest federal court cases came first arranged in reverse chronological order (meaning most recent first). Then came cases from the next highest court, and so on. I expect many judges and practitioners will either be unaware of the new rule or ignore it. These general guidelines are set forth in Rule 36.2 of the *ALWD Guide*.

Practice Pointer

Ask employers whether they have a preference for ordering authority in string citations.

---

12 BLUEBOOK, *supra* ch. 56, note 1, R. 1.4, at 65; *see also* ALWD GUIDE, *supra* ch. 56, note 1, R. 36, at 377.

C. Order of signals (ALWD R. 35.5; BB R. 1.3)

When you use more than one signal to support or contradict a proposition, the signals (along with the cited authorities) should appear in the order shown above on pages 465–466. Signals of the same type (supportive, contradictory, comparative, or background) should be strung together within a single citation sentence and separated by semi-colons. Signals of different types must be grouped in different citation sentences.[13]

Try It: Exercise 57.2

(answers at App. B, at p. 526)

Create a citation using appropriate signals and the following information. You are writing a brief to the Iowa Supreme Court. There are two cases you must cite:

1. Case One

   Appellant: The State of Iowa

   Appellee: Jacob Jones

   Reporter: Volume 900 of the second edition of the North Western reporter

   This case was decided by the Iowa Supreme Court in 2020.

   The case starts on page 783. You are citing page 793.

   This case stands for your point, albeit indirectly.

2. Case Two

   Appellant: TeddyBear Systems Company

   Appellee: Digital Development Systems, Incorporated

   Reporter: Volume 678 of the South Eastern reporter

   This case was decided by the Georgia Supreme Court in 2019.

   This case starts on page 890. You are citing page 927.

   This case states the contrary of your point.

---

13 ALWD GUIDE, *supra* ch. 56, note 1, Rule 35.5, at 373; BLUEBOOK, *supra* ch. 56, note 1, R. 1.3, at 64.

For More Information

Here are some additional resources for learning citation rules according to the *ALWD Guide* and the *Bluebook*. At the time this book was published, some had not yet been updated to include the changes in *Bluebook*'s twenty-first edition (2020) or the *ALWD Guide*'s seventh edition (2021).

Free and online:

Cornell Law, ***Introduction to Basic Legal Citation*** (2019), https://www.law.cornell.edu/citation/.

Georgetown University Law Center, ***Bluebook Guide*** (last updated 6/20) https://guides.ll.georgetown.edu/bluebook.

Loyola Law School, L.A., ***Bluebooking and Legal Citation*** (last updated 9/20), https://guides.library.lls.edu/bluebook.

Online with Lexis subscription:

Lexis's ***Interactive Citation Workstation*** (ICW). ICW is an online tutorial that helps law students build their basic citation skills. It is a good supplement to the instruction provided in introductory legal research and writing courses. To access ICW, login to Lexis Advance and click on the nine dots in the upper left corner, then click on Interactive Citation Workstation. If the link has moved and you cannot find it, just google it.

Print:

Deborah Bouchoux, ***Cite-Checker: Your Guide to Using the Bluebook*** (4th ed. 2016).

Tracy L. Norton, ***Interactive Citation Workbook for The Bluebook: A Uniform System of Citation*** (2020).

Tracy L. Norton, ***Interactive Citation Workbook for ALWD Guide to Legal Citation*** (2020).

Test Your Knowledge: Part XIII

To assess your understanding of the material in this part, click here to take a quiz.

Part XIV

Memory and Delivery

Chapter 58

Reporting to a Supervisor

Aristotle's last two canons of rhetoric are memory and delivery (see Chapter 13.D). Because ancient cultures were primarily oral cultures, a speaker had to be able to memorize a speech to deliver it effectively, especially to a large crowd. In the twenty-first century, it is rare for lawyers to have to memorize oral speeches or arguments (perhaps with the exception of opening statements and closing arguments in a trial-like setting). When a lawyer is required to orally articulate her research findings, analysis, advice, or arguments, she usually has access to written materials.

That said, it's important to recognize and develop the different skills involved in speaking about the law. Regardless of the type of law you practice, you will be required and expected to be able to converse intelligently and effectively about your work. People don't usually speak the way they write. If you were to read a transcript of your everyday conversation, you would probably be shocked at how difficult it is to read. People tend to interrupt one another, speak in fragments, rely on verbal cues, context, tone, etc. to infer meaning.

> **Practice Pointer**
>
> When orally reporting the **results of your research:**
>
> - create a list of talking points
> - take your research with you
> - be prepared to give an opinion on how the law applies to your client's situation
> - take good notes during the meeting
> - do not hesitate to ask questions
> - leave with a clear sense of what you are supposed to do next and when

In fact, one hallmark of a seasoned lawyer is their ability to examine a witness or dictate a brief in complete and coherent sentences. As with predictive and persuasive writing, effective speaking requires *logos*, *pathos*, and *ethos*: it must be logical, sympathetic, and credible.

One of the first experiences you are likely to have in practice is to meet with a supervisor or colleague to report and discuss your research. You may be asked to write a memo, a PowerPoint presentation, or an email and then explain it, or you may be asked to discuss your findings in advance of memorializing them in writing. Either way, the lawyers you are working with are likely to have certain expectations about how those meetings should unfold.

If you have time, create a list of talking points in advance. For example, if you were asked to discuss the likelihood that the Velases could succeed in an action against CSP for false disparagement, you might jot down the known facts, the elements of a claim under Texas law, any unknown facts that would help you analyze the claim, and key cases. These talking points will jog your memory and allow you to speak intelligently about your findings.

Be sure to bring your research with you to the meeting. As already indicated, you will not be expected to have memorized the law. Who could do that? Instead, bring your research—statutes, cases, secondary authority, summaries, charts, etc.—with you, in either print or electronic form. Be sure it is organized in a form you can readily access or consult. You might even send copies of the significant statutes or cases in advance of the meeting for others attending to review.

Do not assume that it will be enough for you to turn your research findings over to your supervisor. Your supervisor will expect you to come with more than just what you found. You will need to synthesize your findings to determine what the law *is* and think through in advance how it applies to your client's situation. Be prepared also to give your opinion. It's okay if your initial instincts turn out to be wrong; the process of talking through your analysis with your supervisor will help you determine the next steps to take.

Take good notes during the meeting. The time your supervisor has set aside to discuss your research is valuable. This may be the only time they have been able to devote to the client this week. Therefore, it is important to maximize that time by listening carefully to your supervisor's responses, ideas, and suggestions. Write them down. If they don't make sense, ask questions. You probably know the law better than they do, and they will expect you to challenge their ideas if they are mistaken or misguided about the law.

For your own sake, do not leave the meeting without knowing what your supervisor expects you to do next and when. Even if you know what you are supposed to do but are unsure about how to go about doing it, ask for guidance. You may not get another opportunity before that assignment is due. Just a few years out of law school, lawyers tend to forget how confusing the law can be and how long it takes to complete good and comprehensive research. So take responsibility for your work but self-advocate as well.

Chapter 59

Client Meetings

Early in your career, you may be called upon to interview or speak with a client before you feel you are ready. This could happen in the course of your work for a clinic, internship, externship, or summer job. Although you may feel comfortable with the legal issues you are dealing with, you may not have much experience speaking with people you don't know, particularly those struggling with legal problems. Meeting with clients calls on your ability to be analytical and empathetic at the same time, and this type of multi-tasking is challenging.

This chapter provides a basic approach for meeting with clients. The specifics of the process will depend on the context and custom of your particular office. In the absence of specific guidance, these principles should help you prepare.

> **Practice Pointer**
>
> When **interviewing** or **meeting** with a client:
>
> - do your homework
> - don't reinvent the wheel
> - greet the client warmly
> - explain the meeting is confidential and privileged
> - listen carefully
> - ask a broad range of questions
> - take good notes
> - resist the temptation to give advice or predict outcome
> - make sure the client leaves knowing what to do and expect next from you

Start by doing your homework. Has the client already retained you or your office? If not, that may affect whether your conversations are privileged. Second, if this is an existing client, check to see if there is a client file or any background information available. Be sure to read it and take notes. If you have some idea of the legal issues involved, do some initial research to help you ask the right questions. If possible, make a list of questions you think might need to be answered.

You don't need to reinvent the wheel. Ask a colleague for advice. Practicing lawyers often forget what it is like to do things for the first time, but they will respect your asking them for advice. Again, depending on the nature of the law office, there may even be an intake or client contact form you should use.

When the client arrives, greet them warmly. As nervous as you might be, your client is likely to be more so. In order for the meeting to be productive, establish a safe and comfortable environment. A firm handshake, a bit of small talk, and direct eye contact—these will go a long way toward helping the client feel at ease. Before the interview starts, consider how you would want to be treated under the same circumstances.

If this is the first meeting with the client, explain the confidential and privileged nature of your conversation.[1] You are permitted to discuss the conversation with colleagues but not with anyone who does not represent the client or anyone outside the office. You also want to make sure the client knows to keep your conversations confidential as well so as to preserve attorney-client privilege.[2] That means the client should not discuss the content of your conversation with family, friends, or other advisors.

As you move into the substance of the conversation, begin with a few broad, open-ended questions: "What brings you here today," "What can I help you with," or "I read your email, and it appears you are having trouble with your landlord. Is that right?" These sorts of questions invite clients to speak freely about the situation in their own way. Let the client give you the whole story. Take good notes throughout and indicate to yourself where you want to follow-up with questions, rather than interrupting your client's story. As you listen, try to remain objective and open-minded. The client is here for your help, not your judgment. Then, you can go into lawyer mode. Ask any follow-up questions, the questions you prepared in advance, and any questions you need to ask to flesh out as much of the story as possible.

For example, assume Christina and Ramon Velas have an appointment to meet with you. You have never met them, and you have no idea what legal problem they will present to you. Having listened to their story, you would want to be sure to fill in any gaps. You can use who, what, when, where, why, and how questions to get at the most critical information:

Who is involved?

> Who are the bean suppliers from Central and South America? Do your clients have their contact information if you need it? May you contact them directly? Who were the old bean suppliers? Who is CSP? Do they know any of the members? Have they had any prior contact with CSP

1 "A lawyer shall not reveal information relating to the representation of a client unless the client gives informed consent." Model Rule 1.6, *supra* ch. 44, note 25.

2 "The principle of client-lawyer confidentiality is given effect by related bodies of law: the attorney-client privilege, the work product doctrine and the rule of confidentiality established in professional ethics. *Id.* at cmt. 3." *See also* Sue Michmerhuizen, *Confidentiality, Privilege: A Basic Value in Two Different Applications* (May 2007), https://www.americanbar.org/content/dam/aba/administrative/professional_responsibility/confidentiality_or_attorney.authcheckdam.pdf (https://perma.cc/3HUT-DUJB)

or its members? Any contact since the newsletter came out? What about the Velases' employees? Have they had any contact or relationship with CSP? What about Starbucks' officers? May you contact them directly?

What happened to you?

Did CSP ever contact or attempt to contact them or any of their employees? How soon after the March newsletter came out did they begin to notice a decline in sales? How is that documented? What did customers say or do? Do they have any proof that the beans are organic? Is it in writing? Have the beans been tested? Do they sell any beans that are not organic? Do they have financial reports or other data indicating the losses incurred so far?

When did it happen?

Try to create a timeline of events. When did your clients enter into the relationship with their current suppliers? Why did they make the switch? When did the newsletter come out? How soon afterward did the Velases begin to notice a decline in sales?

Where did it happen?

Do they have more than one location? Have there been statements about the nature of their coffee beans made anywhere else beside the newsletter? Do they think their customers have repeated the contents of the newsletter to other customers?

Why and how do you think it happened?

Did anything happen before CSP's newsletter was published indicating that CSP questioned the organic nature of the beans? Phone calls, rumors, email, letters, etc.? Is there any reason why anyone involved with CSP would want to damage their business?

Anything else you think I should know or have?

You can conclude by asking this catch-all question. Your questions may have triggered memories or ideas that the client is now primed to share.

Recognize that it can be difficult to listen carefully, connect with your client, and take good notes at the same time. You will get better with practice. Don't hesitate to ask the client to slow down or repeat information. You may find it easier to take written notes and then type them later. You may be able to listen and type without constantly looking down at the screen. You might even tape the interview so you can go over it again later, but get your client's consent to do that.

When you have completed your questions, resist the temptation to give advice or predict an outcome. Presumably, you have some research and consultation to do before you will be in a position to do either one of those things. The risk you run is overstating the client's prospects or promising results you cannot deliver.

Before the client leaves, be sure to schedule next steps. The client should know what you expect them to do before the next meeting, such as send information, documents, contacts, etc. Similarly, the client should have an idea of what you plan to do before your next meeting and how to contact you in the interim.

For example, you might ask the Velases to send you any documents indicating the beans are organic, the contract with the current suppliers, the March 2019 CSP newsletter, and contact information for their employees and their bean suppliers. You might then indicate that before you meet again, you will conduct legal research, review the materials they send, and be in a position to give an assessment of their legal options.

Chapter 60

Oral Advocacy

Oral advocacy takes many forms: talking on the telephone with opposing counsel; negotiating with opposing counsel in person; examining witnesses before or during trial; and arguing before a judge, agency, or arbitration panel, to name a few. But the most formal type of oral advocacy is oral argument before a panel of appellate judges.

You may get an opportunity to practice oral advocacy in your first-year legal research and writing course. For example, you might draft a memorandum in support of a motion (e.g., motion for summary judgment) and argue that motion, or you might draft an appellate brief and make an oral argument. Because the tradition in legal writing courses has been to teach appellate briefs and oral argument, this chapter focuses on appellate oral argument, although much of the advice applies to argument in all contexts.

The opportunity for oral argument in federal and state court is not always automatic. You may need to request it in your appellate brief or be given permission by the court.[1] Since it is not always an automatic right, lawyers are grateful for the opportunity. Oral argument exists primarily for the advocates to answer questions the judges have about the case, not to give them an opportunity to repeat the arguments already made in their briefs. Oral argument is usually limited to a specific amount of time.[2]

A. Typical oral argument

The chief judge (who sits in the middle) usually invites counsel for the appellant to begin the argument. Appellate lawyers usually begin by greeting the court and introducing themselves.

---

1 For example, the United States Court of Appeals for the Fifth Circuit requires the appellant to explain as a preamble to its brief why oral argument would be helpful. If the appellant fails to do so, the opportunity for oral argument is waived. 5th Cir. R. 28.2.3, https://www.ca5.uscourts.gov/docs/default-source/forms-and-documents---clerks-office/rules/federalrulesofappellateprocedure (https://perma.cc/4U3R-RV6Y).

2 For example, the Fifth Circuit usually allots 20 minutes per side, which refers to parties in their position on appeal. *Id.* at R. 34.11.

1. Introduction and reservation of rebuttal time.

A standard introduction would be, "May it please the court, my name is ______________, and I represent the appellant."

If more than one attorney for the same party plans to argue, you can also introduce your co-counsel and explain what each of you plans to argue. The appellant usually indicates at this time whether they wish to reserve rebuttal time and how much (the time you can reserve varies by court). If you don't request rebuttal time, you may waive it. Only the appellant gets an opportunity for rebuttal.

Practice Pointer

Appellate oral argument usually consists of:

- an introduction
- a statement of the issue(s)
- a recitation of facts
- an argument combined with questions and answers
- a conclusion

2. Statement of the case and the issue(s) from the client's perspective.

Counsel for the appellant should strive to open her argument with an attention-getting characterization of the case and the legal issues before the court. Your client's story, your client's character, the nature of the conflict, and your theory of the case will help you frame the opening. From there, you may proceed to state the issues before the court, framed from your client's perspective.

For example, as counsel for the Velases, you might open with:

> "This case is about Christina and Ramon Velas, small business owners who own and operate a successful coffee shop. They have been damaged by CSP's bulldozer approach to protecting the local food supply," or
>
> "Your Honors, the appellee's newsletter has threatened the existence of my client's business for which the appellee claims there is no remedy under Texas law," or
>
> "For years, the Velases have struggled to build a successful small business in the Dallas area. Two years ago, they began to realize that dream when suddenly, out of the blue, CSP sent out its March 2019 newsletter."

You would then proceed to characterize the legal issues:

> "The issue, Your Honors, is whether the Velases, who sell coffee beans and coffee beverages, are protected under a Texas statute that protects sellers of perishable food products against false statements," or

> "This Court must decide whether the Texas legislature intended to protect business owners like the Velases, who sell food products in Texas that cannot be grown in Texas," or
>
> "To resolve this appeal in my client's favor, you need find only that the Velases sell a perishable food product that decays beyond marketability in a limited period of time."

There are countless options, and your theory of the case should guide you.

3. Recitation of the facts.

Next, counsel for the appellant usually offers to recite the relevant facts of the case (from the appellant's perspective of course). If the judges are familiar with the facts or have just read the parties' briefs, they may not need the facts repeated, or they may ask for a quick summary. Counsel for the appellee may take issue with the appellant's version of the facts, but the judges do not usually want to hear a second, full statement of facts.

4. Argument/question and answer period.

Begin your argument by offering reasons why the court should rule in your client's favor. Because your time is limited, keep them simple: based on the arguments in your brief, state the two or three main reasons (elements, factors, policies, key cases, etc.) why the party should prevail. Like a roadmap, this outline gives the judges an idea of what to expect. The outline will also help you keep focused on your goals for the argument.

Proceed to make your arguments in the order you listed them. Most judges expect to hear dispositive issues and strongest arguments first. If the standard of review is also at issue, you might want to argue that first. It makes sense to begin with your strongest arguments. If you don't, and the questioning takes you in a direction you did not anticipate, you may not get an opportunity to make your best argument.

Don't be surprised if the judges quickly interrupt you with questions. That's why you are there: to talk *with* them, not *at* them. Instead of feeling annoyed or flustered, take the questions as a sign that the judges are engaged and interested. Use the questions as a way to make the arguments you planned to make even if in a different order. Your prepared remarks may not end up being as important as answering the judges' questions. The questions may signal the arguments likely to be the most responsive to the judges' concerns.

Judges often ask if you have factual or legal support for your arguments. For that reason, you can take your materials up with you to the lectern. However, resist the temptation to read extensively from them. The judges can read these materials on their own. Different courts have different rules about electronic materials, so ask before you bring up a laptop or tablet. In the event you cannot remember the support for a particular argument, or you do not have the citation for a case you rely on, you may offer to submit that to the court after the argument.

If the judges ask a question to which you don't know the answer, don't pretend to know it. For example, a judge might ask where the record supports a factual statement you just made, what case stands for the proposition of law you just quoted, or whether you are familiar with a case that stands for the opposite proposition of law. Simply admit that you do not know the answer and move on.

Based on the interpretation of the law or the rule you propose the judges accept, the judges may pose a **hypothetical question** to explore the logical extension of your client's position. For example, as counsel for the Velases, you might argue that they are "producers" under the Texas false disparagement statute because they sell the produce essentially in its raw form. At that point, a judge might pose a hypothetical question to test the limits of your argument. The key to answering hypothetical questions is to answer them directly and honestly (even if the hypothetical exposes the limits of your rule), gently remind the judge that your case is not the hypothetical case, and then steer the court back to your argument.

For example, this exchange might take place at oral argument:

> **The Court:** Counsel, am I correct that your clients do not themselves grow the coffee beans?
>
> **You:** Yes, that is correct. They import them from Central and South America.
>
> **The Court:** But your argument is that they are producers under Texas law. How can they be producers if they do not grow the produce?
>
> **You:** I'm glad you raised that issue, Your Honor. Coffee beans do not grow in Texas, so all coffee sold in the United States is imported.
>
> **The Court:** But why then, should coffee sellers in Texas be protected against false statements under the Texas statute? Are you saying that the statute protects all sellers of all food products in Texas without regard to where they are grown? What if the false statements were about beans sold by an organic grocery store, such as Whole Foods Market? Is Whole Foods protected?

At this point, you have no choice but to answer the hypothetical question. Your job here is to acknowledge that certain interpretations of the statute might lead to more liability than the legislature intended, but then you can offer a reason why liability in this case is still warranted:

> **You:** Not necessarily, Your Honor. The legislative history of the Texas statute indicates that it was designed to protect the Texas economy without regard to whether the producer is also the grower. But only producers of

perishable food products are protected under the statute. Whole Foods sells a host of items, some of which do not perish or decay in a limited period of time. In order for Whole Foods to be protected, the statements would have to be about a particular perishable food product. And, as we submit, even if the perishable food product was not grown in Texas, it would make sense to extend the protection of the statute to Whole Foods in that case as well as to plaintiffs like the Velases. Otherwise, there could be a significant number of businesses selling perishable food products in Texas that could be damaged by false statements in a way that harms the local economy.

5. Conclusion

If time permits, you can conclude by summarizing your arguments, underscoring the most important points, and stating the specific relief your client seeks on appeal.

B. Oral argument etiquette

There is a customary etiquette to oral argument. You should always be polite and deferential: address each judge as "your Honor" and don't interrupt a judge who is speaking. You can be assertive (remember the duty of zeal in advocacy), but do not become hostile in your tone or language. Always be open to the judges' questions and honest with your answers. If you cannot recall the name or facts of a case, don't pretend.

> **Practice Pointer**
>
> **Oral argument etiquette:**
>
> - be polite and deferential
> - don't interrupt the judges
> - be assertive but not hostile or argumentative
> - be honest
> - watch the time clock
> - observe local customs
> - try not to fidget, wiggle, or otherwise detract from your argument

Each court keeps advocates apprised of their time limits differently. When you see that your time is running out, pace your arguments accordingly. If you have just one minute or thirty seconds left, use that time to touch on any arguments you have not yet addressed or summarize your arguments. The argument as a whole will be more effective if it appears to have a planned beginning, middle, and end. You don't want to have to stop mid-sentence and then sit down.

Also ask people who have argued before the court what to expect. Some judges do not allow you to walk away from the lectern while speaking; others do. Some will allow you to hand charts or graphs to the judge; others do not allow you to approach the bench at all. And finally, when your time runs out, do not assume you can finish your sentence. It is best to ask the Court if you may finish your sentence or provide a summary statement.

Although first-year legal research and writing courses may expose you to legal argument, they are usually not classes in oral advocacy. You will have many opportunities to hone your speaking skills in other law school courses. Nevertheless, even at this early stage in your career, keep these few tips in mind: try not to fidget, wiggle, or otherwise detract from the substance of your argument. Shifting your weight from one foot to another, playing with a pen, twisting your hair, taking your hands in and out of your pockets—these can all affect the persuasiveness of your argument. Try to avoid excessive use of sentence "fillers," such as "um," "you know," "like," and "right," which can also be distracting. Speak slowly and clearly. Many people speed up their speech when they're nervous, so get a colleague to tell you if you are speaking too fast. Don't be afraid to stop and think before you answer. No one minds the silence but you. Finally, speak with conviction. If you are making a statement, don't make it sound like a question. A rising inflection at the end of a sentence can make it sound like you are not sure that what you're saying is correct, and that is not the impression you want to give the judges.

C. How do I prepare for oral argument?

Remember that oral argument is not a theatrical performance where you have to memorize your lines. It is a conversation with three judges interested in your answers to questions they have about your client's position so they know how to rule. By the time you get to oral argument, you will be so familiar with the record, the procedural history of the case, the legal issues, and the applicable law that you won't need to memorize anything.

> **Practice Pointer**
>
> **To prepare for oral argument:**
>
> - use notes, not a script
> - memorize only your opening paragraph
> - anticipate counterarguments and hypothetical questions
> - practice

You may be tempted to write out a script to take up to the lectern to read. Although it seems like that would provide you with some comfort, detailed scripts tend to be counter-productive. They are not conducive to conversation. And if the judge quickly steers you off script, it can be very difficult to remember where you left off and find your place. If, on the other hand, you have just your opening sentences written out and an outline with bullet or talking points, a quick glance at these can get you back on track.

Your bullets or talking points should include your opening characterization of the case and statement of the legal issues. Then, list the main points you intend to make, and any sub-points or key cases you intend to make or rely on. These will keep you focused. You may even want to write down your conclusion. You can also prepare a binder (or perhaps use an electronic device, but check the court rules first) with the most important cases, tabbed or marked as necessary, for quick reference.

The only part of your argument you might consider memorizing is the opening. It is normal to be nervous when you first stand up to speak, and having that first paragraph memorized can help a great deal. Most lawyers find that once they get past that opening paragraph and into question-and-answer mode with the judges, their nervousness quickly disappears.

As you prepare, be sure to think about the opposing party's position. What arguments are they likely to make? What do the briefs tell you about that? Anticipate the key arguments and cases your opponent will rely on and come up with good answers to as many of those arguments as possible. Also try to anticipate the sorts of hypothetical questions a judge might ask given the weaknesses in your client's position. Remember you may be asking them to create a rule that will apply to many future cases.

Finally, practice, practice, practice. Write out questions you would ask the parties if you were the judge. Find a classmate, colleague, or supervisor and ask them to pose those questions to you. Get their feedback on your opening statements, how convincing your arguments and answers are, and how they might be improved.

For More Information

David C. Frederick, *The Art of Oral Advocacy* (3d ed. 2019).

Bryan A. Garner, *Interviews with Supreme Court Justices*, 13 Scribes J. Leg. Writing (2010) (on writing briefs and oral advocacy).

The Honorable Alex Kozinski, *The Wrong Stuff*, 1992 BYU L. Rev. 325 (1992).

You can listen to oral arguments before the United States Supreme Court at www.oyez.org.

Chapter 61

Public Speaking

Public speaking isn't easy. It makes most of us nervous. But it's a skill you can learn and develop, just like legal writing. With the right tools and plenty of practice, your speaking skills will improve, and your confidence will grow. Try to develop your public speaking skills in law school. Take clinical courses or courses in trial or appellate advocacy, negotiations, etc.

Once out of law school, you will find yourself in a number of situations that call on these skills outside a courtroom, such as convincing a potential client to retain you, explaining your litigation strategy to corporate executives, negotiating a deal, making a speech at a bar association event, presenting at a law conference, or even toasting a colleague at a special event.

A. Can I overcome a fear of public speaking?

In law school, I sat in the back row. I was terrified of being called on. It wasn't until I started teaching that I realized that sitting in the back row put me directly in my professors' sight line. That anxiety extended to my law practice. People were unaware how nervous I was, but I almost always felt sick when I went to court. It was not until I started teaching that I finally overcame my fear of public speaking. Being nervous about speaking in public is normal, and if I conquered it, so can you.

> **Hear It**
>
> See what Jerry Seinfeld has said about the common fear of public speaking:
>
> https://www.youtube.com/watch?v=RrCQnRFBuGc (https://perma.cc/UX2P-9KZJ)

Think about something unrelated to law school that you do consistently well—play an instrument, cook, play basketball, etc.—that also makes you feel good. Even with natural talent, most of us have had to work hard to get to that place. How did you develop those skills? Did you have help? How many hours of coaching or practice did it take? Speaking in public is no different. It takes lots of practice. With practice, you begin to build confidence, and that confidence helps control your nerves.

Try to figure out why public speaking makes you so nervous. What are you afraid will happen? For me, it was the fear of making a mistake or sounding stupid. But I never asked myself what would happen next. Naturally, I would have been embarrassed, but then what? Not much else to be honest. My classmates would have understood. My professors would have understood. And even if they didn't, life goes on.

Next, start practicing. Start by explaining something complicated about the law to someone not in law school and field their questions. Go to your professor's office hours. Risk a conversation with a classmate. Have a conversation with someone at a party you just met. Volunteer to speak in class. By slowly exposing yourself to more and more risk, you will begin to discover that your worst fears rarely come to pass, and even if they do, you can survive them.

B. Principles of effective public speaking

As David Dempsey, a trial lawyer and professor of communications put it:

> There are no born speakers. There is no magic wand that anyone can wave over your head, no magic elixir you can drink, no pill you can swallow to learn the art of speaking. Speaking is a craft that is learned and constantly honed. Reading about speaking will guide you, but it alone will not make you a better speaker. Only practice and experience will do that.[1]

To develop effective speaking skills, you need to learn to anticipate your audience, prepare a well-constructed speech, and deliver it convincingly. Use these principles as a starting point.

1. Anticipate your audience.

Recall Lloyd Bitzer's definition of rhetoric as the use of language to bring about change.[2] Critical to his concept of the rhetorical situation is the importance of the audience that can make the desired change happen and any constraints that limit the possibility of change.[3] These principles are as applicable to public speaking as to written legal argument.

Knowing your audience makes all the difference. Imagine proposing that your clients pursue a course of action that will cost more than they can afford to spend. Or taking fifteen minutes out of a thirty-minute meeting with your client's chief financial

---

1 DAVID J. DEMPSEY, LEGALLY SPEAKING: 40 POWERFUL PRESENTATION PRINCIPLES LAWYERS NEED TO KNOW xviii (2009).

2 *See supra* ch. 8, note 8.

3 *See id.* at 6–8.

officer to explain the history of a legal rule you find fascinating. Or addressing a crowd and telling jokes about a subject they know nothing about or could be offended by.

To be persuasive, you will need to **anticipate your audience**: who they are, how much time they have set aside for your presentation, what other constraints they have, and what they need to make the decision you want them to make. For example, who will you be addressing? Lawyers? Non-lawyers? A combination? Are they going to be there as part of their job? Or will they attend during their free time? How much time have they allotted? What will they be expecting? Are they likely to oppose your views? What will prevent them from agreeing with you or deciding in your favor? What will likely change their minds? Don't think so much about what you want to tell them as what they think they need to decide. Preparing with the audience in mind puts you in a better position to persuade them.[4]

2. Prepare a well-constructed speech.

Preparing a speech is like writing a document. It needs to be well researched, thought through, organized, and delivered well. And it should be logical, credible, and engaging.[5] The principles of classical rhetoric were designed precisely for this purpose. Because your audience is listening, as opposed to reading, your speech should have a distinct beginning, middle, and end to guide them. The introduction should capture the audience's attention, identify the subject matter of your speech, state your specific position or argument, and prepare the audience for what they are going to hear next. In this way, the introduction functions like the statement of the issue and the roadmap in the argument section of a brief.[6]

> **Practice Pointer**
>
> A well-constructed speech has a **distinct beginning, middle, and end:**
>
> **Introduction**—captures attention, states your subject matter or purpose, outlines your main points
>
> **Body**—lays out your main points in more detail, using transition words to move from one point to the next
>
> **Conclusion**—recaps the main points and underscores the reasons for making the proposed decision

The body of the speech should contain the main points you plan to make in support of your position. As with legal writing, use transition words to signal to the audience that you are moving from one point to the next.[7] The conclusion should remind the audience what they have just heard and reinforce why they should make the decision you propose.

4 *See, e.g.*, DEMPSEY, *supra* note 1, at 45.

5 *See supra* ch. 13, on the three modes of artistic appeals.

6 *See supra* chs. 45.A, at 323 and 48.C.2, at 356.

7 *See supra* ch. 53.A.7, at 406.

The best way to capture the audience's attention will depend on your goals, the circumstances, and your creativity. You might open by summarizing the gravity of the issue the audience is facing. Or perhaps you need to open with an anecdote to lighten the mood or ask the audience a question to consider as you proceed with your remarks. Or maybe the best introduction is to get right down to business: *this* is why I am here and what I can offer you.

3. Develop a speaking presence.

First impressions are perhaps more important in public speaking than in written advocacy. Even if you are nervous, you can establish a physical presence that commands your audience's attention. It probably goes without saying, but think about what clothes are appropriate to the situation. Even before you begin speaking, stand straight, with your feet shoulder-width apart, but don't lock your knees. You might want one leg slightly in front of the other to provide stability. Roll your shoulders back (rotating your thumbs forward helps), tuck in your tail, and relax. Own your space. Don't try to be anyone else but you. Breathe normally, make eye contact with your audience, commit, and begin.

4. Use effective body language, gestures, vocal cues, and visual aids.

Your **body language** speaks volumes. If you stand tall and look the audience in the eye, they are more likely to listen and engage. If you slump and look down or away, they will be uncomfortable and less likely to listen carefully. Physically, you want to appear open and receptive, not closed and defensive. Your facial expressions matter too. If you don't have a poker face, practice making sure the audience cannot read impatience, annoyance, or judgment in your face. Taking a video is a great way to get immediate feedback.

The **gestures** you make should support your message, not detract from it. In general, gesture intentionally and in the mid-range; not too high and not too low. Gestures can be used to guide the audience, such as using your fingers to indicate your first, second, and third points. You can even take a step to denote each separate point you make. Gestures can also clarify meaning, such as using your hands to indicate a small or large amount, raising a hand high or low to indicate an increase or decrease, or making a sweeping motion with your arms to include everyone in the room.[8]

Your gestures can also detract from your message. If your arms flail about or you move quickly and erratically, your audience will have a hard time focusing on what you are saying. Distracting gestures tend to be a function of nerves, and you

---

8 *See also* DEMPSEY, *supra* note 1, at 146–50. For a comprehensive list of gestures used in everyday speech, see https://en.wikipedia.org/wiki/List_of_gestures (https://perma.cc/HG5L-C3F5).

can work to eliminate most of them. Remember that audiences tend to be very forgiving as long as you are sincere and not wasting their time. Sometimes, nervousness can be endearing because it signals to the audience how much you care about the subject and hard you are working to achieve your or your client's goals.

The pitch, tone, rate, and volume of your speech also affect your ability to persuade. These non-verbal, **vocal cues** can signal nervousness; a lack of enthusiasm, passion, or preparation; or a speaker who is competent and passionate about the subject matter. Think of your reaction to a professor who speaks too softly, too slowly, and in a monotone voice versus one who can easily be heard but is not yelling, pronounces words so you can understand them, and naturally varies the pitch and tone of their voice.

Practice Pointer

Distracting gestures include

- Bobbing and weaving
- Contorting or touching your body
- Fidgeting
- Hands in pockets
- Hands on hips
- Leaning on the lectern
- Pacing
- Playing with clothing, jewelry, pens
- Playing with hair
- Swaying

See Dempsey, *supra* note 1, at 128–30.

According to Michael Higdon, lawyers are perceived as more persuasive when they speak faster (but not too fast), "with minimal pauses and hesitations, with varied pitch, and with moderate loudness."[9] Although pauses can be used for emphasis,[10] they should be used sparingly. Audiences may interpret excessive pauses as a lack of confidence. Although it is natural to make mistakes, and use filler words like "uh" and "um," most experts advise that you reduce them as much as possible. Words and phrases such as "you know," "like," "right," and "of course," can be distracting, and the audience may find you less credible.[11] In contrast, Barbara Gotthelf has argued that "uh" and "um" act as useful signals for the audience. They indicate that a speaker is temporarily delayed while formulating a complex thought or slowing down to make sure they communicate their thought accurately.[12] President Obama, considered one of our most eloquent Presidents in recent history, consistently used fillers like "uh" and "um."[13]

---

9 Michael J. Higdon, *Oral Argument and Impression Management: Harnessing the Power of Nonverbal Persuasion for a Judicial Audience*, 57 U. KAN. L. REV. 631, 661 (2009); *see also* DEMPSEY, *supra* note 1, at 133–37.

10 *See* DEMPSEY, *supra* note 1, at 139–43.

11 *See* Higdon, *supra* note 9, at 662.

12 *See* Barbara K. Gotthelf, *The Lawyer's Guide to Um*, 11 LEGAL COMMC'N & RHETORIC: JALWD 1, 10–14 (2014).

13 *See, e.g.*, Susmita Baral, *Can't quit saying 'um' and 'ah'? Just learn how to use them better*, QUARTZ (July 25, 2016), https://qz.com/740602/cant-quit-saying-um-and-ah-just-learn-how-to-use-them-better/ (https://perma.cc/9BPE-JZ43).

Finally, **visual aids** can enhance your persuasiveness. "A significant portion of any audience want to see, not just hear, in order to understand."[14] In terms of PowerPoint slides, for the most part, less is more. A few well-designed slides will have more impact than twenty slides jam-packed with information that compete for your audience's attention.[15] Pictures that illustrate the point may be even more effective than text, but either way, make sure the audience can easily see your slides. Other visual aids can be effective too, particularly if you will be seeking audience participation: whiteboards, flip charts, handouts, index cards, and even props. Most important, practice using your visual aids, so they fit well in your presentation and you are confident that you know how to use them.[16]

5. Avoid memorizing the entire speech and reduce reliance on detailed notes.

Hear It

Watch Chris Anderson, TED Talk Curator, discuss how to deliver a successful talk. His four major tips include:

- limit your presentation to one major idea
- give your listeners a reason to care or make them curious
- build your idea "piece by piece" and speak your audience's language
- make your idea worth sharing (brighten the audience's day, explain who it benefits, and inspire them)

https://www.ted.com/talks/chris_anderson_ted_s_secret_to_great_public_speaking?language=en (https://perma.cc/KE8N-EPP2)

As with oral argument,[17] resist the temptation to memorize your speech or write out a detailed script or notes. Memorizing can make you sound stilted or stiff, and if you lose your mental place in the memorized speech, it can be very hard to find your way back to it. Depending on the circumstances, Dempsey suggests memorizing your opening or closing lines, a joke you plan to tell, or the phrasing of key points you plan to make.[18] If you need some notes to guide you, keep them to a minimum, using a short list or bullet points to remind you of the flow of the speech and the points you need to make. Even those who give Ted Talks have a teleprompter on the floor in front of them in case they lose their place, but they try to rely on the prompts as little as possible.

---

14 ROBERT N. SAYLER & MOLLY BISHOP SHADEL, TONGUE-TIED AMERICA: REVIVING THE ART OF VERBAL PERSUASION 92 (3d ed. 2018).

15 *See Perlin*, *supra* ch. 36, note 1.

16 *See generally* SAYLER & SHADEL, *supra* note 14, at 91–105.

17 *See supra* ch. 60.C, at 484.

18 *See* DEMPSEY, *supra* note 1, at 119–20.

6. Pay attention to your audience's response and adapt accordingly.

A successful presentation requires that you pay attention to your audience's reactions. If you are not connecting with the audience, you can make adjustments. You will know you've lost the audience if they seem distracted, start to close their eyes, fidget, or play with their phones. When that happens, make an honest observation (e.g., this is complicated, I know), ask them a question (e.g., Is this making sense? What are you all thinking right now? Am I moving too quickly?), or even make a joke. In some settings, it may help to call on someone you know is engaged or supportive to get their attention back or let them know you care about their reaction.

For More Information

Heidi K. Brown, *Untangling Fear in Lawyering: A Four-Step Journey Toward Powerful Advocacy* (2019).

Jeena Cho & Karen Gifford, *The Anxious Lawyer: An 8-Week Guide to a Joyful and Satisfying Law Practice Through Mindfulness and Meditation* (2016).

Marsha Hunter, Brian K. Johnson & Jami McKeon, *The Articulate Advocate: Persuasive Skills for Lawyers in Trials, Appeals, Arbitrations, and Motions* (2d ed. 2016).

Test Your Knowledge: Part XIV

To assess your understanding of the material in this part, click here to take a quiz.

PART XV

Appendices

Appendix A

Case Briefing

Set forth below is the online version of *Copeland v. District of Columbia Department of Employment Services, Inc.*, 3 A.3d 331 (2010).[1] Re-read the case and then prepare a case brief. Two sample case briefs follow.

A. *Copeland* decision

Case caption

Shirley A. COPELAND, Petitioner,
v.
DISTRICT OF COLUMBIA DEPARTMENT OF EMPLOYMENT SERVICES, Respondent.
No. 09–AA–240.
|
District of Columbia Court of Appeals.

Deciding court and date of decision

Submitted March 25, 2010.
|
Decided Sept. 2, 2010.

Synopsis

Background: Appeal was taken from decision of the Compensation Review Board denying an award of attorney fees in a public sector disability compensation case.

[Holding:] The Court of Appeals, Glickman, J., held that Board erred as a matter of law in concluding that law students' work was not compensable in a reasonable attorney fee award under Comprehensive Merit Personnel Act.

Reversed and remanded.

[1] Used with permission from Thomson Reuters.

West Headnotes (5)

Headnotes and key numbers that will appear in the opinion (see Chapter 26.A.3(b))

[1] **District of Columbia ⊶ Officers, agents, and employees**

In public sector disability compensation case, appellate court will defer to the Compensation Review Board's (CRB) construction of statute if it is a reasonable one, i.e., not plainly wrong or inconsistent with the legislature's intent, but appellate court will not uphold a decision that reflects a misconception of the relevant law or a faulty application of the law.

[2] **District of Columbia ⊶ Officers, agents, and employees**

In a public sector disability compensation case, claimant must utilize the services of an attorney-at-law in the successful prosecution of his or her claim in order to be entitled to statutory award of reasonable attorney fee, but when that threshold requirement is met, it is untenable to argue that a reasonable attorney fee cannot be based on the work of law students and other non-lawyers who assisted in the representation under the attorney's direction. D.C. Official Code, 2001 Ed. § 1–623.27(b)(2).

[3] **District of Columbia ⊶ Officers, agents, and employees**

Fact that law students permissibly performed tasks in a public sector disability compensation case that otherwise would have fallen to full-fledged attorneys was not enough to exclude their work from the purview of the attorney fee statute in Comprehensive Merit Personnel Act, which provided that District of Columbia government employee who utilized services of attorney-at-law in successful prosecution of her claim was entitled to reasonable attorney fee award; critical point was that claimant was not represented before Department of Employment Services by the law students alone, and instead, she was represented by the law students together with a licensed attorney-at-law under whose direction the students did their work. D.C. Official Code, 2001 Ed. § 1–623.27(b)(2).

[4] **Attorney and Client ⚿ What constitutes a retainer**

Attorney and Client ⚿ Acts and omissions of partners and associates

Under the Rules of Professional Conduct, a lawyer, who supervises law students, has an attorney-client relationship with the law students' client and is personally responsible for her representation. Rules of Prof. Conduct, Rule 5.3(b, c).

[5] **District of Columbia ⚿ Officers, agents, and employees**

Claimant utilized the services of an attorney-at-law in the successful prosecution of her public sector disability compensation claim, and the law students who assisted her did so under direction and control of claimant's attorney, and therefore, Compensation Review Board (CRB) erred as a matter of law in concluding that the students' work was not compensable in a reasonable attorney fee award under Comprehensive Merit Personnel Act, which provided that District of Columbia government employee who utilized services of attorney-at-law in successful prosecution of her claim was entitled to reasonable attorney fee award. D.C. Official Code, 2001 Ed. § 1–623.27(b)(2).

Attorneys and Law Firms

*__332__ Jeffrey S. Gutman for petitioner.

Peter J. Nickles, Attorney General for the District of Columbia, Todd S. Kim, Solicitor General, Donna M. Murasky, Deputy Solicitor General, and David A. Hyden, Assistant Attorney General, for appellee.

Before RUIZ, REID, and GLICKMAN, Associate Judges.

Opinion

Court's opinion begins here

GLICKMAN, Associate Judge:

Introduction

This is an appeal of a Compensation Review Board ("CRB") order denying an award of attorney's fees in a public sector disability compensation case. D.C. Code § 1–623.27(b)(2) (Supp. 2010), a part of the Comprehensive Merit Personnel Act, provides that a District Government employee who utilizes the services of an attorney-at-law in the successful prosecution of her claim is entitled to a reasonable attorney's fee award. The CRB interpreted this provision to bar a fee award where the claimant was represented by law students participating in a clinical program under a lawyer's supervision. We conclude that the CRB erred in its application of the statute.

I.

In 1994, petitioner Shirley Copeland, an employee of the District of Columbia Department of Human Services, suffered a work-related injury to her back. She applied for, and received, disability compensation benefits. In June 2007, however, the Office of Risk Management in the Department of Employment Services terminated her benefits on the ground that her medical condition was not causally related to her workplace injury. Seeking to have her benefits reinstated, Ms. Copeland filed a request for an administrative hearing. To represent her in the administrative proceedings, ***333** Ms. Copeland retained the Public Justice Advocacy Clinic (the "Clinic") of the George Washington University Law School. The Clinic is directed by Professor Jeffrey Gutman, who is a member of the District of Columbia Bar. Under Professor Gutman's tutelage and supervision, two third-year law students, Daniel Greenspahn and Kiva Feldman, prepared Ms. Copeland's case. With Professor Gutman in attendance, the students represented her at her hearing.

Summary of legally significant facts

Ms. Copeland prevailed at the hearing, and on November 23, 2007, the administrative law judge entered a compensation order reinstating her benefits. The order identifies Professor Gutman as Ms. Copeland's counsel in the proceeding. Following their victory, Professor Gutman and the two law students applied pursuant to D.C. Code § 1–623.27(b)(2) for an award of reasonable attorney's fees for their work on Ms. Copeland's behalf. They sought fees for only half of the students' 170 hours

Procedural history

(an exercise of "billing judgment," they explained, because some of the students' time was "pedagogical in nature, rather than directly focused on direct client service"), and no fees for Professor Gutman's time. The fee application stated that the fee award would be used for client services provided by the Clinic.

On September 8, 2008, Chief Administrative Law Judge Linda Jory entered an order denying the fee application on the ground that "[t]he plain language of the statute [D.C. Code § 1–623.27(b)(2)] provides for payments to 'attorney-at-law' and does not specify any other class of person eligible to receive such payments." The CRB agreed with this rationale, stating that law students "do not qualify as attorneys-at-law." The CRB rejected the argument that, for purposes of compensation in an attorney's fee award, the law students' work for Ms. Copeland was comparable to paralegal work:

> [It] is important to note that [paralegal] work is performed in support of, pursuant to, and under the direction of, an attorney-at-law. Work performed by a paralegal constitutes the work-product of the attorney of record . . . in a case. Such a circumstance is distinguishable from the instant case as [ ] the two students directly represented Petitioner in court and engaged in the limited practice of law. Paralegals have no authority to do so.

II.

D.C. Code § 1–623.27(b)(2) provides that "[i]f a person utilizes the services of an attorney-at-law in the successful prosecution of his or her claim . . . , there shall be awarded . . . a reasonable attorney's fee, not to exceed 20% of the actual benefit secured, which fee award shall be paid directly . . . to the attorney for the claimant. . . ." Ms. Copeland argues that the CRB erred as a legal matter by construing this statute to preclude recovery as part of a "reasonable attorney's fee" award for any time devoted to the representation by law students and other para-professionals working with the claimant's attorney. The Department of Employment

Discussion of legal issue begins here

Services responds that the CRB did not interpret the statute as barring fee awards for para-professional work in all circumstances; rather, it distinguished between work performed by non-attorneys "in support of, pursuant to, and at the direction of" an attorney who represents a claimant, and work performed by non-attorneys who represent claimants themselves, even if they do so under the supervision of an attorney. The Department argues that the CRB reasonably construed D.C. Code § 1–623.27(b)(2) to preclude an award of attorney's fees only under the second set ***334** of circumstances, and that it reasonably applied that construction to the facts of this case.

[1] The material facts of this case are not in dispute, and the CRB's interpretation and application of § 1–623.27(b)(2) are subject to ***de novo*** review in this court. We will defer to the CRB's construction if it is a reasonable one—i.e., "not plainly wrong or inconsistent with the legislature's intent"[2]—but we will not uphold a decision that "reflects a misconception of the relevant law or a faulty application of the law."[3]

First of five headnotes in text of opinion

[2] There is no question that a claimant must "utilize[ ] the services of an attorney-at-law in the successful prosecution of his or her claim" in order to be entitled to the award of "a reasonable attorney's fee" under § 1–623.27(b)(2). But when that threshold requirement is met, it would be untenable to argue that "a reasonable attorney's fee" cannot be based on the work of law students and other non-lawyers who assisted in the representation under the attorney's direction. The Council of the District of Columbia patterned § 1–623.27(b)(2) on the virtually identical attorney's fee provision of the District of Columbia Workers' Compensation Act, D.C. Code § 32–1530(a) (2001),[4]

Court interprets language of statute

Court uses canon of construction and legislative history (see Chapter 17.B) as tools of interpretation

---

2 Howard Univ. Hosp. v. District of Columbia Dep't of Employment Servs., 952 A.2d 168, 173 (D.C.2008) (internal quotation marks omitted).

3 Georgetown Univ. v. District of Columbia Dep't of Employment Servs., 971 A.2d 909, 915 (D.C.2009) (internal quotation marks omitted).

4 In pertinent part, D.C. Code § 32–1530(a) provides that "[i]f . . . the person seeking benefits . . . utilizes the services of an

which the Department of Employment Services long has construed to cover the services of para-professionals assisting the claimant's attorney.[5] The presumption, absent good reason to think otherwise, is that when a legislature imports language from a statute of settled meaning to a new statute "with an identical stated purpose," it means for the imported language in the new law to be interpreted in the same way ***335** as it is in the old one.[6]

In addition to finding no support in the statute's text or legislative history, an interpretation of § 1–623.27(b)(2) precluding the recognition of para-professional services in attorney's fee awards would render the

Court looks to similar statutes for guidance

---

attorney-at-law in the successful prosecution of his claim, there shall be awarded . . . a reasonable attorney's fee . . . , which shall be paid directly . . . to the attorney for the claimant. . . ." The legislative history of § 1–623.27(b)(2) refers to this provision of the private sector workers' compensation law. *See* COUNCIL OF THE DISTRICT OF COLUMBIA, COMMITTEE ON GOVERNMENT OPERATIONS, REPORT ON BILL 16–238, *the District Government Injured Employee Protection Act of 2006* (2006), page 2. The purpose of each statutory provision is the same, to enable injured employees to obtain "legal services" to assist them with their claims. *Id.* ("Many employees[ ] who are injured on the job[ ] and are forced to seek legal representation find it extremely difficult to obtain legal services.").

5 Since 1986, the Department's regulations have required applications for attorney's fees under the Workers' Compensation Act to specify "the professional status (*e.g.*, attorney, paralegal, law clerk, or other person assisting an attorney) of each person performing the work" for which compensation is sought. 7 DCMR § 224.3(a) (2010). The Director of the Department of Employment Services issued a Policy Directive in 2005 confirming that "a reasonable paralegal fee . . . shall be afforded where appropriate" as part of the award under § 32–1530(a), "in recognition of the increasingly important role of paralegals to the practice of law in the D.C. area, including the practice of workers' compensation law before DOES." *Policy Directive Clarifying the Award of Attorney Fees in the District of Columbia Workers' Compensation Cases* (May 12, 2005). The Policy Directive is available on the Department's web site, at http://www. does.dc.gov/does/frames.asp?doc=/does/lib/does/services/Award_of_Attorney_Fees_OWC_011905.pdf. (last visited Aug. 3, 2010). In accordance with that directive, the CRB has upheld fee awards for para-professional work. *See, e.g., Steadman v. United Parcel Serv.,* CRB No. 05–262, 2005 DC Wrk. Comp. LEXIS 381 (Dec. 14, 2005).

6 *Cannon v. Univ. of Chicago,* 441 U.S. 677, 696–98, 99 S.Ct. 1946, 60 L.Ed.2d 560 (1979).

statute an anomaly among fee-shifting statutes. As the Supreme Court has observed in a case construing one such statute (42 U.S.C. § 1988), the collaborative nature of legal representation implies that "a 'reasonable attorney's fee' cannot have been meant to compensate only work performed personally by members of the bar. Rather, the term must refer to a reasonable fee for the *work product* of an attorney . . . [taking] into account the work not only of attorneys, but also of . . . others whose labor contributes to the work product for which the attorney bills her client."[7] And "reasonable attorney's fee" awards historically have encompassed the work of law students; this court perceived nothing unusual or inappropriate, for example, in approving such an award under the Truth in Lending Act almost three decades ago.[8] An especially noteworthy case for present purposes, because it involved a fee application (under the Freedom of Information Act) for supervised student work in a law school clinic, is *Jordan v. United States Department of Justice.*[9] Rejecting the government's several objections, the D.C. Circuit Court of Appeals stated:

Court analogizes to prior similar case

> The argument that law student services cannot possibly form the basis for an attorneys' fee award merely because law students are not lawyers has only superficial vitality. It loses force drastically when one notes the commonplace use of law students by law firms—usually full-time during summer months, and part-time during the academic year—to perform tasks that otherwise would fall to full-fledged attorneys. And the argument founders completely in the tide of state statutes and court rules authorizing law students, under appropriate circumstances, to undertake functions of licensed attorneys, including actual repre-

7 *Missouri v. Jenkins,* 491 U.S. 274, 285, 109 S.Ct. 2463, 105 L.Ed.2d 229 (1989).

8 See *Frazier v. Franklin Inv. Co., Inc.*, 468 A.2d 1338, 1342 (D.C.1983).

9 223 U.S. App. D.C. 325, 691 F.2d 514 (1982).

> sentation of clients before a court. . . . [W]e cannot condone a concept of attorneys' fees so narrow as to exclude the work of law students simply because they are not yet members of the bar.[[10]]

The Department of Employment Services does not take issue with these principles; it acknowledges that an application for an award of reasonable attorney's fees under § 1–623.27(b)(2) properly may seek compensation for the work of non-attorneys, including law students, who assisted an attorney in the successful prosecution of a claim. The Department disputes only that the law students rendered that type of assistance here. They did not do so, the Department argues, because as the CRB stated, "the two students directly represented [Ms. Copeland] in court and engaged in the limited practice of law" themselves.

[3] **[4]** This analysis is faulty. The fact that, as in *Jordan,* the law students permissibly "perform[ed] tasks that otherwise would [have] fall[en] to full-fledged attorneys" is not enough to exclude their work from the purview of the attorney's fee statute. The critical point is that Ms. ***336** Copeland was not represented before the Department by the law students alone; she was represented by the law students together with Professor Gutman, a licensed attorney-at-law under whose direction the students did their work. This was in accordance with the Rules of this Court. Rule 48 permits eligible law students to engage in "the limited practice of law" and appear before the District's courts and administrative tribunals on behalf of indigent clients, provided they do so as part of a law school clinical program and work under the direction of a "supervising lawyer."[11]co_footnote_B010102022904506_1 The "supervising lawyer" must be an "active" member of the District of Columbia Bar;[12]co_footnote_B011112022904506_1 must "[a]ssume full responsibility for guiding the student's work . . . and for supervising the quality" of that

---

10 *Id.*, 223 U.S. App. D.C. at 332–33, 691 F.2d at 522–23.

11 D.C. App. R. 48(a)(1).

12 *Id.*, R. 48(e)(4).

work;[13] must do everything "necessary in [his or her] professional judgment to insure that the student's participation is effective on behalf of the indigent person represented";[14]co_footnote_B013132022904506_1 and must sign all pleadings and other documents to be filed in the matter.[15] Under the Rules of Professional Conduct, a lawyer having such "direct supervisory authority" over a non-lawyer in the practice of law is obliged to make "reasonable efforts to ensure" that the non-lawyer's conduct is "compatible with" the lawyer's own professional obligations and may be held "responsible for conduct of such a person that would be a violation of the Rules . . . if engaged in by a lawyer."[16] Given these requirements, the "supervising lawyer" clearly has an attorney-client relationship with the law students' client and is personally responsible for her representation.

In this case, the "supervising lawyer" was Professor Gutman. The detailed time records submitted in support of the fee application confirm his assiduous supervision of the law students who handled Ms. Copeland's case.[17] As the administrative law judge recognized in the order reinstating Ms. Copeland's disability benefits, Professor Gutman was her legal counsel.

[5] Thus, contrary to the Department's characterization, this was not a case of lay representation before the Department. Ms. Copeland "utilized the services of an attorney-at-law in the successful prosecution" of her claim, and the law students who assisted her pursuant to Rule 48 did so under that attorney's direction and control. The CRB therefore erred as a matter of law in

Holding

13 *Id.*, R. 48(e)(2).

14 *Id.*, R. 48(e)(3).

15 *Id.*, R. 48(d)(1)(i).

16 D.C. Rules of Prof'l Conduct R. 5.3(b), (c).

17 According to the time records, Professor Gutman devoted considerable time providing his students with guidance and reviewing and correcting their work product. In preparing for Ms. Copeland's hearing, the students had weekly meetings with Gutman to discuss the case. Among other things, Gutman helped them with discovery and pleadings; advised them with respect to legal issues; and prepared them to conduct the hearing.

concluding that the students' work was not compensable in a reasonable attorney's fee award under D.C. Code § 1–623.27(b)(2).

Accordingly, we reverse the decision of the CRB and remand this case for an administrative law judge to consider the fee application on its merits and award a reasonable attorney's fee.[18]

Disposition

---

18 We note that the fee application asks for payment to be made to the George Washington University Legal Clinics ("GWULC"), not to Professor Gutman. The Department has not argued that payment directly to GWULC at Professor Gutman's request would be impermissible in light of the requirement in D.C. Code § 1–623.27(b)(2) that the attorney's fee award be paid directly to the attorney, nor do we suppose it would be. *See Jordan,* 223 U.S. App. D.C. at 328 n. 14, 691 F.2d at 517 n. 14.

B. Sample case briefs

Sample 1

Facts

- D.C. government employee Copeland (C) sustained back injury at work and got benefits
- Department of Employment Services terminated benefits—condition held not related to work injury
- C filed request for administrative hearing
- C represented by two GW law students at Justice Advocacy Clinic under supervision of professor Gutman (G), a member of the D.C. bar
- Hearing judge reinstated benefits
- G and students filed for attorney's fees under D.C. Code § 1–623.27(b)(2) (only half their time)

Procedural History

- 9/8/08 chief hearing judge denied fee application since students not attorneys
- C filed appeal of decision denying fees

Issue

Does D.C. Code 1–623.27(b)(2) prevent an award of attorney's fees where the claimant was represented by law students participating in a clinical program under a lawyer's supervision?

Holding No

Reasoning

- D.C. code permits recovery of fees for work "performed in support of, pursuant to, and under the direction of, an attorney-at-law"
- D.C.'s distinction between non-attorneys working "in support of, pursuant to, and under the direction of" attorneys and non-attorneys who directly represent claimants is untenable
- 623.27(b)(2) is patterned on D.C.'s Workers Compensation Act which has been held to include paralegal work; presumption is that when legislature imports language with settled meaning it intends for it to be interpreted in same way
- 42 U.S.C. § 1988 interpreted to mean more than actual members of the bar
- *Jordan v. United States Department of Justice* involved clinic students under federal law
- Students here acted under G's direction just as paraprofessionals do

Result Reversed and remanded to award appropriate fee

Sample 2

Facts:

- DC employee prevailed in compensation-related suit rep'd by law students in clinic supervised by licensed atty prof
- Students/prof applied for atty's fees (1/2 time only, no time for prof)
- ALJ recognized prof as 'legal counsel'

Procedural History:

- ALJ denied award of atty's fees where plaintiff was represented by law students (supervised by atty.); CRB affirmed

Legal Issue(s):

- Whether work done by supervised law students in representing plaintiff amounted to representation by an attorney or a layperson (under CMPA)
- Whether work done by supervised law students in representing plaintiff amounted to representation by an attorney or a layperson (under CMPA)

Holding:

- CRB erred in concluding law students' work not compensable re atty's fees award under Comp Merit Personnel Act

Reasoning:

- Law student work parallels paralegal work (in that it contributes to work product of supervising atty)
- Law student work parallels 'full-fledged' atty work (in that law students do work that would otherwise fall to full attys during summer assoc/part-time jobs, as long as 'limited practice of law')
- BUT law students DO NOT = lay representation because of teaching, supervision, and review of licensed atty (creating atty-client relationship between prof/plaintiff)
- To exclude law student work would be anomaly among fee-shifting statutes

Result:

- Reversed and remanded for ALJ to consider on merits and award reasonable atty's fees

APPENDIX B

Suggested Answers to Exercises

Part IV

Apply It: Exercise 16.1 (from p. 108)

The **legislative branch** can check the executive branch by overriding a presidential veto by 2/3 majority vote in both houses of Congress. It can also reject Presidential nominations, control the budget, and impeach the President. The legislative branch can check the judicial branch by passing new legislation if the judiciary invalidates a statute as unconstitutional.

The **executive branch** can check the legislative branch by enforcing the law through Executive Orders and agency action. The President can also veto proposed legislation. The President checks the judicial branch by having the power to nominate federal judges.

The **judicial branch** can check the executive branch by declaring Executive Orders unconstitutional. It checks the legislative branch through judicial review of statutes to determine their constitutionality.

Apply It: Exercise 16.2 (from p. 112)

A textualist would likely argue that we should focus on the words as they appear. This would mean that the meaning of the word "dollar" at the time of adoption would not control. Therefore, a textualist would probably say that "dollar" means the current Federal Reserve note. Under this interpretation, your client would be entitled to a jury trial since $42 is greater than $20.

An originalist would consider what the term "dollar" meant at the time of adoption. Therefore, an originalist would probably contend that "dollar" should refer to the modern value of four hundred and sixteen grains of standard silver. Twenty silver dollars were then worth the rough equivalent of $188.[1] Under this interpretation, your client would not be entitled to a jury trial since $42 is less than $188.

---

1 See Jay Marshall Wolman, *The Seventh Amendment Calculator*, THE LEGAL SATYRICON (MARCH 12, 2015), https://randazza.wordpress.com/2015/12/03/the-seventh-amendment-calculator/ (https://perma.cc/B2KH-A3XL).

A living constitutionalist would recognize that the definition of the word "dollar" has changed over time. Considering that almost all courts today interpret "dollar" to mean the Federal Reserve note, a living constitutionalist would likely recognize a "dollar" as the Federal Reserve note. Under this interpretation, your client might be entitled to a jury trial.

In your client's case, then, the best arguments are likely those put forth from a textualist and living constitutionalist perspective, because they might allow your client to gain access to a jury trial under the Seventh Amendment.

Apply It: Exercise 19.1 (from p. 126)

1. *Stare decisis*, the principle of treating like cases alike, ensures fairness and predictability. By treating similar cases similarly, we strive to provide the same outcome to all parties. By discerning patterns of treatment, lawyers can better advise clients on the potential outcome of their case based on precedent.

2. a. Based on the *ratio descedendi* of the case, the insurance company would likely argue that *Wigham* stands for the proposition that falling asleep while operating a vehicle makes the operator automatically liable. This is a broad reading of the case that would make it applicable to your client's case despite the factual differences between them (e.g., your client was not working). The insurance company might also argue as a policy matter that even though your client was not working while operating the vehicle, the underlying purpose of the decision in *Wigham* was to protect the public from unsafe drivers, and that same purpose is served here by holding the driver liable.

b. Based on the legally salient facts in *Wigham*, you might argue that the case stands only for the proposition that train conductors are automatically liable for accidents caused by the conductor falling asleep at the wheel. This narrow reading of the case makes it distinguishable from your client's case on several grounds (i.e., the vehicle was a car, not a train; your client is not a conductor, etc.). You might also argue that *Wigham* was intended to protect passengers who had entrusted their safety to a third-party operator, and the underlying purpose served in that case would not be served by holding your client liable in this case.

Part V

Apply It: Exercise 22.1 (from p. 144)

1. (g), (c), (d), (b), (f), (i), (a), (e), (h). Begin by categorizing the legal authorities as primary or secondary. Then rank within those categories from most to least binding. Primary authorities: The state statute (g) and regulation (c) come first and second. The most binding case is (d) from the Maine Supreme Judicial Court. Next come the two federal cases in order of rank, (b) and (f). The federal rule (i) is arguably last as inapplicable in a Maine court. If you put it at the very end of the list, that would make sense too. The rest is secondary authority. The treatise (a) is likely next because it is specific to Maine law and the subject of the dispute. Next is likely (e) because Restatements are highly respected and this one might fill in missing holes in the Maine approach. The law review article, which represents one author's view on a related subject seems least helpful to the court. Reasonable minds could differ on the suggested ordering of the last four authorities.

2. Yes, under 28 U.S.C. § 1332. Recall that this statute grants federal courts diversity jurisdiction—one form of subject matter jurisdiction—to hear legal disputes between parties from different states. Since the property owners are domiciled in Pennsylvania and the complaining parties reside in Maine, a federal court would likely be able hear the case even if based on state law.

3. (i), (g),(c), (d) and perhaps (b). Federal courts are bound first here by their own procedural rules making (i) first. On the questions of state law, recall that the federal court must apply state court interpretations of state law under the *Erie* doctrine. Therefore, the federal court is next bound and in this order by the zoning statute, the regulation, and the decision by Maine's Supreme Judicial Court. The federal district court might treat (b) as binding as well. Of course, the court might find other helpful, non-conflicting sources persuasive.

4. (g), (c), (d). Here, the Federal Rule of Procedure does not apply in state court. Thus, the state trial court would be bound in this order and only by the zoning statute, the regulation from the Code of Maine Rules, and the decision by Maine's Supreme Judicial Court. Here too, the court might find other helpful, non-conflicting sources persuasive.

Part VI

Apply It: Exercise 24.1 (from p. 157)

1. A suit could be filed in federal court under 28 U.S.C. § 1332 if the parties are citizens of different states.

2. The most binding cases would still be from the Texas Supreme Court because that court has the final say on Texas law, and federal courts are bound by state law decisions when applying state law in diversity cases. However, if the United States Supreme Court or the Fifth Circuit Court of Appeals had dealt with this issue of Texas law before, those cases would be very persuasive. If the federal and state interpretations of Texas law differed, the trial court would need to decide how to reconcile them.

Apply It: Exercise 24.2 (from p. 158)

1. Gather and evaluate the facts:

   who: Troy Bean, Liam Hawke, neighbors of vacation home, guests at the vacation home

   what: complaints from neighbors about guests, potential lawsuit, parties, live band, noise, traffic, cars, late hours, quality of life, use of property

   when: dates of parties? most recent? start and stop times? how many total parties?

   where: clients in PA, home in ME; public road, private homes

   why: interfering with use of property, quality of life

   how: owners absent, not supervising use of home by guests

2. Identify the controlling jurisdiction(s): Maine

3. Determine the law likely to be most binding and persuasive: Maine law and federal cases construing Maine law

4. Draft a research question to guide you: Under Maine law, are absent home owners liable for guests who allegedly interfere with the neighbors' use of their property?

Apply It: Exercise 25.1 (from p. 165)

Remember that there is no one way to brainstorm search terms. This chart is designed to get you to think in different ways about the facts and generate ideas to improve your research results.

1. Brainstorm search terms

Categories of information	Facts	Increased breadth (synonyms or related terms)	Increased depth (varying degrees of abstraction)
Parties involved Describe according to relationships to each other	Troy Bean, Liam Hawke, neighbors, guests	homeowner landowner	property owners residents invitees
Places and things For example: Geographic location Type of location (School? Office?) Tangible objects (automobile) Intangible concepts (vacation)	vacation home Maine guests parties complaints noise band traffic	rental property private home parties events music commotion interference property use cars	hotel, inn, bed and breakfast, receptions, galas, sound, property rights, property enjoyment, zoning, restrictions, occupancy, complaints, objections, notice
Potential claims and defenses If not obvious, consider: Parties' conduct (acts done/ undone) Parties' mental state Injury suffered	zoning violation interfering with property use (is there a specific cause of action?)	ordinance violation homeowner's association?	violation of land use laws, regulations, restrictions interference with land use, enjoyment, rights
Relief sought by the complaining or Injured party	stop having parties; money?		compensation, injunction, other damages

2–4. Your particular circumstances will affect whether you use print or online sources or both. If you had access to Maine statutes and treatises in print, they would likely be easier to use. Knowing nothing about the types of claims a homeowner might make under these facts, I might start with a few secondary sources to get an overview of this area of law, including encyclopedias, treatises, or the Restatements on property law. Given the rising use of private property as Airbnbs, there might be some good law review articles on related liability issues. Having some idea of the potential options would make searching Maine statutes, regulations, and case law more efficient. I would also search for federal cases construing the pertinent Maine law.

Apply It: Exercise 26.1 and 27.1 (from pp. 181 and 187)

This chart represents only a portion of potential research results. Use it to gauge the results you found. Most important is whether you found the nuisance statute and some of the binding Maine cases.

Secondary Source	**Citation**	**Date Found/ Updated**	**Title**	**Notes**	
Restatement 2d on Torts	§ 822	10-12	general rule on private nuisance	liability for interfering with use/ enjoyment of land if unreasonable or otherwise actionable	§ 821D defines private nuisance
Am. Jur. 2d Nuisances	§§ 52–57	10-12	describes conduct leading to liability	harm can arise from act or failure to act; Key Number Nuisance (279) 1, 59	conduct can be intentional, reckless, or negligent
26 Causes of Action 2d 277	Cause of Action for Private Nuisance Caused by Noise	10-12	Noise alone may create a nuisance, Burch, 647 S.E.2d 879 (W. Va. 2007).	279k3(3)	
Law review articles	*Property, Tort, And Contract Law For Managing The Airbnb,* 13 NYU J. Law and Business 295	10-12	landowners of an adjoining parcel may file claim if guests repeatedly cause a disturbance		
Statute	**Citation**	**Date Found/ Updated**	**Elements**	**Result**	**Exceptions**
	tit. 22, § 1561 removal of private nuisance	10-13	Applies only to health hazards		

	tit. 17, § 2701 authorizes civil actions for common law or statutory nuisance	10-13		None of the enumerated nuisances in statute apply	
Maine B&B ordinance	https://www.maine.gov/dps/fmo/plans-review/bbrequirements (https://perma.cc/H47F-F85F)	10-13		need to apply for permit	
Cases	**Citation**	**Date Found/ Updated**	**Facts**	**Issue or Element Discussed**	**Holding**
Darney v. Dragon (D. Me. 2011)	771 F.Supp.2d 91	10-14/ current 11-2; no helpful citing cases	alleged dust and vibrations from cement manufac-turing plant allegedly caused nuisance	common law elements: 1) intent to interfere or failure to act with notice 2) interfer-ence 3) substantial harm that reduces land value, and 4) unreason-able use	not a nuisance since no proof that caused more than minor disturbance or annoyance
Johnston v. Maine Energy (Me. 2010)	997 A.2d 741	10-14/ current 11-2; cites Darney Dist. Ct. case	nuisance claim for odor from waste incinerator plant	granting of motion to dismiss	Court reversed grant of motion since claim satisfied notice pleading requirements
Charlton v. Town of Oxford (Me. 2001)	774 A.2d 366	10-14/ curent 11-2; distin-guished by Johnston	claim based on property improve-ments	restates elements of claim	did not establish element 3) on substantial harm to land value
Stonington v. Galilean Gospel Temple (Me. 1999)	722 A.2d 1269	10-14/ current 11-2; aff'd Eaton v. Cormier 748 A.2d 1006 (2000)	claim based on noise and dust from quarry operations	essence of private nuisance is interference with use and enjoyment of land	allegations sufficient to state claim for private nuisance

Shore v. Maple Lane Farms (Tenn. 2013) Not Binding	411 S.W.3d 405	10-14/ current 11-2; Magness v. Couser 2020 WL 1983797 (Tenn.) Prosser on Torts § 87	claim against farmer for nuisance related to music concerts	noise may be nuisance if it imposes discomfort beyond the reasonable limit dictated by surrounding conditions	allegations of sleep loss, headaches, nausea due to concerts sufficient to state nuisance claim

Part VII

Apply It: Exercise 30.1 (from p. 197)

After Civil Procedure, the rule might have been no cell phone use in class unless there is an emergency, the phone is turned off, or you ask your professor in advance. This broader rule would benefit the student.

After Contracts, these four incidents might be synthesized to form any one of the following rules:

- no cell phones in class unless you have an emergency that affects the life of a family member or your phone is turned off;
- no cell phones in class unless you have a good reason to bring one, which courts have interpreted differently, or your phone is turned off;
- the majority view is that cell phones are permitted as long as you have a good reason to bring one or your phone is turned off.

What other rules can you think of? Are they broad or narrow? To whose advantage?

Apply It: Exercise 30.2 (from p. 202)

1. Second element: Knowledge of falsity includes actual knowledge of falsity as well as a reckless indifference to truth. *Thomas Meats, Inc. v. Safeway, Inc.*, 3 S.W.3d 45, 47 (Tex. 2018).

2. Third element: To state or imply that a perishable food product is unsafe, the defendant must indicate that the product is inherently dangerous in some way. *Green's Grocer & Co. v. Janus*, 4 S.W.3d 94, 95 (Tex. App. 2019).

Test Yourself: Exercise 31.1 (from p. 209)

The syllogism can be validated using this drawing. The outer circle represents all forms of dissemination to the public that might qualify under the Texas statute. The inner circle is based on Thomas Meats, and represents dissemination to at least

100 people. Since CSP emailed its newsletter to more than 100 people, it fits within the second circle, indicating the reasoning (not the premises) is valid.

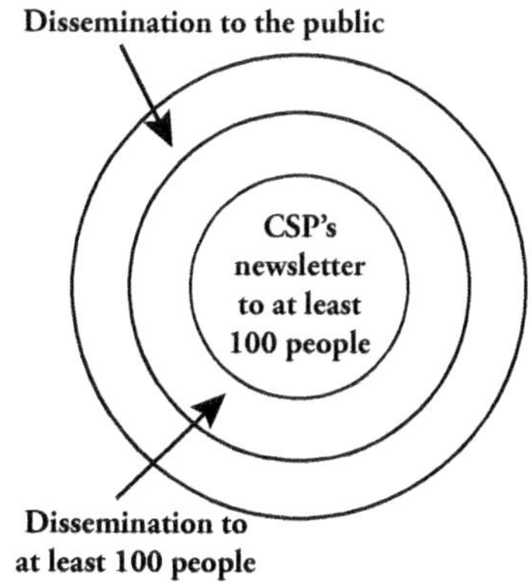

Test Yourself: Exercise 31.2 (from p. 211)

1. Which of the terms in these premises are distributed? The distributed terms are in bold.

A. All **roads** lead to Rome.

B. **Fifth Avenue** is not a **road**.

C. **Fifth Avenue** does not lead to **Rome**.

D. **No roads** lead to **Rome**.

E. **Fifth Avenue** leads to Rome.

F. **To tell information to one person** is not **dissemination in any manner to the public**.

G. **CSP** did not tell just **one person**.

H. **CSP** disseminated information in any manner to the public.

2. Assume the following premises in these syllogisms are reasonably true. Apply the validity test on page 210 to determine whether the logic is sound.

A. All roads lead to Rome.

Fifth Avenue is not a road.

Therefore, Fifth Avenue does not lead to Rome.

This syllogism fails Rule 2(b). Rome is distributed in the conclusion but not the major premise. This is the fallacy of denying the antecedent because there may be other pathways to Rome. See Chapter 31.F.3, at 216. The syllogism would be valid if the major premise were that only roads lead to Rome.

B. No roads lead to Rome.

Fifth Avenue is not a road.

Therefore, Fifth Avenue leads to Rome.

This syllogism fails Rule 2(e). If one premise is negative, the conclusion usually needs to be negative too. This is the fallacy of the double negative. See Chapter 31.F.4, at 217.

C. To tell information to one person is not dissemination in any manner to the public.

CSP did not tell just one person.

CSP disseminated information in any manner to the public.

This syllogism fails Rules 2(d) and (e). Valid conclusions are rarely drawn from two negative premises, and if one premise is negative, the conclusion usually needs to be negative too.

Apply It: Exercise 31.3 (from p. 213)

Troy Bean and Liam Hawke are not likely **(qualifier)** to be liable for nuisance **(claim)** because the music played at their guests' parties can only be heard when the neighbors' windows are open **(datum)**. Although noise, including music, can constitute a nuisance, it must cause discomfort to neighbors beyond that which is reasonable under the circumstances **(warrant)**. Parties are held just two times a week, usually on weekend days, and shut down by midnight **(to anticipate a claim that noise intrudes into neighbors' homes at unreasonable times or days)**, and neighbors need only shut their windows to eliminate the noise. In a vacation spot, where this particular property is located, it is reasonable for guests to hold outdoor parties and play music, as much as it is for their neighbors to do the same **(backing)**.

Apply It: Exercise 33.1 (from p. 231)

1. Since CSP disseminated its newsletter to its subscribers, it disseminated information "in any manner."

This seems reasonable given the breadth of the quoted phrase and the fact that CSP emailed the newsletter, which is a reliable method of delivery.

2. Since CSP disseminated its newsletter to 150 subscribers, it disseminated it "to the public."

This also seems reasonable since we know the Texas court held in *Thomas Meats* that 100 people constituted the public. There is some risk though because in that case, the 100 people saw the sign; they did not need to "open and read it."

3. Assuming the statement that the coffee is grown using pesticides is false, CSP knew it was false.

This is not reasonable. The facts suggest that to our knowledge, CSP did not reach out to the Velases to confirm its story. However, there might be other ways of determining falsity. The legal standard of recklessness gives the Velases a reasonable argument regarding this element.

4. Since the newsletter states that Velas' coffee is grown using pesticides, it states or implies that it is not safe for consumption.

This seems reasonable given the public's typical response to the danger of consuming pesticides.

Apply It: Exercise 35.1 (from p. 241)

1. CSP might argue that the primary goals of the statute are to encourage and protect truthful speech about the quality of our food supply as well as those who ingest and grow the food.

2. As a policy matter, CSP could argue that a finding that 150 people, who are all members of a private organization, constitutes the public would result in more lawsuits (category one relating to an efficient judicial system), discourage valuable speech relating to the safety of our food supply (category two relating to public health and safety), and impermissibly expand liability (category three relating to the branch best suited to make law).

3. CSP might argue that interpreting the "public" more narrowly, to mean the public at random, as in *Thomas Meats*, is more faithful to the legislative intent by not sweeping in circumstances the legislature did not anticipate (category three).

4. In response, Velas might argue that if false statements about the safety of food are made, any increase in lawsuits is acceptable as part of a fair judicial system (category one); under both interpretations of "the public," only those who make false statements will be liable and thus truthful speech will not be discouraged (category two); and the court is in the best position to respond to unique circumstances the legislature cannot anticipate (category three).

Part XII

Try It: Exercise 53.1 (from p. 417)

There are many possible ways to improve these sentences. These are just suggested answers:

1. Assuming *arguendo* that the Velases, doing business as Starbucks, produce a perishable food product, it must be proved that CSP knew that its statements were false or untrue. (28 words)

Revision: Assuming that the Velases produce a perishable food product, they must prove CSP knew its statements were false. (18 words)

Explanation: Latin and unnecessary words omitted, passive voice converted to active, omitted redundancy

2. In its opinion, the United States Court of Appeals for the Ninth Circuit held that thenceforth, any contract to engage in illegal activity would be null, void, and of no effect whatsoever. (32 words)

Revision: Any contract to engage in illegal activity is void. (9 words) [cite Ninth Circuit case].

Explanation: old fashioned-phrase removed, unnecessary words and redundancy omitted

3. The agency cited the respondent for being in violation of the pertinent regulations set forth herein and determined *sua sponte* to assess a fine. (24 words)

Revision: The agency fined the respondent for violating the regulation. (9 words)

Explanation: Latin used in unusual context and removed, old fashioned term and unnecessary words removed, nominalization converted to verb

4. In no way did the defendant contribute or add to the confusing nature of the situation, making it highly unlikely that he had anything whatsoever to do with the cause of the accident. (33 words)

Revision: The defendant behaved legally and thus did not cause the accident. (11 words)

Explanation: unnecessary words omitted, thought clarified using transition word

5. The next section of this memo addresses the three major defenses that were discussed at the meeting. (17 words)

Revision: [Client] may advance three defenses. (5 words)

Explanation: language telling the reader what the writer intends to do removed, unnecessary reference to discussion omitted, sentence now acts an adequate roadmap for the reader

Try It: Exercise 53.2 (from p. 421)

There are many possible ways to improve these sentences. These are just suggested answers:

1. We believe that our opponent's position doesn't make the grade.

Revision: The opponent's argument likely fails.

Explanation: The use of first person was removed, belief was converted to probability, and the contraction and colloquialism were removed.

2. The question clearly becomes, "Did the witness commit perjury?"

Revision: The issue is whether the witness committed perjury.

Explanation: The rhetorical question was converted to a declarative sentence, and the adverb was deleted.

3. The judgement included damages for attorney's fees, for out-of-pocket costs and consequential damages.

Revision: The judgment included attorney's fees, out-of-pocket costs, and consequential damages.

Explanation: The first *e* in judgement and unnecessary repetition were removed, and an Oxford comma was inserted.

4. In that case, the FAA charges United Airlines with violating safety regulations; they are saying the airline mechanics didn't log daily repairs.

Revision: In that case, the FAA charged United Airlines with violating safety regulations; it said the airline mechanics were not logging daily repairs.

Explanation: The cited case is now discussed in the past tense, the FAA is referred to as "it," and the contraction was removed.

5. In so holding, the *Jones* court stated:

> In cases such as these, where the totality of the circumstances is the key to the validity of the stop, the court must look at each factor and then make a determination as to whether or not the officer's belief is reasonable.

Jones, 87 N.W.2d at 75.

Revision: Whether the officer's belief is reasonable depends on the totality of the circumstances. *Jones*, 87 N.W.2d at 75.

Explanation: The paraphrased quotation takes up less space and is equally effective.

Try It: Exercise 54.1 (from p. 432)

Suggested answers:

1. Looking at each element, the plaintiff will not meet it's burden of proof.

Revision: The plaintiff cannot meet its burden of proof.

Explanation: The dangling modifier was removed, and *it's* was converted to the correct possessive form, *its*.

2. If the officer's belief is reasonable they are permitted to conduct a brief investigatory stop without a warrant.

Revision (assuming the officer identifies as male): If the officer's belief is reasonable, he is permitted . . .

Explanation: A comma was properly inserted after the introductory clause, and the noun and pronoun now agree.

3. The court must first terminate the parents rights and then it must determine what is in the child's best interest.

Revision: The court must first terminate the parents' rights, and then it must determine what is in the child's best interest.

Explanation: Plural possessives take an apostrophe after the *s*, and a comma was inserted before the coordinating conjunction, *and.*

4. The frisk, that must be based on a reasonable belief that the suspect is armed and dangerous, must be confined to a weapons search.

Revision: The frisk, which must be based on a reasonable belief . . .

Explanation: *That* was correctly replaced with *which* because the clause is non-restrictive.

5. An employer is not entitled to unilaterally terminate an employee for 'blowing the whistle' on his illegal activities.

Revision: An employer is not entitled to terminate the employee unilaterally for "blowing the whistle" on his illegal activities.

Explanation: The infinitive is not split because it sounds better, and quotation marks should be double for direct quotations.

6. The parties' were unable to agree on contract terms, and thus failed to form an enforceable contract.

Revision: The parties were unable to agree on contract terms and failed to form an . . .

Explanation: *Parties* is plural here, not possessive, and no comma was needed because *and* does not function here as a coordinating conjunction. The verb is compound: *unable to* and *failed.*

7. An employee such as the plaintiff in this case can be fired for any reason and is considered "at will;" however, they cannot be fired for reporting illegal activities to the appropriate authorities.

Revision: An employee, such as Ms. Knox in this case, can be fired for any reason and is considered "at will"; however, she cannot be fired for reporting illegal activities to the appropriate authorities.

Explanation: Commas are used to set off appositives, the semi-colon should be placed outside the quotation marks, and the noun and pronoun now agree.

8. CSP will argue that the Velases coffee beans are not "perishable food products".

Revision: CSP will argue that the Velases' coffee beans are not "perishable food products."

Explanation: *Velases* here takes the plural, possessive form, and the quotation marks belong outside the period.

9. The Joneses primary complaint was that their neighbors were effecting there ability to enjoy their backyard.

Revision: The Jones' [or Joneses'] primary complaint was that their neighbors were affecting their ability to enjoy their backyard.

Explanation: *Joneses* here operates as a plural possessive, and the words *effect* and *there* were misused.

10. Knowledge of falsity can be imputed, constructive, which means the defendant should have known, or actual.

Revision: Knowledge of falsity can be imputed; constructive, which means the defendant should have known; or actual.

Explanation: Items in a series should be separated using semi-colons, where one item contains a comma.

Part XIII

Try It: Exercise 56.1 (from p. 456)

1. *Smith Indus. v. U.S. Dep't of Agric.*, 890 P.3d 300, 342 (Or. 2017). (see ch. 56.E.1–4)

2. *Smith Indus.*, 890 P.3d at 344. (see ch. 56.E.8)

3. *Id.* at 350.

Try It: Exercise 56.2 (from p. 458)

1. 5 U.S.C. § 552.

2. Iowa Code §§ 562.9–.10 (2018). (see ch. 56.F.2–3)

3. 5 U.S.C. § 552. OR § 552. (see ch. 56.F.5)

4. *Id.* § 562.10. (see ch. 56.F.6)

Try It: Exercise 56.3 (from p. 459)

Iowa Const. art. II, § 1. Note that Iowa is spelled out per ALWD App. 3(B) and BB T.10.

Try It: Exercise 56.4 (from p. 461)

F.H. Buckley, *The Fall and Rise of Crown Government*, 68 Drake L. Rev. 252, 265 (2020).

Try It: Exercise 57.1 (from p. 467)

Assume you want to make this proposition in a case governed by Florida law:

"All fresh fruit perishes within a limited period of time."

What signal would you use to introduce the following cited authority?

1. *See.* An inference is required from the specific (banana) to the general (all fruit), so the see signal makes sense here. ALWD Chart 35.1 at 301; BB R. 1.2(a).

2. *See generally.* ALWD Chart 35.1 at 302; BB Rule 1.2(d).

3. *Contra.* This case is directly contrary to the proposition. ALWD Chart 35.1 at 302; BB R. 1.2(c).

4. No signal. Cited authority directly states the proposition. ALWD Chart 35.1 at 301; BB R. 1.2(a).

5. *E.g.*, ALWD Chart 35.1 at 301; BB R. 1.2(a).

6. *See.* An inference is required from the general (all produce) to the specific (fruit). ALWD Chart 35.1 at 301; BB. R. 1.2(a).

7. *Compare . . . with.* ALWD Chart 35.1 at 302; BB R. 1.2(b).

8. *Cf.* Cited authority supports a proposition different from the main proposition but sufficiently analogous to lend support. ALWD Chart 35.1 at 301; BB R. 1.2(a).

9. *See, e.g.*, An inference is required from the cited authorities on specific fruits to all fruit. ALWD Chart 35.1, at 301; BB R. 1.2(a). *E.g.*, can be combined with other signals. ALWD R. 35.5(b); BB R. 1.2(a).

10. *But cf.* Cited authority supports a proposition analogous to the contrary of the main proposition. ALWD Chart 35.1 at 302; BB 1.2(c).

11. *Accord* would be used here to introduce the California case. ALWD Chart 35.1 at 301; BB R. 1.2(a).

12. *But see, e.g.*, Note that *e.g.*, can be combined with other signals. ALWD R. 35.5(b); BB R. 1.2(a).

13. No signal needed with a quotation. ALWD Chart 35.1 at 301; BB R. 1.2(a).

Try It: Exercise 57.2 (from p. 469)

1. *See State v. Jones*, 900 N.W.2d 783, 793 (Iowa 2020).

2. *Contra TeddyBear Sys. Co. v. Digit. Dev. Sys., Inc.*, 678 S.E.2d 890, 927 (Ga. 2019).

Appendix C

CSP Newsletter, March 2019

CSP
Cititzens for Safe Products

THE OBSERVER
The Official Newsletter of Citizens for Safe Products™

Volume 32, No. 10 March 2019

The "Organic Issue"

Dear Dallas Members,

Spring has sprung! We hope you are looking forward to enjoying all the fresh fruits and vegetables the spring has to offer. With fresh basil, beans, berries, corn, cucumbers, lettuce, peppers, radishes, and tomatoes to look forward to, we thought this the perfect time for an issue on organic produce. Whether you are already committed to eating organic or just considering it, this issue focuses on the benefits of growing and eating organic food—from fruits and vegetables to meats and grains—and where to get it here in the Dallas area. Have a safe and productive planting season!

—Lou Fields, President 2018–2020

Local Spotlight

What's Brewin' in Your Beans?

No matter the time of year, we all like to treat ourselves to a nice steaming cup of coffee. Did you know that even coffee can be organic? We sent out our reporters to find the best local stops for organic coffee. Here is their short list:

Brewed + Pressed

3700 McDougal Ave, 75205

Coffee House Café

6150 Beanford Rd, 75251

LaLa Land, Kind Café

5624 Ring Ave, Dallas, 75216

But perk up reader! You know that Starbucks on Commerce Street? The supposedly "organic beans" are not so organic after all. A confidential source reports that the beans are grown using pesticides. We thought you'd want to know what you're drinking. Just another example of how we're working hard to protect our membership.

In This Issue

The Dirty Dozen

Every year, The Environmental Working Group publishes a list of the fruits and vegetables with the highest amount of pesticides when grown conventionally versus organically. Here is this year's list:

Strawberries
Spinach
Kale
Nectarines
Apples
Grapes
Peaches
Cherries
Pears
Tomatoes
Celery
Potatoes

The Clean Fifteen

Here is the Working Group's list of the produce from conventional growers that generally had less residue in the group's tests:

Avocados
Sweet corn
Pineapples
Frozen sweet peas
Onions

(continued on page 2)

Appendix D

Sample Legal Memorandum

To: Kim Janney

From: Ben Golum

Date: February 12, 2020

Re: Knox/WPA Claim

Question Presented

Under the Michigan Whistleblowers' Protection Act (WPA), did Good Hope Hospital commit retaliatory discharge when it fired Kathy Knox after she threatened to report the director of the hospital's blood bank to the FDA for distributing allegedly tainted blood?

Controlling law

Legal question

Legally significant facts

Brief Answer

Probably. The WPA requires that the plaintiff prove three elements, only two of which are at issue: that (1) she was engaged in protected activity, (2) she was discharged, and (3) there is a causal connection between her threat to report to a public body and her discharge. Neither party disputes that Knox has been discharged or that the FDA is a public body.

The Brief Answer begins with a short phrase that telegraphs the ultimate prediction. The writer quickly explains what the elements of the claim are and which need analysis.

With respect to the first element, Knox is likely to establish that she was engaged in "protected activity" under the WPA because she was "about to" report a suspected violation to the FDA. She will also likely establish that she was about to report a "suspected violation" because even though she cannot point to a specific rule violation, she was acting in good faith and

This paragraph states the writer's prediction as to the first element and summarizes their reasoning.

reasonably believed that using blood stored at improper temperatures violated federal regulations.

With respect to the third element, Knox can likely establish a causal connection between her threat to report and her discharge. She was fired within a week of threatening to report; both the director of the blood bank and Knox's supervisor, Kleusing, were upset that she wanted to report; and Knox had an excellent performance record. For these reasons, any legitimate reason the defendant gave for firing Knox is likely a pretext.

This paragraph explains the writer's prediction as to the third element and their reasoning.

Statement of Facts

Kathy Knox is a registered nurse who began working at Good Hope Hospital ("the hospital") in 2010. She was responsible for retrieving blood from and returning unused blood to the hospital's blood bank. Knox routinely kept track of the blood units she received, and placed the blood in the refrigerator for surgical use.

Comma not needed (after "received") with a compound verb. Ch. 54.A.2, at p. 424.

In the summer of 2015, Knox began to notice that the refrigerator was registering a higher temperature than FDA regulations permit. Knox asked the hospital maintenance department to examine the refrigerator and a few days later, they told her it was working properly. However, she still felt certain it was warmer than usual. On June 15, Knox told Mimi Betz, the director of the blood bank, about the potential problem with the refrigerator and suggested that she discard the blood that had been stored in it. The next day, when Knox returned unused blood to the blood bank, Betz told her the maintenance department said the refrigerator was fine, and Knox should focus on her own job.

Strive to be concise: just say "noticed." Ch. 53.B.11, at p. 416.

A comma is needed before "and a few days later" because "and" acts as a coordinating conjunction. Ch. 54.A.2, at p. 424.

The word "she" here is ambiguous; it's better to say "Betz." Ch. 54.A.9, at p. 427.

On June 20, Knox noticed that one of the blood units she suspected was tainted had been given back to her. When she questioned the safety of that particular unit of blood, Betz told Knox she was getting tired of Knox's complaints and that she would not "toss perfectly good product" just because Knox imagined there was some problem with it. Knox said something like: "I care about my patient's safety. If you give me any more bad blood, I am going to the FDA". Within minutes, Betz told Jon Kleusing, Knox's supervisor, about Knox's threat. Kleusing fired Knox one week later, claiming he had received complaints from co-workers that she was difficult to work with. When Knox asked Kleusing whether firing her was due to her interaction with Betz, Kleusing did not respond but reminded Knox that she had been reprimanded once in 2014 for complaints from a patient's parents. According to Knox, all the nurses who cared for that patient received complaints, but none of them was reprimanded or terminated.

Improper quotation placement; it should be: ". . . FDA." Ch. 54.A.11, at p. 427.

Traditionally, a sentence should not end with a preposition. You could just say "was difficult." Ch. 54.A.22, at p. 430.

Ms. Knox would like to know if she can successfully sue her employer for retaliatory discharge under the Michigan Whistleblowers' Act.

Facts conclude by stating the purpose of the memo (i.e., what the client wants to know). Ch. 37.A, at p. 252.

Discussion

Courts analyze claims filed under the WPA using a burden-shifting framework similar to that used in employment-related claims filed under the federal and state Civil Rights Acts. *Schmidli v. City of Fraser*, 784 F. Supp. 2d 794, 801 (E.D. Mich. 2011); *Taylor v. Modern Engineering, Inc.*, 653 N.W.2d 625, 630 (2002). If the plaintiff can make a prima facie claim of retaliatory discharge, the burden shifts to the defendant to articulate a legitimate reason for the discharge. *Roulston v. Tendercare, Inc.*, 608 N.W.2d 525, 530 (2000). If the defendant can establish a legitimate reason, the plaintiff may establish that the reason offered by the defendant is a pretext. *Id.*

The first two paragraphs act as a roadmap of the controlling law and analysis. They succinctly summarize how whistleblower claims are tried and the elements of such a claim, explain the second element as not at issue, and prepare the reader for the analysis of the first and third elements at issue (without the writer having to explain what she is about to do). Ch. 53.B.3, at p. 412.

To state a prima facie claim under the WPA, the plaintiff must show that (1) she was engaged in a protected activity as defined by the Act, (2) the defendant discharged her, and (3) a causal connection exists between the protected activity and the discharge. *See* Mich. Comp. Laws Ann. § 15.362 (West 2020); *Kuhn v. Washtenaw Cnty.*, 709 F.3d 612, 629 (6th Cir. 2013); *Farha v. Cogent Healthcare of Mich.*, 164 F. Supp. 3d

This citation indicates that these elements have not changed under Michigan law over time and that federal and state courts have construed the statute.

974, 992 (E.D. Mich. 2016); *Whitman v. City of Burton*, 831 N.W.2d 223, 229 (Mich. 2013). Neither party disputes that Knox was discharged or that FDA is a public body. The remaining issues are whether Knox can prove she was engaged in a protected activity and whether she was fired because of her threat to report to the FDA.

> The topic sentence indicates this paragraph will begin the discussion of the first element. Note the writer could have included her prediction here as well. Ch. 38.B, at p. 266.

The first element requires that Knox prove she was "about to" report a violation or suspected violation of law to a public body. § 15.362; *Shallal v. Catholic Soc. Servs.*, 566 N.W.2d 571, 579 (Mich. 1997). Unlike other states Michigan protects conscientious employees who intend to report but are fired before they have a chance. *Shallal*, 566 N.W.2d at 575. About to report means "on the verge of" doing so. *Id.* In cases construing the WPA, the United States District Court for the Eastern District of Michigan has held that a plaintiff must prove that she was about to report, verbally or in writing, and 2) that the person who fired her was "objectively aware" that she was about do report before she was fired. *See, e.g., Robinson v. Radian, Inc.*, 624 F. Supp. 2d 617, 629 (E.D. Mich. 2008); *see also Kaufman & Payton, P.C. v. Nikkila*, 503 N.W.2d 728, 732 (Mich. Ct. App. 1993) (noting a defendant's right to objective notice of a report or a threat to report by a whistleblower). This must be shown by clear and convincing evidence. *Shallal*, 566 N.W.2d at 575.

> Comma needed after "states" because this word completes an introductory phrase to the sentence. Ch. 54.A.1, at p. 423.

> This paragraph includes a general and synthesized rule (the major premise) on "about to" report. Note that it took several sentences to explain this complex rule. That's fine. It also uses an explanatory parenthetical to add authority without length. Ch. 53.B.7, at p. 414.

In *Shallal*, an employee of a social service agency told her supervisor that she was going to report his misuse of agency funds to the Department of Social Services if he did not "straighten up." In addition to making the threat, she discussed her plan to report her supervisor with her co-workers and a member of her employer's Board of Directors. In a suit against her supervisor under the WPA, the court noted that the plaintiff had discussed reporting with third parties, but it held that the express threat to report—made directly to her supervisor—was sufficient. *Id.* at 579. In this case, Knox confronted Betz and explicitly told her she would report her to the FDA if she gave Knox any more potentially tainted blood. That threat was communicated directly to Kleusing via Betz. Kleusing was thus "objectively aware" that Knox was about to report.

> The second paragraph begins with an explanation of the rule from *Shallal*; it explains the key facts, holding, and reasoning of the court in that case.

> Em dashes can be used for emphasis. Ch. 53.C.13, at p. 420.

> The last two sentences of this paragraph state the facts of Knox's case (the minor premise) and analogize Knox's case to *Shallal*.

Cases where plaintiffs have failed to establish they were about to report are likely distinguishable. In some cases, the plaintiff failed to make an actual threat. *See, e.g., Schmidli*, 784 F. Supp. 2d at 801 (holding that the plaintiff's collected documentation, inquiries to public bodies, and disagreements with her supervisor did not amount to a threat). In other cases, the plaintiff failed to make the threat known to the supervisor, or the supervisor denied a threat was ever made and there was no corroborating evidence of the threat. *See, e.g., Richards v. Sandusky Cmty. Schs.*, 102 F. Supp. 2d 753, 760 (E.D. Mich. 2000) (holding that plaintiff's concerns and intent to report were not known to the defendant as required under the WPA); *Hays v. Lutheran Soc. Servs.*, 832 N.W.2d 433, 438 (Mich. Ct. App. 2013) (holding the plaintiff was not "about to report" when she told no one about her intent to report); *Pope v. Brinks Home Sec. Co.*, Nos. 294600 & 294609, 2011 WL 711133, at *7 (Mich. Ct. App. March 1, 2011) (holding the plaintiff was not "about to" report when the defendant denied she made the alleged threat and no one else had allegedly heard it). In this case, Betz communicated the threat directly to Kleusing, who does not dispute having been aware of it.

In this paragraph, the writer anticipates the defendant's counterarguments by distinguishing cases where the plaintiff failed to establish "about to" report. Notice the writer anticipates the defendant's arguments without having to say "the defendant may claim" or "the defendant may cite." Ch. 38.C, at p. 268.

Having examined the potential counterarguments, the writer concludes on this sub-issue.

As part of the first element, Knox must also prove that she was about to report a "suspected violation" because she had been told that the refrigerator used to store the blood was functioning properly. *See* § 15.362; *Melchi v. Burns Int'l Sec. Serv., Inc.*, 597 F. Supp. 575, 583 (E.D. Mich. 1984). A suspected violation is behavior that an employee, acting in good faith, reasonably believes is against the law. *Smith v. Gentiva Health Serv. Inc.*, 296 F. Supp. 2d 758, 762 (E.D. Mich. 2003); *Melchi*, 597 F. Supp. at 583–84. In *Melchi*, a security guard of a nuclear facility observed the defendant destroy and falsify security records. Although the plaintiff could not establish that this behavior violated any law, the court held the guard had acted in good faith and his belief was reasonable because of "the pervasive regulation of the nuclear power industry by state and federal agencies." *Melchi*, 597 F. Supp. at 583–84.

Topic sentence here indicates a transition to the second sub-issue under the first element. The writer includes a synthesized rule on "suspected violation" that explains the element and how it has been interpreted.

The writer states the synthesized rule (major premise) for "suspected violation."

Explanation of the rule with key facts, holding, and court's reasoning.

Like in Melchi, Knox likely acted in good faith and her belief was likely reasonable. The healthcare industry is as highly regulated as the nuclear power industry, and the FDA has strict regulations relating to blood storage. Thus, Knox could reasonably believe it was unlawful to use blood she thought had been stored improperly. Unlike the security guard in *Melchi*, who was certain that the defendant had destroyed documents, Knox was not certain that the refrigerator was malfunctioning. However, in view of the health risks to patients from contaminated blood and Knox's experience, a Michigan court is likely to hold that Knox acted in good faith and with a reasonable belief of a "suspected violation."

Analogy to *Melchi*.

The writer anticipates how the hospital might try to distinguish *Melchi*.

Conclusion.

To prove the third element, that a causal connection exists between the protected activity and Knox's discharge, Knox must show a causal, not just a temporal, connection between her protected activity and her termination. *See West v. Gen. Motors Co.*, 665 N.W.2d 468, 473 (Mich. Ct. App. 2003); *Taylor v. Modern Eng'g, Inc.*, 653 N.W.2d 625, 630 (Mich. Ct. App. 2002); *Roulston v. Tendercare, Inc.*, 608 N.W.2d 525, 530 (Mich. Ct. App. 2000). However, the burden of establishing a prima facie case is not intended to be onerous. If a reasonable juror could conclude that Knox would not have been fired if she had not threatened to report, the causal requirement is met. *See West*, 665 N.W.2d at 473 (stating that a whistleblower plaintiff must show the adverse action "was in some manner influenced by the protected activity"); *cf. Nguyen v. City of Cleveland*, 229 F.3d 559, 563 (6th Cir. 2000) (discussing the causal connection in a failure to promote case under Title VII).

This topic sentence transitions the reader from the first to the third element and reminds the reader what the third element is.

Here, the writer explains the synthesized rule on causal connection.

In *Roulston*, the plaintiff, a social services director at a nursing home, was fired within hours of reporting suspected abuse to state regulators. The court held that the extent of her supervisor's anger, his harsh language, his watching her collect her belongings, and her performance record suggested the plaintiff had been fired because she had reported. *Roulston*, 608 N.W.2d at 530. The court also noted that if the defendant could establish a legitimate reason for the dis-

This paragraph explains how the rule was applied in *Roulston*.

charge, the plaintiff would have an opportunity to show that the defendant's stated reason was a pretext, and pretext can be shown even where the defendant acts from mixed motives (e.g., both a legitimate and a retaliatory reason). *Id; see also Melchi*, 597 F. Supp. at 583.

Like Roulston, Knox is likely to establish a causal connection between her threat to report and her discharge. First, Knox was also fired soon after she threatened to report, roughly one week later, even though she had worked at the hospital for roughly five years. Second, like Roulston's supervisor, Betz's reaction to Knox's concerns was anger, which she would have communicated to Kleusing, who fired her. Finally, Knox's performance record—she was reprimanded just one in five years—suggests her threat to report motivated Kleusing, at least in part, to fire her. As long as the threat to report contributed to Knox being discharged, she is likely to prove causation.

> The writer compares Knox's case (the minor premise) to *Roulston*. They also explain that once a prima facie claim is established, Knox can likely establish pretext.

> The writer states a conclusion on the third element.

Conclusion

Knox is likely to succeed in her whistleblower claim against the hospital under Michigan's Whistleblowers' Protection Act. Knox's threat to Betz, who conveyed it to Kleusing, establishes that Knox was "about to" report. There is no indication that either Betz or Kleusing will deny those statements. Because the storage of blood for hospital use is highly regulated by the FDA, Knox can also establish that she acted in good faith and reasonably believed that Betz's use of potentially tainted blood was against the law. Finally, Knox can probably prove that a causal connection exists between her threat to report and her discharge. In addition to Knox being discharged within just one week of the threat, both Betz and Kleusing were upset about the threat, and Knox had an excellent performance record. For these reasons, any reason the defendant states for firing Knox is likely to be considered a pretext.

> The conclusion recaps for the reader how the writer reached the conclusion, explaining why Knox will probably succeed in proving the disputed elements of the claim.

Appendix E

Sample Appellate Brief

United States Circuit Court of Appeals
For The Fourth Circuit

Case No. CF–20–298

United States,

Appellant,

v.

Paul Woods,

Appellee.

On Appeal from the United States District Court
for the Eastern District of Virginia

Brief for the Appellee

Carlton Jones
Jones & Associates
345 Main Street
Richmond, VA 22320

Table of Contents

Table of Authorities

Jurisdictional Statement

The Court has jurisdiction of this matter under 18 U.S.C. § 3731.

Statement of the Issue Presented for Review

Under the United States Constitution, did police violate Paul Woods' Fourth Amendment rights when they stopped and frisked him for standing outside a 7-Eleven late at night with his hands in his pockets while waiting for a ride?

> The Statement of the Issue characterizes the facts from the appellee's point of view and suggests a positive answer. Ch. 45.A, at p. 323. It also hints at the role the client plays here as "the innocent." Ch. 47.A.1, at p. 342.

Statement of the Case

On October 12, 2019, the United States District Court for the Eastern District of Virginia granted Woods' pretrial motion to suppress evidence, concluding that the stop and frisk conducted by police officers Kim and Nelson violated his Fourth Amendment rights. Order at 1. The government appeals this ruling.

> The Statement of the Case opens with the procedural history, which happens to favor the appellee. The use of "violated" here is stronger than the nominalization "in violation of." Ch. 53.B.5, at p. 413.

Shortly before 11:00 p.m. on June 13, 2019, Paul Woods stopped at his neighborhood 7-Eleven for a pint of cream for his morning coffee and a cherry Slurpee. When he got back in his car, Woods discovered that the battery had died. He called a friend to pick him up and waited outside the store for his friend to arrive. Although 7-Eleven stores were named to indicate they are open from 7:00 a.m. to 11:00 p.m. seven days a week, many 7-Elevens are now open twenty-four hours a day, including this one. As Officers Leila Kim and James Nelson drove by the store in their patrol car, they observed Woods standing outside the storefront under a lamp with his hands in his pockets. R. at 2.

> The story begins in a state of relative calm and frames the defendant as a normal person engaging in normal activities on his way home. And who doesn't love a Slurpee? But then, a series of complicating incidents occurs: Woods' car battery dies, and he has to call a friend to come get him. Now the police have observed him standing outside the 7-Eleven. He's not doing anything, but that may be a problem.

Kim testified that Woods attracted their attention because of the late hour in a relatively high-crime area, with his overall "nervous appearance" and hands in his pockets. As Kim drove into the store parking lot, Woods walked away from them toward his car. R. at

> The quotation marks call the officer's characterization of the defendant's behavior into question, suggesting that Woods has a different story to tell.

12. Kim also testified that as Woods turned his back to them, she noticed he matched the description of a suspect in a robbery the day before at a jewelry store two miles away. R. at 13, 19. The eyewitness description was of a "young black male, tall and thin, wearing dark clothing." R. at 15. Other than this description, the officers had no knowledge of Woods or his ever having engaged in criminal activity. R. at 17.

Notice that facts are supported by citations to the record on appeal. Ch. 47, at p. 341; *see also* ALWD R. 25.5; BB R. B17.2 & 10.8.3.

Officer Kim stopped the car for Officer Nelson to get out and then drove directly behind Woods as he walked around and behind the store. R. at 15. Within a minute or so, Officer Nelson approached Woods with his gun drawn, waved him over, and ordered him to "Stop," and "Come here, let me talk to you." R. at 33. Frightened and confused, Woods stopped when Nelson ordered him to do so. R. at 34.

Woods doesn't run, but he does try to separate himself from whatever is happening. The goal is for the reader to sympathize with Woods' response. When Nelson draws his weapon and orders Woods to stop, Woods does not flee, get angry, act nervous or otherwise suspicious. He simply complies and submits to the frisk.

Nelson told Woods that he matched the description of the suspect in a recent robbery and instructed him to place his hands on the hood of the police car so that he could be searched for weapons. R. at 35. Nelson testified that the frisk was necessary because they had seen Woods's hands in his pockets and he was evasive. R. at 36. When told to put his hands on the car to be searched for weapons, Woods immediately cooperated, stating repeatedly that he had none. R. at 37. Although Nelson felt nothing that resembled a weapon, he reached in and pulled out an eyedropper and two glass vials of phencyclidine. R. at 37. Nelson then arrested Woods for possession of a controlled substance.

Although no weapons are found, the officers seize illegal drugs and paraphernalia. Phencyclidine is also known as angel dust, but the writer uses this less inflammatory term. What officers seized here is less important as a legal matter than how they seized it. The story leaves us with the rising action concluded just before the climax and resolution in the argument. Ch. 47.A.3, at p. 344.

Summary of Argument

The officers violated Woods' Fourth Amendment rights, and the motion to suppress the evidence was properly granted. The Fourth Amendment of the Constitution guarantees the right to be free from unreasonable searches and seizures. When the officers subjected Paul Woods to a *Terry* stop and frisk without reasonable suspicion that Paul was involved in a crime or that he was armed and dangerous, they violated that right.

The Summary opens by reiterating the basic claim as framed by the Issue Statement: Woods' rights were violated by the stop and frisk. Ch. 53.A.2, at p. 403 (on avoiding elegant variation). Here, "properly" splits the infinitive, but the writer could decide that this sounds better than saying "was granted properly." Ch. 54.A.19, at p. 429.

A *Terry* stop is unlawful unless officers have reasonable, articulable suspicion that the person stopped is engaging or about to engage in criminal activity. As the lower court held, the fact that officers observed Woods in a high-crime area, late at night, with his hands in his pockets was insufficient to suspect Woods was engaged in a crime. He stood still under a lit lamp of an open convenience store, waiting for a friend to pick him up. When Officer Kim followed behind him in her car, Woods did not flee, otherwise evade the officers, or act in a suspicious or excessively nervous manner. Without any explanation for their presence, he simply tried to avoid interacting with them.

This paragraph summarizes the argument that the stop was illegal, touching on each of the factors argued later in detail. Ch. 48.C.2, at 356. It also reminds the reader what the lower court held on these facts. Notice the rule is framed from Woods' point of view: The stop is unlawful unless . . . (as opposed to: *Terry* stops are lawful when . . .). Ch. 48.E, at p. 358. Note that citations are not needed in the Summary of Argument.

The frisk here was unlawful because the officers had no reason to stop Woods. But even if the stop was lawful, the frisk was not. The officers did not have reasonable, articulable suspicion that Woods was armed and dangerous. Without more, the fact that Woods had his hands in his pockets while waiting for a ride, was insufficient for Nelson to believe he was in danger, particularly since Woods cooperated immediately when told to stop and submitted voluntarily to the frisk.

Similarly, this paragraph summarizes the argument that the frisk was illegal, arguing in the alternative and emphasizing that Woods did not engage in any threatening behavior.

Standard of Review

The issue before the court is whether the trial court erred in suppressing the evidence; the underlying facts are not in dispute. The circuit court reviews legal conclusions regarding reasonable suspicion for a *Terry* stop and frisk de novo. *United States v. Arvizu*, 534 U.S. 266, 275 (2002); *United States v. Curry*, 965 F.3d 313, 319 (4th Cir. 2020).

Since this is a legal question, the review is de novo. Common Latin phrases in legal writing are not italicized. Ch. 53.A.3, at p. 404; ALWD R. 1.3(f); BB R. 7(b). Cases are arranged in the string cite in a logical order from highest to lowest federal courts. Ch. 57.B, at p. 468; ALWD R. 36.3; BB R. 1.4.

Argument

> The major heading echoes the wording of the Statement of the Issue and the Summary of Argument, encapsulates the argument on both the stop and frisk, and prepares the reader for an argument on each.

The Officers Violated Woods' Fourth Amendment Rights Because They Lacked Reasonable, Articulable Suspicion to Stop and Frisk Mr. Woods.

No reasonable, articulable suspicion existed to justify the stop and frisk of Mr. Woods. The Fourth Amendment guarantees the "right of the people to be secure in their persons, houses, papers, and effects, against unreasonable searches and seizures." U.S. Const. amend. IV. Absent a warrant, police may conduct only a brief investigatory stop if they have reason to believe that an individual is engaged in or about to engage in criminal activity. *Terry v. Ohio*, 392 U.S. 1, 30 (1968); *Curry*, 965 F.3d at 320. If the stop is lawful, police may then conduct a brief pat down of outer clothing only if they have reason to believe the individual is armed and presently dangerous. *Terry*, 392 U.S. at 30; *Curry*, 965 F.3d at 320. In this case, neither the stop nor the frisk was based on reasonable suspicion, and the motion to suppress was properly granted.

> This introductory paragraph begins the climax of the story. It begins with a topic sentence that argues the overall legal conclusion. It then provides some context for the reader—Fourth Amendment stop and frisk law—and states the general rules of law for each, framed from Woods' point of view. It also acts as an implicit roadmap for the argument as a whole, without saying first I will argue *x*, and then I will argue *y*. Ch. 48.C.2, at p. 356 and Ch. 53.B.3, at p. 412. It concludes by reminding the court to affirm, the ultimate resolution of the story.

A. The stop was unlawful because the officers lacked reasonable, articulable suspicion that Woods was engaging in or about to engage in criminal activity.

> The first minor heading argues that the stop was unlawful and why.

The officers here had no reason to believe that Woods was involved in a crime. To conduct a *Terry* stop, officers must rely on more than a "gut feeling" or hunch. *See Terry*, 392 U.S. at 27; *United States v. Slocumb*, 804 F.3d 677, 682 (4th Cir. 2015); *United States v. Pittman*, 102 F. App'x 315, 320 (4th Cir. 2004) (stating an officer's "subjective sense about impending criminal activity is completely irrelevant"). "[T]he Constitution requires 'a *particularized* and objective basis for suspecting *the particular person stopped* of criminal activity.' " *Slocumb*, 804 F.3d at 682 (quoting *United States v. Massenburg*, 654 F.3d 480, 486 (4th Cir. 2011). Yet the officers here can state no facts in support of a belief that Woods was or was about to be engaging in criminal activity.

> This paragraph begins with a strong topic sentence arguing that the stop was not based on adequate suspicion to implicate Woods and provides more detail on what level of suspicion is required. Combined with the next paragraph, it acts as a mini-roadmap for this section, laying out the test and factors for determining reasonable suspicion.

To assess the reasonableness of police suspicion, this Court reviews the totality of circumstances, including 1) the nature of the area, including whether it is a high crime area, the individual's location in that area, and the time of day; 2) the officers' experience and knowledge of the individual's prior or any other nearby criminal activity; and 3) the individual's conduct and response to officers, including evasive and nervous behavior. *See, e.g., Illinois v. Wardlow*, 528 U.S. 119, 124 (2000); *Terry*, 392 U.S. at 23; *Slocumb*, 804 F.3d at 682; *United States v. Bumpers*, 705 F.3d 168, 175 (4th Cir. 2013); *Massenburg*, 654 F.3d at 489; *United States v. Foster*, 634 F.3d 243, 246 (4th Cir. 2011). Although seemingly innocent factors may in the aggregate amount to the requisite suspicion, *Arvizu*, 534 U.S. at 277–78, "[t]he government 'must do more than simply label a behavior as "suspicious" to make it so.' " *Slocumb*, 804 F.3d at 684 (quoting *Massenburg*, 654 F.3d at 491).

The test for reasonable suspicion is a totality of circumstances test determined on the basis of factors, but courts do not consistently list the same factors in the same order in this area of Fourth Amendment law. Here, the writer has selected those factors relevant to Woods' case and grouped and numbered them in a logical way. The reader is now primed to expect three arguments, one for each factor. The factors argued might be different on a different set of facts.

Regarding the first factor, neither the nature of the surrounding area nor Woods' location at the front of the store at 11:00 p.m. contributed to reasonable suspicion. Although the 7-Eleven is in a relatively high crime neighborhood, being present in the area was not enough to suspect Woods was committing a crime. *See Wardlow*, 528 U.S. at 124 ("presence in an area of expected criminal activity, standing alone, is not enough to support a reasonable, particularized suspicion that the person is committing a crime"); *Slocumb*, 804 F.3d at 682. In *Slocumb*, the defendant was helping a woman with an infant transfer a car seat from one car to another. As officers approached, Slocumb appeared to be hurrying the woman and avoided eye contact with them. He mumbled some of his answers to their questions but explained that his girlfriend's car had broken down. In defending the stop and subsequent frisk, the government argued in part that Slocumb was in a high-crime area, late at night, and the business had been closed for hours. The court held these facts alone did not amount to reasonable suspicion because they did not support a particularized suspicion as to the defendant. *See Slocumb*, 804 F.3d at 684.

This paragraph opens with transition words to signal to the reader that the argument on the first factor is beginning. It combines those transition words with an argument on that factor. **[C]** It begins with the rule that being in a high-crime area is not enough to suspect a particular individual. **[R]** Notice the writer relies on more than one case per rule to demonstrate the breadth of the research and the reliability of the rule. Then the rule is explained using *Slocumb*, including key facts, holding and reasoning. **[E]**

Similarly, Woods was stopped in a high-crime area, late at night, in the parking lot of a commercial business with a malfunctioning car. Slocumb was picking up his girlfriend because her car had died, and Woods was waiting for a ride for the same reason. Unlike in *Slocumb,* the 7-Eleven was still open and would remain open all night. Woods stood still under a lit lamp outside the storefront of the 7-Eleven waiting for his friend to arrive, and he was two miles away from the jewelry store that had been robbed the day before. Thus, these facts do not support reasonable suspicion for the stop.

The rule is applied by comparing Woods' case to *Slocumb* to require the same outcome. As the writer points out, the facts of Woods' case are even stronger for the defense than in *Slocumb*. **[A]** The writer then re-concludes on this factor. **[C]** *See* Ch. 29, at p. 193 (on the analytical paradigm in legal argument).

As for the second factor, the officers had no knowledge of Woods or whether he had ever committed a crime. The generic description of the suspect who allegedly robbed the jewelry store cannot establish reasonable suspicion for stopping Woods. Descriptions of suspects can contribute to reasonable suspicion when a crime has just occurred, but the description must come from a reliable source, be specific, and connect the defendant to an ongoing or recent crime. *United States v. Brown*, 401 F.3d 588, 596 (4th Cir. 2005); *United States v. Swann*, 149 F.3d 271, 274 (4th Cir. 1998). In *Brown*, police officers received an anonymous tip that a short, black male with glasses was carrying a firearm outside an apartment complex. Because the tip did not contain sufficient indicia of reliability, the description of the man was brief and general, and the defendant did not act in a suspicious manner prior to the stop, the Court held the defendant's *Terry* stop invalid. *Brown*, 401 F.3d at 596.

The argument on the second factor is structured similarly: argument, rule, explanation, application, and conclusion.

Again, the writer relies on a case with a favorable outcome and analogizes Woods' case.

In this case, despite repeated requests, the government has failed to provide any evidence of the reliability of the description provided by the eyewitness. Like in *Brown*, the description was brief and general and could have applied to numerous individuals. In a predominantly black neighborhood, a "tall, thin man in dark clothing" is not sufficiently specific. *See Swann*, 149 F.3d at 274 (holding a *Terry* stop was valid where police were investigating a recent theft on the scene; encountered individuals meeting the description of two black male suspects, one wearing "a black

In a sense, the writer anticipates the counterargument that the description was specific enough by comparing it to the more specific description in *Swann*.

leather jacket"; and the suspects acted in a threatening and nervous manner prior to the stop). Moreover, when the police encountered Brown outside the apartment complex, he did nothing to suggest he was carrying a firearm. *Brown*, 401 F.3d at 596. Similarly, Woods did nothing to suggest he was involved with the recent robbery or any other "sinister activity." *Slocumb*, 804 F.3d at 684.

As for the third factor, Woods was not evasive, suspicious, or nervous in ways that might justify the stop here. In the absence of flight or other evasive measures, suspicious behaviors, or extreme nervousness, an individual's response to police cannot justify a *Terry* stop. *Id.* at 682–83; *United States v. Sprinkle*, 106 F.3d 613, 617–18 (4th Cir.1997). Where police lack reasonable suspicion to stop, a citizen is not obligated to stop or answer police questions, and his failure to do so does not equate to evasion. *See Florida v. Royer*, 460 U.S. 491, 497–98 (1983).

The third factor (the defendant's conduct) is comprised of three discrete sub-factors that the writer addresses in turn: evasiveness, suspicious behavior, and extreme nervousness. Ch. 48.B.1, at p 352. This paragraph acts as a mini-roadmap preparing the reader for the three arguments.

Behaviors considered evasive include taking off in "headlong flight," *Wardlow*, 528 U.S. at 124, "walking away 'at a fast pace,' " *Bumpers*, 705 F.3d at 168, or exiting the area. *United States v. Mayo*, 361 F. 3d 802 (4th Cir. 2004). In *Bumpers*, officers approached two men trespassing on private property on a December evening around 7:30 p.m. They were standing near garbage dumpsters near the back of a side lot of a convenience store. As the officers approached, the men started to walk away "at a fast pace," trying "to get away from the area." *Bumpers*, 705 F.3d at 170. In conjunction with the fact that the area was known for trespassing, multiple shootings, and countless drug arrests, the court held the stop was valid. *Id.* at 176.

For this and the next sub-factor, the rule is explained using the most similarly factual case with an adverse outcome. That means the writer must distinguish it. This not only explains the rule but anticipates the appellant's potential reliance on this case and demonstrates why it is not controlling here.

Unlike Bumpers, Woods was not trespassing or otherwise engaging in criminal activity when Kim and Nelson observed him at the 7-Eleven. Uncertain as to why the police had entered the parking lot or why Kim would follow behind him in her car, Woods naturally attempted to avoid interacting with them. He did not take off in "headlong flight," walk away from them at a fast pace in an attempt to dodge them, or attempt to shield his activity. In fact, he had no obligation to stay there, but he cooperated immediately as soon as Nelson ordered him to stop.

Nor was Woods' behavior suspicious. Furtive gestures and other behaviors such as putting one's hands in their pockets may contribute to reasonable suspicion, *see, e.g.*, *Massenburg*, 654 F.3d at 491; *Mayo*, 361 F. 3d at 807. In *Mayo*, officers observed Mayo in the middle of the street talking to someone. When Mayo noticed the officers, he put his hand in his left jacket pocket and pushed down as though he had something heavy in it or was controlling a weapon while moving at the same time. In holding the subsequent stop and frisk lawful, the court noted that Mayo was walking in a high crime area, his response to the officers indicated he had a concealed weapon (in itself a crime), he evaded police, and was palpably nervous. *Id.* at 807–08. Unlike in *Mayo*, Woods already had his hands in his pockets—a common stance while waiting—when Kim and Nelson first observed him standing outside the 7-Eleven. He did not place them there in response to the officers' presence.

The types of excessively nervous behaviors that lead to reasonable, articulable suspicion include heavy breathing, heavy sweating, pulsing of the carotid artery, and shaky hands. *See, e.g.*, *id.*; *United States v. Foreman*, 369 F.3d 776, 784 (4th Cir. 2004). However, this Court has acknowledged that some nervousness in the presence of police is normal. *Slocumb*, 804 F.3d at 683–84 (finding that avoiding eye contact and mumbling are consistent with situations where one might expect citizens to be upset in the presence of police). Despite the officers' description of Woods as nervous, he did not exhibit any of these behaviors. At most, the government points to Woods walking away, which under the circumstances was neither flight nor extreme nervousness. Instead, his response was consistent with a situation where a person, particularly a black man, might be expected to be upset in the presence of police.

Taken together, these factors do not add up to reasonable suspicion for a *Terry* stop. Although it was late at night in a high-crime area, that alone was inadequate to suspect Woods of a crime. Woods had just stopped to make a purchase at his neighborhood 7-Eleven. Discovering that his car battery had died, he waited for a friend to come get him. The police did not know Woods or whether he had a criminal record, and he was not engaging in any suspicious or excessively nervous behavior. Finally, his response to the patrol car was in the normal range, consistent with what we might expect citizens to do when unexpectedly confronted by police late at night. As the *Slocumb* court has so eloquently stated, "his seizure had 'no connection with the individual seized, the activity [he was] involved in, [his] mannerisms, or [his] suspiciousness; rather the seizure [was] a mere happenstance of geography.' " *Slocumb*, 804 F.3d at 684.

Since this is a totality test, the writer concludes by summing up the totality of the factors and arguing why they do not amount to reasonable suspicion. Depending on the facts and factors, this sort of summary may not be necessary.

B. Even if the stop was lawful, the frisk was unlawful because Officer Nelson lacked reasonable, articulable suspicion to believe Woods was armed or dangerous.

The second minor heading argues that the frisk was unlawful and why.

Officers Kim and Nelson lacked reasonable, articulable suspicion to stop Woods, but even if they had reason to stop Woods, the frisk was unlawful. To conduct a frisk following a *Terry* stop, the police must be able to articulate particular facts leading them to believe a suspect was armed and dangerous. *Terry*, 392 U.S. at 27; *United States v. Burton*, 228 F.3d 524, 528 (4th Cir. 2000). Unless "a reasonably prudent man in the circumstances would be warranted in the belief that his safety or that of others was in danger," a frisk is unlawful. *Terry*, 392 U.S. at 27.

As you read this section, try to identify the components of the argument (in terms of the analytical paradigm). Put another way, where is the C-R-E-A-C?

In *Burton*, the defendant stood outside a pay phone at a convenience store, with his right hand in his pocket. As officers approached, they asked him for identification and ordered him to take his hand out of his pocket, but Burton did neither. A frisk produced a handgun, which the defendant attempted to fire at the officers. Holding the stop and frisk invalid, the court emphasized that an officer may not frisk a citizen merely because he feels uneasy about his safety. *Id.* at 528–29. Without reasonable suspicion that Burton was engaging in criminal activity, the officers were obliged to avoid a person [they] consider[ed] dangerous." *Terry*, 392 U.S. at 32. Similarly, the officers in this case had no reason to stop Woods in the first place, and even if they had, Woods did nothing to suggest the officers were in danger. His clothing did not suggest he had a concealed weapon, he did not threaten them in any way, and his hands were no longer in his pockets. Thus, the frisk was unlawful.

Conclusion

For the reasons stated above, the district court's granting of the motion to suppress was proper and should be affirmed.

Conclusion states in one sentence the precise relief sought.

Respectfully submitted,

Carlton Jones

March 12, 2020

Bibliography

Articles

Rakefet Ackerman & Morris Goldsmith, *Metacognitive Regulation of Text Learning: On Screen Versus on Paper*, 17 J. Experimental Psychol.: Applied 18 (Mar. 2011).

Ruggero J. Aldisert, Stephen Clowney & Jeremy D. Peterson, *Logic for Law Students: How to Think Like a Lawyer*, 69 Univ. Pitt. L. Rev. 1 (2007).

Akhil Reed Amar, *The Supreme Court, 1999 Term—Foreword: The Document and the Doctrine*, 114 Harv. L. Rev. 26 (2000).

Susmita Baral, *Can't quit saying 'um' and 'ah'? Just learn how to use them better* (July 25, 2016), https://qz.com/740602/cant-quit-saying-um-and-ah-just-learn-how-to-use-them-better/.

Jane B. Baron, *Law, Literature, and the Problems of Interdisciplinarity*, 108 Yale L. J. 1059 (1999).

Mary Beth Beazley, *Writing (and Reading) Appellate Briefs in the Digital Age*, 15 J. App. Prac. & Process 47 (2014).

Linda L. Berger, *A Revised View of the Judicial Hunch*, 10 Legal Commc'n & Rhetoric: J. ALWD 1 (2013).

Linda L. Berger, *Applying New Rhetoric to Legal Discourse: The Ebb and Flow of Reader and Writer, Text and Context*, 49 J. Legal Educ. 155 (1999).

Linda Berger, *How Embedded Knowledge Structures Affect Judicial Decision Making: An Analysis of Metaphor, Narrative, and Imagination in Child Custody Disputes*, 18 S. Cal. Interdisc. L.J. 259 (2009).

Linda L. Berger, *The Lady, or the Tiger? A Field Guide to Metaphor and Narrative*, 50 Washburn L. J. 275 (2011).

James A. Berlin, *Contemporary Composition: The Major Pedagogical Theories*, 44 Coll. Eng. 765 (1982).

James Berlin, *Rhetoric and Ideology in the Writing Class*, 50 Coll. Eng. 477 (1988).

Mitchell N. Berman, *Originalism is Bunk*, 84 N.Y.U. L. Rev. 1 (2009).

Ann E. Berthoff, *From Problem-Solving to a Theory of Imagination*, 33 C. English 636 (1972).

Lloyd F. Bitzer, *The Rhetorical Situation*, 1 PHILOSOPHY & RHETORIC 1 (1968).

Patricia Bizzell, *Cognition, Convention, and Certainty: What We Need to Know About Writing*, 3 PRE/TEXT 213 (1982).

William J. Brennan, Jr., *Reason, Passion, and "the Progress of the Law,"* 10 CARDOZO L. REV. 3 (1988).

Guido Calabresi, *Some Thoughts on Risk Distribution and the Law of Torts*, 70 YALE L.J. 499 (1961).

Guido Calabresi & Jon T. Hirschoff, *Toward a Test for Strict Liability in Torts*, 81 YALE L.J. 1055 (1972).

Kenneth D. Chestek, *Competing Stories: A Case Study of the Role of Narrative Reasoning in Judicial Decisions*, 9 LEGAL COMMC'N & RHETORIC: JALWD 99 (2012).

Kenneth D. Chestek, *The Plot Thickens: The Appellate Brief as Story*, 14 J. LEG. WRITING 127 (2008).

Ronald H. Coase, *The Problem of Social Cost*, 3 J.L. & ECON. 1 (1960).

Robert J. Connors, *The Rise and Fall of the Modes of Discourse*, 32 COLL. COMPOSITION & COMMC'N 444 (1981).

Kimberlé Crenshaw, *Demarginalizing the Intersection of Race and Sex: A Black Feminist Critique of Antidiscrimination Doctrine, Feminist Theory and Antiracist Politics*, 1989 U. CHI. LEGAL F. 139 (1989).

Kimberlé Crenshaw, *Mapping the Margins: Intersectionality, Identity Politics, and Violence Against Women of Color*, 43 STANFORD L. REV. 1241 (1993).

Clare Dalton, *Where We Stand: Observations on the Situation of Feminist Legal Thought*, 3 BERKELEY WOMEN'S L.J. 1 (1988).

Frances DeLaurentis, *When Ethical Worlds Collide: Teaching Novice Legal Writers to Balance the Duties of Zealous Advocacy and Candor to the Tribunal*, 7 DREXEL L. REV. 1 (2014).

Harold Demsetz, *Toward a Theory of Property Rights*, 57 AM. ECON. ASS'N 347 (1967).

Christy DeSanctis, *Narrative Reasoning and Analogy: The Untold Story*, 9 LEG. COMMC'N & RHETORIC: J. ALWD 149 (2012).

Lisa Ede & Andrea Lunsford, *Audience Address/Audience Invoked: The Role of Audience in Composition Theory and Pedagogy*, 35 COLL. COMPOSITION & COMMC'N 155 (1984).

Linda H. Edwards, *Speaking of Stories and Law*, 13 LEGAL COMMC'N & RHETORIC 157 (2016).

Linda H. Edwards, *The Convergence of Analogical and Dialectic Imaginations in Legal Discourse*, 20 Leg. Stud. Forum 7 (1996).

Robert C. Ellickson, *Property in Land*, 102 Yale L.J. 1315 (1993).

Elizabeth Fajans, *Legal Writing in the Time Of Recession: Developing Cognitive Skills for Complex Legal Tasks*, 49 Duq. L. Rev. 613 (2011).

Lucinda M. Finley, *Transcending Equality Theory: A Way Out of the Maternity and the Workplace Debate*, 86 Colum. L. Rev. 1118 (1986).

Brian Foley & Ruth Anne Robbins, *Fiction 101: A Primer for Lawyers on How to use Fiction Writing Techniques to Write Persuasive Facts Sections*, 32 Rutgers L. J. 459 (2001).

Judith D. Fischer, *Bareheaded and Barefaced Counsel: Courts React to Unprofessionalism in Lawyers' Papers*, 31 Suffolk U. L. Rev. 1 (1997).

Judith D. Fischer, *The Role of Ethics in Legal Writing: The Forensic Embroiderer, the Minimalist Wizard, and Other Stories*, 9 Scribes J. Legal Writing 77 (2003–2004).

Linda Flower & John R. Hayes, *The Cognition of Discovery: Defining a Rhetorical Problem*, 31 Coll. Composition & Commc'n 21 (1980).

Mignon Fogarty, *Bad Versus Badly*, http://www.quickanddirtytips.com/education/grammar/bad-versus-badly?page=1 (last accessed March 2016).

Lawrence M. Friedman, *The Law and Society Movement*, 38 Stan. L. Rev. 763 (1986).

Bryan A. Garner, *Interviews with Supreme Court Justices*, 13 Scribes J. Leg. Writing (2010).

Bryan A. Garner, *The Legal Writing Skills Test*, 5 Scribes J. Leg. Writing 107 (1995).

Jane Kent Gionfriddo, *Thinking Like A Lawyer: The Heuristics of Case Synthesis*, 40 Tex. Tech L. Rev. 1 (2007).

Charles J. Goetz & Robert E. Scott, *Enforcing Promises: An Examination of the Basis of Contract*, 89 Yale L.J. 1261 (1980).

George D. Gopen, *The State of Legal Writing: Res Ipsa Loquitur*, 86 Mich. L. Rev. 333 (1987).

Barbara K. Gotthelf, *The Lawyer's Guide to Um*, 11 Legal Commc'n & Rhetoric: JALWD 1 (2014).

Jamal Greene, *Pathetic Argument in Constitutional Law*, 113 Colum. L. Rev. 1389 (2013).

Janet Gusdorff, *Inferences explained: Using and rebutting inferences* (Dec. 2019), https://www.advocatemagazine.com/images/issues/2019/12-december/reprints/Gusdorff_article.pdf.

Gillian K. Hadfield, *Judicial Competence and the Interpretation of Incomplete Contracts*, 23 J. LEGAL STUD. 159 (1994).

Jonathan Haidt, *The Emotional Dog and Its Rational Tail: A Social Intuitionist Approach to Moral Judgment*, 108 PSYCHOL. REV. 814 (2001).

Janet Halley, *The Politics of Injury: A Review of Robin West's Caring for Justice*, 1 UNBOUND: HARV. J. LEGAL LEFT 65 (2005).

Henry Hansmann, *Condominium and Cooperative Housing: Transactional Efficiency, Tax Subsidies, and Tenure Choice*, 20 J. LEGAL STUD. 25 1991).

Lillian B. Hardwick, *Classical Persuasion Through Grammar and Punctuation*, 3 LEGAL COMMC'N & RHETORIC (formerly J. ALWD) 75 (2006).

Richard L. Hasen, *The Efficient Duty to Rescue*, 15 INT'L REV. L. & ECON. 141 (1995).

Michael J. Higdon, *Oral Argument and Impression Management: Harnessing the Power of Nonverbal Persuasion for a Judicial Audience*, 57 U. KAN. L. REV. 631 (2009).

Oliver Wendell Holmes, *The Path of the Law*, 10 HARV. L. REV. 457 (1897), http://moglen.law.columbia.edu/LCS/palaw.pdf.

Oliver Wendell Holmes, Jr., *The Theory of Legal Interpretation*, 12 HARV. L. REV. 417 (1889).

Dan Hunter, *No Wilderness of Single Instances: Inductive Inference in Law*, 48 J. LEG. EDUC. 365 (1998).

Joseph C. Hutcheson, Jr., *The Judgment Intuitive: The Function of the 'Hunch' in Judicial Decision*, 39 S. TEX. L. REV. 889 (1998), *reprinted from* 14 CORNELL L. Q. 274 (1929).

Vicki Jackson, *Holistic Interpretation: Fitzpatrick v. Bitzer and Our Bifurcated Constitution*, 53 STAN. L. REV. 1259 (2001).

Pam Jenoff, *The Self-Assessed Writer: Harnessing Fiction-Writing Processes to Understand Ourselves as Legal Writers and Maximize Legal Writing Productivity*, 10 LEGAL COMMC'N & RHETORIC: J. ALWD 187 (2013).

Steven J. Johansen, *Was Colonel Sanders a Terrorist? An Essay on the Ethical Limits of Applied Legal Storytelling*, 7 J. ALWD 63 (2010).

Christine Jolls, Cass R. Sunstein & Richard Thaler, *A Behavioral Approach to Law and Economics*, 50 STAN. L. REV. 1471 (1998).

Daniel Kahneman & Gary Klein, *Conditions for Intuitive Expertise: A Failure to Disagree*, 64 AM. PSYCHOLOGIST 515 (2009).

Jeanne M. Kaiser, *When the Truth and Story Collide: What Legal Writers Can Learn from the Experience of Non-Fiction Writers about the Limits of Storytelling*, 16 J. LEG. WRITING 163 (2010).

William A. Kaplin, *The Process of Constitutional Interpretation: A Synthesis of the Present and a Guide to the Future*, 42 RUTGERS L. REV. (1990).

Duncan Kennedy, *Cost Benefit Analysis of Entitlement Problems*, 33 STAN. L. REV. 387 (1981).

Laurie Rose Kepros, *Queer Theory: Weed or Seed in the Garden of Legal Theory?* 9 L. & SEXUALITY 279 (2008).

Orin S. Kerr, *How to Read a Legal Opinion: A Guide for New Law Students*, 11 GREEN BAG 2D 51 (2007).

Derek H. Kiernan-Johnson, *Telling Through Type: Typography and Narrative in Legal Briefs*, 7 COMMC'N & RHETORIC: JALWD 87 (2010).

Phillip C. Kissam, *Thinking (By Writing) About Legal Writing*, 40 VAND. L. REV. 135 (1987).

The Honorable Alex Kozinski, *The Wrong Stuff*, 1992 BYU L. REV. 325).

Charles Lane, *Book review: 'Failing Law Schools' by Brian Z. Tamanaha*, WASH. POST, Aug. 3, 2012.

Christopher C. Langdell, *Teaching Law as a Science*, 21 AM. L. REV. 123 (1887).

Katrina June Lee, *Process Over Product: A Pedagogical Focus on Email as a Means of Refining Legal Analysis*, 44 CAP. UNIV. L. REV. 655 (2016).

Karl N. Llewellyn, *Remarks on the Theory of Appellate Decision and the Rules or Canons About How Statutes Are to Be Construed*, 3 VAND. L. REV. 395 (1950).

Harold Anthony Lloyd, *Cognitive Emotion and the Law*, 41 LAW & PSYCHOL. REV. 53 (2016).

Andrea A. Lunsford, *Cognitive Development and the Basic Writer*, 41 COLL. ENGLISH 1979).

William Lutz, *Notes Toward a Description of Doublespeak (Revised)*, 13 Q. REV. DOUBLESPEAK (1987).

Anne Mangen, Bente R. Walgermo & Kolbjørn Brønnick, *Reading Linear Texts on Paper versus Computer Screen: Effects on Reading Comprehension*, 58 INTL. J. OF EDUC. RESEARCH 61 (2013).

Ellie Margolis, *Closing the Floodgates: Making Persuasive Policy Arguments in Appellate Briefs*, 62 MONT. L. REV. 59 (2001).

Ellie Margolis, *Is the Medium the Message?* 12 LEGAL COMMC'N. & RHETORIC: JALWD 1 (2015).

Mari J. Matsuda, *When the First Quail Calls: Multiple Consciousness as Jurisprudential Method*, 14 WOMEN'S RTS. L. REP. 297 (1992).

Lisa T. McElroy & Christine N. Coughlin, *The Other Side of the Story: Using Graphic Organizers to Counter the Counter-Analysis Quandary*, 39 U. Balt. L. Rev. 227 (2010).

Joseph W. Mead, *Stare Decisis in the Inferior Courts of the United States*, 12 NEV. L. J. 787 (2012).

Sue Michmerhuizen, *Confidentiality, Privilege: A Basic Value in Two Different Applications* (May 2007), https://www.americanbar.org/content/dam/aba/administrative/professional_responsibility/confidentiality_or_attorney.authcheckdam.pdf.

Johnathan T. Molot, *The Rise and Fall of Textualism*, 106 COLUM. L. REV. 1 (2006).

Jenny Morgan, *Feminist Theory as Legal Theory*, 16 MELB. U. L. REV. 743 (1988), *reprinted in* 1 FEMINIST LEGAL THEORY (Frances E. Olsen ed., 1995).

Brandon J. Murrill, Cong. Research Serv., R45129, *Modes of Constitutional Interpretation* (2018), https://fas.org/sgp/crs/misc/R45129.pdf.

Kathleen Dillon Narko, *How Do I Look? Design Your Documents for Greater Legibility and Persuasion*, 33-DEC CBA REC. 38 (2019).

Laurel Currie Oates, *Leveling the Playing Field: Helping Students Succeed By Helping Them Learn to Read As Expert Lawyers*, 80 St. John's L. Rev. 227 (2006).

Herman Oliphant, *A Return to Stare Decisis*, 14 ABA J. 71 (1928).

Robyn Painter, Kate Mayer & Kate Mathews, *Which Court Is Binding?: Binding vs. Persuasive Cases*, Georgetown Law Writing Center (2d ed. 2017), https://www.law.georgetown.edu/wp-content/uploads/2018/07/Which-Court-is-Binding-HandoutFinal.pdf.

Stephen Paskey, *The Law is Made of Stories Erasing the False Dichotomy Between Stories and Legal Rules*, 11 LC&R: J. ALWD 51 (2014).

Sondra Perl, *Understanding Composing*, 31 COLL. COMPOSITION & COMMC'N 363 (1980).

Jonah Perlin, *Making Your Power(Point): An Introductory Guide to Digital Presentation Design for Lawyers*, 18 LEGAL COMMC'N & RHETORIC __ (forthcoming 2021).

Todd E. Pettys, *The Emotional Juror*, 76 FORDHAM L. REV. 1609 (2007).

Eric A. Posner, *Law and the Emotions*, 89 GEO. L.J. 1977 (2001).

Richard A. Posner, *What Do Judges and Justices Maximize? (The Same Thing Everyone Else Does)*, 3 SUP. CT. ECON. REV. 1 (1993).

H. Jefferson Powell, *The Original Understanding of Original Intent*, 98 HARV. L. REV. 885 (1985).

Katie Rose Guest Pryal, *The Genre Discovery Approach: Preparing Law Students to Write Any Legal Document*, 59 WAYNE L. REV. 351 (2013).

William H. Rehnquist, *The Notion of a Living Constitution*, 54 TEX. L. REV. 693 (1976).

Charles Reich, *Mr. Justice Black and the Living Constitution*, 76 HARV. L. REV. 673 (1963).

James A. Reither, *Writing and Knowing: Toward Redefining the Writing Process*, 47 COLL. ENGLISH 620 (1985).

Christopher Rideout & Jill Ramsfield, *Legal Writing: A Revised View*, 69 WASH. L. REV. 35 (1994).

David T. Ritchie, *The Centrality of Metaphor in Legal Analysis and Communication: An Introduction*, 58 MERCER L. REV. 839 (2007).

Roberts: "My Job is to Call Balls and Not to Pitch or Bat," CNN (Sept. 12, 2005), https://www.cnn.com/2005/POLITICS/09/12/roberts.statement/.

Ruth Anne Robbins, *Harry Potter, Ruby Slippers, and Merlin: Telling the Client's Story Using the Characters and Paradigms of the Archetypal Hero's Journey*, 29 SEATTLE U. L. REV. 767 (2006).

Mark Sableman, *Typographic Legibility: Delivering Your Message Effectively*, 17 SCRIBES J. LEGAL WRITING 9 (2017).

Ann C. Scales, *The Emergence of Feminist Jurisprudence: An Essay*, 95 YALE L.J. 1373 (1986).

Louis B. Schwartz, *With Gun and Camera Through Darkest CLS-Land*, 36 STAN. L. REV. 413 (1984).

Stacy Rogers Sharp, *Crafting Responses to Counterargument: Learning from the Swing-Vote Cases*, 10 LEGAL COMMC'N & RHETORIC: JALWD 201 (2013).

David Segal, *Is Law School A Losing Game?*, N.Y. TIMES, Jan. 9, 2011.

David Segal, *What They Don't Teach Law Students: Lawyering*, N.Y. TIMES, Nov. 20, 2011.

Steven Shavell, *Criminal Law and the Optimal Use of Nonmonetary Sanctions as a Deterrent*, 85 COLUM. L. REV. 1232 (1985).

Ann Sinsheimer & David J. Herring, *Lawyers at Work: A Study of the Reading, Writing, and Communication Practices Of Legal Professionals*, 21 J. LEGAL WRITING 63 (2016).

Michael R. Smith, *Levels of Metaphor in Persuasive Legal Writing*, 58 MERCER L. REV. 919 (2007).

Lawrence B. Solum, *Legal Theory Lexicon 077: Living Constitutionalism*, LEGAL THEORY LEXICON (Nov. 25, 2018), https://lsolum.typepad.com/legal_theory_lexicon/2017/05/legal-theory-lexicon-077-living-constitutionalism.html.

Lawrence B. Solum, *Originalism versus Living Constitutionalism: The Conceptual Structure of the Great Debate*, 113 NW. U. L. REV. 1243 (2019).

Nancy Sommers, *Revision Strategies of Student Writers and Experienced Adult Writers*, 31 COLL. COMPOSITION & COMMC'N 378 (1980).

Kathryn M. Stanchi, *Playing With Fire: The Science of Confronting Adverse Material in Legal Advocacy*, 60 RUTGERS L. REV. 381, 429 (2008).

Kathryn M. Stanchi, *The Power of Priming in Legal Advocacy: Using the Science of First Impressions to Persuade the Reader*, 89 OR. L. REV. 305 (2010).

Toby J. Stern, *Federal Judges and Fearing The "Floodgates Of Litigation,"* 6 UNIV. PA. J. CONST. LAW 377 (2003).

Donald Stewart, *Some History Lessons for Composition Teachers*, 3 RHETORIC REV. 134 (1985).

Cass R. Sunstein, Commentary, *On Analogical Reasoning*, 106 HARV. L. REV. 741 (1993).

Kristen Konrad Tiscione, *Feelthinking Like A Lawyer: The Role of Emotion in Legal Reasoning and Decisionmaking*, 54 WAKE FOREST L. REV. 1159 (2019).

Kristen Konrad Robbins-Tiscione, *From Snail Mail to E-Mail: Traditional Legal Memoranda in the Twenty-First Century*, 58 J. LEGAL EDUC. 32 (2008).

Kristen K. Robbins (now Tiscione), *Paradigm Lost: Recapturing Classical Rhetoric to Validate Legal Reasoning*, 27 VT. LAW REV. 483 (2003).

Kristen K. Robbins (now Tiscione), *The Inside Scoop: What Federal Judges Really Think About the Way Lawyers Write*, 8 J. LEGAL WRITING 257 (2002).

Kristen K. Tiscione, *The Rhetoric of Email*, 92 OR. L. REV. 575 (2013).

Jennifer Sheppard, *The "Write" Way: A Judicial Clerk's Guide to Writing for the Court*, 38 U. BALT. L. REV. 73 (2008).

Michael R. Smith, *The Sociological And Cognitive Dimensions Of Policy-Based Persuasion*, 22 J.L. & POL'Y 35 (2013).

Kevin M. Stack, *First Principles for Interpreting Regulation*, THE REGULATORY REVIEW (Feb 11, 2013), https://www.theregreview.org/2013/02/11/11-stack-regulation-interpretation.

Kevin M. Stack, *Interpreting Regulations*, 111 Mich. L. Rev. 355, 361 (2012), https://repository.law.umich.edu/mlr/vol111/iss3/2.

Paul T. Wangerin, *Skills Training in "Legal Analysis": A Systematic Approach*, 40 Univ. Miami L. Rev. 409 (1986).

D. Don Welch, *Ruling with the Heart: Emotion-Based Public Policy*, 6 S. Cal. Interdisc. L. J. 55 (1997).

Web Design Debate: Do I Really Need to Use Sans Serif Fonts?, https://designshack.net/articles/typography/web-design-debate-do-i-really-need-to-use-sans-serif-fonts/.

Robin West, *Communities, Texts, and Law: Reflections on the Law and Literature Movement*, 1 Yale J. L & Humanities 129 (1989).

Melissa H. Weresh, *Morality, Trust & Illusion: Ethos as Relationship*, 9 Legal Commc'n & Rhetoric (formerly J. ALWD 229 (2012).

James Boyd White, *Law as Rhetoric, Rhetoric as Law: The Arts of Cultural and Communal Life*, 52:3 Univ. Chicago L. Rev. 684 (1985).

Jennifer Will, *Call It an E-Convo: When an E-Memo Isn't Really a Memo at All*, 24 J. Leg. Writing 269 (2020).

Wendy W. Williams, *The Equality Crisis: Some Reflections on Culture, Courts, and Feminism*, 7 Women's Rts. L. Rep. 175 (1981–82).

Colin E. Wrabley, *Applying Federal Court of Appeals' Precedent: Contrasting Approaches to Applying Court of Appeals' Federal Law Holdings and Erie State Law Predictions*, 3 Seton Hall Cir. Rev. 1 (2006).

Books & Book Chapters

Ruggero J. Aldisert, Logic For Lawyers: A Guide To Clear Legal Thinking (3d ed. 2001).

Am. Bar Ass'n, 2020–2021 Standards and Rules of Procedure for Approval of Law Schools (2020), https://www.americanbar.org/content/dam/aba/administrative/legal_education_and_admissions_to_the_bar/standards/2020-2021/2020-21-aba-standards-and-rules-chapter3.pdf.

Am. Bar Ass'n, Task Force on Law Schools and the Profession: Narrowing the Gap (1992).

Andrew Altman, Critical Legal Studies: A Liberal Critique (1990).

Am. Jurisprudence Legal Forms 2d.

Dionne Anthon, The Bluebook Uncovered: A Practical Guide to Mastering Legal Citation (Twenty-First Edition of The Bluebook), http://dionneanthon.com/bbu/Anthon%20Bluebook%20Uncovered%20(21st%20Edition%20of%20Bluebook)%202020.08.06.pdf.

ANTOINE ARNAUD & PIERRE NICOLE, LOGIC, OR THE ART OF THINKING (Jill Vance Buroker ed., 1996).

ARISTOTLE, ON SOPHISTICAL REFUTATIONS (E. S. Forster, trans. 1955).

ARISTOTLE, THE RHETORIC OF ARISTOTLE (Lane Cooper, trans., 1932), also at http://www.perseus.tufts.edu/hopper/text.jsp?doc=Perseus:text:1999.01.0060.

1-2 ARISTOTLE, THE ORGANON (Harold P. Cooke & Hugh Tredennick eds., Harv. Univ. Press 1960).

ARISTOTLE, THE WORKS OF ARISTOTLE (W.D. Ross ed., Clarendon Press 1952).

GILBERT AUSTIN, CHIRONOMIA, OR A TREATISE ON RHETORICAL DELIVERY (Mary Margaret Robb and Lester Thonssen, eds., 1806).

AUTHOR UNKNOWN, AD C. HERENNIUM (RHETORICA AD HERENNIUM) (Harry Caplan trans., Harv. Univ. Press 1954), also at https://archive.org/stream/adcherenniumdera00capluoft?ref=ol#page/n15/mode/2up.

FRANCIS BACON, SELECTED WRITINGS OF FRANCIS BACON (Hugh C. Dick ed., 1955).

FRANCIS BACON, THE NEW ORGANON (Lisa Jardine & Michael Silverthorne eds., Cambridge Univ. Press 2000) (1620).

ALEXANDER BAIN, ENGLISH COMPOSITION AND RHETORIC (Scholars' Facsimiles & Reprints 1996) (1871).

CAROL M. BALDWIN, PLAIN LANGUAGE AND THE DOCUMENT REVOLUTION (1999).

COLEEN BARGER, ALWD GUIDE TO LEGAL CITATION (6th ed. 2017).

DERRICK BELL, RACE, RACISM AND AMERICAN LAW (4th ed. 2000).

JEREMY BENTHAM, THE WORKS OF JEREMY BENTHAM (John Bowring ed., 1843).

JAMES A. BERLIN, RHETORIC AND REALITY: WRITING INSTRUCTION IN AMERICAN COLLEGES 1900–1985 (1987).

BLACK'S LAW DICTIONARY (11th ed. 2019).

HUGH BLAIR, LECTURES ON RHETORIC AND BELLES LETTRES (1833).

THE BLUEBOOK: A UNIFORM SYSTEM OF CITATION (21st ed. 2020), https://www.legalbluebook.com/bluebook.

ROBERT H. BORK, THE TEMPTING OF AMERICA: THE POLITICAL SEDUCTION OF THE LAW (1990).

DEBORAH BOUCHOUX, CITE-CHECKER: YOUR GUIDE TO USING THE BLUEBOOK (4th ed. 2016).

HEIDI K. BROWN, UNTANGLING FEAR IN LAWYERING: A FOUR-STEP JOURNEY TOWARD POWERFUL ADVOCACY (2019).

JEROME BRUNER, ACTUAL MINDS, POSSIBLE WORLDS (1986).

BRITANNICA CONCISE ENCYCLOPEDIA (2006).

KENNETH BURKE, A RHETORIC OF MOTIVES (1950).

STEVEN J. BURTON, AN INTRODUCTION TO LAW AND LEGAL REASONING (3d ed. 2007).

JUDITH BUTLER, GENDER TROUBLE: FEMINISM AND THE SUBVERSION OF IDENTITY (1990).

MATTHEW BUTTERICK, TYPOGRAPHY FOR LAWYERS: ESSENTIAL TOOLS FOR POLISHED AND PERSUASIVE DOCUMENTS (2d ed. 2018)

GEORGE CAMPBELL, PHILOSOPHY OF RHETORIC (Charles Ewer ed., 1823), also at https://books.google.ht/books?id=CGqsjgEACAAJ&printsec=frontcover&hl=-fr&source=gbs_ge_summary_r&cad=0#v=onepage&q&f=false.

JOSEPH CAMPBELL, JOSEPH CAMPBELL, THE HERO WITH A THOUSAND FACES, ch. 3 (Robert Walter & David Kudler, eds., 3d ed. 2008).

MARTHA CHAMALLAS, INTRODUCTION TO FEMINIST LEGAL THEORY (1999).

STUART CHASE, THE POWER OF WORDS (1953).

GEOFFREY CHAUCER, THE CANTERBURY TALES (Jill Mann ed., Penguin Classics 2005).

JEENA CHO & KAREN GIFFORD, THE ANXIOUS LAWYER: AN 8-WEEK GUIDE TO A JOYFUL AND SATISFYING LAW PRACTICE THROUGH MINDFULNESS AND MEDITATION (2016).

CICERO, CICERO IN TWENTY-EIGHT VOLUMES (H.M. Hubbell trans., Harv. Univ. Press 1971).

2 CICERO, DE INVENTIONE (H.M. Hubbell trans., 1968) (c. 87 B.C.), also at https://archive.org/details/in.ernet.dli.2015.189092.

3-4 CICERO, DE ORATORE (E.W. Sutton trans., 1967) (c. 55 B.C.), also at https://archive.org/details/cicerodeoratore01ciceuoft/page/n5/mode/2up.

CICERO, DIVISIONS OF ORATORY (H. Rackham trans., Harv. Univ. Press 2004).

5 CICERO, ORATOR (H.M. Hubbell trans., 1971) (c. 46 BCE), also at https://archive.org/details/orator00aubegoog.

M. TULLIUS CICERO, *Against Catiline*, *in* THE ORATIONS OF MARCUS TULLIUS CICERO (C.D. Yonge, trans. 1856) (c. 63 BCE), also at http://data.perseus.org/citations/urn:cts:latinLit:phi0474.phi013.perseus-eng1:1.1.

LANE COOPER, THE RHETORIC OF ARISTOTLE (1932).

EDWARD P.J. CORBETT, CLASSICAL RHETORIC FOR THE MODERN STUDENT (1971).

EDWARD P.J. CORBETT & ROBERT J. CONNORS, CLASSICAL RHETORIC FOR THE MODERN STUDENT (4th ed. 1999).

MARTIN CUTTS, THE PLAIN ENGLISH GUIDE (1995).

ANTONIO R. DAMASIO, DESCARTES' ERROR: EMOTION, REASON, AND THE HUMAN BRAIN (1994).

ANTONIO DAMASIO, SELF COMES TO MIND: CONSTRUCTING THE CONSCIOUS BRAIN (2010).

WAYNE A. DAVIS (with the GEORGETOWN LOGIC GROUP), AN INTRODUCTION TO LOGIC (2011).

DAVID J. DEMPSEY, LEGALLY SPEAKING: 40 POWERFUL PRESENTATION PRINCIPLES LAWYERS NEED TO KNOW (2009).

RENÉ DESCARTES, DISCOURSE ON METHOD AND THE MEDITATIONS (John Veitch trans., Prometheus Books 1989).

MARY L. DUNNEWOLD, BETH A. HONETSCHLAGER, & BRENDA L. TOFTE, JUDICIAL CLERKSHIPS: A PRACTICAL GUIDE (8th ed. 2010).

TESSA L. DYSART, LESLIE H. SOUTHWICK & RUGGERO J. ALDISERT, BETTER BRIEFS AND ORAL ARGUMENT: WINNING ON APPEAL (3d ed. 2017).

LINDA H. EDWARDS, LEGAL WRITING AND ANALYSIS (4th ed. 2015).

PETER ELBOW, WRITING WITHOUT TEACHERS (2d ed. 1998).

ENCYCLOPEDIA OF RHETORIC (Oxford Univ. Press 2001).

JANET EMIG, THE COMPOSING PROCESS OF TWELFTH GRADERS (1971).

ANNE ENQUIST & LAUREL CURRIE OATES, JUST WRITING: GRAMMAR, PUNCTUATION, AND STYLE FOR THE LEGAL WRITER (5th ed. 2017).

DESIDERIUS ERASMUS, DE RATIONE STUDII AC LEGENDI INTERPRETANDIQUE AUCTORES (ON THE METHOD OF STUDY), IN 24 COLLECTED WORKS OF ERASMUS (Craig R. Thompson, ed. 1978) (1513), also at https://college.holycross.edu/faculty/wziobro/ClassicalAmerica/ErasmusdeRationeHP.html.

DESIDERIUS ERASMUS, DE DUPLICI COPIA VERBORUM AC RERUM IN 24 COLLECTED WORKS OF ERASMUS (Craig R. Thompson ed. 1978) (1528).

ESSAYS ON CLASSICAL RHETORIC AND MODERN DISCOURSE (Robert J. Connors et al. eds., 1984).

FEDERAL JUDICIAL CENTER, LAW CLERK HANDBOOK: A HANDBOOK FOR LAW CLERKS TO FEDERAL JUDGES (4th ed. 2020), https://www.fjc.gov/content/345912/law-clerk-handbook-handbook-law-clerks-federal-judges-fourth-edition.

STEPHEN M. FELDMAN, AMERICAN LEGAL THOUGHT FROM PREMODERNISM TO POSTMODERNISM: AN INTELLECTUAL VOYAGE (2000).

JENNIFER FLETCHER, TEACHING ARGUMENTS: RHETORICAL COMPREHENSION, CRITIQUE, AND RESPONSE (2015).

DAVID C. FREDERICK, THE ART OF ORAL ADVOCACY (3d ed. 2019).

DANIEL FOGARTY, ROOTS FOR A NEW RHETORIC (1959).

W.W. FORTENBAUGH, ARISTOTLE ON EMOTION (2d ed. 2002).

JEROME FRANK, LAW AND THE MODERN MIND (1949).

DAVID C. FREDERICK, THE ART OF ORAL ADVOCACY (2d ed. 2011).

MICHAEL H. FROST, INTRODUCTION TO CLASSICAL LEGAL RHETORIC (2005).

MARY JO FRUG, POSTMODERN LEGAL FEMINISM (1992).

IAN GALLACHER, A FORM AND STYLE MANUAL FOR LAWYERS (2005).

JAMES A. GARDNER, LEGAL ARGUMENT: THE STRUCTURE AND LANGUAGE OF EFFECTIVE ADVOCACY (2d ed. 2007).

BRYAN A. GARNER, LEGAL WRITING IN PLAIN ENGLISH (2d ed. 2013).

BRYAN A. GARNER, THE ELEMENTS OF LEGAL STYLE (2d ed. 2002).

BRYAN A. GARNER, THE REDBOOK: A MANUAL ON LEGAL STYLE (3d ed. 2013).

BRYAN A. GARNER, THE WINNING BRIEF: 100 TIPS FOR PERSUASIVE BRIEFING IN TRIAL AND APPELLATE COURTS (3d ed. 2014).

JOHN F. GENUNG, PRACTICAL ELEMENTS OF RHETORIC (1885).

CAROL GILLIGAN, IN A DIFFERENT VOICE: PSYCHOLOGICAL THEORY AND WOMEN'S DEVELOPMENT (1982).

JAMES L. GOLDEN, GOODWIN F. BERQUIST, WILLIAM E. COLEMAN & J. MICHAEL SPROULE, THE RHETORIC OF WESTERN THOUGHT: FROM THE MEDITERRANEAN WORLD TO THE GLOBAL SETTING (9th ed. 2009).

JAMES L. GOLDEN & EDWARD P.J. CORBETT, THE RHETORIC OF BLAIR, CAMPBELL, AND WHATLEY (1968).

WILLIAM GOLDMAN, ADVENTURES IN THE SCREEN TRADE: A PERSONAL VIEW OF HOLLYWOOD AND SCREENWRITING (1983).

ROSS GUBERMAN, POINT MADE: HOW TO WRITE LIKE THE NATION'S TOP ADVOCATES (2d ed. 2014).

JONATHAN HAIDT, THE RIGHTEOUS MIND: WHY GOOD PEOPLE ARE DIVIDED BY POLITICS AND RELIGION (2012).

H.L.A. HART, THE CONCEPT OF LAW (1961).

JACK HART, STORY CRAFT: THE COMPLETE GUIDE TO WRITING NARRATIVE NONFICTION (2011).

RICHARD HUGHES & ALBERT DUHAMEL, PRINCIPLES OF RHETORIC (1967).

WILSON HUHN, FIVE TYPES OF ARGUMENT (2d ed. 2014).

DAVID HUME, A TREATISE OF HUMAN NATURE (David Fate Norton & Mary J. Norton eds., Oxford Univ. Press 2000).

DAVID HUME, AN ENQUIRY CONCERNING HUMAN UNDERSTANDING (Tom L. Beauchamp ed., Oxford Univ. Press 2000).

MARSHA HUNTER, BRIAN K. JOHNSON & JAMI MCKEON, THE ARTICULATE ADVOCATE: PERSUASIVE SKILLS FOR LAWYERS IN TRIALS, APPEALS, ARBITRATIONS, AND MOTIONS (2d ed. 2016).

JOHN IRVING, A PRAYER FOR OWEN MEANY (1989).

MARGARET Z. JOHNS & CLAYTON S. TANAKA, PROFESSIONAL WRITING FOR LAWYERS (2d. ed. 2012).

SISTER MIRIAM JOSEPH, THE TRIVIUM: THE LIBERAL ARTS OF LOGIC, GRAMMAR, AND RHETORIC (Marguerite McGlinn ed., Paul Dry Books 2002) (1937).

THE COLLECTED WORKS OF C. G. JUNG (Sir Herbert Read, Michael Fordham, & Gerhard Adler, eds. 1966).

DANIEL KAHNEMAN, THINKING, FAST AND SLOW (2011).

IMMANUEL KANT, CRITIQUE OF PURE REASON (F. Max Müller trans., Anchor Books 1966) (1781).

Duncan Kennedy, *Legal Education as Training for Hierarchy*, *in* POLITICS OF LAW: A PROGRESSIVE CRITIQUE (David Kairys ed., 1982).

ENCYCLOPEDIA OF RHETORIC (Oxford Univ. Press 2001).

GEORGE A. KENNEDY, CLASSICAL RHETORIC & ITS CHRISTIAN AND SECULAR TRADITION FROM ANCIENT TO MODERN TIMES (2d ed. 1999).

GEORGE KENNEDY, THE ART OF PERSUASION IN GREECE (1963).

JAMES L. KINNEAVY, A THEORY OF DISCOURSE (1971).

THOMAS J. KINNEY, THE COMMON TOPICS (2003–04).

GARY A. KLEIN, SOURCES OF POWER: HOW PEOPLE MAKE DECISIONS (1999).

WILLIAM P. LAPIANA, LOGIC & EXPERIENCE: THE ORIGIN OF MODERN AMERICAN LEGAL EDUCATION (1994).

LAW AND ECONOMICS (Jules Coleman & Jeffrey Lange eds., 1992).

Charles Lawrence III, *The Id, the Ego, and Equal Protection Reckoning with Unconscious Racism*, *in* CRITICAL RACE THEORY: THE KEY WRITINGS THAT FORMED THE MOVEMENT (Kimberlé Crenshaw et al. eds., 1995).

TERRI LECLERCQ & KARIN MIKA, LEGAL WRITING WITH STYLE (2016).

EDWARD H. LEVI, AN INTRODUCTION TO LEGAL REASONING (1949).

NANCY LEVIT AND ROBERT R. M. VERCHICK, FEMINIST LEGAL THEORY: A PRIMER (2d ed. 2016).

KARL N. LLEWELLYN, THE BRAMBLE BUSH: ON OUR LAW AND ITS STUDY (1960).

ANDREA A. LUNSFORD AND JOHN J. RUSZKIEWICZ, EVERYTHING'S AN ARGUMENT (8th ed. 2018).

CATHERINE A. MACKINNON, FEMINISM UNMODIFIED: DISCOURSES ON LIFE AND LAW (1987).

Terry A. Maroney, *Judicial Emotion as Vice or Virtue: Perspectives Both Ancient and New*, *in* ARISTOTLE ON EMOTIONS IN LAW AND POLITICS (Liesbeth Huppes-Cluysenaer & Nuno M.M.S. Coelho eds., 2018)

RUTH ANN MCKINNEY & KATIE ROSE GUEST PRYAL, CORE GRAMMAR FOR LAWYERS, https://coregrammarforlawyers.com.

RUTH ANN MCKINNEY, READING LIKE A LAWYER (2d ed. 2012).

DAVID MELLINKOFF, THE LANGUAGE OF THE LAW (1963).

NOAH MESSING, THE ART OF ADVOCACY: BRIEFS, MOTIONS, AND WRITING STRATEGIES OF AMERICA'S BEST LAWYERS (2013).

PHILIP N. MEYER, STORYTELLING FOR LAWYERS (2014).

JAMES J. MURPHY, A SHORT HISTORY OF WRITING INSTRUCTION: FROM ANCIENT GREECE TO TWENTIETH CENTURY AMERICA (1990).

JAMES J. MURPHY, RHETORIC IN THE MIDDLE AGES: A HISTORY OF RHETORICAL THEORY FROM SAINT AUGUSTINE TO THE RENAISSANCE (1974).

JAMES J. MURPHY & RICHARD A. KATULA, A SYNOPTIC HISTORY OF CLASSICAL RHETORIC (3d ed. 2003).

James J. Murphy, *Rhetorical History as a Guide to the Salvation of American Reading and Writing: A Plea for Curricular Courage*, *in* THE RHETORICAL TRADITION AND MODERN WRITING (James J. Murphy ed., 1982).

TRACY L. NORTON, INTERACTIVE CITATION WORKBOOK FOR THE BLUEBOOK: A UNIFORM SYSTEM OF CITATION (2020).

TRACY L. NORTON, INTERACTIVE CITATION WORKBOOK FOR ALWD GUIDE TO LEGAL CITATION (2020).

MARTHA NUSSBAUM, UPHEAVALS OF THOUGHT: THE INTELLIGENCE OF EMOTIONS (2001).

JOYCE CAROL OATES, RAPE: A LOVE STORY (2003).

OED ONLINE (June 2020), at www.oxfordreference.com.

THE OXFORD CLASSICAL DICTIONARY (Simon Hornblower, Antony Spawforth & Esther Eidinow eds., 4th ed. 2012).

CHAIM PERELMAN, JUSTICE, LAW, AND ARGUMENT (1980).

CHAIM PERELMAN & LUCIE OLBRECHTS-TYTECA, THE NEW RHETORIC: A TREATISE ON ARGUMENTATION (1958).

CHAIM PERELMAN, THE REALM OF RHETORIC (William Kluback trans., Univ. of Notre Dame Press 1982).

LES PERELMAN, *The Medieval Art of Letter-Writing: Rhetoric as an Institutional Expression, in* TEXTUAL DYNAMICS OF THE PROFESSIONS (Charles Bazerman & James Paradis eds., 1991).

PLATO, COMPLETE WORKS (John M. Cooper ed., Hackett Pub. Co. Inc. 1997).

RICHARD A. POSNER, ECONOMIC ANALYSIS OF LAW (7th ed. 2007).

WILLIAM H. PUTMAN, LEGAL ANALYSIS AND WRITING (3d ed. 2009)

QUINTILIAN, INSTITUTIO ORATORIO (Donald A. Russell trans. & ed., Harv. Univ. Press 2001) also at http://www.perseus.tufts.edu/hopper/text?doc=Perseus%3Atext%3A2007.01.0069%3Abook%3D12.

JACK RAKOVE, ORIGINAL MEANINGS: POLITICS AND IDEAS IN THE MAKING OF THE CONSTITUTION (1996).

PETER RAMUS, LOGIKE (1574).

MARY RAY & JILL J. RAMSFIELD, LEGAL WRITING: GETTING IT RIGHT AND GETTING IT WRITTEN (6th ed. 2018).

WAYNE A. REBHORN, RENAISSANCE DEBATES ON RHETORIC (2000).

I.A. RICHARDS & C.K. OGDEN, THE MEANING OF MEANING (1923).

I.A. RICHARDS, THE PHILOSOPHY OF RHETORIC (1936).

JOSEPHY RICKABY, S.J., SCHOLASTICISM (1908).

RUTH ANNE ROBBINS, STEVE JOHANSEN, & KEN CHESTEK, YOUR CLIENT'S STORY: PERSUASIVE LEGAL WRITING (2d ed. 2018).

WILL ROGERS, *The Lawyers Talking, in* 6 WILL ROGERS' WEEKLY ARTICLES: THE ROOSEVELT YEARS, 1933–1935 (Steven K. Gragert ed., Will Rogers Mem'l Museums rev. ed. 2011) (1982).

Charles Rollin, The Method of Teaching and Studying the Belles Lettres (A. Bettesworth & C. Hitch trans., 1734).

Marjorie Dick Rombauer, Legal Problem Solving: Analysis, Research, and Writing (1991).

W. D. Ross, Aristotle's Prior and Posterior Analytics (Leonardo Taran ed., Garland Publishing, Inc. 1980) (1949).

Annette T. Rottenberg, The Structure of Argument (3d ed. 2000).

Ronald Rotunda, Original Intent, the View of the Framers, and the Role of the Ratifiers, 41 Vand. L. Rev. 507 (1988).

Robert N. Sayler & Molly Bishop Shadel, Tongue-Tied America: Reviving the Art of Verbal Persuasion 92 (3d ed. 2018).

Antonin Scalia, *Common-Law Courts in a Civil-Law System: The Role of United States Federal Courts in Interpreting the Constitution and Laws, reprinted in* A Matter of Interpretation: Federal Courts and the Law (Amy Gutmann ed., 1997).

Antonin Scalia & Bryan Garner, Making Your Case: The Art of Persuading Judges (2009).

Hon. Antonin Scalia, *Common-Law Courts in a Civil-Law System: The Role of United States Federal Courts in Interpreting the Constitution and Laws, in* A Matter of Interpretation: Federal Courts and the Law (Amy Gutmann ed., 1997).

Karen A. Schriver, Dynamics in Document Design (1997).

A Select Library Of The Nicene And Post-Nicene Fathers Of The Christian Church: St. Augustine's City Of God And Christian Doctrine (Phillip Schaff, ed., 1956).

William Shakespeare, Hamlet (New Folger ed., Wash. Square Press 2003).

William Shakespeare, Romeo and Juliet (New Folger ed., Wash. Square Press 2004).

William Shakespeare, The Second Part of King Henry VI (New Folger ed., Wash. Square Press 1988).

Helene S. Shapo Et Al., Writing And Analysis In The Law (5th ed. 2008).

Thomas Sheridan, A Course of Lectures on Elocution (1968) (1762).

Amy E. Sloan, Basic Legal Research: Tools And Strategies (7th ed. 2018).

Amy E. Sloan, Researching the Law: Finding What You Need When You Need It (3d ed. 2020).

MICHAEL R. SMITH, ADVANCED LEGAL WRITING: THEORIES AND STRATEGIES IN PERSUASIVE WRITING (3d ed. 2012).

DONALD C. STEWART, THE AUTHENTIC VOICE: A PRE-WRITING APPROACH TO STUDENT WRITING (1972).

SAINT AUGUSTINE, CONFESSIONS (Henry Chadwick trans., 1998).

ROY STUCKEY AND OTHERS, BEST PRACTICES FOR LEGAL EDUCATION: A VISION AND A ROAD MAP (2007).

WILLIAM M. SULLIVAN ET AL., EDUCATING LAWYERS: PREPARATION FOR THE PRACTICE OF LAW 13 (2007).

JONATHAN SWIFT, THE BATTLE OF THE BOOKS (Sir Henry Craik ed., 1912).

JONATHON SWIFT, A PROPOSAL FOR CORRECTING, IMPROVING AND ASCERTAINING THE ENGLISH TONGUE (R.C. Alston ed., Scolar Press 1969) (1712).

DAVID A. STRAUSS, THE LIVING CONSTITUTION (2010).

BRIAN Z. TAMANAHA, FAILING LAW SCHOOLS (2011).

STEPHEN E. TOULMIN, THE USES OF ARGUMENT (Cambridge Univ. Press updated ed. 2003) (1958).

BRIAN VICKERS, IN DEFENCE OF RHETORIC (1988).

GIAMBATTISTA VICO, ON THE STUDY METHODS OF OUR TIME (Elio Gianturco ed., Cornell Univ. Press 1990), available at https://cornellup.degruyter.com/view/title/552063?language=en.

GIAMBATTISTA VICO, THE ART OF RHETORIC (Giorgio A. Pinton & Arthur W. Shippee trans. & eds., 1996) (c. 1711–44).

GIAMBATTISTA VICO, THE NEW SCIENCE OF GIAMBATTISTA VICO (Thomas Goddard Bergin & Max Harold Fisch trans., Cornell Univ. Press 3d ed. 1984) (1744).

2 JOHN WALKER, ELEMENTS OF ELOCUTION (R.C. Alston ed., Scolar Press 1969) (1781).

RICHARD H. WEISBERG, POETHICS AND OTHER STRATEGIES OF LAW AND LITERATURE (1992).

MELISSA H. WERESH, LEGAL WRITING: ETHICAL AND PROFESSIONAL CONSIDERATIONS (2d ed. 2009).

WEST'S LEGAL FORMS.

RICHARD WHATELY, ELEMENTS OF RHETORIC (Douglas Ehninger ed., 1963).

JAMES B. WHITE, HERACLES' BOW: ESSAYS ON THE RHETORIC AND POETICS OF THE LAW (1985).

Carolyn Williams, ALWD, ALWD Guide to Legal Citation (7th ed. 2021).

Joseph Williams & Joseph Bizup, Style: Lessons in Clarity and Grace (12th ed. 2016).

Thomas Wilson, The Art of Rhetoric (Peter Medine ed., Penn. State Univ. Press 1994) (1560).

Christopher G. Wren & Jill R. Wren, The Legal Research Manual: A Game Plan For Legal Research And Analysis (2d ed. 1986).

The Writing Teacher's Sourcebook (Gary Tate & Edward P.J. Corbett eds., 2d ed. 1988).

The Writing Teacher's Sourcebook (Gary Tate, Edward P.J. Corbett & Nancy Myers eds., 3d ed. 1994).

The Writing Teachers' Sourcebook (Edward P.J. Corbett, Nancy Myers & Gary Tate eds., 4th ed. 2000).

Richard C. Wydick & Amy E. Sloan, Plain English for Lawyers (6th ed. 2019).

Richard Young, Paradigms and Problems: Some Needed Research in Rhetorical Invention, Research on Composing: Points of View of Departure (Charles R. Cooper & Lee Odell eds., 1978).

Richard E. Young & Alton L. Becker, *Toward a Modern Theory of Rhetoric, reprinted in* Contemporary Rhetoric: A Conceptual Background with Readings (W. Ross Winterowd ed., 1975).

Cases

Aguimatang v. California State Lottery, 286 Cal. Rptr. 57 (Cal. Ct. App. 1991).

Baker v. Nelson, 409 U.S. 810 (1972).

Brown v. Bd. of Educ., 347 U.S. 483 (1954).

Clementson v. State, 492 S.W.3d 802 (Tex. App. 2016).

Coffin v. United States, 156 U.S. 432 (1895).

Copeland v. D.C. Dep't of Emp. Servs., 3 A.3d 331 (D.C. 2010).

Denny v. Radar Industries, 184 N.W.2d 289 (Mich. Ct. App. 1970).

Dixie Carpet Installations, Inc. v. Residences at Riverdale, S.W.3d 618 (Tex. App. 2020).

Erie Railroad Co. v. Tompkins, 304 U.S. 64 (1938).

Etheridge v. Opitz, 580 S.W.3d 167 (Tex. App. 2019).

Fashion 21 v. Coalition for Humane Immigr. Rts. of L.A., 12 Cal. Rptr. 3d 493 (Cal. Ct. App. 2004).

Hudson Distributors, Inc. v. Eli Lilly & Co., 209 N.E.2d 234 (C.P. 1965).

J & J Ventures Gaming, LLC v. Wild, Inc., 38 N.E. 194, 201 (Ill. App. Ct. 2015), *aff'd*, 67 N.E.3d 243 (2016).

Jenkins v. State, 493 S.W.3d 583 (Tex. Crim. App. 2016).

Kubbernus v. ECAL Partners, 574 S.W.3d 444 (Tex. App. 2018).

Korematsu v. United States, 323 U.S. 214 (1944).

Lake River Corp. v. Carborundum Co., 769 F.2d 1284 (7th Cir. 1985).

Marbury v. Madison, 5 U.S. 137 (1803).

Plessy v. Ferguson, 63 U.S. 537 (1896).

In re Estate of Scott, 601 S.W.3d 77 (Tex. App. 2020).

Roe v. Wade, 410 U.S. 113 (1973).

Texas Beef Grp. v. Winfrey, 11 F. Supp. 2d 858 (N.D. Tex. 1998).

Trump v. Hawaii, 585 U.S. ___ (2018).

Van Horn v. Chambers, 970 S.W.2d 542 (Tex. 1998).

Speeches

Closing Argument of Atticus Finch, To Kill a Mockingbird, https://www.youtube.com/watch?v=tNxrnOC_WTs.

Summation for the Prosecution by Justice Robert Jackson, The Nuremburg Trials (July 26, 1946), https://famous-trials.com/nuremberg/1933-jacksonsummation.

Martin Luther King, Jr., *I Have a Dream* (Aug. 28, 1963), https://www.youtube.com/watch?v=smEqnnklfYs.

Abraham Lincoln, *The Gettysburg Address* (November 19, 1863), http://showcase.netins.net/web/creative/lincoln/speeches/gettysburg.htm.

General Mattis, *Acceptance Speech for the Semper Fidelis Award* (Feb. 22, 2014), http://battlerattle.marinecorpstimes.com/2014/03/03/mad-dog-mattis-just-gave-what-may-be-the-most-motivating-speech-of-all-time/.

Barack Obama, *DNC Keynote Address* (July 27, 2004), https://www.youtube.com/watch?v=eWynt87PaJ0.

Oral Argument of Petitioner, *in Obergefell v. Hodges* (Mary L. Bonauto, April 28, 2015), https://www.oyez.org/cases/2014/14-556.

Statutes, Orders, Rules & Model Laws

Am. Bar Ass'n, Model Rules of Pro. Conduct (2020), https://www.americanbar.org/groups/professional_responsibility/publications/model_rules_of_professional_conduct/model_rules_of_professional_conduct_table_of_contents/.

D.C. Rules of Pro. Conduct, https://www.dcbar.org/for-lawyers/legal-ethics/rules-of-professional-conduct.

Exec. Order No. 12,044, 3 C.F.R. 152 (1978).

Exec. Order No. 12,174, 3 C.F.R. 462 (1980).

Fed. R. App. P.

Fed. R. Civ. P.

U.S. Const. art. III, § 2; art. VI, ¶ 2.

U.S. Const. amend. VII.

15 U.S.C. § 78d.

28 U.S.C. §§ 1251, 1254, 1291, 1292, 1331, 1332.

Plain Writing Act of 2010, Pub. L. No. 111–274, 124 Stat. 2861.

Tex. Civ. Prac. & Rem. Code Ann. §§ 96.001–.004 (2020).

Index

References are to pages; pages in bold indicate where the term is primarily discussed or defined.